VERBAL ADVANTAGE

10 EASY STEPS TO A POWERFUL VOCABULARY

CHARLES HARRINGTON ELSTER

Random House
Reference

This book is available for special discounts for bulk purchases for sales promotions or premiums. Special editions, including personalized covers, excerpts of existing books, and corporate imprints, can be created in large quantities for special needs. For more information, write to Random House, Inc., Special Markets/Premium Sales, 1745 Broadway, MD 6-2, New York, NY, 10019 or e-mail *specialmarkets@randomhouse.com*.

Please address inquiries about electronic licensing of reference products, for use on a network or in software or on CD-ROM, to the Subsidiary Rights Department, Random House Reference, fax 212-572-6003.

Visit the Random House Reference Web site at www.randomwords.com

Typeset and printed in the United States of America.

Library of Congress Cataloging-in-Publication Data
Elster, Charles Harrington.
    Verbal advantage : 10 easy steps to a powerful vocabulary / Charles Harrington Elster.—1st ed.
        p. cm.
    Includes bibliographical references and index.
    ISBN 0-375-70932-0
        1. Vocabulary—Problems, exercises, etc.   I. Title.
    PE1449 .E454 2000
    428.1—dc21

                                                                        00-059188

0 9 8 7 6

ISBN: 0-375-70932-0

New York Toronto London Sydney Auckland

Table of Contents

Key to Pronunciation

Vowel Sounds

A, a—flat, back, pass, exact
AH, ah—spa, father, hot, mop
AHR, ahr—car, jar, farm, alarm
AIR, air—hair, stare, bear, where
AY, ay—hay, wait, came, state
AW, aw—raw, all, walk, thought
E, e—yes, let, step, echo
EE, ee—see, beat, key, she
EER, eer—fear, pier, beer, mere
I, i—in, hit, sip, mix, pick
Y, y and EYE, eye—by, nice, pie, right, aisle
Note: Y is used in combination with other letters to form a syllable: SLYT-lee (*slightly*).
    EYE is used when this sound by itself forms a syllable: EYE-land (*island*).
OH, oh—go, sew, coat, approach
OO, oo—do, ooze, rule, true
OR, or—for, door, born, war
OOR, oor—poor, tour, allure, obscure
OW, ow—cow, out, tower, doubt
OY, oy—oil, loin, boy, annoy
UH, uh—up, dull, some, color; also ago, allow, about
UR, ur—turn, stir, were, learn
UU, uu—pull, full, good, took, would

Obscure or Unstressed Vowel Sounds

a̲—final, woman, elephant, balsam, librarian
e̲—item, taken, moment, novel, difference
i̲—edible, policy, charity, nation, imminent
o̲—connect, polite, gallop, carrot, summon
u̲—focus, lettuce, singular, column, raucous

Consonant Sounds

B, b—boy, cab, bubble
CH, ch—chip, catcher, peach
D, d—dog, add, sudden
F, f—fat, effort, staff

G, g—get, bigger, bogus, tag
H, h—hit, hope, behind
HW, hw—wheat, whither, whet
J, j—jug, juice, tragic, age
K, k—king, cup, take, actor, pack
L, l—leg, also, bell
'l—temple, ladle, cattle, turtle, apple, pedal
M, m—my, humble, gem
'm—spasm, bosom, album, schism
N, n—no, knee, end, winner
'n—hidden, cotton, open, satin, reason
NG, ng—sing, anger, tank
P, p—pen, pepper, pop
R, r—red, arrive, car
S, s—sit, ask, pass
SH, sh—she, rush, nation, conscious
T, t—top, sit, bitter, party
TH, th—thin, thirst, nothing, bath
T̲H̲, t̲h̲—there, this, brother, bathe
V, v—very, even, live
W, w—will, wait, power
Y, y—yes, you, layer
(Y), (y)—indicates that some speakers employ the Y sound of *you* and others do not: N(Y)OO (*new*); D(Y)OO-tee (*duty*); uh-ST(Y)OOT (*astute*).
Z, z—zoo, daze, please
ZH, zh—vision, measure, azure, or French *je*

Foreign Sounds

K̲H̲, k̲h̲—as in German *ach*, Scottish *loch*, Hebrew *l'chaim*.
     A guttural sound like that of clearing the throat.
(N), (n)—as in French *vin, blanc, bon, garçon*.
     A nasalized sound. The N is stopped in the nose.

Stress/Accent

- Syllables are separated by a hyphen [-].
- Syllables printed in CAPITAL letters are stressed.
- Syllables printed in lowercase (small) letters are not stressed.
- Words of one syllable are printed in CAPITALS.
- Words of two syllables in which each syllable receives roughly equal stress are also printed in CAPITALS: AY-MEN (*amen*), SHORT-LYVD (*short-lived*).
- Words of more than two syllables that have primary and secondary stress are transcribed in the following manner: The syllable with secondary stress is printed in CAPITALS, and the syllable with primary stress is printed in **BOLD CAPITALS**: pruh-NUHN-see-**AY**-shin (*pronunciation*).

List of Keywords in *Verbal Advantage*

Level 3

39. INDIGENT
40. CLAIRVOYANT
41. ADROIT
42. PLATITUDE
43. FASTIDIOUS
44. VENDETTA
45. LUCID
46. SALIENT
47. CATEGORICAL
48. INSCRUTABLE
49. CONSTRUE
50. ALLUDE

Level 4

1. PROVIDENT
2. IMPUTE
3. ASTUTE
4. NEOPHYTE
5. ENIGMA
6. CREDENCE
7. VENERATE
8. GARRULOUS
9. TRENCHANT
10. AUTONOMOUS
11. PANACEA
12. EPHEMERAL
13. ONEROUS
14. LAITY
15. PUNGENT
16. PROSAIC
17. CHARLATAN
18. PERFUNCTORY
19. MORASS
20. SOPHISTRY
21. PROLIFIC
22. MUNDANE
23. MYRIAD
24. DISSIDENT

25. LAUDABLE
26. INIMITABLE
27. JADED
28. MYOPIC
29. DEMONSTRABLE
30. CALLOW
31. ACQUIESCE
32. PONTIFICATE
33. DELETERIOUS
34. AMBIVALENT
35. PENSIVE
36. IMPROMPTU
37. CONJECTURE
38. SURREPTITIOUS
39. EXEMPLARY
40. IMPECCABLE
41. ATTEST
42. COPIOUS
43. FALLACIOUS
44. STOIC
45. RECRIMINATION
46. AFFINITY
47. VOLATILE
48. SQUALID
49. EXPEDITE
50. ABJECT

Level 5

1. VOLUBLE
2. COMMISERATE
3. DILEMMA
4. TRANSITORY
5. PHILANTHROPIC
6. LETHARGY
7. EXONERATE
8. PUGNACIOUS
9. CONTRITION
10. ABROGATE

39. MALINGER
40. AVER
41. CACOPHONY
42. REFRACTORY
43. ICONOCLAST
44. ENERVATE
45. LEVITY
46. EQUANIMITY
47. STRICTURE
48. OPULENT
49. DISPARAGE
50. DISCURSIVE

Level 7

1. REDRESS
2. ANOMALOUS
3. OBSEQUIOUS
4. DIDACTIC
5. TRUNCATE
6. ABSTEMIOUS
7. ETHEREAL
8. BOMBASTIC
9. SENESCENT
10. PERNICIOUS
11. CATHOLIC
12. OBJURGATION
13. EFFUSIVE
14. UMBRAGE
15. VICISSITUDE
16. CONTENTIOUS
17. OBEISANCE
18. ASSIDUOUS
19. DUPLICITY
20. INSOUCIANT
21. MYRMIDON
22. NASCENT
23. ACCEDE
24. MAGNANIMOUS

25. NONAGE
26. INVECTIVE
27. MACHINATION
28. DOCILE
29. REDOUBTABLE
30. PROGNOSTICATE
31. ENGENDER
32. FETID
33. PEDANTIC
34. CAPITULATE
35. INCHOATE
36. EXPONENT
37. MENDACIOUS
38. STRIDENT
39. OLIGARCHY
40. REFULGENT
41. NEPOTISM
42. RIBALD
43. AVUNCULAR
44. SUPPLICATE
45. IRASCIBLE
46. INEXORABLE
47. PARVENU
48. SALUBRIOUS
49. HYPERBOLE
50. SANCTIMONIOUS

Level 8

1. ALACRITY
2. OBVIATE
3. EMOLUMENT
4. INTRANSIGENT
5. MORDANT
6. SAGACIOUS
7. ACERBIC
8. VARIEGATED
9. SUCCOR
10. IMPORTUNE

11. PALLIATE
12. WIZENED
13. CAPTIOUS
14. EMENDATION
15. TRUCULENT
16. EXPURGATE
17. REPROBATE
18. SPURIOUS
19. VOLITION
20. INTERPOLATE
21. ADDUCE
22. MISCREANT
23. QUIXOTIC
24. SUPPURATE
25. MARTINET
26. COMPUNCTION
27. MERCURIAL
28. NOSTRUM
29. PROPITIATE
30. EFFICACY
31. TANTAMOUNT
32. PARIAH
33. GERMANE
34. LICENTIOUS
35. SUPERANNUATED
36. EGREGIOUS
37. VAPID
38. CROTCHET
39. EPIGRAPH
40. EXPATIATE
41. SINECURE
42. PREDILECTION
43. IMBROGLIO
44. INEFFABLE
45. STOLID
46. OFFAL
47. LISSOME
48. MELLIFLUOUS
49. SURFEIT
50. BLANDISHMENT

Level 9

1. PROLIX
2. APOCRYPHAL
3. CUPIDITY
4. VERNAL
5. TEMERITY
6. RAPPROCHEMENT
7. DISQUISITION
8. PROSCRIBE
9. MUNIFICENCE
10. PROBITY
11. PUISSANT
12. PECULATE
13. DIFFIDENT
14. VENAL
15. PARSIMONIOUS
16. PUSILLANIMOUS
17. EXTANT
18. MERETRICIOUS
19. XENOPHOBIA
20. QUOTIDIAN
21. EXIGENCY
22. PULCHRITUDE
23. DENOUEMENT
24. FUGACIOUS
25. TURBID
26. INDEFEASIBLE
27. DISINGENUOUS
28. SCURRILOUS
29. RECRUDESCENCE
30. DEFENESTRATE
31. DILATORY
32. VILIFY
33. PHLEGMATIC
34. ADVENTITIOUS
35. DESICCATED
36. COMITY
37. SPECIOUS
38. NOISOME

39. CALUMNY
40. EXCORIATE
41. LASSITUDE
42. TRADUCE
43. DISHABILLE
44. SATURNALIA
45. EXTIRPATE
46. FLAGITIOUS
47. PERIPATETIC
48. CACHINNATE
49. MANUMIT
50. EXPIATION

Level 10

1. JEJUNE
2. PAUCITY
3. MINATORY
4. PUTATIVE
5. LUCUBRATION
6. TROGLODYTE
7. ALEATORY
8. FARRAGO
9. CYNOSURE
10. BADINAGE
11. HIERATIC
12. SATURNINE
13. EXECRATE
14. VITIATE
15. VENIAL
16. RISIBLE
17. LIONIZE
18. CONTRETEMPS
19. RODOMONTADE
20. HEBETUDE
21. SANGUINE
22. DEIPNOSOPHIST
23. FRANGIBLE
24. APODICTIC
25. FULMINATE

26. SCARIFY
27. HEBDOMADAL
28. DIVAGATE
29. IATROGENIC
30. TERGIVERSATION
31. NACREOUS
32. FAINEANT
33. HISPID
34. LONGANIMITY
35. SCIOLIST
36. PROPINQUITY
37. FACTITIOUS
38. PLEXIFORM
39. SUSURRUS
40. TRITURATE
41. PROTEAN
42. CREPITATE
43. NOCTIVAGANT
44. FULIGINOUS
45. HORTATORY
46. HELIOLATRY
47. SCIAMACHY
48. GLABROUS
49. PETTIFOGGER
50. EPICENE

Introduction

Let me guess why you picked up this book. You want to become a better writer and speaker. You want to use the English language correctly and with confidence.

You're looking for something that will help you learn more words and learn them swiftly—something that's not just informative but also interesting and fun to read.

You don't want word games. You want results.

Stop right here.

Verbal Advantage is precisely what you're looking for: the most comprehensive, accessible, and effective vocabulary-building program available today.

Here's what you can expect from *Verbal Advantage*:

By the time you finish reading this book you will have more than tripled your normal rate of learning vocabulary. And when you have mastered all the words in the program, your vocabulary level will be in the top 5 percent of all educated adults. You will also know how to avoid common errors of grammar, usage, and pronunciation, and you will possess the tools to continue building your verbal skills for the rest of your life.

Throughout the *Verbal Advantage* program I will be your personal guide on a tour of the English language, a tour that I guarantee will help you improve your word power dramatically and permanently. Along the way I will also coach you in how to use the language with greater clarity,[1] precision, and style.

Let me tell you a bit about myself.

I am an author, journalist, and radio commentator who specializes in writing about the English language. Like most serious writers, I care deeply about words—where they came from, what they mean, how they are used and pronounced. In fact, I think it's fair to say that I'm afflicted with a terminal passion for words.

Allow me to explain how I contracted this most pleasant malady.[2]

For as long as I can remember I have been in love with the beauty, rhythm, subtlety, and power of language, and from an early age I aspired[3] to a career

---

[1] *clarity* (KLAR-i-tee) clearness, state of being clear to the eye or to the understanding
[2] *malady* (MAL-uh-dee) ailment, sickness, disorder
[3] *aspire* (uh-SPY-ur) to strive to achieve, seek ambitiously

working with words. Like many writers, I acquired my affection for words from my parents. Although both my father and mother are retired professional musicians, they have always been avid[4] readers with a fine ear for language as well as music.

When I was young they read me stories and poems at bedtime, and as I grew older they encouraged me to read widely on my own. I often had lengthy discussions with them about books and language, and whenever we had a question or a dispute about a word, the hefty unabridged dictionary in our living room was the final authority.

The consequence of this verbally intensive upbringing was that two parents who loved language but made music for a living wound up with a son who loves music but makes his living with words.

But that's enough about me, because this book is not about me and my writing credentials. It's about you, and how you can achieve the verbal advantage.

Verbal Advantage is about definitions, so let's begin by defining the phrase "verbal advantage." What exactly is a "verbal advantage"? Does it suggest what smart, successful people know about language? Does it refer to the words they use in conversation and writing?

Yes, in part. But in this book, "verbal advantage" encompasses something more than just what educated people already know about using the language. It also means what educated people *ought* to know about using the language—and how using it well can help them succeed.

In short, a "verbal advantage" is the ability to use words in a precise and powerful manner, to communicate clearly, correctly, and effectively in every situation, both on and off the job. In this book I intend to take your ability with words and turn it into mastery.

Numerous studies have shown that there is a correlation between career and financial success and an above-average vocabulary, and that the level of success people achieve is linked to the number of words they command. You may be on the right track, but are you as productive and successful as you know you can be? In the long run all your hard work and all the knowledge you gain from experience may not produce the results you expect if you lack the confidence that comes from an accompanying mastery of words.

As the syndicated columnist William Raspberry once put it, "Good English, well spoken and well written, will open more doors than a college degree. . . . Bad English will slam doors you don't even know exist."

---

[4] *avid* (AV-id) enthusiastic, eager, dedicated

Verbal Advantage will give you most of the linguistic tools you need to communicate more effectively and confidently, and I will show you how to use them with precision. If you like, consider *Verbal Advantage* an apprenticeship to a second career—one that can help you immeasurably and enhance your chances of success. When you finish reading this book, you'll be on your own. But I think you'll find yourself prepared to meet the challenge of achieving and maintaining a verbal advantage.

Improving your verbal skills is not an easy task, but it doesn't have to be a chore. In fact, it can be one of the most rewarding activities you will ever undertake. Few things can equal the satisfaction that comes from using the right word at the appropriate moment or realizing that the way you have chosen to express something has moved or gratified or persuaded your audience.

Let's begin, then, with a brief summary of what you stand to gain from reading this book.

You will learn about vocabulary building and why it is indispensable to your personal development. I will teach you the principles and techniques of building a large and exact vocabulary and introduce you to words that will add clarity to your writing and infuse your conversation with style. You will also discover how to put your powerful new vocabulary into action right away, and how to make the words you've learned serve you well for the rest of your life.

Throughout this book we will also explore the subject of usage versus "abusage"—in other words, how to use, not abuse, the language. You will learn how usage changes, why it changes, and why certain changes have been accepted and others have not. I will also cover some perplexing problems of usage that trouble even the best writers and speakers. Finally, I will address the issue of rules—good rules versus bad rules—and discuss how you can strike a balance between current standard usage and what seems natural and correct to you.

Building a powerful vocabulary and learning how to use words properly require that you also develop your knowledge of a related subject: pronunciation.

It is a sad fact that many educated people who have invested a great deal of time and energy building impressive vocabularies have not bothered to learn how to pronounce the words they have acquired. That deficiency leads to a twofold tragedy. First, to those who look up to the speaker as a more knowledgeable person, the mispronouncer does the disservice of passing along his or her mispronunciations. Second, to those who know something about words and how they should be pronounced, the mispronouncer, no matter how intelligent, will appear uneducated, even foolish.

The point is, if you have taken the time to learn the meaning of a word and how to use it properly, then why not also learn how to pronounce it correctly?

With *Verbal Advantage*, not only will you learn the proper pronunciation of words that are new to you, you will also learn to avoid common mispronunciations of familiar words—ones you may be mispronouncing right now without realizing it. In addition, I will teach you some simple techniques that will help you continue to improve your speech on your own.

Building your vocabulary is the primary goal of this program, and research has shown that the most effective way to build your word power rapidly and permanently is to learn words in their order of difficulty. Certain words are harder than others; therefore it stands to reason that you have to know the easier words before you can learn and retain the harder ones. When you know what *reckless* and *rash* mean, you're ready to learn the more difficult synonyms *impulsive*, *imprudent*, and *impetuous*. And when you have those words under your belt, then you can tackle the challenging synonyms *precipitate* and *temerarious*.

In short, you are far more likely to remember words if you are exposed to them in ascending order of difficulty. That is why I have made *Verbal Advantage* a graduated vocabulary-building program, which means the words get harder as you go along.

You will proceed through ten levels of vocabulary, each level more challenging than the last. For example, Level 1 contains words familiar to about 60 to 70 percent of adults—that is, words known to many high school graduates and most college graduates. By the end of Level 5 you will have raised your vocabulary to about the 75th percentile—the top quarter of all educated adults. By the end of Level 8 your vocabulary will have surpassed that of most executives and professionals, including those with advanced degrees. And when you complete the tenth and final level you will have progressed beyond 95 percent of the entire population. You will command an armory of words that only a handful of people in every thousand can match.

Each level of *Verbal Advantage* focuses on specially selected "keywords" essential to educated discourse. But those words constitute only a fraction of what you'll learn from this book. Carefully study all the keyword discussions and you will learn scores of useful related words and a plethora (PLETH-uh-ruh, great number or quantity, abundance) of challenging synonyms and antonyms. You will also discover where the words you are learning come from and how their history has influenced their current meaning.

In addition to building your vocabulary, *Verbal Advantage* will guide you in the subtleties of using the language properly and precisely. Each level contains interludes on commonly misused words, commonly confused words, and commonly mispronounced words. You will learn how to avoid various errors of grammar, diction, and pronunciation that vex even the most educated adults. I will show you how to eliminate redundancies—flabby, repetitive phrases—from your writing and speech, and help you heed the advice of Mark Twain, who said, "Use the right word, and not its second cousin." Finally, the synonym studies in the keyword discussions will develop your ability to distinguish wisely between words of similar meaning.

Let's return now to the link between vocabulary and success.

The theory that knowing more words can help you succeed is nothing new. Since the early twentieth century, researchers have documented the connection between a strong vocabulary and academic and professional success.

Professor Dean Trembly of the Testing and Counseling Center at California Polytechnic State University, San Luis Obispo, supports the thesis that building your vocabulary enhances your chances of success. In his book *Learning to Use Your Aptitudes*, Trembly explains that "a large vocabulary is more than knowing the difficult words; it is knowing the easier words more thoroughly and using them with greater precision. . . . A powerful vocabulary gives you the facility to use the easier words more smoothly. . . . As with grades in school," writes Trembly, "money earnings are related to vocabulary. Within each occupation, those with larger vocabularies are more likely to profit. Put a dollar sign in front of each additional word you learn."

Perhaps the most influential researcher to explore the connection between vocabulary and achievement was Johnson O'Connor, founder of the Human Engineering Laboratory, now called the Johnson O'Connor Research Foundation.

O'Connor was a Harvard-educated engineer who devoted his life to identifying and measuring human aptitudes and studying their relationship to a knowledge of English vocabulary. After more than twenty years of testing thousands of Americans of all ages, occupations, and levels of education, O'Connor concluded that "an exact and extensive vocabulary is an important concomitant of success. . . . Furthermore, such a vocabulary can be acquired. It increases as long as a person remains in school or college, but without conscious effort does not change materially thereafter."

Margaret E. Broadley is an authority on Johnson O'Connor's work and the author of several books on human aptitudes. In *Your Natural Gifts* she explains how, as far back as the 1930s, O'Connor's Human Engineering Laboratory discovered, as Broadley puts it, "a close relationship between a large, precise knowledge of English words and achievement in life."

"Worldly success, earnings and management status," writes Broadley, "correlated with vocabulary scores. In follow-up studies of persons tested as much as twenty or thirty years ago, a limited vocabulary is proving an important factor in holding men and women back from achieving the position which their aptitudes showed they should have gained."

Broadley continues: "A low vocabulary is a serious handicap. Ambitious and energetic persons can push ahead in their jobs just so far, but then they reach a plateau caused by low vocabulary. They never advance. And while youthful zest and high aptitudes can enable us to forge ahead despite low vocabulary, when we become mature the world expects us to know something and we are judged on knowledge rather than our possibilities. The world doesn't see our aptitudes, but it pays for knowledge because that can be seen."

Broadley then gets down to the nitty-gritty. "Studies show that at middle-age the low-vocabulary persons are stuck in routine jobs. Furthermore, when big companies have their shakedowns and mergers, too often the low-vocabulary persons find themselves out on the street. Too often they place the blame on prejudice, inside politics, and personal antagonism when the truth can be traced to low vocabulary. . . .

"Only about 3,500 words separate the high vocabulary person from the low," Broadley concludes. "Yet these 3,500 words can mean the difference between success and failure."

It is worth noting here that company presidents and upper-level business executives have consistently achieved the highest scores in the vocabulary tests administered by the Johnson O'Connor Research Foundation. As a group, executives score better than editors, writers, college professors, scientists, doctors, lawyers, psychologists, architects, and engineers—all high-vocabulary occupations.

The foundation's researchers are not quite sure what to make of that finding, but they do know one thing: If you wish to succeed in your career, your vocabulary level must at least equal the average level of the members of your profession. If you wish to excel, your vocabulary must surpass that of your colleagues.

As Johnson O'Connor said, "Words are the instruments of thought by which men and women grasp the thoughts of others, and with which they do most of their thinking."

To paraphrase that: Words are the tools of thought, and it follows that if your tools aren't the sharpest ones in the shed, you can't expect to have an edge in the struggle for success.

There is one other point about vocabulary and success that I would like to clarify before we go any further. Researchers and language experts have known for many years that vocabulary is the key to success, but what does that really mean? It is true that various studies have shown that, particularly among business executives, English vocabulary level often correlates with salary level. However, there are many wealthy people who have low vocabularies and lack ability with language, just as there are many people who earn modest salaries but who have excellent vocabularies and a wide knowledge of the world.

The point is, if your only ambition in life is to make wads of money, there are ways to do that without building your vocabulary. Therefore it is important that you do not equate building a large vocabulary only with padding your bank balance and diversifying your stock portfolio. Vocabulary is the key to success, but wealth is not the only yardstick of success.

What I am talking about is a definition of success that encompasses more than salaries and investments. What I am talking about is your career—what you do and how well you do it—and also your personal development—how you can make the most of your natural abilities and achieve your goals in life. That is where a powerful vocabulary can help you. That is where knowing the precise meanings of many words gives you an invaluable advantage—a *Verbal Advantage*.

What it boils down to can be expressed in two words: career satisfaction.

Building a powerful vocabulary can help you advance your career, because as you improve your skill with language you will become a better speaker, a better writer, a better reader, and a better listener. And if you are all of those things, then you probably will be a more successful person.

I would be remiss in my duty as your instructor and guide if I neglected to underscore the fact that building your vocabulary takes time and dedication. True and lasting knowledge is not acquired overnight. That's why most of us spend the first quarter of our lives in school, presumably learning to be intelligent, productive members of society.

Verbal Advantage will boost your vocabulary and enhance your verbal skills, but remember that your verbal development did not start with this book and it should not end with it. Think of this program as the beginning of a lifelong process of self-education; or, if you like, think of yourself as an athlete—an intellectual athlete—embarking on a challenging conditioning program for your mind.

Verbal Advantage will give you the tools and show you how to use them, but it's up to you to decide what to build with those tools, and the responsibility for keeping them clean and sharp ultimately lies with you.

Therefore you will get the most out of this book if you follow the three R's of verbal development: *routine, repetition,* and *review.*

Effective vocabulary building begins with establishing a routine and sticking to it. You should read *Verbal Advantage* for a set amount of time every day, preferably at least thirty minutes. If you currently watch an hour or more of television each day, why not cut a half-hour out of that time and devote it to something more productive: reading this book. However you decide to work it into your day, for best results you should make *Verbal Advantage* a regular part of your schedule.

As the saying goes, practice makes perfect, and when it comes to building your vocabulary, repetition and review are essential if you wish to retain the words you learn. You will make best use of this book if you go over the material a second time—and even a third time as the words get more difficult—before forging ahead.

I also recommend that when you finish each level in the program you review the entire level in one or two sessions, focusing your attention on the words and concepts you had trouble remembering when you read the material the first time.

Although reviewing will be your responsibility, I have incorporated regular review sections into the program to help reinforce your comprehension.

After every ten keyword discussions there is a brief, informal quiz designed to fix in your mind the words you've just learned. When you take these quizzes, keep track of how many correct and incorrect answers you make, and which words are most challenging for you.

If you get some answers wrong the first time around, don't worry about it. Mistakes and missteps are a natural part of learning. However, if you're reviewing the material and you miss three or more answers in a quiz, you should go back and read all ten keyword discussions again.

To help you further gauge your progress, I have also included a review test for each level of *Verbal Advantage*. Here you will find questions pertaining to all the additional information in the program—including synonyms, antonyms, related words, and word origins, along with advice on usage, pronunciation, and using a dictionary. After you have read and reviewed a level and mastered its keyword quizzes, take the review test before moving ahead.

One last thing to remember: Don't rush. Take your time. The Johnson O'Connor Research Foundation has found that when you engage in a conscientious study of vocabulary, your rate of improvement is "related less to how fast you cover the material and more to how thoroughly you study the material step-by-step in order of difficulty."

One word of caution: If you're the eager-beaver type, you may be tempted to skip around or jump ahead. That is your prerogative, but I do not recommend taking any shortcuts. In the long run you will only shortchange yourself. To get the full benefit of the *Verbal Advantage* program, I urge you to start at the beginning and read straight through to the end.

Keep in mind that this is a graduated vocabulary-building program designed to improve your knowledge of words step by step in the most effective way possible. Although you may know some of the keywords in the early levels, right from the start the discussions cover many more difficult synonyms and related words.

Also, *Verbal Advantage* contains a great deal of information about language that anyone, at any level, will find useful. As the vocabulary-building experts Maxwell Nurnberg and Morris Rosenblum once put it, "You learn more words by learning more about words." That's exactly what *Verbal Advantage* is designed to do: build your vocabulary by teaching you a lot more about words than just their definitions.

To sum up: I encourage you to read this book for a set amount of time each day, read it straight through, and always review what you've learned before moving on. By the time you finish I think you'll agree that *Verbal Advantage* is a challenging program designed for people who are committed to improving their vocabularies and serious about translating their verbal skills into personal success.

Are you ready to begin your journey toward a more powerful and precise command of the English language?

Let's go. I'll be with you all the way.

An Important Note Before You Begin

To help you chart your vocabulary development, *Verbal Advantage* includes two diagnostic tests: a pretest and a posttest.

You should take the pretest before you begin reading *Verbal Advantage*. You should take the posttest only after reading and reviewing the entire program.

Don't worry about your score on the pretest. The test is not a measure of your intelligence or your ability to learn new words. It is simply a device you can use to assess your current vocabulary level before you begin the *Verbal Advantage* program.

Here's what you should do: Take the following pretest, calculate your score, and then put it out of your mind. Then read this book slowly and carefully from beginning to end, reviewing the material often. When you have finished reading and reviewing the whole book, take the posttest. Then compare your two scores.

In this way you will have a reasonable measure of your vocabulary development and you will see how much *Verbal Advantage* has improved your knowledge of the English language. I have no doubt that you will be delighted with your progress.

A Note on Pronunciations Recommended in This Book

This book and your dictionary are strikingly different in how they approach pronunciation. Your dictionary records whatever pronunciations are common among literate people, without evaluating them and without indicating preference. This book will exhort you to be more discriminating and it will express strong preferences. You may find that some of these preferences differ from what you are accustomed to, what you often hear, or what happens to be listed first in your dictionary. I assure you, however, that every pronunciation recommended in this book is based on cultivated usage and sound authority.

—*Charles Harrington Elster*

Verbal Advantage: Pretest

Directions: Each test word is printed in CAPITAL letters in a phrase or sentence. From the five answer choices directly beneath the phrase or sentence, select the one that comes nearest to the precise meaning of the test word.

1. Do not DIGRESS.
   disagree   hesitate   wander   object   give up

2. Their CREED.
   mistake   confusion   goal   desire   belief

3. ARDUOUS tasks.
   repetitive   difficult   unusual   routine   easy

4. UNSCRUPULOUS people.
   dirty   unjust   reliable   dishonorable   persistent

5. A COMMODIOUS place.
   private   uncomfortable   familiar   important   spacious

6. CLANDESTINE circumstances.
   special   unreasonable   secret   inevitable   obvious

7. TACIT approval.
   silent   complete   unquestioning   expected   outspoken

8. The ACME.
   bottom   reason   symbol   peak   example

9. IMPETUOUS behavior.
   strange   careful   hasty   unpredictable   perfect

10. That is INCONGRUOUS.
    relevant   uncalled for   necessary   out of place   uneven

11. DIURNAL responsibilities.
    routine   daily   never-ending   extraordinary   unpleasant

12. SOLICITOUS about it.
    pleased   confused   concerned   angry   curious

13. A noticeable DEARTH.
    loss   difference   likeness   misfortune   lack

14. Always CIRCUMSPECT.
risky   clever   cautious   indirect   prepared

15. Their QUANDARY.
opportunity   ineffectiveness   uncertainty   question   choice

16. He is ADROIT.
skillful   effective   correct   clumsy   deceitful

17. A SALIENT feature.
standard   interesting   hidden   conspicuous   unattractive

18. TRENCHANT analysis.
critical   penetrating   painstaking   superficial   deep

19. An EPHEMERAL thought.
foolish   sudden   persistent   passing   profound

20. PERFUNCTORY speech.
mechanical   hesitant   perfect   powerful   spontaneous

21. LAUDABLE behavior.
amusing   noticeable   questionable   inappropriate
praiseworthy

22. Will she ACQUIESCE?
listen   agree   understand   refuse   answer

23. Heard him PONTIFICATE.
make objections   answer clearly   speak pompously
argue vehemently   make excuses

24. Is it DELETERIOUS?
shorter   better   abusive   harmful   obvious

25. It was FALLACIOUS.
impossible   misleading   unbelievable   ridiculous   pleasant

26. To EXPEDITE it.
refuse   object to   prevent   avoid   hasten

27. Her VOLUBLE friend.
obnoxious   attractive   talkative   intelligent   shy

28. He is PUGNACIOUS.
stubborn   quarrelsome   stocky   easygoing   funny

29. An OFFICIOUS coworker.
hardworking   ambitious   meddlesome   efficient   overbearing

30. Her EBULLIENCE.
enthusiasm   rudeness   flexibility   persistence   reluctance

31. Was it a CHIMERA?
wonderful event   lost cause   strange experience   waste of time
foolish fancy

32. JUXTAPOSE them.
switch   replace   separate   evaluate   put side by side

33. ESOTERIC information.
useful   important   confidential   insignificant   accessible

34. AUSPICIOUS circumstances.
special   favorable   unpredictable   sinister   difficult

35. I will ESCHEW it.
avoid   consider   not allow   investigate   accept

36. Astonishing LEGERDEMAIN.
wit   speed   determination   verbal ability   sleight of hand

37. VACUOUS remarks.
brief   empty   confusing   insightful   comprehensive

38. ADMONISH them.
warn   seize   ignore   reward   punish

39. He was OSTRACIZED.
misunderstood   reprimanded   perplexed   expelled
depressed

40. Note the PLETHORA.
variety   scarcity   objection   difference   excess

41. It was INCESSANT.
intense   useless   constant   annoying   irregular

42. ODIOUS people.
submissive   detestable   irritating   foul-smelling   polite

43. His PECCADILLO.
hobby   weakness   complaint   secret activity   slight offense

44. A REFRACTORY child.
naughty   stubborn   abnormal   obedient   impolite

45. She was ENERVATED.
surprised   stimulated   insulted   weakened   determined

46. Complete EQUANIMITY.
confidence   fairness   chaos   similarity   composure

47. Thoroughly DIDACTIC.
entertaining   deceptive   offensive   instructive   unfair

48. SENESCENT leaders.
wise   fearless   unresponsive   dictatorial   aging

49. EFFUSIVE speech.
garbled   gushing   angry   persuasive   slow

50. ASSIDUOUS employees.
industrious   intelligent   loyal   lazy   inefficient

51. An INSOUCIANT attitude.
uncooperative   arrogant   carefree   aggressive   serious

52. It was MAGNANIMOUS.
very large   noble   polite   dishonorable   hilarious

53. INCHOATE ideas.
undeveloped   irrelevant   perfected   complicated   impossible

54. STRIDENT voices.
strong   subdued   angry   shrill   insistent

55. It was REFULGENT.
disgusting   brilliant   delicious   gloomy   unnecessary

56. Will you PROGNOSTICATE?
refuse   agree   delay   answer   predict

57. HYPERBOLIC statements.
anxious   demanding   exaggerated   humble   firm

58. With ALACRITY.
promptness   bitterness   emptiness   resentment   sorrow

59. He was INTRANSIGENT.
aloof   obliging   passionate   uncompromising   unreliable

60. A SAGACIOUS decision.
hasty   wise   careful   unexpected   foolhardy

61. The WIZENED man.
peculiar   rational   shriveled   tired   old

62. This is SPURIOUS.
exceptional   unnecessary   authentic   offensive   false

63. TANTAMOUNT to it.
next   suited   exposed   unrelated   equivalent

64. Was it EGREGIOUS?
tedious   flagrant   inappropriate   pleasant   satisfactory

65. Thoroughly DRACONIAN.
hardworking   unheard of   unfair   severe   nasty

66. It was BROBDINGNAGIAN.
weird   impossible   outrageous   out of control   enormous

67. His SINECURE.
property   solution   cushy job   personal problem
recommendation

68. Another IMBROGLIO.
unfortunate outcome   foolish idea   difficult task   predicament
connection

69. INEFFABLE ideas.
inexpressible   unworkable   undeveloped   unclear   intricate

70. To take UMBRAGE.
time   cover   offense   advantage   interest

71. They seemed OMNISCIENT.
familiar   hostile   superior   all-knowing   all-powerful

72. PEDESTRIAN writing.
rambling   ordinary   wordy   old-fashioned   energetic

73. An UNCTUOUS smile.
ugly   pleasant   insincere   radiant   meek

74. A TRACTABLE employee.
stubborn   honest   difficult   competent   manageable

75. PLATITUDINOUS remarks.
long-winded   trite   impressive   pointed   meaningless

76. This is APOCRYPHAL.
sacred   abnormal   destructive   illegitimate   unbelievable

77. Her TEMERITY.
recklessness   bashfulness   caution   cruelty   inquisitiveness

78. PARSIMONIOUS people.
intolerant   outgoing   self-righteous   whining   stingy

79. PUSILLANIMOUS actions.
noble   sudden   violent   cowardly   charitable

80. A DILATORY response.
evasive   verbose   tardy   inaccurate   immediate

81. SPECIOUS arguments.
unreasonable   deceptive   penetrating   shallow   persuasive

82. She found it NOISOME.
injurious   irritating   wholesome   overwhelming   loud

83. A COMPLAISANT manner.
smug   haughty   unconcerned   lazy   obliging

84. This is FRIABLE.
changeable   easily done   easily crumbled   flawed   edible

85. FUGACIOUS thoughts.
deceptive   dismal   fleeting   vicious   scandalous

86. A MINATORY statement.
essential   complicated   brief   threatening   advisory

87. It was FLAGITIOUS.
obvious   wicked   insulting   extraordinary   explosive

88. PERIPATETIC tourists.
foreign   wealthy   sightseeing   traveling by train   walking about

89. An ALEATORY event.
historic   unpredictable   unknown   important   strange

90. She heard the OBLOQUY.
sermon   ceremony   conference   contradiction   defamation

91. It's a FARRAGO.
mixture   mess   disaster   lucky event   humorous situation

92. HIERATIC writings.
philosophical   indecipherable   priestly   ancient   popular

93. Will it be VITIATED?
corrupted   abused   freed   exposed   explained

94. Their HEBETUDE.
routine   childhood   silence   stupidity   bashfulness

95. An entertaining DEIPNOSOPHIST.
lecturer   actor   musician   comedian   conversationalist

96. Another FULMINATION.
objection   delay   speech   explosion   addition

97. CREPUSCULAR sounds.
indistinct   creaking   insect   twilight   grunting

98. His TERGIVERSATION.
excuse   desertion   reasoning   scheme   decisive action

99. They watched the SCIAMACHY.
riot   debate   shadowboxing   religious festival
outdoor concert

100. A GLABROUS surface.
smooth   sticky   shiny   wet   icy

Verbal Advantage: Pretest Answer Key

1. DIGRESS: wander
2. CREED: belief
3. ARDUOUS: difficult
4. UNSCRUPULOUS: dishonorable
5. COMMODIOUS: spacious
6. CLANDESTINE: secret
7. TACIT: silent
8. ACME: peak
9. IMPETUOUS: hasty
10. INCONGRUOUS: out of place
11. DIURNAL: daily
12. SOLICITOUS: concerned
13. DEARTH: lack
14. CIRCUMSPECT: cautious
15. QUANDARY: uncertainty
16. ADROIT: skillful
17. SALIENT: conspicuous
18. TRENCHANT: penetrating
19. EPHEMERAL: passing
20. PERFUNCTORY: mechanical
21. LAUDABLE: praiseworthy
22. ACQUIESCE: agree
23. PONTIFICATE: speak pompously
24. DELETERIOUS: harmful

25. FALLACIOUS: misleading
26. EXPEDITE: hasten
27. VOLUBLE: talkative
28. PUGNACIOUS: quarrelsome
29. OFFICIOUS: meddlesome
30. EBULLIENCE: enthusiasm
31. CHIMERA: foolish fancy
32. JUXTAPOSE: put side by side
33. ESOTERIC: confidential
34. AUSPICIOUS: favorable
35. ESCHEW: avoid
36. LEGERDEMAIN: sleight of hand
37. VACUOUS: empty
38. ADMONISH: warn
39. OSTRACIZED: expelled
40. PLETHORA: excess
41. INCESSANT: constant
42. ODIOUS: detestable
43. PECCADILLO: slight offense
44. REFRACTORY: stubborn
45. ENERVATED: weakened
46. EQUANIMITY: composure
47. DIDACTIC: instructive
48. SENESCENT: aging

49. EFFUSIVE: gushing
50. ASSIDUOUS: industrious
51. INSOUCIANT: carefree
52. MAGNANIMOUS: noble
53. INCHOATE: undeveloped
54. STRIDENT: shrill
55. REFULGENT: brilliant
56. PROGNOSTICATE: predict
57. HYPERBOLIC: exaggerated
58. ALACRITY: promptness
59. INTRANSIGENT: uncompromising
60. SAGACIOUS: wise
61. WIZENED: shriveled
62. SPURIOUS: false
63. TANTAMOUNT: equivalent
64. EGREGIOUS: flagrant
65. DRACONIAN: severe
66. BROBDINGNAGIAN: enormous
67. SINECURE: cushy job
68. IMBROGLIO: predicament
69. INEFFABLE: inexpressible
70. UMBRAGE: offense
71. OMNISCIENT: all-knowing
72. PEDESTRIAN: ordinary
73. UNCTUOUS: insincere
74. TRACTABLE: manageable
75. PLATITUDINOUS: trite
76. APOCRYPHAL: illegitimate
77. TEMERITY: recklessness
78. PARSIMONIOUS: stingy
79. PUSILLANIMOUS: cowardly
80. DILATORY: tardy
81. SPECIOUS: deceptive

82. NOISOME: injurious
83. COMPLAISANT: obliging
84. FRIABLE: easily crumbled
85. FUGACIOUS: fleeting
86. MINATORY: threatening
87. FLAGITIOUS: wicked
88. PERIPATETIC: walking about
89. ALEATORY: unpredictable
90. OBLOQUY: defamation
91. FARRAGO: mixture
92. HIERATIC: priestly
93. VITIATED: corrupted
94. HEBETUDE: stupidity
95. DEIPNOSOPHIST: conversationalist
96. FULMINATION: explosion
97. CREPUSCULAR: twilight
98. TERGIVERSATION: desertion
99. SCIAMACHY: shadowboxing
100. GLABROUS: smooth

Verbal Advantage: Pretest Evaluation

90–100: Very high vocabulary.

75–89: Above-average vocabulary.

60–74: Good, but could be considerably better.

40–59: Your vocabulary should and can be stronger.

25–39: There is ample room for improvement. Apply yourself.

Below 25: It is essential that you improve your vocabulary.

Level 1

Word 1: PARAPHRASE (PAR-uh-frayz)

To restate, put what someone else has expressed into different words.

The noun a *paraphrase* is a restatement of a text or passage to give the sense of the original in fuller terms. The verb to *paraphrase* means to restate something, giving the meaning in another form.

To *quote* and to *paraphrase* are sharply distinguished. To *quote* is to use or repeat the words of someone else, giving acknowledgment to the source. To *paraphrase* is to restate in different words what someone else has said or written.

Word 2: OSTENSIBLE (ah-STEN-si-bul)

Apparent, appearing or seeming to be true, professed or declared as true without being demonstrated or proved.

More difficult synonyms of ostensible include *plausible* (PLAW-zi-bul) and *specious* (SPEE-shus). *Specious*, however, has the negative suggestion of using deception to make something false appear true. A specious argument is one that looks good on the surface but is flawed underneath.

Ostensible is often used in opposition to *real* or *actual*. An ostensible motive is not necessarily a real motive; an ostensible advantage is not necessarily an actual advantage. *Ostensible* means apparent, stated as true but not necessarily proved.

Word 3: DIGRESS (di-GRES *or* dy-GRES)

To wander, stray from the point, ramble, deviate, go off in another direction.

Digress comes from the Latin *digressus*, which comes in turn from the prefix *dis-*, apart, and *gradi*, to go, walk, step. *Digress* means literally to go apart, walk away. From the same Latin source come *ingress* (IN-gres), the place you walk in, the entrance; and *egress* (EE-gres), the place you walk out, the exit.

Digress once was used of a physical wandering or turning aside, but that sense is now archaic (ahr-KAY-ik), which means old-fashioned. Today we do not say, "She turned right and digressed down Main Street." Instead, *digress* is used of speaking or writing that departs from the main point or subject at hand and wanders off in another direction: "In a business report or an oral presentation, it's important to stick to the facts and not digress"; "If she hadn't digressed so much, her lecture would have been more interesting."

The corresponding noun is *digression* (di-GRESH-un or dy-GRESH-un): "The old man's story was full of humorous digressions."

Word 4: UNCANNY (uhn-KAN-ee)

Eerie, strange, weird, mysterious: "an uncanny experience."

Uncanny may refer to something that is strange in an unnatural or unearthly way, something whose strangeness is unsettling or even frightening.

Uncanny may also be used to mean beyond what is normal or expected, strange in a remarkable or marvelous way, as "an uncanny resemblance," or "uncanny ability."

Word 5: CANDOR (KAN-dur)

Frankness, openness, sincere expression.

Synonyms include *straightforwardness*, *outspokenness*, *forthrightness*, and *ingenuousness*. *Candor* is the noun; the adjective is *candid*, frank, open, sincere.

The *candid* person expresses his or her thoughts frankly and openly, with no hesitation. The *forthright* person speaks directly to the point, plainly and sometimes bluntly, in a no-nonsense manner. The *ingenuous* (in-JEN-yoo-us) person speaks honestly and sincerely, with no hint of evasiveness or deception.

Word 6: MOROSE (muh-ROHS)

Gloomy, moody, glum, grumpy, ill-tempered, depressed. "After weeks of futile job-hunting, he became morose."

More difficult synonyms of *morose* include *dolorous* (DOH-luh-rus), which means mournful, full of sadness; *lugubrious* (luh-GOO-bree-us), which means extremely gloomy or dismal; and *saturnine* (SAT-ur-nyn), which means having a bitter disposition or sour outlook on life.

Antonyms—words opposite in meaning—include *optimistic*, *jovial* (JOH-vee-ul), and *sanguine* (SANG-gwin), which means having a cheerful, confident outlook on life.

Sullen (SUHL-in) and *morose* are close in meaning. When you refuse to speak or associate with people because you're in a bad mood, you are being sullen. When you are depressed and silent because you are feeling bitter or resentful, you are morose. *Merriam-Webster's Collegiate Dictionary*, tenth edition, says that morose suggests "bitterness or misanthropy." *Misanthropy* (mis-AN-thruh-pee) is hatred of humankind, a spiteful or pessimistic attitude about the human race. *Moroseness* is ill-tempered, bitter gloominess.

Word 7: ADEPT (uh-DEPT)

Skilled.

Synonyms include *handy*, *clever*, *able*, *deft*, *expert*, *adroit*, *dexterous* (DEK-strus, also DEK-stur-us), and *proficient* (pruh-FISH-int, not proh-).

Adept comes from the Latin *adeptus*, an alchemist who has learned how to do the impossible—change base metals into gold. The noun an *adept* (AD-ept) means a highly skilled person, an expert. The adjective *adept* means skilled, dexterous, proficient: "He was adept at managing his investments, and they always turned a handsome profit."

Word 8: SATURATED (**SACH**-uh-RAY-tid)

Soaked, thoroughly wet, full of moisture.

Synonyms include *drenched*, *steeped*, *permeated* (**PUR**-mee-AY-tid), *impregnated*, *imbued* (im-BYOOD), and *sodden* (SAHD-'n).

Sodden may mean heavy with moisture, soggy, or dull, stupefied, expressionless, as from drinking too much liquor. To *saturate* means to soak or wet thoroughly, either literally, as in "My french fries are saturated with oil," or figuratively: "The company saturated the media with ads for its new product." *Saturation* is the corresponding noun.

Word 9: PRAGMATIC (prag-MAT-ik)

Practical, having to do with actual practice, concerned with everyday affairs as opposed to theory or speculation.

Pragmatic comes from the Latin *pragmaticus*, which means skilled in business or law. The lawyer is concerned with evidence and proof; the businessperson is concerned with facts and figures. Both have little time for idle speculation or harebrained schemes. Both must be *pragmatic*, concerned with practical, everyday affairs.

Word 10: CONGENIAL (kun-JEE-nee-ul)

Sympathetic, agreeable, compatible, kindred, harmonious, having the same taste, nature, or temperament.

Congenial persons have similar or sympathetic tastes, interests, or personalities. Congenial things agree, go well together.

Antonyms, or opposites, of *congenial* are *alien*, *dissident* (DIS-uh-dint), and *incongruous* (in-KAHNG-groo-us).

Let's review the ten keywords you've just learned. Consider the following questions and decide whether the correct answer is yes or no. Answers appear on page 22.

1. When you paraphrase something, can you change the wording?
2. Is an ostensible reason always a true reason?
3. Would someone who speaks with candor be likely to digress?
4. Would seeing a UFO or finding a million dollars in the street be an uncanny experience?
5. Can you describe a morose person as congenial?
6. Does an adept worker do a job well?
7. Would a pragmatic person be likely to make a business decision based on a hunch?
8. Can the market ever be saturated with competing products?

Here are the next ten keywords in Level One:

Word 11: CAPRICIOUS (kuh-PRISH-us)

Unpredictable, tending to change abruptly for no apparent or logical reason.

Synonyms of *capricious* include *flighty, changeable, impulsive,* and *fickle.* More difficult synonyms include *erratic, whimsical* (W(H)IM-zi-kul), *volatile* (VAHL-uh-tul), and *mercurial* (mur-KYUR-ee-ul).

A *caprice* (kuh-PREES) is a sudden change of mind or change in the emotions. A person or a thing that is capricious is subject to caprices—to abrupt, unpredictable changes: "He's so capricious, his mood changes with the wind"; "New England has a capricious climate"; "The stock market is notoriously capricious."

Did you notice that my recommended pronunciation for *capricious* is kuh-PRISH-us, the second syllable rhyming with *wish?* You will hear educated speakers say kuh-PREE-shus, a pronunciation based on the corresponding noun *caprice* (kuh-PREES). This variant has been recognized by American dictionaries since the 1960s. But authorities have preferred kuh-PRISH-us since the 18th century, when pronunciation was first recorded. Current American dictionaries list kuh-PRISH-us first, and it is the only pronunciation in the *Oxford English Dictionary.* Have you ever heard anyone put an *E* in the middle of *suspicious, judicious,* or *avaricious?* Rhyme *capricious* with *delicious.*

Word 12: BLATANT (BLAYT-'nt)

Noisy, disagreeably or offensively loud, boisterous, clamorous: "the blatant sound of horns honking in heavy traffic."

Blatant is also used to mean sticking out in a glaring way, obtrusive, flagrant, as in "a blatant lie," "a blatant error," "a blatant attempt to impress the boss."

In either sense, *blatant* suggests something conspicuous and disagreeable.

Word 13: OBLIGATORY (uh-BLIG-uh-tor-ee)

Required, necessary, binding, mandatory.

Obligatory duties are those you must perform to fulfill an obligation or responsibility. Doing miscellaneous paperwork is an obligatory function of the clerical worker.

Do not pronounce the initial *o* in *obligatory* like the *o* in *open.* Pronounce it like the *a* in *above.*

Word 14: NEGLIGIBLE (NEG-li-ji-bul)

Unimportant, trifling, of little consequence.

That which is negligible can be neglected. A negligible concern can be disregarded; it is so trivial and insignificant that it warrants little or no attention.

Word 15: ADAMANT (AD-uh-mint)

Unyielding, immovable, inflexible, refusing to give in, unshakable, unrelenting, implacable. "She was adamant in her opposition to the plan."

The adjective *adamant* comes from the noun *adamant*, which refers to a hard substance or stone, such as a diamond, that in ancient times was believed to be unbreakable. There is an old word *adamantine* (AD-uh-**MAN**-tin), still listed in current dictionaries but not often used; it means like adamant, very hard, unbreakable. The adjective *adamant*, which has replaced *adamantine* in current usage, means hard in the sense of inflexible, immovable, unyielding.

Word 16: SPORADIC (spuh-RAD-ik *or* spor-AD-ik)

Occasional, infrequent, irregular, not constant, happening from time to time, occurring in a scattered or random way.

A business venture may have sporadic success. A gambler's luck may be sporadic. Sporadic crimes are crimes scattered throughout a city or neighborhood. Sporadic outbreaks of a disease in the population are occasional, isolated outbreaks.

Antonyms of *sporadic* include *constant*, *incessant* (in-SES-int), and *unremitting*.

Word 17: VANGUARD (VAN-gahrd)

The forefront of an action or movement, leading position or persons in a movement: "They were in the vanguard of the war on poverty."

In its strict military sense, *vanguard* means the troops moving at the head of an army, the part of the army that goes ahead of the main body, an advance guard.

Word 18: CONCUR (kun-KUR)

To agree, be in accord with, unite in opinion.

Concur comes from the Latin *con-*, together, and *currere*, to run, flow, and means literally to run or flow together, go along with. That derivation has led to three slightly different meanings of the word.

First, *concur* may be used to mean to act together, combine in having an effect, as "Time and chance concurred in our success."

Second, *concur* may be used to mean happen together, occur at the same time, coincide, as "His pay raise concurred with his promotion."

The third and most common meaning of *concur* is to agree, as "Your story concurs with theirs"; "We concurred on almost every point of negotiation."

Word 19: PRECOCIOUSNESS (pruh-KOH-sh<u>u</u>s-n<u>is</u>)

Early development or maturity, especially in mental ability.

The noun *precociousness* and the adjective *precocious* come from the Latin *praecox*, which means premature, or literally, "ripening before its time." *Precocious* is most often used of children whose intellectual or emotional development is unusually advanced. *Precociousness*, early development, is the opposite of *retardation*, slowness in development.

Word 20: ALOOF (uh-LOOF)

Apart, at a distance, removed, withdrawn, not wishing to speak or associate with others.

The aloof person is emotionally reserved and keeps a cool distance from others. *Aloofness* means reluctance to get involved or take an interest in something.

Synonyms of *aloof* include *unsympathetic*, *unapproachable*, *standoffish*, and *indifferent*.

Let's review the ten keywords you've just learned. Consider the following statements and decide whether each one is true or false. Answers appear on page 23.

1. The capricious person is always predictable.
2. A blatant attempt is quiet and inconspicuous.
3. When attendance at a company function is obligatory, that means you have to go whether you want to or not.

4. Something negligible can be disregarded.
5. An adamant person refuses to compromise.
6. Something sporadic occurs at regular intervals.
7. If you take the lead on an important project, you are in the vanguard.
8. When two people concur, they argue or disagree.
9. Precociousness in a child may be a sign of above-average intelligence.
10. An aloof person is unwilling to associate with others.

Let's proceed to the next ten keywords in Level 1.

Word 21: CREED (rhymes with *need*)

Belief, professed faith or opinion, especially a system of religious belief. Synonyms include *doctrine* and *dogma.*

In the United States it is illegal to discriminate against someone based on race or creed, belief.

Creed comes from the Latin *credo,* "I believe," the source of the English word *credo* (KREE-doh or, like the Latin, KRAY-doh). A credo is a declared set of beliefs or opinions.

Credo and *creed* are synonymous. *Credo* is the more learned (LUR-nid) word, usually reserved for a formal declaration of belief. *Creed* is used more generally of any professed faith or opinion.

The Latin *credo* is also the source of *incredible,* not believable, *credible,* believable, and *credulous* (KREJ-uh-lus). *Credulous* means inclined to believe, willing to accept something as true without questioning. *Credulous* and *gullible* are synonymous. To a credulous person, even the most outrageous tall tales seem credible.

Word 22: TAWDRY (TAW-dree, rhymes with *Audrey*)

Cheap and showy, gaudy, garish, sleazy.

Legend has it that *tawdry* comes from the phrase "tawdry lace," a corruption of "Saint Audrey lace," a type of lace sold at Saint Audrey's fair in England. Apparently the lace was of inferior quality, thus over time the word *tawdry* came to mean cheap and showy. Today the word may be used both literally and figuratively. A person may wear tawdry clothing or have a tawdry reputation.

Word 23: PEEVISH (PEE-vish)

Irritable, cross, complaining, fretful, ill-humored and impatient, difficult to please.

There are peevish moods, peevish remarks, and peevish looks. A *peeve* is something that irritates or annoys: "Her pet peeve is a wet towel left on the bed." *Peevish* means irritable, ill-humored, full of complaints.

Word 24: ARDUOUS (AHR-joo-<u>us</u>)

Very difficult, hard to achieve or accomplish, requiring great effort. "Compiling the annual report is an arduous task." "Raising children is an arduous responsibility."

Synonyms of *arduous* include *strenuous*, *laborious*, and *toilsome*.

Word 25: PERSONABLE (PUR-suh-nuh-buul)

Attractive, pleasing in appearance, handsome, comely, fair, presentable.

In recent years, *personable* has come to be used to mean having a nice personality. You should avoid using the word in that way. The words *sociable*, *affable*, and *amiable* already suggest people who are friendly, pleasant, and approachable. There is no need for *personable* to take over this sense. An awkward or unbecoming person, no matter how friendly and pleasant, cannot correctly be personable. Reserve *personable* for someone who is either attractive in appearance or attractive both in appearance and personality.

Word 26: RESOLUTE (REZ-uh-loot)

Firmly determined or settled, resolved, having a set opinion or purpose, steadfast, unwavering, persevering.

Resolute comes from the Latin *resolvere*, the source also of the verb to *resolve*, which means to decide, determine, settle once and for all: "After much debate, the board of directors resolved to go ahead with the five-year plan." "The lawyers tried to resolve the case out of court." *Resolute* means resolved in one's opinion or purpose: "He was resolute about earning a master's degree and starting a successful business."

Antonyms of *resolute* include *irresolute*, *unsteady*, and *vacillating* (VAS-<u>i</u>-lay-ting).

Word 27: SUPPOSITION (SUHP-uh-ZISH-in)

An assumption, theory, hypothesis.

To *suppose* means to assume as true, put something forward for consideration. A *supposition* is something supposed, an idea put forward for consideration.

A *hypothesis* (hy-PAHTH-uh-sis), a *conjecture* (kun-JEK-chur), and a *supposition* are all assumptions or theories.

A *hypothesis* is a preliminary or incomplete theory based on insufficient evidence: "There are conflicting hypotheses about the origin of the universe." (The plural, *hypotheses*, is pronounced hy-PAHTH-uh-seez.)

A *conjecture* is an assumption based on so little evidence that it is merely an educated guess: "Every week we hear different conjectures about trends in the stock market."

A *supposition* may be based on ample evidence or no evidence at all, and may be either sensible or irrational: "His suppositions about the company's financial condition proved consistent with the facts."

Word 28: ARBITRARY (AHR-bi-TRAIR-ee *or* -TRER-ee)

Unreasoned, based on personal feelings or preferences rather than on reason, logic, or law: "An arbitrary price for a product is not necessarily a fair price"; "His arbitrary decisions have cost the company a lot of money."

Arbitrary comes from the same Latin source as the words *arbiter* (AHR-bi-tur) and *arbitrator* (AHR-bi-TRAY-tur). *Arbiter* and *arbitrator* both mean a judge or umpire who makes a final decision or resolves a dispute. *Arbitrary* means making discretionary judgments or decisions that may or may not be fair or reasonable.

Arbitrary has two other useful meanings. It may mean determined or arrived at in a random or illogical manner. For example, the arrangement of furniture in a room may be arbitrary, without an evident theme or pattern; arbitrary decisions are arrived at in a hasty, haphazard way. *Arbitrary* may also mean exercising unrestrained or absolute power: an arbitrary government has no regard for individual liberty.

Word 29: MONOTONOUS (muh-NAHT-uh-nus)

Lacking variety, tediously uniform, unvarying and dull.

Monotonous means literally having one continuous sound or tone. It combines the word *tone* with the prefix *mono-*, one, single. The prefix *mono-* appears in many English words, including *monogamy* (muh-NAHG-uh-mee), marriage to one person; *monocle* (MAHN-uh-kul), a single eyeglass; and *monogram* (MAHN-uh-gram), two or more letters woven into one.

That which is monotonous is boring because it lacks variety. A monotonous speaker says the same thing again and again in the same tone of voice. Monotonous music is dull and repetitive. A monotonous job is one where the routine never changes. The corresponding noun is *monotony* (muh-NAHT'n-ee), a tedious lack of variety.

Word 30: LEGACY (LEG-uh-see)

Something handed down from the past, an inheritance.

Legacy may be used in two ways. It may mean a gift of money or property provided by a will, an inheritance, bequest: "Her wealthy uncle left her a generous legacy." It may also mean anything inherited or passed down through time: "The cultural legacy of ancient Greece and Rome has shaped Western civilization."

Let's review the ten keywords you've just learned.

This time we're going to play the synonym-antonym game: Decide if the pairs of words below are synonyms—words with the same or almost the same meaning (*beautiful* and *lovely*)—or antonyms, words opposite in meaning (*love* and *hate*). Answers appear on page 23.

1. *creed* and *faith* are . . . synonyms or antonyms?
2. *tawdry* and *elegant* are . . .
3. *fretful* and *peevish* are . . .
4. *strenuous* and *arduous* are . . .
5. *personable* and *unbecoming* are . . .
6. *resolute* and *wavering* are . . .
7. *hypothesis* and *supposition* are . . .
8. *arbitrary* and *rational* are . . .
9. *varied* and *monotonous* are . . .
10. *legacy* and *bequest* are . . .

Let's take a break from the keyword lessons and look at a few commonly mis-pronounced words and redundancies (ri-DUHN-din-seez), repetitive phrases.

If your business has anything to do with real estate, or if you ever do business with a real-estate broker, there is one word you should be careful to pronounce correctly: *Realtor* (which usually has a capital *R* because it is a trademark).

How do you pronounce this word?

The correct pronunciation is REE-ul-tur. The mispronunciation, which is very common even among Realtors themselves, is REE-luh-tur. Most dictio-naries do not recognize the pronunciation REE-luh-tur; the few that do label it "nonstandard" or "unacceptable to many." If you now mispronounce this word, it's not hard to correct the error once you train your ear to discriminate be-tween the right and wrong pronunciations. REE-luh-tur puts the sound of the *l* before the *a*, as though the word were spelled *r-e-l-a-t-o-r*. The proper pronun-ciation sounds like the word *real* plus the *tur-* in *turnip*.

You should also take care to pronounce the word *realty* correctly. Don't stick the *l* sound where it doesn't belong and say REE-luh-tee. The word should be pronounced like *real* plus *tea*. For practice, try repeating this sen-tence: "A Realtor sells realty."

Now let's expose some of the many redundancies that clutter our writing and speech.

When referring to the size, height, length, or width of something, it is not necessary to use these words. Don't say big in size, small in size, large in size, or little in size. Don't say tall in height or short in height, short or long in length, or wide or skinny in width. Those are all redundancies. Just say something is big, small, large, little, tall, short, long, wide, or slender, and leave it at that.

Getting rid of redundancy—or verbiage (pronounce it with three syllables, VUR-bee-ij)—in your speech and writing is like going on a diet. It takes some work to stick to it, but when you shed those unwanted pounds, or unneces-sary words, you feel better and look better.

Now let's return to the vocabulary for ten more keywords.

Word 31: MANIFOLD (MAN-i-fohld)

Numerous and varied, consisting of many kinds, containing many elements, features, or characteristics: a large company with manifold operations and divi-sions; a challenging executive position with manifold responsibilities.

Manifold may sound like a fancy substitute for *many*, but it's not. While *many* simply means much, a lot, *manifold* emphasizes variety, diversity. If your job has manifold duties then the things you do are both numerous and varied.

Equally difficult synonyms of *manifold* are *multifarious* (MUHL-ti-**FAIR**-ee-us) and *multitudinous* (MUHL-ti-**T(Y)OO**-di-nus). Both *manifold* and *multifarious* mean having great variety or diversity: The human race is multifarious, and human nature is even more complex and manifold. *Multitudinous* means containing a multitude, consisting of a great number of persons or things: "After his promotion to management, Bob was sometimes overwhelmed by mountains of paperwork and multitudinous administrative chores."

Word 32: PLIANT (PLY-int)

Bending easily, flexible, adaptable, workable.

Pliant comes from the French *plier*, to bend, the same source as *pliers*, the tool commonly used for bending or manipulating wires or metal pieces.

Pliant, *pliable*, and *supple* all mean bending or moving easily. *Pliant* and *pliable* usually refer to objects that are easily workable. *Supple* may apply to material things or to a human body that is flexible and limber.

Word 33: RETORT (ri-TORT)

A quick reply, especially one that is cutting or witty.

A *retort* and a *rejoinder* are similar in meaning but not quite synonymous. *Rejoinder* may be used generally to mean any answer or response, but specifically it means a counterreply, an answer to a reply. A *retort* is a swift, pointed response.

Retort comes from the prefix *re-*, back, and the Latin *torquere*, to twist, turn, and means literally "something turned back." In its most precise sense, a retort is a quick reply that counters or turns back a statement or argument: "Phil's clever retorts kept his opponent on the defensive."

Word 34: OBSTINATE (AHB-sti-nit)

Stubborn, inflexible, unwilling to give in or compromise, not yielding to argument or persuasion.

The obstinate person stubbornly adheres to a purpose or opinion, often regardless of the consequences: "First we reasoned with him, then we pleaded with him, but no matter what we said he remained obstinate and determined to have his way."

Obstinate is sometimes mispronounced as if it were spelled *obstinant*, with an *n* slipped in before the final *t*. Take care to spell and pronounce this word correctly.

Synonyms of *obstinate* include *hidebound*, *intractable*, *intransigent*, and *adamant* (word 15 of Level 1).

Word 35: LACERATE (LAS-uh-rayt)

To tear, cut roughly, rend, mangle: "The sharp thorn lacerated his thumb."

Lacerate may also be used figuratively to mean to wound, afflict, cause pain: "Her husband's vicious retort lacerated her pride and made her burst into tears."

Word 36: OMNIPOTENT (ahm-NIP-uh-tint)

All-powerful, almighty, having unlimited power or authority.

Omnipotent is formed from the word *potent*, powerful, and the combining form *omni-*, all. Whenever you see *omni-* in a word you have a good clue to its meaning, for you know that half the word means "all."

For example, *omnidirectional* (AHM-nee-di-**REK**-shi-nul) means all-directional, as an omnidirectional microphone, one that picks up signals from all directions. *Omnipresent* (AHM-ni-**PREZ**-int) means all-present, present everywhere at once. *Omniscient* (ahm-NISH-int) means all-knowing, having universal knowledge. *Omnivorous* (ahm-NIV-uh-rus) means eating all kinds of food or taking in everything: "She is an avid reader with an omnivorous mind." Our keyword, *omnipotent*, means all-powerful, almighty.

Word 37: UNSCRUPULOUS (uhn-SKROO-pyuh-lus)

Untrustworthy, dishonorable, deceitful, corrupt, lacking integrity or moral principles: "The commission issued a report on unscrupulous business practices in the industry."

A *scruple* is something that causes hesitation or doubt in determining what is appropriate and proper. *Scrupulous* means having scruples; hence, taking pains to do something exactly right. The scrupulous person is precise, careful, and honest. *Unscrupulous* means without scruples; hence, untrustworthy, unreliable, deceitful, and corrupt. Unscrupulous people will do almost anything, no matter how dishonorable, to get what they want.

Word 38: RENAISSANCE (ren-uh-SAHNS *or* REN-uh-sahns)

A revival, rebirth, resurgence, renewal of life or vigor.

The Renaissance was a revival of classical forms and motifs in art, architecture, literature, and scholarship that began in Italy in the fourteenth century, spread throughout Europe, and continued into the seventeenth century. Historically, the Renaissance marked the end of the medieval era and the beginning of the modern world.

The word *renaissance* comes from a French verb meaning to be born again. When spelled with a small or lowercase *r*, *renaissance* may refer to any renewal or resurgence of life, energy, or productivity. Many types of renaissance are possible: a cultural renaissance, a moral renaissance, a spiritual renaissance, and even a renaissance in the economy. A renaissance is a revival, rebirth, resurgence.

Word 39: GENESIS (JEN-uh-sis)

A coming into being, beginning, origin, birth, creation.

The first book of the Judeo-Christian Bible is called Genesis because it describes God's creation, the origin of the universe and humankind. In current usage *genesis* may refer in a general sense to any creation or process of coming into being: the genesis of an idea; the genesis of a work of art; the genesis of an important social movement; the genesis of a distinguished career.

Word 40: WARRANT (WAHR-int)

To justify, give good reason for, authorize, sanction: the circumstances do not warrant such extraordinary measures; the evidence warrants further investigation; these safety procedures are warranted (WAHR-in-tid) by company regulations.

Warrant may also mean to guarantee, promise, give formal assurance of: the Postal Service will not warrant delivery on a specific day; the manufacturer warrants the safety of the product.

The adjective *unwarranted* means without good reason or authorization, unjustifiable: the U.S. Constitution protects citizens against unwarranted search and seizure; people resent unwarranted government interference in private enterprise.

Let's review the ten words you've just learned.

This time we're going to play a version of the *Sesame Street* game "One of These Things Is Not Like the Others" called "One of These Definitions Doesn't Fit the Word."

In each statement below, a word is followed by three apparent—or ostensible—synonyms. Two of the three words or phrases are true synonyms; one is unrelated in meaning. Which ostensible synonym doesn't fit the word? Answers appear on page 24.

1. *Manifold* means complicated, numerous, varied.
2. *Pliant* means flexible, supple, graceful.
3. *Retort* means a reply, comment, response.
4. *Obstinate* means nasty, stubborn, uncompromising.
5. *Lacerate* means to disrupt, mangle, tear.
6. *Omnipotent* means all-powerful, almighty, all-knowing.
7. *Unscrupulous* means selfish, untrustworthy, corrupt.
8. *Renaissance* means revival, reevaluation, rebirth.
9. *Genesis* means creation, origin, completion.
10. *Warrant* means to justify, guarantee, obligate.

Now let's learn the final ten keywords in Level 1.

Word 41: CANTANKEROUS (kan-TANGK-uh-r<u>u</u>s)

Difficult to deal with, disagreeable, argumentative, quick to quarrel or to exhibit ill will.

A cantankerous old man is ill-tempered and disagreeable. Cantankerous relatives are argumentative and hard to get along with.

Cantankerous comes from a Middle English word meaning strife, contention. Synonyms of cantankerous include *contentious* (k<u>u</u>n-TEN-sh<u>u</u>s), which means quarrelsome, prone to argue or dispute; *malicious*, which means mean-spirited, nasty, spiteful; and *irascible* (i-RAS-uh-b<u>u</u>l), which means quick-tempered, easily angered, extremely irritable.

Word 42: FLIPPANT (FLIP-'nt)

Disrespectful in a frivolous way, treating something serious in a trivial manner.

Flippant refers to speech or writing that trivializes or makes fun of something that deserves respect. Flippant language is inappropriately lighthearted or disrespectful: "Everyone at the meeting gasped when Harry made a flippant remark about the board of directors."

Although flippant expression generally causes dismay or offense, occasionally it may be humorous, depending on your point of view. For example, many talk show hosts today are adept at making flippant comments to dismiss guests or callers with opposing points of view.

Synonyms of *flippant* include *cheeky*, *fresh*, *thoughtless*, and *impertinent*. Antonyms include *solemn*, *sober*, *sedate*, and *grave*.

Word 43: SUBJUGATE (SUHB-juh-gayt)

To conquer, defeat, vanquish, overwhelm completely, bring under rigid control, make submissive, dominate, enslave.

Subjugate comes from the Latin *sub-*, under, and *jugum*, a yoke, and means literally to place under a yoke. It is related to the noun a *subject*, which in one of its senses means a person under the control of a ruler, as a subject of the king. A subject is someone who has been subjugated, made submissive, brought under control, enslaved.

The words *defeat*, *conquer*, and *subjugate* are generally synonymous but are used in slightly different ways. *Defeat* suggests winning or beating an opponent in a single engagement; you can defeat a person in an argument, a contest, a game, or a fight. *Conquer* suggests achieving a final victory or gaining complete control over an opponent after a series of contests: "After a long and arduous campaign, Caesar conquered the Gauls." *Subjugate* adds to *defeat* and *conquer* the suggestion of domination, bringing the vanquished opponent under complete and rigid control: "During World War II, Hitler conquered most of Europe and then brutally subjugated its people."

Subjugation need not apply only to war; it may also refer to psychological domination. For example, you may subjugate an addiction, subjugate an impulse, or subjugate an emotion—yoke it, make it submit to your will, bring it under complete control.

Word 44: WRY (like *rye*)

Twisted, crooked, lopsided, askew, distorted in an odd, amusing way.

By derivation *wry* means twisted, but in modern usage it has come to imply twisted in a peculiar and often humorous manner.

A wry smile or grin is crooked, lopsided, and therefore comical. A wry remark has a funny or sarcastic twist to it. A person with a wry sense of humor is capable of twisting or distorting things in a laughable way.

Word 45: URBANE (ur-BAYN)

Polished, sophisticated, suave, cosmopolitan.

Urbane is related to the adjective *urban*, pertaining to or living in a city. *Urbane* suggests the polite, polished style of a sophisticated city dweller. The word may be used either of suave, socially refined behavior or of expression that is polished and elegant: "Mary's stunning designer dresses and witty, urbane conversation made her a popular guest at all the high-society parties."

Word 46: JARGON (JAHR-gun)

Specialized and often pretentious language; speech or writing that is highly technical and difficult to understand.

Jargon refers especially to the specialized language or private vocabulary used and understood only by members of a particular group or profession. Medical jargon is the specialized vocabulary used by doctors; computerese is the jargon or highly technical language of computer science; legal jargon comprises the particular stock of Latin terms and complex phraseology used by lawyers.

Jargon develops initially as a means for the members of a particular group to communicate precisely and efficiently; its inevitable consequence, however, is to confuse and exclude those who are not members of the group and who are unfamiliar with the jargon. In current usage, therefore, jargon has come to mean any pretentious speech or writing that seems unnecessarily difficult to understand: "Savvy businesspeople know that using a lot of professional jargon will only alienate clients."

Word 47: PRUDENT (PROO-dint)

Cautious, careful, planning wisely, exercising sound judgment in practical matters.

Synonyms include *discreet* (di-SKREET), *judicious* (joo-DISH-us), and *circumspect* (SUR-kum-spekt).

Prudent may also mean spending carefully, using one's resources wisely. Synonyms of *prudent* in this sense include *thrifty*, *economical*, and *frugal*.

Prudent and *circumspect* both refer to people who proceed cautiously. *Circumspect* comes from the Latin *circum-*, around, and *specere*, to look, observe. The circumspect person looks around carefully to make sure that no unforseen circumstance will frustrate a plan of action. *Prudent* comes from the same Latin source as the verb to *provide*. Prudent people are concerned with protecting their personal interest and providing for a rainy day. They are characterized by their sound, careful judgment in handling practical matters, especially money.

Word 48: INVIOLABLE (in-VY-ul-uh-bul)

Secure, safe from assault, infringement, or destruction, sacred, untouchable, unassailable, incorruptible.

Inviolable combines the prefix *in-*, not, the suffix *-able*, and the verb to *violate*, and means literally "not able to be violated." An inviolable peace between nations cannot be broken or disrupted. An inviolable contract cannot be breached, altered, or revoked. An inviolable oath or promise is sacred, secure, incorruptible. Inviolable rights cannot be abused or taken away; they are safe from infringement or assault. An inviolable place cannot be violated or trespassed upon; it is safe, secure, unassailable.

Word 49: COMMODIOUS (kuh-MOH-dee-us)

Spacious, having plenty of room, comfortably convenient. Synonyms of *commodious* include *ample* and *capacious* (kuh-PAY-shus).

Commodious comes through French from the Latin *commodus*, convenience, suitability, the source also of *commode*, a euphemism for *toilet* that means literally "something convenient or suitable." From the same Latin *commodus*, convenience, come the verb *accommodate* and the noun *accommodations*, sleeping quarters, lodging. If you find your *accommodations* accommodating—convenient, suitable to your needs—then chances are they are also *commodious*, spacious, roomy, comfortable, and convenient.

Word 50: PROXIMITY (prahk-SIM-i-tee)

Nearness, closeness, the state of being in the vicinity of something.

Proximity may be used either of persons or things to mean nearness in place, time, or relation: the proximity of their houses; the proximity of historic events; the proximity of two ideas. In modern society, marriage between first cousins is forbidden because of their proximity of blood relation. However, if you marry the girl or boy next door, it might be said that proximity was the deciding factor.

You will often hear *proximity* used in the phrase "close proximity." That is a redundancy. *Proximity* means closeness, nearness; therefore "close proximity" means "close closeness" or "near nearness." According to the second college edition of *The American Heritage Dictionary*, "the expression *close proximity* says nothing that is not said by *proximity* itself."

Usage tip: Drop *close* and let *proximity* do its work alone.

Let's review the ten keywords you've just learned—the last ten words in Level 1. This time the review word will be followed by three words or phrases, and you decide which of those three answer choices comes nearest the meaning of the review word. Answers appear on page 24.

1. Does *cantankerous* mean stubborn, disagreeable, or violent?
2. Does *flippant* mean disrespectful, outrageous, or peculiar?
3. Does *subjugate* mean to request, to calm down, or to conquer?
4. Does *wry* mean wrong, twisted, or painful?
5. Does *urbane* mean awkward, aloof, or sophisticated?
6. Does *jargon* refer to a humorous reply, a confusing remark, or a specialized vocabulary?
7. Does *prudent* mean cautious and thrifty, stiff and formal, or hasty and thoughtless?
8. Does *inviolable* mean secure, vague, or not allowed?
9. Does *commodious* mean appropriate, spacious, or friendly?
10. Does *proximity* mean relation, distance, or nearness?

Let's wind up Level 1 with a lighthearted look at a grave grammatical pitfall.

Lie Down and I'll Lay It on You

Failure to distinguish between the verbs to *lay* and to *lie* is one of the most common errors among educated adults. It is a relatively simple distinction that is not hard to grasp, and once learned it becomes second nature. Furthermore, those who observe the difference have the distinct advantage of speaking properly and sounding perfectly natural at the same time. You will never be considered affected or pretentious for using these verbs correctly.

Now, since this *lay* and *lie* lesson has been *laid* down countless times before, and since I would rather that you sit up and take note of what I am saying rather than *lie* down and go to sleep, I have composed an illustrative (i-LUHStruh-tiv) anecdote to once more give the *lie* to *lay*. (In this story, when you see *lie* and *lay* used without *italics*, it's wrong.)

I would like to say I was just *lying* around one day, but actually I was leaving a restaurant with some friends after *laying* down a generous tip. As we strolled toward our car, we passed a man barking at his dog, which, in my experience, happens rather more often than the other way around.

"Lay down," the man said.

The dog sat, his tongue lolling.

"Lay down," said the man again, growing impatient.

The dog continued to sit, looking curiously at his master.

Overhearing this, one of my friends said, under his breath, "Maybe if you told that dog to *lie* down, he might do what you want."

"Lay down," the dog's master bellowed, as if to silence my friend's criticism. Then, perhaps feeling guilty for raising his voice in public, the man begged his pet softly, "Please lay down."

The plea fell upon large, floppy, obstinate ears.

"Why won't you lay down?" the man groaned as my friends and I climbed into our car.

The answer is, my friend was right: That dog was dead set against *lying* down for a master who didn't know how to *lay* down the law with good diction. The master may be the one blessed with the faculty of speech, but the dog was the better judge of what constitutes correct English.

Here's the difference:

To *lie* means to rest, recline, be situated. You *lie* on a bed, rest there, recline on it.

To *lay* means to put, place, set. You *lay* a book on a table, put or set it there; you *lay* your head on a pillow, place it on the pillow. Whatever you can put down you can also *lay* down. You can *lay* something down, but you can't lay down, rest, recline. You can *lie* down, but you can't lie something down. That's simple, right?

Now, here's where it gets a bit tricky.

The past tense of *lie* is *lay*: "Last night I *lay* in bed." It is wrong to say that you laid in bed, because *laid* is the past tense of the verb to *lay*, which means to put, place. You wouldn't say "Last night I put in bed," would you? (If you laid in bed last night, you are a chicken.)

Here's how the tenses break down for the verb to lay (put, place): You *lay* a book down today; you *laid* it down yesterday; and you have *laid* it down anytime in the past.

Here's how the tenses break down for the verb *to lie* (rest, recline): When you're tired you *lie* down; when you were tired yesterday you *lay* down; and when you have been tired in the past you have *lain* down. (*Lain* is always preceded by *have* or *had*.)

Okay, here's a pop quiz (answers appear below):

1. Which verb means to put, place, prepare?
2. Which verb means to rest, recline, be situated?
3. Do you lay something down or lie it down?
4. On weekends do you lay or lie around the house?
5. Were you laying in bed last night or lying in bed?
6. Have you laid in bed before or lain in bed before?
7. Have you lain books on the sofa or have you laid them there?

Here's the final, sixty-four-thousand-dollar question: Do you lay down on a bed or lie down on it? (Well, if you're a dog, you'd better lie down on the rug if you know what's good for you.)

Answers:

on a bed, of course!
have laid them there. Sixty-four-thousand-dollar question: You lie down
you. 7. You have lain there before. 6. Your bed is full of eggs. 7. You
chicken and your bed is full of eggs. 6. You have lain there before. 7. You
lying in bed last night. If you were laying in bed last night, you are a
were you. 5. You lie around the house. 4. You lay it down. 3. Lie. 2. Lay. 1.

And with that dogged account of the distinction between *lay* and *lie*, we come to the end of Level 1. I hope you've enjoyed the material so far. You may have found some of the keywords familiar, but keep going because there are more challenging levels to come, each chock-full of useful information on hundreds of English words.

By now you should have established your vocabulary-building routine. I cannot overemphasize the fact that review is essential to ensure full comprehension and retention of what you've learned. For best results, I recommend that you spend at least one or two reading sessions going over this entire level again before proceeding to Level 2, which begins with a discussion of the relationship between vocabulary building and reading.

Answers to Review Quizzes for Level 1

Keywords 1–10

1. Yes. To *paraphrase* is to put what someone else has expressed into different words.
2. No. *Ostensible* means apparent, appearing or seeming to be true but not necessarily true.
3. No. Someone who speaks with *candor*, frankness, openness, sincerity, would not be likely to *digress*, stray from the point, wander away from the subject.
4. Yes, indeed. *Uncanny* means beyond what is normal or expected, strange in a remarkable or unsettling way.
5. No. *Morose* and *congenial* suggest opposite moods. A person who is *morose*, gloomy, bitterly depressed, is not likely to be *congenial*, sympathetic, willing to agree or get along.
6. Yes. *Adept* means skilled, handy, proficient.
7. No. *Pragmatic* means practical, based on practice rather than speculation.
8. Yes, it can. To *saturate* means to soak thoroughly, drench completely, permeate, either literally or figuratively.

Keywords 11–20

1. False. *Capricious* means fickle, inconstant, changeable.
2. False. *Blatant* means unpleasantly noisy and conspicuous.
3. True. *Obligatory* means required, necessary, mandatory.
4. True. *Negligible* means unimportant, of little consequence.
5. True. *Adamant* means inflexible, unyielding, unwilling to give in.
6. False. *Sporadic* means occasional, irregular, happening every now and then.
7. True. The *vanguard* is the forefront of an action or movement, the leading position.
8. False. To *concur* is to agree, be in accord.
9. True. *Precociousness* means early development or maturity, especially in mental ability.
10. True. *Aloof* means apart, at a distance, emotionally reserved and unapproachable.

Keywords 21–30

1. Synonyms. *Creed* means belief, especially a system of religious belief.
2. Antonyms. *Tawdry* means cheap and showy, of inferior quality.
3. Synonyms. *Peevish* means irritable, cross, complaining.

4. Synonyms. *Arduous* means difficult, hard to accomplish.
5. Antonyms. *Personable* means attractive.
6. Antonyms. *Resolute* means unwavering, determined, resolved.
7. Synonyms. A *supposition* is an assumption, theory, idea put forward for consideration.
8. Antonyms. *Arbitrary* means unreasoned, based on personal feelings or preferences rather than on reason, logic, or law.
9. Antonyms. *Monotonous* means lacking variety, unvarying, uniform and dull.
10. Synonyms. A *bequest* is a gift made through a will; a *legacy* is an inheritance, something handed down from the past.

Keywords 31–40

1. *Complicated* doesn't fit. *Manifold* means numerous and varied.
2. *Graceful* doesn't fit. *Pliant* means bending easily, flexible, supple.
3. *Comment* doesn't fit. A *retort* is a quick reply, especially one that is cutting or witty.
4. *Nasty* doesn't fit. *Obstinate* means stubborn, uncompromising.
5. *Disrupt* doesn't fit. *Lacerate* means to tear, mangle, wound.
6. *All-knowing* doesn't fit; *omniscient* means all-knowing. *Omnipotent* means all-powerful, having unlimited power.
7. *Selfish* doesn't fit. A selfish person may or may not be *unscrupulous,* untrustworthy, unreliable, dishonest, corrupt.
8. *Reevaluation* doesn't fit. *Renaissance* means rebirth, revival, resurgence.
9. *Completion* doesn't fit. The *genesis* of something is its creation, beginning, origin, process of coming into being.
10. *Obligate* doesn't fit. To *warrant* means to justify, authorize, or guarantee.

Keywords 41–50

1. *Cantankerous* means disagreeable, argumentative, difficult to deal with.
2. *Flippant* means disrespectful in a frivolous way, treating something serious in a trivial manner.
3. *Subjugate* means to conquer, overwhelm completely, bring under rigid control.
4. *Wry* means twisted or distorted in an odd, amusing way.
5. *Urbane* means polished, sophisticated, suave, cosmopolitan.
6. *Jargon* is a specialized and often pretentious vocabulary, language that is highly technical and difficult to understand.
7. *Prudent* means cautious, exercising careful judgment in practical matters, thrifty, spending carefully.
8. *Inviolable* means secure, safe, not able to be violated.
9. *Commodious* means spacious, roomy, comfortably convenient.
10. *Proximity* means nearness, closeness.

Review Test for Level 1

1. Which word means to restate in different words?

(a) attribute
(b) repeat
(c) quote
(d) paraphrase

2. Which word is an antonym of *ostensible*?

(a) avowed
(b) plausible
(c) specious
(d) demonstrable

3. *Digress*, *ingress*, and *egress* all come from the Latin *gradi*, which means

(a) to stay
(b) to run
(c) to walk
(d) to enter

4. Which word is *not* a synonym of *morose*?

(a) dolorous
(b) saturnine
(c) sullen
(d) jovial
(e) lugubrious

5. Select the nearest synonym of *whimsical*, *volatile*, and *mercurial*.

(a) arbitrary
(b) capricious
(c) cantankerous
(d) abrupt

6. Which word is an antonym of *sporadic*?

(a) incessant
(b) occasional
(c) temporary
(d) intermittent

7. Which is *not* an accepted meaning of *concur*?

(a) agree
(b) act together

(c) arrive together

(d) happen together

8. *Credible* and *credulous* come from the Latin *credo*, which means

   (a) I know

   (b) I believe

   (c) I hope

   (d) I am

9. Who is associated with the origin of *tawdry*?

   (a) the Bard of Avon

   (b) King Arthur

   (c) Saint Andrew

   (d) Saint Audrey

10. Which word is an antonym of *resolute*?

    (a) vacillating

    (b) peevish

    (c) rational

    (d) careless

11. Which is *not* an accepted meaning of *arbitrary*?

    (a) random

    (b) illogical

    (c) consistent

    (d) exercising unrestrained power

12. Which prefix means "one, single"?

    (a) auto-

    (b) mono-

    (c) proto-

    (d) mini-

13. The phrases *large in size* and *small in size* are objectionable because

    (a) they are monotonous

    (b) they are vague

    (c) they are redundant

    (d) they are inaccurate

14. Which word is a synonym of *supple*?

    (a) flimsy

    (b) flexible

    (c) fragile

    (d) rigid

15. In *retort* and *rejoinder*, the prefix *re-* means
   (a) toward
   (b) against
   (c) back
   (d) twice

16. Which pair of words is *not* synonymous?
   (a) hidebound, intransigent
   (b) stubborn, adamant
   (c) intractable, unyielding
   (d) obstinate, circumspect

17. Which word means all-knowing, having universal knowledge?
   (a) omniscient
   (b) omnivorous
   (c) omnipresent
   (d) omnipotent

18. Which word is *not* a synonym of *renaissance*?
   (a) revival
   (b) reproduction
   (c) renewal
   (d) resurgence

19. Which word does *not* describe a cantankerous person?
   (a) malicious
   (b) affable
   (c) irascible
   (d) contentious

20. Which word means inappropriately lighthearted or disrespectful?
   (a) wry
   (b) tawdry
   (c) flippant
   (d) urbane

21. Which word means old-fashioned, belonging to an earlier time?
   (a) obsolete
   (b) adamantine
   (c) precocious
   (d) archaic

22. Which word means hatred of humankind?
   (a) moroseness

(b) impertinence

(c) misanthropy

(d) cantankerousness

23. Which word is a synonym of *aloof*?

   (a) indifferent

   (b) sullen

   (c) urbane

   (d) flippant

24. What is a *peeve*?

   (a) something interesting and different

   (b) something negligible

   (c) something conspicuous and disagreeable

   (d) something that irritates or annoys

25. Which is the proper pronunciation of *Realtor*?

   (a) REE-luh-tur

   (b) REE-<u>ul</u>-tur

26. Which phrase is redundant?

   (a) in proximity

   (b) in close proximity

27. Which word means having great variety or diversity?

   (a) multifarious

   (b) multitudinous

   (c) multifaceted

28. What is a *digression*?

   (a) an effect or feeling

   (b) an injury or offense

   (c) a straying from the point

   (d) a double meaning

29. What does the prefix *omni-* mean?

   (a) all

   (b) above

   (c) many

   (d) everywhere

30. Which word is *not* a synonym of *subjugate*?

   (a) enslave

   (b) battle

(c) conquer

(d) defeat

31. Which word does *not* describe jargon?

    (a) specialized

    (b) technical

    (c) pretentious

    (d) candid

32. *Laborious* and *toilsome* are synonyms of which word?

    (a) monotonous

    (b) commodious

    (c) arduous

    (d) credulous

33. Which word means trivial, insignificant?

    (a) wry

    (b) unwarranted

    (c) inviolable

    (d) negligible

34. What is a *scruple*?

    (a) a guarantee or promise

    (b) something that causes hesitation or doubt

    (c) something mean-spirited or nasty

    (d) a judgment based on little evidence

35. Which word does *not* properly describe a renaissance?

    (a) refinement

    (b) renewal

    (c) resurgence

    (d) revival

Answers

1. d 2. d 3. c 4. d 5. b 6. a 7. c 8. b 9. d 10. a 11. c 12. b 13. c
14. b 15. c 16. d 17. a 18. b 19. b 20. c 21. d 22. c 23. a 24. d 25. d
26. b 27. a 28. c 29. a 30. b 31. d 32. c 33. d 34. b 35. a

Evaluation

A score of 30–35 is excellent. If you answered fewer than thirty questions in this test correctly, review the entire level and take the test again.

Level 2

In the introduction to this program I discussed the importance of building a powerful vocabulary. Now let's take a moment to discuss how powerful vocabularies are built.

There are many ways to enrich your knowledge of words. You may have seen the feature "It Pays to Enrich Your Word Power" that has been running for years in *Reader's Digest*. Its vocabulary quizzes are fun, but unless you review the words several times and put them to work right away in your conversation and writing, the definitions are soon forgotten and you are back where you started. Moreover, the words are not presented in order of difficulty. They are a miscellaneous assortment, with easier words mixed in with more difficult ones.

If you already know the easier words, testing you on them does nothing but flatter your ego. Likewise, if the harder words are beyond your vocabulary level, then your chances of retaining them are slim. In such a random quiz, designed for a mass audience, it's doubtful that more than two or three of the words in each month's list will be challenging and useful to you. Not to mention that a month is a long time to wait to learn a handful of new words.

So, what else can you do to improve your knowledge of words? Well, any disciplined and structured study of words is always more beneficial than casual exposure. And if you have the discipline, *Verbal Advantage* will provide the structure. Unlike most other vocabulary-building books and programs, which force-feed you a random selection of words and definitions that you must learn by rote, this one introduces you to words in their order of difficulty, accompanied by relevant information on where they come from, how they are properly used, and how to avoid common errors of usage and pronunciation.

But there is another way to build your vocabulary that is even more effective than *Verbal Advantage*. Vocabulary-building books and courses are an excellent start, but they cannot cover everything you need to know, and both must at some point come to an end. That is where the primary method of vocabulary building comes in.

Have you guessed what it is? It's reading. Simple, but oh-so-true.

If you wish to continue to build your vocabulary after completing this program—in fact, if you want to retain the words you know right now—you must start reading more, reading widely, and reading something—even if it's just a few pages at first—every single day.

That, of course, requires discipline. You need to set aside some time each day to read. An hour is great, but most of us have a hard time finding an hour when we can be undisturbed. You should be able to schedule thirty minutes, though, without too much trouble, and even fifteen minutes of reading a day will help, provided you stick to it and choose your material with an eye toward building your knowledge of words.

What should I read? is the next question. Well, let's start with what you read now.

Most people spend fifteen or twenty minutes a day reading a newspaper. But the newspaper is not the best place to find new words, simply because most newspapers are written in elementary, everyday language. That is no accident, nor is it a comment on the inferior abilities of the nation's journalists. Newspapers must serve the general public, and the general public consists mostly of low-vocabulary readers. However, some newspapers contain excellent writing—*The New York Times*, the *Los Angeles Times*, *The Wall Street Journal*, and *The Christian Science Monitor* are particularly well written. Also, certain sections within any given newspaper are generally written better than others.

For instance, in the editorial pages you will read some of your paper's most talented writers and the syndicated columns of some of the finest journalists in the nation as well. Regardless of which newspaper you read, you will not do much for your vocabulary if you read only the sports section, the society page, the advice columns, or the funnies. If you're looking for interesting, useful words to add to your vocabulary, how about trying the theater, book, movie, and restaurant reviews? Many people also find the crossword puzzle a helpful vocabulary-building tool.

Weekly news magazines such as *Time*, *Newsweek*, and *U.S. News and World Report* can also provide a nutritious diet of good writing and challenging words, as well as the added benefit of keeping you up-to-date without taking up a lot of your time. And while you're at it, be sure to note the headlines of all the articles you read; they can be a veritable gold mine of new words. Headline writers must find the shortest, sweetest way to capture the essence of a story, and often that means dredging up such stumpers as *eschew*, *aver*, *impugn*, *distaff*, and *bruit*.

Are you familiar with those words? Let's take a brief look at them. *Eschew* (es-CHOO, like letter *s* + *chew*) means to avoid, shun, as to eschew alcohol. *Aver* (uh-VUR) means to assert, declare, state positively, as to aver one's faith or innocence. *Impugn* (im-PYOON) means to oppose in words, attack by argument, question or criticize the truth or integrity of, as to impugn authority or impugn someone's reputation. *Distaff* (DIS-taf) means female, pertaining to women, as in the distaff side of a family, which is opposed to the *spear* side, the male line of descent. Finally, to *bruit* (like *brute*) means to report widely, spread the word, as the scandal was bruited (BROO-tid) in the media.

If you have a hobby or particular area of interest outside of your occupation, you should subscribe to a publication that specializes in it. Articles on hunting, fishing, gardening, mechanics, parenting, cooking, antiques, travel, and a host of other subjects frequently contain uncommon words. For example, did you know that a stamp collector is called a *philatelist* (fi-LAT-uh-list, with -LAT- as in *flat*), a coin collector is a *numismatist* (n(y)oo-MIZ-muh-tist), and the word for a magician who specializes in sleight-of-hand is *prestidigitator* (PRES-ti-**DIJ**-i-tay-tur)?

In an article on exercise in a health magazine you might run across a medical term like *pulmonary* (PUUL-muh-ner-ee or PUHL-muh-ner-ee), pertaining to the lungs, or *vascular* (VAS-kyuh-lur), pertaining to the blood vessels. In magazines specializing in food and wine you may find such delicious words as *gastronome* (GAS-truh-nohm), a lover and connoisseur of fine food; *indigenous* (in-DIJ-i-nus), belonging or native to a particular country or region; and *sommelier* (suhm-ul-YAY, also sawm-), the wine steward in a restaurant.

Recently I read an article on the nineteenth-century French painter Edgar Degas (de-GAH). It was published in a national fashion magazine that does not have a reputation for catering to a high-vocabulary audience. In just the first two pages, however, I found the following high-vocabulary words: *vignette* (vin-YET), a literary sketch, short composition; *redolent* (RED-uh-lint), which means exuding a fragrance, aromatic; *simian* (SIM-ee-in), which means pertaining to or resembling an ape; *libido* (li-BEE-doh), which means sexual drive; *misogyny* (mi-SAHJ-i-nee), which means hatred of women; *salacious* (suh-LAY-shus), which means arousing sexual desire; *assiduous* (uh-SIJ-oo-us), which means careful and persistent; and *ennui* (ahn-WEE), which means boredom or a state of weary dissatisfaction.

The point is, interesting, challenging, and useful words are everywhere in your everyday reading if you want to find them. The key is to keep your eyes and ears open and don't let any of them slip by.

So whenever you read, make a conscious effort to *look for words you don't know*, and *keep a dictionary handy* while you're reading so you can look them up right away. If you can't always read with a dictionary beside you, then highlight or underline the unfamiliar words in your reading, or dog-ear the pages on which they occur, so you can look up the words later. Reading with an eye for unfamiliar words and reading with a dictionary are the two best ways you can continue to enrich your vocabulary after you finish this program.

Now let's delve into the second level of the *Verbal Advantage* vocabulary. Here are the first ten keywords:

Word 1: ADVOCATE (AD-vuh-kayt)

To support, plead for, be in favor of, defend by argument; especially, to speak or write in favor or in defense of a person or cause. Synonyms include *champion*, *endorse*, and *espouse* (e-SPOWZ).

Advocate comes from the Latin *ad-*, to, and *vocare*, to call, summon. You can hear the Latin *vocare* in the English words *vocation* (voh-KAY-shin), a calling, profession; avocation, a hobby, sideline, subordinate occupation; and *vocational*, pertaining to an occupation or trade.

Combine the Latin *vocare*, to call, with the prefix *con-*, together, and you get the more difficult English words *convoke* (kun-VOHK), which means to call together, and *convocation* (KAHN-vuh-**KAY**-shin), the act of calling together or a group that has been summoned. Combine the single-letter prefix *e-*, which is short for the Latin *ex-*, out, with *vocare*, to call, and you get the English words *evoke*, to call out, call forth, summon, and *evocative* (i-VAHK-uh-tiv), calling forth a response, especially an emotional response. *Vocare* also can be heard in the common word *vocal*, spoken, oral, inclined to speak out.

An advocate is a vocal supporter or defender of a cause, a champion: "He is an outspoken advocate of handgun control." An advocate may also be a person who speaks for another, for example, a lawyer who pleads a case before a court. To *advocate* means to support, plead for, defend by argument: "Their organization advocates educational reform."

Word 2: DELEGATE (DEL-uh-gayt)

To entrust with authority or power, deliver to another's care or management, hand over to an agent or representative: "The executive director delegated various managerial duties to her assistant"; "Our department chief has trouble letting go of the reins and delegating responsibility."

Word 3: UNPRECEDENTED (uhn-PRES-i-den-tid)

Unheard-of, novel, new, having no precedent or parallel, having no prior example.

A *precedent* is an authoritative example, something done or said that may serve as a reason to justify a later act or statement. *Precedent* is often used specifically of a legal decision or case used as an example or as authorization in a subsequent decision or case. *Unprecedented* means without a precedent, without prior example or justification, and so unheard-of, novel, new.

Word 4: POIGNANT (POYN-yint)

Piercing, sharp, biting, penetrating, keen.

Poignant is used to mean piercing, sharp, or penetrating in three ways. First, it may mean keenly affecting the senses: a poignant odor, poignant beauty, a poignant look. Second, it may mean piercing or penetrating to the feelings, emotionally touching, painfully moving: a poignant drama, a poignant family reunion. Third, it may mean biting, cutting, acute, piercingly effective: poignant wit, poignant delight, a poignant critique.

The odd spelling of *poignant*, with its silent *g*, comes from French; the word ultimately comes from the Latin *pungere*, to pierce or prick. *Pungere* is also the source of *puncture*, to pierce; *pungent* (PUHN-jint), piercing to the smell or taste; and *expunge* (ek-SPUHNJ), to punch out, erase, delete: "The editor expunged all potentially offensive and derogatory material from the book."

Poignant means piercing or penetrating to the senses, to the emotions, or to the intellect.

Word 5: NEBULOUS (NEB-yuh-lus)

Unclear, vague, obscure, hazy, indefinite, indistinct.

In astronomy the word *nebula* (NEB-yuh-luh) refers to a cloudy mass of dust or gas visible between stars in space. The plural is *nebulae* (NEB-yuh-lee).

The adjectives *nebular* and *nebulous* both come from a Latin word meaning cloudy, misty, foggy, like a nebula, and according to dictionaries both words may still be used in this sense. It is probably best, however, to let *nebular* take over the meaning cloudy, misty, vaporous, and to use *nebulous* in its more popular sense of vague, indefinite, hazy, unclear, as in nebulous writing, a nebulous idea, a nebulous purpose or goal.

Word 6: CLANDESTINE (klan-DES-tin)

Kept secret, done in secrecy, especially for an evil, immoral, or illegal purpose: a clandestine affair; a clandestine business deal; a clandestine intelligence operation.

Synonyms include *private, concealed, covert* (properly KUH-vurt but now often KOH-vurt), *underhand, sly, stealthy, furtive* (FUR-tiv), and *surreptitious* (SUR-up-**TISH**-us).

Clandestine is sometimes pronounced klan-DES-tyn, klan-DES-teen, KLAN-des-tyn, or KLAN-des-teen. You should avoid all these recent variants. The traditional and preferred pronunciation is klan-DES-tin (DES-tin as in *destiny*).

Word 7: TIRADE (TY-rayd)

A long-drawn-out speech, especially a vehement and abusive one: "After suffering through yet another one of his boss's frequent tirades, Joe decided it was time to quit and move on."

Tirades have three characteristics: they are *protracted* (proh-TRAK-tid), drawn out to great length; they are *vituperative* (vy-T(Y)OO-pur-uh-tiv), full of harsh, abusive language; and they are *censorious*, meaning that they tend to *censure* (SEN-shur), to blame or condemn.

Tirade may also be pronounced with the accent on the second syllable: ty-RAYD.

Word 8: RECUR (ri-KUR)

To happen again, occur again, especially at intervals or after some lapse of time.

In *The Careful Writer*, Theodore M. Bernstein explains the difference between the words *recur* and *reoccur*: Both mean to happen again, he says, but *reoccur* "suggests a one-time repetition," whereas *recur* "suggests repetition more than once." Thus you would say "the revolt is not likely to reoccur," but "as long as these skirmishes recur, the revolt will continue."

Here's another example: If economists predict that a recession will reoccur in this decade, that means they're predicting it will happen only one more time. If economists predict that recession recurs on average every ten years, then they're predicting it happens again and again at intervals.

"It is the ability to feel a fine distinction such as this," writes Bernstein, "and to choose the word that precisely expresses the thought that marks the writer of competence and taste."

Word 9: TACIT (TAS-it)

Unspoken, silent, implied or understood without words.

Tacit is most often used to mean done or made in silence, not expressed or declared openly. Tacit consent is approval given without words, perhaps with a look or a nod. A tacit agreement is an unspoken understanding, one arrived at in silence. *Tacit* comes from the Latin *tacere*, to be silent, hold one's tongue, the source also of the word taciturn, reserved, uncommunicative, inclined to hold one's tongue.

Word 10: ALLEGATION (AL-uh-GAY-shin)

An assertion or declaration, especially one made without proof.

In law, an allegation is an assertion of what one intends to prove. Often the word implies an unsupportable assertion: "The judge dismissed the allegations, citing lack of evidence to support them." "A spokesperson for the company today denied the allegations of wrongdoing regarding the firm's hiring practices."

Let's review the ten words you've just learned. Read the following questions. After each one, decide whether the correct answer is yes or no. Answers appear on page 63.

1. Can someone advocate an unworthy cause?
2. Can you seize or maintain control by delegating it?
3. If something has happened before, is it unprecedented?
4. Can a strong odor, a passionate and persuasive speech, and an emotionally moving story all be described as poignant?
5. Can a poignant sensation or thought be nebulous?
6. Are clandestine arrangements made in public?
7. Are tirades ever delivered in a clandestine manner?
8. Could an unprecedented event ever recur?
9. Is an oral agreement also a tacit agreement?
10. Can a tirade contain an allegation?

Let's move on now and learn the next ten keywords in Level 2. Here they are:

Word 11: GULLIBLE (GUHL-uh-bul)

Easily deceived, fooled, or cheated.

A more difficult synonym of *gullible* is *credulous* (KREJ-uh-lus). *Credulous* comes from the Latin *credere*, to believe, and means inclined to believe, willing to accept something as true without questioning.

To *gull* is to take advantage of someone who is foolish, unwary, or inexperienced. The gullible person is easily gulled, fooled, cheated. To *dupe* and to *gull* both mean to take advantage of. *Dupe* suggests unwariness on the part of the victim; *gull* suggests a willingness or readiness to be deceived.

Word 12: BENIGN (bi-NYN, rhymes with *resign*)

Kindly, good-natured, gracious, mild, having or showing a gentle disposition, as a benign old man, a benign smile, a benign intention, a benign government.

That is the first meaning of *benign* listed in dictionaries, and probably the most common. The word is also used in several other ways. It may mean favorable, positive, propitious: a benign omen; a benign view. It may be used of the weather or climate to mean healthful, wholesome, salubrious. And in medicine *benign* means mild, not deadly or severe, as a benign tumor or disease.

Word 13: PERIPHERAL (puh-RIF-uh-rul)

External, outer, lying at or forming the outside or boundary of something; hence, not essential, irrelevant.

The noun *periphery* means the boundary, the external surface or area. It may be used literally, as in "exploring the periphery of the polar icecap," "situated on the periphery of the combat zone"; or it may be used figuratively, as in "the periphery of consciousness," "the periphery of one's sphere of influence."

Peripheral may mean external in the literal sense of lying at the edge or on the boundary, or external in the figurative sense of irrelevant, nonessential, as peripheral issues, a peripheral point, or peripheral considerations.

Word 14: REBUFF (ri-BUHF)

To refuse bluntly, reject sharply, turn down abruptly, snub, spurn.

In colloquial terms—that is, in informal, conversational language—*rebuff* means to give the cold shoulder to, slam the door on, nix. A *rebuff* is an abrupt refusal or rejection, especially of a request, an offer to help, or a person making advances. To *rebuff* means to refuse or reject bluntly.

Word 15: ANIMOSITY (AN-i-MAHS-i-tee)

Ill will, hostility, antagonism, strong dislike or hatred: "There was long-standing animosity between the two families." "After her coworker apologized for his rude remarks, she resolved not to harbor any animosity toward him."

More difficult synonyms of *animosity* include *malice* (MAL-is), *aversion* (uh-VER-zhun), *malevolence* (muh-LEV-uh-lints), *antipathy* (an-TIP-uh-thee), *rancor* (RANG-kur), and *enmity* (EN-mi-tee).

Word 16: TENUOUS (TEN-yoo-us)

Thin, slender, slight, flimsy, weak, not dense or substantial, lacking a strong basis.

At high altitudes, air is *tenuous*, thin. In chemistry, certain fluids or compounds are said to be *tenuous*, not dense. In general, nonscientific usage, *tenuous* refers to something weak or flimsy, that has little substance or strength: a tenuous grip, a tenuous proposal, a tenuous argument, or tenuous construction.

Word 17: COMPLACENT (kum-PLAY-sint)

Self-satisfied, smug, overly pleased with oneself.

Complacent suggests being so satisfied with one's abilities, advantages, or circumstances that one lacks proper concern for the condition of others and is unaware of the situation around one. A complacent smile is a smug, self-satisfied smile. Complacent behavior is self-centered and disregards others' concerns. A complacently ignorant person is completely satisfied with his ignorance; he does not know he lacks knowledge and would not care if he did.

Complacent and *complaisant* (kum-PLAY-zint) should be distinguished in spelling, pronunciation, and meaning. *Complaisant*, with a *z* sound for the *s* in the final syllable, means inclined to please, gracious, obliging, courteous, affable (AF-uh-bul), urbane (ur-BAYN). It has a positive connotation. *Complacent*, with an *s* sound for the *c* in the final syllable, has a negative connotation. *Complacent* means self-satisfied, smug, overly pleased with oneself.

Word 18: ACME (AK-mee)

The peak, highest point, summit, zenith, especially the point of culmination, the highest possible point in the development or progress of something.

Here's a funny story about vocabulary development.

I learned the word *acme* as a young boy watching the "Roadrunner" cartoons on television, in which Wile E. Coyote uses various products made by the "ACME" company in his obsessive quest to capture the Roadrunner. Of course the coyote's plans always backfire, and he usually winds up flying headlong over some precipitous cliff. Through the power of association I have since connected the height of those cliffs with the word *acme*, the peak, highest point.

You see, even watching television can help you build your vocabulary. However, reading *Verbal Advantage* along with a regular diet of general reading is a far more effective method.

Acme comes directly from a Greek word meaning the highest point, extremity. The word is often used figuratively to mean the highest point in the development or progress of something, as in "the acme of his career," "a company at the acme of the industry." The corresponding adjective is *acmatic* (ak-MAT-ik): "Albert Einstein's theory of relativity was an acmatic scientific breakthrough." The antonym of the acme is the *nadir* (NAY-dur), the lowest point.

Word 19: DEFUNCT (di-FUHNGKT)

Dead, extinct, obsolete; no longer in existence, effect, operation, or use.

Defunct comes from the Latin *defunctus*, dead, departed, finished. A defunct law is no longer in existence or effect; a defunct organization is no longer functioning or doing business; a defunct factory is no longer in operation; a defunct procedure is no longer in use; a defunct species is extinct; a defunct expression is no longer in use; a defunct idea is no longer useful or popular; and a defunct person is dead.

Word 20: ABET (uh-BET)

To encourage, support, help, aid, promote, assist in achieving a purpose.

Some dictionaries note that *abet* means especially to encourage or assist in wrongdoing, as in the legal cliché "to aid and abet," meaning to assist a criminal in the commission of a crime. That sense is perhaps more common, but *abet* may also be used favorably, as "to abet the cause of justice," "to abet the committee's efforts to get the plan approved."

Let's review the ten words you've just learned. Decide whether the following statements are true or false. Answers appear on page 64.

1. A gullible person is hard to fool.
2. A benign expression is a gentle, good-natured expression.
3. If something's peripheral, it's essential.
4. To rebuff a request or proposal is to reconsider it.
5. A benign person is full of animosity.
6. A tenuous grasp of the facts is weak or insubstantial.
7. Complacent people are thoughtful and considerate of others.
8. The peak of a person's career is the acme.
9. A defunct corporation is likely to grow and turn a profit.
10. You can abet a criminal or abet a worthy cause.

Let's take a moment to debunk a widely held superstition about good usage. (By the way, *debunk*, pronounced di-BUHNGK, means to expose as false, deceitful, or exaggerated, to prove that something is *bunkum* [BUHNGK-um], foolish and insincere.)

Do you remember the old rule, "Don't end a sentence with a preposition"? Well, it's too bad it was ever taught, for it is wrong, wrong, wrong. If you think I'm cracked, that I don't know what I'm talking about, then I dare you to say, "You don't know about what you're talking."

Some time ago, while visiting relatives, I met a woman who was studying to be a teacher. She had just received a misguided lecture on the evils of ending a sentence with a preposition. "How long are you staying for?" she asked me. Then, embarrassed, she changed that perfectly natural sentence to "For how long are you staying?"—which made her sound like Eliza Doolittle practicing for her next pinky-in-the-air tea party.

"For years Miss Thistlebottom has been teaching her bright-eyed brats that no writer would end a sentence with a preposition," says Theodore M. Bernstein in *The Careful Writer* (1965), a book that anyone who puts words on paper should keep close at hand. "The truth," Bernstein asserts, "is that no good writer would follow Miss Thistlebottom's rule, although he might occasionally examine it to see if there was any merit in it."

Bernstein was assistant managing editor of *The New York Times*, an associate professor in Columbia University's School of Journalism, and a respected arbiter on English usage. Bernstein maintains that sentences that end with prepositions are "idiomatic and have been constructed that way from Shakespeare's 'We are such stuff as dreams are made on' to today's 'Music to read by.' They are a natural manner of expression. Examine a handful: 'It's nothing to sneeze at'; 'Something to guard against'; 'You don't know what I've been through'; 'He is a man who can be counted on'; 'I'm not sure what the cake was made of.' Surely there is nothing amiss with these idiomatic constructions. Woe to Miss Thistlebottom if she tries to 'correct' them. She won't have a leg on which to stand."

Back in 1926, the legendary English grammarian H. W. Fowler, in his classic guide *Modern English Usage*, called the rule about prepositions "a cherished superstition." According to Fowler, "Those who lay down the universal principle that final prepositions are 'inelegant' are unconsciously trying to deprive the English language of a valuable idiomatic resource, which has been used freely by all our greatest writers except those whose instinct for English idiom has been overpowered by notions of correctness derived from Latin standards.

"The legitimacy of the prepositional ending in literary English must be uncompromisingly maintained," says Fowler. "In respect of elegance or inelegance, every example must be judged not by any arbitrary rule, but on its own merits, according to the impression it makes on the feeling of educated English readers."

Hundreds of great writers from Chaucer, Shakespeare, and Milton to Herman Melville, Mark Twain, Ernest Hemingway, and Toni Morrison all have written intelligible, graceful, idiomatic sentences that ended with a preposition. To say those writers were wrong is like saying everyone in baseball's Hall of Fame didn't know a thing about how to play the game. The best contemporary writers also do not hesitate to let a preposition end a sentence when it pleases the ear, and they avoid doing so when it does not.

So the next time some nitpicking Miss Thistlebottom says you mustn't end a sentence with a preposition, try this retort: "You, dear sir or madam, may twist your syntax into knots if you like, but please refrain from telling the rest of us what to end our sentences with."

And that, as the saying goes, is what it all boils down to.

Let's move on now to the next ten keywords in Level 2.

Word 21: HAGGARD (HAG-urd)

Worn out, tired, gaunt (GAWNT), drawn, emaciated (i-**MAY**-shee-AY-tid). A person who is haggard has a wild-eyed and wasted look, as from exhaustion, illness, or grief.

Haggard is another word whose meaning I remember through the power of association. When I read *King Solomon's Mines* by H. Rider Haggard, I imagined the author as being as worn out and wild-eyed as his characters were by the end of their harrowing adventure. But you don't need to go through a death-defying experience to look or feel haggard. Long hours at work, lack of sleep, or inadequate nutrition can easily make you *haggard*, worn out, tired, wasted, gaunt.

Word 22: WAIVE (WAYV, like *wave*)

To relinquish voluntarily, give up, forgo.

To *relinquish* implies giving up something one doesn't want to part with, either out of necessity or because one has been compelled or forced: to relinquish possession, to relinquish command. To *waive* implies a voluntary refusal to insist on one's right or claim to something: to waive one's right to a trial by jury; to waive one's claim on a title or property.

Waive may also mean to postpone, defer, or dispense with, as to waive discussion, or to waive formalities and get on with business.

Word 23: CARNAL (KAHR-nal)

Bodily, pertaining to the flesh as opposed to the spirit, sensual, corporeal.

Carnal is not used to mean bodily in a general or neutral sense; we do not say carnal functions or carnal aches and pains. *Carnal* refers to the basic physical appetites of the body, especially the sexual appetite. We speak of carnal desires, carnal lust, carnal knowledge.

Word 24: SANCTION (SANGK-shun)

To approve, allow, permit, authorize, certify, ratify.

To *sanction*, *certify*, and *ratify* all mean to approve. *Ratify* means to officially approve something done by a representative: to ratify a treaty. *Certify* means to officially approve compliance with requirements or standards: a certified public accountant. *Sanction* means to give authoritative approval: the company's board of directors sanctioned the merger; many religions do not sanction unmarried sexual relations; the law sanctions free speech but not antisocial behavior.

Word 25: AMBIGUOUS (am-BIG-yoo-us)

Uncertain, unclear, doubtful, dubious, questionable, puzzling, having an obscure or indefinite meaning.

By derivation, *ambiguous* means having two or more possible meanings, capable of being understood in more than one way. An ambiguous intention is uncertain, difficult to determine, and therefore questionable, dubious. An ambiguous statement is puzzling because it can be interpreted in more than one way; it is unclear and indefinite.

More difficult synonyms of *ambiguous* include *enigmatic* (EN-ig-**MAT**-ik), *cryptic* (KRIP-tik), and *equivocal* (i-KWIV-uh-k<u>u</u>l). Antonyms of *ambiguous* include *distinct*, *apparent*, *evident*, *conspicuous*, and *manifest*.

Word 26: SPENDTHRIFT (rhymes with *bend lift*)

Wasteful, spending extravagantly or foolishly, squandering one's resources: "His spendthrift habits will put the company out of business."

You may use *spendthrift* either as an adjective meaning wasteful, spending extravagantly, or as a noun to mean a wasteful person, someone who foolishly squanders money or resources: "There isn't a thrifty bone in his body. He's a gambler and a spendthrift to the core."

The words *improvident*, *prodigal*, *profligate*, and *spendthrift* all mean wasteful, spending thoughtlessly or squandering one's resources.

Improvident (im-PRAHV-i-dent) means literally not provident, not providing for the future; the improvident person does not save money for retirement or for a rainy day.

Prodigal (PRAH-di-gal) is a close synonym of *spendthrift* and means spending money in a reckless or extravagant way, usually to support a lavish or luxurious lifestyle. In the Bible, the famous parable about the prodigal son tells of a young man who wasted his inheritance but was forgiven by his father.

Profligate (PRAHF-li-git) means extremely prodigal or spendthrift; it refers specifically to a person who spends money with reckless abandon and lives a life shamelessly devoted to pleasure: a profligate Hollywood movie star who squandered his fortune in exclusive nightclubs and casinos.

Spendthrift means wasteful, spending extravagantly: "The taxpayers want a more efficient and less spendthrift government."

Word 27: MOLLIFY (MAHL-uh-fy)

To calm, soothe, pacify, appease, soften in feeling or tone, make less harsh or severe: "Nothing mollified his anger."

Mollify comes from the Latin *mollis*, soft, and *facere*, to make, and means literally "to make soft." Also from the Latin *mollis*, soft, comes the word *emol-*

lient (i-MAHL-y<u>i</u>nt). As an adjective, *emollient* means softening, soothing, mollifying; as a noun it means a softening or soothing agent, such as a lotion or cream for the skin.

The verb to *mollify* once meant literally to make soft or tender, as to mollify meat, tenderize it. That sense is now obsolete and *mollify* today is used to mean to soften in feeling or tone, calm, soothe, make less harsh or severe: "The union leaders decided to mollify their demands"; "A good manager should be adept at mollifying conflicts that can damage morale"; "The plaintiff's attorney said that only a million-dollar settlement would mollify her client"; "He was furious, and nothing she said mollified him."

Word 28: UNEQUIVOCAL (UHN-i-**KWIV**-uh-k<u>u</u>l)

Clear and direct, definite, straightforward, certain, having a single, obvious meaning, capable of being interpreted in only one way.

Unequivocal, clear and direct, and *ambiguous*, uncertain, unclear, are antonyms.

Unequivocal combines the common prefix *un-*, which means not, with the word *equivocal*, a synonym of *ambiguous*. Equivocal language can be interpreted in several ways; it is deliberately vague, evasive, or ambiguous. Unequivocal language is clear, straightforward, and direct: "Reporters are so accustomed to equivocal answers from government officials that they are often surprised and suspicious when they get an unequivocal response."

Now that you know the meaning of *unequivocal* I'd like to caution you about how you pronounce it. I have heard many educated speakers add a syllable to the word and say "unequivocable," and I have even seen the word misspelled that way in books and magazines. No matter whom you hear saying "unequivocable," it's incorrect—a beastly mispronunciation. *Unequivocal* ends with *-vocal*, not *-vocable*, and has five syllables: un-e-quiv-o-cal.

Word 29: MALLEABLE (MAL-ee-uh-b<u>u</u>l)

Capable of being shaped, able to be molded or manipulated, adaptable, impressionable.

Certain metals, such as gold and iron, are malleable; they can be molded or shaped. In a figurative sense, *malleable* can also apply to a person or abstract thing that can be molded or shaped. For example, a young person's mind may be malleable, impressionable, capable of being shaped, or an idea may be malleable, adaptable, capable of being shaped to fit various purposes.

Malleable and the challenging word *tractable* (TRAK-tuh-bul) are close in meaning. *Malleable* comes from the Latin *malleare*, to hammer, and means literally "capable of being hammered into a desired shape." *Tractable* comes from the Latin *tractare*, to handle, manage, haul or drag along. From the same source comes the familiar word *tractor*, the farm vehicle used to pull wagons, mowers, and other agricultural equipment. By derivation that which is *tractable* can be pulled or hauled; hence, a tractable person is manageable, easily handled. A *malleable* person or thing is easily hammered into shape, and therefore is adaptable, impressionable.

Antonyms of *malleable* and *tractable* include *inflexible*, *unyielding*, *stubborn*, *obstinate* (AHB-sti-nit), and *intransigent* (in-TRAN-zi-jint).

Word 30: VERBOSE (vur-BOHS)

Wordy, having too many words, long-winded, full of verbiage (VUR-bee-ij). More difficult synonyms of *verbose* include *garrulous* (GAR-uh-lus), *loquacious* (loh-KWAY-shus), *voluble* (VAHL-yuh-bul), and *prolix* (PROH-liks).

Verbose refers to speech or writing that uses more words than necessary to get the point across. The corresponding noun is *verbosity*, wordiness, long-windedness, an overabundance of words.

Whenever you see *verb-* at the beginning of a word, you can safely assume that the meaning of the whole word has something to do with words. That's because most English words containing *verb-* come from the Latin *verbum*, word. From this *verbum* come the English words *verbal*, pertaining to or expressed in words; *verbatim*, expressed in precisely the same words; *verbiage*, an excess or overabundance of words; and *verbose*, wordy, long-winded, using more words than necessary to get the point across.

Since I'm already waxing verbose about words from the Latin *verbum*, word, allow me to digress even further and proffer a few words of advice on the words *verbal* and *verbiage*. (Are you familiar with the verb to *proffer*, pronounced PRAHF-ur? It means to put forward for acceptance, present as a gift, as to proffer one's services, or to proffer friendship.)

But back to the word *verbiage* (VUR-bee-ij), which is often mispronounced VUR-bij, as if it had only two syllables. *Carriage* and *marriage* have two syllables, but *verbiage* and *foliage* (FOH-lee-ij) have three. Try not to say VUR-bij and FOH-lij, or even worse, FOY-lij. You will hear many educated people mispronounce these words, but believe me when I say that careful speakers consider the two-syllable variants beastly mispronunciations. Take care to pronounce these words in three syllables: VUR-bee-ij and FOH-lee-ij.

Now for a word to the wise on the proper use of *verbal*. You will often hear or read such phrases as "a verbal agreement" or "a verbal understanding." Have you ever stopped to ask yourself exactly what they mean? If you're like most people, you probably figured that a verbal agreement or a verbal understanding meant one that was arrived at through conversation, one that was spoken but not written down—and therein lies the problem.

The word *oral* means spoken, not written, and the precise meaning of *verbal* is expressed in words, either orally or in writing. Too often *verbal*, expressed in words, is used to mean *oral*, spoken, and the message that results from that confusion is usually ambiguous. For example, listen to this sentence, which I found recently in the business section of my local newspaper: "Ensure all promises made verbally are included, in writing, in the contract." As written, the sentence means that we should make sure that all promises, both spoken and written, are included in the contract. The writer wants to say that we should put all spoken promises in writing, but to convey that meaning precisely the sentence should read like this: "Ensure all promises made orally are included in the contract."

In the future, whenever you refer to promises, agreements, or understandings, remember that if they are expressed in speech, they are *oral*, and if they are expressed in words, whether spoken or written, they are *verbal*. Of course, if they are expressed in too many words, like most long-winded legal contracts, then they are *verbose*, full of verbiage.

Let's review the ten keywords you've just learned. This time I'm going to give you two words, and you decide if they are synonyms or antonyms. Answers appear on page 64.

1. *Energetic* and *haggard* are . . . synonyms or antonyms?
2. To *waive* and to *relinquish* are . . .
3. *Spiritual* and *carnal* are . . .
4. To *sanction* and to *prohibit* are . . .
5. *Doubtful* and *ambiguous* are . . .
6. *Miserly* and *spendthrift* are . . .
7. To *mollify* and to *irritate* are . . .
8. *Unequivocal* and *ambiguous* are . . .
9. *Adaptable* and *malleable* are . . .
10. *Verbose* and *long-winded* are . . .

Did you remember to calculate your score on this quiz? If you answered eight or more questions correctly, read on. If not, review the last ten keywords.

Let's continue now with the *Verbal Advantage* vocabulary. Here are the next ten keywords in Level 2:

Word 31: TRANSIENT (TRAN-sh<u>i</u>nt)

Temporary, passing away with time, lasting only a short while, momentary, fleeting, short-lived—in which *-lived* is commonly mispronounced with a short *i* as in *give*, when it should have a long *i* as in *strive*.

Does that pronunciation pronouncement surprise you? In *short-lived* and *long-lived*, the *-lived* does not come from the verb to *live*, as many think. It is formed from the noun *life* plus the suffix *-ed*. That is why pronunciation authorities and careful speakers have long preferred short-LYVD and long-LYVD, and why nearly all current American dictionaries give priority to the long-*i* pronunciation.

Since we're discussing pronunciation I should point out that you will often hear educated speakers pronounce our keyword, *transient*, as TRAN-zee-<u>i</u>nt or TRAN-see-<u>i</u>nt, especially when the word is used as a noun to mean a homeless person, vagrant, or vagabond. Despite the popularity of these three-syllable variants, I recommend TRAN-sh<u>i</u>nt, with two syllables, because it is the traditional American pronunciation and the one listed first in all the major current American dictionaries. Remember, *transient* sounds like *ancient*.

Challenging synonyms of the adjective *transient* include *transitory*, *evanescent*, *ephemeral*, *fugitive*, and *fugacious*. All of these words mean lasting only a short while, but let's examine the fine distinctions in their meanings.

Transitory (**TRAN**-si-**TOR**-ee *or* **TRAN**-zi-) applies to something that by its nature is bound to pass away or come to an end. All life must by nature end; therefore life is transitory. When Andy Warhol said everyone will be famous for fifteen minutes, he was describing the transitory nature of fame—here one moment and gone the next.

Evanescent (EV-uh-**NES**-<u>i</u>nt) applies to that which fades away like vapor or vanishes as if into thin air: the evanescent beauty of springtime flowers. A shooting star creates an evanescent trail of light. An intense experience, no matter how brief and evanescent, can become a lifelong memory.

Ephemeral (<u>e</u>-FEM-uh-r<u>u</u>l) by derivation means literally "living or lasting for only a day." Newspaper writing used to be called "ephemeral literature" because the articles had a lifespan of only one day, with one day's reportage ostensibly erased by the next day's edition. From this original sense of lasting only a day, *ephemeral* has evolved to mean short-lived, existing for a short while. If when you meet people you have trouble remembering their names ten minutes later, you could say that you have an ephemeral memory for names.

Fugitive (FYOO-ji-tiv) and *fugacious* (fyoo-GAY-sh<u>u</u>s) come from the Latin *fugere*, to flee, run or fly away, the source also of the Latin expression *tempus fugit* (TEM-p<u>u</u>s FYOO-jit), "time flies." By derivation *fugitive* and *fugacious* mean fleeting, disposed to fly away or disappear. A *fugitive*, from the same Latin *fugere*, to flee, is a person who eludes pursuit, who flees from captivity or danger. The adjectives *fugitive* and *fugacious* both refer to things that are elusive, that are hard to catch or perceive because they happen or pass by so quickly: a fugitive smile; the fugitive colors of the sunset; our fugacious memories of childhood. We may pursue happiness, but it is fugacious.

Our keyword, *transient*, applies to anything that lasts temporarily or that is in the process of passing on. A transient guest stays for a while and moves on. A transient event is fleeting, momentary. A transient condition lasts for a short time.

Antonyms of *transient* include *permanent*, *timeless*, *eternal*, and *everlasting*.

Word 32: NETTLE (NET-'l)

To irritate, annoy, vex, harass (HAR-is *or* huh-RAS), pester, provoke: Their supervisor constantly nettled them about trivial or irrelevant details.

You may be familiar with the plant called the *nettle*, which has tiny hairs that sting and irritate the skin. The verb to *nettle* means to sting like a nettle, hence to irritate or annoy. Someone who is nettled is irritated to the point of silent anger or resentment.

Word 33: REPUDIATE (ri-PYOO-dee-ayt)

To reject, cast off, disown, renounce, refuse to accept as one's own; also, to reject as false, deny the authority of, refuse to accept as true.

Repudiate suggests a formal, often vehement (VEE-uh-mint, the *h* is silent) rejection. You can repudiate a child, reject or disown the child; you can repudiate a belief, cast it off or renounce it; you can repudiate a claim, deny its authority; and you can repudiate a charge, reject it as untrue.

Word 34: IMPETUOUS (im-PECH-oo-<u>us</u>)

Hasty, rash, overeager, acting in a sudden, vigorous, emotional way, with little thought: "The impetuous shopper buys on impulse rather than out of necessity"; "A prudent investor is not likely to make impetuous decisions."

The words *rash*, *impulsive*, and *impetuous* all refer to hasty or sudden actions or to people who act first and think later. *Rash* suggests reckless haste and foolish daring: In the arena of international relations, rash statements can lead to war. *Impulsive* suggests an ungovernable inner force that drives one to act without thinking: He is an impulsive talker who often puts his foot in his mouth. *Impetuous* suggests great energy, eagerness, or impatience. Children are often *impetuous*, prone to act suddenly without thinking. Impetuous behavior in an adult is often considered overemotional or immature.

Antonyms of *impetuous* include *prudent* and *circumspect*. For more on those two words, review the discussion of *prudent*, keyword 47 in Level 1.

Word 35: FRUGAL (FROO-g<u>ul</u>)

Spending carefully and wisely, thrifty, economical.

Frugal comes directly from a Latin word meaning economical, and ultimately from the Latin *frux*, fruit, produce. Frugal people are cautious and sparing with the fruit of their labors.

Thrifty, *economical*, *provident*, and *parsimonious* all mean *frugal*, spending carefully and wisely, but in slightly different ways and degrees.

Thrifty implies hard work and good management as a means to prosperity. The thrifty person spends only what is necessary and diligently saves the rest.

Economical implies the use of money or resources in the most advantageous way. An economical car uses fuel efficiently. An economical investment is one that generates a higher return.

Provident suggests providing for the future. The provident person spends carefully with a mind toward what may be needed later.

Parsimonious means extremely frugal, stingy, miserly. The parsimonious person keeps a wary eye on every nickel and dime.

Frugal, spending carefully, may also be used to mean involving little expense, not wasteful or lavish. A frugal meal is an economical, no-frills meal. Flying coach rather than first-class is a more frugal way to travel.

Word 36: INCONGRUOUS (in-KAHNG-groo-wu̲s)

Out of place, inappropriate, inconsistent, unsuitable, lacking harmony of parts or agreement in character.

Incongruous comes from a Latin verb meaning to come together, fit in. From the same source come the adjectives *congruous* (KAHNG-groo-wu̲s) and *congruent* (KAHNG-groo-i̲nt), which mean coming together harmoniously, fitting in consistently. The *in-* at the beginning of *incongruous* is called a privative (PRIV-uh-tiv) prefix, which means it deprives or takes away the meaning of what follows. Thus, *incongruous* means not congruous, not appropriate, not consistent, out of place.

An incongruous remark is one that is inappropriate or not in keeping with the conversation. An incongruous element is out of place, not consistent with the elements around it. An incongruous action is unsuitable to the occasion or situation. An incongruous mixture lacks harmony or agreement.

Word 37: ASSUAGE (uh-SWAYJ, rhymes with *a stage*)

To relieve, ease, allay (uh-LAY), mitigate (MIT-i̲-gayt), make less severe or intense; also, to satisfy, appease (uh-PEEZ), make content.

When you assuage someone's grief, assuage someone's anger, assuage someone's pain, or assuage someone's fears, you relieve those conditions, allay them, make them less severe or intense. When you assuage your hunger or thirst, you relieve it by providing food or drink. When you assuage a need or desire, you satisfy it by procuring what is needed or desired.

Assuage is sometimes mispronounced uh-SWAYZH or uh-SWAHZH. These recent variants have made their way into a few current dictionaries, but the traditional and proper pronunciation, countenanced by all dictionaries, is uh-SWAYJ.

Word 38: CORROBORATE (kuh-RAHB-uh-rayt)

To confirm, support, make more certain or believable: "Six witnesses corroborated the victim's account of the crime."

Corroborate comes from a Latin verb meaning to strengthen. In modern use *corroborate* means to strengthen by providing additional evidence or proof. When you corroborate a story, you strengthen it, support it, help to establish it as true.

Authenticate, *verify*, *substantiate*, and *corroborate* all mean to confirm in slightly different ways.

To *authenticate* is to establish something as authentic or genuine: You authenticate a document, a signature, or a work of art.

To *verify* is to establish as true, confirm the accuracy of: Reporters have a responsibility to verify facts and quotations.

To *substantiate* is to support by supplying reliable evidence or proof: Scholars and scientists must substantiate their theories. The investigation uncovered several key facts that substantiated the case against the company.

To *corroborate* is to substantiate what someone else has said by supplying additional evidence or proof. When you corroborate another person's statement, you make it more certain or believable.

Word 39: EMBELLISH (em-BEL-ish)

To decorate, dress up, adorn, enhance with ornamentation, make more beautiful, elegant, or interesting.

Embellish comes from an Old French verb meaning to make beautiful and has been traced back to the Latin *bellus*, pretty. By derivation, *embellish* means to beautify, make pretty. An *embellishment*, the corresponding noun, is a decoration, ornament, something that beautifies.

Embellish may be used in numerous ways to mean to decorate, make more beautiful or interesting. You can embellish your home by decorating it with beautiful things. You can embellish an outfit with ornaments or accessories. You can embellish your speech or writing with interesting words and elegant phrases. And you can embellish a story, dress it up with entertaining details or even things that aren't true: "Over the years the old fisherman had added many fanciful embellishments to his tale about 'the big one that got away.'"

Word 40: AVARICIOUS (AV-uh-RISH-us)

Greedy, money-grubbing, miserly, consumed with a selfish desire to accumulate money or property. The corresponding noun is *avarice* (AV-uh-ris), greed, an inordinate desire for wealth.

Greedy, *covetous*, and *avaricious* all apply to people who eagerly want to acquire more than they have or are entitled to have.

Greedy is the general term for an excessive desire for anything. A person can be greedy for approval, greedy for success, or a greedy eater.

Covetous (KUHV-i-tus) suggests an excessive and sometimes immoral desire for what another person has: "Steve wasn't sure if his neighbor Dave was more covetous of his new sports car or his attractive wife"; "When Anne was promoted to vice president, she could tell that most of her former coworkers in middle management were covetous of her spacious office and impressive salary."

Avaricious implies an excessive and selfish drive to accumulate wealth and valuable possessions, and often suggests an accompanying desire to hoard them: "Any observant person could see plainly that the city was run not by the people or the politicians but by a few avaricious developers who controlled most of the real estate, and a few avaricious bankers who were tight with credit and charged outrageous interest rates."

Let's review the ten words you've just learned. This time we're going to play "One of These Definitions Doesn't Fit the Word." In each statement below, a word is followed by three ostensible synonyms. (*Ostensible* means "apparent," remember?) Two of the three are true synonyms; one is unrelated in meaning. You must decide which one of the three ostensible synonyms doesn't fit the word. Answers appear on page 65.

1. *Transient* means temporary, passing, portable.
2. To *nettle* means to puzzle, irritate, annoy.
3. To *repudiate* means to renounce, revoke, reject.
4. *Impetuous* means impulsive, hostile, rash.
5. *Frugal* means prudent, economical, spendthrift.
6. *Incongruous* means inappropriate, inadequate, inconsistent.
7. To *assuage* means to sympathize, ease, relieve.
8. To *corroborate* means to confirm, explain, support.
9. To *embellish* means to make beautiful, dress up, show off.
10. *Avaricious* means lustful, covetous, greedy.

Let's take a break now from the *Verbal Advantage* vocabulary for an exposé of two commonly confused words and one commonly misused word.

What is the distinction between *sensual* and *sensuous*? Is there a difference in meaning when you say "*sensuous* feelings" and "*sensual* feelings"?

Yes, there is indeed a difference. *Sensuous* refers favorably to things experienced through the senses: sensuous music, sensuous colors, the sensuous beauty of the forest, the sensuous aroma of fine food. *Sensual* refers, usually unfavorably, to the gratification of the senses or physical appetites, especially in a self-indulgent or sexual way: the sensual excesses of the glutton, the sensual nightlife of the city; the sensual atmosphere of a singles bar; the sensual cravings of a drug addict. The controversial 1969 bestseller *The Sensuous Woman* would have been more accurately titled *The Sensual Woman* because its explicit subject matter concerns the unabashed gratification of sexual desire.

Here's how you can keep the two words straight: If you mean lovely, pleasurable, or experienced through the senses, use *sensuous*; if you mean self-gratifying or pertaining to physical desires, use *sensual*. Sensuous thoughts have a pleasant effect on your senses as well as your mind. Sensual thoughts are erotic, sexually arousing, maybe even lewd.

Here's a sentence that can help you remember the distinction: The *sensuous* feeling of silk against her skin filled her with *sensual* desire.

Now, before that sensuous sentence makes you break out in a sensual sweat, let's take a quick look at a commonly misused word: *comprise*. In strict usage, *comprise* means to include, contain, consist of, be composed of. It should not be used to mean to make up. Do not say the United States is comprised of fifty states, or that fifty states comprise the United States.

The rule for *comprise* is that "the whole *comprises* (contains) its parts; the parts *compose* (make up) the whole." Therefore you should say the United States *comprises* (*contains* or *consists of*) fifty states, or fifty states *compose* (*constitute* or *make up*) the United States. When you mean "to make up," use that phrase or *compose* or *constitute*. Use *comprise* only when you mean to include or contain: Our city comprises a million residents; they watched a TV miniseries comprising five episodes; the report comprised three different proposals.

Now let's proceed to the final ten keywords in Level 2.

Word 41: CURSORY (KUR-sur-ee)

Quick, hasty, not methodical, done rapidly with little attention to detail, passing quickly over or through something that deserves closer examination.

Synonyms of *cursory* include *hurried*, *haphazard*, *slapdash*, and *superfi-*

cial. Antonyms include *thorough*, *careful*, *exhaustive*, *prolonged*, and *protracted*.

Don't be fooled by the sound of the word *cursory*; it has nothing to do with curses or cursing. *Cursory* comes through the Latin *cursorius*, running, from the Latin *currere*, to run. This Latin *currere*, to run, is also the root of the words *course*, a path on which one moves or runs; *curriculum*, a course of study; and *courier*, a messenger who runs here and there delivering important documents or urgent news.

By derivation, *cursory* means "running about, not standing still," and the word was once used in this sense. Today, however, *cursory* is used to mean done rapidly with little attention to detail, passing quickly over or through something that deserves closer examination.

A cursory glance is a quick, passing glance. A cursory reading is a hasty, superficial reading. A cursory explanation is a hurried explanation, one that covers the subject in a haphazard way. A cursory investigation is not methodical; it is done rapidly with little attention to detail.

Word 42: VACILLATE (VAS-i-layt)

To waver, fluctuate, be indecisive, show uncertainty, hesitate in making up one's mind: The strong leader is decisive; the weak leader vacillates.

Vacillate comes from a Latin verb meaning to sway to and fro. When you vacillate you go back and forth mentally on an issue or question. The person or group that vacillates has difficulty coming to a conclusion or expressing a firm opinion.

Word 43: CLEMENT (KLEM-int)

Mild, calm, tranquil, moderate, temperate, not severe or extreme; also, merciful, lenient, inclined to pardon or forgive.

Clement comes from the Latin *clemens*, mild, and may be used to mean mild in two ways. You may say the weather is clement when it's mild or temperate; when it's rough or stormy it's *inclement* (in-KLEM-int), not clement, not mild and calm. *Clement*'s second sense applies to a mild state of mind, one in which the person is inclined to be lenient or forgiving. A convicted criminal can only hope for a clement judge. If you screw up at work, you hope your boss will be *clement*, lenient, merciful.

The corresponding noun is *clemency*, mildness, leniency, compassion: "The lawyers asked the governor to show clemency and stay the execution."

Word 44: LUCRATIVE (LOO-kruh-tiv)

Profitable, producing wealth, money-making, financially productive, remunerative (ri-MYOO-nur-uh-tiv).

You've probably heard the phrase "filthy lucre," which comes from Shakespeare. *Lucre* (LOO-kur) is an old word for money, profit, wealth. In modern usage *lucre* used alone usually implies *filthy lucre*, tainted money, ill-gotten gains.

Lucre and the useful adjective *lucrative* come from the Latin *lucrum*, gain, profit. That which is lucrative is likely to make money, turn a profit. A lucrative job pays well; a lucrative business deal is profitable; a lucrative enterprise is a money-making enterprise.

Word 45: ALLOCATE (AL-uh-kayt)

To assign, designate, earmark, set aside for a specific purpose.

Allocate comes from a Latin verb meaning to locate, determine the place of. That which is allocated has been assigned a special place or purpose. A person might allocate a bedroom in the house as a home office. Busy parents try to allocate time to spend with their children. Voters pass bond measures to allocate funds for education, parks, or libraries. One measure of a successful company is how much money it allocates for product development.

Word 46: RECONCILE (REK-un-syl)

To make friendly again, restore friendly relations between, settle, resolve, bring into harmony or agreement.

Reconcile comes from the Latin *reconciliare*, to make good again, restore, repair. When estranged partners reconcile, they make their relationship good again by restoring it, repairing what was wrong with it. When two parties in a dispute reconcile their differences, they settle them and restore friendly relations. The corresponding noun is *reconciliation*, a settlement, resolution, the act of restoring harmony or agreement.

Reconcile also has two other useful senses. It may mean to bring into agreement, make consistent: "The jury found it hard to reconcile the defendant's confession of guilt the night of the murder with his profession of innocence during the trial." *Reconcile* may also mean to resign oneself to accept something undesirable: "Nancy didn't want to live with her mother-in-law, but she reconciled herself to it and tried to get on with her life."

Word 47: PARAGON (PAR-uh-gahn)

A model of excellence, perfect example.

Paragon applies to a person or thing so excellent that it serves as a model or example of perfection. The inventor Thomas Alva Edison is a paragon of American ingenuity. In her Camelot days, Jacqueline Kennedy Onassis was considered a paragon of beauty and style. The Gettysburg Address is a paragon of forceful, eloquent speechwriting.

A *paragon* is a model of excellence, a perfect example.

Word 48: ANALOGOUS (un-NAL-uh-gus)

Similar, akin, comparable (KAHM-pur-uh-buul), corresponding partially, sharing some aspects of form, function, or content.

An *analogy* is a partial similarity, likeness, or resemblance that allows for a comparison between things: You can draw an analogy between the human brain and a computer, between the human heart and a mechanical pump, or between an airplane and a bird.

When we see an analogy between two things, we say they are *analogous*, similar but not entirely alike, comparable in some respects. *Analogous* does not apply to things that are identical. For example, brains and computers and birds and airplanes differ markedly in all but a few ways, but in those ways they are analogous.

When things are analogous they share certain features or particulars; they are similar enough to form the basis for a comparison. If you say your company's management style is analogous to Japanese management style, you mean the styles are alike in some respects but not in others. If you tell a coworker that your job descriptions are analogous, you mean they are similar, comparable, alike in certain ways.

Word 49: DIURNAL (dy-UR-nul)

Daily, recurring each day, performed or happening in the course of a day.

Diurnal comes from the Latin *diurnus*, belonging to or lasting for a day. The ocean's tides and the rotation of the earth are diurnal; their cycles are completed in the course of a day. At work your diurnal duties are the tasks you perform every day. If your coworker Joanne complains every day about not getting a raise, that's her diurnal complaint. Perhaps if Joanne made reading

Verbal Advantage part of her diurnal routine, she might eventually get that raise and get off your back.

Diurnal is also used to mean active during the day, as opposed to *nocturnal,* active during the night.

Word 50: PRETEXT (PREE-tekst)

An excuse, ostensible reason or motive, professed purpose.

Pretext comes through the Latin *praetextum,* an ornament, from the verb *praetexere,* to pretend, literally "to weave in front." By derivation a *pretext* is a front, a façade, something used for cover. As the *Century Dictionary* (1914) puts it, a pretext is "that which is assumed as a cloak or means of concealment; something under cover of which a true purpose is hidden."

Tyrannical leaders often invent pretexts for invading or declaring war on other countries. Irresponsible employees will invent pretexts for not coming to work. A supervisor who hates an employee's guts may try to come up with a pretext for firing the person. A pretext is an excuse, an ostensible reason designed to hide the real reason.

Let's review the ten keywords you've just learned. This time I'm going to give you the review word followed by three words or phrases, and you decide which of those three answer choices comes nearest the meaning of the review word. Answers appear on page 65.

1. Does *cursory* mean unnecessary, offensive, or superficial?
2. Does *vacillate* mean to lubricate, to waver, or to deceive?
3. Does *clement* mean gracious, fair, or mild?
4. Does *lucrative* mean profitable, prudent, or unethical?
5. Does *allocate* mean to place, to assign, or to support?
6. Does *reconcile* mean to examine closely, to deduce from evidence, or to make friendly again?
7. Is a *paragon* a reproduction, a model of excellence, or the highest point?
8. Does *analogous* mean similar, identical, or out of proportion?
9. Does *diurnal* mean daily, occasional, or constant?
10. Is a *pretext* an introduction, an opportunity, or an excuse?

By the way, did you keep track of your answers in this quiz? How about for each of the review quizzes in this level?

Review is the key to retaining the words you learn, and as the words in this program get more difficult, the amount of time you spend reviewing will determine whether you will fix those words in your vocabulary for life or forget them by tomorrow morning. So remember: Be sure to reread each set of keyword discussions until you can answer at least eight of the questions in the corresponding quiz correctly.

In the introduction to Level 2 we discussed how you can use newspapers and magazines—otherwise known as periodical literature—to build your vocabulary. Now let's talk about how to get you reading more books.

In recent years, many busy professionals have begun listening to tape-recorded books while commuting or driving to and from appointments. That's certainly better than reading two books a year—the average for American college-educated adults—or reading no books at all. Listening to a book on tape is also convenient and can save you valuable time. However, when it comes to vocabulary building, audio books won't help you very much. It's too easy to concentrate just on getting the gist of what's being said and to ignore the words you don't know. On top of that, you may be hearing mispronunciations and absorbing them without realizing it.

What it comes down to is this: If you currently read fewer than six books a year—one every two months—then you need to rediscover the wonderful world of books and make recreational reading a part of your life. (Note that I used the word *recreational*. I'm talking about reading for *fun* as well as for self-improvement.)

Here's how you can start: Read your local newspaper's book reviews or subscribe to a magazine or out-of-town paper that reviews books. Not only will that help you find books you will enjoy, but the reviews themselves are often an excellent source of expressive words.

Another way to get yourself on a regular schedule of reading is to join a book club, where you are obligated to order a certain number of books each year. That can be an incentive to finish the books you start and also to read more widely.

The next time you order a book or browse in a bookstore, be daring. Let your curiosity get the best of you. Try something on a subject that you don't know much about but that piques your interest. (Is the verb to *pique* familiar to you? It's pronounced like *peek* and means to prick, stimulate.) If you have trouble making that leap, how about reading a biography of someone you respect or admire? Also, let's not forget the value of fine fiction. Ask a friend or someone in the office to recommend a good novel. If you like it, try reading other books by the same author.

Now, I should caution you that when it comes to fiction, I don't put much stock in thrillers, romances, westerns, and war novels. With the exception of mysteries, which are generally written by better-than-average writers for a higher-caliber audience, most genre or category fiction provides plenty of diversion but little edification (ED-i-fi-**KAY**-shin). Look it up now if it's unfamiliar. What, no dictionary handy? Tsk, tsk.

These days there are few popular novelists who truly know their craft. I'll never forget the time I heard a radio interview with a best-selling author of westerns. When the interviewer asked him to explain a few unusual words from the book, the author gave the wrong definitions. What can you expect to learn from reading a book by someone like that?

Finally, I encourage you to take advantage of the public library. Becoming a regular patron of your local library is the simplest and least expensive way to broaden your knowledge of the world. When was the last time you checked out a book? If you can't remember, then you're overdue for a visit. Go down and get reacquainted with the Dewey Decimal System. And if you have kids, take them with you and introduce them to the children's section. You have nothing to lose and everything to gain by making the quest for new words, good books, and useful knowledge an integral part of your personal and professional life.

So now that I've told you what to read, let me say a few things about how to read. Here are five principles to follow.

Principle 1: *Read outside of your specialty or area of expertise*

It may sound strange, but most of what you read should not be directly related to your work. By all means, keep up with what's going on in your profession, but don't limit your reading to subjects you already know well.

Are you familiar with Tom Peters? Peters is the author of, among other books, the best-selling management guide *On Excellence*; he also writes a syndicated column with the same title. In one of those columns he discussed his strategies for making "learning in the workplace" a "continuous exercise," strategies he felt would work even for those whose schedules are "crammed from dawn till dusk."

Peters concurs with me in recommending that you avoid reading too much in areas where you are "already reasonably well versed." "The most effective professionals," he says, "know their own turf cold, to be sure. But their special added value, for clients and colleagues, is their ability to draw upon analogous ideas from disparate fields to form analyses about problems closer to home."

Not only does Peters make an important point, but in making it he also uses two fine words: *analogous*, which we discussed as word 48 of Level 2, and *disparate* (DIS-puh-rit). As you now know, *analogous* means similar, comparable, alike in certain ways. Do you know what *disparate* means? As you probably deduced from the quotation, *disparate* means different, distinct, having incompatible elements or natures. Occasionally you will hear educated people pronounce the word dis-PAR-it, with the accent on the second syllable. This relatively recent variant has made its way into the dictionaries and is now standard. Careful speakers, however, use the traditional and preferred pronunciation, which places the stress on the first syllable.

Principle 2: *Go for variety*

Remember the old saying, Variety is the spice of life? To paraphrase that *adage* (AD-ij), variety is also the spice of reading. With each book you read, try a different subject, or choose a subject you want to know more about and make a three- or four-book study of it. Alternating between nonfiction and fiction is also a good way to keep things interesting. And remember, in selecting your reading material, don't let yourself be manipulated by other people's tastes. You don't have to have all the bestsellers or all the classics on your shelf. You're not reading to keep up with the Joneses; you're reading to become a more informed, articulate, and successful person.

Principle 3: *Read what you enjoy*

This is very important. You won't learn much from a book you force yourself to read. If something doesn't hold your interest, put it down and read something else. Reading shouldn't be a chore. It should be a pleasure.

Principle 4: *Read with a dictionary*

If your dictionary is in the other room, it's too easy to get lazy and say the heck with it. When your dictionary's right beside you, you can look up an unfamiliar word immediately. You don't have to lug your dictionary around wherever you go, either. Every educated person should own at least two dictionaries—not the paperback variety, either, mind you; too many of the words you'll look up won't be in there. One dictionary should be on your desk at the office, or wherever you do most of your writing and paperwork. The other dictionary should be at home, within reach of the books and magazines you are currently reading.

As you read, underline or highlight words you don't know and words you aren't entirely sure of and look them up. If you can't or don't want to mark up the text, or if you don't care to interrupt the flow of your reading, simply jot down any unfamiliar words on a bookmark or a slip of paper—along with the page number—and look them up at the end of your reading session. Don't forget to write down the number of the page on which the word appears so you can find the word again and study how it is used in context.

I don't work for any dictionary publishers, and I'm not trying to sell you a bill of goods here. I can vouch from experience and unequivocally guarantee that promptly checking the dictionary definition of unfamiliar words will greatly improve your reading comprehension and do wonders for your vocabulary. (By the way, did you pronounce *unequivocally* correctly? See Level 2, word 28.)

Principle 5: *Don't cheat yourself*

You should never "read around" words you don't know or that you *think* you can figure out from context. Bypassing a word you think you know because you've seen it once or twice before, or because you can figure out what the sentence means, is a bad habit—one that in the long run can be detrimental to your vocabulary.

Unfortunately, most people read around difficult words without realizing it. I have even had the disturbing experience of meeting people who express pride that they can discern the general meaning of a passage without knowing the precise meanings of the words it contains. That, I'm afraid, is a delusion.

Being able to read around words is not a sign of intelligence; it is a sign of laziness. Furthermore, the consequences of guessing what a word means can be quite serious. First, you cheat yourself out of a precise knowledge of the language, and second, because the margin for error is so great, more often than not you will make the wrong guess. You know what you are doing then? Building a vocabulary filled with incorrect definitions! That kind of vocabulary leads straight to bad usage and embarrassment. So you see what I mean when I say that reading around words is nothing but a colossal waste of time.

Also, the words you read around are often the words at the border of your vocabulary, the ones you are most receptive to learning and the ones you most need to check in a dictionary right away. They are the words you could pick up rapidly with a minimum of effort. However, if you skip over them, they remain locked forever in your passive vocabulary. Then you never extend the boundary of your vocabulary and pave the way for learning more difficult words.

So that's why I say *don't cheat yourself* when it comes to using the dictionary to abet your vocabulary development. If you have the slightest doubt about what a word means, or how the writer used it, look it up. If you find that the definition you had in mind is the correct one, that's cause for celebration. You have just added a new word, or a new definition of a familiar word, to your permanent active vocabulary.

Now, before we move on to Level 3, I'd like to take a moment to tell you about two special techniques you can use to continue building your vocabulary after you've completed the *Verbal Advantage* program. They require a modest investment of your time and energy, but they are extremely effective.

You're probably familiar with the first technique, the classic "flashcard method." It's as simple as it sounds. All you do is write every new word you find in reading or hear in conversation on an index card. On one side write the word, and on the other side write the dictionary definition. (You should also note how the word is pronounced, and perhaps include a sample phrase or sentence that illustrates how the word is used.) Carry as many of these word cards with you as is convenient, and take them out and test yourself several times a day for a few days, until you have memorized the meanings of all the words and feel comfortable with them. Then file the cards for future reference, and start in on a new batch.

My father used the flashcard method while attending the Curtis Institute of Music in Philadelphia, probably the most prestigious and exclusive conservatory in the country. He knew that the trade-off for training ten hours a day to become a top-flight professional musician was missing out on a well-rounded, liberal arts college education. To make up for it, he took summer classes at the University of Chicago, read widely on his own, kept a record of any unfamiliar words he came across, and tested himself rigorously with the flashcards. Entirely on his own he acquired an excellent vocabulary, which undoubtedly was an important factor in his later becoming the principal harpist of the Metropolitan Opera Orchestra in New York City, a position he held for thirty-eight years until his retirement in the 1980s.

Perhaps intuitively my father understood that a powerful vocabulary will help you achieve more in life—even if your career doesn't appear to require strong verbal skills. In short, I believe my father is living proof of Johnson O'Connor's theory that whatever your occupation, the level of your vocabulary is closely linked to the level of your professional success.

Now for the second vocabulary-building technique, which I call the "personal dictionary." With this method, you simply record all the new words you come across on a legal pad or in a notebook. If you have a computer, you can start a personal dictionary file, which is easy to update and keep in alphabetical order.

You can arrange your personal dictionary in any number of ways. You can show the words you've learned each month, show the words you've learned from each book you've read, or show which words you've learned from conversing with friends and business associates. However you choose to organize it, your personal dictionary is your individual record of progress, a measure of how much you've read, heard, and absorbed.

To sum up what we have discussed so far: Carefully reading and reviewing each level of *Verbal Advantage*, in the proper order, will put your vocabulary development into high gear. But if you want to keep your verbal skills humming along smoothly after you finish the program, you need to read more, use your dictionary, keep track of the words you learn, and review them frequently.

And with that unambiguous tirade, we come to the end of Level 2. Be sure to review this level so you'll be fully prepared to take on the more challenging words ahead. And while you're at it, maybe you should also find your dictionary and give it a thorough dusting. It wouldn't hurt to start consulting it while you're reading the rest of the *Verbal Advantage* program.

Answers to Review Quizzes for Level 2

Keywords 1–10

1. Yes. To *advocate* means to support, be in favor of, defend by argument. One may advocate any cause, either worthy or unworthy.
2. No. To *delegate* means to entrust with authority or power, hand over management or control to another.
3. No. *Unprecedented* means unheard-of, novel, new, having no precedent or prior example.
4. Yes. *Poignant* means piercing, sharp, keen, penetrating to the senses, the mind, or the emotions.
5. No. *Nebulous* means unclear, hazy, vague, indistinct, obscure.
6. No. *Clandestine* means kept secret, done in secrecy, especially for an evil, immoral, or illegal purpose.
7. No. A *tirade* is a long-drawn-out speech, especially a vehement and abusive one.
8. No. *Unprecedented* means unheard-of, never having happened before. *Recur* means to happen again, especially at intervals or after some lapse of time.

9. No. *Oral* means expressed through spoken words. *Tacit* means unspoken, silent, implied or understood without words.
10. Yes. An *allegation* is an assertion or declaration, especially one made without proof.

Keywords 11–20

1. False. *Gullible* means easily deceived, fooled, or cheated.
2. True. *Benign* means kindly, good-natured, gracious, mild.
3. False. *Peripheral* means external, on the outside or boundary of something; hence, not essential, irrelevant.
4. False. *Rebuff* means to refuse bluntly, reject sharply, snub, spurn.
5. False. A *benign* person is gracious, good-natured. *Animosity* means hatred, hostility, ill will, strong dislike.
6. True. *Tenuous* means thin, weak, flimsy, lacking substance or strength.
7. False. *Complacent* means self-satisfied, smug, overly pleased and concerned with oneself.
8. True. *Acme* means the peak, summit, highest point.
9. False. *Defunct* means dead, extinct, obsolete; no longer in existence, effect, operation, or use.
10. True. To *abet* is to encourage, support, assist in achieving a purpose. It may be used of offering aid to good people or purposes as well to those that are bad.

Keywords 21–30

1. Antonyms. *Haggard* means worn-out, tired, gaunt, emaciated.
2. Synonyms. *Waive* means to relinquish or give up voluntarily.
3. Antonyms. *Carnal* means pertaining to the flesh as opposed to the spirit, bodily, sensual, corporeal.
4. Antonyms. *Sanction* means to approve, allow, permit, authorize.
5. Synonyms. *Ambiguous* means uncertain, unclear, doubtful, having an obscure or indefinite meaning.
6. Antonyms. *Miserly* means hoarding money; the miserly person is a pennypincher, cheapskate, skinflint. *Spendthrift* means wasteful, spending extravagantly; a spendthrift is a person who thoughtlessly wastes money.
7. Antonyms. To *mollify* means to calm, soothe, pacify, appease.
8. Antonyms. *Ambiguous* means uncertain, unclear, indefinite. *Unequivocal* means clear and direct, definite, straightforward, having a single, obvious meaning, capable of being interpreted in only one way.
9. Synonyms. *Malleable* means adaptable, capable of being shaped or molded.
10. Synonyms. *Verbose* means wordy, long-winded.

Keywords 31–40

1. *Portable* doesn't fit. *Transient* means temporary, passing, lasting a short time.
2. *Puzzle* doesn't fit. *Nettle* means to irritate, annoy.
3. *Revoke* doesn't fit. *Revoke* means to take back, withdraw, cancel. *Repudiate* means to reject, refuse, renounce, deny.
4. *Hostile* doesn't fit. *Impetuous* means hasty, impulsive, rash, acting suddenly with little or no thought.
5. *Spendthrift* doesn't fit. *Spendthrift* means wasteful, spending extravagantly. *Frugal* means economical, spending carefully.
6. *Inadequate* doesn't fit. *Incongruous* means inappropriate, inconsistent, out of place.
7. *Sympathize* doesn't fit. To *assuage* means to relieve, ease, make less severe or intense.
8. *Explain* doesn't fit. To *corroborate* means to confirm, support, substantiate, make more certain or believable.
9. *Show off* doesn't fit. To *embellish* means to decorate, dress up, adorn, make more beautiful, elegant, or interesting.
10. *Lustful* doesn't fit. *Avaricious* means greedy, miserly, covetous, driven to accumulate wealth and possessions.

Keywords 41–50

1. *Cursory* means hasty and superficial, done quickly with little attention to detail.
2. *Vacillate* means to waver, show uncertainty, hesitate in making up one's mind.
3. *Clement* means mild, temperate, not severe or extreme. *Clement* may also mean merciful, lenient, inclined to forgive.
4. *Lucrative* means profitable, money-making, producing wealth.
5. *Allocate* means to assign, designate, earmark, set aside for a specific purpose.
6. *Reconcile* means to make friendly again, settle, resolve, bring into harmony or agreement.
7. A *paragon* is a model of excellence, perfect example.
8. *Analogous* means similar, comparable, alike in some respects.
9. *Diurnal* means daily, recurring each day.
10. A *pretext* is an excuse, ostensible reason, a professed purpose designed to hide the real purpose.

Review Test for Level 2

1. Remember the five principles for effective reading? Fill in the missing words:

    (1) Read _____ of your specialty or area of expertise.

    (2) Go for _____.

    (3) Read what you _____.

    (4) Read with a _____.

    (5) Don't _____ yourself.

2. When you read, the best thing you can do to help build your vocabulary is

    (a) look for words you don't know

    (b) try to guess what words mean from context

    (c) read around words you don't know

    (d) read books with difficult words

3. Which word means exuding a fragrance, aromatic?

    (a) adamant

    (b) redolent

    (c) poignant

    (d) ambient

4. Which one of the following words denotes a coin collector?

    (a) prestidigitator

    (b) philatelist

    (c) sommelier

    (d) numismatist

5. Which word means to report widely, spread the word?

    (a) aver

    (b) eschew

    (c) bruit

    (d) impugn

6. Which word means softening, soothing?

    (a) enervating

    (b) emollient

    (c) ebullient

    (d) effervescent

7. Which word means belonging or native to a particular country or region?

    (a) indigenous

    (b) ingenuous

    (c) inviolable

    (d) innocuous

8. Which word means arousing sexual desire?

    (a) clandestine
    (b) carnal
    (c) avaricious
    (d) salacious

9. Which word means means careful and persistent?

    (a) monotonous
    (b) impetuous
    (c) assiduous
    (d) incessant

10. Which pair of words is *not* synonymous?

    (a) antagonism, animosity
    (b) rudeness, rancor
    (c) malice, malevolence
    (d) antipathy, enmity

11. What is the proper pronunciation of *poignant*?

    (a) POY-int
    (b) POYN-yint
    (c) POYG-nint
    (d) POYN-int

12. In *convocation*, the prefix *con-* means

    (a) together
    (b) against
    (c) additional
    (d) same

13. Which of the following is *not* characteristic of a tirade?

    (a) It is protracted.
    (b) It is censorious.
    (c) It is enigmatic.
    (d) It is vituperative.

14. What is the proper pronunciation of *clandestine*?

    (a) klan-DES-tyn
    (b) klan-DES-teen
    (c) klan-DES-tin
    (d) KLAN-des-tyn
    (e) KLAN-des-teen

15. *Vocal*, *vocational*, and *evocative* come from the Latin *vocare*, which means

    (a) to call

(b) to speak

(c) to feel

(d) to describe

16. Who wrote the classic guide, *Modern English Usage*?

    (a) Noah Webster

    (b) Theodore M. Bernstein

    (c) H. W. Fowler

    (d) Mark Twain

17. In which phrase is *periphery* used figuratively?

    (a) the periphery of experience

    (b) the periphery of town

18. What is the *nadir*?

    (a) the lowest point

    (b) the highest point

    (c) the beginning

    (d) the end

19. In modern usage, *lucre* usually implies

    (a) a great fortune

    (b) ill-gotten gains

    (c) a profitable venture

20. In which part of a newspaper are you most likely to come across words you can add to your vocabulary?

    (a) the sports section

    (b) the society page

    (c) the editorial page

    (d) the advice columns

21. Which of the following is *least* likely to make a person haggard?

    (a) working too hard

    (b) eating too much

    (c) lack of sleep

    (d) malnutrition

22. *Improvident*, *prodigal*, *profligate*, and *spendthrift* all mean

    (a) foolish

    (b) unlucky

    (c) poor

    (d) wasteful

23. Which word is *not* a synonym of *verbose*?

   (a) prolix

   (b) voluble

   (c) garrulous

   (d) taciturn

   (e) loquacious

24. The phrase "a paragon of American ingenuity" would best describe which person?

   (a) Abraham Lincoln

   (b) Thomas Alva Edison

   (c) Ernest Hemingway

   (d) Martin Luther King, Jr.

25. What is the preferred pronunciation of *-lived* in *short-lived* and *long-lived*?

   (a) with a short *i* as in *give*

   (b) with a long *i* as in *strive*

26. Which of the following is a privative prefix meaning "not"?

   (a) sub-

   (b) con-

   (c) mis-

   (d) in-

27. What is the traditional and proper pronunciation of *assuage*?

   (a) uh-SWAYZH

   (b) uh-SWAYJ

   (c) uh-SWAHZH

28. Three of the following words are related in meaning. Find the unrelated word:

   (a) investigate

   (b) authenticate

   (c) corroborate

   (d) substantiate

29. Which sentence illustrates the precise and proper use of *comprise*?

   (a) New York City comprises five boroughs.

   (b) New York City is comprised of five boroughs.

30. Which word properly refers to things experienced through the senses?

   (a) sensuous

   (b) sensual

31. *Cursory, course, curriculum,* and *courier* all come from the Latin *currere,* which means
    (a) to examine
    (b) to deliver
    (c) to run
    (d) to be steady

32. *Enigmatic, cryptic,* and *equivocal* are synonyms of which word?
    (a) reticent
    (b) ambiguous
    (c) ambivalent
    (d) tenuous

33. Which word is an antonym of *cursory*?
    (a) protracted
    (b) haphazard
    (c) slapdash
    (d) superficial

34. Someone who *vacillates*
    (a) puts things off
    (b) is reluctant to speak
    (c) has difficulty making a decision
    (d) rushes ahead without thinking

35. *Clement* comes from a Latin word that means
    (a) sweet
    (b) friendly
    (c) mild
    (d) light

Answers

1. outside; variety; enjoy; dictionary; cheat.
2. a 3. b 4. d 5. c 6. b 7. a 8. d 9. c 10. b 11. b 12. a 13. c 14. c 15. a 16. c 17. a 18. a 19. b 20. c 21. b 22. d 23. d 24. b 25. b 26. d 27. b 28. a 29. a 30. a 31. c 32. b 33. a 34. c 35. c

Evaluation

A Score Of 30–35 is excellent. If you answered fewer than thirty questions correctly in this test, review the entire level and take the test again.

Level 3

Welcome to Level 3 of *Verbal Advantage*. Let me begin by asking you an important question: Do you know the name of your dictionary?

Think about it for a moment. Can you remember the full name?

Here's why I ask: In the professional workshops I've taught I've found that most people haven't the slightest idea what the name of their dictionary is. "Webster's," they tell me, and I shoot back: "Did you know that the name *Webster* is in the public domain, and there are easily over a dozen dictionaries called 'Webster's' on the market? Which Webster do you own?"

Most people don't know the name of their dictionary or who publishes it. They may know if it's old or new, but they generally don't know if it's abridged or unabridged, or what its strengths and weaknesses are. That has always struck me as strange. Would you buy a car without knowing the name of the company that made it, or a tool without knowing how to use it? Most people agree that a dictionary is an essential resource—one that everyone should own—but they rarely take advantage of all it has to offer.

The average college-educated person probably consults a dictionary once or twice a month. In my workshops I've found that secretaries use a dictionary once or twice a week. Their bosses, on the other hand—the managers, executives, and professionals—may crack the binding of a wordbook as infrequently as once or twice a year. As I'm sure you can guess by now, that spells disaster for anyone who wants to use the language with precision.

The Dictionary Habit

Part of achieving the verbal advantage is developing what I call "the dictionary habit." I can assure you it is a beneficial addiction. No harm will come to you from using a dictionary to increase your knowledge of words.

You should own at least two dictionaries—keep one at work and one at home—and make an effort to consult them regularly. (If you work on a computer, you can use a dictionary on CD-ROM if you find that more convenient.) Look up any challenging words you come across in reading—especially those you think you know and have been reading around, as we discussed earlier. You should also use the dictionary when you write.

Let me underscore that last point. If you write without consulting a dictionary, all sorts of embarrassing errors can slip by into the finished product. A report, proposal, or memo in which words are misused or misspelled is irritating to read, and we all know that when it comes to making the right impression, even a little irritation can damage your credibility.

I should also stress that relying only on your computer's spelling and grammar checker is not enough. Spelling and grammar checkers are notoriously fallible. They often fail to expose common errors—for example, using *it's* for *its*, *their* for *there*, and *effect* for *affect*—and they frequently suggest "corrections" that are erroneous and sometimes ludicrous. Your checker will help you catch some mistakes, but it is no substitute for diligent use of a dictionary.

I once edited a book on business leadership by a prominent management consultant who has a doctoral degree. Throughout the book, the author used the phrase "a decisional criteria." Does anything about that phrase strike you as objectionable? If you're thinking "That sounds like jargon" (word 46 of Level 1), you're right. It's an example of specialized, unnecessarily technical language. Beyond that objection, I suspect that most readers would find the phrase innocuous.

Now there's a fine word: *innocuous* (i-NAHK-yoo-us). It means harmless, not producing any ill effect, as an innocuous drug or an innocuous remark. Look it up and see if I'm right.

And now let's get back to the phrase "a decisional criteria." It may seem innocuous, but in fact it contains two serious errors.

First, the word *criteria* is the plural of *criterion*. "A criteria" is wrong. You must say "This is my *criterion*" (singular), and "These are my *criteria*" (plural). With a quick peek into a dictionary, the author could have corrected the mistake. In checking the definition of *criterion*, he also could have avoided the second blunder: redundancy—for even if the phrase were corrected to "a decisional criterion," it would still be redundant.

A *criterion* is a standard on which a judgment or decision is based. "Decisional criterion" repeats the idea conveyed by the meaning of *criterion* alone. Translate the author's words into clear and simple English and you have the ridiculous phrase "a standard for decision-making that pertains to making decisions."

So you see, writing isn't easy, and even well-educated people can make mistakes if they don't take the time to examine their diction—their choice of words—and check their usage and spelling in a dictionary.

Don't delegate this task to a secretary or assistant. You will learn a great deal from editing your own writing, you will avoid the embarrassment of turning out a shoddy product, and you will save yourself the time spent rectifying things down the line. The more paperwork you have, the easier it is to overlook small but significant errors; therefore it's essential that you make time to revise everything you write—not just the reports and proposals and briefs, which usually get the most attention, but also your everyday letters and memoranda.

Here's something helpful you can do your next day on the job: Ask a coworker whose language skills you trust to look over what you have written before it goes out the door. In asking this favor you can offer to return it, and so begin to set up an editorial system that can wind up improving the quality of writing in the entire office or department.

A second and even third pair of eyes never hurt a piece of writing; in fact, every book, before it gets bound and published, is scrutinized by at least four persons—the author, editor, copy editor, and proofreader. Even then, a few errors still may appear in the finished product. Nobody's perfect, but the more conscientious you are about checking your writing and the more help you can get correcting it, the better off you will be. In the long run it will pay off in many ways—from making the right impression to satisfying clients or customers to getting others to understand your point of view.

Which Dictionary Should I Use?

So now that you are going to develop "the dictionary habit," the next question to resolve is "Which dictionary should I use?" Although every dictionary has its strengths and weaknesses, for general purposes just about any current, hardcover dictionary will do. Paperback dictionaries, which are sometimes called "pocket" dictionaries, have limited vocabularies and are best used for checking spelling and pronunciation. Come to think of it, I could also say that their vocabularies are *circumscribed*, a word you will soon meet as keyword 11 of this level.

Hardcover dictionaries come in two sizes: abridged and unabridged. Unabridged dictionaries contain up to four times as many words as abridged dictionaries, but they can be bulky and cumbersome, and unless you have a large desk, they are not well suited for use at the office. However, I am unequivocal (word 28 of Level 2), adamant (word 15 of Level 1), and even obstinate (word 34 of Level 1) in my belief that every self-respecting, word-conscious person should own an unabridged dictionary because of the breadth of information it contains. The best place for one is on a table or counter in the living room or family room, where you can lay it open and thumb through it easily.

For general purposes, the best American unabridged dictionary currently on the market is *The Random House Dictionary of the English Language*, second edition, published by Random House. If you become a serious word collector and you want to study the origin and development of words, you may want to acquire the second edition of the great *Oxford English Dictionary*, or *OED*, which is available in a compact, micrographic edition.

In the office most people use an abridged dictionary, usually called a "desk dictionary" or "college dictionary." Desk dictionaries are easy to handle and contain most of the linguistic information you will need on the job. Of the many on the market today, the four most reputable are *Random House Webster's College Dictionary*, published by Random House; *Merriam-Webster's Collegiate Dictionary*, tenth edition, published by Merriam-Webster; *Webster's New World Dictionary*, fourth college edition, published by IDG; and *The American Heritage Dictionary*, third edition, published by Houghton Mifflin, an oversized desk dictionary masquerading as unabridged.

How to Read a Dictionary

Now I'd like to share with you a few tips on how to read a dictionary—in other words, how to get the most out of what it contains.

A dictionary is an extraordinarily detailed and comprehensive source of knowledge about language, a one-volume reference library. Not only does your dictionary define words, it also shows how they're pronounced, it explains where they came from, and it provides information on grammar, usage, and style.

When you look up a word, the first thing the entry tells you is the thing people most often overlook: pronunciation. Don't skip over the pronunciation to get to the definition. The task of learning how to use a word begins with knowing how to say it right. If you have trouble deciphering some of the symbols used to indicate pronunciation, don't worry. I'll be giving you some help with that in Level 5.

The next thing the dictionary tells you is the part of speech—whether the word is a noun (*n.*), verb (*v.* or *vb.*), adjective (*adj.*), adverb (*adv.*), and so on. Mainly, this helps you save time finding the right entry or part of an entry. For example, if you look up the word *level* you will find three listings: for the noun *a level*, the verb *to level*, and the adjective *level*. The part-of-speech label directs you quickly to the definition you need.

Usually before but sometimes after the word is defined there is another useful bit of information that most people unfortunately can't be bothered with: the etymology (ET-uh-**MAHL**-uh-jee). *Etymology* is the history of a word or the study of the history of words. It is often confused in pronunciation with *entomology* (EN-tuh-**MAHL**-uh-jee), which means the study of insects. I have heard numerous college-educated professionals say *entomology* when they meant *etymology*. You see how a little slip of the tongue can result in a serious mistake? Remember, there is no *en-* in *etymology*.

If you are committed to building a powerful vocabulary, you should take the time to read the etymology of each word you look up in the dictionary. At first the foreign words will seem strange, but soon you will begin to see patterns and recognize relationships that will give you deeper insight into the language and help you decipher the meanings of unfamiliar words.

For example, the combining form *mal-* comes from the Latin *malus*, bad, evil. In English, when *mal-* appears in a word it means bad, inadequate, or abnormal, as in *malpractice*, bad practice, *maladjustment*, inadequate adjustment, and *malformation*, abnormal formation. Once you're familiar with *mal-*, you have a clue to help you deduce the meanings of the harder words *malefactor* (**MAL**-uh-FAK-tur), a bad person, evildoer, criminal; *maladroit* (MAL-uh-**DROYT**), inadequately skilled, clumsy, awkward; and *malapropos* (MAL-ap-ruh-**POH**), not normal or appropriate to the situation, not apropos (ap-ruh-POH). If vocabulary is the key to success, then etymology—word history—is the key to successfully building a large and exact vocabulary.

Now let's talk about the information everyone associates with a dictionary: definition. I want to stress here that you should always read all the definitions of the word you are looking up. Most people tend to skip to the definition that fits whatever they have just read or written. Don't sell yourself short. (Remember, from Level 2, my fifth principle for effective vocabulary building? "Don't cheat yourself.") Read the entire entry. A word may have two or three or even ten different senses. Learning the other meanings of a word is like learning several new words instead of just one.

While we're on the subject of definition, let me introduce you to the words *denotation* (DEE-noh-**TAY**-shin) and *connotation* (KAHN-uh-**TAY**-shin). The *denotation* of a word is its precise, explicit meaning, its dictionary definition. The *connotation* of a word is its implied meaning, including all the ideas, images, and emotions the word suggests.

The corresponding verbs are *denote* (di-NOHT) and *connote* (kuh-NOHT). In *The Careful Writer*, Theodore M. Bernstein nicely distinguishes the two words. "*Denote* means, *connote* implies," writes Bernstein. "To *denote* is . . . to furnish a factual, exact definition. To *connote* . . . embraces all the overtones, flavors, and suggestions that are not explicit in the purely minimal dictionary definitions." In short, knowing the denotation of a word helps us use it with precision and clarity. Grasping its connotation helps us use it to better effect—with greater sensitivity, wit, or power.

Dictionary definitions stick chiefly to denotation; the connotation is something you'll have to wrestle with on your own. As you acquire new words and learn what they denote, take care to consider what they connote, not only to you but to others.

Two more useful features in today's dictionaries are usage notes and synonym studies. Most desk dictionaries include brief remarks on the proper and improper use of certain controversial words. If you see a usage note after a dictionary entry, be sure to read it. But bear in mind that the opinions given in usage notes vary from dictionary to dictionary. Some are more strict and others more permissive. If possible, compare notes in two or more dictionaries, and when in doubt, take the cautious route—be circumspect (word 21 of this level)—and avoid any usage that seems questionable or that you think other educated people may find objectionable.

Now, let me ask you this: Off the top of your head can you differentiate the words *gather*, *collect*, *assemble*, *congregate*, *accumulate*, *amass*, *marshal*, and *rally*? Reading your dictionary's synonym studies will help you gain insight into the subtle differences in meaning among these and other groups of closely related words, which in turn will help you make precise distinctions in your choice of words.

The last dictionary feature I'd like to bring to your attention is the supplement (or sometimes supplements) on style. Most current desk dictionaries have one, yet most people have no idea this invaluable resource is there. Check your dictionary's table of contents to find out where these few priceless pages are hidden. The style guide explains in simple terms the rudiments of punctuation, capitalization, documentation of source material in footnotes and bibliographies, and proper forms of address. (And while you're checking your dictionary for the whereabouts of the style guide, do you also need to check on the word *rudiments*?)

I cannot overemphasize the importance of this information. Anyone who commits words to print (and even e-mail) must have a solid sense of where to place commas and semicolons, how to use single and double quotation marks, and when and when not to hyphenate and capitalize. Don't be caught with your periods or commas outside your quotation marks. Consult your dictionary's style guide whenever you have the slightest doubt about the mechanics of writing.

The point of all this talk about what's inside your dictionary is to impress upon you how much more you can learn from that book than simply what words mean and how they are spelled. The dictionary is there to help you at every step of your journey toward mastery of the language—so use it often and enjoy the process of discovery! And while you're exploring the dictionary, if you're confused by any of the symbols, abbreviations, or labels you come across, all you have to do is consult the explanatory notes printed in the front of the book.

Now let's get back to the business of building your vocabulary. Here are the first ten keywords in Level 3:

Word 1: DEFRAY (di-FRAY)

To pay, provide money for, cover the cost or expenses of.

Pay and defray are synonymous, but they are not interchangeable. You pay for a meal in a restaurant, you don't defray it. You pay your bills, you don't defray them. In current usage defray means to cover the cost or expense of something, especially to provide money for a portion of that cost or expense. For example, you might use an income tax refund to help defray the expense of a trip to Europe. A nonprofit corporation that receives a grant or donation might use it to defray the cost of office equipment and supplies.

Word 2: TACITURN (TAS-i-turn)

Silent, not talkative, holding one's tongue, reserved, uncommunicative, reticent (RET-i-sint).

Challenging antonyms of taciturn include garrulous (word 8 of Level 4), loquacious (loh-KWAY-shus), effusive (e-FYOO-siv, word 13 of Level 7), and voluble (VAHL-yuh-bul, word 1 of Level 5).

Taciturn comes from the same Latin root as tacit (word 9 in Level 2). Tacit means unspoken, done or made in silence. Taciturn means silent by nature, preferring not to speak.

Taciturn and reticent both mean not talkative, uncommunicative. Reticent suggests a disinclination to express one's feelings or supply information. Taciturn refers to a person who is habitually silent and withdrawn.

A word of caution about reticent. Though you increasingly hear people use reticent to mean reluctant, in careful usage these words are not synonymous. Reluctant means unwilling, hesitant, disinclined. Reticent means reluctant to speak.

Word 3: TERSE (rhymes with *worse*)

Brief and to the point, free of superfluous words, expressed in a pointed and polished way.

More difficult synonyms of terse include concise, pithy (PITH-ee), succinct (suhk-SINGKT), and laconic (luh-KAHN-ik, word 18 of this level).

Antonyms include *long-winded*, *redundant*, *verbose* (word 30 of Level 2), and *prolix* (word 1 of Level 9).

Concise, *succinct*, and *terse* all suggest brevity, expressing something in a brief and direct way. *Concise* implies eliminating anything unnecessary or superfluous: "Her presentation was persuasive and concise." *Succinct* implies getting the point across in the fewest possible words: "An effective letter to the editor must be succinct."

By the way, I'm sure you've heard the beastly mispronunciation suh-SINGKT, which in recent years has become widespread among educated speakers. Good speakers don't say ASS-uh-dent for *accident*, uh-SEPT for *accept*, or suh-SEED for *succeed*, so there's no logical reason for saying suh-SINGKT. Take care to pronounce the *cc* in *succinct* like *k-s*: suhk-SINGKT.

But let's get back to our keyword, *terse*. Terse writing or speech is brief, pointed, and polished. It communicates smoothly and effectively, without digressions or excess words. *Terse* may also suggest expression that is blunt or brusque (rhymes with *dusk*). A terse reply is brief and pointed, but it stops just short of being rude.

Word 4: BOON (rhymes with *moon*)

A blessing, timely and welcome benefit, something beneficial bestowed upon one, something to be thankful for.

A *boon* once meant a favor or request. In stories of yore—of time long past—knights, courtiers, and all manner of supplicants would bow before their kings and queens and say, "As your humble servant, I beseech you to grant me this boon." Are you wondering what *supplicant* means? A *supplicant* (SUHP-li-kint) is a person who begs for something, and *supplication* is the act of begging for something humbly and earnestly.

Getting back to *boon*, the meaning "favor, request" is now archaic (ahr-KAY-ik), or old-fashioned, and today *boon* is used to mean a blessing, a timely and welcome benefit, something to be thankful for, as in "This good weather is a boon"; "His efforts were a boon to their enterprise."

Word 5: PROLETARIAT (PROH-luh-**TAIR**-ee-it)

The working class, especially the industrial wage-earning class, which earns its living by manual labor. The adjective is *proletarian* (PROH-luh-**TAIR**-ee-in), of or relating to the working class.

In the philosophy of Karl Marx, the famous exponent (ek-SPOH-nint; do you need to look it up?) of communism, the proletariat comprises those members of society without property or capital who must sell their labor to survive. *Proletariat* comes through French from the Latin *proletarius*, which means a Roman citizen of the lowest class. Today the word is still used to mean the lowest and poorest class of people in any society.

Word 6: HETEROGENEOUS (HET-uh-roh-JEE-nee-u̱s)

Varied, composed of parts of different kinds, made up of unrelated or diverse elements, mixed, dissimilar, miscellaneous.

The opposite of *heterogeneous* is *homogeneous* (HOH-moh-**JEE**-nee-u̱s, five syllables), of the same or similar nature or kind.

The prefix *homo-* means same, similar, like, as in *homosexual*, attracted to the same sex; *homogenize*, to blend, make similar or homogeneous; and *homonym* (HAHM-uh-nim), a word that is pronounced the same as another word but that has a different origin and meaning, such as *fair* and *fare*.

The prefix *hetero-* means other, different, unlike, as in *heterosexual*, attracted to the other sex; *heterodox* (HET-ur-uh-dahks), having an opinion different from the accepted opinion, the opposite of *orthodox* (OR-thuh-dahks); and *heterogeneous*, varied, dissimilar, diverse, consisting of different elements or kinds.

Word 7: PITTANCE (PIT-'ns)

A small amount, portion, or share, especially a small or meager amount of money. "Her inheritance was only a pittance"; "He received a pittance for his services"; "Some people will work for a pittance if the job is rewarding."

Think of the pit of a fruit, which is small and hard, and you'll easily remember that a *pittance* is a *small* amount of money that is *hard* to live on.

Word 8: GLIB (rhymes with *rib*)

Smooth-spoken, speaking in a ready, fluent manner, with natural or offhand ease, talkative in a nonchalant way.

Synonyms of *glib* include *suave*, *facile*, *bland*, *voluble* (word 1 of Level 5), *flippant*, and *unctuous* (UHNGK-choo-u̱s).

By the way, I really like the word *unctuous*. It comes from the Latin *ungere*, to anoint, which is also the source of the English word *unguent* (UHNG-gwe̱nt), a medicinal ointment, salve (SAV or SAHV). By derivation *unctuous* means oily, fatty, having a greasy or soapy feel, and today *unctuous* is used to mean having a slimy, slippery, or smarmy manner. The unctuous person appears agreeable or earnest, but in an affected, self-serving, and insincere way.

Our keyword, *glib*, also has a slightly unpleasant aroma. In general *glib* refers to the ability to speak or to something spoken in a smooth, easy, nonchalant way, but the word usually suggests a manner that is too smooth and easy to be convincing. Glib answers may be thoughtless, ill-considered; glib proposals or solutions may be superficial; and a glib salesperson or a glib politician may be persuasive but insincere.

Word 9: PENCHANT (PEN-chint)

A liking, leaning, strong inclination, decided taste: "a penchant for sports," "a penchant for poetry," "a penchant for spicy food."

More difficult synonyms of *penchant* include *propensity*, a profound, often irresistible inclination; and *proclivity*, a strong natural or habitual tendency, especially toward something objectionable or wicked. Career criminals have a proclivity for violence. Successful businesspeople have a propensity for discerning the bottom line and making a profit. And many people have a penchant for chocolate, a strong liking, decided taste.

Word 10: SOLICITOUS (suh-LIS-i-tus)

Concerned, showing care and attention, especially in a worried, anxious, or fearful way.

Solicitous suggests great concern, usually displayed by thoughtful care or hovering attention. In this sense *solicitous* may be followed by the prepositions *of*, *for*, or *about*: one may be solicitous *about* the outcome of an event, solicitous *of* a child, or solicitous *for* the welfare of another.

Solicitous may also be used to mean eager, full of desire, willing. In this slightly different sense it is followed by the preposition *to* and still conveys anxious concern: solicitous to gain the advantage; solicitous to know the results of the election; solicitous to go ahead with the plan.

Let's review the ten keywords you've just learned. Consider the following questions and decide whether the correct answer is yes or no. Answers appear on page 110.

1. Would a year-end bonus help defray your holiday expenses?
2. Is a garrulous or loquacious person also taciturn?
3. Is a terse speaker long-winded and tedious?
4. Would winning the lottery be a boon?
5. Is the aristocracy the opposite of the proletariat?
6. Is American society heterogeneous?
7. Will some people work for a pittance if the job is rewarding?
8. Is a glib speaker earnest and excited?
9. When you have a penchant for something, do you find it irritating or disagreeable?
10. Can you be solicitous about someone's health?

A Dictum on Diction

Because you are such an exemplary (word 39 of Level 4) student of vocabulary, I know you have just looked up the word *dictum* and discovered that it comes from the Latin *dicere*, to say, speak; that it means a formal pronouncement, an official opinion or decree; and that the plural is *dicta*.

Did you also check the word *diction*? It comes from the Latin *dictus*, the past participle of *dicere*, to say, speak, and it is often used today to mean vocal expression, specifically one's enunciation, the clarity and distinctness of one's speech. But the traditional meaning of the word, which is still in good standing, refers to one's selection of words with regard to clarity, accuracy, and variety.

Your diction is your choice of words, manner of expression. It differs from your vocabulary, which is the entire stock of words you possess. Good diction means using language that is clear, accurate, varied, and apposite (AP-uh-zit), which means both relevant and appropriate. (Take a moment to look up *apposite*.) Poor diction means using a word or phrase in the wrong way or the wrong place, creating an inappropriate or illogical effect.

Irregardless is a classic example of poor diction. Grammarians have railed against this nonstandard word for years, but like a hardy cockroach it continues to crawl out of the illiterate woodwork into the light of conversation, and occasionally into the pages of the newspaper. The proper word is *regardless*, which means without regard. Adding the privative, or negative, prefix *ir-* to *regardless* creates a double negative. *Irregardless* therefore means not without regard, or, more simply, with concern for. Of course, that's just the opposite of what those who use *irregardless* intend it to mean.

Peruse (puh-ROOZ) also has become the victim of mounting abuse. *Peruse* once meant to use up, wear out, for the prefix *per-* means thoroughly, throughout, through to the end. You can see the prefix *per-* at work in the familiar words *perfect*, which combines *per-*, thoroughly, with the Latin *facere*, to make; and *perennial*, from *per-*, throughout, and the Latin *annus*, a year. Thus by derivation *perfect* means thoroughly made, and *perennial* means throughout the year.

But let's get back to *peruse*. In its traditional and still correct sense, *peruse* is a lovely word that means to read carefully and critically, examine closely, read through to the end.

But in recent years people have begun using *peruse* to mean skim, browse, dip into or glance through.

Here's a sentence that misuses *peruse*, which I found in a newspaper story on book collectors: "Buying at the rate of 50 books a week has clearly made it impossible for him to read most of his purchases, though he strives at least to peruse each one." Properly, the sentence should read like this: "Buying at the rate of 50 books a week has clearly made it impossible for him to *peruse* most of his purchases, though he strives at least to *skim* each one."

Poor diction is painfully apparent in the trendy substitution of the word *reticent* for *reluctant*. We discussed *reticent* earlier. Do you remember what it means? Not talkative, not disposed to speak one's mind. It's a synonym of *taciturn* (keyword 2 of this level), which you just learned means habitually silent or reserved.

Reticent has come to be used by many educated speakers in place of the word *reluctant*. They say, "I am reticent to talk about it," or "He is reticent to take action." This substitution is a prime example of what I call the "sounds-like syndrome," where a fancier word that sounds like a simpler word gradually takes over the simpler word's meaning, and sometimes loses its own specific meaning.

The confusion between *reticent* and *reluctant* is now so common that some dictionaries list them as synonyms. You should interpret that as recognition of the frequency of the error rather than as justification for committing it yourself. Don't use *reticent* when you mean *reluctant*. You cannot be "reticent to do something" or "reticent to speak." You can only be reluctant. A reluctant person is hesitant, disinclined, unwilling to do something. A reticent person is reluctant to speak.

Another error of diction I am not reluctant to expose is the use of *loathe* for *loath*. I have heard some of the most prominent broadcasters on radio and TV confuse and mispronounce these words, and I have often seen the words confounded in print—even in the pages of such prestigious publications as *The New York Times*. The adjective *loath* (no *e* at the end) is a strong synonym of *reluctant*. When you are loath to do or say something, you are reluctant almost to the point of aversion or disgust. The verb to *loathe* (with an *e* at the end) means to hate, despise. When you loathe something, you find it disgusting or despicable.

Loath and *loathe* are distinguished not only in spelling and meaning but also in pronunciation. The *th* in these words has a different sound. *Loathe* (LOH<u>TH</u>) has a "voiced" *th* and rhymes with *clothe*. *Loath* (LOHTH) has a "voiceless" *th* and rhymes with *both*. Do not say you are loathe (LOH<u>TH</u>) to do something. Say you are loath (LOHTH) to do it.

Last but not least, the words *emulate* and *imitate* are frequently confused. To *imitate* is to follow the example of, take as a model. If you imitate a person you act the same way that person acts. To *emulate* means to strive to equal or excel. If you emulate a person you try to surpass or outdo that person's ability or achievement. Thus, a son may imitate his father's mannerisms, but emulate his skill in driving a car. A painter may imitate a masterpiece, or attempt to emulate the master.

Your diction is important because it reflects the way you think. In many situations, people judge you on your choice of words. If you loathe ignorance but are loath to learn, you're not going to go very far. To make a favorable impression, you must avoid imitating the poor habits of others and emulate the writers and speakers you admire. And one of the best ways to improve your diction is to read widely and peruse the dictionary.

Let's return now to the *Verbal Advantage* vocabulary. Here are the next ten keywords in Level 3:

Word 11: CIRCUMSCRIBE (sur-k<u>u</u>m-SKRYB *or* SUR-k<u>u</u>m-skryb)

To limit, restrict, confine, hem in, fix the boundaries of.

The *scribe* in *circumscribe* means to write, draw, and *circum-* means around. Literally, *circumscribe* means to draw a line around, encircle; figuratively, it means to enclose within narrow limits, restrict, confine: the circumscribed routine of daily life; a law that circumscribes certain rights.

You can see the combining form *circum-* at work in many English words. *Circumstance* combines *circum-*, around, with the Latin *stare*, to stand, and means literally "that which stands around"; hence, a condition or factor influencing a situation or surrounding an event. *Circumcision* combines *circum-* with *incision* to mean literally "a cutting around." *Circumvent* combines *circum-*, around, with the Latin *venire*, to go, and means to go around, bypass, especially in a clever or resourceful way: "She had to circumvent a lot of red tape to get the job done." From this somewhat circumlocutory (SUR-k<u>u</u>m-**LAHK**-yuh-tor-ee), or roundabout, discussion, can you guess the meaning of *circumnavigate*? That's right: It means to navigate or sail around, as to circumnavigate the earth.

Our keyword, *circumscribe*, means literally to draw a line around; hence, to enclose within narrow limits, fix the boundaries of: "A limited vocabulary can circumscribe your career and undermine your chances for success."

Word 12: DEARTH (rhymes with *earth*)

A lack, scarcity, insufficiency, inadequate supply of something needed.

A more difficult synonym of *dearth* is *paucity* (PAW-si-tee, word 2 of Level 10). Antonyms of *dearth* include *abundance*, *surplus*, *excess*, *superfluity* (SOO-pur-**FLOO**-i-tee), *plethora* (PLETH-uh-ruh, word 19 of Level 6), and *surfeit* (SUR-fit, word 49 of Level 8).

Dearth is a noun formed from the adjective *dear*. Something dear is precious, costly, highly valued. Literally, a dearth is a lack of something dear. *Dearth* is now used of any serious insufficiency or inadequate supply: a dearth of supplies; a dearth of hope; a dearth of opportunities in the job market.

Word 13: INGRATIATING (in-**GRAY**-shee-AY-ting)

Flattering, attempting to win approval or curry favor, trying to gain acceptance, done to charm or please another.

The word *unctuous* (UHNGK-choo-us), which was discussed under *glib*, keyword 8 in this level, is a close synonym of *ingratiating*.

Ingratiating comes from the Latin *in*, which means in or into, and *gratia*, grace. By derivation *ingratiating* means getting into the good graces of another.

Dictionaries and thesauruses often give *charming*, *pleasing*, and *agreeable* as synonyms of *ingratiating*, but today the word is rarely used in a positive sense. Invariably it has the negative suggestion of charming in an insincere way, pleasing in an attempt to win approval or curry favor, agreeable so as to get into the good graces of another: "Every time Don walked by the boss's office or passed him in the hallway, he would flash a fake, ingratiating smile. That, and other unctuous gestures, soon made Don's coworkers loathe him."

Word 14: MERCENARY (**MUR**-suh-NER-ee)

Greedy, done for payment only, motivated by a selfish desire for money or other reward. Synonyms include *covetous* and *avaricious*, which are discussed in word 40 of Level 2.

Mercenary is also close in meaning to the challenging word *venal* (VEE-nul). *Venal* means corruptible, capable of being bribed or bought off: a venal social climber; a venal politician.

The noun a *mercenary* denotes a hired soldier, one who fights not for a cause or for love of country but for money. The adjective *mercenary* means done for payment only, motivated by greed: "Harry's interest in the deal was strictly mercenary."

Word 15: EXTEMPORIZE (ek-STEM-puh-ryz)

To improvise, to speak or compose with little or no preparation or practice, perform something in an offhand or unpremeditated way: "She delivered her speech using notes, but during the question-and-answer session she extemporized."

To *improvise* is the general word meaning to make up on the spur of the moment. You can improvise a speech, a tune on the piano, or a plan of action. *Extemporize* usually refers specifically to speaking in an offhand, spontaneous way. The corresponding adjective *extemporaneous* means spoken or composed with little or no preparation or practice. Extemporaneous remarks are impromptu, made up on the spur of the moment.

Word 16: ERUDITE (traditionally, **ER**-uh-DYT; now usually **ER**-yuh-DYT)

Learned, scholarly, possessing extensive knowledge acquired chiefly from books.

Erudite comes from the Latin *erudire*, to instruct, educate, polish, free from roughness or rudeness. The corresponding noun is *erudition*, extensive knowledge acquired from reading books: "He displayed his erudition with wit and grace."

People and things can both be erudite. For example, erudite professors often write erudite studies of obscure subjects. Reading *Verbal Advantage* will help you build an erudite vocabulary, which in turn will help you become a more erudite person, someone who possesses a wide store of knowledge.

I should point out that my pronunciation of *erudite* and *erudition* is slightly different from most educated speakers. Today most people pronounce these words with a long *u*: **AIR**-yoo-DYT (or **AIR**-yuh-) and AIR-yoo-**DISH**-un (or AIR-yuh-). The interesting thing is that the speakers who prefer these long-*u* pronunciations rarely take pains to preserve the traditional long-*u* sound in *duty*, *assume*, *student*, *opportunity*, or *prelude* (properly PREL-yood, not PRAY-lood). Yet they have trained themselves to say **AIR**-yoo-DYT and AIR-yoo-**DISH**-u̱n presumably because the cultivated sound of the long *u* complements the meaning of these words.

The long-*u* pronunciations of *erudite* and *erudition* are not incorrect. In fact, they have been acceptable for several decades and all current dictionaries list them. However, to my hypercritical ear they smack of pseudosophistication, or sham erudition, because they ignore the etymologically significant *rude* dwelling within these words and illogically transform a short Latin *u* into a long English *u*. And so I remain faithful to the older, though now less popular, pronunciations **ER**-uh-DYT and ER-uh-**DISH**-u̱n. (For more on the pronunciation of *erudite*, see my *Big Book of Beastly Mispronunciations*.)

Word 17: AUSTERE (aw-STEER)

Severe, somber, stern, serious, grim, grave, dour (properly rhymes with *poor*, not *sour*).

Austere may mean severe or stern in appearance, manner, or practice. An austere person is forbidding, somber, grave. An austere lifestyle is characterized by strict self-discipline or severe self-denial. Austere surroundings have a dearth of creature comforts or decoration; they are grim and barren.

Word 18: LACONIC (luh-KAHN-ik)

Using few words, briefly and often bluntly expressed.

Laconic comes from the Greek *lakonikos*, a Spartan, a resident of the ancient city state of Sparta, which was renowned for its austere and warlike people. By derivation *laconic* refers to the Spartans' reputation for rigorous self-discipline and reticence.

Synonyms of *laconic* include *succinct*, *concise*, *terse*, and *pithy*. We discussed some of these words earlier in this level, under *terse* (word 3), but it's worth going over them again so you can clearly distinguish their meanings.

Succinct means expressed in the briefest, most compressed way possible: a succinct update on the issue. *Concise* implies expression that is free from all superfluous words: a concise letter of resignation. *Terse* adds to concise the suggestion of pointedness and polish: a terse presentation. *Pithy* refers to concise expression that is full of meaning and substance, that is both brief and profound: pithy advice.

Laconic expression may be either terse or pithy, but it also implies an abruptness that can seem brusque or indifferent. Julius Caesar's three-word pronouncement, "*Veni, vidi, vici*" (I came, I saw, I conquered), is one of the most famous laconic statements of all time. There is also the anecdote about Calvin Coolidge, the thirtieth president of the United States, who was legendary for his taciturnity, extreme reluctance to speak. As the story goes, someone once approached Coolidge and said, "Mr. President, I bet I can make you say more than three words." Without hesitating or even cracking a smile, Coolidge shot back, "You lose." Now that's laconic wit.

Like the ancient Spartans, the laconic speakers and writers of today are determined to use no more words than are necessary to get the point across, even at the risk of giving offense.

Word 19: AMELIORATE (uh-MEEL-yuh-rayt)

To make or become better or more tolerable, improve, amend, correct, reform, rectify, raise the condition or state of.

Ameliorate is used chiefly of improving something that needs help because it is inferior, oppressive, or intolerable. City officials may decide to ameliorate a run-down neighborhood. A charitable organization may work to ameliorate the hapless condition of the homeless or the poor.

Word 20: EXPUNGE (ek-SPUHNJ)

To erase, delete, cancel; punch, strike, or wipe out; eradicate, obliterate.

To *erase* means literally to rub or scratch out. You erase a blackboard or a pencil mark. To *cancel* means literally to cross out with lines. You cancel a check or a clause in a contract. To *delete* means to remove written material. On a computer you can delete a word, a paragraph, or an entire document with a few keystrokes or clicks of the mouse. To *expunge* means to wipe out something completely so it appears as though it had never existed: to expunge a name from a list; to expunge all record of an event; to expunge a word from your vocabulary.

Let's review the ten words you've just learned. Consider the following statements and decide whether each one is true or false. Answers appear on page 111.

1. Listening to *Verbal Advantage* will circumscribe your vocabulary.
2. If a country has a dearth of food, its people may be starving.
3. The ingratiating person uses flattery to win approval.
4. Mercenary motivations are high-minded and generous.
5. When you speak off the cuff, you extemporize.
6. An erudite person lacks knowledge and cultivation.
7. The happy-go-lucky person has an austere outlook on life.
8. A laconic speaker is long-winded and boring.
9. If you ameliorate something, you make it better.
10. When you expunge something, you remove all trace of it.

Did you remember to keep track of your answers and calculate your score? Don't read ahead in the program until you can answer at least eight questions in these review quizzes correctly.

Here are the next ten keywords in Level 3:

Word 21: CIRCUMSPECT (SUR-k<u>u</u>m-spekt)

Careful, cautious, wary, watchful, carefully considering all circumstances before acting or making a judgment.

Synonyms of *circumspect* include *discreet*, *vigilant*, and *prudent* (word 47 of Level 1).

Earlier in this level you learned the word *circumscribe*, to limit, confine, restrict. As in that word, the *circum-* in *circumspect* means around. The second half of *circumspect* comes from the Latin *specere*, to look at carefully, observe.

The Latin *specere* is also the source of the words *spectator*, one who looks on; *spectacle*, something unusual to look at, an impressive display; and *spectacular*, wonderful to behold. By derivation, *circumspect* means looking around carefully before making a decision or taking action, and that's the meaning of the word today.

Careful implies close attention and concern; one is careful to pronounce words properly. *Cautious* implies guarding against danger and risk; you should be cautious when crossing the street. *Circumspect* implies a worried care, a nervous, wary cautiousness. The circumspect person is concerned about unforseen circumstances and unfavorable consequences, and so is careful to avoid making an ill-considered move.

Word 22: QUIESCENT (kwy-ES-int)

Still, quiet, tranquil, inactive, at rest or repose.

Antonyms of *quiescent* include *vigorous*, *animated*, *sprightly*, *vivacious*, and *ebullient* (i-BUHL-yint or i-BUUL-yint).

The words *latent*, *dormant*, and *quiescent* are related in meaning. *Latent* applies to something that has not yet been revealed: a latent ability, a latent desire. *Dormant* applies to something inactive or that seems asleep: a dormant volcano, a dormant power. *Quiescent* suggests a temporary cessation of activity, a period of rest or repose: the sea was quiescent after the storm.

Word 23: FOIBLE (FOY-bul)

A weak point, slight fault or flaw, minor failing, especially a weakness in a person's character.

By derivation *foible* means the weak part of a sword, and it is related to the word *feeble*, weak, frail.

A foible is not a serious defect in character but rather a minor flaw or weakness that is usually forgivable: "A penchant for rich desserts is her only foible."

Word 24: FERVENT (FUR-vint)

Passionate, having or showing great warmth or intensity of feeling, fiery, earnest, impassioned.

Synonyms of *fervent* include *vehement*, *ardent*, *fervid*, and *zealous* (ZEL-us).

Antonyms of *fervent* include *lukewarm*, *listless*, *apathetic*, *indifferent*, *impassive*, and *phlegmatic* (fleg-MAT-ik, word 33 of Level 9).

Fervent and *fervid* both come from the Latin *fervere*, to boil, glow, and both are still used to mean very hot, boiling, glowing, burning. When used of feelings, *fervent* suggests great warmth and earnestness. *Fervid* is stronger and suggests intense, even violent emotion. A fervent speech or a fervent belief is fiery and passionate, but a fervid debate or a fervid protest is vehement, overheated, boiling over with passionate intensity.

Word 25: PROTRACT (proh-TRAKT)

To draw out, drag out, extend in time, lengthen, prolong, especially to excess.

Antonyms of *protract* include *abbreviate*, *condense*, *curtail*, and *truncate* (TRUHNG-kayt).

Prolong and *protract* both refer to increasing the duration of something. *Prolong* suggests making it longer than usual, lengthening it beyond ordinary limits: to prolong a meeting, a prolonged illness. *Protract* comes from the Latin *tractare*, to draw, drag around. It suggests drawing or dragging something out needlessly, often to the point of irritation or boredom. A protracted trial is long and tedious. A protracted debate seems to drag on forever. And now, before you accuse me of protracting this discussion, I shall curtail it—cut it short—and move on to the next word.

Word 26: OSTENTATIOUS (AHS-t<u>e</u>n-**TAY**-sh<u>u</u>s)

Showy, extremely conspicuous, extravagant, flamboyant; specifically, displayed or done in a flashy, vain manner.

Antonyms of *ostentatious* include *simple*, *plain*, *modest*, and *unassuming*.

Pretentious, *pompous*, and *ostentatious* all refer to persons or things that are showy, extravagant, and self-important. All three words are often used of style, as in writing, speech, fashion, art, music, or architecture.

Pretentious means laying claim to a level of distinction or worth that is undeserved. The pretentious person asserts his self-importance in a demanding, arrogant way. That which is pretentious draws attention to itself by strutting and bragging.

Pompous means puffed up with exaggerated self-importance. The pompous person is full of solemn reverence for himself or his opinions. That which is pompous takes itself too seriously.

Ostentatious emphasizes conspicuousness and vanity. The ostentatious person puts on an extravagant show to impress others. Ostentatious clothing parades itself. An ostentatious display of wealth is an exaggerated, unnecessary show of wealth.

Word 27: QUANDARY (KWAHN-duh-ree *or* KWAHN-dry)

A state of uncertainty, perplexity, or doubt.

Predicament, *dilemma*, and *quandary* all apply to situations or conditions that are difficult and perplexing.

A *predicament* is a situation that is especially unpleasant or unfortunate: "Larry looked at his smashed-up car lying in the ditch, then at his mistress who was more smashed than his car, and he wondered how he had gotten himself into this predicament."

Dilemma (word 3 of level 5) is often used today of any difficult problem or troublesome situation, but many good writers and speakers object to that as loose usage. *Dilemma* comes from the greek *di-*, meaning two, and *lemma*, a proposition, and by derivation means a choice between two propositions. Strictly speaking, *dilemma* should be used only of situations in which one faces a choice between equally undesirable alternatives, as "The soldiers who defended the Alamo faced a terrible dilemma: to surrender or die."

A *quandary* is a state of uncertainty or confusion that renders one unable to act. To be "in a quandary" means to be puzzled, full of doubts, and not sure what to do: "Julie was in a quandary over whether to look for a better job"; "the thought of buying a new house put them in a quandary: they wanted a nicer place with more room for the kids, but could they afford it?"

Word 28: CENSURE (SEN-shur)

To blame, condemn, find fault with, criticize harshly, express stern disapproval of.

Synonyms of *censure* include *denounce*, *reprimand*, and *reprehend* (rep-ri-HEND). Antonyms include *commend*, *extol* (ek-STOHL), and *laud* (rhymes with *sawed*).

Censure is often used today to mean to reprimand formally, blame or condemn in an official manner, as "The Senate censured one of its members for unethical conduct." But you may also use *censure* less formally to mean to express stern disapproval of, criticize harshly, as to censure an employee for lackadaisical performance. *Censure* usually implies condemnation of irresponsible behavior rather than condemnation of character.

Be careful not to confuse the words *censure* and *censor*. To *censor* (SEN-sur) is to suppress or delete something objectionable, as to censor a book, or to censor unpopular opinions. To *censure* (SEN-shur) is to blame, condemn, find fault with.

Word 29: CAVIL (KAV-ul)

To criticize or complain unnecessarily, point out petty flaws, raise trivial or frivolous objections.

Synonyms of *cavil* include *nitpick*, *niggle*, *carp*, and *quibble*. All these words suggest making unnecessary criticisms or complaining about trivial things. A good editor corrects your grammar and punctuation but doesn't nitpick every sentence. A boss who niggles about every detail will eventually exasperate the employees. Husbands and wives often carp at each other about household expenses and domestic chores. Professors quibble with their colleagues about minor points of scholarship. Newspaper critics will often cavil in their reviews just to assert their authority as critics.

To *cavil* means to complain unnecessarily, point out petty flaws, raise trivial or frivolous objections.

Word 30: ASSIMILATE (uh-SIM-i-layt)

To absorb, take in, incorporate, appropriate.

In physiology, *assimilate* means to absorb into the body, convert to nourishment, digest. In general use, *assimilate* has two senses. It may mean to absorb or take into the mind, comprehend, as to assimilate ideas, to assimilate new words into your vocabulary. It is also commonly used to mean to adapt to or become absorbed by a system or culture: "American society is composed of generations of immigrants, some more assimilated than others." "He feared that if he accepted the job, he would have to assimilate into the faceless machine of the bureaucracy."

Let's review the ten keywords you've just learned. This time I'm going to give you two words, and you decide if they are synonyms or antonyms. Answers appear on page 111.

1. *Circumspect* and *cautious* are . . . synonyms or antonyms?
2. *Animated* and *quiescent* are . . .
3. *Flaw* and *foible* are . . .
4. *Fervent* and *impassive* are . . .
5. To *protract* and to *curtail* are . . .
6. *Flamboyant* and *ostentatious* are . . .
7. *Quandary* and *predicament* are . . .
8. To *censure* and to *commend* are . . .
9. To *cavil* and to *quibble* are . . .
10. To *absorb* and to *assimilate* are . . .

The Express Lane to Better Diction

To keep you on your toes about using the language properly, here's a little quiz I think you'll enjoy. I'm going to ask you three questions, and in each one I will make the same error of diction—my choice of words. See if you can tell which word I'm misusing. Here we go:

1. Would you say there are more cars on the road now than there were five years ago, or are there less?
2. Do you think a stronger economy will cause less U.S. companies to manufacture their products in foreign countries? (I don't care whether you answer yes or no. Just try to tell which word I'm misusing.)
3. The last time you bought groceries, did you buy less than you did the time before, or more?

Okay, did you catch which word I abused? If you guessed *less*, you're right. In each question I failed to make the proper distinction between *less* and *fewer*, a distinction that unfortunately is observed less and less these days by fewer and fewer people.

Many people incorrectly use *less* when *fewer* is required. Here's the difference.

Less modifies quantities, abstractions, things that are considered single or whole—*less* food, *less* time, *less* money. *Fewer* modifies things that can be itemized, enumerated, broken down into separate elements or parts—*fewer* thoughts, *fewer* words, *fewer* mistakes. In the questions I posed a moment ago, instead of saying *less* I should have said *fewer* cars, *fewer* companies, and *fewer* groceries, because cars, companies, and groceries all can be considered individually.

The use of *less* in place of *fewer* is so common nowadays that to many speakers *fewer* has come to sound stilted, even if they know it's correct. I once edited a business manual that contained the following sentence: "As prices increase, producers will offer more products for sale; as prices decrease, producers will offer less (or fewer) products." The author couldn't decide whether to use *less* or *fewer*, and so used both in a desperate attempt to satisfy all parties—those who erroneously offer less products, and those who properly offer fewer of them.

If you think I'm just nitpicking or caviling about this *fewer/less* distinction, let me assure you that the error has a far-reaching effect on our daily lives. William Safire, who for years has been writing about language for *The New York Times Magazine*, has said that "the most power-intensive moment" in the history of his column "came when Safeway Stores was criticized for 'Express Lane—Ten Items or Less' and promptly rectified the mistake." Safire boasted that "millions of mothers take their tots through the checkout counters at that fine company under signs that now read 'Ten Items or Fewer.'"

I never saw that correction in the Safeway stores where I live. However, they did make one small change in the express-lane sign: It went from reading "ten items or less" to "nine items or less." Perhaps out of guilt for compounding the error, a short while later Safeway sold out to the giant supermarket chain Vons.

All was not lost, however. After the Vons people finished relocating the butter and spaghetti, rearranging the meat, and decorating the store with double-coupon banners, they finally got around to the wording on the express-lane signs.

But instead of changing "nine items or less" to "nine items or fewer," they simply ducked the diction issue altogether. The express-lane signs now read, "No more than nine items."

I hope you will take this little lesson on *less* and *fewer* to heart. The ability to distinguish between these words is one sign of a careful writer and speaker. Using them properly won't make you less attractive or cause you to have fewer friends. And remember, the people who have less trouble in life are the ones who make fewer mistakes. So take care to use *less* when you're talking about quantities, abstractions, or things that are considered single or whole, and use *fewer* when you're talking about things that can be itemized, considered individually, or broken down into elements or parts.

And now it's time to move on and learn no fewer than the next ten keywords in Level 3.

Word 31: RESCIND (ri-SIND)

To cancel, take back, take away, remove; also, to render void, annul, repeal.

Rescind comes from a Latin verb meaning to cut, and by derivation means to cut back or away; hence, to remove, cancel, take back something one has said or done. When you rescind an order, rescind a contract, or rescind a law, you cancel it, make it void. When you rescind a statement you take it back, remove it from the record.

Word 32: DISCERNIBLE (di-SURN-i-bul)

Recognizable, detectible, perceptible, capable of being recognized by the senses or by the mind.

Synonyms of *discernible* include *apparent*, *evident*, *distinguishable*, and *manifest* (MAN-i̱-fest). Antonyms of *discernible* include *obscure*, *invisible*, *indistinct*, and *imperceptible*.

Discernible and the related words *discern*, *discernment*, and *discerning* come from a Latin word meaning to sift, separate, distinguish between, and all of these words pertain to sifting or separating things in order to distinguish them.

The verb to *discern* means to recognize with the senses or the mind, especially to perceive something hidden or obscure: the philosopher's goal is to discern the truth; the doctor's job is to discern the cause of a disease; the numismatist—n(y)oo-MIZ-muh-tist, an expert on coins—can discern the genuine from the counterfeit.

The noun *discernment* denotes the ability to make accurate distinctions or discriminate keenly and wisely. Discernment is what enables a good manager to hire the most capable, loyal employees. The psychologist and the detective both must show discernment in reading people's character and assessing their motives. Challenging synonyms of *discernment* include *astuteness*, *acumen* (uh-KYOO-me̱n), and *perspicacity* (PUR-spi-**KAS**-i̱-tee).

The adjective *discerning* means having or showing discernment, revealing knowledge or insight: a wine taster must have a discerning palate; the person with a discerning eye has an exceptional ability to make subtle judgments or distinctions.

The adjective *discernible*, our keyword, means distinguishable, perceptible, capable of being discerned: "The faint light of dawn was barely discernible on the horizon"; "Industry analysts concluded that there was no discernible difference between the company's performance before and after the merger."

Word 33: CATACLYSM (KAT-uh-KLIZ-'m)

A disaster, great mishap, catastrophe, violent upheaval.

A *disaster*, a *catastrophe*, a *calamity*, a *debacle*, and a *cataclysm* all refer to accidents, misfortunes, and sudden or violent changes. Let's examine these words in order.

The negative prefix *dis-* denotes the absence or reverse of what follows: *dislike* is an absence of affection, *discomfort* is the absence of comfort, and *disadvantage* is the reverse of an advantage. In the word *disaster*, *dis-* combines with the Latin *astrum*, a star, to mean literally a reversal of the stars, an unfavorable horoscope; hence, an absence of luck, misfortune. Today *disaster* refers to a great misfortune involving ruinous loss of life or property. The sinking of the Titanic and the stock market crash of 1929 were disasters.

Catastrophe (kuh-TAS-truh-fee) combines the Greek *kata-*, down, with *strophe*, turn, to mean literally a down-turning. Originally *catastrophe* referred to the final turning point in a Greek tragedy where things go down the drain. Today *catastrophe* is used interchangeably with *disaster*, but properly *disaster* emphasizes the unforeseen, unlucky aspect of an event and *catastrophe* emphasizes its tragic and irreversible nature: The stock market crash of 1929 was a disaster for Wall Street, but it was only the beginning of the economic catastrophe we now call the Great Depression.

A *calamity* (kuh-LAM-i-tee) is an event that produces great distress, hardship, or misery, particularly on a personal level: The death of a loved one is always painful, but there is no greater calamity than the death of a child.

Debacle (di-BAH-kul) refers by derivation to a violent breaking up of ice in a river. It is often used today of any violent disruption or breakdown that leads to collapse or failure: "The breakup of the former Soviet Union was the debacle of communism"; "When Colosso Corporation laid off 20 percent of its workforce, company executives called it downsizing but employees called it a debacle."

Our keyword, *cataclysm*, comes from a Greek verb meaning to wash away or dash over. In its original sense, still in good standing today, a *cataclysm* is a great flood, a deluge (DEL-yooj), specifically the biblical flood that inundated the earth for forty days and forty nights. (By the way, to *inundate*— pronounced IN-uhn-dayt or, less often, in-UHN-dayt—means to overflow or overwhelm.)

In current usage, *cataclysm* most often refers to a violent upheaval that causes great destruction and change. The adjective is *cataclysmic* (KAT-uh-**KLIZ**-mik). A cataclysmic event may be geological—such as a devastating earthquake, fire, or flood—or it may be social or political. Many would say that World War II was the greatest cataclysm in the tumultuous course of twentieth-century history.

Word 34: NARCISSISM (**NAHR**-si-SIZ-'m)

Self-love, excessive admiration of oneself.

Synonyms of *narcissism* include *vanity*, *conceit*, *egotism*, and *amour-propre* (ah-MOOR PRAWP-ruh or PRAWP-ur). Antonyms include *humbleness*, *modesty*, and *humility*.

Narcissism comes from Narcissus (nahr-SIS-us), a character in Greek mythology who fell in love with his reflection in a pool of water. A *narcissist* is a person afflicted with narcissism, self-love, excessive admiration of one's appearance, abilities, or achievements. *Narcissistic* is the adjective: "Amy was sick of dating narcissistic men whose only topic of conversation was me, me, me."

Word 35: INCRIMINATE (in-KRIM-uh-nayt)

To charge with a crime, accuse of wrongdoing, implicate, present evidence or proof of involvement in a wrongful act.

You can see all but the last letter of the word *criminal* in the spelling of *incriminate*. When you incriminate someone, you accuse that person of doing something illegal or unethical. Incriminating evidence corroborates a person's involvement in a wrongful act. An incriminating statement is a statement that makes one appear guilty of wrongdoing.

Word 36: STIGMA (STIG-muh)

A mark of shame or disgrace, a moral blemish, a stain on one's character or reputation.

Stigma comes directly from Greek, and means literally a mark, brand, tattoo. In its original but no longer common sense, *stigma* refers to a brand or scar made with a red-hot iron in the flesh of slaves and criminals. Later it came to be used of anything that branded a person as unwholesome or disgraceful, a mark of shame, stain on one's character or reputation: the stigma of divorce; the stigma of a bad credit rating. The corresponding verb is *stigmatize* (STIG-muh-tyz), to brand as shameful, set a mark of disgrace upon: The media rarely have an indifferent view of celebrities and politicians; they either praise them or stigmatize them.

The plural of *stigma* is either *stigmas* or *stigmata* (preferably STIG-muh-tuh; I'll elaborate in a moment). *Stigmas* is the anglicized plural—to *anglicize* means to make English, conform to English modes of spelling, pronunciation, and usage. *Stigmata*, the Latinate plural, is also an interesting word by itself. Specifically, *stigmata* refers to marks resembling the wounds on the crucified body of Jesus Christ that are believed to have been supernaturally impressed on the bodies of certain persons, such as St. Francis of Assisi.

Now for a word of advice on pronunciation. For the plural *stigmata*, STIG-muh-tuh, with the stress on the first syllable, follows the Latin and Greek accentuation and is the traditional English pronunciation. The alternative pronunciation stig-MAH-tuh, with the accent on the second syllable, has been around since the 1920s; it is now standard and listed first in some dictionaries. Despite its popularity, however, stig-MAH-tuh is a pseudoclassical pronunciation; in other words, those who say it that way probably think they are following the proper classical accentuation. Although stig-MAH-tuh is not wrong, it carries a slight stigma of affectation. There is no such stigma associated with the pronunciation STIG-muh-tuh, which I recommend as having a longer tradition and greater authority.

Word 37: BREVITY (BREV-i-tee)

Shortness, briefness, as the brevity of life, the brevity of a child's attention span.

Brevity may also mean brief expression, shortness of speech, as "Forcefulness and brevity are the most important characteristics of a good speaker." Synonyms of brevity in this sense include conciseness, succinctness (suhk-SINGKT-nis), terseness, and pithiness.

Brief and brevity both come from the Latin brevis, short, the source also of the unusual word breve (BREEV, rhymes with leave and grieve). A breve is one of the diacritical marks or symbols used to indicate pronunciation. It's a small curve, like a tiny smile, placed over a vowel to indicate a short sound, as in the e in pet or the a in cat. You've probably seen the breve many times in your dictionary without realizing what it is. Well, now when you see it again you'll know what it's called, and you will also know that the breve is a symbol for brevity, shortness, briefness.

Word 38: PERQUISITE (PUR-kwi-zit)

A benefit, incidental gain or reward; specifically, an expected or promised benefit, privilege, or advantage received in addition to one's normal salary or wages.

You may not have heard the word perquisite before, but I'll bet you're familiar with the noun perk, as in the phrase "a job with good perks," meaning a job with good benefits and privileges. Just as the word bennies has today become the popular, informal substitute for benefits, the word perk was created as a shorter, snappier, and informal synonym for perquisite. But unlike benny meaning benefit, which is recent slang and has yet to make it into a dictionary, perk dates back to the 1820s. Nevertheless, perk did not appear in an American dictionary until the 1960s, when Merriam-Webster's Third New International recorded it along with the label "chiefly British." Since then, however, perk has become fully standard in American usage, and because it has retained its informal flavor it is now more widely used than the original word, perquisite.

Perquisite comes from a Latin noun meaning acquisition, and ultimately from a Latin verb meaning to ask or search for diligently. In modern usage, *perquisite* refers to a benefit or privilege accompanying a position. The perquisites of a job are the nice things you expect or that have been promised in addition to your salary. An expense account, a company car, a commodious office, and a profit-sharing plan all are nice perquisites—if you can get them.

Word 39: INDIGENT (IN-di-jint)

Poor, needy, penniless, impoverished, down-and-out.

Challenging synonyms of *indigent* include *destitute* and *impecunious* (IM-pe-**KYOO**-nee-us). The impecunious person has little or no money: "Many great writers have suffered through long periods of impecunious obscurity"; "He is a lazy, impecunious wretch posing as a gentleman." The destitute person has no visible means of support: "Ralph's addiction to booze and gambling eventually left his family destitute"; "the starving, destitute refugees of a war-torn nation."

Indigent comes from the Latin *indigentis*, in need, wanting. The indigent person is down-and-out and in need of assistance or relief: "They built a new shelter for the homeless and the indigent"; "Some people resent paying taxes to support the indigent members of society."

Word 40: CLAIRVOYANT (klair-VOY-int)

Having exceptional powers of perception, unusually clear-sighted or discerning; specifically, able to see objects or events that others cannot, having extrasensory perception or the power of divination.

Clairvoyant comes through French from the Latin *clarus*, clear, and *videre*, to see. By derivation *clairvoyant* means having the power to see clearly what others cannot. The corresponding noun *clairvoyance* means exceptional insight or perception, the ability to see things others can't. *Clairvoyant* may also be used to mean a person who supposedly possesses the power to see into the future, a medium, soothsayer.

With the advent of modern science, clairvoyance has fallen into disrepute. Yet economists continually attempt to be clairvoyant (though they rarely are), and many ordinary people experience occasional clairvoyant moments full of startling, exceptional insight.

Let's review the ten words you've just learned in another round of "One of These Definitions Doesn't Fit the Word." In each statement below, a word is followed by three ostensible synonyms. Two of the three are true synonyms; one is unrelated in meaning. Decide which one of the three ostensible synonyms doesn't fit the word. Answers appear on page 112.

1. To *rescind* means to seize, cancel, remove.
2. *Discernible* means recognizable, perceptible, familiar.
3. A *cataclysm* is an uproar, catastrophe, disaster.
4. *Narcissism* means self-knowledge, self-admiration, self-love.
5. To *incriminate* means to charge, expose, accuse.
6. A *stigma* is a design, mark, stain.
7. *Brevity* means shortness, briefness, rudeness.
8. A *perquisite* is a benefit, favor, privilege.
9. *Indigent* means needy, poor, unlucky.
10. *Clairvoyant* means uncanny, clear-sighted, discerning.

Did you keep track of your answers and calculate your score? With eight or more correct answers, you may read on. Otherwise, review the last ten keyword discussions.

Now let's learn the final set of keywords in Level 3.

Word 41: ADROIT (uh-DROYT)

Skillful, clever, dexterous; specifically, showing skill in using one's hands or in using one's brains.

Synonyms of *adroit* include *deft*, *resourceful*, *ingenious*, *artful*, and *adept* (word 7 of Level 1). Antonyms of *adroit* include *awkward*, *clumsy*, *inept*, and *maladroit* (MAL-uh-**DROYT**).

Adroit comes from Latin through the French *droit*, right, and means literally "to the right." Historically, the English language has always favored the right hand as the better, more skillful hand. Yes, I know that's unfair to southpaws, but my job is not to "say it ain't so" but to "call 'em like I see 'em." The fact is, a bias for right-handed words is ingrained in the language, which is one reason we don't say "out in right field" to mean crazy, weird, unorthodox.

Let's take a brief look at some of these "handy" English words.

The Latin *dexter* means on the right side, skillful. From *dexter* we inherit the word *dexterous*, skilled with the hands or body. Now, here's where things get sinister for lefties. The Latin *sinister* means left, on the left side, and also wrong, evil, unfavorable, adverse, the meaning of the English word *sinister* today. People who are ambidextrous are equally skillful or dexterous with both hands. Can you guess what the opposite of *ambidextrous* is? The unusual word *ambisinister* means literally having two left hands, equally awkward with both hands.

Latin is not the only language that favors righties and disdains lefties. The French *gauche* (GOHSH) means left, but also crooked, awkward, clumsy. *Gauche* entered English in the eighteenth century, and since then it has been used to refer to a person who is awkward, crude, or blundering, or to behavior that lacks culture or social grace. On the other hand (so to speak), from French we have also assimilated the word *adroit*, done with the right hand, and therefore skillful, clever, dexterous.

Adroit may refer to physical dexterity, but it is also often used of mental ingenuity; for example, you can make an adroit maneuver in a wrestling match or in a game of chess. *Adroit* also often implies exhibiting either physical or mental dexterity to elude danger or extricate oneself from a difficult situation.

Word 42: PLATITUDE (PLAT-i-t(y)ood)

A flat, dull, ordinary remark, a trite statement or hackneyed saying, especially one uttered as if it were original or profound: "Phil thought the management seminar was a big waste of time because the instructor kept repeating the same old platitudes he had heard many times before."

Platitude comes from the French word for flat, and means literally "a flat remark." Synonyms of *platitude* include *cliché*, *truism* (TROO-iz-'m), and *bromide* (BROH-myd).

Platitude also has several useful relatives. The adjective *platitudinous* (PLAT-i-**T(Y)OO**-di-nus) refers to speech or expression that is dull, ordinary, commonplace, insipid, banal. The verb to *platitudinize* (PLAT-i-T(Y)OO-di-nyz) means to utter platitudes. And a *platitudinarian* (PLAT-i-T(Y)OO-di-**NAIR**-ee-in) is a person who habitually utters platitudes—flat, dull, ordinary remarks.

In Shakespeare's *Hamlet*, the character Polonius is considered a platitudinarian. In bidding leave to his son Laertes, the pompous old adviser cannot resist sharing his favorite precepts, among them "Neither a borrower nor a lender be," "To thine own self be true," and "The apparel oft proclaims the man."

These and many other expressions from Shakespeare have since become platitudes—dull, ordinary statements uttered as if they were still meaningful and fresh.

Word 43: FASTIDIOUS (fa-STID-ee-us)

Extremely delicate, sensitive, or particular, especially in matters of taste or behavior; dainty, fussy, finicky, overnice: fastidious table manners; a fastidious dresser; a fastidious worker who agonizes over every detail of the job.

Fastidious may also mean hard to please, extremely picky or demanding, exacting, critical to a fault: a fastidious ear for music; fastidious in one's choice of friends; a fastidious client for whom a good job is never good enough.

Fastidious descends from Latin words meaning squeamish, disgusted, disdainful, and conceited. More than a trace of these unpleasant words remains in the way *fastidious* is used today. The fastidious person is so excessively concerned with details that he may become squeamish or disgusted if things are not just right. The fastidious person may also be so hard to please, so critical and demanding, that she appears contemptuous of others. According to the great *Century Dictionary* (1914), "Fastidious almost always means a somewhat proud or haughty particularity; a fastidious person is hard to please, because he objects to minute points or to some point in almost everything."

Scrupulous, *meticulous*, *punctilious*, and *fastidious* all suggest demanding standards and careful attention to every aspect or detail.

Scrupulous (SKROO-pyuh-lus) means having scruples or principles; hence, rigorously careful and exact about doing what is correct and proper: "City officials called for a scrupulous investigation into the alleged embezzlement of public funds"; "All employees must follow company regulations scrupulously."

Meticulous (muh-TIK-yuh-lus) is often used today to mean painstaking, taking pains to attend to details or exercise care, as in "The report showed meticulous research," or "Doctors must wash their hands meticulously before examining patients." Bear in mind, however, that *meticulous* comes through the Latin *meticulosus*, timid, from *metus*, fear, and by derivation properly suggests exaggerated attention to details or unimportant matters out of nervousness or timidity: "Albert dressed for the interview with meticulous care, all the while reminding himself that making a good first impression was the key to getting the job."

Punctilious (puhngk-TIL-ee-us) comes from the Latin *punctum*, a point.

From the same Latin *punctum* comes the English word *punctilio* (puhngk-TIL-ee-oh), a fine point, nice detail. By derivation, *punctilious* means exact and often excessive attention to punctilios, to fine points or minute details, especially in observing customs, ceremonies, or procedures: "The new executive director seemed to have *Robert's Rules of Order* memorized, for she cited chapter and verse as she guided the board through each item on the agenda with a stern and punctilious hand."

Fastidious means having extremely delicate, sensitive, or particular tastes; fussy, picky, or demanding in a condescending way. As *Webster's New International Dictionary,* second edition (1934), puts it, *fastidious* suggests "a certain disdainfulness in rejecting what is displeasing to one's taste."

Word 44: VENDETTA (ven-DET-uh)

A bitter, protracted feud or rivalry.

Vendetta comes through Italian from the Latin *vindicta,* revenge, vengeance, the source also of the English word *vindictive* (word 39 of Level 5), vengeful, seeking revenge. The vindictive person feels he has been wronged and is disposed to retaliate; in certain cases this may lead to a *vendetta,* a long, bitter, and often violent feud.

Vendetta refers specifically to the violent tradition, formerly practiced in Italy, Sicily, and Corsica, of revenging the murder of a relative by killing the murderer or a member of his family. Of course, such private, extralegal vengeance usually leads to further retaliation, until a murderous rivalry ensues. Both in Italian and in English, these protracted blood feuds are known as *vendettas.* Anyone who's seen the *Godfather* film trilogy knows that vendettas are still common among the American Mafia, and they can last for generations.

In English, *vendetta* may also be used more generally to mean any long, bitter feud or rivalry, not necessarily between families and not necessarily attended by bloodshed: "The mayor accused her opponent of waging a vendetta instead of a campaign." "At first Steve was excited about his new managerial position with Eye-for-an-Eye Incorporated, but he soon realized that the company was run by backstabbing executives engaged in vicious departmental vendettas."

Word 45: LUCID (LOO-sid)

Clear, easy to see or understand, plainly expressed. *Lucid* is also commonly used to mean clear of mind, mentally sound, rational, sane: "His ninety-year-old mother is senile, but she still has some lucid days."

Synonyms of *lucid* in the first sense—clear, easy to understand—include *intelligible*, *comprehensible*, *limpid* (LIM-pid), and *perspicuous* (pur-SPIK-yoo-us).

Antonyms include *murky*, *obscure*, *befuddled*, *nebulous* (word 5 of Level 2), *ambiguous* (word 25 of Level 2), and *abstruse* (ab-STROOS, word 5 of Level 6), which means complicated, hard to understand.

Anything that is clearly understood or plainly expressed can be described as lucid: a lucid explanation; a lucid question; a lucid account of the issues. The unusual but useful word *pellucid* (puh-LOO-sid) intensifies the meaning of *lucid*; *pellucid* means exceptionally clear, extremely easy to see or understand.

Word 46: SALIENT (SAY-lee-int)

Conspicuous, noticeable, prominent; sticking or jutting out.

Synonyms of *salient* include *protruding*, *manifest* (MAN-i-fest), *obtrusive* (uhb-TROO-siv), and *protuberant* (proh-T(Y)OO-bur-int). Antonyms include *inconspicuous*, *unassuming*, *unobtrusive*, *indiscernible*, and *unostentatious* (uhn-AHS-ten-**TAY**-shus).

Salient comes from the Latin verb *salire*, to leap, jump, spring. That which is *salient* seems to leap out at you, jump into view, or spring forward to command your attention. People often have salient noses or other salient physical features. A salient characteristic is a person's most conspicuous or noticeable characteristic. A salient wit is forceful and prominent.

Salient may apply to things that are attractive or unattractive. Salient beauty and salient ugliness are both striking and conspicuous; they leap out at you with equal force.

Word 47: CATEGORICAL (KAT-uh-GOR-i-kul)

Absolute, unqualified, explicit; without exceptions, conditions, or qualifications. Antonyms of *categorical* include *ambiguous* (word 25 of Level 2), and *doubtful*, *dubious*, *indefinite*, *enigmatic*, and *equivocal*.

In the philosophy of logic, a categorical proposition affirms something absolutely without resorting to conditions or hypothesis. In the philosophy of ethics, Immanuel Kant's famous categorical imperative is, as the third edition of *The American Heritage Dictionary* puts it, "an unconditional moral law that applies to all rational beings and is independent of any personal motive or desire."

In general usage, *categorical* refers to statements or assertions that are absolute, unqualified, direct and explicit. A categorical reply is direct and explicit; a categorical refusal is complete and unconditional; a categorical denial is absolute and unqualified.

Although *categorical* may be used of any utterance that is absolute and unqualified, today it often suggests a statement or state of mind that is rigid, narrow, arrogant, or arbitrary. A categorical decision may seem universal to some but unfair and arbitrary to others. And when someone calls a creed or opinion categorical, the implication is that some assert that it is absolute while others believe it is narrow-minded or false.

Word 48: INSCRUTABLE (in-SKROO-tuh-bul)

Incomprehensible, unfathomable, extremely difficult to understand, not open to investigation or analysis.

Synonyms of *inscrutable* include *mysterious*, *impenetrable*, *esoteric* (ES-uh-**TER**-ik, word 29 of Level 5), *arcane* (ahr-KAYN), and *abstruse* (word 5 of Level 6). Antonyms include *comprehensible*, *lucid* (word 45 of this level), and *perspicuous* (pur-SPIK-yoo-us).

Inscrutable combines the negative prefix *in-*, which means not, with the Latin *scrutari*, to examine, inspect, search thoroughly. *Scrutari* is also the source of the English words *scrutinize*, to investigate, examine closely, and *scrutiny*, a close examination. By derivation *inscrutable* means incapable of being scrutinized, not able to be examined or investigated.

Anything that cannot be fathomed, that does not open itself readily to the understanding, may be called inscrutable. Many of the workings of nature are inscrutable, even to biologists. Human nature and the functions of the mind are still inscrutable to psychiatrists and neurologists. And even to philosophers and theologians the meaning of life is still—and probably always will be—inscrutable.

Now for some advice on usage: Chances are you've heard *inscrutable* used in the phrase "an inscrutable smile." That's a cliché, a hackneyed expression. Unless you're trying to be humorous, it's best to avoid it altogether. When you use *inscrutable*, strive for an original turn of phrase.

And one other word of caution: In the past, perhaps because of the popularity of the fictional characters Fu Manchu and Charlie Chan, the word *inscrutable* was often applied to Asians or to the Asian race. You should be aware that today this use is considered not only cliché but also derogatory and offensive.

Word 49: CONSTRUE (k<u>u</u>n-STROO)

To interpret, explain the meaning or intention of.

Construe comes from the same Latin source as the familiar words *construct* and *construction*. One less common meaning of the word *construction* is an explanation or interpretation; in this sense, to put a construction on something—such as a statement or an action—means to assign a meaning to it, explain its significance or intent. For example, in every case decided by the United States Supreme Court, the role of the justices is to put their particular construction on how the Constitution shall influence the law of the land.

By derivation, the verb to *construe* means to put a particular construction on something, to interpret it, explain its underlying meaning or intention. Silence is often construed as agreement. An ambiguous reply is difficult to construe. Some men insist on construing that when a woman says no, she really means yes. If your boss asks you why you were late to work three days in a row, while you dream up an excuse you can buy time by responding, "I'm not sure how to construe your question."

Word 50: ALLUDE (uh-LOOD)

To refer to something indirectly, make a casual reference.

Synonyms of *allude* include *suggest*, *hint*, *insinuate*, and *intimate* (IN-ti-mayt). Antonyms include *indicate*, *specify*, *detail*, and *enumerate* (i-N(Y)OO-mur-ayt).

To *allude* and to *refer* are synonymous but differ markedly in usage. To *refer* is to mention something specifically, point it out distinctly: The Declaration of Independence refers to "life, liberty, and the pursuit of happiness" as "unalienable rights." To *allude* is to refer to something indirectly or casually, without mentioning it. A political candidate might allude that an opponent has a skeleton in the closet. In a report or proposal you might allude to a study that supports your point without citing it directly. Someone who is afraid of heights might allude to a disturbing childhood experience as the source of the phobia.

The corresponding noun is *allusion* (uh-LOO-zh<u>u</u>n). An *allusion* is an indirect, casual, or passing reference: "The novel contains many allusions to Shakespeare"; "Only by allusion did the article suggest that the company was in financial trouble."

Let's review the ten keywords you've just learned. This time I'm going to give you the review word followed by three words or phrases, and you decide which of those three answer choices comes nearest the meaning of the review word. Answers appear on page 112.

1. Is an *adroit* maneuver skillful, quick, or deceptive?
2. Is a *platitude* a strong opinion, a trite statement, or an embarrassing error?
3. Is a *fastidious* person thoughtful and patient, pushy and obnoxious, or fussy and demanding?
4. Is a *vendetta* a bitter feud, an official reprimand, or an apology?
5. Is a *lucid* remark humorous, clear, or insightful?
6. Does *salient* mean superior, well known, or conspicuous?
7. Is a *categorical* statement contradictory, argumentative, or absolute?
8. Would something *inscrutable* be irreparable, incomprehensible, or unusual?
9. Does *construe* mean to assemble, to interpret, or to agree?
10. When you *allude* to something, do you reveal it, run away from it, or refer to it indirectly?

Remember that if you answered fewer than eight of the questions correctly, you should review the keyword discussions for this last section before moving on to Level 4.

Putting Your New Words to Work

Now let's talk about the final stage in the process of vocabulary building: putting your new words into action. What are you going to do with all these new words you are working so hard to learn?

I mentioned earlier how words are the tools of thought. They are, in fact, like finely engineered pieces of machinery in the sense that they are designed to perform a specific function with precision. If a carpenter drives a large nail into a slender piece of wood, the wood will split. So it is with sentences. If a word is too complicated or too simple, if it is forced or awkward, or if its meaning does not fit the context exactly, the sentence becomes faulty and useless, like that split piece of wood.

There's an anecdote my family has passed down for generations that illustrates this point.

My great-grandfather was a dyed-in-the-wool Yankee from Andover, New

Hampshire. He divided his time between practicing law, dabbling in state politics, and running a small farm on which he employed, from time to time, a handyman named George.

Well, one day George decided to build himself a new house. So that spring he went to work, sawing and hammering, and by harvest time the dwelling was finished. George invited my great-grandfather over to admire his handiwork. My great-grandfather walked slowly around the place, inspecting everything. Then he stepped back and examined the structure from a distance.

"Well, whaddaya think?" George asked, worried by my great-grandfather's puzzled expression.

"George," said my great-grandfather, "does that doorframe look a bit crooked to you?"

"By golly it does, now that you mention it."

"And that window, there. It seems to be lower than the one next to it."

"You know, you're right," George replied. "I never noticed that before."

"And George, look at the roof. Seems to be sagging some, wouldn't you say?" The poor handyman had to agree.

"Well?" said my great-grandfather.

George was silent for a moment. "You know, I can't understand it," he said finally. "Them tools was all new."

Words are like tools also in the sense that if you care about them, keep them in good working order, and use them conscientiously, they will perform beautifully and never wear out. But if, like George, your tools are all new but you don't know how to use them properly, you are setting yourself up for a few unpleasant surprises. That's the challenge of taking the step from acquiring a new word to using it in your writing and conversation. How and when you use the words you learn will of course be your decision and your responsibility. But I can offer you some guidelines that will help you put your new vocabulary into action right away, and help you enjoy doing it right and doing it well.

The first thing you should do with every new word is try it out silently in your mind several times before using it in speech or writing. Say you're in the middle of a telephone conversation and you think of an adroit way to slip in one of the words you've just learned. Great! You're on your way to mastering the word. But wait—don't use it yet. Let it pass this time, and make a mental note to check *Verbal Advantage*, and your dictionary, to be sure that your usage and pronunciation were correct. If they were, then the next time you can use the word with assurance. If you didn't get it quite right, listen to the keyword discussion again, then record the word and the definition on a flashcard and review it until you feel confident you can use it precisely.

Sometimes the hardest part of learning new words is putting them in context. The problem with acquiring a miscellaneous assortment of words is that they tend to remain miscellaneous, floating in the gray matter of your passive vocabulary instead of being catalogued in the proper cubbyhole of your active memory. You need to create a vivid, personal context for each word you learn, and this is where the power of association can help you. Try making a list of a dozen or so new words, and next to each one write something that particular word brings to mind. Examples might include people you know, places you've been, books you've read, experiences you've had, or some image the word evokes from you.

One effective method I have employed in my own vocabulary building is associating a word with the circumstances in which I first encountered it. Where did I read it? Who said it? What was my reaction to the way it sounded or the way it was used? By using this method, I have found I can remember where and when I learned a certain word, even as far back as my childhood. Another helpful method is to keep a journal or personal notebook in which, as you record your thoughts and experiences, you occasionally test out some of your new words, and so gain practice with them before putting them to more public use.

Here are a few other pragmatic suggestions to help you build confidence in employing your new vocabulary:

Jot down three or four words you want to use on a given day, and on the way to work imagine a conversation with a coworker in which you use them, or try to incorporate them into a letter or report you have to write. In your office, place your list of new words by the phone, the typewriter, or the computer, so you can refer to it as you conduct your business. Finally, if you encounter a new word in your reading and the passage in which you found it is especially interesting or meaningful to you, you might try memorizing the passage and quoting it in something you write or at an opportune moment in a meeting.

One very important thing you must do with each word you learn is decide if it is better used in writing or in speech, or if you are comfortable using it either way. For example, a word like *lachrymose* (LAK-ri-mohs) doesn't occur often in speech, and has a literary and somewhat old-fashioned flavor. Therefore, in conversation, *tearful*, *mournful*, or even *lamentable* would be more appropriate. On the other hand, the words *lucid* and *perspicuous* can be used either in writing or conversation where the simpler word *clear* would not have the same power, precision, or style.

In conclusion, let me offer you a few words of advice on what *not* to do when you put your vocabulary into action.

Don't try to use a new word too soon, before you have studied it and tested it repeatedly in your mind. Wait until you feel entirely comfortable with a word; otherwise you run the risk of misusing it and embarrassing yourself.

Don't use a new word just for the sake of using it. If you suspect that a familiar word may be more appropriate in a given situation, use the familiar word. Be patient and the time for the new word will come.

Also, don't lard your sentences with difficult words simply for the effect. I assure you that this sort of exercise is exciting only for you, never for your listener or reader. Remember that the goal of communication is to be lucid, not inscrutable. Like your wardrobe, your diction doesn't have to be ostentatious to look good.

The final and very important "don't" is don't use your vocabulary to impress people. That's like flashing a wad of bills to show everyone how flush you are. The person who shows off with words only annoys or intimidates others. The big word is not always the better word; certain words are more appropriate in a given situation than in others. When choosing your words, always consider the intelligence, education, interests, and concerns of the person you are speaking to or the people who will read what you write.

That's not to say that you'll never be able to use many of the words you learn. On the contrary, a large vocabulary will make you a more capable and versatile user of the language because you will have a greater selection of words to choose from and a better understanding of how to use them precisely.

A powerful vocabulary will help you communicate more effectively than ever before, provided you are sensitive to the subtleties of using the right word in the right place at the right time. I assure you that if you continue with this program and make a conscious effort to read more and consult your dictionary, using your new vocabulary soon will become as natural as riding a bicycle or tying your shoes.

Answers to Review Quizzes for Level 3

Keywords 1–10

1. Yes, it certainly would. *Defray* means to pay, provide money for, cover the cost or expenses of.
2. No. *Garrulous* and *loquacious* mean talkative. *Taciturn* means habitually silent, uncommunicative, reticent.
3. No. *Terse* means brief and to the point, expressed in a pointed and polished way.
4. Yes, you bet it would. A *boon* is a blessing, something to be thankful for, a timely and welcome benefit.
5. Yes. *Aristocracy* means literally "rule by the best persons"; the aristocracy comprises the wealthiest and most powerful members of society. The

proletariat is the working or wage-earning class, which comprises the poorest and least powerful members of society.

6. Yes, it is. *Heterogeneous* means varied, mixed, composed of different kinds, made up of unrelated or diverse elements.
7. Yes. A *pittance* is a small amount of money.
8. No. *Glib* means smooth-spoken, speaking fluently in an easy, offhand manner, talkative in a nonchalant way.
9. No. A penchant is a liking, strong inclination, decided taste for something.
10. Yes. *Solicitous* means concerned, showing care and attention, especially in a worried, anxious, or fearful way.

Keywords 11–20

1. Utterly false. *Circumscribe* means to enclose within narrow limits, restrict, confine. The goal of *Verbal Advantage* is to broaden your knowledge of words.
2. True. *Dearth* means a lack, scarcity, insufficiency, an inadequate supply of something needed.
3. True. *Ingratiating* means flattering, attempting to win approval or gain acceptance, done to charm or please another.
4. False. *Mercenary* means greedy, done for payment or reward.
5. True. To *extemporize* means to improvise, speak without preparation, compose on the spur of the moment.
6. False. *Erudite* means learned, scholarly, possessing extensive knowledge acquired chiefly from books.
7. False. *Austere* means severe, stern, somber, grim, serious in appearance or character.
8. False. *Laconic* means using few words, briefly and often bluntly expressed.
9. True. *Ameliorate* means to improve, make more tolerable, rectify, raise the condition or state of.
10. True. To *expunge* means to eradicate; obliterate; punch, strike, or wipe out completely.

Keywords 21–30

1. Synonyms. *Circumspect* means cautious, discreet, carefully considering all circumstances before acting or making a judgment.
2. Antonyms. *Animated* means lively, energetic. *Quiescent* means still, quiet, tranquil, at rest or repose.
3. Synonyms. A *foible* is a weak point, slight fault or flaw, especially a weakness in a person's character.
4. Antonyms. *Impassive* means showing no sign of feeling. *Fervent* means passionate, earnest, showing great warmth or intensity of feeling.

5. Antonyms. To *curtail* means to abbreviate, cut short. To *protract* means to drag out, lengthen, prolong.

6. Synonyms. *Ostentatious* means showy, extremely conspicuous, extravagant, flamboyant.

7. Synonyms, but not exact synonyms. A *predicament* is an unpleasant or unfortunate situation. A *quandary* is a state of uncertainty, perplexity, or doubt.

8. Antonyms. To *censure* means to blame, condemn, find fault with, criticize harshly, express stern disapproval of.

9. Synonyms. To *cavil* means to criticize or complain unnecessarily, point out petty flaws, raise trivial or frivolous objections.

10. Synonyms. To *assimilate* means to absorb, take in.

Keywords 31–40

1. *Seize* doesn't fit. To *rescind* is to cancel, take back, remove, render void, annul.

2. *Familiar* doesn't fit. *Discernible* means recognizable, detectible, perceptible, capable of being recognized by the senses or by the mind.

3. *Uproar* doesn't fit. A *cataclysm* is a disaster, great mishap, catastrophe, violent upheaval.

4. *Self-knowledge* doesn't fit. *Narcissism* means self-love, excessive admiration of oneself.

5. *Expose* doesn't fit. *Incriminate* means to charge with a crime, accuse of wrongdoing, implicate, present evidence or proof of involvement in a wrongful act.

6. *Design* doesn't fit. A *stigma* is a mark of shame or disgrace, a stain on one's character or reputation.

7. *Rudeness* doesn't fit. *Brevity* means shortness, briefness, or brief expression, shortness of speech.

8. *Favor* doesn't fit. A *perquisite* is an expected or promised benefit, privilege, or advantage received in addition to one's normal salary or wages.

9. *Unlucky* doesn't fit. *Indigent* means poor, needy, penniless, impoverished, down-and-out.

10. *Uncanny* doesn't fit. *Uncanny*, word 4 in Level 1, means eerie, strange, mysterious. *Clairvoyant* means having exceptional powers of perception, unusually clear-sighted or discerning; specifically, able to see objects or events that others cannot.

Keywords 41–50

1. An *adroit* maneuver is skillful, clever, dexterous. *Adroit* means showing skill in using one's hands or in using one's brains.

2. A *platitude* is a flat, dull, ordinary remark, a trite statement, especially one uttered as if it were original or profound.
3. *Fastidious* means fussy and demanding; hard to please, finicky; extremely delicate, sensitive, or particular, especially in matters of taste or behavior.
4. A *vendetta* is a bitter, protracted feud or rivalry.
5. A lucid remark is clear. *Lucid* means clear, easy to see or understand, plainly expressed. It may also mean clear of mind, rational, sane.
6. *Salient* means conspicuous, noticeable, prominent; sticking or jutting out.
7. A categorical statement is absolute. *Categorical* means without exceptions, conditions, or qualifications.
8. Something *inscrutable* is incomprehensible, unfathomable, extremely difficult to understand, not open to investigation or analysis.
9. *Construe* means to interpret, explain the meaning or intention of.
10. When you *allude* to something you refer to it indirectly, make a casual reference to it.

Review Test for Level 3

1. What does *innocuous* mean?
    (a) not guilty
    (b) unhealthy
    (c) harmless
    (d) secret

2. Which pair of phrases shows the proper singular and plural forms?
    (a) this criteria, these criterion
    (b) this criterion, these criterias
    (c) this criteria, these criterions
    (d) this criterion, these criteria
    (e) this criteria, these criterias

3. Which word means one's choice of words, manner of expression?
    (a) grammar
    (b) enunciation
    (c) diction
    (d) syntax

4. The vocabulary coverage of paperback, or pocket, dictionaries is
    (a) anglicized
    (b) obsolete

(c) categorical

(d) circumscribed

5. Which word means the history of a word or the study of the history of words?

(a) entomology

(b) etymology

6. Which is *not* a meaning of the prefix *mal-*

(a) unusual

(b) abnormal

(c) inadequate

(d) bad

7. *Connotation* refers to

(a) the explicit meaning of a word

(b) the implied meaning of a word

(c) the earliest meaning of a word

(d) the various meanings of a word

8. *Garrulous*, *loquacious*, and *voluble* are antonyms of

(a) platitudinous

(b) caviling

(c) taciturn

(d) punctilious

9. In careful usage, which word is *not* synonymous with *reluctant*?

(a) hesitant

(b) disinclined

(c) unwilling

(d) reticent

10. Which word is an antonym of *terse*?

(a) pithy

(b) verbose

(c) succinct

(d) laconic

11. Which is the proper pronunciation of *succinct*?

(a) suhk-SINGKT

(b) suh-SINGKT

12. Which word means the act of begging for something humbly and earnestly?

(a) extemporizing

(b) supplication
(c) ingratiation
(d) amelioration

13. In good usage, which preposition does *not* properly follow *solicitous*?

(a) on
(b) to
(c) of
(d) for
(e) about

14. Which word means having an opinion different from the accepted opinion?

(a) mercenary
(b) indigent
(c) heterodox
(d) stigmatized

15. Which pair of words is *not* synonymous?

(a) voluble, glib
(b) unctuous, suave
(c) bland, facile
(d) ostentatious, flippant

16. *Propensity* and *proclivity* are synonyms of

(a) foible
(b) quandary
(c) penchant
(d) perquisite

17. By derivation, *clairvoyant* means

(a) having the ability to speak well
(b) having the power to see clearly
(c) having exceptional intelligence
(d) having no doubt or fear

18. *Diction* and *dictum* come from the Latin *dicere*, which means

(a) to know
(b) to say
(c) to write
(d) to choose

19. Which word means relevant and appropriate?

(a) apposite

(b) fastidious

(c) pellucid

(d) gauche

20. What is the traditional and precise meaning of *peruse*?

    (a) to skim

    (b) to use up

    (c) to read carefully

    (d) to puzzle over

21. Which sentence is correct?

    (a) I am loath to do it.

    (b) I am loathe to do it.

    (c) I am loathed to do it.

22. The prefix *circum-* means

    (a) within

    (b) between

    (c) around

    (d) under

23. Which word is an antonym of *dearth*?

    (a) brevity

    (b) perquisite

    (c) paucity

    (d) plethora

24. Which word is *not* a synonym of *mercenary*?

    (a) avaricious

    (b) scrupulous

    (c) covetous

    (d) venal

25. Extemporaneous remarks are

    (a) verbose

    (b) impromptu

    (c) rehearsed

    (d) digressive

26. Which word denotes the opposite of *laconic*?

    (a) concise

    (b) succinct

    (c) garrulous

    (d) reticent

27. *Circumspect*, *spectacular*, and *spectacle* come from the Latin *specere*, which means
   (a) to enjoy
   (b) to look at
   (c) to be amazed
   (d) to wonder

28. Which pair of words is *not* antonymous (opposite in meaning)?
   (a) impassive, ardent
   (b) phlegmatic, zealous
   (c) vehement, listless
   (d) lukewarm, indifferent
   (e) fervid, apathetic

29. By derivation, *dilemma* means
   (a) a puzzle
   (b) a problem without a solution
   (c) a choice between two propositions
   (d) an unlucky turn of events

30. Which statement is true?
   (a) "We want fewer taxes" is correct usage.
   (b) "We want less taxes" is correct usage.
   (c) "We want fewer taxes" and "We want less taxes" are both correct usage.

31. *Perspicacity* and *acumen* are synonyms of
   (a) impecuniousness
   (b) discernment
   (c) meticulousness
   (d) salience

32. Which word means to make English?
   (a) anglicize
   (b) extemporize
   (c) homogenize
   (d) platitudinize

33. Which word by derivation means a reversal of the stars, unfavorable horoscope?
   (a) catastrophe
   (b) calamity
   (c) cataclysm
   (d) disaster

34. Which word comes directly from a Latin word that means left, on the left side?

(a) ambiguous

(b) sinister

(c) salient

(d) adroit

35. Which word is an antonym of *inscrutable*?

(a) abstruse

(b) incomprehensible

(c) lucid

(d) esoteric

Answers

1. c 2. d 3. c 4. d 5. b 6. a 7. b 8. c 9. d 10. b 11. a 12. b 13. a
14. c 15. d 16. c 17. b 18. b 19. a 20. c 21. a 22. c 23. d 24. b 25. b
26. c 27. b 28. d 29. c 30. a 31. b 32. a 33. d 34. b 35. c

Evaluation

A score of 30–35 is excellent. If you answered fewer than thirty questions correctly in this test, review the entire level and take the test again.

Level 4

Congratulations! Why are congratulations in order? Because you are making terrific progress.

Since you began reading this book you have probably more than doubled your normal rate of vocabulary growth. You have also absorbed more useful information on language than most people learn in a year of college or several years on the job. At the rate you're proceeding, your verbal skills soon will match those of the most intelligent and successful people you know. So keep reading, and remember always to review the material before moving ahead.

Word 1: PROVIDENT (PRAHV-i-dint)

Thrifty, economical, saving or providing for future needs.

Synonyms of *provident* include *prudent*, word 47 of Level 1, and *frugal*, word 35 of Level 2.

Provident and the verb to *provide* both come from the same Latin root. One meaning of the verb to *provide* is to prepare for some anticipated condition in the future, as to provide for a rainy day. *Provident* means providing for the future, especially in the sense of saving money for some anticipated need: "After the birth of their first child, Sam and Sarah vowed to be provident and start putting aside some money every month for college and retirement."

Word 2: IMPUTE (im-PYOOT)

To charge or attribute, especially with a fault or misconduct, lay the responsibility or blame upon, ascribe, assign.

Unlike the verb to *credit*, which has a favorable connotation, and the verbs to *assign* and to *ascribe* (uh-SKRYB), which are neutral, the verb to *impute* often has a negative connotation. According to the famous eighteenth-century essayist and lexicographer Samuel Johnson, "We usually ascribe good, but impute evil." (Do you need to look up *lexicographer*?)

To *impute* means to charge with something bad, attribute the blame for, lay the responsibility on: "They imputed their fourth-quarter losses to sagging sales and fluctuations in the stock market"; "Some critics impute the decline in verbal skills among young people today to watching too much television."

The corresponding noun is *imputation*, a charge or accusation, the act of imputing, as "Company officials vigorously denied the imputation of mismanagement."

Word 3: ASTUTE (uh-ST(Y)OOT)

Shrewd, clever, perceptive, discerning, acute, keenly aware, quick-witted.

More difficult synonyms of *astute* include *sagacious* (suh-GAY-shus, word 6 of Level 8), *perspicacious* (PUR-spi-KAY-shus), and *sapient* (SAY-pee-int).

Astute usually is used in a positive sense to mean showing keen intelligence and a shrewd ability to protect one's interests or avoid being deceived: an astute investor; an astute negotiator; an astute observer of human behavior. Occasionally it has the negative suggestion of clever in a cunning or self-serving way, as an astute self-promoter, an astute political operator.

Word 4: NEOPHYTE (NEE-uh-fyt, like *knee a fight*)

A beginner, novice, amateur, tyro; specifically, a new member of or convert to a religion.

There are several interesting words for various types of inexperienced persons.

Tyro (TY-roh) comes from a Latin word meaning a recruit in the Roman army, a newly enlisted soldier. *Tyro* is used today to mean a raw beginner, one who may be eager to learn but who is utterly incompetent.

Amateur (AM-uh-tur or -chur) comes from the Latin *amare*, to love. By derivation an amateur is a person who does something for the love of it rather than for money. An amateur may or may not be skilled, but the word often implies a lower level of competence than expert or professional.

A *dilettante* (**DIL**-uh-TAHNT or DIL-uh-**TAHNT**) is an amateur practitioner of an art, such as music, painting, acting, dancing, or literary composition. *Dilettante* is often used disparagingly of someone who dabbles in something and lacks the serious discipline necessary to excel.

Like *tyro*, both *novice* and *neophyte* refer to a person just starting out at something. *Tyro* emphasizes the beginner's incompetence; *novice* emphasizes the beginner's inexperience; and *neophyte* emphasizes the beginner's enthusiasm.

Word 5: ENIGMA (i-NIG-muh)

A mystery, puzzle, riddle, perplexing problem, something or someone hard to understand or explain.

Anything baffling, inexplicable (preferably in-EK-spli-kuh-buul, commonly IN-ek-SPLIK-uh-buul), or inscrutable (word 48 of Level 3) may be described as an enigma: "She is an enigma to me"; "Their motives are still an enigma"; "The case presents us with one enigma after another."

Word 6: CREDENCE (KREE-dints)

Belief, acceptance, especially belief in a published report or acceptance of another's opinion or testimony: "In recent years many medical studies have shown that reducing fat intake can help prevent heart disease, and there is now widespread credence among the public that a low-fat diet is more healthful."

Credence, *creed*, *credible*, and *credulous* all come from the Latin *credere*, to believe. *Credible* means believable, and *credulous* means willing to believe without questioning. *Creed*, word 21 of Level 1, refers to a declared belief or formal set of opinions: "Conservatism is his creed." *Credence* refers to belief itself, to acceptance of something stated or heard: "It is dangerous to give credence to gossip."

Credence is often used with the verbs to *give* or *lend*. "She gave no credence to their claims." "His neat appearance and confident manner lent credence to his story."

Word 7: VENERATE (VEN-uh-rayt)

To respect deeply, revere, regard with awe and adoration.

In a strict sense, to *venerate* means to regard as holy or sacred; to *revere* means to regard with great respect and honor. We revere great leaders, thinkers, and artists; we venerate holy persons, sacred writings, and religious or moral principles.

The adjective *venerable*, worthy of veneration, of being venerated, is more loosely applied. It is often used of something or someone old or long-established: a venerable tradition is an old and deeply respected tradition; a venerable cause is longstanding and worthy of profound respect.

Word 8: GARRULOUS (GAR-uh-l<u>u</u>s)

Talkative, especially in a rambling, annoying, pointless, or long-winded way.

Garrulous comes from the Latin *garrire*, to chatter, babble, talk in a rambling and tiresome way. In zoology (properly pronounced zoh-AHL-uh-jee, *not* zoo-) there is a genus of birds called *Garrulus*. This genus contains several of the common jays, which are known for their harsh, chattering call. Both by derivation and by association, *garrulous* means chattering like a jaybird. The garrulous person talks for the sake of talking, usually about trivial matters, and often babbles on when no one else is interested in listening.

Synonyms of *garrulous* include *verbose* (word 30 of Level 2), *loquacious*, *voluble* (word 1 of Level 5), and *prolix* (word 1 of Level 9). Antonyms of *garrulous* include *reserved*, *reticent*, *taciturn* (word 2 of Level 3), and *laconic* (word 18 of Level 3).

Word 9: TRENCHANT (TREN-ch<u>i</u>nt)

Keen, penetrating, vigorously effective, sharp and to the point.

Synonyms of *trenchant* include *forceful*, *acute*, and *incisive*.

Incisive (in-SY-siv) applies to expression that gets right to the point or penetrates the heart of the matter. *Cutting* and *biting* imply harsh or sarcastic expression that hurts the feelings. *Trenchant*, which comes from a French verb meaning to cut, suggests both the forcefulness of *incisive* and the sharp, painful implication of *cutting* and *biting*.

A trenchant analysis is keen and vigorous; a trenchant style is sharp and clear; a trenchant remark displays penetrating insight and has the ability to wound.

Word 10: AUTONOMOUS (aw-TAHN-uh-m<u>u</u>s)

Independent, self-governing, not under the control of something or someone else.

Autonomous comes from the Greek *autos*, self, and *nomos*, law, and means literally self-ruling. From the Greek *autos*, self, comes the English combining form *auto-*, which also means self. *Auto-* appears in many English words, including *autobiography*, a story of oneself, of one's own life; *autograph*, one's own signature; *automobile*, literally a self-moving vehicle; *automatic*, literally self-thinking, done without conscious thought; and *autocracy* (aw-TAHK-ruh-see), not self-government but rule by one self or one person—hence, dictatorship, tyranny, despotism (DES-puh-tiz-'m).

The corresponding noun *autonomy* (aw-TAHN-uh-mee) means self-government, independence.

The heart is an autonomous organ; it functions by itself. An autonomous company is independent, not a subsidiary (suhb-SID-ee-ER-ee—five syllables, not four) of another corporation. When the United States won its independence from Great Britain, it became an autonomous nation.

Let's review the ten keywords you've just learned. Consider the following questions and decide whether the correct answer is yes or no. Answers appear on page 156.

1. Does the provident person save for a rainy day?
2. Can you impute an error to carelessness?
3. Would an astute observation point out the obvious?
4. Is a neophyte experienced?
5. Is an enigma easy to understand?
6. Can an unsupported rumor gain the public's credence?
7. When you venerate something, do you criticize it?
8. Is a garrulous speaker charming and sophisticated?
9. Can trenchant humor be both sarcastic and insightful?
10. Is an autonomous decision made independently?

Now let's forge ahead and learn the next ten keywords in Level 4. Here they are:

Word 11: PANACEA (PAN-uh-SEE-uh)

A cure-all, universal antidote, remedy for all diseases and difficulties.

Panacea comes from the Greek *pan-*, all, and *akos*, cure, and today retains its literal meaning, cure-all. From the same Greek *pan-*, all, comes the English prefix *pan-*, which appears in front of a number of English words: a *panorama* (PAN-uh-**RAM**-uh) is literally a view all around; *pantheism* (PAN-thee-iz-'m), from the Greek *theos*, god, is the belief that all things are God, that God is universal; and a *pantheon* (PAN-thee-un or -on) is a temple dedicated to all the gods, or all the gods worshiped by a given people. In current usage *pantheon* may also mean any group of highly respected or revered persons. When novelist Toni Morrison won a Nobel Prize in 1993, she earned a place beside such esteemed writers as Ernest Hemingway, William Faulkner, and Mark Twain in the pantheon of American literature.

You have probably heard the common phrase "a panacea for all ills." The expression is redundant, because *panacea* by itself means a cure for all ills, a universal remedy. You may use *panacea* to mean either a cure-all for physical ailments or an antidote for worldly woes: "His lawyer emphasized that filing for bankruptcy would not be a panacea for his financial troubles."

Word 12: EPHEMERAL (i-FEM-uh-rul)

Short-lived, passing, fleeting, lasting for a short time. (By the way, did you remember that *short-lived* should rhyme with *strived*? If you've forgotten why this pronunciation is preferred, see *transient*, word 31 of Level 2.)

Ephemeral comes from a Greek word meaning daily, lasting or living only for a day. *Ephemeral* is sometimes used in this literal sense, as in the phrase "ephemeral literature," publications that come out every day, such as newspapers. Ephemeral literature is opposed to periodical literature, which refers to anything published periodically—weekly, monthly, and so on. In fact, the familiar word *journalism* by derivation means ephemeral literature, writing that pertains to the events of the day. *Journalism* and *journal* come from the French *jour*, day, as in the restaurant menu item soup *du jour*, soup of the day. Thus the common expression "daily journal" is redundant, for by derivation *journal* means something written or published each day.

Today *ephemeral* is most often used in a general sense to mean conspicuously brief in duration. Ephemeral ideas are popular for only a brief while; the jokes of late-night TV comedians are ephemeral, here today and gone tomorrow; an ephemeral trend in the economy or in fashion is one that passes swiftly away.

More difficult synonyms of *ephemeral* include *transitory* (word 4 of Level 5), *evanescent*, *fugitive*, and *fugacious* (word 24 of Level 9). For more on these words, review the discussion of *transient*, word 31 of Level 2.

Word 13: ONEROUS (AHN-ur-us, like *honor us*)

Burdensome, troublesome, oppressive, hard to bear, difficult to accomplish or endure: an onerous task, an onerous assignment.

Onerous comes from the Latin *onus*, a load, burden. Directly from the Latin comes the English word *onus* (OH-nus), a burden, obligation, especially a disagreeable responsibility. *Onerous* means like an *onus*, and therefore burdensome, troublesome, difficult to accomplish or endure.

Word 14: LAITY (LAY-i-tee)

Nonprofessionals, laypeople collectively, all the people outside of a given profession or specialized field.

The adjective *lay* means nonprofessional, not belonging to a particular profession. A lay opinion of a legal case is an opinion from someone who is not a lawyer or a judge. A lay diagnosis of a disease is a diagnosis proffered by someone who is not a medical professional.

In its original and most precise sense, *laity* refers to all who do not belong to the clergy, to religious worshipers in general. Today *laity* may be used either in this way or to mean those who do not belong to a given profession.

Word 15: PUNGENT (PUN-jint)

Sharp, penetrating, biting, acrid, caustic.

Pungent comes from the same Latin source as *poignant* (POYN-yint) and *expunge*—the Latin *pungere*, to pierce, prick. *Pungent* may refer to a literal piercing, to that which is sharp to the sense of taste or smell, or it may refer to a figurative piercing, to that which penetrates the mind or emotions.

A pungent sauce is sharp to the taste, perhaps spicy, sour, or bitter. A pungent critique or pungent humor is sharp and sometimes bitterly worded; it penetrates the mind or pierces the emotions in a direct and often painful way.

Word 16: PROSAIC (proh-ZAY-ik)

Dull, ordinary, uninteresting, unimaginative.

Synonyms of *prosaic* include *commonplace*, *humdrum*, *tedious*, *dry*, *stale*, *mediocre*, and *matter-of-fact*. And those are only the prosaic synonyms of *prosaic*. More difficult and interesting synonyms include *insipid*, which means tasteless, bland; *pedestrian*; *vapid* (rhymes with *rapid*), word 37 of Level 8; and *jejune* (ji-JOON), word 1 of Level 10.

Prosaic may be used literally to mean consisting of prose or of the nature of prose, as opposed to poetry. Because poetry is considered lovely and lyrical and prose is considered uninteresting and unimaginative, *prosaic* has come to be used figuratively to mean dull and ordinary. Today *prosaic* is most often used in this figurative sense. A prosaic performance is mediocre; a prosaic style is dry and stale; a prosaic explanation is humdrum, tedious, or matter-of-fact.

Word 17: CHARLATAN (SHAHR-luh-tin)

A fake, quack, imposter, fraud, humbug; specifically, a person who pretends to have a special skill or knowledge.

The words *charlatan* and *mountebank* are close in meaning and were once synonymous. *Mountebank* (like *mount a bank*) comes from the Italian *montambanco*, one who gets up on a bench. By derivation a *mountebank* is a person who mounts a bench or platform and delivers a flamboyant sales pitch to attract customers and hawk his wares. In its earliest sense, a *charlatan* was a huckster who made elaborate and fraudulent claims about his merchandise. In olden days, charlatans and mountebanks would travel about selling trinkets, relics, and panaceas; they were the proverbial snake-oil salesmen.

Since the early nineteenth century, however, *charlatan* has been used to mean a fake or a quack, someone who pretends to have a special skill or knowledge and who covers up the fraud with an elaborate and sometimes intimidating verbal display. In *The Wizard of Oz*, the Wizard is a classic example of a charlatan.

Today charlatans and mountebanks continue to thrive not only at carnivals and on the street corner but in the office and the boardroom as well. They're the ones who are always giving you the glad hand and handing you a line. The difference between them is that the mountebank makes an impressive verbal display in an attempt to sell you a bill of goods, while the charlatan makes an impressive verbal display to hide the fact that he doesn't have the skill or knowledge he claims to possess.

Word 18: PERFUNCTORY (pur-FUHNGK-tur-ee)

Mechanical, routine, listless, done merely as a duty, performed in an indifferent, halfhearted, superficial, and often careless way, without interest or enthusiasm.

Perfunctory comes from a Latin verb meaning to get through, be done with. The perfunctory worker is just trying to get through doing the job; the perfunctory teacher just wants to be done with the lesson; a perfunctory speech is mechanical, routine, delivered in a halfhearted, listless manner.

Word 19: MORASS (muh-RAS, rhymes with *alas*)

Literally, a swamp, marsh, bog; figuratively, something that traps, confines, or confuses, a sticky situation or troublesome state of affairs: "There was always a morass of paperwork on his desk"; "She penetrated the morass of red tape at city hall"; "Some people consider middle age the morass of life"; "The project got bogged down in a morass of trivial details."

Word 20: SOPHISTRY (SAHF-i-stree)

Deceptive reasoning, subtle and misleading argument: "Voters today want candidates who address the issues, not ones who engage in mudslinging and sophistry."

Sophistry comes ultimately from the Greek *sophos*, clever, wise, the source also of the word *sophisticated*. The corresponding adjective is *sophistic* (suh-FIS-tik) or *sophistical* (suh-FIS-ti-kul).

In ancient Greece, the Sophists (SAHF-ists) were teachers of rhetoric, politics, and philosophy who were notorious for their deceptive and oversubtle method of argumentation. The Sophists eventually came into contempt for accepting payment for their instruction. The word *sophistry* retains the stigma imputed to the clever Sophists so long ago. Today *sophistry* refers to speech or writing that is clever and plausible but marred by false or deceptive reasoning.

Let's review the ten keywords you've just learned. Consider the following statements and decide whether each one is true or false. Answers appear on page 156.

1. There is no such thing as a panacea for the world's troubles.
2. An ephemeral comment lingers in your mind.
3. An onerous job is interesting and enjoyable.
4. To a doctor, lawyers and engineers are members of the laity.
5. Pungent food is mild and bland.
6. A prosaic story is original and lively.

7. A charlatan is capable, sincere, and reliable.
8. When an employee's work is perfunctory, it's outstanding.
9. When you're in a morass, you are swamped, stuck, or confused.
10. A speaker who is adept at sophistry may be a charlatan.

Humpty Dumpty and Miss Thistlebottom

Up to this point we have examined a number of specific questions of usage. Now I'd like to explore the concept of usage itself.

Usage, like politics, is a passionate and controversial subject. Any discussion of it is bound to bring out the prejudices of all involved. Everyone, it seems, has an opinion about how words should or should not be used, and like most opinions, some are more logical and sensible than others.

Some people, for instance, embrace a do-as-you-please policy about language. They say, "As long as we communicate, what difference does it make?" Others maintain that anyone who has scruples about usage wants to standardize the language and is opposed to change. They believe that change is evidence that the language is living and growing, thus all change must be good. The most adamant among this group become self-appointed advocates of change, and whenever someone questions a particular change they cry out that no one has the right to tamper with this natural evolutionary process.

On the other side of the issue are the people who insist that rules are rules, tradition is tradition, and that any deviation from what should be or what has always been is yet another sign that the language is going down the tubes. These folks are the self-appointed guardians of the mother tongue.

The do-as-you-please, "language must change" folks constitute the permissive party. Permissivists don't make value judgments about usage because they believe it's undemocratic. Of course, they teach their children the difference between good and bad manners, and when driving they obey the rules of the road, but for some reason when it comes to language they believe it's unfair to insist that there is such a thing as right and wrong.

The rules-are-rules people constitute the purist party. Purists are cruel, grammar-worshiping taskmasters committed to upholding inflexible standards and imposing them on everyone else. They cling obstinately to the ways of the past and revel in telling the rest of us to tuck in our verbal shirttails.

Somewhere between these two extremes are the moderates who maintain that change is inevitable but not always sensible or for the better. These people believe that each case must be considered individually, and wherever possible and reasonable, standards should be upheld, distinctions should be drawn, and the integrity of the language should be preserved.

As you may have guessed by now, I consider myself a moderate purist. I don't believe all change is good and that anything goes, but I also don't believe that rules are rules and that the English language is doomed because people aren't observing them. In short, I am neither a Humpty Dumpty nor a Miss Thistlebottom. Allow me to explain those terms.

In Lewis Carroll's *Through the Looking Glass*, the sequel to *Alice's Adventures in Wonderland*, Alice and Humpty Dumpty have a conversation in which she criticizes how the eggman uses a certain word.

"When I use a word," Humpty Dumpty chides her, "it means just what I choose it to mean, neither more nor less."

"The question is," says Alice, "whether you can make words mean so many different things."

"The question is," cries Humpty Dumpty, "which is to be Master—that's all."

To be master or not to be master, and what kind of master to be—these are indeed the questions. Humpty is clearly heading for a fall if he thinks he controls the meanings of words and can use them any way he likes. On the other hand, anyone who believes usage is fixed and that the rules never change is equally cracked.

The caricature of this hidebound type is Miss Thistlebottom, the creation of the late Theodore M. Bernstein, the distinguished editor who for many years wrote a column called "Watch Your Language" for *The New York Times*. Miss Thistlebottom is the ruler-wielding schoolmarm of your childhood nightmares, the evil exponent of English grammar who plucked prepositions from the ends of your sentences, had a cow when you said "ain't," and read you the riot act for using double negatives like "I don't know nothin'." But with her sanctimonious (word 50 of Level 7) adherence to arbitrary (word 28 of Level 1) rules, Miss Thistlebottom instilled in you as many falsehoods and as much confusion as the empty-headed Humpty Dumpty would have, had he been your instructor.

What is needed in any debate about usage is a compromise between the ideological extremes of Miss Thistlebottom and Humpty Dumpty. We need to be aware of how words are actually used and at the same time improve our understanding of how they are best used. And we need to draw a distinction between usage and abusage—one based on what seems natural as well as on what most people consider correct. That is a difficult row to hoe, for it means we must resist being arbitrary and instead investigate each issue and decide for ourselves. It means each of us must rise above the temptation to make snap judgments and become more knowledgeable and scrupulous users of the language.

So how the heck do I do that? you're wondering. How do I become a "knowledgeable, scrupulous user of the language"? (If you need to brush up on the precise meaning of *scrupulous*, see word 37 of Level 1.) Don't worry. It's not as daunting as it seems. There's plenty of help out there if you want it, and the first step is to find out where to look for it and what to expect.

Advice on usage falls into one of two categories—either *prescriptive* or *descriptive*. Let's start with the latter term.

When you open a dictionary, you are looking at a descriptive document. By that I mean the dictionary is a description of the words of a language at a given time. Dictionary editors, who are also called lexicographers, try to make their wordbooks objective records of the language. As they see it, their job is not to make judgments but to hold up a mirror to the language and show you its reflection. The dictionary gives you the facts, and then you decide how to interpret them.

That's all fine and dandy; however, what the dictionary doesn't tell you is how you can use words with subtlety and style, and it doesn't teach you what distinguishes good writers and speakers from bad ones. A dictionary contains almost everything you need to know about words except how to use them effectively. You could read the entire book and still be unable to create a dynamic sentence. And you could learn a hundred words a week, but if you have no idea what they connote or how to use them accurately, you will have no way of judging whether your usage is cultivated or crass. That is where prescriptive advice can help you.

To prescribe is to set down as a rule or direction—not to lay down an arbitrary law but to clarify what works and expose what does not. To use the lingo of business, the prescriptive approach takes words out of the warehouse of the dictionary, puts them on the open market, and then hands us a sales report: Are these words useful? Do they do what they were made to do? Can they compete with what's already on the shelf? The business of usage requires good management and constant evaluation, and a wise prescriptivist, like a smart consultant, can tell you which verbal moves will succeed and which will lead to ruin.

The proper goal of the prescriptive approach is not to dictate but to evaluate, not to cavil but to rectify, not to condemn but to ameliorate. *Verbal Advantage* will help you clean up your diction and clarify many nebulous distinctions, but I urge you to build on what you learn here by exploring the works of some of the best commentators on style, past and present.

A short list of them would include H. W. Fowler, Bergen Evans, William Strunk and E. B. White (who wrote the famous handbook *The Elements of Style*), Rudolph Flesch, Wilson Follett, Jacques Barzun, Theodore M. Bernstein, Harry Shaw, Norman Lewis, Edward D. Johnson, William and Mary Morris, J. N. Hook, James J. Kilpatrick, William Zinsser, Constance Hale, Patricia T. O'Conner, Barbara Wallraff, Richard Lederer, Bryan A. Garner, and William

Safire. These are some of the experts who have enlightened me, and much of the advice I am sharing with you in this program I have learned from them.

To sum up, the way you use words makes a telling statement about the kind of person you are. And if you want your words to manifest intelligence and confidence, then along with building your vocabulary you must make good usage a priority.

I should also point out that the difference between building your vocabulary and improving your usage is like the difference between buying a piano and knowing how to play it. Possessing the instrument of language does not ensure that you will be able to make music with it. Reading, using your dictionary, and studying *Verbal Advantage* will give you the linguistic tools you need to tackle the job of communication. But to refine your skill with those tools you will need to heed the advice of the distinguished author, historian, and professor Jacques Barzun.

In his book *Simple and Direct: A Rhetoric for Writers* (1985), Barzun writes that "the price of learning to use words is the development of an acute self-consciousness.

> Nor is it enough to pay attention to words only when you face the task of writing—that is like playing the violin only on the night of the concert. You must attend to words when you read, when you speak, when others speak. Words must become ever present in your waking life, an incessant concern, like color and design if the graphic arts matter to you, or pitch and rhythm if it is music, or speed and form if it is athletics. Words, in short, must be *there*, not unseen and unheard, as they probably are and have been up to now.

And with that priceless piece of advice, let's return now to the *Verbal Advantage* vocabulary and discuss ten more keywords.

Word 21: PROLIFIC (proh-LIF-ik)

Fruitful, fertile, productive.

Antonyms of *prolific* include *unproductive*, *barren*, *sterile*, *impotent* (IM-puh-tint), and *effete* (i-FEET).

Prolific comes from a Latin word meaning offspring, children, progeny. *Prolific* may mean producing many offspring or much fruit, as a prolific family or a prolific orchard. It may also mean producing many products of the mind, as a prolific writer, a prolific composer. A prolific worker is a productive worker, one whose labor bears much fruit. A prolific period is a fruitful period, one marked by inventiveness and productivity.

Word 22: MUNDANE (MUHN-dayn *or* muhn-DAYN)

Of the world, worldly, earthly, material as distinguished from spiritual.

Synonyms of *mundane* include *terrestrial*, *temporal* (TEM-puh-rul, stress the first syllable), and *secular*. An unusual and literary synonym is *sublunary* (suhb-LOO-nur-ee). *Sublunary* means literally beneath the moon, and so of the world; sublunary beings are creatures who abide on Earth.

Antonyms of *mundane* include *lofty*, *heavenly*, *sublime*, *celestial*, *ethereal* (word 7 of Level 7), and *extraterrestrial*, which means literally beyond the earth.

Mundane is often used today to mean ordinary, humdrum, commonplace, banal, unimaginative, prosaic. All current dictionaries list this meaning, but some commentators on usage object to it. They argue that *mundane's* specific meaning should be protected, and the word should not be lumped with the many other words that mean ordinary and dull. It is a criticism I would advise you not to take lightly.

Jacques Barzun offers this sentence as an example of the debasement of *mundane*: "A mundane sex life can be compared to a TV dinner, but it's not a gourmet banquet." According to Barzun, "sex life, of whatever kind, is inescapably mundane, and so is a gourmet banquet."

In strict usage, *mundane* is reserved for things that are worldly as opposed to heavenly, material as opposed to spiritual, secular as opposed to religious. Mundane affairs are worldly affairs, not ordinary affairs. Mundane writing is not unimaginative or prosaic; it is concerned with worldly matters. Business is by nature mundane because it deals with concrete, material things rather than nebulous spiritual values. Politics is also mundane because it focuses on the issues and problems of the world.

Word 23: MYRIAD (MIR-ee-id)

Countless, innumerable, infinite, consisting of a great or indefinite number.

Originally, the noun a *myriad* specified ten thousand; in ancient Greece a *myriad* was a military division composed of ten thousand soldiers. Today the noun *myriad* is most often used to mean a great or indefinite number, as a myriad of troubles, a myriad of details to attend to.

The adjective *myriad* means countless, innumerable, infinite, consisting of a great or indefinite number. "On a clear night you can see myriad stars twinkling in the sky"; "A chief executive officer has myriad responsibilities."

Word 24: DISSIDENT (DIS-i-d<u>e</u>nt)

Disagreeing, disaffected, dissenting, nonconformist.

Dissident comes from the Latin *dis-*, apart, and *sedere*, to sit, and by derivation means to sit apart; hence, to withdraw one's approval or belief, disagree.

The noun a *dissident* refers to a person who disagrees with a prevailing opinion, method, or doctrine. The word is commonly used today in politics and journalism of someone who opposes the policies and practices of his government. The adjective *dissident* refers to the nonconforming and disaffected attitude of the dissident. A dissident opinion expresses disagreement; it does not conform to accepted opinion. Dissident activities are activities undertaken in opposition to a prevailing doctrine or authority.

Word 25: LAUDABLE (LAW-duh-b<u>u</u>l)

Praiseworthy, commendable, worthy of approval or admiration.

Synonyms of *laudable* include *meritorious* (MER-i-**TOR**-ee-<u>u</u>s), *exemplary* (ig-ZEM-pluh-ree, word 39 of this level), and *estimable* (ES-ti-muh-b<u>u</u>l). Antonyms of *laudable* include *contemptible*, *deplorable* (di-PLOR-uh-b<u>u</u>l), and *ignominious* (IG-nuh-MIN-ee-<u>u</u>s).

The verb to *laud* (LAWD, rhymes with *sawed*) means to praise, commend, extol (ik-STOHL). The adjective *laudable* means commendable, worthy of praise. Laudable actions, laudable motives, and laudable goals all are praiseworthy, commendable, deserving of approval or admiration.

In *Macbeth*, Shakespeare writes, "I am in this earthly world, where to do harm / Is often laudable, to do good sometime / Accounted dangerous folly."

Word 26: INIMITABLE (i-NIM-i-tuh-b<u>u</u>l)

Unable to be imitated, copied, or reproduced; beyond compare.

Synonyms of *inimitable* include *matchless*, *unrivaled*, *peerless*, *unparalleled*, and *surpassing*.

The prefix *in-* often means "in" or "into," as in the words *inhale*, to breathe in; *ingrain*, to rub in, fix in the mind; and *ingress* (IN-gres), the way in, the entrance. However, *in-* is just as often privative (PRIV-uh-tiv); that is, it deprives or takes away the meaning of the word to which it is affixed. Like the prefix *un-*, the prefix *in-* often means "not," as in the words *informal*, not formal; *inaudible*, not audible, unable to be heard; and *injustice*, something that is not fair or just. Our keyword, *inimitable*, combines this privative prefix *in-* with the somewhat unusual word *imitable*, able to be imitated, to mean "not able to be imitated."

You may use *inimitable* to describe anything that is one-of-a-kind, individual, unique. An inimitable style cannot be imitated or copied. An inimitable performance is unrivaled, incomparable (stress on *-com-*). An inimitable achievement surpasses all other achievements; it is matchless, beyond compare.

Word 27: JADED (JAY-did)

Worn out, tired, fatigued, weary, exhausted; specifically, worn out by overwork or overindulgence.

One meaning of the noun a *jade* is a worn-out or broken-down horse, a nag. The verb to *jade* means to be or become like a worn-out or broken-down horse. The adjective *jaded* means like that broken-down horse; specifically, worn out from overwork or overindulgence. When you drive your mind too hard or abuse your body, you become jaded; but you can also become jaded from too much of a good thing, as "Their lovemaking left him jaded."

In current usage *jaded* often suggests weariness accompanied by an insensitivity or immunity to something unpleasant: children jaded by abuse; seeing the consequences of so much violent crime had left the detective jaded.

Word 28: MYOPIC (my-AHP-ik, rhymes with *dry topic*)

Short-sighted; not able to see the long-range picture; having a narrow or circumscribed view; lacking discernment, foresight, or perspective.

Synonyms of *myopic* include *narrow-minded*, *purblind* (PUR-blynd, rhymes with *her kind*), and *obtuse* (uhb-T(Y)OOS). Antonyms of *myopic* include *broad-minded*, *liberal*, *tolerant*, *catholic* (note the lowercase *c*), and *latitudinarian* (LAT-i-T(Y)OO-di-NAIR-ee-in).

The adjective *myopic* comes from the noun *myopia* (my-OH-pee-uh), the common medical disorder known as nearsightedness. In its literal sense, *myopic* means nearsighted, affected with myopia. In its figurative sense, myopic suggests mental nearsightedness, a lack of long-range vision, a mental outlook that is limited or narrow. The myopic person lacks perspective and foresight; he can't see the big picture. A myopic approach to solving a problem is short-sighted; it lacks imagination and does not address long-term needs or goals. A myopic opinion is narrow-minded and prejudiced; it reflects only what the person who expresses it wants to see.

The words *purblind*, *obtuse*, and *myopic* are close in meaning. *Purblind* means partly blind, dim-sighted; like *myopic*, *purblind* may be used literally to mean half-blind or figuratively to mean lacking insight or imagination. *Obtuse* comes from a Latin word meaning dull, blunt, and in modern usage *obtuse* is used to mean mentally dull, slow to recognize or understand something. *Myopic* means short-sighted, having a limited perspective or narrow view.

Word 29: DEMONSTRABLE (di-MAHN-struh-buul)

Capable of being demonstrated, able to be proved.

Demonstrable is the noun corresponding to the verb to *demonstrate*. Demonstrable facts can be demonstrated, presented clearly and shown to be true. A demonstrable statement or opinion is one that can be proved.

Because that which is demonstrable can be demonstrated or proved, the word has also come to be used to mean obvious, apparent, self-evident, as in a demonstrable liar, a demonstrable fool: "When Joe asked Sheila if she would have dinner with him, she took it as a sign of his demonstrable interest in her."

Word 30: CALLOW (KAL-oh)

Immature, inexperienced, unsophisticated, green, naive, lacking experience in and knowledge of the world.

Callow comes from a Middle English word meaning bald, and the word was formerly used of very young birds to mean without feathers, unfledged. Today both *callow* and the word *fledgling* are used of persons, behavior, or things that are immature or inexperienced. A fledgling is a young bird that has just acquired its feathers and is learning to fly. From that original sense, *fledgling* has come to refer either to a young and inexperienced person or to something that is just getting off the ground, as a fledgling enterprise. *Callow* suggests an immaturity or inexperience manifested by a lack of sophistication. People who are callow know little of the ways of the world; they are green, still wet behind the ears.

Because *callow* means immature, it sometimes also suggests childishness or foolishness. For example, a callow remark may be not only unsophisticated but also downright silly. Synonyms of *callow* in this unfavorable sense include *juvenile* (preferably JOO-vuh-nil, but now also JOO-vuh-nyl, which was originally British), *sophomoric* (SAHF-uh-MOR-ik), and *puerile* (PYOOR-ul).

Let's review the ten keywords you've just learned. I'll give you two words, and you decide if they are synonyms or antonyms. Answers appear on page 156.

1. *Prolific* and *barren* are . . . synonyms or antonyms?
2. *Earthly* and *mundane* are . . .
3. *Innumerable* and *myriad* are . . .
4. *Dissident* and *conforming* are . . .
5. *Laudable* and *deplorable* are . . .
6. *Matchless* and *inimitable* are . . .
7. *Exhausted* and *jaded* are . . .
8. *Short-sighted* and *myopic* are . . .
9. *Demonstrable* and *unverifiable* are . . .
10. *Callow* and *inexperienced* are . . .

Did you remember to keep track of your answers and calculate your score? If you answered fewer than eight questions correctly, review the last ten keywords.

Just Between Us, This One's for You and Me

Now for another "Word to the Wise." This time we have a cautionary tale of good grammar gone awry. (*Awry* is pronounced uh-RY to rhyme with *apply*. Do you know what it means?)

Here's the question I'd like you to consider: Why is it that so many people insist on using the nominative rather than the objective case with the prepositions *for* and *between*?

Nominative? Objective? What the heck is he talking about? you're thinking.

All right, I'll put it in plain English. Why do people say "for you and I" and "between you and I" when good grammar requires "for you and me" and "between you and me"?

Believe me, this is not an error the ordinary person makes. It's a mistake committed almost exclusively by educated folks who ought to know better.

Talk to any Joe Blow on the street and I'll bet he'll say, "Just between you and me, pal, there's somethin' screwy goin' on at city hall." Or sit down next to him at a bar and he'll say to the bartender, "Hey Mac, howzabout a round for my friend and me?" But give him a college degree, a professional position, and a house in the suburbs, and by golly the next minute you'll hear, "Let's keep this information between you and I," or "I think this is a good investment for you and I."

So, just between you and me, why is it that so many upwardly mobile types say "just between you and I"? Did their sixth-grade teachers give them a demerit for saying "it's me" instead of "it is I"? Did their mothers dock their allowance for telling a friend, "You and me should go out and play"?

Whatever the reason, if you are one of the many who have graduated from the unpretentious and proper "just between you and me" to the overrefined, pinky-in-the-air erroneousness of "just between you and I," it's high time to get reeducated—or *dee*ducated, as the case may be.

In *The Careful Writer*, Theodore M. Bernstein says that "uncomprehending souls who have heard strictures about 'It is me' tend to think of 'me' as a naughty word, particularly when it is associated with 'you,' which they mistake for a nominative case. Thinking they are leaning over backward to be correct, they somersault onto their faces and come up with 'between you and I.'"

Think of the nominative case as being the subject of a sentence. In the sentence "I am going," *I* is the subject and in the nominative case. In the sentence "You and I are going," *you and I* is a compound subject, and both words are in the nominative case. In the sentence "It is for you," *it* is now the subject, and *you* is in the objective case. In the sentence "It's for you and me," the subject is still *it*, and *you and me* are in the objective case. The problem is caused by the word *you*, which can be either nominative or objective, but which in our misguided attempt to be proper we tend to treat as a nominative.

If all this grammar is so much linguistic jargon to your ear, just remember this rule of thumb: Whenever something is *between* someone else and you, or *for* someone else and you, say *me*, not *I*: "There's no difference between you and *me*"; "The boss had only the highest praise for Pamela, Gregg, and *me*."

Or try this little trick: Eliminate the other people in the sentence and see how it sounds. If you're about to say "It's for him and I," take out *him* and you'll hear that "it's for I" sounds wrong, which it is. I know you would never say "That's for I, not her," so take care to say "That's for her and me."

If you observe this rule, you will never sound unnatural or pretentious. And that's my guarantee—just between you and me.

Now let's return to the *Verbal Advantage* vocabulary for the next ten keywords in Level 4.

Word 31: ACQUIESCE (AK-wee-ES)

To agree without protest, accept without argument or resistance, give in quietly.

Synonyms of *acquiesce* include *consent*, *comply*, *submit*, *assent*, and *accede* (ak-SEED). The corresponding noun is *acquiescence* (AK-wee-**ES**-ints). *Acquiescence* means the act of acquiescing, passive agreement, quiet acceptance.

Assent, *accede*, and *acquiesce* all mean to agree in slightly different ways. *Assent* implies agreement reached after careful consideration or deliberation: "The president of the company predicted that the stockholders would assent to the proposed merger." *Accede* implies agreement in which one person or party gives in to persuasion or yields under pressure: "Management is not likely to accede to the union's demands." *Acquiesce* implies agreement offered in spite of tacit reservations. The person who acquiesces often is unwilling to agree but lacks the will or energy to resist: "Despite her doubts about the plan, Lucy acquiesced"; "Bob wasn't happy with the salary that Mercenary Media had offered him, but he knew he would have to either acquiesce or take an even lower-paying job."

Acquiesce is sometimes followed by the preposition *in*: "One member of the jury remained obstinate and would not acquiesce in the verdict"; "The chief executive officer acquiesced in the board of directors' decision."

Word 32: PONTIFICATE (pahn-TIF-i-kayt)

To speak in a pompous and overbearing way, make pretentious or categorical statements, express one's opinion as though it were an official, authoritative decree.

The Roman Catholic pope is also known by two other names: the Bishop of Rome and the pontiff (PAHN-tif). *Pontiff* comes from the Latin *Pontifex Maximus*, the high priest of Rome. As the leader of the Roman Catholic Church, the pontiff is responsible for interpreting religious doctrine, or dogma, and issuing official decrees, called papal bulls. To these official decrees the pontiff affixes a seal called a bulla (BUUL-uh).

In its original sense, to *pontificate* means to be a pontiff, to fulfill the office of a pope and issue official decrees on church doctrine or dogma. From this the word came to apply in a disparaging way to anyone who speaks as if he were the pope issuing an official decree.

Because only the pontiff has the absolute right to pontificate, *pontificate* now means to express opinions or make judgments in a categorical, dogmatic way. I'll save you the trouble of looking up *dogmatic*, which is pronounced dawg-MAT-ik (or dahg-). It means opinionated, dictatorial, expressing an opinion as if it were fact.

If your boss pontificates in a meeting, that means he or she is speaking dogmatically, in a pompous, pretentious, dictatorial manner. The person who pontificates expresses an opinion as though it were an official, authoritative decree: "Teenagers don't respond well when their parents or teachers pontificate."

The corresponding noun is *pontification* (pahn-TIF-i-**KAY**-shin).

Word 33: DELETERIOUS (DEL-i-**TEER**-ee-u̱s)

Harmful, destructive, injurious, detrimental; especially, harmful to health or well-being.

Synonyms of *deleterious* include *ruinous*, *noxious*, *pernicious* (pur-NISH-u̱s, word 10 of Level 7), and *malignant* (muh-LIG-ni̱nt). Antonyms include *healthful*, *advantageous*, *wholesome*, and *salutary* (**SAL**-yuh-TER-ee).

Deleterious comes from a Greek word meaning destructive and may be applied to something that has a detrimental effect upon a person's health or well-being or to anything harmful or destructive. Smoking is deleterious, harmful to health. A divorce may be deleterious to children, injurious to their psychological well-being. An impetuous statement may have deleterious consequences. For example, you may daydream about stomping into your boss's office and giving the old pontificating windbag a piece of your verbally advantaged mind, but doing that probably would be deleterious to your career.

Word 34: AMBIVALENT (am-BIV-uh-li̱nt)

Uncertain, indecisive, having conflicting feelings or desires, simultaneously drawn in opposite directions, attracted to and repulsed by something at the same time.

The corresponding noun is *ambivalence*, a state of uncertainty or indecisiveness.

One meaning of the combining form *ambi-* is "both," as in the words *ambidextrous* (AM-bi-DEK-str̠us), skilled with both hands, and *ambivert* (AM-bi-vurt), a person who is both *introverted*, inner-directed, and *extroverted*, outer-directed. *Ambivalent* combines *ambi-*, both, with the Latin *valere*, to be strong. When you are ambivalent on an issue, you have strong feelings both ways; you are simultaneously drawn in opposite directions. The ambivalent person has conflicting feelings or desires, and therefore is uncertain, indecisive.

Word 35: PENSIVE (PEN-siv)

Thoughtful, absorbed in thought, especially in a deep, dreamy, or melancholy way.

Synonyms of *pensive* include *reflective*, *meditative*, *wistful*, and *contemplative* (kun-TEM-pluh-tiv).

Pensive comes through an Old French verb meaning to think from the Latin *pensare*, to ponder, consider, weigh in the mind. When you are pensive, you are thinking deeply about something, pondering it, weighing it in your mind.

Pensive, *contemplative*, and *wistful* all mean thoughtful, but in different ways.

Wistful, which is related to the word *wishful*, suggests thoughtfulness marked by a strong and often sad longing or desire. When two lovers are apart, they are often wistful.

Contemplative (stress the second syllable), the adjective corresponding to the noun *contemplation*, suggests profound reflection usually directed toward achieving deeper understanding or enlightenment. Philosophers and prophets are contemplative.

Pensive suggests a deep, dreamy, and often melancholy thoughtfulness. A pensive mood is characterized by dreamy seriousness. When you grow pensive you become lost in thought, and probably have a slightly sad, faraway look in your eyes.

The corresponding noun is *pensiveness*: "The most salient characteristic in the poetic temperament is pensiveness."

Word 36: IMPROMPTU (im-PRAHMP-t(y)oo)

Made up or done on the spur of the moment, uttered or performed without preparation, improvised for the occasion.

Synonyms of *impromptu* include *offhand*, *spontaneous*, and *extemporaneous* (ek-STEM-puh-**RAY**-nee-us).

Impromptu comes from a Latin phrase meaning in readiness, at hand. By derivation, something impromptu lies close at hand, ready to use when the occasion arises. In modern usage *impromptu* may apply to either spontaneous expression or activity: an impromptu response is an offhand or off-the-cuff response; an impromptu performance is improvised for the occasion; an impromptu party is thrown on the spur of the moment.

Here's an image you can associate with the word *impromptu* that may help you remember what it means: Imagine yourself at a dinner party or wedding reception, chatting amiably with the people around you, when suddenly everyone in the room turns toward you and starts chanting "Speech, speech!" Although you are unprepared, you rise to the occasion and deliver a few urbane remarks. When your audience laughs at the right moment and applauds at the end, you are delighted. Your speech not only was impromptu, it was a triumph.

Word 37: CONJECTURE (kun-JEK-chur)

To guess; especially, to make an educated guess; to form an opinion or make a judgment based on insufficient evidence.

Familiar synonyms of *conjecture* include to *suppose*, *imagine*, *suspect*, and *presume*.

To *guess*, to *speculate*, to *surmise*, and to *conjecture* all mean to form an opinion or reach a conclusion based upon uncertain or insufficient evidence.

To *guess* is the least reliable and most random of these words. When you guess you have a roughly equal chance of being right or wrong, and there is ample room for doubt about your opinion.

To *speculate* means to make a judgment based on observation and reasoning. When you speculate you form a reasonable opinion by evaluating whatever facts are at hand, however dubious they may be.

To *surmise* means to come to a conclusion by using one's intuition or imagination. When you surmise, you use your instinct and power of insight to make a judgment based on slender evidence.

Our keyword, *conjecture*, comes from the Latin *con-*, together, and *jacere*, to throw, and by derivation means to throw something together. In modern usage to *conjecture* means to take whatever evidence is available and quickly construct an opinion based on one's knowledge and experience—in short, to make an educated guess.

The corresponding noun a *conjecture* means an educated guess, an assumption or conclusion based on insufficient evidence.

Word 38: SURREPTITIOUS (SUR-up-TISH-us)

Stealthy; characterized by secrecy and caution; done, made, obtained, or enjoyed in a secret and often sly or shifty manner, so as to avoid notice.

Synonyms of *surreptitious* include *crafty*, *furtive* (FUR-tiv), *covert* (traditionally and properly KUH-vurt, but now usually KOH-vurt), *underhand*, and *clandestine* (klan-DES-tin, word 6 of Level 2). Antonyms include *evident*, *unconcealed*, *overt*, *aboveboard*, and *manifest*.

Stealthy, *furtive*, *clandestine*, *covert*, and *surreptitious* all mean secret, hidden from the knowledge or view of others. Let's examine their connotations in order.

Stealthy is used of any secret or deceptive action that is careful, quiet, slow, and designed to conceal a motive: a cat stalks its prey in a stealthy manner; she heard the stealthy footsteps of a prowler outside the house.

Furtive adds to *stealthy* the suggestion of quickness and cunning. The word comes from the Latin *furtum*, theft, and that which is furtive exhibits the craftiness, dishonesty, and evasiveness of a thief: "Their furtive glances at each other during the meeting convinced Jim that there was something fishy about the deal"; "Suzanne knew her date with Arnold was going to be a disaster when she caught him making a furtive attempt to look down the front of her dress."

Clandestine applies to that which is done secretly to conceal an evil, immoral, or illicit purpose: a clandestine love affair; a clandestine plot to overthrow the government.

Covert applies to anything deliberately covered up or disguised, and often suggests an effort to conceal something illegal or unethical. When we speak of an undercover operation, we usually mean a secret operation sanctioned by law, but when we speak of a covert operation, we usually mean one that is kept secret because it is criminal or corrupt.

I'd like to take a moment to explain why I prefer and recommend the pronunciation KUH-vurt. This is the traditional pronunciation, and it was the only way of saying the word recognized by dictionaries until the 1960s. Since then—and especially since the Watergate scandal in the early 1970s, when "KOH-vurt operation" was heard repeatedly on radio and television—the variant KOH-vurt has become so popular that several dictionaries now list it first.

Although few people today are aware that KUH-vurt was the earlier and only standard pronunciation, dictionaries still list KUH-vurt and many older educated speakers prefer KUH-vurt out of respect for the word's tradition, which dates back to the fourteenth century. If you'd rather go with the flow on this issue, that's fine—no one can say you're wrong; however, keep in mind that while KOH-vurt is recognized by current dictionaries, another popular variant, koh-VURT, is often not listed at all. On the other hand, if you are not afraid to distinguish yourself as a cultivated speaker at the risk of raising a few eyebrows, then I invite you to join me in the righteous cause of preserving the traditional pronunciation, KUH-vurt.

And now let's wind up this not-so-undercover discussion with a look at our keyword, *surreptitious*. It comes from a Latin word meaning stolen, kidnapped, and ultimately from the Latin verb *surripere*, to snatch, pilfer, take away or withdraw secretly. By derivation *surreptitious* means snatched while no one is looking, and in modern usage the word combines the deliberate, cautious secrecy suggested by *stealthy* with the crafty, evasive secrecy suggested by *furtive*. That which is surreptitious is done or acquired under the table, in a sly or shifty way, so as to avoid detection: "For years Paul was so surreptitious about his drinking that no one at work knew he had a problem"; "The general decided to launch a surreptitious attack under cover of darkness"; "Larry was afraid the IRS would find out about his surreptitious real estate deals."

Word 39: EXEMPLARY (ig-ZEM-pluh-ree)

Worthy of imitation, praiseworthy, commendable, serving as a model of excellence, appropriateness, or correctness.

Synonyms of *exemplary* include *ideal*, *admirable*, *meritorious* (MER-i-**TOR**-ee-us), *estimable* (ES-ti-muh-buul), and *laudable* (word 25 of Level 4). Antonyms include *shameful*, *disreputable*, *contemptible*, *deplorable* (di-PLOR-uh-buul), *ignominious* (IG-nuh-**MIN**-ee-us), *odious* (OH-dee-us), and *heinous* (HAY-nis, rhymes with *anus*).

By the way, *heinous* means reprehensible, wicked, evil, as a heinous crime, a heinous lie. I have heard scores of educated people mispronounce it as HEE-nis, HEE-nee-us, and HAY-nee-us. The best I can say about these pronunciations is that they are creative but wrong. The only pronunciation recognized by dictionaries is HAY-nis, and anything else is utterly *heinous*, evil, wicked, reprehensible.

Now back to our more pleasant keyword, *exemplary*, which comes from the same Latin source as the word *example*. By derivation, something exemplary sets an example, and is therefore worthy of imitation. Exemplary conduct is praiseworthy. An exemplary performance is commendable. *Verbal Advantage* teaches you how to use words in an exemplary manner.

Word 40: IMPECCABLE (im-PEK-uh-buul)

Perfect, faultless, flawless; free from faults or imperfections. Also, unable to do wrong, incapable of sin.

Equally challenging synonyms of *impeccable* include *unimpeachable* and *irreproachable*. Challenging antonyms of *impeccable* include *reprehensible*, *censurable* (SEN-shur-uh-buul), and *culpable* (KUHL-puh-buul).

Earlier in this level I told you about the prefix *in-*, which may mean "in" or "into" or have a privative function, depriving or taking away the meaning of what follows. *Impeccable* combines this privative prefix *in-*, meaning "not," with the Latin *peccare*, to make a mistake, do wrong, blunder, sin. By derivation, *impeccable* means not able to make a mistake, incapable of sinning or doing wrong; hence, perfect, faultless.

Now, if you've been reading carefully I bet you're wondering why in the world I'm talking about the prefix *in-* when the prefix in *impeccable* is *im-*. Well, my verbally advantaged friend, your exemplary guide through the oddities of the English language has the answer, and here it is:

When the prefix *in-* is attached to a word beginning with the letter *b*, *p*, or *m*, the *n* changes to an *m*. Thus, *imbalanced* means not balanced; *impossible* means not possible; and *immutable* means not mutable, not changeable, fixed. Similarly, when the prefix *in-* appears before a word beginning with *l* or *r*, the *n* changes to an *l* or an *r*: *illogical* means not logical; *irreproachable* means not reproachable, without fault or blame, and therefore *impeccable*, perfect, flawless.

So now that you know how the spelling of the prefix *in-* changes, I suppose you're wondering *why* it changes. The answer is simple: ease of pronunciation. If we had to say *in*peccable and *in*reproachable, it would be not only *in*logical but also nearly *in*possible. The altered spelling of the prefix makes these and dozens of other words easier to pronounce.

Now let's take a look at the closely related words *impeccable*, *immaculate*, and *infallible*, all of which employ the privative prefix *in-*, meaning not.

The adjective *fallible* comes from the Latin verb *fallere*, to deceive, lead astray, cause to make a mistake. In modern usage *fallible* means capable of error or likely to be wrong, as human beings are fallible creatures. Attach the prefix *in-* to *fallible* and you have the word *infallible*, not fallible, not capable of making an error, unable to fail. As your infallible guide through *Verbal Advantage*, I assure you that this program is an infallible method of building your vocabulary.

The unusual noun *macula* (MAK-yuh-luh) means a spot or stain. Its direct Latin root, *macula*, meant either a physical spot or blotch or a moral blemish, a stain on one's character. In current usage *macula* refers specifically either to a blemish on the skin or to a sunspot; the corresponding adjective *maculate* means stained, blemished, impure, corrupt. Attach the prefix *in-* to the adjective *maculate* and you have the word *immaculate*, not maculate, unstained, spotless. An immaculate house is spick-and-span; an immaculate complexion has no blemishes; an immaculate reputation or background is spotless, clean as a whistle. In Roman Catholicism, the Immaculate Conception is the doctrine that the Virgin Mary was miraculously conceived without the moral stain of original sin.

And now for our keyword, *impeccable*. From its Latin root, *peccare*, to make a mistake, blunder, sin, English has also inherited three other words: the noun *peccadillo* (PEK-uh-DIL-oh) means a small sin, minor fault or flaw; the adjective *peccant* (PEK-int) means guilty, sinful, culpable; and the adjective *peccable* (PEK-uh-buul) means liable to sin or do wrong. Slap the privative prefix *in-* onto the unfortunate *peccable* and you have its more pleasant antonym, *impeccable*, incapable of sin, unable to do wrong, and therefore free from all faults or imperfections. Impeccable taste is faultless; impeccable speech is flawless; an impeccable performance is perfect.

Let's review the ten keywords you've just learned by playing "One of These Definitions Doesn't Fit the Word." In each statement below, a keyword (in *italics*) is followed by three definitions. Two of the three are correct; one is unrelated in meaning. Decide which definition doesn't fit the keyword. Answers appear on page 157.

1. To *acquiesce* means to agree, make do, give in.
2. To *pontificate* means to speak pompously, speak powerfully, speak pretentiously.
3. *Deleterious* means unnecessary, injurious, detrimental.
4. *Ambivalent* means uncertain, indecisive, inconsistent.
5. *Pensive* means concerned, thoughtful, reflective.
6. *Impromptu* means improvised, spontaneous, unpredictable.
7. To *conjecture* means to suppose, presume, plan.
8. *Surreptitious* means furtive, wicked, stealthy.
9. *Exemplary* means salient, commendable, meritorious.
10. *Impeccable* means perfect, fantastic, flawless.

Get with the Pronunciation Program

The program is getting quite challenging now, don't you agree? Well, for a respite let's take a brief look at some commonly mispronounced words.

And you just read one of them—*respite*, which is properly pronounced RES-pit, with the accent on the first syllable, but which is often mispronounced ruh-SPYT, with the accent shifted to the second syllable. A *respite* is an interval of rest or relief, a lull, hiatus, as "a vacation is a respite from work." Take care to stress this word on the first syllable: RES-pit.

How do you pronounce the *-gram* in *program*? Many speakers today slur it and say PROH-grum. Current dictionaries now countenance this slurred pronunciation, so I can't say categorically that it's wrong, but I can state my dogmatic opinion: PROH-gr*u*m is illogical and sloppy. The vast majority of speakers don't slur the -*gram* in *telegram*, *anagram*, *cryptogram*, *monogram*, *kilogram*, *milligram*, and *diagram*, so it only makes sense to be consistent and preserve the -*gram* in *program*. Pronounce the second syllable to rhyme with *ham*.

One of the most common speaking errors is misplacing the accent or stress in a word. Misplaced accents are rife among educated speakers today. Just for fun, try this little test:

Do you say *in*fluence or in*flu*ence; *af*fluent or af*flu*ent; su*per*fluous or superfluous; *pref*erable or pre*fer*able; *com*parable or com*par*able; *for*midable or for*mid*able; *in*tegral or in*teg*ral; *hos*pitable or ho*spit*able; *ap*plicable or ap*plica*ble; and last but not least, do you say *ex*quisite or ex*quis*ite?

In every case, the first pronunciation is preferred. If you check these words in a dictionary, you will find some of the second pronunciations listed, simply because so many speakers now misplace the accent in these words that dictionary editors feel compelled to record the practice. However, take it from me: *in*fluence, for*mid*able, pre*fer*able, and all the rest are either trendy or flat-out wrong. The traditional and cultivated pronunciations are *in*fluence, *af*fluent, su*per*fluous, *pref*erable, *com*parable, *for*midable, *in*tegral, *hos*pitable, *ap*plicable, and *ex*quisite.

Now let me ask you this: When you make a mistake, do you AIR or do you UR? Properly, the verb to *err* should rhyme with *sir*, not with *hair*. Dictionaries have recorded pronunciation for about two hundred years. The variant AIR for *err* did not appear in a dictionary until the 1960s; since then, it has become the dominant pronunciation. Although some commentators argue in favor of AIR on the grounds that it links the verb phonically with the noun *error*, many cultivated speakers and current authorities still prefer UR, and I stand firmly with them. In my book, to AIR is human, to UR divine.

If you're clever and you prefer to be right, then answer me this: When management and labor try to hammer out a contract, would you say they are engaged in nego-*see*-ations or in nego-*shee*-ations? When people have strong, opposing views on an issue, would you describe the issue as contro-ver-*see*-al or controver-*shal*? If you would have said nego-*see*-ations and con-trover-*see*-al, ask yourself this: Have you always pronounced these words like that, or did you unconsciously change your pronunciation at some point because you heard so many friends, coworkers, and broadcasters pronouncing them that way?

Nego-*see*-ate and controver-*see*-al are vogue pronunciations, by which I mean they are trendy and pseudosophisticated. To borrow a phrase from the great authority on language H. W. Fowler, they owe their vogue, or popularity, "to the joy of showing that one has acquired them." Why have so many people recently decided to say nego-*see*-ate and controver-*see*-al? Beats me. All I know is that these pronunciations, to quote one noted authority on language, are "prissy." There is no good reason to follow the herd and adopt them. Stick with controver-*shal* and nego-*shee*-ate, which have served us for generations, and no one will ever stick it to you.

And that goes for the word *species* too. The alternative pronunciation SPEE-seez, now used by many educated speakers, has been heard since the mid-twentieth century. The traditional pronunciation, SPEE-sheez, has been around since the word came into the language in the fourteenth century. Nevertheless, because of its popularity today among the overrefined, SPEE-seez is recognized by current dictionaries. Not one, however, lists it first. That makes my heart glad, for to my ear this sibilant SPEE-seez sounds SOH-see-uh-lee am-BIS-ee-us and intellectually SOO-pur-FIS-ee-ul. In my opinion, SPEE-seez is just too PRES-ee-us for words.

To sum up: As you can see, when it comes to pronunciation I am a creature of an altogether different species (SPEE-sheez). I have my own program (don't slur -*gram*). I don't think all pronunciations are comparable (stress on *com*-); I believe some are preferable (stress on *pref*-) to others. When I hear someone err (rhymes with *sir*), it hurts my exquisitely (stress on *ex*-) sensitive ears. I have formidable (stress on *for*-) opinions, I am not often willing to negotiate (nego-*shee*-ayt), and I am certainly not afraid of being controversial (four syllables, with -sh<u>ul</u> at the end). All that may not make me popular or affluent (stress on *af*-), but at least I've done my homework and I know what I'm talking about. If you choose to follow my advice on pronunciation, no one can rightfully accuse you of slovenly speech.

But that's enough pontification about pronunciation. Now let's take a look at some commonly confused words.

First, consider the verbs to *imply* and to *infer*, which hordes of well-educated people have a murderous time distinguishing.

To *imply* is to suggest, hint, indicate indirectly: a person may say one thing and imply another, or someone may think you are implying something when you are not. For example, if you ask a coworker out for lunch, the person may think you are implying, hinting, that you want to get intimate when all you want is some company so you don't have to stare at the wall while you chew.

To *infer* means to deduce, conclude, draw a conclusion. You can infer, draw a logical conclusion, from evidence or known facts; you can also infer something from what someone implies. For example, if a client says he needs to think about an offer you have just made, he might be implying that he is unhappy with it, and you might infer that he may go to someone else. As Theodore M. Bernstein puts it in *The Careful Writer*, "The implier is the pitcher; the inferrer is the catcher." Someone who implies throws out a hint, a suggestion. Someone who infers catches that suggestion and makes a conclusion, deduction.

Now let's differentiate between the words *disinterested* and *uninterested*. No one ever has a problem with *uninterested*—it simply means not interested. The trouble starts when people use *disinterested* to mean the same thing as *uninterested*. *Disinterested* means impartial, unbiased, not influenced by selfish motives. In court you want a disinterested judge, not an uninterested one, and at work you want a disinterested boss—a fair, impartial boss—not an uninterested one.

Finally, let's distinguish between the words *anxious* and *eager*. *Eager* is rarely misused, but you will often hear *anxious* used in place of *eager* in such phrases as "Mike is anxious to see the new movie," or "Amanda was anxious to get a promotion." *Anxious* means full of anxiety, worried, nervous, concerned. *Eager* means showing keen interest or impatient desire. In his helpful guide, *The Appropriate Word*, J. N. Hook explains that "we are anxious (worried) about harmful things that may happen, eager about things we want to happen." Thus, Mike should be eager to see the new movie, but anxious about whether he'll be able to get a good seat. Amanda should be eager to get a promotion, but anxious about handling the greater responsibility of the job.

And now, after that long-winded lecture on pronunciation and usage, I'll bet you're eager to learn more words, so before you get anxious, let's return to the *Verbal Advantage* vocabulary for the final ten keywords in Level 4.

Word 41: ATTEST (uh-TEST)

To affirm to be true, genuine, or correct; certify or authenticate officially; stand as proof or evidence of.

Attest comes from the Latin *ad*, to, and *testari*, to bear witness, and ultimately from *testis*, a witness. From the same Latin *testis*, witness, English has inherited a number of other words, including *testify*, *testimony*, *testimonial*, and the legal terms *testator* (TES-tay-tur), a person who has made a valid will, and *intestate* (in-TES-tayt), which means not having made a legal will.

By derivation, *attest* means to bear witness to, give testimony, and today the word may be used in this literal sense, as to attest to someone's whereabouts, to furnish references who will attest to your skills and qualifications. (Note that in this sense *attest* is followed by *to*.) *Attest* is also used to mean to affirm to be true, genuine, or correct, or to stand as proof or evidence of: "Many studies attest the deleterious effects of saturated fat and cholesterol";

"Michelangelo's *David* is but one of many masterpieces that attest the greatness of this Renaissance artist."

Word 42: COPIOUS (KOH-pee-us)

Abundant, plentiful, large in amount or number.

Synonyms of *copious* include *ample*, *bountiful*, and *profuse* (pruh-FYOOS). Antonyms include *scanty*, *meager*, *sparse*, and *paltry* (PAWL-tree).

Copious comes from the Latin *copia*, abundance, plenty, and means literally abundant, plentiful. From the same Latin *copia*, plenty, and *cornu*, a horn, comes the English word *cornucopia* (KORN-(y)uh-**KOH**-pee-uh), a horn of plenty. Historically, a *cornucopia* is a symbol of abundance and prosperity in the form of a goat's horn overflowing with fruit, flowers, and grain. In modern usage, *cornucopia* is often applied to any overflowing stock or supply, as a cornucopia of menu selections, or a cornucopia of products and services.

The adjective *copious* may be used of anything that exists or is provided in abundance. Copious praise is abundant praise; a copious harvest is a plentiful harvest; copious information is a great supply of information; copious speech overflows with words.

Word 43: FALLACIOUS (fuh-LAY-shus)

False, misleading, deceptive, invalid, based on a fallacy.

Synonyms of *fallacious* include *erroneous* (i-ROH-nee-us), *spurious* (SPYOOR-ee-us), *untenable* (uhn-TEN-uh-buul), *illusory* (i-LOO-suh-ree), and *sophistical* (suh-FIS-ti-kul).

The noun *fallacy* (FAL-uh-see) means a false or misleading idea, statement, or argument. *Fallacy* and *sophistry* (SAHF-i-stree, word 20 of this level) are close in meaning. A *fallacy* is a misleading or deceptive argument that violates the laws of reasoning. *Sophistry* refers to reasoning that deliberately uses fallacies, misleading arguments, to confuse or deceive.

Both *fallacy* and the adjective *fallacious* come from the Latin *fallere*, to deceive, lead astray. That which is fallacious is based on a fallacy, and is therefore misleading, deceptive, false. To the skeptical person, all statements, assumptions, and notions are fallacious until clearly proved otherwise.

Word 44: STOIC (STOH-ik)

Showing no feelings, unemotional, unaffected by pleasure or pain, bearing pain or suffering without complaint.

Synonyms of *stoic* include *impassive, dispassionate, indifferent, apathetic* (AP-uh-**THET**-ik), *placid* (PLAS-id), *languid* (LANG-gwid), *phlegmatic* (fleg-MAT-ik, word 33 of Level 9), and *imperturbable*.

Antonyms of *stoic* include *ardent, vehement* (VEE-uh-mint), *zealous* (ZEL-us), *fervid,* and *fervent* (word 24 of Level 3).

Stoic and *stoicism* (**STOH**-i-SIZ-'m) come from the Greek *stoa,* a porch or covered walkway—specifically, the famous Painted Porch in ancient Athens where the doctrine of Stoicism was born. In his *English Vocabulary Builder,* Johnson O'Connor explains that "STOICISM . . . was a school of philosophy founded by Zeno about 308 B.C. . . . STOICISM is so named because Zeno expounded his philosophy from the Painted Porch, one of the covered walks about the Agora (AG-uh-ruh), the public square of ancient Athens. A STOIC . . . was a follower of Zeno, one who believed that men should be free from passion, unmoved by joy or grief, and submit without complaint to the unavoidable necessity by which all things are governed."

In modern usage, *stoicism* means indifference to pleasure or pain; the noun *stoic* refers to anyone who exhibits rigorous self-control; and the adjective *stoic* means showing no feelings, unemotional, bearing pain or suffering without complaint.

Word 45: RECRIMINATION (ri-KRIM-uh-**NAY**-shin)

A countercharge or counteraccusation.

Recrimination combines the prefix *re-,* which means "back" or "again," with the Latin verb *criminari,* to accuse, bring a charge against, and means literally to accuse in return, accuse again. The great *Webster's New International Dictionary,* second edition (1934), defines recrimination as "an accusation brought by the accused against the accuser."

Recriminations, or countercharges, are perhaps most often heard today in political campaigns, international relations, and legal proceedings. In modern usage, when we speak of mutual recriminations the word usually suggests a series of bitter denunciations exchanged in the course of fervid debate.

Recrimination is the noun. The corresponding verb is *recriminate,* to bring a countercharge against, denounce in return. The corresponding adjective has two forms: *recriminative* (ri-**KRIM**-uh-NAY-tiv) and *recriminatory* (ri-KRIM-i-nuh-tor-ee).

Word 46: AFFINITY (uh-FIN-i-tee)

Close resemblance or relationship, a strong likeness, similarity, or connection, as the affinity of the Italian, French, and Spanish languages, an affinity among the painters of the Impressionist school, an affinity between the blues and early rock and roll.

Affinity may also mean a natural attraction to, or liking for, a person or thing, as an affinity for classical music, an affinity for the freewheeling literature of the Beat Generation, an affinity among neighbors in a close-knit community.

Synonyms of *affinity* in the sense of "close resemblance or relationship" include *kinship*, *correspondence*, *compatibility*, and *consanguinity* (KAHN-sang-GWIN-i-tee). Synonyms of *affinity* in the sense of "liking or attraction" include *penchant* (word 9 of Level 3), *propensity*, and *proclivity*.

Affinity comes from a Latin word meaning "relationship by marriage," and dictionaries still recognize this literal sense although the word is not often used in that way. In current usage *affinity* usually means either a close relationship or likeness, or a natural attraction to or liking for a person or thing.

Word 47: VOLATILE (VAHL-uh-tul; British say VAHL-uh-tyl)

Changeable, unstable, inconstant, likely to change or shift rapidly and unpredictably: The stock market is often volatile; a person may have volatile moods; the weather in New England is notoriously volatile.

Synonyms of *volatile* include *fickle*, *flighty*, *capricious* (kuh-PRISH-us, word 11 of Level 1), *erratic*, *protean* (PROH-tee-in), and *mercurial* (mur-KYUR-ee-ul).

Antonyms include *stable*, *fixed*, *steadfast*, *invariable*, *immutable*, and *quiescent* (kwy-ES-int, word 22 of Level 3).

Volatile, which entered English in the early 1600s, has a volatile history, full of many shifts and changes in meaning. The word comes from the Latin *volare*, to fly, and its original meaning was "flying" or "having the power to fly." Today *volatile* is rarely used in this sense, and instead we have the word *volant* (VOH-lant), which came into the language shortly before *volatile* from the same Latin *volare*, to fly. *Volant* means flying, able to fly, or quick, nimble, agile.

The fickle, unpredictable *volatile* then came to mean evaporating quickly, easily vaporized, as a volatile oil or liquid. In the science of chemistry it is still used in this way, and today it would be unusual but not outlandish for an essayist to write about the volatile morning dew, or for a weathercaster to speak of volatile fog or clouds, or for a TV chef to discuss the volatile nature of wine used in cooking.

By the mid-seventeenth century the inconstant *volatile* had acquired its most durable meaning: changeable, unstable, inconstant, likely to change or shift rapidly and unpredictably. In this sense it is a close synonym of *capricious* and *mercurial*. Out of this notion of changeability and inconstancy, *volatile* gained two more meanings: fleeting, vanishing swiftly, transient, ephemeral; and also lighthearted, lively and carefree, whimsical, prone to flights of fancy.

In the second half of the twentieth century *volatile* took on yet another meaning: explosive, likely to erupt into violence. You will often hear *volatile* used this way in news reports about domestic or international affairs characterized by tension and sporadic conflict. This sense is an outgrowth of the meaning "unstable, unpredictable," for when a situation is unstable or unpredictable it is often likely to explode or erupt in violence.

Finally, in the 1990s *volatile* acquired one more sense. According to *Webster's New World Dictionary*, third college edition, in the jargon of computer science *volatile* is used to mean pertaining to "memory that does not retain stored data when the power supply is disconnected."

Despite its capricious, changeable history, *volatile* has remained close to its roots. For as I'm sure you can see, all the various senses of *volatile* incorporate the notions of flight, flightiness, and swift, unpredictable change suggested by the word's Latin root, *volare*, to fly. When you see or hear *volatile* used, and when you use it yourself, remember that in all of its senses the word describes that which can swiftly fly away from one condition or mood into another.

Volatile is the adjective; the corresponding noun is *volatility*.

Word 48: SQUALID (SKWAHL-id)

Dirty and run-down as a result of poverty or neglect, foul or filthy from lack of care, wretched, miserable, degraded.

Synonyms of *squalid* include *seedy*, *unkempt*, *slovenly* (SLUHV-un-lee), and *dilapidated* (di-**LAP**-i-DAY-tid—take care to pronounce the last two syllables -*dated*, not -*tated*).

Antonyms include *unsullied*, *immaculate*, and *pristine* (PRIS-teen or pri-STEEN).

Squalid is the adjective; the corresponding noun is *squalor* (SKWAHL-ur). *Squalor* means filthiness, foulness, degradation, a wretched, miserable condition resulting from poverty or neglect.

Squalid comes from the Latin verb *squalere*, which has various meanings, including to be rough or scaly; to be covered with filth; to be overgrown or dirty from neglect; and to wear mourning clothes. In modern usage *squalid* has retained a taste of all these senses. Squalid attire is rough and unkempt— or, to use an informal term, grungy. Squalid language is filthy or foul. A squalid neighborhood is slummy, dilapidated, dirty and run-down from neglect. And just as a person in mourning is sad and forlorn, squalid people or squalid conditions are wretched and miserable because they are poor, degraded, and pitiable.

The adjectives *squalid* and *sordid* (SOR-did) are close in meaning. Both words mean dirty, filthy, and run-down, but *squalid* applies to that which is dirty and miserable because of poverty or neglect, while *sordid* suggests a filthy wretchedness resulting from a degraded or debased character.

Word 49: EXPEDITE (EK-spi-dyt)

To speed up, hasten, facilitate, accelerate the progress of, handle or perform quickly and efficiently: "The company decided to expand its workforce to expedite production of its new product."

Antonyms of *expedite* include *delay*, *postpone*, *hinder*, *retard*, *slacken*, and *protract* (word 25 of Level 3).

Expedite comes from the Latin verb *expedire*, to set free, disentangle, get ready for action. When you expedite something, you free it from all hindrances or obstructions; you disentangle it from whatever is delaying its progress so that action can proceed. In current usage, when you expedite a plan or a project it means you speed up its progress, hasten its completion. And when the boss says to you, "Please expedite the matter," that means the boss wants you to take care of the matter as quickly and efficiently as possible.

Word 50: ABJECT (AB-jekt *or* ab-JEKT)

Degraded, brought low in condition or status; hence, lacking self-respect, contemptible, wretched.

The corresponding noun is *abjection* (ab-JEK-shin), a degraded, wretched, contemptible state.

Synonyms of *abject* include *debased* (di-BAYST), *despicable* (DES-pik-uh-buul; the stress properly is on the first syllable), *ignoble*, *groveling* (GRAH-vul- or GRUH-vul-), *servile* (SUR-vil), and *squalid* (word 48 of this level). Antonyms of *abject* include *noble*, *dignified*, *lofty*, *majestic*, *eminent*, and *illustrious* (i-LUHS-tree-us).

In Middle English *abject* meant "outcast." The word comes ultimately from the Latin *ab*, meaning "away" or "off," and the verb *jacere*, to throw, and means literally "thrown away, cast off." The abject members of society are the outcasts, the undesirables, and the indigent—the people who have been thrown away or cast off because they seem to have no social place or worth.

This literal sense of thrown away or cast off led to the modern meaning of *abject*: brought low in condition or status— hence, degraded, wretched, or contemptible.

Abject poverty is utterly wretched poverty. Abject conditions are hopeless and degrading conditions. An abject coward is thoroughly contemptible. An abject person has fallen so low that he has lost all self-respect.

If you behave toward someone in an abject manner, you are behaving in a groveling, servile manner, like a defeated dog that bares its neck and belly to the vanquishing dog.

Let's review the ten keywords you've just learned. This time I'm going to give you the review word followed by three words or phrases, and you decide which of those three answer choices comes nearest the meaning of the review word. Answers appear on page 158.

1. When you *attest* something, or *attest to* it, do you pass judgment on it, affirm it as true, or examine it?
2. Is a *copious* supply meager, excessive, or abundant?
3. When a statement is *fallacious*, is it silly, misleading, or clever?
4. Would a *stoic* person be unemotional, unpredictable, or inarticulate?
5. When two people exchange *recriminations*, do they exchange compliments, insults, or countercharges?
6. When things have an *affinity*, do they have a luxurious appearance, a close relationship, or a refined quality?
7. Is a *volatile* situation unstable, unusual, or unwholesome?
8. Is a *squalid* environment confined and uncomfortable, noisy and distracting, or dirty and run-down?
9. When you *expedite* something, do you throw it away, speed it up, or observe it closely?
10. Are *abject* conditions troublesome, degraded, or offensive?

Remember that if you answered fewer than eight of the questions correctly in this quiz, you should read the last ten keyword discussions again. Also, don't forget to review this entire level at least once before moving on to Level 5.

Now that we're almost done with Level 4, it's time to—wait a minute! Did you notice anything wrong with what I just said?

Does anything about the phrase "now that we're almost done with Level 4" sound incorrect to you? If so, you may be an untapped member of the

League of Inflexible Super-Purists—for which the acronym, quite appropriately, is LISP.

For years hard-core purists have criticized the use of the word *done* to mean finished, as in the sentence "I'm just trying to get the job done." It's true, as they assert, that using *done* in this way is informal, but that in itself does not make it incorrect. Sometimes informal usage is inappropriate or objectionable, but as Rudolph Flesch argues persuasively in his classic guide, *The Art of Readable Writing* (1949), most good, clear writing and speech is largely composed of everyday, practical words. Moreover, it's a mistake to assume that every rule about language is a good rule, and the best writers know that it's sometimes necessary to break a rule to achieve a desired effect.

So now let me tell you the story of *done* versus *finished*.

In 1965, the eminent usage commentator Theodore M. Bernstein echoed the sentiments of many educated speakers who had been pilloried by their parents and teachers for allegedly misusing *done*. "The word should not be used in good writing to mean finished or completed," Bernstein stated in *The Careful Writer*. "It is proper to say, 'The roast is done,' but this does not mean it is finished; it means the roast is sufficiently cooked."

By 1977, however, Bernstein had changed his "don't" to a "maybe." In *Dos, Don'ts, and Maybes of English Usage*, he noted that in 1969 "the usage panel of the American Heritage Dictionary split 53 to 47 percent in favor of . . . done to mean completed or finished."

Bernstein continues: "Webster's unabridged, second edition [1934] labels it colloquial, but the third edition [1961] finds nothing wrong with it. Neither do Webster's New World, the Random House and the big Oxford English Dictionary. The verdict would seem to be that done in the sense of finished is well on the way to acceptability, if it has not already arrived." Discerning observers of the language like Bernstein know that it's essential to question change and resist it when it seems objectionable, but they also know that it's obstinate and myopic to maintain that something is unacceptable in the face of overwhelming evidence to the contrary.

In 1987, the *Random House Dictionary of the English Language*, second edition, unabridged, confirmed Bernstein's conjecture in unequivocal terms with a usage note that said, "In the adjectival sense, 'completed, finished, through,' *done* dates from the 14th century and is entirely standard." Other current dictionaries concur and list the "finished, completed" definition without comment.

Based on that evidence, it would seem that the acceptability of *done* meaning "finished" is a done deal. And with that pronouncement, we are now done with Level 4.

Answers to Review Quizzes for Level 4

Keywords 1–10

1. Yes. *Provident* means thrifty, economical, saving or providing for future needs.
2. Yes. To *impute* means to charge or attribute, especially with a fault or misconduct, lay the responsibility or blame upon.
3. No. *Astute* means shrewd, clever, perceptive, discerning.
4. No. A *neophyte* is a beginner, novice, amateur, tyro; specifically, a new member of or convert to a religion.
5. No. An *enigma* is a mystery, puzzle, riddle, perplexing problem, something or someone hard to understand or explain.
6. Yes. *Credence* means belief, acceptance, especially belief in a published report or acceptance of another's opinion.
7. No. To *venerate* means to respect deeply, revere, regard with awe and adoration.
8. No. *Garrulous* means talkative in a rambling, annoying, pointless, or long-winded way.
9. Yes. *Trenchant* means keen, penetrating, vigorously effective, sharp and to the point.
10. Yes. *Autonomous* means independent, self-governing, not under the control of something or someone else.

Keywords 11–20

1. True. A *panacea* is a cure-all, universal antidote, remedy for all diseases and difficulties.
2. False. *Ephemeral* means short-lived, passing, fleeting, lasting for a short time.
3. False. *Onerous* means burdensome, troublesome, oppressive, hard to bear, difficult to accomplish or endure.
4. True. *Laity* means all the people outside of a given profession or specialized field, nonprofessionals.
5. False. *Pungent* means sharp, penetrating, biting, acrid.
6. False. *Prosaic* means dull, ordinary, uninteresting, unimaginative.
7. False. A *charlatan* is a fake, quack, imposter, fraud, a person who pretends to have a special skill or knowledge.
8. False. *Perfunctory* means mechanical, routine, listless; done without interest or enthusiasm; performed in an indifferent, halfhearted, superficial, and often careless way.
9. True. Literally, a *morass* is a swamp, marsh, bog; figuratively, a *morass* is

something that traps, confines, or confuses, a sticky situation or troublesome state of affairs.
10. True. *Sophistry* is deceptive reasoning, subtle and misleading argument.

Keywords 21–30

1. Antonyms. *Prolific* means fruitful, fertile, productive.
2. Synonyms. *Mundane* means of the world, earthly, material as distinguished from spiritual.
3. Synonyms. *Myriad* means countless, innumerable, infinite, consisting of a
   great or indefinite number.
4. Antonyms. *Dissident* means disagreeing, disaffected, dissenting, nonconformist.
5. Antonyms. *Deplorable* means wretched, grievous, lamentable, worthy of
   severe disapproval. *Laudable* means praiseworthy, commendable, worthy
   of approval or admiration.
6. Synonyms. *Inimitable* means unable to be imitated, copied, or reproduced; matchless, peerless, beyond compare.
7. Synonyms. *Jaded* means worn out by overwork or overindulgence, tired,
   fatigued, weary, exhausted.
8. Synonyms. *Myopic* means not able to see the long-range picture, having
   a narrow or circumscribed view, short-sighted.
9. Antonyms. *Unverifiable* means unable to be tested or proved true.
   Demonstrable means capable of being demonstrated or proved.
10. Synonyms. *Callow* means immature, inexperienced, unsophisticated.

Keywords 31–40

1. *Make do* doesn't fit. To *acquiesce* means to agree without protest, accept
   without argument or resistance, give in quietly.
2. To *speak powerfully* doesn't fit. Powerful speech is either strong, clear,
   and persuasive, or simply loud. To *pontificate* means to speak in a
   pompous and overbearing way, make pretentious or categorical statements, express one's opinion as though it were an official decree.
3. *Unnecessary* doesn't fit. *Deleterious* means harmful, destructive, injurious,
   detrimental; especially, harmful to health or well-being.
4. *Inconsistent* doesn't fit. *Ambivalent* means uncertain, indecisive, having
   conflicting feelings or desires, simultaneously drawn in opposite directions.
5. *Concerned* doesn't fit. *Pensive* means thoughtful, reflective, especially in a
   deep, dreamy, or melancholy way.
6. *Unpredictable* doesn't fit. *Impromptu* means made up or done on the
   spur of the moment, improvised for the occasion, spontaneous.

7. *Plan* doesn't fit. To *conjecture* means to make an educated guess; to suppose, presume; form an opinion or make a judgment based on insufficient evidence.

8. *Wicked* doesn't fit. *Surreptitious* means stealthy, furtive, shifty, sly, characterized by secrecy and caution.

9. *Salient* doesn't fit. *Salient* means conspicuous, prominent, sticking out. *Exemplary* means worthy of imitation; hence, praiseworthy, commendable, meritorious.

10. *Fantastic* doesn't fit. *Fantastic* means like a fantasy, and therefore strange, extravagant, or wonderful. *Impeccable* means perfect, faultless, flawless, incapable of error or sin.

Keywords 41–50

1. To *attest* means to affirm to be true, genuine, or correct; certify or authenticate officially; stand as proof or evidence of.

2. A copious supply is a plentiful supply; *copious* means abundant, large in amount or number.

3. A *fallacious* statement is misleading, false, deceptive, invalid, based on a fallacy.

4. A stoic person is unemotional; *stoic* means showing no feelings, unaffected by pleasure or pain.

5. They exchange countercharges. A *recrimination* is a countercharge or counteraccusation.

6. An *affinity* is a close resemblance or relationship, a strong likeness, similarity, or connection. *Affinity* may also mean a natural attraction to, or liking for, a person or thing.

7. A volatile situation is changeable, unstable, inconstant; *volatile* means likely to change or shift rapidly and unpredictably.

8. A *squalid* environment is dirty and run-down as a result of poverty or neglect, foul or filthy from lack of care.

9. When you *expedite* something you speed it up, hasten its progress, handle or perform it quickly and efficiently.

10. Abject conditions are degraded. *Abject* means brought low in condition or status; hence, lacking self-respect, contemptible, wretched.

Review Test for Level 4

1. Which word means specifically an amateur practitioner of an art?
   (a) tyro
   (b) novice

    (c) neophyte

    (d) dilettante

2. Which word is an antonym of *garrulous*?

    (a) verbose

    (b) laconic

    (c) loquacious

    (d) voluble

3. The combining form *auto-* means

    (a) other

    (b) alone

    (c) self

    (d) only

4. The combining form *pan-* means

    (a) one

    (b) all

    (c) over

    (d) through

5. Which phrase is *not* redundant?

    (a) a daily journal

    (b) the nonprofessional laity

    (c) a panacea for all ills

    (d) all of the above phrases are redundant

6. Which is *not* an accepted meaning of *pantheon*?

    (a) a collection of the best examples of something

    (b) all the gods worshiped by a given people

    (c) a temple dedicated to all the gods

    (d) any group of highly respected or revered persons

7. *Insipid*, *vapid*, and *jejune* are synonyms of

    (a) abject

    (b) myopic

    (c) prosaic

    (d) deleterious

8. Which pair of words is *not* synonymous?

    (a) fraud, fake

    (b) humbug, charlatan

    (c) imposter, dissident

    (d) quack, mountebank

9. *Mechanical*, *routine*, and *listless* are synonyms of
    (a) jaded
    (b) onerous
    (c) ambivalent
    (d) perfunctory

10. Which statement does *not* apply to *sophistry*?
    (a) it is clever
    (b) it is confusing
    (c) it is plausible
    (d) it is deceptive

11. Miss Thistlebottom, the hidebound grammarian, is the creation of
    (a) Theodore M. Bernstein
    (b) H. W. Fowler
    (c) William Safire
    (d) Lewis Carroll

12. What is a lexicographer?
    (a) a writing instructor
    (b) an author of usage guides
    (c) a maker of dictionaries
    (d) an expert on word origins

13. Which word is a synonym of *mundane*?
    (a) sublunary
    (b) celestial
    (c) sublime
    (d) ethereal

14. In ancient Greece a *myriad* was
    (a) a temple dedicated to all the gods
    (b) a period of fasting followed by a feast
    (c) a division of ten thousand soldiers
    (d) a marathon

15. Which pair of words is synonymous?
    (a) laudable, deplorable
    (b) meritorious, ignominious
    (c) commendable, contemptible
    (d) exemplary, estimable

16. Which of the following is least likely to make someone jaded?

    (a) abuse
    (b) inactivity
    (c) overwork
    (d) overindulgence

17. Which word is a synonym of *latitudinarian*?

    (a) purblind
    (b) obtuse
    (c) catholic
    (d) myopic

18. Which sentences illustrate proper usage? (This question has *two* correct answers.)

    (a) This is between you and me.
    (b) This is between you and I.
    (c) This is for Mary and me.
    (d) This is for Mary and I.

19. By derivation, the word *pontificate* is related to

    (a) the Stoic philosophers
    (b) the Pope
    (c) snake-oil salesmen
    (d) the Sophists

20. Which word means expressing opinion as if it were fact?

    (a) diurnal
    (b) disparaging
    (c) dogmatic
    (d) demonstrable

21. In *ambivalent* and *ambidextrous*, the combining form *ambi-* means

    (a) around
    (b) through
    (c) other
    (d) both

22. To *speculate*, *surmise*, and *conjecture* all mean

    (a) to risk
    (b) to guess
    (c) to examine
    (d) to take for granted

23. Which word is an antonym of *surreptitious*?

    (a) manifest
    (b) furtive
    (c) clandestine
    (d) covert

24. Which is the proper pronunciation of *heinous*?

    (a) HEE-n<u>i</u>s
    (b) HAY-n<u>i</u>s
    (c) HEE-nee-<u>u</u>s
    (d) HAY-nee-<u>u</u>s

25. Which word is an antonym of *impeccable*?

    (a) perfunctory
    (b) extemporaneous
    (c) culpable
    (d) jaded

26. Which word means a small sin, minor fault or flaw?

    (a) stigma
    (b) idiosyncrasy
    (c) macula
    (d) peccadillo

27. Which word means a lull, hiatus?

    (a) jade
    (b) respite
    (c) abjection
    (d) acquiescence

28. In *preferable*, *formidable*, *comparable*, and *applicable*, where does the stress properly fall?

    (a) on the first syllable
    (b) on the second syllable

29. The question "What are you inferring?" means

    (a) What are you deducing or concluding?
    (b) What are you suggesting or indicating indirectly?
    (c) What are you explaining or defining?
    (d) What precisely are you saying?

30. "Amanda was _____ to improve her verbal skills." In careful usage, which word properly should fill the blank in that sentence?

(a) anxious

(b) eager

31. By derivation, a *cornucopia* is

(a) an official decree

(b) a horn of plenty

(c) a worker of miracles

(d) an artistic masterpiece

32. Which word is an antonym of *stoic*?

(a) apathetic

(b) astute

(c) ardent

(d) ambivalent

33. Which pair of words are synonyms?

(a) immutable, erratic

(b) protean, mercurial

(c) capricious, invariable

(d) flighty, quiescent

34. *Unsullied*, *immaculate*, and *pristine* are antonyms of

(a) onerous

(b) impeccable

(c) volatile

(d) squalid

35. *Conjecture* and *abject* both come from the Latin verb *jacere*, which means

(a) to accept

(b) to judge

(c) to throw

(d) to make a mistake

Answers

1. d 2. b 3. c 4. b 5. d 6. d 7. c 8. c 9. d 10. b 11. a 12. c 13. a
14. c 15. d 16. b 17. c 18. a + c 19. b 20. c 21. d 22. b 23. a 24. b
25. c 26. d 27. b 28. a 29. a 30. a 31. b 32. c 33. b 34. d 35. c

Evaluation

A score of 30–35 is excellent. If you answered fewer than thirty questions correctly in this test, review the entire level and take the test again.

Level 5

Welcome to Level 5 of *Verbal Advantage*. If you've been reviewing the material diligently, by now I imagine you are comfortable with many of the words you've learned, and you probably have also noticed a marked improvement in your verbal awareness.

But guess what? We're not even halfway through the program yet. There's plenty of useful information and there are a lot more challenging words to come—so keep reading and reviewing and you will soon enjoy an even greater *Verbal Advantage*.

Becoming a Cultivated Speaker

Let's begin this level with a brief overview of the subject of pronunciation. My aim in broaching this topic is twofold: to make you more aware of the importance of good pronunciation and to help you become a more careful, conscientious speaker.

Is there a right way and a wrong way to pronounce a word? Do words sometimes have more than one correct pronunciation? If so, are certain pronunciations better—or more correct—than others?

The answer to these questions, in my opinion, is yes. Just as there are good and bad ways to use words, there are right and wrong ways to pronounce them. In some cases there is even a good, better, and best way, along with bad, worse, and worst.

Many linguists and lexicographers (dictionary editors) would disagree with me. Being descriptive rather than prescriptive in their approach, they do not believe we should make value judgments about meaning, usage, or pronunciation. The truth, however, is that they often do. Many times a certain pronunciation will not be listed in a dictionary, or it will appear with a cautionary label such as "nonstandard" or "substandard." Clearly, that constitutes a value judgment. It implies, "We don't recognize this pronunciation as legitimate, prevalent, or proper in educated speech."

Dictionary editors don't like to admit that they make these sorts of judgment calls, perhaps because they're afraid of being labeled "undemocratic" or "snobbish." But when it comes to pronunciation, I don't think people want to be told that anything goes. Most of us are well aware that in many situations people will judge us by the way we speak, and for that reason most of us want to say it right.

Therefore, when people consult a dictionary they expect to find what is considered acceptable and correct, and they appreciate whatever reliable advice they can get. This awareness of the importance of using standard pronunciation is the first step in becoming what is often called a "cultivated speaker," someone who cares enough about speaking well to invest some time and energy in learning how to pronounce words properly.

One meaning of the verb to *cultivate* is to devote special attention to with the aim of improving, and the adjective *cultivated* means refined by study and training, marked by skill and taste. Cultivated speakers are those who have arrived at their pronunciation not by imitation or guesswork but by study and practice. Cultivated speech means the manner in which such conscientious speakers concur on how words should be pronounced, and how that agreement is represented in the dictionaries.

The first goal of *Verbal Advantage* is to add more words to your vocabulary; the second is to teach you how to use them properly and precisely; and the third is to set you on the path to becoming a cultivated speaker of the language. This last goal is just as important as the others, especially if you do any public speaking or conduct a good deal of your business orally.

It's fine to know lots of words and how to use them, but you must also be able to pronounce them properly if you wish to avoid sounding eccentric, or even worse, foolish. People will understand you, but they will not consider you a careful speaker if you say . . .

- HYTH instead of HYT (rhymes with *kite*) for *height*
- WAHRSH instead of WAHSH (with no *r* sound) for *wash*
- mis-CHEE-vee-us instead of MIS-chi-vus for *mischievous* (the word has three syllables, not four, and the stress is on *mis-*)
- AK-ur-it instead of AK-yur-it for *accurate*
- DROWN-did instead of DROWND for *drowned*
- eye-DEER instead of eye-DEE-uh for *idea*
- i-REV-uh-lint instead of i-REL-uh-vint for *irrelevant*
- JOO-luh-ree instead of JOO-wuul-ree for *jewelry*
- thee-AY-tur instead of THEE-uh-tur for *theater*
- NOO-kyuh-lur instead of N(Y)OO-klee-ur for *nuclear*

In each case above, the first pronunciation is a sign of a careless speaker.

I should also point out that of the three goals of this program, good pronunciation is the easiest to achieve. It may take a while to learn the precise meaning and proper use of a given word, but you can memorize and master its pronunciation in a minute. In fact, knowing how to pronounce a word can sometimes help you remember its meaning. But the most challenging task isn't learning how to pronounce unfamiliar words. The real work begins with learning to avoid mispronouncing words you already know.

The advice on pronunciation I have included throughout *Verbal Advantage* will help. When you have finished this program, however, you will have to commit yourself to improving your pronunciation on your own. To prepare yourself for that, you need to do three things:

1. Start paying closer attention to how other people speak.
2. Make sure to check the pronunciation of every word you look up in the dictionary.
3. Learn how to interpret diacritical marks—the symbols dictionaries use to indicate pronunciation.

First, pay attention to every word you read in this program. When you see an unfamiliar word, note the transcription of the pronunciation I give for it and try saying the word to yourself several times. Then the next time you have a dictionary handy, look up the word and read the pronunciation, the definition, and the etymology (ET-uh-**MAHL**-uh-jee, a word you met in Level 2), the part of the entry that covers the origin of the word.

As you train your ear to pay closer attention to pronunciation, bear in mind that accent is a natural part of cultivated speech. In a large, diverse country like the United States, people from different regions are bound to pronounce certain words a bit differently. Some people make the mistake of assuming that a different accent constitutes mispronunciation. There is indeed a general American standard for pronunciation, but in most cases it takes into account our regional differences.

For example, although I have lived in southern California for almost twenty years, I was born and raised in New York City and I have also lived in New England. Because I spent my formative years in the East, my accent is, for the most part, an eastern one.

Depending on where you're from, you may pronounce the adjective *merry*, the verb to *marry*, and the name *Mary* all in the same way: MAIR-ee (rhymes with *hairy*). Because of my Eastern background, I employ three distinct pronunciations: for *merry* I say MER-ee (*e* as in *met*); for *marry* I say MAR-ee (*a* as in *mat*), and for *Mary* I say MAIR-ee (rhyming with *dairy*). The point is, these are differences in accent, not mispronunciations; both ways of pronouncing these words are acceptable in cultivated speech.

The second thing you need to do to become a cultivated speaker is to pay close attention to the way words are pronounced by the people around you and by people on the airwaves. When you listen to the radio or watch television, take note of people's pronunciation, and if something strikes you as different or unusual, jot it down and look it up later. If you hear a friend or coworker use an unfamiliar pronunciation, take the time to check and see if it's in a dictionary.

It's best if you can check the word in more than one dictionary so you can compare their opinions on pronunciation. Dictionaries don't differ much in their treatment of definition, but they can vary considerably in how they record pronunciation.

By doing this, not only will you learn the right way to pronounce the words you add to your vocabulary, you will also ameliorate your pronunciation of the words you already know.

To sum up: If you wish to become a better speaker, you must listen critically to the way you and others speak, and you must check your pronunciation in the dictionary—not just the pronunciation of the new words you learn but also of the words you know and think you are pronouncing correctly.

Having made that effort myself, I can tell you it's a sobering moment when you discover you've been mispronouncing a familiar word for years. On the other hand, there's a profound satisfaction in knowing that you've uncovered an error and corrected it.

Finally, there are two bad habits you must eschew at all costs. (*Eschew*— a word you met briefly in Level 2 and that you will meet again as keyword 47 of this level—means to avoid, abstain from, shun. It is not pronounced e-SHOO, as a growing number of educated adults today mistakenly believe. The traditional and proper pronunciation is es-CHEW, like the letter *s* plus the word *chew*.)

First, don't invent your own pronunciations. When you come across a new word, don't guess how it's pronounced; that's like reading around an unfamiliar word and guessing what it means. (That's also probably how people started putting an erroneous *shoe* in *eschew*.)

Second, don't blindly imitate other people's pronunciation. "Monkey-hear, monkey-say" is a risky game.

But don't just take my word for it. Take it from the nineteenth-century American lexicographer Noah Webster, whose name appears prominently on the covers of so many of our dictionaries. In his *Dissertations on the English Language*, Webster wrote that people tend to model their speech after those "whose abilities and character entitle [their] opinions to respect, but whose pronunciation may be altogether accidental or capricious." (By the way, *capricious* is properly pronounced kuh-PRISH-u̲s, not, as you frequently hear, kuh-PREE-shu̲s. The second syllable should rhyme with *wish*, not *we*.)

Mimicking the pronunciation of people you admire may be the natural thing to do, but more often than not it will lead you into error. Then you will mislead someone else, and that person will mislead someone else, until half the country is saying it wrong and dictionary editors eventually list it as standard.

The point is, just because a person is intelligent or accomplished doesn't mean he or she is also a cultivated speaker. Let me share an anecdote with you that illustrates what I mean.

Not long ago a fan of my *Big Book of Beastly Mispronunciations* called me to relate a disturbing story. She said she was in her last year of medical school, and recently one of her professors had ridiculed her in front of the entire class for her pronunciation of a certain medical term. I had researched the word and written about it, concluding that her pronunciation was correct and the professor's was wrong. The professor may be an authority on medicine, but that doesn't make him an expert on pronunciation. Moreover, it's horrifying to think that he abused his authority by going out of his way to humiliate someone who, as it turned out, knew more about what she was saying than he did.

The lesson here is, don't take your own or anyone else's pronunciation for granted. When in doubt, go to the dictionary.

Understanding Diacritical Marks

The last thing you need to do to become a more cultivated speaker is learn how to interpret the diacritical marks or symbols that dictionaries use to show pronunciation. (The word *diacritical* means "serving to distinguish.")

Unfortunately, most people are baffled by diacritical marks, and because they are baffled they simply give up and ignore the whole question of pronunciation altogether—which, as you can imagine, puts them at a distinct verbal disadvantage.

The truth is that learning to interpret diacritical marks is much easier than learning to read music or use a word-processing program. In fact, if you can balance your checkbook and operate a VCR, then with a minimum of effort you can familiarize yourself with diacritical marks. Knowing how to decipher these symbols will help you become a better speaker, so let me wind up this discussion by teaching you some of the most common ones.

Most people recognize the macron and the breve.

The *macron* (MAY-krahn or MAY-kru̲n) is a horizontal line or dash placed over a vowel: ā, ē, ī, ō, ū. The macron represents the "long" sound of the vowel: ā as in *date* and *fate*; ē as in *even* and *meter*; ī as in *ice* and *night*; ō as in *over* and *total*; and ū as in *music* and *cute*.

The *breve* (BREEV, rhymes with *leave*) is a small curved mark, like a tiny smile, placed over a vowel to represent the "short" sound of the vowel: ă as in *cat* and *hat*; ĕ as in *pet* and *let*; ĭ as in *hit* and *sit*; ŏ as in *hot* and *not*; and ŭ as in *up* and *butter*.

The diacritical mark people seem to have the most trouble with is the *schwa* (SHWAH). The schwa looks like a small letter *e* turned on its head—in other words, printed upside-down and backwards: ə. The schwa is a versatile symbol used to indicate an unstressed vowel sound that is neither long nor short but lightened or obscure. For example, to represent the sound of *a* in *ago*, *e* in *item*, *i* in *sanity*, *o* in *comply*, and *u* in *focus*, dictionary editors use a *schwa* (ə-gō, ī-təm, săn-ə-tē, kəm-plī, fō-kəs).

The last two symbols you should know are the dieresis and the circumflex.

A *dieresis* (dy-ER-i-sis) is two dots printed over a vowel; it is also called an *umlaut* (UUM-lowt). The dieresis most often is used over an *a* to indicate an open or broad vowel sound, as in *car* (cär) and *father* (fä-<u>th</u>ur); it may also appear over a *u* to represent an OO sound, as in *flute* (flüt) or *roof* (rüf).

The *circumflex* (SUR-k<u>u</u>m-fleks) looks like the tip of a tiny arrow, or like an equilateral triangle with the horizontal bottom line removed: ∧. More precisely, it's a small *caret* (pronounced like *carrot*), a mark used in copyediting to indicate that something needs to be inserted.

The circumflex sits on top of a vowel like a little hood. Depending on the dictionary you use, it may appear over the vowels â, î, ô, or û when they are followed by the letter *r* to indicate that the sound of the vowel blends into the *r*.

For example, âr is pronounced like *air*, as in *care* (kâr); îr is pronounced like *ear*, as in *dear* (dîr) and *pier* (pîr); ôr is pronounced like *or*, as in *store* (stôr) and *door* (dôr); and ûr is pronounced like *ur* in *fur* or *ir* in *fir* (fûr).

And now for an extremely important piece of advice: Whenever you check a pronunciation in a dictionary, remember to look for the accent mark (or marks) and note where the primary stress falls. Many mispronunciations occur because people stress the wrong syllable. As my mother was fond of saying when she corrected my pronunciation, "Don't put your accent on the wrong syl-LAH-ble."

Many speakers mistakenly say adMIRable, forMIDable, and comPAIRable when the words *admirable*, *formidable*, and *comparable* are properly pronounced ADmirable, FORmidable, and COMparable. These mispronunciations could be corrected easily by consulting a dictionary.

There are dozens more mispronunciations in which the error is simply a matter of misplaced stress. For example, *impotent* (properly IM-puh-t<u>i</u>nt) is often mispronounced im-POH-t<u>i</u>nt; *disparate* (properly DIS-puh-rit) is often

mispronounced dis-PAR-it; *gondola* (properly GAHN-duh-luh) is often mispronounced gahn-DOH-luh; *superfluous* (properly soo-PUR-floo-u̲s, stress on
-*per*-) is often mispronounced SOO-pur-**FLOO**-us, with primary stress on -*flu*-)
and *influence* (properly IN-floo-i̲nts) is often mispronounced in-FLOO-i̲nts.

You must become keenly aware of where the stress falls in a word, for it
seems that almost every day some new error of this type crops up and gains
currency. In recent years I have heard numerous broadcasters pronounce
mayoral and *electoral* with second- and third-syllable stress, respectively. The
traditional and proper pronunciations are MAY-ur-ul, with first-syllable stress,
and i̲-LEK-tur-ul, with second-syllable stress. If you make sure to note which
syllable receives the primary stress every time you look up a word, you won't
be misled by these or any other eccentric or erroneous pronunciations you
may hear.

Finally, spend some time studying your dictionary's pronunciation key.
Though most dictionaries use the symbols I have just discussed, there are always variations, and each key is individual. Read the section on pronunciation
in the guide to your dictionary, which is part of the front matter—the material
preceding the vocabulary. When you think you have a basic understanding of
the key, turn to any page in the dictionary, find a word you don't know, and try
to pronounce it. Do the symbols make sense right away, or do you have to
refer to the key for help?

If your dictionary doesn't have a condensed pronunciation key printed at
the bottom of each or every other page (a very helpful feature), I suggest that
you either affix a Post-it note or "sticky" on the page in the dictionary's guide
that contains the key or make a photocopy of the key and paste it to the inside
cover of the dictionary. That way you'll easily be able to refer to the pronunciation key whenever you look up a word.

Now that you know what to do to become a more conscientious speaker
of the language, it's time to give you some more words you can use to embellish your cultivated speech. So, without further ado, here are the first ten keywords of Level 5.

Word 1: VOLUBLE (VAHL-yuh-bu̲l)

Talkative, talking much and easily, characterized by a great and continuous
flow of words.

Synonyms of *voluble* include *long-winded*, *glib* (word 8 of Level 3), *garrulous* (GAR-uh-lu̲s), *loquacious* (loh-KWAY-shu̲s), *verbose* (word 30 of Level 2),
and *effusive* (e̲-FYOO-siv).

Antonyms include *reticent*, *terse* (word 3 of Level 3), *laconic* (word 18 of Level 3), and *taciturn* (TAS-i̯-turn).

Voluble refers to a person who talks freely and easily, and usually at great length. It may also mean characterized by a great and continuous flow of words; in this sense either speech or writing may be voluble.

Word 2: COMMISERATE (kuh-MIZ-uh-rayt)

To sympathize, feel or express sympathy, show sorrow or pity for.

A somewhat unusual synonym of *commiserate* is the verb to *condole* (kun-DOHL), which means to grieve in sympathy, express condolence.

To *commiserate* comes from a Latin verb meaning to pity, and by derivation *commiserate* means to share someone else's misery. *Commiserate* is often followed by *with*: "When Sally lost her job, her coworkers commiserated with her."

Word 3: DILEMMA (di-LEM-uh)

A predicament. In general, any difficult problem or unpleasant situation; specifically, a predicament in which one must choose between equally undesirable alternatives.

As I mentioned in my discussion of *quandary* (keyword 27 of Level 3), *dilemma* is often used today of any difficult problem or troublesome situation, but many good writers and speakers object to that as loose usage.

Dilemma comes from the Greek *di-*, meaning two, and *lemma*, a proposition, and by derivation means a choice between two propositions. Strictly speaking, *dilemma* should be used only of situations in which one faces a choice between equally undesirable alternatives: Elected officials often face the dilemma of either voting for what their constituents want and going against their conscience, or voting their conscience and losing the support of their constituents.

Quandary (KWAHN-duh-ree), *quagmire* (KWAG-myr, rhymes with *bag liar*), and *dilemma* all refer to complicated and perplexing situations from which it is hard to disentangle oneself.

Quandary emphasizes confusion and uncertainty; someone in a quandary has no idea what to do to get out of it.

Quagmire emphasizes hopelessness and impossibility. Literally, a *quagmire* is a bog, a tract of soft, wet ground. When used in a figurative sense, *quagmire* refers to an inextricable difficulty. Someone in a quagmire feels hopelessly stuck and unable to get out.

By derivation, a *dilemma* is a choice between two equally undesirable, unfavorable, or disagreeable propositions. Hamlet's famous dilemma was "to be or not to be."

Colloquial or informal expressions for the state of being in a dilemma include "in a fix," "in a pickle," "between a rock and a hard place," and "between the devil and the deep blue sea."

Word 4: TRANSITORY (**TRAN**-si-TOR-ee *or* **TRAN**-zi-TOR-ee)

Passing, temporary, fleeting, not permanent or enduring.

The words *transitory*, *transient*, *ephemeral*, and *evanescent* all mean passing, temporary.

Evanescent (EV-uh-**NES**-int) comes from the Latin verb *evanescere*, to vanish, disappear, and refers to something that appears briefly and then fades quickly away: evanescent memories, evanescent joy.

Ephemeral (e-FEM-uh-rul) means literally lasting only a day, but in a broad sense it refers to anything conspicuously short-lived: Our precious youth is ephemeral—lasting, it would seem, but a day. (Did you remember that *short-lived* is properly pronounced so that *-lived* rhymes with *strived*?)

Transient (TRAN-shint, not TRAN-zee-int) refers to anything that lasts or stays only for a short while: a transient occupant, a transient event.

Transient and our keyword *transitory* both come from the Latin *transire*, to go or pass over, the source also of the familiar words *transit* and *transition*. *Transitory* refers to something that by nature must pass or come to an end: Life is transitory, and sometimes so is love.

Word 5: PHILANTHROPIC (FIL-un-**THRAHP**-ik)

Charitable, benevolent, humane; motivated by or done out of a desire to help or improve the welfare of others.

The corresponding noun *philanthropy* means a desire to help others, especially through charitable giving.

Philanthropy and *philanthropic* both come from the Greek *philein*, to love, and *anthropos*, man. *Philanthropy* means literally "love of mankind"; the adjective *philanthropic* means literally "loving mankind."

You can see the Greek *philein*, to love, in such words as *philosophy*, literally love of wisdom; and *philharmonic*, literally loving or devoted to music. You can see the Greek *anthropos*, man, in *anthropology*, the study of mankind, of human customs, habits, and traditions; and *anthropomorphic* (AN-throh-puh-**MOR**-fik), shaped like or resembling a man or human being.

The words *philanthropic*, *humanitarian*, *altruistic* (AL-troo-**IST**-ik), and *charitable* all mean helping others. *Charitable* refers specifically to giving money to help others. *Altruistic* suggests unselfish giving. *Humanitarian* applies to persons or organizations devoted to reducing the pain and suffering of others. *Philanthropic* literally means motivated by a desire to help others; today the word is used chiefly of persons or organizations that make large charitable gifts, fund endowments, or finance humanitarian or cultural institutions.

Word 6: LETHARGY (LETH-ur-jee)

Lack of energy, sluggishness, dullness, apathy, stupor; an abnormally dull, drowsy, inactive condition or state of mind.

The corresponding adjective is *lethargic*, which means sluggish, drowsy, dull, apathetic: "Dan always felt lethargic after a big business lunch"; "Whenever we visit the zoo, the bears and the lions seem lethargic"; "Weeks after getting over the flu, Emily still felt lethargic."

According to the third edition of *The American Heritage Dictionary* (1992), *lethargy* "may be caused by factors such as illness, fatigue, or overwork, but it manifests itself in drowsy dullness or apathy."

Apathy (AP-uh-thee) and *lethargy* are close in meaning. *Apathy* suggests an indifferent state of mind, a thorough lack of emotion or concern: "Analysts predict that voter apathy will result in a low turnout for the election." *Lethargy* is a prolonged state of dullness, inactivity, or lack of energy, a sluggish condition either of body or of mind: "The Renaissance roused Europe from the intellectual lethargy of the Middle Ages"; "As every college professor knows, nothing can penetrate or cure the lethargy of the college student who has partied too hard the night before."

More difficult synonyms of *lethargy* include *torpor* (TOR-pur), *somnolence* (SAHM-nuh-lints), *lassitude* (LAS-i-t(y)ood), *languor* (LANG-gur), and *stupefaction* (ST(Y)OO-puh-**FAK**-shin).

Word 7: EXONERATE (eg-ZAHN-ur-ayt)

To free from blame, free from a charge or the imputation of guilt, declare blameless or innocent.

Synonyms of *exonerate* include *acquit*, *absolve*, and *exculpate* (ek-SKUHL-payt or EK-skul-payt).

Exculpate comes from the Latin *ex-*, meaning "out," and *culpa*, blame, and means literally to free from blame. The word *onerous* (AHN-ur-us, like *honor us*, not OH-nur-us) means burdensome, and the corresponding noun an *onus* (OH-nus) means a burden. *Exonerate* combines the Latin *ex-*, out, with *onus*, a burden, to mean removing a burden—in modern usage, removing the burden of guilt.

Word 8: PUGNACIOUS (puhg-NAY-shus)

Given to fighting, combative (kum-BAT-iv), quarrelsome, ready and willing to fight.

Challenging synonyms of *pugnacious* include *contentious* (kun-TEN-shus), *belligerent* (buh-LIJ-ur-int), and *bellicose* (BEL-i-kohs). Antonyms include *peaceable*, *clement* (KLEM-int, word 43 of Level 2), and *amicable* (AM-i-kuh-bul).

Pugnacious comes from the Latin *pugnare*, to box, fight with the fists, and still has the connotation of someone ready to put up his dukes. From the same Latin *pugnare*, to fight, we inherit the word *pugilist* (PYOO-ji-list), a boxer, someone who fights with his fists.

Word 9: CONTRITION (kun-TRISH-in)

Remorse, penitence, repentance, deep and devastating sorrow for one's sins or for something one has done wrong.

Penitence is sorrow for having sinned or done wrong; it is often temporary. The penitent person may say "I'm sorry" today and sin again tomorrow.

Remorse is deep sorrow. The remorseful person is tortured by a sense of guilt, and wishes he could erase what he has done.

Contrition is even more intense than remorse. It comes from a Latin verb meaning to crush, and by derivation means a crushing sense of guilt accompanied by a sincere, earnest desire to repent, make amends, and change for the better.

Contrition is the noun; the corresponding adjective is *contrite* (kun-TRYT, rhymes with *a light*), remorseful, penitent, full of guilt, regret, and sorrow for one's sins or offenses: "When Larry's wife found out about his mistress and his sleazy real estate deals and threatened to leave him, Larry was contrite and swore he'd mend his ways."

Word 10: ABROGATE (AB-ruh-gayt)

To abolish by legal or authoritative action or decree.

Synonyms of *abrogate* include *cancel*, *revoke*, *repeal*, *annul*, *nullify*, and *rescind* (ri-SIND, word 31 of Level 3).

To *abolish* means to do away with: to abolish slavery, abolish cruel and unusual punishment.

Rescind, *revoke*, and *repeal* all suggest a formal withdrawal. *Rescind* means literally to cut off: you rescind an order. *Revoke* means literally to call back: you revoke a contract. To *repeal* means literally to call back on appeal, and applies to something canceled that formerly was approved: we repeal a law or an amendment.

To *annul* (uh-NUHL) and to *abrogate* mean to cancel or make void. A marriage may be annulled. Rights and privileges are abrogated, abolished by authoritative action or decree.

Let's review the ten keywords you've just learned. Consider the following questions and decide whether the correct answer is yes or no. Answers appear on page 209.

1. Would a voluble person also be reticent?
2. Can you commiserate with someone who is unhappy?
3. If you are faced with choosing between the lesser of two evils, are you in a dilemma?
4. Could the blooming of springtime flowers be described as transitory?
5. Is making money the goal of a philanthropic institution?
6. Does lethargy mean a state of excitement or agitation?
7. When a jury pronounces someone guilty, is the person exonerated?
8. Is a pugnacious person likely to pick a fight with you?
9. Is contrition a state of quiet contemplation?
10. Can your house and property be abrogated?

Here are the next ten keywords in Level 5:

Word 11: OFFICIOUS (uh-FISH-us; do not say oh-FISH-us)

Pronounce the initial *o* of *officious* like the *a* in *ago*.

Meddlesome, nosy, intrusive, interfering, prying; specifically, offering unwanted advice or unnecessary services, especially in a high-handed, overbearing way.

The officious person butts in and tries to tell others what to do, or offers help that others do not need. The officious person is a meddler, a busybody: "Lucy was sick and tired of her officious supervisor, who would constantly peer over her shoulder and in a single breath tell her what to do, offer to help her do it, and then upbraid her for not doing it right away." (Do you know the precise meaning of *upbraid*? If you have the slightest doubt, look it up now.)

A more difficult and unusual word for this type of unpleasant person is *quidnunc* (KWID-nuhngk, second syllable rhyming with *skunk*). *Quidnunc* comes directly from Latin and means literally "What now?" The quidnunc always wants to know what's going on, the busybody is always sticking his or her nose into your business, and the officious person is always trying to manage your affairs.

Word 12: INTRACTABLE (in-TRAK-tuh-bul)

Hard to manage or control, stubborn, unruly.

Antonyms of *intractable* include *obedient*, *compliant* (kum-PLY-int), *malleable* (MAL-ee-uh-bul), *docile* (DAHS-'l), and *tractable*.

The antonyms *tractable* and *intractable* come from the Latin *tractare*, to drag around, haul, and also to manage, control. The familiar words *traction* and *tractor* come from the same source.

Both *tractable* and *intractable* are used chiefly of persons rather than things: *Tractable* means obedient, compliant, easily managed; *intractable* means stubborn, unruly, hard to manage or control.

Word 13: ALTRUISM (AL-troo-iz-'m)

Selflessness, unselfish concern for the welfare of others.

In the philosophy of ethics, *altruism* refers to the doctrine that promoting the welfare of society is the proper and moral goal of the individual. In this sense, *altruism* is opposed to *egoism* (EE-goh-iz-'m), self-centeredness, specifically the doctrine that self-interest is the proper goal of the individual, that the only sensible thing to do in life is look out for number one.

Egoism is distinguished from *egotism* (EE-guh-tiz-'m), both in spelling and meaning. *Egotism* is extreme self-involvement, excessive reference to oneself in speech or writing; the *egotist* (EE-guh-tist) cannot stop talking about himself. *Egoism* implies self-centeredness, concern for oneself; the *egoist* (EE-goh-ist) cares only about his own needs, concerns, and goals. Egoism is unpleasant but less intense and disagreeable than egotism.

On the opposite end of the spectrum is *altruism*. The *altruist* is selfless, highly moral, and puts the needs of others and of society first. *Altruism* is unselfish concern for others.

Word 14: ACCOLADE (ak-uh-LAYD *or* AK-uh-layd)

An award; sign of respect or esteem; expression of praise; mark of acknowledgment; anything done or given as a token of appreciation or approval: "At the ceremony she received an accolade from the president for her work"; "He was showered with accolades after the success of his project."

Here's an interesting word story for you: *Accolade* comes through French and Italian from the Latin *accollare*, to embrace, which comes in turn from *ad-*, meaning "to," and *collum*, the neck, the source of the word *collar*.

Originally, an *accolade* was an embrace, specifically the ritual embrace used in conferring knighthood. At one time this consisted of a ceremonial kiss and a light blow on each shoulder with the flat side of a sword. Later the embrace was dropped and the ceremony was limited to the tap on each side of the collar with a sword. From this ritual the word *accolade* has come to mean any special recognition of merit, achievement, or distinction.

My preferred pronunciation for *accolade* is ak-uh-LAYD (last syllable like *laid*), but there are no fewer than three other established, acceptable pronunciations: AK-uh-layd, with the stress on the first syllable; ak-uh-LAHD, final syllable rhyming with *rod*; and AK-uh-lahd, stress on the first syllable.

Word 15: VERNACULAR (vur-NAK-yuh-lur)

The native language of a people, especially, the common, everyday language of ordinary people as opposed to the literary or cultured language.

The noun *vernacular* may refer to a native language as opposed to a foreign one, and the adjective *vernacular* may mean native as opposed to foreign, as: English is my vernacular tongue. More often, though, *vernacular* is used of the common, everyday language of ordinary people. A vernacular expression is a popular expression, one used by ordinary folk. Vernacular literature is either popular literature or literature written in everyday as opposed to formal language. The phrase "in the vernacular" means in ordinary and unpretentious language.

"I'm not going to do it" is formal language. "I ain't gonna do it" is in the vernacular. "He doesn't wish to speak with anyone" is formal language. "He don't wanna talk to nobody" is vernacular.

These examples of vernacular English are considered ungrammatical and substandard, and I want to be careful not to give you the impression that bad English is the only form of vernacular English. The vernacular comprises all language that is common and informal, any word or expression that ordinary people use—whether it is considered bad or good, acceptable or improper.

In *Modern English Usage*, H. W. Fowler describes the vernacular as "the words that have been familiar to us for as long as we can remember, the homely part of the language, in contrast with the terms that we have consciously acquired."

Calling someone a "sharp cookie" is the vernacular way of calling someone intelligent, perceptive, judicious (joo-DISH-us, the next keyword in this level), or sagacious (suh-GAY-shus, word 6 in Level 8). Saying someone is a "phony" is the vernacular way of saying someone is a sham, an imposter, or a charlatan (SHAHR-luh-tin, word 17 of Level 4). The vernacular of the East differs from the vernacular of the West, and often residents of different parts of the same state or city have their own vernacular—common, informal, everyday language.

Word 16: JUDICIOUS (joo-DISH-us)

Wise and careful, having or showing sound judgment.

Synonyms of *judicious* include *sensible*, *levelheaded*, *prudent* (word 47 of Level 1), and *discreet*. Antonyms include *thoughtless*, *foolhardy*, *impetuous* (im-PECH-oo-us), and *temerarious* (TEM-uh-**RAIR**-ee-us).

Judicious comes through the Latin *judicium*, judgment, from *judex*, a judge. *Judex* and the Latin verb *judicare*, to judge, pass judgment, are also the source of the English words *judge*, *judgment*, *judicial*, pertaining to a judge or to a judgment, and *judiciary* (joo-**DISH**-ee-ER-ee), judges collectively or the judicial branch of government.

As long as we're passing judgment on all these words, here's a spelling tip: Everyone knows the word *judge* has an *e* at the end, but many Americans don't seem to realize that there is no *e* in the middle of the word *judgment*. The British (and many Canadians who follow British usage) prefer to retain this medial *e* and spell the word *judgement*. The preferred American spelling, however, is *judgment*.

Our keyword, *judicious*, means having or showing sound judgment. A judicious decision is a wise and careful decision. A judicious course of action is a sensible, levelheaded, prudent course of action.

Word 17: CHRYSALIS (KRIS-uh-lis)

The pupa of a butterfly; the stage in the development of the insect between the larval and adult stages, during which the insect is enclosed in a case or cocoon.

Chrysalis is now also used in a figurative sense to mean a sheltered and undeveloped state or stage of being: "Promising young artists and writers have always had to break out of their creative chrysalis to achieve the recognition they deserve"; "After four years at college she emerged from her chrysalis in the ivory tower into the wide-open world, fully mature and ready to accomplish great things."

In this general sense, *chrysalis* is a useful word that can add a nice touch of style to your expression. Be careful, however, to use it precisely. The danger lies in confusing *chrysalis* with the words *transformation* and *metamorphosis* (MET-uh-**MORF**-uh-sis).

Listen to this sentence, which was written by a theater critic about a performance of George Bernard (BUR-nurd) Shaw's *Pygmalion*: "Dirickson is convincing and eminently likable as Eliza, deftly handling the chrysalis from street urchin to lady while, along the way, growing in confidence and independence."

You cannot "handle" a sheltered and undeveloped state "from" one thing to another. What the critic meant to describe was a change that resembled the transformation a butterfly undergoes from its larval (LAHR-vul) stage, when it is but a caterpillar, through its chrysalis, its stage of development in the shelter of the cocoon, and then to fully formed adulthood. The proper word for that transformation is *metamorphosis*. *Chrysalis* means a sheltered state or undeveloped stage of being.

Word 18: GENTEEL (jen-TEEL)

Refined, polite, well-bred, sophisticated, elegantly stylish or fashionable, pertaining or belonging to high society.

Genteel came into English in the early seventeenth century from the French *gentil*, which at the time meant noble, polite, graceful. Originally *genteel* meant possessing the qualities of those of high birth and good breeding. That definition is still listed in current dictionaries, but today *genteel* usually suggests an excessive or affected refinement, and the word is often applied to someone or something that is trying to appear socially or intellectually superior.

Word 19: JOVIAL (JOH-vee-ul)

Merry, full of good humor, hearty and fun-loving, jolly, convivial (kun-VIV-ee-ul).

The exclamation "by Jove!" means literally "by Jupiter," the name of the chief deity (properly pronounced DEE-i-tee, not DAY-i-tee) in Roman mythology, called Zeus by the ancient Greeks. From Jove, who was renowned for his love of feasting and merriment, we inherit the word *jovial*, literally like Jove, merry, good-humored, convivial.

Word 20: SUBTERFUGE (SUHB-tur-fyooj)

A deception, trick, underhanded scheme.

Synonyms of *subterfuge* include *stratagem*, *artifice* (AHRT-i-fis), and *ruse* (properly pronounced ROOZ to rhyme with *news*, not ROOS to rhyme with *loose*).

By derivation *subterfuge* means to flee secretly, escape. In modern usage the word applies to any secret or illicit plan or activity designed to conceal a motive, escape blame, or avoid something unpleasant: "Mystery and spy novels abound with myriad examples of the art of subterfuge."

Don't soften the *g* in this word and say SUHB-tur-fyoozh. The final syllable, *-fuge*, should rhyme with *huge*.

Let's review the ten keywords you've just learned. Consider the following statements and decide whether each one is true or false. Answers appear on page 209.

1. An officious person is industrious and reliable.
2. It's hard to get an intractable person to do what you want.
3. If more people were motivated by altruism, the world would be a better place.
4. Winning an outstanding service award or being selected as employee of the month would be an accolade.
5. "Expressed in the vernacular" means expressed in polite, formal language.
6. Driving under the influence of alcohol is a judicious act.
7. When something emerges from a chrysalis, it is transformed.
8. Genteel conversation is lively and good-natured.
9. A jovial person is haughty and domineering.
10. If you discover that a coworker has been doing nasty, sneaky things behind your back to make you look bad, then you are a victim of subterfuge.

Did you remember to keep track of your score? Don't read ahead in the program until you have answered at least eight of the preceding questions correctly.

It's time now for a word to the wise on English plurals—specifically, the formation of English plurals for words derived from Latin and Greek. Is the plural of *octopus* "octopi" or "octopuses"? Should you say "the media is" or "the media are"? Is the word *bacteria* singular or plural?

The answers are not always simple and clear, and for those who have had no instruction in classical languages—in other words, for most of us—intuition is often the only guide. Here, then, is some advice to direct you through this pluralistic maze.

Words that end in *-is* in the singular change to *-es* in the plural: *basis* becomes *bases*; *thesis* becomes *theses*; *crisis* becomes *crises*; and *neurosis* becomes *neuroses*. In each instance, the second syllable of the plural form is pronounced *-eez* (like the word *ease*). Take care not to say "this crises" (KRY-seez) when you mean "this crisis" (KRY-sis).

Another word of caution here: Don't get confused and apply this rule to the plural noun *processes*, for which the mispronunciation "process-eez" is now often heard. *Process* is of Latin origin and not analogous (uh-NAL-uh-g<u>u</u>s, word 48 of Level 2) to words of Greek origin that end in *-is*. Furthermore, most dictionaries do not recognize the pronunciation "processeez," and no pronunciation authority with a reputation to lose would countenance this faddish affectation. Pronounce the singular *process* as PRAH-ses (the pronunciation PROH-ses is British) and the plural *processes* as PRAH-ses-iz.

The plurals of a number of English words that come from Latin end with the letter *a*: *media* and *bacteria* are common examples. The phrase "a deadly bacteria" is wrong because *bacteria* is the plural of *bacterium*. It should be "a deadly bacterium." Likewise with *media*. The *media* are plural, so don't say "the media is." TV is one medium, radio another medium, and print yet another medium. Together they constitute the media. Never, ever say "medias."

In the case of the word *data*, however, we have a draw. Traditionally, *data* is a plural noun, like *facts*, and the singular is *datum*. Until fairly recently, careful writers and editors followed the traditional rule of treating *data* as a plural, preferring "These data are conclusive" over "This data is conclusive," and "We'll decide when all the data are in" instead of "We'll decide when all the data is in." Today, however, the use of *data* as a singular noun is so prevalent among educated speakers—including scientists and researchers, who compile data for a living—that in 1992, 60 percent of the esteemed Usage Panel of the *American Heritage Dictionary* sanctioned the use of *data* with a singular verb, and 77 percent accepted it in the sentence "We have very little data on the efficacy of such programs." (*Efficacy*, pronounced EF-i-kuh-see, means effectiveness. It is keyword 30 of Level 8.)

Purists may be upset by that vote, but there's no denying that a decided majority of educated speakers and writers now use *data* as a synonym of *information*. I'm still not wholly comfortable using *data* with a singular verb, but I have to concede that the folks who prefer to say "the data is" have a persuasive case. After all, *agenda* ("things to be done") started out as the plural of *agendum*, an item on an *agenda*, but now *agendum* is nearly defunct (word 19 of Level 2) and everyone uses *agenda*, with the newly manufactured English plural *agendas*, as a singular noun meaning "a list of things to do or a plan of action." As the prolific (word 21 of Level 4) writer and professor Isaac Asimov remarked in the 1985 edition of *The Harper Dictionary of Contemporary Usage*, "What's the use of saying 'These data are' when to say it will cause everyone who hears it to consider you illiterate? 'Data' is plural in Latin, singular in English."

Now it's up to you to decide what seems natural and correct. In the meantime, here are some quick rulings on a few more problematic plurals:

For the word *syllabus*, the English plural *syllabuses* and the Latin plural *syllabi* (SIL-uh-by) are both acceptable.

For *octopus*, the English plural is *octopuses*, which I recommend. The Greek plural, now rarely heard, is *octopodes* (ahk-TAHP-uh-deez). *Octopi* (AHK-tuh-py), which is neither English nor Greek but pseudo-Latin, is improper but recognized by many dictionaries.

For the word *formula*, the English *formulas* is most common, with the Latin *formulae* (FORM-yuh-lee) now a rather pretentious alternative. The same goes for *forum* and *stadium*. The anglicized *forums* and *stadiums* are preferred over the Latin plurals, *fora* and *stadia* (unless you happen to be talking about ancient Greece and Rome). However, when you write more than one *memorandum*, you may call them either *memoranda* or *memorandums*. (I prefer *memoranda*.)

When you are talking about insects and you want to say they have more than one antenna, the plural you need is *antennae* (an-TEN-ee, last syllable rhyming with *see*, not *fly*). However, if you are referring specifically to the media reception contraption, the preferred plural is *antennas*.

For the plural of *index*, both *indexes* and *indices* (IN-di-seez) are acceptable, although most usage authorities now consider *indices* pretentious in ordinary, nontechnical contexts.

Finally, for *appendix*, the English plural *appendixes* and the Latin plural *appendices* (uh-PEN-di-seez) are both correct, with usage being about evenly divided between them. It is not true that appendices belong in books and appendixes in bodies. Usage experts are divided in their recommendations, editors and doctors prefer one form or the other, and no formal differentiation has yet been made. (For the record, my money's on *appendixes* for both books and bodies.)

And now let's return to the *Verbal Advantage* vocabulary for the next ten keywords in Level 5.

Word 21: EBULLIENCE (i-BUHL-yints *or* i-BUUL-yints)

Lively enthusiasm, high spirits, bubbly excitement. Synonyms include *exuberance*, *exhilaration*, and *effervescence* (EF-ur-**VES**-ints).

The words *ebullition* (EB-uh-LISH-in), *ebullient* (i-BUHL-yint or i-BUUL-yint), and *ebullience* all come from the Latin verb *ebullire*, to boil, bubble.

The noun *ebullition* literally means a boiling or bubbling up. It may be used figuratively of an emotional outburst, as "Lisa was delighted with her husband's amorous ebullition on their anniversary."

The adjective *ebullient* means bubbling with enthusiasm, overflowing with high spirits: "The stadium was packed with thousands of ebullient fans."

The noun *ebullience* means bubbly enthusiasm, seething excitement, irrepressible exuberance: "When Jack won the lottery, he could not contain his ebullience."

Ebullience and *ebullient* are often mispronounced. Don't say i-BOOL-yints and i-BOOL-yint, or i-BYOO-lee-ints and i-BYOO-lee-int. The BOOL and BYOOL sounds (which rhyme with *fool*) are wrong. Also, take care to eschew (es-CHOO, remember?) the sloppy mispronunciations EB-yuh-lints and EB-yuh-lint, which move the stress to the first syllable.

In *ebullience* and e*bullient*, the stress should fall on the second syllable, *-bul-*, in which the *u* may have the sound of the *u* in *bulk* or *bull*.

Word 22: IMPERVIOUS (im-PURV-ee-us)

Impenetrable, incapable of being entered or passed through; hence, unable to be moved or affected by something.

Synonyms of *impervious* include *impassable*, *impermeable* (im-PUR-mee-uh-bul), and *opaque* (oh-PAYK). Antonyms include *penetrable* (PEN-i-truh-bul), *passable*, *accessible*, *permeable*, *translucent* (tranz-LOO-sint), and *diaphanous* (dy-AF-uh-nus).

An impervious substance cannot be penetrated: certain fabrics are impervious to water; a recording studio must be well insulated and impervious to external noise. If you are impervious to pain, then pain does not penetrate your consciousness. And if your mind is impervious to reason, that means you cannot be moved or affected by any argument, no matter how persuasive.

Word 23: REMONSTRATE (ri-MAHN-strayt)

To object, protest, reprove, rebuke, argue or plead against.

To *expostulate* (ek-SPAHS-chu-layt) and to *remonstrate* are close in meaning. To *expostulate* suggests an earnest and sometimes passionate attempt to change someone's views or behavior by pleading and argument. To *remonstrate* suggests a calmer and more reasoned attempt to show that someone is wrong or blameworthy.

Word 24: EFFACE (e-FAYS)

To rub out, wipe out, obliterate, erase, expunge: "Time gradually effaced the memory of the tragedy."

To *efface* may also mean to make oneself inconspicuous, keep oneself out of the limelight: "During the celebration, he effaced himself so his partner would get all the attention." The self-effacing person stays in the background and behaves in a modest, retiring fashion.

Take care to distinguish the words *deface* and *efface*. To *deface* means to spoil the appearance of, ruin, disfigure, mar. To *efface* means to rub out, wipe out, erase, or to withdraw from notice, make oneself inconspicuous.

Word 25: CHIMERA (ky-MEER-uh)

A foolish fancy, fantastic notion or idea, figment of the imagination.

Synonyms of *chimera* include *whimsy* (WHIM-zee), *crotchet* (KRAHCH-it), *maggot*, and *caprice* (discussed in word 11 of Level 1).

In Greek mythology, the Chimera was a fire-breathing monster with the head of a lion, the body of a goat, and the tail of a serpent. In modern usage *chimera* may refer to that monster or a similar fabulous creature, but more commonly it means an absurd and fabulous creation of the mind. A *chimera* is a vain or idle fancy, an impossible or visionary idea. The corresponding adjective is *chimerical* (ki-MER-i-kul), which means imaginary, fantastic, preposterous, absurd.

Word 26: INCORRIGIBLE (in-KOR-ij-uh-bul *or* in-KAHR-)

Bad beyond correction or reform, hopeless, irreformable; also, unruly, unmanageable, difficult to control.

Synonyms of *incorrigible* in the sense of "bad beyond correction or reform" include *irredeemable*, *irreclaimable*, *unrepentant*, *inveterate* (in-VET-uh-rit), and *unregenerate* (UHN-ri-**JEN**-uh-rit).

Synonyms of *incorrigible* in the sense of "unruly, difficult to control" include *obstinate* (word 34 of Level 1), *willful*, and *intractable* (word 12 of this level).

The adjective *corrigible* means "capable of being corrected, amended, or reformed." By adding the privative (PRIV-uh-tiv, meaning "depriving" or "canceling") prefix *in-*, meaning "not," to the adjective *corrigible*, we get its antonym, *incorrigible*, not capable of being corrected, amended, or reformed—and therefore hopelessly bad, irreformable, as an incorrigible drinker, an incorrigible practical joker.

Because incorrigible behavior cannot be corrected or reformed, it also cannot be managed or controlled, and from that logical inference grew the second meaning of *incorrigible*: unruly, unmanageable, difficult to control. Wild, unruly teenagers and spoiled children who will not mind their parents are often called incorrigible.

Word 27: JUXTAPOSE (JUHK-stuh-**POHZ** *or* JUHK-stuh-POHZ)

To place side by side or close together, especially so as to compare or contrast.

The first half of the word *juxtapose* comes from the Latin *juxta*, which means "near, close by." The second half, *-pose*, comes from the Latin *ponere*, to put, place, the source also of the familiar word *position* and the more challenging word *posit* (PAHZ-it). To *posit* means to put forward as true, set down as a fact, as the Declaration of Independence posits that "all men are created equal." By derivation the verb to *juxtapose* means "to place near, put close by."

When you juxtapose two or more things you place them side by side, usually for the purpose of comparing or contrasting them. Painters often juxtapose colors for a striking effect; philosophers and scientists juxtapose ideas so as to evaluate them; a consumer might juxtapose two products, place them side by side, to decide which one is better.

The corresponding noun is *juxtaposition* (JUHK-stuh-puh-**ZISH**-in).

Word 28: CONVERSANT (kun-VUR-sint)

Familiar, acquainted, well-informed or well-versed.

Conversant comes from the Latin *conversari*, to associate with, the source also of the verb to *converse* and the noun *conversation*. When you are conversant with something you have had a conversation with it; you have associated with it, and therefore you are familiar or well acquainted with it. The person who is conversant with astronomy or folklore or Russian history or the microcomputer industry is well informed and able to speak knowledgeably about the subject.

Conversant and *versed* are close synonyms. *Conversant* is usually followed by *with*; *versed* is usually followed by *in*. *Versed* often suggests the familiarity that comes from experience. You can be versed in the ways of life, versed in the techniques of marketing or public relations, or versed in the culture of a foreign country. *Conversant* often suggests the familiarity that comes from having studied something or acquired information about it. You can be conversant with the work of a certain writer, conversant with economics, conversant with modern art, or conversant with current events.

Word 29: ESOTERIC (ES-uh-TER-ik)

Intended for or designed to be understood only by a select group, known only by a few people; hence, not public, secret, confidential.

Synonyms of *esoteric* include *mysterious*, *impenetrable*, *inscrutable* (word 48 of Level 3), *cryptic* (KRIP-tik), *abstruse* (ab-STROOS, word 5 of Level 6), *arcane* (ahr-KAYN), and *recondite* (REK-un-dyt).

Antonyms of *esoteric* include *plain*, *apparent*, *accessible*, *manifest*, *discernible* (word 32 of Level 3), *lucid* (word 45 of Level 3), and *perspicuous* (pur-SPIK-yoo-us).

Esoteric comes from a Greek word meaning "inner," and by derivation means intended for or known only by an inner circle. According to the 1914 edition of the great *Century Dictionary*, the word *esoteric* "originally applied to certain writings of Aristotle of a scientific, as opposed to a popular, character, and afterward to the secret . . . teachings of Pythagoras; hence, [*esoteric* has come to mean] secret; intended to be communicated only to the initiated."

Because *esoteric* refers to that which is secret or understood only by a few select people, in recent years the word has come to be used more generally to mean beyond most people's knowledge or understanding, highly complex and difficult to comprehend, as an esoteric theory or the esoteric language of computer programming.

Many educated people now use the word in this more general way, and there is nothing wrong with that—except that I suspect most people who use *esoteric* today are not aware of the word's original, more specific meaning. Thus, you will have a leg up on them if you keep in mind the precise meaning of *esoteric*: intended to be communicated only to the initiated.

An esoteric theory is complex and impenetrable because it is designed to be understood only by a select group. An esoteric purpose is secret and mysterious because it is known only by a few chosen people.

The antonym or opposite of *esoteric* is *exoteric* (EKS-uh-**TER**-ik). *Exoteric* begins with the prefix *exo-*, which means "outer, outside." *Exoteric* means external, popular, of the outside world or open to public view. Exoteric writing is intended for the world at large; it is communicated to or suitable for the general public. Esoteric writing is intended for an inner circle; it is understood only by a few people.

Word 30: AUSPICIOUS (aw-SPISH-us)

Favorable, fortunate, marked by favorable circumstances or good fortune, conducive to success, boding well.

The ancient Romans were, by modern standards, a highly superstitious people who believed in supernatural signs and omens and who often consulted oracles, astrologers, clairvoyants (klair-VOY-ints), and soothsayers (the *sooth-* rhymes with *truth*) when they wanted to know what the future held in store for them. One of the most popular fortune-tellers in ancient times was the *auspex* (AW-speks), who practiced a form of divination known in Latin as *auspicium*, which meant the act of predicting the future by observing the flight of birds.

In English, the word *auspice* (AW-spis) means an omen or sign, especially a favorable one. From that sense *auspice* came to be used in the plural, *auspices* (AW-spi-siz), to mean protection, guardianship, or sponsorship, as an investigation conducted under the auspices of the government. Both the noun *auspice* and the adjective *auspicious* come from the Latin *auspicium*, which in turn comes from *avis*, bird, and *specere*, to look at, observe. By derivation *auspicious* refers to that which an *auspex*, or bird-watcher, has said will have a favorable outcome.

In modern usage *auspicious* applies to anything marked by favorable circumstances or good fortune. An auspicious debut is a favorable debut, one conducive to future success. When the telephone rings and the caller wants to buy your product or pay for your services, that's an auspicious call, one marked by good fortune. And when you meet someone at a party who later turns out to be an important business contact, that meeting can only be described as *auspicious*, favorable, fortunate.

The adjectives *auspicious* and *propitious* (pruh-PISH-us) are close in meaning. *Propitious* by derivation means rushing forward or striving after something—in the vernacular (word 15 of this level) or in colloquial (word 43 of this level) terms, "going for it." In current usage *propitious* usually refers to favorable conditions or a favorable time for doing something: fishermen hope for propitious weather; stockbrokers are always looking for the propitious moment to buy or sell. *Auspicious* means favorable in the sense of boding well, giving indication of success. An auspicious event is one that seems an omen of success, good fortune, or prosperity.

Let's review the ten keywords you've just learned. Decide if the pairs of words below are synonyms or antonyms. Answers appear on page 210.

1. *Ebullience* and *exuberance* are . . . synonyms or antonyms?
2. *Impervious* and *accessible* are . . .
3. To *remonstrate* and to *acquiesce* are . . .
4. To *efface* and to *obliterate* are . . .
5. *Chimera* and *fantasy* are . . .
6. *Irreformable* and *incorrigible* are . . .
7. *Separate* and *juxtapose* are . . .
8. *Unfamiliar* and *conversant* are . . .
9. *Esoteric* and *mysterious* are . . .
10. *Unfavorable* and *auspicious* are . . .

Unique is Weak

When people use words loosely, with no regard for their precise meanings, it can lead, as Johnson O'Connor put it, "to serious mistakes of understanding and judgment." If your boss tells you to *peruse* a report, how do you know whether the boss means skim it or read it carefully and critically? If someone says he's *disinterested*, does that mean he's not interested or that he's fair-minded and impartial? When people use *reticent* to mean *reluctant*, *comprised of* to mean *composed of*, or *verbal* to mean *oral*, they are not being clever, novel, or stylish. They are being either lazy or pretentious. Good usage begins with learning the precise meanings of words and ends with respecting those meanings in your writing and speech.

Take, for example, the word *unique*. Aren't you thoroughly sick of it? Haven't you had enough of *unique* this, *unique* that, everything being *so very unique*? I certainly have. Why? Because *unique* is so overused its uniqueness has worn out.

Wherever you turn these days people are trying to be unique by saying *unique* and they are proving only that they have mastered the art of monotonous diction. They're being unique on television talk shows, on every page of the newspaper, in every advertising circular, and at every happy hour. Yes, everywhere intelligent people are inserting *unique* into their sentences as swiftly and predictably as a computer chip gets clapped onto a printed circuit board in an assembly line. But while a chip can store a great deal of information and instantaneously perform a variety of tasks, the word *unique*, soldered to a sentence today, does only one thing: bore, bore, bore.

As if the repetition of this word day in and day out is not enough, people have aggravated the situation by qualifying just how unique whatever they're talking about is. They say, "My child is *very* unique"; "Ours is the *most* unique product of its kind"; "This program is *completely* unique." (You will notice, please, that not once have I called the *Verbal Advantage* program unique. I prefer to think of it as exceptional or peerless.)

At any rate, all these flaccid (FLAK-sid, not FLAS-id, meaning "limp and weak") modifications of *unique* say just one thing to me: Most people tacitly acknowledge that *unique* isn't unique anymore, but they can't seem to come up with anything better.

I suppose it won't make much difference if I point out that, properly, *unique* should not be qualified. *The American Heritage Dictionary* contains this example of the gross (and laughable) misuse of *unique*: "Omaha's most unique restaurant is now even more unique." The sentence comes from advertising copy, where some of the most flagrant transgressions of the language occur. Something may be more unusual, or the most exceptional, but it cannot be more or most unique.

Unique comes from the Latin *unicus*, one, only, sole, from *unus*, one, and means unlike anything else, unmatched, one-of-a-kind. A thing cannot be more or less unique than another thing; it is simply unique. The restaurant in Omaha either is unique or is not—and most probably it is not.

Of course, if you consult the recent editions of *Merriam-Webster's Collegiate Dictionary* and *Random House Webster's College Dictionary* on this issue, you will find lengthy usage notes devoted to rationalizing the current in-fatuation with modifying *unique*. Merriam-Webster says, "In modern use both comparison and modification are widespread and standard," and Random House concludes, "Such comparison, though criticized, is standard in all vari-eties of speech and writing." What both dictionaries fail to note in their defense of modifying *unique* is something any decent usage guide will tell you: that *unique* now needs modifiers because the word is addictive and its users re-quire increasing doses of uniqueness.

Unique has been used so often as an elegant variation for *unusual* and *un-common* that it is no longer unusual or uncommon, and hardly elegant. *Unusual* and *uncommon* mean out of the ordinary, rare. They can be modified. Something can be *very* unusual, or *rather* uncommon, but it can't logically be very *unique*, unmatched, incomparable, without equal or peer.

Merriam-Webster says something else interesting in its usage note: "Unique dates back to the 17th century but was little used until the end of the 18th when, according to the Oxford English Dictionary, it was reacquired from French. H. J. Todd entered it as a foreign word in his edition (1818) of Johnson's Dictionary, characterizing it as 'affected and useless.'"

It doesn't surprise me that in the last two hundred years the word's stand-ing has not improved. Through widespread acceptance *unique* has exchanged affectation for tedium, and through widespread use its uselessness has only been affirmed. That *unique* must now be dressed up to do its duty proves how feckless it has become. (By the way, *feckless* means weak, feeble, ineffective. It combines the Scottish word *feck*, effect, with the privative suffix *-less* to mean literally "without an effect.")

But back to *unique*. If you agree with me that this feckless word is over-worked and deserves a vacation, then join me in boycotting *unique* wherever to use it would be weak.

Here's how you can do it: The next time *unique* is about to spring from your lips, pause for a moment and make the effort to summon another word—can you think of anything better right now? How about *unrivaled*, *matchless*, *peerless*, *unparalleled*, *incomparable*, *singular*, or the delicious *inimitable* (i-NIM-i-tuh-bul)?

These are truly elegant variations. They will make your sentence sparkle. They will awaken interest in your audience. They will set you apart from the humdrum herd of "uniquealaliacs."

By the way, don't bother trying to find *uniquealaliac* (pronounced yoo-NEEK-uh-**LAY**-lee-ak) in a dictionary. It's my nonce-word, a word I made up for the occasion. I created it by affixing *unique* to the combining form *-lalia*, which comes from a Greek word meaning "talk, chat," and in modern medicine is used to denote a speech disorder. For example, *rhinolalia* (RY-noh-**LAY**-lee-uh) is an abnormally strong nasal tone in a person's speech; *echolalia* (EK-oh-**LAY**-lee-uh) is the habit of repeating what other people say.

So I hope you will develop a temporary case of echolalia and repeat what I've said about *unique* to as many people as you can. If together we can manage to stem the tedious tide of uniquealalia, it would be a singular, and perhaps even inimitable, achievement.

Now let's return to the *Verbal Advantage* vocabulary for the next ten keywords.

Word 31: ITINERANT (eye-TIN-ur-int)

Wandering, traveling about, moving from place to place, especially to perform work.

Synonyms of the adjective *itinerant* include *migratory*, *wayfaring*, *vagrant*, *nomadic* (noh-MAD-ik), *ambulatory* (AM-byuh-luh-tor-ee), and the interesting word *peripatetic* (PER-i-puh-**TET**-ik). I'll discuss *peripatetic* further in the tenth and final level of the program, so keep reading!

Itinerant is also a noun meaning an itinerant person, a wanderer, wayfarer, someone who travels from place to place.

The words *itinerant* and *itinerary* (eye-TIN-uh-rair-ee) come from the Late Latin verb *itinerari*, to travel, go on a journey. An *itinerary* is a route, a course taken on a journey, especially a detailed plan or list of places to visit while traveling, as "The travel agent prepared an itinerary for their trip to Europe, noting their transportation schedule and the hotels where they planned to stay."

In current usage *itinerary* is sometimes used loosely as a synonym of *agenda*, but these words should be sharply distinguished. An *agenda* is a list of things to be done or dealt with, especially a list of items to be addressed in a meeting. An *itinerary* is a list of places to go, a detailed plan for a journey.

The words *itinerant*, *nomadic*, *vagrant*, and *ambulatory* all mean moving or traveling about.

Ambulatory, from the Latin *ambulare*, to walk, means walking, able to walk around: "When Kevin broke his leg the doctor said it would be at least three months before he'd be ambulatory again."

Vagrant comes ultimately from the Latin *vagari*, to wander, and means wandering about with no fixed purpose. *Vagrant* is usually applied to people, such as hobos and tramps, who have no home or job and who wander about in a shiftless way.

Nomadic applies not to individuals but to tribes or groups of people who lack a permanent home, and who wander together from place to place to sustain themselves: "The nomadic tribes of the desert must move from oasis to oasis to provide enough water for themselves and their livestock."

Itinerant applies to people who travel from place to place to work or seek work, and the word usually suggests traveling on a regular course or circuit. An itinerant preacher goes from town to town, spreading the gospel. Itinerant laborers must travel from place to place to do their work. In the past, the legal system had many itinerant judges who traveled on a regular circuit to adjudicate (uh-JOO-di-kayt) cases in various far-flung districts.

Word 32: CULL (rhymes with *dull*)

To pick out, select from various sources, gather, collect.

Cull comes from the Latin *colligere*, to gather, the source also of the familiar words *collect* and *collection*.

The verbs to *cull* and to *glean* are close in meaning.

Glean (rhymes with *spleen*) was originally used in farming to mean to gather up the stray bits and pieces of a crop that remained after the reapers or gatherers had done their work. From that sense, *glean* came to mean to collect or gather mentally, especially to learn or discover something bit by bit, in a laborious fashion: the investigator gathers facts to glean information; the historian gleans knowledge about the past by studying old records and documents.

The unusual noun a *cull* means something picked out or rejected as inferior or worthless, and in its original sense the verb to *cull* means to eliminate culls, as to cull livestock, to separate inferior specimens from the herd, or to cull lumber, to pick out and remove defective pieces. From that sense, *cull* came to mean to pick out so as to collect and keep, to select with an eye for retaining rather than rejecting.

Today we speak of culling useful information or culling ideas, meaning we gather that information or those ideas from various sources. When you cull flowers from a garden you select and gather them, and when you cull interesting words from reading, you pick them out and collect them in your mind.

Word 33: PROMULGATE (pruh-MUHL-gayt *or* PRAHM-ul-gayt)

To make known, publish, proclaim, make public in an official manner.

You may pronounce this word with the accent either on the second syllable or on the first. Pruh-MUHL-gayt is the original American pronunciation;

PRAHM-ul-gayt was imported from Britain in the 1920s. Since the 1960s, PRAHM-ul-gayt has steadily eclipsed the traditional pruh-MUHL-gayt, and today PRAHM-ul-gayt is sanctioned by all dictionaries and preferred by many educated speakers. (My sympathies, however, remain with pruh-MUHL-gayt.)

Synonyms of *promulgate* include *announce, advertise, broadcast, disseminate* (di-SEM-i-nayt), and *bruit* (BROOT, like *brute*). All of these words share the meaning of bringing something to the attention of the public, making it widely known.

The verb *promulgate* has two corresponding nouns: *promulgation* (PRAHM-ul-**GAY**-shin or PROH-mul-**GAY**-shin) is the act of making something public or widely known; a *promulgator* (**PRAHM**-ul-GAY-tur or, traditionally but now less often, pruh-MUHL-gay-tur) is a person who makes something widely known, who proclaims or publicizes it.

Promulgate comes from the Latin *promulgare*, to publish, proclaim. The word applies chiefly to making something known in a formal or official way: the government promulgates a new law or policy; religions promulgate their doctrine or creed; a corporation promulgates its financial status in an annual report to stockholders; and people often promulgate their opinions on radio talk shows and on the editorial pages of the newspaper.

Word 34: GRATUITOUS (gruh-T(Y)OO-i-tus)

Free, given without charge or obligation; also, without legitimate cause or reason, uncalled-for, unjustified, baseless, unwarranted.

Gratuitous comes from the Latin *gratuitus*, meaning not paid for, unprovoked, or spontaneous. Related English words include the adjective *gratis* (GRAT-is, not GRAH-tis), which means free, without charge, and the noun a *gratuity*, a gift or favor given in return for a service. After dining in a fancy restaurant, you leave the waiter a gratuity; after eating in a greasy spoon, you leave the server a tip.

In modern usage, *gratuitous* may be used to mean either given without charge or obligation, or given without legitimate cause or reason.

When your boss gives you an unexpected pay raise, it's a gratuitous blessing; if a friend offers you a free pair of tickets to a ballgame, they're gratuitous. On the other hand, a gratuitous remark or gesture is not given freely; it's uncalled-for, unwarranted. Likewise, a gratuitous assumption is baseless, and a gratuitous criticism is unjustified.

Whenever you see or hear *gratuitous* used, be sure to consider the context carefully to determine in which sense you should construe the word.

I shall conclude this discussion by offering you some gratuitous advice on usage. After you hear it, you may decide whether it was gratuitous in the sense of "given freely" or gratuitous in the sense of "unjustified, uncalled-for."

Have you ever received a "free gift" or been given something "for free"? Of course you have, but are you also aware that when you accepted that "free gift" or that whatnot "for free," you acquiesced in two of the most preposterous redundancies in the English language?

Think about it for a moment. A *gift* is something given free, a present. You wouldn't say a "free present," would you? That would sound ridiculous, which it is. Similarly, "free gift" is ridiculous because the phrase literally means "something given free without charge." So why do so many people insist on saying "free gift" when a gift already is free?

I'll tell you why: because for years marauding hordes of advertising copy-writers and marketers have assaulted us with this redundant phrase in every sleazy, gratuitous pitch they make on radio or television or drop into our mailboxes, until our brains are so saturated with it that we can't look a gift horse in the mouth without calling it free. That, in a word, is mind control.

The question now is, Shall we continue to let ourselves be subjugated by the mind-numbing mannikins of Madison Avenue, or shall we strike a blow for freedom in our own writing and speech by striking *free* from the redundant "free gift"?

I hope you will consider that question the next time someone offers you "something free for nothing."

Likewise with the phrase "for free" used to mean "for nothing." William Safire, the columnist on language for *The New York Times Magazine*, calls "for free" a joculism (JAHK-yoo-liz-'m), which he defines as "a word or phrase intended to be an amusing error that is taken up as accurate by the unwary." Safire posits that this joculism arose from a joke line from the 1930s: "I'll give it to you free for nothing." Just as *irregardless* began as a jocular play on the words *irrespective* and *regardless* and then weaseled its way into the speech of those who didn't realize *irregardless* was a joke and not a legitimate word, so did the joke-phrase "for free" mutate from a facetious usage into a widely accepted one.

Everywhere you turn today you hear educated speakers saying "I'll give it to you for free" or "Only a fool works for free" without giving a second thought to the fact that, as Safire puts it, "something is either free or for nothing—not both." To that I would add that if the pure and simple word *free* by itself doesn't satisfy your verbal appetite and you yearn for something more verbose, then use the formal "without charge," the trendy "cost-free," or the emphatic "at no cost to you."

So remember, my verbally advantaged friend, that there's no such thing as a free lunch, and there's no such thing as a "free gift," because nothing in this world is "for free." When it comes to language, one word is almost always better than two, even when they're free, without charge, and at no cost to you.

Word 35: NOMENCLATURE (NOH-men-KLAY-chur)

A system of names, especially a system of names used in a science, art, or branch of knowledge.

Nomenclature combines the Latin *nomen*, meaning "name," with *calare*, to call, and by derivation means "name-calling," not in a negative but in a neutral, disinterested sense. From the same source comes the unusual English word *nomenclator* (**NOH**-men-KLAY-tur). According to the *Century Dictionary*, "in ancient Rome candidates canvassing for office . . . were attended each by a nomenclator, who informed the candidate of the names of the persons they met, thus enabling him to address them by name." From that sense *nomenclator* came to be used to mean one who invents names for things, specifically a person who assigns technical names in scientific classification.

Nomenclature is the system of names used by a *nomenclator*, the whole vocabulary of names or technical terms used in a given science, art, or branch of knowledge. Engineering, philosophy, economics, and chemistry all have distinct nomenclatures, as do music, carpentry, computer science, and plumbing. In the eighteenth century, the Swedish botanist Carolus Linnaeus (KAR-uh-lus li-NEE-us) founded the binomial (by-NOH-mee-ul, "two-name") system of nomenclature, which has since been adopted by many sciences.

Word 36: DROLL (rhymes with *bowl*)

Amusing, humorous, comical; especially, funny or witty in an odd or outrageous way.

Synonyms of *droll* include *ridiculous*, *ludicrous*, *farcical*, and *waggish*. Antonyms include *sober*, *sedate, staid* (pronounced like *stayed*), and *austere* (word 17 of Level 3).

Droll comes from a French word meaning a buffoon, a jester, or a wag. *Droll* was once used as a noun to mean a buffoon, someone who clowns around telling jokes and performing amusing tricks—the kind of person that today we might describe as "the life of the party." The noun a *droll* is now old-fashioned, and in current usage *droll* is used as an adjective to mean amusing or witty in a quirky, eccentric way. A droll person has a playful, lively sense of humor; a droll expression is an oddly comical expression; a droll remark is humorous in an offbeat way.

The corresponding noun is *drollery* (DROH-lur-ee), which may denote either an oddly amusing quality or something said or done in a slightly outrageous and amusing way.

Word 37: INSATIABLE (in-SAY-shuh-bul *or* in-SAY-shee-uh-bul)

Greedy, hungry, unable to be satisfied or appeased.

Synonyms of *insatiable* include *ravenous*, *voracious* (vor-RAY-shus), *unquenchable*, and *unappeasable*. The direct antonym is *satiable*, capable of being satisfied.

From the Latin *satis*, which means "enough, sufficient," English has inherited the antonyms *insatiable* and *satiable*, the verbs to *satisfy* and to *satiate* (SAY-shee-ayt), and the challenging noun *satiety* (suh-TY-i-tee).

To *satiate* means to satisfy completely or somewhat to excess. When you fill your hungry belly with a hearty meal, you are satiated with food. If you occasionally feel that *Verbal Advantage* is stuffing your brain with more words than it can comfortably contain, then you're feeling satiated with words. But don't worry. I don't think you'll reach the point of satiety. The noun *satiety* means a state of excessive gratification, satisfaction beyond what one normally desires.

Our keyword, *insatiable*, means incapable of being satiated, not able to achieve satiety, unable to be satisfied or appeased— in short, greedy, hungry, ravenous.

The human animal can be insatiable in many ways. You can have an insatiable appetite for food, or drink, or sex; you can have an insatiable desire to make money or achieve fame; you can have an insatiable hunger for attention; you can have an insatiable longing for the way things were; and you can have an insatiable thirst for knowledge or for learning new words.

Word 38: BEGUILE (be-GYL)

To deceive, delude, or mislead; also, to charm, amuse, or delight.

Synonyms of *beguile* in the sense of "deceive, delude, or mislead" include *dupe* and *gull*, which were discussed in word 11 of Level 2, and also *hoodwink*, *swindle*, *bamboozle*, *ensnare*, and *cozen* (KUZ-'n, like *cousin*). Synonyms of *beguile* in the sense of "charm, amuse, or delight" include *enchant*, *enrapture*, *enthrall* (en-THRAWL), and *ensorcel* (en-SOR-sul), also spelled *ensorcell*, a poetic word that by derivation means to practice sorcery upon.

The word *guile* (rhymes with *mile*) comes to us through Old French, probably from an Old English word meaning sorcery or divination. The notion that the practitioners of sorcery are evil wizards has led to the modern meaning of *guile*: deceitful craftiness, treacherous cunning.

The prefix *be-* at the beginning of the verb to *beguile* is an intensifier meaning "completely, thoroughly." You can see this intensifying prefix *be-* in the words *besmirch*, to smirch or stain thoroughly; *befuddle*, to completely fuddle or confuse; and *beware*, to be completely wary of, to be thoroughly on one's guard.

In its original sense the verb to *beguile* means to deceive completely by means of *guile*, crafty, treacherous cunning. In Genesis, the first book of the Old Testament, Eve tells God, "The serpent beguiled me, and I did eat." Since Shakespeare's time *beguile* has also been used in a far less sinister way to mean to completely capture the attention of, to thoroughly divert or distract, and so to charm, amuse, or delight.

Depending on the motives of the beguiler, when you are beguiled you may either be thoroughly charmed and enraptured or completely distracted and deceived. Beguiling eyes are captivating, fascinating eyes; beguiling words are crafty, deceptive, misleading words.

Word 39: VINDICTIVE (vin-DIK-tiv)

Seeking or wanting revenge, vengeful, characterized by a desire to get even.

Vengeful and *vindictive* are close in meaning, and both words are used of people who have a strong desire for revenge or retribution. (*Retribution* means repayment—specifically, repayment in the form of punishment in return for a wrong.)

The *vengeful* person wants to inflict an equivalent degree of suffering upon the wrongdoer in accordance with the famous code of Hammurabi (HAH-muu-**RAH**-bee), the ancient Babylonian king, which stipulated "an eye for an eye, a tooth for a tooth."

The *vindictive* person is less rational and more fervent. When a vindictive person feels wronged he is driven to retaliate at all costs. Consequently, *vindictive* often suggests gratuitous or unjustified retaliation for an offense that is imagined rather than actual.

Word 40: REPLETE (ri-PLEET)

Fully or richly supplied, well-stocked, chock-full, filled to capacity.

Synonyms of *replete* include *stuffed*, *crammed*, *gorged*, *abounding*, *brimming*, *teeming*, *laden*, and *surfeited* (SUR-fi-tid).

Replete comes from the Latin *replere*, to refill, fill again, from *re-*, meaning "again," and *plere*, to fill. From the Latin *plere*, to fill, and the adjective *plenus*, full, come the familiar English words *plenty* and *plentiful*, and the more challenging words *plenitude* (PLEN-i-t(y)ood), an abundance, ample amount, and *plenary* (PLEE-nuh-ree), which means full or complete in all respects. Plenary powers are complete powers; a plenary session of Congress is a fully attended session of Congress.

Our keyword, *replete*, by derivation means filled to capacity, well-stocked, abounding. A river may be replete with fish; a house may be replete with furniture; a conversation may be replete with humor; a book may be replete with insight; a mind may be replete with wisdom; and a life may be replete with experience. *Verbal Advantage*, of course, is replete with words.

The words *replete* and *fraught* (rhymes with *caught*) are close in meaning but are used in different ways.

Fraught comes from Middle English and Middle Dutch words meaning "loaded, freighted, full of cargo." By derivation *fraught* suggests carrying a heavy load. That which is fraught is burdened or weighted down: a situation may be fraught with danger; a person's face may be fraught with worry; a life may be fraught with pain and suffering. *Fraught* suggests great weight or emotional intensity, and is usually used of that which is burdensome or distressful. *Replete*, on the other hand, suggests great volume or mass, and may be used of any abundant supply. A train overflowing with passengers is replete with passengers, not fraught with them, but a relationship full of conflict is fraught with conflict, not replete with it.

Recently, *replete* has come to be used to mean complete. The words are not synonymous or interchangeable. *Complete* means lacking nothing, having all necessary elements, ingredients, or parts. *Replete* means well-stocked, fully or richly supplied. A multivitamin may come complete with all the minimum daily requirements. When your body absorbs those vitamins, it is replete with them.

Let's review the ten keywords you've just learned by playing "One of These Definitions Doesn't Fit the Word." Of the three ostensible synonyms in each statement below, two are true synonyms and one is unrelated in meaning. Which one does not fit the word?

Circle your choice. Answers appear on page 210.

1. *Itinerant* means wandering, traveling, lost.
2. To *cull* means to select, deceive, gather.
3. To *promulgate* means to make known, make certain, make public.
4. *Gratuitous* means unsound, uncalled-for, unjustified.
5. *Nomenclature* means a system of classification, a system of rules, a system of names.
6. *Droll* means amusing, incredible, comical.
7. *Insatiable* means greedy, desperate, hungry.
8. To *beguile* means to expose, deceive, mislead.
9. *Vindictive* means wanting to win, wanting to get even, wanting revenge.
10. *Replete* means well-stocked, well-done, well-supplied.

Remember that if you answered fewer than eight questions correctly in this quiz, you should read the keyword discussions again before moving ahead in the program.

Here are the final ten keywords in Level 5:

Word 41: PRECLUDE (pri-KLOOD)

To prevent, make impossible, exclude or shut off all possibility of something happening.

Synonyms of *preclude* include *avert*, *obviate* (AHB-vee-ayt), and *forestall*. Antonyms include *incite*, *instigate* (IN-sti-gayt), and *engender* (en-JEN-dur).

Preclude comes from the Latin *prae-*, meaning "before," and *claudere*, to shut, close up. By derivation *preclude* means to take steps beforehand to shut off or close the door on something.

In modern usage, *preclude* suggests preventing something by excluding or shutting off all possibility of its happening: Immunization can preclude many fatal diseases. An alarm system may decrease the chance that your car will be stolen, but it will not preclude it. The framers of the U.S. Constitution adopted the Bill of Rights as a means of precluding the passage of any law that would infringe upon or abrogate the basic rights of citizens in a democracy.

Word 42: CASTIGATE (KAS-ti-gayt)

To punish or criticize severely.

Synonyms of *castigate* include *chasten* (CHAY-sin), *chastise* (chas-TYZ or CHAS-tyz), *rebuke*, *reprimand*, *reprove*, and *censure* (SEN-shur, word 28 of Level 3).

Antonyms of *castigate* include *approve*, *reward*, *praise*, *commend*, *laud* (LAWD), *extol* (ek-STOHL), and *eulogize* (YOO-luh-jyz).

The verbs to *chasten*, to *chastise*, and to *castigate* all mean to punish in slightly different ways.

Chasten is related to the word *chaste*, pure, and by derivation to *chasten* means to punish in order to purify or make chaste. In modern usage *chasten* usually suggests purifying by subjecting to harsh discipline, inflicting pain or suffering to improve the character of someone or something. Military recruits are chastened during basic training; a preacher may chasten a congregation for its sinful ways; a mild heart attack may chasten the workaholic to slow down and take better care of himself. You may also chasten your mind or chasten your style, purify or subdue it by subjecting it to harsh discipline.

The verb to *chastise* was once used as a dignified word for inflicting corporal punishment—in other words, to punish by whipping or beating. In the nineteenth century, teachers were permitted—and often expected—to chastise students who misbehaved in class, and for much of the twentieth century, before the concept of the "time-out" became popular, spanking was considered an acceptable way of disciplining a naughty or obstreperous child. (Do you need to look up *obstreperous*? Quick—grab your dictionary and do it now.)

Today *chastise* may still be used to mean to inflict corporal punishment, but more often the word suggests administering a strong verbal rebuke. When a teacher chastises a student today, it's with harsh words, not a hickory stick. The corresponding noun *chastisement* may be pronounced either CHAS-tiz-ment or chas-TYZ-ment. CHAS-tiz-ment is the traditional pronunciation; chas-TYZ-ment has been recognized by American dictionaries since the late 1940s.

Castigate comes from the Latin *castigare*, to punish with words or blows. Like *chastise*, *castigate* was once used of corporal punishment, but today the word is nearly always used to mean to beat up verbally, criticize severely, especially to subject to harsh public criticism. Politicians often castigate their opponents during a campaign. Some reviewers may praise a book for its controversial ideas, while others may castigate it. If the boss reads you the riot act in front of the whole office, consider yourself castigated. The corresponding noun is *castigation*, as "a pugnacious radio talk show host with a vicious penchant for castigation."

Word 43: COLLOQUIAL (kuh-LOH-kwee-ul)

Conversational; pertaining to, characteristic of, or used in spoken language; hence, informal, casual, natural.

Colloquial, colloquium (kuh-LOH-kwee-um), and *colloquy* (KAHL-uh-kwee) all come from the Latin *loqui*, which means to speak, converse. *Loqui* is also the source of the word *loquacious* (loh-KWAY-shus), extremely talkative.

The noun *colloquy* is a dignified synonym for *conversation*, but while *conversation* may apply to any exchange of spoken words, *colloquy* usually refers to a more formal or intellectual discussion, the kind of talk that occurs between scholars or on television shows where journalists analyze the news. When you or I talk with people at a party or over dinner, that's a conversation, but when William F. Buckley, Jr., talked with his guests on "Firing Line," that was a colloquy.

The noun *colloquium* means a gathering in which a *colloquy* takes place, a conference or meeting for discussion, specifically a relatively informal meeting for the purpose of exchanging views on a subject.

The adjective *colloquial* means conversational, of the spoken language, and therefore informal or casual. Remember *vernacular*, word 15 of this level? Colloquial speech is speech that uses the vernacular, the common, everyday language of ordinary people.

The corresponding noun *colloquialism* (kuh-LOH-kwee-ul-iz-'m) means a colloquial expression, a bit of vernacular language, a word or phrase used in common, everyday, informal speech. There are many thousands of colloquialisms in the language, and you probably use dozens—maybe even hundreds—of them every day without thinking twice about it. For example, every time you say *yeah* instead of *yes* you are using a colloquialism, an expression more appropriate to informal speech than to more formal speech and writing.

Here's a dictionary usage tip: The next time you look up a word and preceding the definition you see the abbreviation *coll.* or *colloq.*, that means the word—or the word used in that particular sense—is a colloquialism, and you may reasonably infer that it is characteristic of colloquial or conversational language.

In concluding this discussion, I would like to stress that colloquial speech and colloquialisms are not necessarily substandard or illiterate, as some ultrapurists might have you believe. To begin with, without the colloquial the English vocabulary would be circumscribed (word 11 of Level 3) and stiff, and if there were some way to outlaw the use of colloquialisms then communication between people of different backgrounds and levels of education would soon become impossible. Then it probably would not be long before English went the way of Latin—into extinction. Most of our communication is spoken, not written, and a liberal dose of colloquial or conversational words and expressions is what keeps a language fluid, fresh, and vital.

Of course, not all colloquialisms are useful or acceptable to all speakers. Some colloquialisms are objectionable because they suggest uneducated or coarse informality. A classic example of that sort is the word *ain't*. Other colloquialisms are objectionable because they're illogical, and here perhaps the best example is the expression "I could care less," which is commonly used in colloquial or informal speech to mean "I could *not* care less." If you can care less, then that means you still have some caring left in you, whereas if you cannot care less, then you do not care at all, which is the sense those who use the improper colloquialism mean to convey.

The point is, there are relatively few examples of exceptionable (do you need to look that up?) colloquial language. The vast majority of colloquial or informal expressions are not only acceptable but also useful and even necessary in conducting our day-to-day communication.

Word 44: OBFUSCATE (ahb-FUHS-kayt or AHB-fuh-skayt)

To make obscure, cloud over, darken, make unclear or indistinct.

Synonyms of *obfuscate* include *confuse, complicate, muddle, bewilder, shroud, eclipse,* and *adumbrate* (ad-UHM-brayt or AD-um-brayt). Antonyms of *obfuscate* include *expose, unveil, clarify,* and *elucidate* (i-LOO-si-dayt).

The corresponding noun is *obfuscation* (AHB-fuh-**SKAY**-shin). Have you ever heard the joke-phrase "Please eschew obfuscation"? That's an ironic way of advising someone to avoid jargon and communicate in clear and simple terms.

Obfuscate comes from the Latin *obfuscare*, to darken, and by derivation means to deprive of light, make dark or dim. In modern usage *obfuscate* may mean either to make something obscure or indistinct, or to make it confused, muddled, or unclear. You can obfuscate the truth, obfuscate your meaning, or obfuscate your intentions. Think of *obscure* when you think of the verb to *obfuscate.*

Obfuscate may be pronounced ahb-FUHS-kayt or AHB-fuh-skayt. The latter pronunciation, which has been heard in American speech since the early twentieth century, was originally British. Although AHB-fuh-skayt was criticized and called erroneous by authorities of the 1920s and 1930s, it is now fully standard and preferred by many cultivated speakers.

Word 45: FACILE (FAS-'l, rhymes with *castle*)

Easy, easily done; performed or achieved in an easy, effortless way; working or acting in a smooth, free, and unrestrained manner.

Synonyms of *facile* include *quick, ready, fluent, nimble, dexterous, expert,* and *adroit* (word 41 of Level 3).

Antonyms of *facile* include *difficult, awkward, unwieldy, laborious, irksome, obstinate* (word 34 of Level 1), *onerous* (AHN-ur-us), *intractable* (word 12 of this level), and *refractory* (ri-FRAK-tur-ee).

The adjective *facile*, the noun *facility*, and the verb to *facilitate* all come through the Latin *facilis*, meaning "easy to do," from the verb *facere*, which means "to make" or "to do." All three words suggest ease of performance or action.

Facilitate means to make easier, help along, as "She was hired to facilitate the project." When using *facilitate*, remember that the word applies to an action or operation, not to the performer of it. Installing new production equipment will not facilitate the workers on an assembly line; it will facilitate assembly of the product.

The noun *facility* means dexterity, aptitude, ease of movement or action. The word usually suggests a practiced ability to do something with quick, skillful ease: he plays the piano with facility; her facility in handling a tricky situation; an impressive facility with words.

Our keyword, *facile*, is often used of speech or the mind to mean able to perform quickly and smoothly, as "a facile wit," or "a facile tongue." *Facile* is now often used in a negative sense to mean done or arrived at too easily, without sufficient care or effort: a facile answer is smooth and easy to the point of being glib (word 8 of Level 3); a facile solution is simplistic or superficial.

In *Modern English Usage*, the classic guide by H. W. Fowler, first published in 1926, Fowler notes that the value of *facile* "as a synonym for *easy* or *fluent* or [*dexterous*] lies chiefly in its depreciatory implication. A *facile* speaker or writer is one who needs to expend little pains (& whose product is of correspondingly little import). A *facile* triumph or victory is easily won (& comes to little)."

Word 46: CONVIVIAL (kun-VIV-ee-ul)

Sociable, merry, festive.

Synonyms of *convivial* include *jovial* (word 19 of this level), and also *genial* (JEE-nee-ul), *companionable, affable* (AF-uh-bul), and *gregarious* (gruh-GAIR-ee-us). Antonyms include *unsociable, reserved, solitary,* and *aloof* (word 20 of Level 1).

Convivial comes from the Latin *convivium*, a feast, banquet, which in turn comes from the prefix *con-*, meaning "together," and *vivere*, to live. By derivation *convivial* means gathering together to eat, drink, and be merry. In modern usage *convivial* may mean either "pertaining to a feast or festive occasion" or "fond of eating, drinking, and good company." A convivial atmosphere is a merry, festive atmosphere; a convivial person is a friendly, sociable person, especially someone who likes to socialize while eating and drinking.

Word 47: ESCHEW (es-CHOO, like *s* plus the word *chew*)

To avoid, shun, abstain from; keep away from something harmful, wrong, or distasteful.

Don't be misled by the sound and spelling of *eschew*; the word has nothing to do with the act of chewing—for which the fancy synonym, by the way, is *mastication* (MAS-ti-**KAY**-shin). When you masticate your food, you chew it thoroughly.

Eschew comes through Middle English from Old French and Old High German words meaning to shun, avoid, or dread. According to the third edition of *The American Heritage Dictionary*, *eschew* suggests avoiding or abstaining from something "because to do otherwise would be unwise or morally wrong." Morally upright people eschew evil, teetotalers eschew alcohol, nonsmokers eschew tobacco, and vegetarians eschew meat—which doesn't mean they masticate it but that they avoid eating it.

In recent years some people have begun pronouncing *eschew* as es-SHOO, like *s* plus *shoe*, so that in 1993 one dictionary, *Merriam-Webster's Collegiate Dictionary,* tenth edition, recognized this mispronunciation along with the even more eccentric e-SKYOO (almost like *askew*). For a thorough account of why you should eschew these variants, see the entry for *eschew* in my *Big Book of Beastly Mispronunciations*. In the meantime, remember that there is no *shoe* in *eschew* (and no *skew* either). Put a *chew* in it.

You may recall that in the introduction to this level I noted that there are two bad habits you must eschew at all costs. First, don't invent your own pronunciations, and second, don't blindly imitate the way other people pronounce words. If you follow those two guidelines, you will have no trouble eschewing objectionable pronunciations and mastering the correct ones.

Word 48: PRODIGIOUS (pruh-DIJ-us)

Enormous, huge, tremendous, immense; extraordinary in size, extent, force, or degree.

Synonyms of *prodigious* include *mammoth*, *monumental*, *colossal*, *gargantuan*, *elephantine*, *herculean*, and *Brobdingnagian*.

The last four synonyms are interesting words worthy of brief comment.

Gargantuan (gahr-GAN-choo-i̯n) comes from the name *Gargantua*, the hero of the famous satirical romance by François Rabelais, published in 1532. *Gargantua*, says the *Century Dictionary*, is "a giant of inconceivable size, who could drink a river dry. The name is doubtless from Spanish *garganta*, [throat], gullet." In modern usage *gargantuan* sometimes suggests gluttony, as a gargantuan feast, but it is perhaps most often used as a stronger synonym of *gigantic* or *enormous*, as a gargantuan house or a gargantuan achievement.

Elephantine (EL-uh-**FAN**-tin, also EL-uh-**FAN**-teen or EL-uh-**FAN**-tyn) may mean pertaining to an elephant, but the word is most commonly used to mean resembling an elephant, and therefore huge, heavy, and awkward. A person may be of elephantine proportions or walk with an elephantine gait. A king-sized bed or an overlarge couch might also be described as *elephantine*, suitable for an elephant, immense.

The adjective *herculean* (hur-KYOO-lee-i̯n or HUR-kyoo-**LEE**-i̯n) comes from the name *Hercules*, the famous hero of Greek mythology renowned for his great feats of strength and courage. By derivation *herculean* means worthy or characteristic of the mighty Hercules. A herculean task demands all your strength and stamina; a herculean effort is a mighty, powerful effort. (The word is now usually spelled with a small *h*.)

The unusual word *Brobdingnagian* (BRAHB-ding-**NAG**-ee-i̯n, don't forget to pronounce the *ding*) refers to the gigantic inhabitants of the imaginary land of Brobdingnag (BRAHB-ding-nag) in Jonathan Swift's *Gulliver's Travels*, or to anyone or anything equally enormous. Because of its literary flavor and peculiar sound, *Brobdingnagian* (always spelled with a capital *B*) is probably best reserved for situations in which you want to achieve a humorous or satirical effect. For example, when your very large, very formidable Aunt Eloise makes her thunderous entrance at your next family reunion, you might greet her by saying, "My dear, you look positively Brobdingnagian this evening!" The antonym of *Brobdingnagian* is the more familiar word *Lilliputian* (LIL-i̯-**PYOO**-shi̯n), which also comes to us from Swift's *Gulliver's Travels*.

And now back to our keyword. *Prodigious* comes through the Latin *prodigiosus*, strange, wonderful, marvelous, from *prodigium*, an omen, portent, sign. From the same source we have inherited the word *prodigy* (PRAH-di̯-jee), a person of marvelous talent or wonderful ability.

Since about 1600, *prodigious* has been used to mean huge, enormous, of extraordinary size or extent, and also marvelous, wonderful, phenomenal, causing wonder or amazement. In modern usage the context often suggests both senses: a prodigious talent is both enormous and amazing; a prodigious accomplishment is both phenomenal and huge; prodigious energy is both astonishing and tremendous; and a prodigious event or a prodigious undertaking is often both extraordinary and wonderful.

When you think of the word *prodigious*, consider this: William Shakespeare composed twenty of his plays in only ten years, an output that can only be described as prodigious.

Word 49: IDIOSYNCRASY (ID-ee-oh-**SING**-kruh-see)

A peculiarity, distinctive characteristic of a person or group, an identifying trait or mannerism.

An *idiosyncrasy*, an *eccentricity* (EK-sen-**TRIS**-i-tee), and a *quirk* (KWURK, rhymes with *shirk*) all designate behavior that is peculiar or distinctive.

Quirk is a mild term for any unusual trait, characteristic, or mannerism. Constant use of *um*, *like*, and *y'know* is a quirk of adolescent speech. Old people often have quirks, odd preferences or strange ways of doing things.

An *eccentricity* is a habit or characteristic that seems strange or peculiar because it differs from what is considered usual or normal. A friend of mine who is also a writer prefers to spell his name without the customary period after the middle initial. Of course, every time he publishes an article he winds up in a battle with some copyeditor who insists on "correcting" this eccentricity.

Our keyword, *idiosyncrasy*, comes from Greek and means literally "one's own peculiar temperament, habit, or bent." In modern usage the word suggests a distinctive characteristic or identifying trait that sets a person apart. An idiosyncrasy may appear somewhat strange or odd, or it may simply mark someone or something as individual and different from others: a writer may have certain stylistic idiosyncrasies; a wine connoisseur can tell you the idiosyncrasies of a particular vintage; and to a person from the Midwest, the speech of someone from New England is full of idiosyncrasies, peculiar or distinctive characteristics.

Idiosyncrasy is the noun; the corresponding adjective is *idiosyncratic* (ID-ee-oh-sin-**KRAT**-ik), peculiar, distinctive, odd.

Word 50: APPROBATION (AP-roh-**BAY**-shin)

Approval, acceptance; especially, official approval or authorization.

Synonyms of *approbation* include *commendation*, *endorsement*, *sanction*, *ratification*, and *acclamation* (AK-luh-**MAY**-shin).

Antonyms include *rejection*, *opposition*, *disapprobation*, *renunciation*, *repudiation*, *disavowal*, and *abjuration* (AB-juu-**RAY**-shin).

The noun *approbation* comes from the Latin *approbare*, to approve, and by derivation means approval. However, because of its Latin derivation, *appro-*

bation is more formal and dignified than *approval*. Children seek the approval of their parents; the president of the United States seeks the approbation of Congress or the electorate. When you want the go-ahead on a plan, you ask your boss for approval. When your plan succeeds and your boss rewards you with a raise or a promotion, that's approbation.

Let's review the ten keywords you've just learned. In the questions below, the review word is followed by three words or phrases. Decide which of those three answer choices comes nearest the meaning of the review word. Answers appear on page 211.

1. When you *preclude* something, do you incorporate it, prevent it, or avoid it?
2. Is a person who is *castigated* criticized severely, treated unfairly, or expelled?
3. When something is expressed in *colloquial* terms, is it incomprehensible, illiterate, or informal?
4. If someone *obfuscates* an issue, does that mean the person is evading it, making it unclear, or misinterpreting it?
5. Is *facile* speech effortless, fast, or unclear?
6. Is a *convivial* person excitable, sociable, or silly?
7. If you *eschew* something, do you consider it, eliminate it, or avoid it?
8. Is a *prodigious* task or a *prodigious* accomplishment unusual, enormous, or impossible?
9. Is an *idiosyncrasy* a similar characteristic, a peculiar characteristic, or an obvious characteristic?
10. If you receive *approbation* for something, does that mean you get noticed for it, get punished for it, or gain approval for it?

I'd like to conclude Level 5 with an important reminder on the subject of review.

In his years of testing the aptitudes and vocabularies of thousands of Americans, Johnson O'Connor discovered three general principles, or laws, of vocabulary development. O'Connor's first law states that it is possible to arrange the words of the language in order of difficulty. The second law posits that people know all or most of the words of the language in order of difficulty up to a certain point, or degree of difficulty, beyond which they recognize few or no words at all. The third law is that your rate of learning—your ability to absorb and retain new words—is greatest at the borderline, or boundary, of your vocabulary.

Therefore, if you wish to extend the boundary of your vocabulary with maximum efficiency and permanent results, you must spend at least as much time reviewing what you have learned as you spend learning it. As with any other subject, in vocabulary building, review is the key to retention.

Consider the *modus operandi* (MOH-dus AHP-uh-**RAN**-dy or -dee)—a Latin phrase meaning "the method of operation"—of the athlete in training. Most of it is review, going over the basics again and again so they become ingrained and automatic. The tennis player hits a thousand routine groundstrokes before attempting to perfect a lob or refine a topspin on a serve. The baseball player takes batting practice every day to review the fundamentals of hitting. And before the weightlifter can raise five hundred pounds, he must develop the muscle tone and stamina to do it by hefting four hundred and ninety pounds over and over again.

So it is with raising the level of your vocabulary. Practice—routine and methodical practice—makes perfect.

As you proceed through *Verbal Advantage* and beyond into a regular schedule of reading and vocabulary building, be sure to review what you have learned at every step of the way—not just once, but as many times as it takes for the knowledge to become instinctive.

If you've assimilated all the keywords, synonyms, antonyms, and related words that I've discussed up to this point, then you can give yourself a hearty pat on the back, because you have raised your vocabulary level to at least the 75th percentile—the top quarter of all educated adults. And if you've absorbed all the additional information on usage, pronunciation, grammar, connotation, and synonym distinctions that I've presented so far, then your level of verbal awareness has probably surpassed that of many of your friends and coworkers.

As you continue reading the program, I hope you will keep this in mind: The difference between having verbal skills and having a verbal advantage is like the difference between the layperson and the expert, or the amateur and the professional. It is the difference between competence and excellence. In my experience, the person who cares about using language precisely is also the person who strives—at all times and in every endeavor—for excellence.

Whatever your occupation, if you wish to succeed in it you must study and practice it seriously. But practical knowledge is only one-half of a complete, well-rounded professional development. By now I'm sure you know what the other half is: knowledge of words and the ability to use them wisely and well.

In the remaining challenging levels of *Verbal Advantage*, I will present a great deal more pragmatic information and introduce you to hundreds more useful words. You've made it this far with flying colors, so don't stop here. Join me as we take the next exciting step on the path to becoming a confident and conscientious user of the language.

Answers to Review Quizzes for Level 5

Keywords 1–10

1. No. *Reticent* means reluctant to speak. *Voluble* means talkative, characterized by a great and continuous flow of words.
2. Yes. To *commiserate* is to sympathize, show sorrow or pity for.
3. Yes. A *dilemma* is a predicament; specifically, a predicament in which one must choose between equally undesirable alternatives.
4. Yes. *Transitory* means passing, temporary, fleeting, not permanent or enduring.
5. No. *Philanthropic* means charitable, benevolent, humane; motivated by or done out of a desire to help or improve the welfare of others.
6. No. *Lethargy* means lack of energy, sluggishness, an abnormally dull, drowsy, inactive condition or state of mind.
7. No. To *exonerate* means to free from blame, declare blameless or innocent.
8. Yes. *Pugnacious* means combative, quarrelsome, ready and willing to fight.
9. No. *Contrition* is remorse, penitence, repentance, deep and devastating sorrow for something one has done wrong.
10. No—or at least let's hope not. To *abrogate* means to abolish by legal or authoritative action or decree.

Keywords 11–20

1. False. *Officious* means meddlesome, nosy, intrusive; specifically, offering unwanted advice or unnecessary services, especially in a high-handed, overbearing way.
2. True. *Intractable* means hard to manage or control, stubborn, unruly.
3. Definitely true. *Altruism* is selflessness, unselfish concern for the welfare of others.
4. True. An *accolade* is an award, sign of respect or esteem, anything done or given as a token of appreciation or approval.
5. False. The *vernacular* is the common, everyday language of ordinary people as opposed to the literary or cultured language.
6. False. *Judicious* means wise and careful, having or showing sound judgment.

7. True. A *chrysalis* is the pupa of a butterfly, the stage during which the insect is enclosed in a cocoon. Figuratively, a *chrysalis* is a sheltered and undeveloped state or stage of being.
8. False. *Genteel* means refined, polite, sophisticated, elegantly stylish or fashionable, belonging to high society.
9. False. *Jovial* means merry, full of good humor, hearty and fun-loving, jolly, convivial.
10. Sad but true. *Subterfuge* means a deception, trick, underhanded scheme.

Keywords 21–30

1. Synonyms. *Ebullience* means lively enthusiasm, high spirits, bubbly excitement.
2. Antonyms. *Impervious* means impenetrable, incapable of being entered or passed through; hence, unable to be moved or affected by something.
3. Antonyms. To *acquiesce*, word 31 of Level 4, means to agree without protest, accept without argument. To *remonstrate* is to object, protest, argue or plead against.
4. Synonyms. To *efface* is to rub out, wipe out, obliterate, erase, expunge.
5. Synonyms. A *chimera* is a foolish fancy, fantastic notion or idea, figment of the imagination.
6. Synonyms. *Incorrigible* means bad beyond correction or reform, hopeless, irreformable; also, unruly, unmanageable, difficult to control.
7. Antonyms. To *juxtapose* is to place side by side or close together, especially so as to compare or contrast.
8. Antonyms. *Conversant* means familiar, acquainted, well-informed or well-versed.
9. Synonyms. *Esoteric* means intended for a select group, known only by a few people; hence, secret, confidential, or mysterious.
10. Antonyms. *Auspicious* means favorable, fortunate, marked by favorable circumstances or good fortune.

Keywords 31–40

1. *Lost* doesn't fit. *Itinerant* means wandering, traveling about, moving from place to place, especially to perform work.
2. *Deceive* doesn't fit. To *cull* means to pick out, select from various sources, gather, collect.
3. *Make certain* doesn't fit. To *promulgate* means to make known, publish, proclaim, make public in an official manner.
4. *Unsound* doesn't fit. *Gratuitous* means without legitimate cause or reason, uncalled-for, unjustified; also, free, given without charge or obligation.

5. *A system of rules* doesn't fit. *Nomenclature* means a system of names or a system of classification, especially a system of names used in a science, art, or branch of knowledge.

6. *Incredible* doesn't fit. *Droll* means amusing, humorous, comical, witty, especially in an odd or outrageous way.

7. *Desperate* doesn't fit. *Insatiable* means greedy, hungry, unable to be satisfied or appeased.

8. *Expose* doesn't fit. To *beguile* means to deceive, delude, or mislead; also, to charm, amuse, or delight.

9. *Wanting to win* doesn't fit. *Vindictive* means vengeful, seeking revenge, wanting to get even.

10. *Well-done* doesn't fit. *Replete* means fully or richly supplied, well-stocked, chock-full, filled to capacity.

Keywords 41–50

1. When you *preclude* something you prevent it, make it impossible, shut off all possibility of its happening.

2. To *castigate* someone means to punish or criticize that person severely.

3. *Colloquial* means conversational; pertaining to or characteristic of spoken language; hence, informal, casual, natural.

4. To *obfuscate* means to make obscure, make unclear or indistinct.

5. *Facile* means easy or easily done; performed or achieved in a smooth, effortless way.

6. A *convivial* person is sociable. A *convivial* occasion or gathering is merry, festive.

7. When you *eschew* something you avoid it, shun it, abstain from it. *Eschew* means to keep away from something harmful, wrong, or distasteful.

8. *Prodigious* means enormous; extraordinary in size, extent, force, or degree.

9. An *idiosyncrasy* is a peculiar or distinctive characteristic of a person or group; an identifying trait or mannerism.

10. You gain approval for it. *Approbation* means approval, acceptance; especially, official approval or authorization.

Review Test for Level 5

1. Which word means refined by study and training, marked by skill and taste?

   (a) judicious
   (b) cultivated

(c) facile

(d) eccentric

2. What is the correct pronunciation of *mischievous*?

   (a) MIS-chi-vus

   (b) mis-CHEE-vus

   (c) mis-CHEE-vee-us

3. On which syllable does the stress properly fall in *superfluous*?

   (a) su-

   (b) -per-

   (c) -flu-

4. Which group of three words contains two antonyms and one synonym of *voluble*?

   (a) taciturn, verbose, garrulous

   (b) loquacious, terse, effusive

   (c) glib, laconic, reticent

5. Which word is *not* a synonym of *transitory*?

   (a) transient

   (b) ephemeral

   (c) itinerant

   (d) evanescent

6. The *phil-* in *philanthropy* and *philharmonic* comes from the Greek *philein*, which means

   (a) to love

   (b) to give

   (c) to sing

   (d) to celebrate

7. Which pair contains a word that is not a synonym of *lethargy*?

   (a) torpor, stupefaction

   (b) lassitude, languor

   (c) apathy, acquiescence

   (d) somnolence, sluggishness

8. *Pugnacious* comes from a Latin word that means

   (a) to argue

   (b) to be unruly

   (c) to be rude

   (d) to fight with the fists

9. What is a *quidnunc*?

    (a) an itinerant person

    (b) an incorrigible person

    (c) a vindictive person

    (d) an officious person

    (e) a convivial person

10. Which word comes from the ritual of conferring knighthood?

    (a) exonerate

    (b) accolade

    (c) judicious

    (d) altruism

11. Which statement is *never* true of vernacular language?

    (a) It is familiar.

    (b) It is common.

    (c) It is scholarly.

    (d) It is grammatical.

12. The Roman god Jupiter is the source of which word?

    (a) judgment

    (b) jovial

    (c) justice

    (d) juxtapose

13. What is the proper plural of *medium*?

    (a) medias

    (b) mediums

    (c) media

14. Which are the two cultivated pronunciations of *ebullient*? (This question has *two* correct answers.)

    (a) i-BUHL-yint

    (b) i-BOOL-yint

    (c) i-BYOO-lee-int

    (d) i-BUUL-yint

    (e) EB-yuh-lint

15. Which word is an antonym of *impervious*?

    (a) diaphanous

    (b) tractable

    (c) opaque

    (d) obfuscated

16. *Imaginary*, *fantastic*, and *preposterous* are synonyms of
- (a) droll
- (b) chimerical
- (c) auspicious
- (d) prodigious

17. *Posit* and *juxtapose* come from the Latin *ponere*, which means
- (a) to tell, explain
- (b) to resist, oppose
- (c) to put, place
- (d) to give, offer

18. Which word is *not* a synonym of *esoteric*?
- (a) abstruse
- (b) inscrutable
- (c) arcane
- (d) idiosyncratic
- (e) cryptic

19. *Auspicious* is related to *auspex*, a soothsayer of ancient Rome who made predictions
- (a) by interpreting dreams
- (b) by casting dice
- (c) by observing the stars
- (d) by observing the flight of birds

20. Which word is a synonym of *promulgate*?
- (a) chasten
- (b) glean
- (c) bruit
- (d) expostulate
- (e) adjudicate

21. Why will you never, ever write or utter the odious phrase *free gift*?
- (a) Because it is redundant, hackneyed, and ridiculous.
(The answer to this question is gratuitous. You may have it free, or for nothing.)

22. What does the *nomen-* in *nomenclature* mean?
- (a) law
- (b) words
- (c) name
- (d) knowledge

23. The noun *satiety* denotes

- *(a)* thorough devotion
- *(b)* excessive gratification
- *(c)* utter confusion
- *(d)* unquenchable desire

24. Which set of words contains a word that is *not* a synonym of *beguile*?

- *(a)* ensnare, obfuscate, swindle
- *(b)* bamboozle, enrapture, enchant
- *(c)* dupe, hoodwink, ensorcel
- *(d)* gull, cozen, enthrall

25. The Latin adjective *plenus*, the source of *replete* and *plenary*, means

- *(a)* all
- *(b)* many
- *(c)* full
- *(d)* every

26. Which word is an antonym of *preclude*?

- *(a)* engender
- *(b)* cull
- *(c)* permit
- *(d)* obviate

27. *Chastise* and *castigate* were both formerly used of

- *(a)* religious purification
- *(b)* corporal punishment
- *(c)* public humiliation
- *(d)* political debate

28. Which word means a vernacular expression?

- *(a)* obfuscation
- *(b)* chrysalis
- *(c)* idiosyncrasy
- *(d)* colloquialism

29. *Facile*, *facility*, and *facilitate* all come from the Latin verb *facere*, which means

- *(a)* to work
- *(b)* to simplify
- *(c)* to flow smoothly
- *(d)* to make or do

30. Which words are synonyms?

    (a) aloof, affable

    (b) genial, convivial

    (c) gregarious, solitary

    (d) reserved, jovial

31. What is the traditional, proper pronunciation of *eschew*?

    (a) es-CHOO

    (b) es-SHOO

    (c) e-SKYOO

32. Which word comes from a character in a satirical romance by François Rabelais?

    (a) elephantine

    (b) prodigious

    (c) gargantuan

    (d) Brobdingnagian

33. Which word comes from Jonathan Swift's *Gulliver's Travels*?

    (a) herculean

    (b) Brobdingnagian

    (c) gargantuan

    (d) prodigious

34. Which word is *not* a synonym of *idiosyncratic*?

    (a) habitual

    (b) quirky

    (c) distinctive

    (d) peculiar

35. Which word is a synonym of *approbation*?

    (a) repudiation

    (b) disavowal

    (c) acclamation

    (d) abjuration

Answers

1. b 2. a 3. b 4. c 5. c 6. a 7. c 8. d 9. d 10. b 11. c 12. b 13. c
14. a+d 15. a 16. b 17. c 18. d 19. d 20. c 21. a 22. c 23. b 24. a
25. c 26. c 27. b 28. d 29. d 30. b 31. a 32. c 33. b 34. a 35. c

Evaluation

A score of 30–35 is excellent. If you answered fewer than thirty questions correctly in this test, review the entire level and take the test again.

Level 6

Welcome to Level 6, and the beginning of the second half of *Verbal Advantage*. So far in our climb up the ladder of language we have ascended from words known by most college graduates all the way to words unknown to three-quarters of adults. If you felt edified by what you learned in the first half of *Verbal Advantage*, then I'm sure that by the time you finish reading the second half you will feel verbally transformed.

I hope you're ready for an exciting intellectual challenge, because from here on in the ascent will be steep and even more demanding. Level 6 begins at about the 75th percentile of the English vocabulary. When you have mastered all the words through Level 8, your vocabulary will equal or exceed that of most executives and professionals, including those with advanced degrees. And when you complete the tenth and final level you will have progressed beyond 95 percent of the entire population. Only a handful of people in every thousand will share your command of words.

"That's terrific," you're thinking, but another voice inside you may be wondering, "Why do I need to know all these difficult, unusual words? What good are they to me if 85 or 95 percent of the population doesn't understand them?"

Possessing a large and exact vocabulary is pleasurable and reassuring for the same reason that it's pleasurable and reassuring to have money in the bank—it's there when you need it, and you can rest easy that you'll never have to ask for a handout. To take that analogy one step further, if words are like dollars, would you rather live on a tight budget, watching every nickel and dime and worrying about where the next dollar's coming from, or would you rather have a walletful of words in all denominations that you can spend at your discretion?

Many of the words you will learn in the second half of *Verbal Advantage* are not ones you are likely to need every day, and the keywords in Levels 9 and 10 are so advanced that you probably will use them only once in a great while. Infrequency of use, however, is not always a fair measure of a word's utility. In figure skating the triple Lutz is an extremely difficult maneuver, not often performed, but when a skater successfully accomplishes that jump it is the crowning moment of the program. The same can be said of adding challenging and unusual words to your verbal repertoire. You may not use them often, but when the need arises you know that you can call upon them with confidence to provide an appropriate and even spectacular effect.

How We Acquire Our Vocabularies

Children, much more than adults, have a natural ability for learning language. They are biologically programmed to pick up words, concepts, and impressions at a rapid rate. Because of their receptivity to language, children, and particularly preschoolers, can easily learn a second and even a third language. All youngsters have this remarkable talent. The problem begins when the child goes to school and the so-called process of socialization begins. Then one language dominates, and the other, unless it is cultivated at home or in school, is gradually forgotten. There is a lesson to be learned from this about language acquisition and development.

When you are a child, you learn hundreds—even thousands—of words each year. At a tender age, nearly every word is new, and the mind absorbs them all like a sponge. As you learn to read, you come across scores of new words that express more complex ideas and subtle shades of thought. By the time you finish high school, however, you have learned most of the words you know today, and the rate at which your vocabulary increases has slowed to only about one or two hundred words a year.

In college your vocabulary continues to grow, but at this slower rate. Many of the words you learn in college are more common in writing than in speech, and in your academic writing you refine your ability to use them. In graduate or professional school, vocabulary growth becomes even more restricted and specialized, for at that point you are no longer exposed to words from a variety of disciplines but are instead focusing your attention on words related to a specific field, such as law, medicine, psychology, or economics.

In our professional lives, most of our reading and writing is confined to the workplace, where the problem usually is not how to improve the quality and clarity of our communication but how to get it all done and out the door on time. Let's face it: Most people have time to read only what is required in the day-to-day performance of the job, and much of that material, I'm sorry to say, is badly written, overwritten, and dull. There's precious little continuing education to be found in a quarterly report, a sales contract, a standard business letter, or a department memorandum. Simply put, what you read, write, and hear at work probably won't do much to improve your vocabulary.

To make matters worse, the average college-educated American reads only two books a year. Judging by what sells in the publishing world I'd wager that those two books are either how-to manuals or popular fiction. That kind of material may provide some relief from the daily grind, or some advice on how not to get pulverized in the daily grind, but as I mentioned in the first half of this program, it will do little or nothing for your vocabulary. Not only that, it may actually be deleterious, for many of today's bestsellers and mass-market books are so poorly written and edited that they may only reinforce certain bad language habits you have picked up over the years and encourage you to become lazy about learning new words.

Thus, environment tends to confine our attention to familiar words and second-rate writing, and circumstance makes it difficult to do much serious reading outside the job. Consequently, our vocabulary growth rate slows way down because we are rarely exposed to new words, and because we are no longer actively using many of the words we learned in school, we start to forget some of them. As the British novelist Evelyn Waugh once wrote, "One forgets words as one forgets names. One's vocabulary needs constant fertilisation or it will die."

Yes, sad to say, you can indeed forget words you once knew. What happens is this: Gradually, as you grow older, certain words you learned when you were younger begin to drop out of your active vocabulary and enter your passive vocabulary. (By *active vocabulary* I mean the words you are able to call upon from memory to use in conversation or in writing. Your *passive vocabulary* is your warehouse of inactive words, which include the words that are "just on the tip of your tongue" as well as those you know you've seen or heard before but can't quite remember.) This disappearing process does not affect your everyday vocabulary. You will not forget the meaning of *food*, *clothing*, and *shelter*. The words you lose will be the ones in your passive vocabulary and the ones at the threshold or boundary of your active vocabulary.

The good news is that, unlike your physical abilities, which begin to decline in your thirties and forties, research has shown that your vocabulary can and does continue to grow throughout your life. The bad news is that the growth usually is so slow and gradual that it is hardly noticeable—only a trickle of new words each year. In short, once you are out of school, your vocabulary growth rate, which was so rapid in the early part of your life, becomes slow, unremarkable, and at times even stagnant. Clearly such sluggish verbal development is unlikely to improve your chances of success or have any lasting influence on your career.

Therefore, if you are convinced, as I am, that vocabulary level is an important factor in determining personal satisfaction and career success, then you must make a concerted effort to seek out and learn new words, beginning with *Verbal Advantage* and continuing throughout the rest of your life. If you strive conscientiously to build your knowledge of words, you can double and even triple your normal vocabulary growth rate, add countless words to your active vocabulary, and rescue from oblivion words that have slipped into your passive vocabulary.

All it takes is a modicum of commitment and self-discipline, just a little bit of effort every day toward the goal. The process is not unlike exercising the muscles of your body to retard the aging process and maintain optimum physical ability for your age. The brain is, after all, like a muscle—the one that commands the whole organism. It, too, needs exercise and nourishment to function at its peak. And that nourishment must be in the form of words and ideas.

I have designed *Verbal Advantage* to help you preserve the words you are in danger of losing, teach you many more new ones, and show you how best to use those words to express your ideas. As you read the second half of the program, I think you'll find yourself paying closer attention to words and caring more about how you use them. And by the time you're finished I think you'll agree that building your vocabulary is not only productive but also enjoyable.

So, are you ready to begin the second half of your ascent to the acme of verbal facility? Here are the first ten keywords in Level 6:

Word 1: LEGERDEMAIN (LEJ-ur-duh-**MAYN**)

Sleight of hand, a cleverly executed trick or deception.

In a general sense, the simple word *magic* is a synonym of *legerdemain*. More challenging synonyms of *legerdemain* include *prestidigitation* and *thaumaturgy*, which I'll discuss (and pronounce) in a moment, after I tell you about the expression "sleight of hand."

The word *sleight* (SLYT, like *slight*) is related to the word *sly*, and "sleight of hand" means literally slyness of the hand, a clever trick or illusion done with the hands.

Legerdemain, *prestidigitation* (PRES-ti-DIJ-i-**TAY**-shin), and *thaumaturgy* (**THAW**-muh-TUR-jee) all refer to magic or deception, but each word has a more specific and precise meaning. *Thaumaturgy* comes from the Greek word for miracle, and by derivation means the working of miracles. The *presti-* in *prestidigitation* comes ultimately from the Italian *presto*, meaning nimble, quick; the *digit* in the middle of *prestidigitation* is the word *digit* (DIJ-it), which in one of its senses means "a finger." By derivation *prestidigitation* is nimbleness with the fingers, quick-fingeredness. *Prestidigitation* is used as a general synonym for *legerdemain*, sleight of hand, but sometimes it refers specifically to the art of juggling.

Legerdemain comes from a Middle French phrase meaning "light of hand." Today the word may refer specifically to adroitness with the hands, as in performing magic tricks, or to any display of clever skill and adroitness. For example, a surgeon, a musician, and an athlete all may display legerdemain. In current usage *legerdemain* may also denote a cleverly executed trick or deception: "Larry hired a sleazy accountant who promised he could outwit the IRS by performing financial legerdemain"; "The first lesson of politics is 'Watch out for dirty tricks and other unscrupulous forms of legerdemain.'"

When you spell *legerdemain*, remember that it does *not* have an *e* at the end.

Word 2: PUERILE (PYOOR-ul *or* PYOO-ur-ul)

Childish, immature; hence, foolish, silly.

Puerile comes through the Latin *puerilis*, meaning youthful, childish, from *puer*, a child.

Synonyms of *puerile* in the sense of "childish or immature" include *infantile* and *juvenile*. Synonyms of *puerile* in the sense of "foolish or silly" include *inane* (i-NAYN), *frivolous*, *asinine*, *fatuous* (FACH-oo-us), *sophomoric* (SAHF-uh-**MOR**-ik), and *callow* (word 30 of Level 4).

Infantile, *juvenile*, and *puerile* all may be used in a general way to mean pertaining to childhood. Specifically, however, *infantile* means pertaining to infancy, to babyhood or very early childhood; *puerile* means pertaining to the childhood years, the time between infancy and puberty; and *juvenile* means pertaining to preadulthood, the teenage years.

You can see the words used in this specific way in the phrases "infantile paralysis," "juvenile court," and "puerile respiration," which is a respiratory murmur heard in healthy children that in adults is considered a sign of disease.

These three words may also be used in a general sense to mean childish, immature, foolish, characteristic of youth. In this sense, *juvenile* is the least negative; *puerile* implies harsher judgment; and *infantile* is the strongest, suggesting the most disagreeable characteristics of childhood—extreme silliness and immaturity. For example, juvenile desires may be simply youthful desires, childlike thoughts in an older head. Puerile behavior is childish and inappropriate behavior, unbecoming of one's years; it may refer to children who act younger than they are, and it may only be temporary. Infantile behavior, however, is extremely childish, and an infantile remark is foolish and stupid.

Puerile has two corresponding nouns: *puerilism* (PYOOR-ul-iz-'m or PYOO-ur-ul-iz-'m) and *puerility* (pyuu-RIL-i-tee or PYOO-uh-**RIL**-i-tee). *Puerilism* is a psychiatric term for the abnormal appearance of childish behavior in an adult. In my considered but medically unsubstantiated opinion, puerilism is the chief occupational disorder of writers and actors. *Puerility* may be used in a general sense to mean childishness, immaturity; in civil law, *puerility* refers to the status of a child between infancy and puberty. Between puberty and the established legal age of maturity, the child is a juvenile.

Word 3: COMPLICITY (kum-PLIS-i-tee)

Conspiracy, partnership in wrongdoing, criminal participation, direct association in guilt, the state of being an accomplice.

Conspiracy, *confederacy*, *collusion*, and *complicity* all refer to partnership or participation in disreputable or illegal activities.

Conspiracy means the act of plotting and cooperating secretly, especially to achieve an unlawful, evil, or treacherous purpose, as a conspiracy to commit murder.

Confederacy refers to people, groups, states, or nations united for a common purpose. It may be used neutrally to mean simply an alliance, as "OPEC is a confederacy of Middle Eastern oil-exporting countries." Quite often, however, *confederacy* is used in a negative sense to mean an alliance in wrongdoing, as "a confederacy of terrorists bent on overthrowing the government."

A *collusion* is a specific type of conspiracy: a secret understanding in which one person or group plays into another's hands with the aim of defrauding a third party. For example, if witnesses in a legal trial or parties to a negotiation are in collusion, they are cooperating secretly while appearing to be adversaries.

Here it seems appropriate to digress for a moment to discuss the noun *connivance* and the verb to *connive*, which today are often used interchangeably with *collusion* and the verb to *collude*. Strictly and traditionally, however, these words are not synonymous.

Connivance and *connive* come from the Latin *connivere*, to wink at, and by derivation suggest the act of winking at wrongdoing. Originally, and in my opinion properly, to *connive* is not to conspire or cooperate secretly in an unlawful act but to wink at it, to pretend not to see it or know about it and so give tacit consent or encouragement: "They bribed the doorman so he would connive at the burglary"; "The police department connived at organized crime in the city."

In like manner, *connivance* properly means the act of conniving, feigning ignorance of wrongdoing: "Illegal gambling would not exist in this town without the connivance of the authorities"; "When investigators exposed the plot to embezzle company funds, they accused the vice president of connivance."

I should point out here that my opinion of how *connive* and *connivance* should be used is puristic, and to a certain extent wishful thinking. All current dictionaries countenance *scheme*, *plot*, and *conspire* as synonyms of *connive* and sanction *conspiracy* as a synonym of *collusion*. My point in raising this issue is not so much to condemn a minor implosion of language as it is to make you aware of the traditional definitions of *connive* and *connivance*, which current dictionaries also countenance but which you may not have known until now. My aim is not to prevent you or anyone else from using *connive* to mean to plot or conspire. My simple, earnest hope is only that you will learn and remember its other, original meaning: "to feign ignorance of wrongdoing."

And now back to our keyword, *complicity*. It comes from the Latin *complicare*, to fold up or fold together, the source also of the words *complicate*, which means literally "to fold or twist together," and *accomplice*, which means literally "a person who is folded up" and therefore involved.

Whereas *connivance* suggests passive cooperation in something unlawful, *complicity* denotes active participation or partnership in wrongdoing, the state of being an accomplice: "When charged with conspiracy, the defendant professed his innocence and denied any complicity in the plot."

Word 4: TRANSMUTE (tranz-MYOOT *or* trans-MYOOT)

To transform; specifically, to change from one nature, form, or substance into another, especially to a higher, better, or more refined one.

The verb *transmute* combines the prefix *trans-*, meaning "across" or "beyond," with the Latin *mutare*, to change. Literally, *transmute* means "to change across the board" or "to change something beyond what it is."

Transmute was once used in the primitive science of alchemy (AL-kuh-mee), which preceded modern chemistry, to refer to the changing of base metals or common elements into a higher form, as to transmute iron into gold. Today the word is used generally to mean to completely change the nature or substance of something, especially to change it to a more refined or more desirable state: You can transmute an idea into a reality, transmute sorrow into joy, or make a modest investment that over thirty years transmutes into a substantial nest egg for retirement.

Word 5: ABSTRUSE (ab-STROOS)

Difficult to understand, hard to grasp mentally, deep, profound, incomprehensible, unfathomable.

Antonyms of *abstruse* include *manifest*, *discernible* (word 32 of Level 3), *lucid* (word 45 of Level 3), and *perspicuous*, which I'll discuss later in this level.

Challenging synonyms of *abstruse* include *inscrutable* (word 48 of Level 3), *esoteric* (word 29 of Level 5), and also *occult, cryptic, enigmatic, arcane, recondite,* and *acroamatic.*

Let's take a closer look at some of those rather abstruse synonyms, all of which apply to things that are secret and mysterious or difficult to understand.

By derivation *esoteric* (ES-uh-**TER**-ik) means understood by a select group, intended only for the knowledge of a few; hence, secret, confidential, or beyond most people's knowledge or understanding.

Occult (uh-KUHLT, first syllable like *a* in *ago*) by derivation means hidden or concealed. Today *occult* may be used either of that which is secret because it is hidden from view or of that which is secret because it is mysterious or incomprehensible.

Cryptic (KRIP-tik) comes from the Greek *kryptos*, hidden, which comes in turn from the verb *kryptein*, to hide. The familiar word *crypt* comes from the same source and means a burial chamber hidden underground. In modern usage *cryptic* applies to that which has a hidden meaning: cryptic ideas are mystifying ideas; a cryptic message is an incomprehensible or coded message.

The noun *enigma* (i-NIG-muh) and the adjective *enigmatic* (EN-ig-**MAT**-ik) come from a Greek verb meaning "to speak in riddles." An *enigma* is something or someone like a riddle, a mystery, puzzle. *Enigmatic* means like an enigma, and therefore perplexing, puzzling, ambiguous, or incomprehensible. *Enigmatic* is perhaps most often used of something written or stated, but the word may also apply to actions and to people.

Arcane (ahr-KAYN) comes from the Latin *arcana*, meaning "shut, closed," or "secret," and ultimately from *arca*, a box or chest, especially a money chest. By derivation *arcane* means shut or closed up, and, like *esoteric, arcane* is now used of that which is known only to a few people. The word usually applies to knowledge or information, as an arcane theory.

Recondite (REK-un-dyt) comes from the Latin *recondere*, to put away, conceal. In modern usage *recondite* applies to that which is beyond the grasp of the ordinary person. To most people, for example, particle physics is a recondite subject.

Acroamatic (AK-roh-uh-**MAT**-ik) is an abstruse and unusual synonym of *esoteric*—so unusual that you won't find it listed in most dictionaries. Historically, *acroamatic* applies to certain writings by the ancient Greek philosopher Aristotle (**AR**-i-STAHT-'l) that were addressed to his disciples as opposed to his exoteric (EKS-uh-**TER**-ik) writings, which were intended for a popular audience. *Acroamatic* comes from the Greek *akroamatikos*, which means "designed for hearing only." According to the encyclopedic *Century Dictionary* (1914), Aristotle's acroamatic writings "were addressed to 'hearers,' that is, were intended to be read to his disciples or were notes written down after his lectures." In a general sense, *acroamatic* may refer to that which is *esoteric*, intended for and understood by a select group, *recondite*, beyond the grasp of the average person, and *abstruse*, extremely hard to understand.

By derivation *abstruse* means put or pushed away, and today the word connotes that which has been pushed out of the realm of comprehension. Scholars and scientists are fond of using abstruse academic jargon to discuss abstruse subjects and ideas. If you buy a computer, the user's manual probably will be so abstruse that you'll wind up having to call the customer service hotline for help.

Word 6: EDIFY (ED-i-fy)

To instruct, improve, teach, enlighten; especially, to instruct or improve intellectually, morally, or spiritually.

Anything that improves the mind, the character, or the spirit can be described as edifying. If you find an experience instructive, eye-opening, or uplifting, you can say that it edified you or that you found it edifying. You can be edified by a movie, a play, a book, a conversation, by traveling, or by working on an interesting project. As I noted in the first half of the program, if you want to learn more about the world and learn more words, then reading is the best way to edify yourself. But even entertainment can be edifying, although some forms of entertainment, such as watching reruns of "Wheel of Fortune," probably won't edify you at all.

The corresponding noun is *edification*, which means enlightenment—intellectual, moral, or spiritual improvement: "Public libraries exist for the benefit and edification of all people"; "He was a philanthropist devoted not only to the material betterment of less fortunate members of society but also to their edification."

Except when used humorously, the phrase "for your edification" should probably be avoided. It has become a cliché, and often has a condescending overtone.

Word 7: SUPERCILIOUS (SOO-pur-**SIL**-ee-us)

Haughty, proud, scornful, contemptuous, disdainful.

Supercilious comes from the Latin *super-*, meaning "over, above," and *cilium*, eyebrow; by derivation it means with raised eyebrows, and therefore proud, haughty, disdainful. *Supercilious* suggests the proud, contemptuous attitude or expression of someone who thinks he's superior and who looks down at others with scorn: "Lucy's new supervisor had seemed quite amiable in her interview, but to her dismay she soon found out he had a supercilious way of assigning her a project and then telling her, 'If I were you, I'd do it like this.'"

Word 8: DISSEMBLE (di-SEM-buul)

To disguise; conceal under a false appearance; speak or behave hypocritically; cover up the facts or one's true feelings or motives; mask under a pretense or deceptive manner.

Synonyms of *dissemble* include to *feign*, *affect*, *simulate*, *camouflage*, *equivocate* (i-KWIV-uh-kayt), and *prevaricate* (pri-VAR-i-kayt).

To *disguise* is the general word meaning to give something a false appearance so it won't be recognized. We disguise our physical appearance, disguise facts, or disguise intentions.

To *feign* (rhymes with *rain*) means to represent falsely, pretend that something exists or is real, as to feign interest, feign illness, feign innocence, or feign sleep.

To *affect* (uh-FEKT) means to put on a false appearance to make a certain impression, as to affect knowledge, affect a cultivated pronunciation, affect social superiority, or affect a carefree manner when your heart is breaking.

Our keyword, *dissemble*, comes from an Old French verb meaning "to appear different," and by derivation means to make something appear different from what it is. When you dissemble the facts or dissemble your feelings, you conceal them under a false appearance. The person who dissembles speaks or behaves hypocritically so as to cover up the truth.

Word 9: VACUOUS (VAK-yoo-us)

Empty, vacant; devoid of substance, interest, intelligence, expression, or meaning.

Synonyms of *vacuous* include *blank*, *unintelligent*, *shallow*, *stupid*, *senseless*, *inane*, and *fatuous*. The corresponding noun is *vacuity* (va-KYOO-i-tee), emptiness, an absence of matter or intellectual content.

Vacuous comes from the Latin *vacuus*, empty. In modern usage *vacuous* is not used where *empty* or *vacant* would be appropriate. An empty box or a vacant apartment cannot be described as vacuous. *Vacuous* usually applies to a figurative lack of content, meaning, or interest. We speak of vacuous eyes, a vacuous discussion, a vacuous mind, a vacuous remark, or a vacuous proposal.

Word 10: CAPACIOUS (kuh-PAY-shus)

Roomy, spacious, ample, able to contain or hold a great deal.

Capacious may be used either literally or figuratively. When used literally it is a synonym of *spacious* and *roomy*: a capacious house; their capacious office; an overcoat with capacious pockets. When used figuratively, it is a synonym of *broad* and *comprehensive*: a capacious intellect; a capacious embrace; a capacious view; a capacious treatment of a subject.

Let's review the ten keywords you've just learned. Consider the following questions and decide whether the correct answer is yes or no. Answers appear on page 261.

1. Could the takeover of a company by another company be described as a feat of corporate legerdemain?
2. Is a puerile remark likely to be taken seriously?
3. If three people are involved in a crime, could one be charged with the crime and the other two with complicity?
4. Can you transmute a thought into words?
5. Is abstruse writing clear and easy to understand?
6. Can eating well and getting enough sleep edify you?
7. Could a supercilious gesture also be described as puerile?
8. If you dissemble the truth, do you explain or reveal it?
9. Is a vacuous look an interested or intense look?
10. Can a capacious room and a capacious memory both hold many things?

Because your mind is capacious and not vacuous, I think you'll find the next ten keywords in Level 6 edifying and not abstruse. Here they are:

Word 11: MNEMONIC (ni-MAHN-ik)

Helping or pertaining to the memory, assisting or improving the ability to recall.

The odd spelling of *mnemonic*, with its initial *mn*, comes from Greek. Ultimately, *mnemonic* comes from a Greek verb meaning to remember, and by derivation means "mindful." In Greek mythology, *Mnemosyne* (ni-MAHS-uh-nee) is the goddess of memory and the mother of the nine Muses who preside over literature, the arts, and the sciences.

The adjective *mnemonic* means assisting or pertaining to the memory. A mnemonic device is a memory aid, something that helps one to remember. For example, the old rhyme, "Thirty days hath September, April, June, and November" is a mnemonic device for remembering the number of days in a given month. The term *mnemonics* refers to any technique or system for improving the memory.

Now, if you can remember all that, you're doing well.

Word 12: SONOROUS (suh-NOR-us *or* SAHN-uh-rus)

Resonant; deep, full, and rich in sound; having, or capable of producing, a powerful, impressive sound: a sonorous voice; a sonorous speaker; the sonorous bells of a cathedral.

The pronunciation SAHN-uh-rus, with the accent on the first syllable, is a British import that began making its way into American speech in the late 1800s. The traditional American pronunciation is suh-NOR-us, with the stress on the second syllable. When it comes to American versus British pronunciation, my policy is that British speakers should use British pronunciations and American speakers should use American pronunciations. Perhaps indicating agreement with that dictum, the four leading current American dictionaries all list suh-NOR-us first. Nevertheless, it must be said that first-syllable stress in *sonorous* is more commonly heard today, and probably will prevail.

Word 13: ADMONISH (ad-MAHN-ish)

To warn or notify of a fault or error, especially in conduct or attitude; to criticize or reprove gently but earnestly.

Synonyms of *admonish* include *advise*, *counsel*, *caution*, *apprise* (uh-PRYZ, like *a prize*), *exhort* (eg- or ig-ZORT), and *expostulate* (ek-SPAHS-chuh-layt). The corresponding noun is *admonishment*, a gentle warning or mild criticism.

To *admonish* comes from the Latin verb *admonere*, to warn, remind; the word suggests putting someone in mind of something he has forgotten, done wrong, or disregarded by giving him a strong but gently expressed warning or reminder. You can admonish an employee for tardiness or for overlooking an error; you can admonish a small child to obey a rule; or you can admonish a friend who is working too hard to take it easy.

Word 14: PARADIGM (PAR-uh-dim *or* PAR-uh-dym)

An example, model, or pattern.

Paradigm, which gets its unusual spelling from Greek, is used of an example that serves to illustrate or explain something or that serves as a model or pattern. Scholars develop paradigms for their theories; a novel may be a paradigm of contemporary morality; an important experience can serve as a paradigm for evaluating later experiences; and the successful strategy of one corporation may be the paradigm for another corporation's plan to restructure itself and redefine its goals.

The corresponding adjective is *paradigmatic* (PAR-uh-dig-**MAT**-ik), which means exemplary, typical, serving as a model or pattern.

PAR-uh-dim is the original pronunciation, preferred by authorities of the eighteenth and nineteenth centuries. The alternative pronunciation PAR-uh-dym came along sometime before 1900 and appears to have originated in Britain; it is now preferred by most educated speakers on both sides of the Atlantic. Modern authorities and current dictionaries countenance both pronunciations, and you may say the word as you please.

Word 15: CIRCUITOUS (sur-KYOO-i-t<u>u</u>s)

Roundabout, indirect, not straightforward, following a roundabout and often extended course.

Challenging synonyms of *circuitous* include *devious*, *meandering* (mee-AN-dur-ing), *sinuous* (SIN-yoo-<u>u</u>s), *tortuous* (TOR-choo-<u>u</u>s), *serpentine* (SUR-pin-teen or -tyn), and *labyrinthine* (LAB-uh-**RIN**-thin), which means like a labyrinth or maze.

The adjective *circuitous* is formed by adding the suffix *-ous* to the familiar noun *circuit*. A circuit is a line or route that goes around and returns to where it started. Literally, *circuitous* means like a circuit, going around, following a roundabout and often lengthy course: "They took a circuitous route to avoid traffic"; "His argument was circuitous, going round and round and never getting to the point"; "Looking back on her career, Pamela realized that her path to success had been circuitous."

Word 16: VINDICATE (VIN-di-kayt)

To clear from blame, free from suspicion of wrongdoing or dishonor, uphold or maintain the truth or innocence of something or someone in the face of criticism or imputations of guilt.

If you are accused of something but later the charge is dropped, then you have been vindicated. You can vindicate your good name or your reputation by clearing it from blame or suspicion. You can also vindicate a claim of ownership or your right to something by defending or upholding the truth of it.

The corresponding noun is *vindication*: "In a civil lawsuit, the plaintiff seeks restitution for an alleged wrong, and the defendant seeks vindication from the charges."

To *vindicate*, to *exonerate* (eg- or ig-ZAHN-ur-ayt), and to *acquit* all mean to free from blame. *Acquit* refers specifically to a judicial decision to release someone from a charge. *Exonerate* implies removing the burden of guilt for a wrongdoing that may or may not have been committed. *Vindicate* means to clear from blame, criticism, or suspicion of guilt by bringing forth evidence and proving the unfairness of the charge. Someone may be acquitted by a jury and exonerated by his family and friends, but never vindicated in the eyes of the community.

Word 17: BUCOLIC (byoo-KAHL-ik)

Rural, rustic, of or pertaining to country life.

Synonyms of *bucolic* include *pastoral* (PAS-tur-ul, be sure to stress the first syllable), *provincial* (pruh-VIN-shul), *agrarian* (uh-GRAIR-ee-in), *idyllic* (eye-DIL-ik), and *Arcadian* (ahr-KAY-dee-in). Antonyms include *urban*, *municipal*, *civic*, *metropolitan*, and *cosmopolitan*.

Bucolic comes from Latin and Greek words meaning a herdsman, shepherd, which in turn come from the Greek *bous*, an ox. *Bucolic* may mean either *pastoral*, pertaining to shepherds, or *rustic*, pertaining to farming and country life. Bucolic poetry is poetry about the country or country folk; bucolic scenery is rural or rustic scenery. Sometimes *bucolic* is used in a depreciatory sense to poke fun at people who live in the country. When supercilious city dwellers speak of bucolic manners or bucolic customs, they mean to imply that those manners or customs are crude or unsophisticated.

Word 18: OSTRACIZE (AHS-truh-syz)

To banish, send into exile, expel from a place; to bar, exclude, or reject from a group or from acceptance by society: "His questionable conduct led to his being ostracized by the other members of his profession"; "After the embarrassing incident her friends began to avoid her, and eventually they ostracized her from their social life."

The verb to *ostracize*, the corresponding noun *ostracism* (AHS-truh-siz-'m), and the related word *petalism* (PET-'l-iz-'m) share an interesting history. Ostracism and petalism were forms of banishment employed by the ancient Greeks. *Ostracize* and *ostracism* come from the Greek *ostrakon*, a potsherd, a piece of broken pottery. Ostracism was practiced by the ancient Athenians as a way of removing from the city people considered dangerous or embarrassing to the state. Citizens would vote by writing the name of the person to be expelled on a potsherd (PAHT-shurd) or earthenware tablet. Banishment was for a period of ten years, after which time the person was considered vindicated and free to return.

Petalism was a similar mode of expulsion practiced in ancient Syracuse. Petalism differed from ostracism only in the method of voting, which was done by writing on an olive leaf instead of on a piece of clay, and in the length of the exile, which was for five instead of ten years. The *Century Dictionary* (1914) notes that petalism was eventually repealed "on account of its deterring the best citizens from participating in public affairs."

Word 19: PLETHORA (PLETH-uh-ruh)

An excess, surplus, overabundance, oversupply.

Synonyms of *plethora* include *superabundance*, *profusion*, *superfluity* (SOO-pur-**FLOO**-i-tee), and *surfeit* (SUR-fit).

Antonyms of *plethora* include *scarcity*, *insufficiency*, *dearth* (word 12 of Level 3), and *paucity* (PAW-si-tee): "The worst kind of boss is the one who offers a plethora of advice and a paucity of assistance."

Plethora comes from the Greek *plethein*, to be full. In medicine the word is used to mean an excess of blood in the body; in general usage *plethora* may refer to any excess, surplus, or overabundance: "This report contains a plethora of dull statistics." "Throughout her career she was blessed with a plethora of opportunities." "American consumers no longer give the bulk of their business to small, specialized retailers, but instead prefer to shop at superstores that offer a plethora of merchandise at discount prices."

Plethora is the noun; the corresponding adjective is *plethoric* (ple-THOR-ik). A plethoric harvest is an overabundant harvest, a bumper crop. Plethoric wealth is excessive wealth. Plethoric writing is verbose, inflated writing; it overflows with words or puffed-up self-importance. When used of language, *plethoric* is synonymous with the words *bombastic* (bahm-BAS-tik) and *turgid* (TUR-jid).

Plethora is sometimes mispronounced with the stress on the second syllable, ple-THOR-uh. Dictionaries do not recognize this variant. Be sure to stress the first syllable: PLETH-uh-ruh.

Word 20: PROCLIVITY (pro-KLIV-i-tee *or* proh-)

An inclination, liking, leaning; a strong natural bent or tendency, often toward something disagreeable, objectionable, or wicked.

Synonyms of *proclivity* include *partiality* (PAR-shee-**AL**-i-tee), *penchant* (PEN-chint, word 9 of Level 3), *predisposition*, *predilection* (PRED-i-**LEK**-shin), and *propensity* (pro-PEN-si-tee).

By derivation *proclivity* means a sloping forward or downward; hence, a leaning, tendency, or inclination. In current usage the word may have a neutral connotation, as a proclivity to study, a proclivity for music. More often, however, *propensity* is used in this neutral sense, and *proclivity* usually suggests a strong natural bent or inclination toward something bad or wrong. For example, a person may have a proclivity for drinking or gambling, a proclivity to lie, or antisocial proclivities.

Let's review the ten keywords you've just learned. Consider the following statements and decide whether each one is true or false. Answers appear on page 262.

1. A mnemonic device helps you remember something.
2. The squeak of a mouse or the squeal of a pig is a sonorous noise.
3. It's illegal to admonish a child.
4. The United States has served as a paradigm for many later democracies.
5. When you take a circuitous route, you proceed in a roundabout manner.
6. A person who feels vindicated feels wrongfully blamed for something.
7. A bucolic lifestyle is an unwholesome lifestyle.
8. Most people would consider it a great honor to be ostracized.
9. When you have a plethora of food, you don't have enough.
10. Some people's proclivities are difficult to tolerate.

Did you remember to keep track of your answers and calculate your score? If you answered eight or more questions correctly, you may continue with Level 6. Otherwise, reread the last ten keyword discussions.

It's Greek to Thee

If some of the words I've talked about so far in this level sound like Greek to you, that's because they are! In fact, some of the most delightful words in the English language are derived from Greek, and particularly from Greek names.

One of my all-time favorites is *Procrustean* (pro-KRUHS-tee-in). Procrustes (pro-KRUHS-teez) was a robber of Attica, says the *Century Dictionary* (1914), "who tortured his victims by placing them on a certain bed, and stretching them or lopping off their legs to adapt the body to its length." Many were maimed upon Procrustes' bed until the Greek hero Theseus (THEE-syoos) tied the old bugger to his own bedposts for a permanent snooze. Today *Procrustean* means producing conformity by cruel or violent means, and to place someone on a Procrustean bed is to use ruthless measures to make him conform.

No less murderous in his manner of making people toe the line was Draco (DRAY-koh), a statesman of Athens whose legendary code of laws was unquestionably Procrustean. Draco "prescribed the penalty of death for nearly all crimes," says the *Century*, "for smaller crimes because they merited it, and for greater because he knew of no penalty more severe." From this arbitrary administrator of Attic justice comes the word *draconian* (dra-KOH-nee-in), meaning ruthlessly severe.

A more pleasant influence on the language was exercised by the philospher Epicurus (EP-i-**KYUUR**-us), the source of the word *epicurean* (EP-i-**KYUUR**-ee-in or EP-i-kyuu-**REE**-in). According to the *Century Dictionary*, Epicurus held that "pleasure is the only possible end of rational action, and the ultimate pleasure is freedom from disturbance." Although Epicurus has come to be thought of as a votary (VOH-tuh-ree—do you need to look it up?) of unrestrained indulgence, in a strict sense *epicureanism* (main stress on -*cure*- or on -*re*-) is distinguished from *hedonism* (HEE-duh-niz-'m), which in common parlance (PAHR-lunts) means living for the moment. Epicurus advocated the renunciation of momentary pleasures in favor of more permanent ones, and his *summum bonum* (SUUM-um BOH-num), or greatest good, was the pursuit of pleasure through the practice of virtue. The word *epicure* (EP-i-kyoor), once used disparagingly of one devoted to sensual pleasure, is today used to describe a person with fastidious tastes, especially in food or wine.

Ancient Greece was also home to Pyrrho (PIR-oh), one of the great skeptic philosophers. His doctrine, says the *Century*, "was that there is just as much to be said for as against any opinion whatever; that neither the senses nor the reason are to be trusted in the least; and that when we are once convinced we can know nothing, we cease to care, and in this way alone can attain happiness. It is said that Pyrrho would take no ordinary practical precautions, such as getting out of the way of vehicles." In modern English, *Pyrrhonism* (PIR-uh-niz-'m) means absolute skepticism, universal doubt, and a *Pyrrhonist* (PIR-uh-nist) is a person who doubts everything.

English has also gained some gems from the geography of ancient Greece. The rural region of Boeotia (bee-OH-shuh), says the *Century*, was known for its torpid climate, which was "supposed to communicate its dullness to the intellect of the inhabitants." Although three of Greece's greatest men of letters—Hesiod (HEE-see-id), Pindar (PIN-dur), and Plutarch (PLOO-tahrk)—were native Boeotians, Athenian city slickers reveled in reviling these bucolic folk. Today the noun *Boeotian* (bee-OH-shin, like *be ocean*) means a dull, ignorant person, and the adjective *Boeotian* means stupid, boring, obtuse. According to Brewer's *Dictionary of Phrase and Fable*, *Boeotian ears* are "ears unable to appreciate music or rhetoric."

The supercilious Athenians also disparaged the inhabitants of Arcadia (ahr-KAY-dee-uh) and Soloi (SOH-loy).

Like the Boeotians, the Arcadians were a pastoral people, fond of music and dancing. They were considered the least intellectual of all the Greeks. The Greek equivalent of the word *Arcadian* meant a shepherd or farmer, but it had the pejorative (pi-JOR-uh-tiv—is your dictionary handy?) connotation of simple-minded bumpkin. Arcadia's reputation has since been vindicated. Today the word *Arcadian* is a poetic or literary way of referring to the simplicity and innocence of rustic life.

Soloi was an ancient Greek colony in Cilicia (si-LISH-uh), Asia Minor, whose citizens were renowned for their horrible habits of speech. That they spoke a corrupt form of Attic—the Athenian dialect—probably only made things worse for them. The Greeks thought the people of Soloi rude, pushy, and foul-mouthed, and coined the word *soloikos* to mean speaking or acting like an inhabitant of Soloi—by extension, speaking incorrectly or behaving in an unrefined fashion. From the Greeks' bad-mouthing of these B.C. boors we inherit the word *solecism* (**SAHL**-uh-SIZ-'m), which usually means a gross grammatical error, but which may also denote a social impropriety, as when someone sneezes in your face or belches audibly in public.

Another city of Asia Minor, Laodicea (LAY-ah-di-**SEE**-uh), became infamous among early Christians for its lip service to the Lord. According to Brewer, the Laodiceans were "indifferent to religion, caring little or nothing about the matter." When it came to believing in a higher power, Laodiceans responded with a primal shrug. Today the word *Laodicean* (LAY-ah-di-**SEE**-in) may be used either as a noun to mean an indifferent or complacent person, or as an adjective to mean indifferent or lukewarm, especially in matters of religion.

Well, my Laodicean pupil, just think of all the solecisms you have already learned to avoid by reading *Verbal Advantage* and tell me that my edifying interlude on Hellenisms has fallen happily upon your Boeotian ears. And with that plethora of information on interesting words that have come to us from ancient Greece, let's return to the *Verbal Advantage* vocabulary for the next ten keywords in Level 6.

Word 21: COMMENSURATE (kuh-MEN-shur-it *also* kuh-MEN-sur-it)

Proportionate, corresponding in amount, measure, or degree; also, equal, of the same size or extent: "She wants to find a job commensurate with her abilities and experience"; "His paycheck was not commensurate with the number of hours he had worked."

By derivation *commensurate* means "measured together," and therefore corresponding or proportionate.

Word 22: INCESSANT (in-SES-int)

Constant, uninterrupted, continuous, unceasing.

Incessant combines the privative prefix *in-*, meaning "not," with the Latin *cessare*, to stop, cease, and means literally not ceasing, never-ending.

Synonyms of *incessant* include *interminable*, *relentless*, and *unremitting*. Antonyms of *incessant* include *occasional*, *irregular*, *intermittent*, *incidental*, *sporadic* (word 16 of Level 1), *fitful*, and *erratic*.

Dictionaries often list the words *continuous* and *continual* as synonyms, and today many educated speakers use them interchangeably. They are not interchangeable, however, and the ability to distinguish *continual* and *continuous* precisely is one sign of a careful user of the language. *Continual* means happening again and again at short intervals. We speak of continual reminders, continual attempts, continual laughter, or the continual ringing of the telephone. *Continuous* means uninterrupted or unbroken. We speak of continuous noise, continuous rain, a continuous effort, or the continuous rotation of the earth.

Continuous and *incessant* are close synonyms. The *Century Dictionary* (1914) explains that "*continuous* means unbroken, and is passive; *incessant* means unceasing, and is active." On one level that distinction is simple: we say a railroad track or telephone cable is continuous, not incessant, because tracks and cables are inactive. But on another level the distinction can be quite subtle and subjective. For example, we may say that a fever is continuous or incessant depending on whether we perceive it as a state or an activity. Similarly, the flow of a waterfall is continuous if viewed as a passive condition of a bucolic scene; it is incessant if looked upon as an active condition within that scene. The bland background music we typically hear in elevators, restaurants, and waiting rooms is continuous to those who don't mind it; but to those who are distracted or irritated by it, it's incessant, unceasing, constant, never-ending.

Word 23: SYCOPHANT (SIK-uh-f<u>u</u>nt; the last syllable, *-phant*, as in *elephant*)

A flatterer, parasite, toady, fawning follower, hanger-on.

No one knows the precise origin of the words *sycophant* and *toady*, but various theories and folk etymologies abound. According to most sources, the word *toady* is related to *toad*. As the etymologist Joseph T. Shipley recounts the story in his *Dictionary of Word Origins* (1945), the charlatans and mountebanks of medieval times usually traveled with an assistant who would swallow, or seem to swallow, a live toad, "so that the master could display his healing powers. These helpers were called *toad-eaters*; then the term came to mean a flattering follower," and "the word has been shortened to *toady*."

Sycophant is thought to come from a Greek word meaning to show figs. As the legend goes, the Athenians passed a law prohibiting the export of figs from their city. Like many laws, this one was rarely enforced, but "there were always found mean fellows," says Brewer's *Dictionary of Phrase and Fable*, "who, for their own private ends, impeached those who violated it; hence *sycophant* came to signify first a government toady, then a toady generally." Although by derivation *sycophant* means an informer, today the word refers to people who attempt to gain influence or advancement by ingratiating themselves through flattery and servility: "Joanne warned Lucy her first day on the job that Ralph and Diane were the office sycophants, always sucking up to the boss and stabbing people in the back."

The corresponding adjective is *sycophantic* (SIK-uh-**FAN**-tik).

Word 24: TANGENTIAL (tan-JEN-sh<u>u</u>l)

Not closely related, only slightly connected, digressive, divergent.

In geometry, the word *tangent* refers to a line that touches a curve but does not intersect it. When you "go off on a tangent" you make an abrupt change of course in what you are saying; you diverge, digress. *Tangential* may mean going off on a subject that is only slightly connected to the one under consideration, or it may mean slightly connected to or touching lightly on a subject. Tangential remarks diverge from the subject in question; they are only slightly connected to it. Tangential information touches lightly on the subject but is not closely related or essential to it.

Word 25: TENABLE (TEN-uh-buul)

Defensible, reasonable; able to be defended, maintained, or upheld.

Tenable comes from the Latin *tenere*, to hold, grasp. From the same source come the unusual noun *tenaculum* (te-NAK-yuu-lum), a pointed, hooked instrument used in surgery for lifting and holding parts, such as blood vessels, and the useful adjective *tenacious* (te-NAY-shus), which means holding firmly, as a tenacious grip or a tenacious memory.

Tenable means defensible, able to be maintained or upheld. The logic behind a course of action may be *tenable*, defensible, or *untenable*, indefensible. The legislature may pass a tenable law, one that can be upheld in the courts, or an untenable law, one that will be struck down. A tenable reason is a reason that can be defended, maintained, or upheld.

Word 26: IMPALPABLE (im-PAL-puh-buul)

Incapable of being felt or understood, not able to be perceived either by the sense of touch or by the mind.

Synonyms of *impalpable* include *untouchable*, *imperceptible*, and *intangible* (in-TAN-ji-buul). Antonyms include *palpable* (PAL-puh-buul), *perceptible*, *manifest*, and *tangible* (TAN-ji-buul).

The adjective *palpable* means capable of being touched or felt, easily perceived or discerned. *Palpable* may be used either literally, as a palpable pulse or palpable heat, or figuratively, as a palpable error or palpable desire.

Impalpable combines *palpable* with the privative prefix *im-*, meaning "not," and means not able to be felt or grasped, either with the fingers or by the mind. An impalpable pulse is a sign of heart failure; an impalpable breeze is so faint as to be imperceptible; an impalpable idea is not easily grasped by the mind.

Both *palpable* and *impalpable* come from the Latin *palpare*, to touch or stroke gently, the source also of the verb to *palpate* (PAL-payt). *Palpate* is used chiefly in medicine to mean to examine or explore by touch, as to palpate a limb or an organ. The corresponding noun is *palpation* (pal-PAY-shin), the act of palpating, examining by touch.

Word 27: ODIOUS (OH-dee-us)

Hateful, detestable, offensive, revolting, arousing strong dislike or aversion.

The English language has a plethora of words that mean hateful or offensive, so *odious* has many synonyms. Here is a selection of them, ranging from the familiar to the not-so-familiar: *disgusting*, *obnoxious*, *objectionable*, *disagreeable*, *contemptible*, *repellent*, *repugnant* (ri-PUHG-nint), *loathsome* (LOHTH-sum), *abominable*, *abhorrent* (ab-HOR-int), *heinous* (HAY-nis), *oppro-*

brious (uh-PROH-bree-<u>us</u>), *flagitious* (fluh-JISH-<u>us</u>, word 46 of Level 9), and last but not least, the thoroughly damning word *execrable* (EK-si-kruh-buul). By derivation *execrable* means expressing a curse, and today the word applies to that which is so horrible or wicked that it deserves to be cursed or damned.

Odious comes from the Latin *odiosus*, hateful, which in turn comes from *odium*, hatred, the direct source of the English noun *odium* (OH-dee-<u>um</u>). *Odium* and *hatred* are synonymous, but *odium* refers less frequently to hatred directed toward someone or something else and more often to hatred experienced or incurred: "Alan's supervisor was a supercilious, draconian tyrant who did not seem to care that her employees regarded her with odium."

The adjective *odious* refers either to that which arouses hate, disgust, or displeasure or to that which is regarded as hateful, detestable, or offensive. An odious remark is extremely unpleasant or offensive; an odious practice is a disagreeable or disgusting practice; an odious person is a person that others find hateful or detestable.

The corresponding noun *odiousness* means the state or quality of being odious, as the odiousness of the crime.

Be careful to distinguish *odious* from *odorous* both in spelling and usage. *Odorous* means emitting an odor, having a distinct aroma or smell. *Odious* means hateful, detestable, revolting. Odorous armpits or odorous garbage may be odious, but there is nothing odious, hateful or offensive, about odorous flowers.

Word 28: UBIQUITOUS (yoo-BIK-w<u>i</u>-t<u>us</u>)

Existing or seeming to exist everywhere at the same time.

Ubiquitous and *nonexistent* are antonyms. Synonyms of *ubiquitous* include *ever-present*, *universal*, *pervading*, and *omnipresent* (AHM-ni-**PREZ**-<u>i</u>nt). The corresponding noun is *ubiquity* (yoo-BIK-wi-tee), the state of being or seeming to be everywhere at once, omnipresence.

Ubiquitous comes from the Latin *ubique*, everywhere. Its closest synonym, *omnipresent*, links the combining form *omni-*, meaning "all," with *present* to mean present in all places at once.

Because few things other than the air we breathe can accurately be described as ubiquitous, existing everywhere at the same time, ubiquitous is often used to mean seeming to exist everywhere at once, extremely widespread. For example, when telephones and televisions first came on the market they were considered novelties and luxury items, but today we see them everywhere, so we could say they are ubiquitous. In George Orwell's classic novel *1984*, which depicts the horrors of life in a futuristic totalitarian state, the image of the dictator, Big Brother, and the slogan "Big Brother is watching you" are ubiquitous; they seem to be in all places at once.

Ubiquitous is also often used to achieve an exaggerated effect. For example, a writer might state that the cockroach is a ubiquitous insect, or that graffiti has become ubiquitous in a neighborhood, or that fast-food restaurant chains are now ubiquitous in our society. And if you ever have the experience of running across a certain person nearly everywhere you go, you could say that person is ubiquitous.

Word 29: RUMINATE (ROO-mi̱-nayt)

To turn over in the mind, think about again and again, consider carefully or at length.

Synonyms of *ruminate* include to *ponder*, *contemplate*, *meditate*, *deliberate*, *muse* (MYOOZ), *cogitate* (KAH-ji̱-tayt), and *mull* (rhymes with *dull*).

The etymology of the verb to *ruminate* may surprise you. It comes from the Latin *ruminare*, to chew the cud, and by derivation means to chew over and over again. In the science of zoology (which is properly pronounced zoh-AHL-uh-jee, *not* zoo-) the word *ruminant* (ROO-mi̱-ni̱nt) is used of animals that chew their cud, such as cows, oxen, sheep, goats, deer, giraffes, and camels. These ruminant creatures have multichambered stomachs, the first chamber of which is called the rumen (ROO-mi̱n). When a ruminant chews its cud, it is chewing food that has been swallowed, partially digested in the rumen, and then regurgitated into the mouth for thorough mastication. (As you may recall from Level 5, *mastication* means the act of chewing.) By a logical extension, the verb to *ruminate* has come to mean to chew the cud mentally, to regurgitate a thought and turn it over and over in the mind.

Just as we often say that we chew on something, we often say that we ruminate on something: "Aging athletes may ruminate on the triumphs of their youth"; "When John heard the rumor of impending layoffs, he went back to his office and ruminated on his future with the company."

Word 30: REMUNERATION (ri-**MYOO**-nuh-**RAY**-shi̱n)

Payment, compensation, or reward.

Remuneration is a suitable payment or reward for a service or something one has provided: "It is rare that the effort a writer expends in writing a book is commensurate with the remuneration received for writing it"; "When people volunteer their services for a cause, the satisfaction they get from doing something they believe in is more than enough remuneration"; "Mark took the job even though he knew the salary was not sufficient remuneration for the work he would have to do."

Synonyms of *remuneration* include *reimbursement*, *recompense* (**REK**-<u>u</u>m-PENTS), *consideration*, *indemnification* (in-DEM-nuh-fi-**KAY**-sh<u>i</u>n), and *emolument* (i-MAHL-yuh-m<u>i</u>nt, word 3 of Level 8).

The corresponding verb is *remunerate* (ri-MYOO-nuh-rayt), to pay or compensate for services rendered, trouble taken, or goods provided.

Let's review the ten keywords you've just learned. I'll give you two words, and you decide if they are synonyms or antonyms. Answers appear on page 263.

1. *Proportionate* and *commensurate* are . . . synonyms or antonyms?
2. *Incessant* and *intermittent* are . . .
3. *Sycophant* and *toady* are . . .
4. *Tangential* and *unrelated* are . . .
5. *Indefensible* and *tenable* are . . .
6. *Tangible* and *impalpable* are . . .
7. *Odious* and *detestable* are . . .
8. *Ubiquitous* and *nonexistent* are . . .
9. To *ruminate* and to *meditate* are . . .
10. *Compensation* and *remuneration* are . . .

If you answered fewer than eight of the questions correctly in this quiz, remember to review the keyword discussions before moving ahead in the program.

Now let's return to the *Verbal Advantage* vocabulary for the next ten keywords in Level 6.

Word 31: PECCADILLO (PEK-uh-**DIL**-oh)

A small sin, slight offense, minor fault or flaw.

Peccadillo means literally "a small sin." It comes through Spanish and Italian ultimately from the Latin *peccare*, to make a mistake, blunder, sin. From the same source English has also inherited three other useful words: *peccant*

(PEK-int), which means guilty, sinful, culpable; *peccable* (PEK-uh-buul), which means liable to sin or do wrong; and its antonym *impeccable* (word 40 of Level 4), which means incapable of sin, unable to do wrong, and therefore free from all faults or imperfections.

Synonyms of *peccadillo* include *failing*, *frailty*, and *foible* (word 23 of Level 3). All these words suggest a weakness, imperfection, or defect of character or habit. *Failing* implies a relatively minor but noticeable shortcoming: Parents are never perfect; all have their failings. *Frailty* implies a weakness that can be exploited or that leads one to yield to temptation: Frailties are an inescapable part of human nature. *Foible* suggests a harmless or trivial weakness or flaw that can be easily overlooked: You may regret your failings and try to keep your frailties in check, but you can laugh about your foibles. Our keyword, *peccadillo*, is a small sin or slight offense that is easily forgiven: A good manager knows how to distinguish between an employee who commits peccadilloes and an employee who causes problems.

The plural of *peccadillo* is *peccadilloes*, which is preferred by most American authorities and listed first in American dictionaries, or *peccadillos*, the British preference.

Word 32: SUPINE (soo-PYN, like *sue pine*)

Lying down on the back, with the face turned upward: "He preferred to sleep in a supine position."

Supine, *prone*, *prostrate* (PRAHS-trayt), and *recumbent* (ri-KUHM-bent) all mean lying down in various ways.

Supine takes its meaning directly from the Latin *supinus*, lying on the back with the face up.

From the Latin *pronus*, leaning forward, we inherit the word *prone*, which may mean inclined or tending toward something, as in the phrase "prone to error," or it may mean lying on the belly, stretched out face downward: "The dog lay prone on the rug, its chin resting on its paws."

Prostrate means lying flat, stretched out, either prone or supine. Because the word comes from the Latin *prosternere*, to throw down in front, cast down, in modern usage *prostrate* denotes lying down flat either as the result of physical or emotional exhaustion, or as an expression of submission, humble adoration, humiliation, or helplessness.

Be careful not to confuse *prostrate* with *prostate* (PRAHS-tayt), the gland in men that contributes to the production of semen and helps control urination. After age forty, men should have regular checkups for prostate cancer, not prostrate cancer.

Recumbent comes from the Latin *recumbere*, to lie back, recline. When you are recumbent you are lying down in a comfortable position, usually supine or on your side: The ancient Greeks and Romans assumed a recumbent posture when taking their meals. Visit any art museum and you are likely to see a portrait of a recumbent nude.

Word 33: BANAL (BAY-nul *or* buh-NAL)

Common, ordinary, unoriginal; flat, dull, and predictable; lacking freshness or zest.

Synonyms of *banal* include *trite*, *commonplace*, *conventional*, *humdrum*, *hackneyed*, *shopworn*, *stereotyped*, *insipid* (in-SIP-id), *vapid* (rhymes with *rapid*), and *bromidic* (bro-MID-ik), which means like a *bromide* (BROH-myd), a statement or idea that is stale and dull.

Antonyms of *banal* include *creative*, *imaginative*, *unconventional*, *unorthodox*, *ingenious*, *innovative*, *novel*, and *pithy* (PITH-ee).

Banal, which came into English from French in the mid-eighteenth century, originally referred to the facilities shared in common by the serfs and tenants of a feudal manor—such as the mill, the ovens, and the wine-press. In this now obsolete sense, *banal* meant "shared by all; used by the whole community." From this notion of commonality, *banal* soon came to be used as a synonym of *common* in its sense of ordinary and unoriginal. Today *banal* is used of anything that is flat, dull, and predictable, that lacks freshness or zest: a television show, a song, a book, a movie, a remark, a conversation, a desire, a relationship, and even a person can be described as banal. When you consider how many things in this world are dull, ordinary, and unoriginal, *banal* suddenly becomes a useful word to add to your vocabulary.

Most educated American speakers pronounce *banal* either BAY-nal (rhymes with *anal*) or buh-NAL (rhymes with *canal*). The variant buh-NAHL, the British preference, is less frequently heard in American speech. The variant BAN-ul (rhymes with *channel*), preferred by several older authorities, is nearly obsolete.

The corresponding noun is *banality* (buh-NAL-i-tee), which means the quality or state of being common, ordinary, and unoriginal, as the banality of prime-time TV, or the banality of workaday life.

Word 34: HETERODOX (HET-ur-uh-dahks)

Having or expressing an opinion different from the accepted opinion; not in agreement with established doctrine or belief.

As you may recall from the discussion of *heterogeneous*, keyword 6 of Level 3, the prefix *hetero-* means other, different, unlike: *heterosexual* means attracted to the other sex; *heterogeneous* means consisting of different elements or kinds, diverse; and *heterodox* means having another opinion or different beliefs.

The *-dox* in *heterodox* comes from the Greek *doxa*, an opinion, which in turn comes from the verb *dokein*, to think. From the same source come the rare English words *doxy* (DAHK-see), an opinion or doctrine, especially a religious opinion, and *doxastic* (dahk-SAS-tik), which means pertaining to opinion or to the formation of an opinion. I wouldn't expect you to know those unusual words, but you may be familiar with *doxology* (dahk-SAHL-uh-jee), which combines the Greek *doxa*, opinion, with the verb *legein*, to speak. *Doxology* is used in Christian worship to mean an expression of praise to God, usually in the form of a brief hymn or chant.

The antonym of *heterodox* is *orthodox*, agreeing with established opinion, adhering to accepted beliefs. A heterodox custom or a heterodox view goes against the prevailing norm; an orthodox custom or view is considered proper or correct.

The prefix *ortho-* means right, upright, proper, or correct. *Ortho-* appears in a number of useful English words. *Orthodontics* (OR-thuh-**DAHN**-tiks) is the dental specialty of correcting irregularities of the teeth. *Orthoscopic* (OR-thuh-**SKAHP**-ik) means having normal or correct vision. *Orthography* (or-THAHG-ruh-fee), which comes from *ortho-*, right, correct, and the Greek verb *graphein*, to write, means correct spelling; an orthographic (OR-thuh-**GRAF**-ik) error is a misspelled word or typographical mistake. Finally, the word *orthoepy* (OR-thoh-uh-pee or or-THOH-uh-pee or **OR**-thoh-EP-ee), which comes from *ortho-* and the Greek *epos*, meaning "word," refers to the study of the proper pronunciation of words. By the way, did you notice that there are no fewer than *three* acceptable pronunciations of *orthoepy*? It just goes to show you that when it comes to pronunciation, even the experts don't always agree. But that still doesn't mean you should embrace heterodox pronunciations, ones different from those acceptable to most educated speakers.

The adjectives *heterodox* and *heretical* (huh-RET-i-kul) both mean having or expressing a controversial opinion or belief, but the words differ in their intensity. *Heterodox* applies to that which differs in a way that does not necessarily challenge or threaten the norm. *Heretical* applies to that which differs from the norm in a way perceived as dangerously false, subversive, or evil.

The corresponding noun is *heterodoxy* (**HET**-ur-uh-DAHK-see), an opinion or belief contrary to what is accepted and established.

Word 35: GRANDILOQUENT (gran-DIL-uh-kwint)

Characterized by lofty, high-flown language; full of grand or high-sounding words.

Synonyms of *grandiloquent* include *bombastic* (bahm-BAS-tik, word 8 of Level 7), *grandiose* (GRAN-dee-ohs), *florid* (FLOR-id), and *turgid* (TUR-jid). All these words suggest speech or writing that is inflated, affected, or extravagant.

Antonyms of *grandiloquent* include *plain-spoken*, *forthright*, *unaffected*, and *candid*.

Grandiloquent combines the word *grand* with the suffix *-iloquent*, which comes from the Latin *loqui*, meaning "to speak." By derivation, *grandiloquent* means "speaking in a grand manner." The Latin *loqui* is also the source of *loquacious*, talkative, and *colloquial* (word 43 of Level 3), which means pertaining to informal speech or conversation.

Believe it or not, the English language has more than twenty words that incorporate the suffix *-iloquent* and designate different ways of speaking. Of course, most of them reside quietly in the depths of unabridged dictionaries and are rarely used, but here are a few you may find useful: *Magniloquent* (mag-NIL-uh-kwint) comes from the Latin *magnus*, meaning "great, large," and means speaking pompously, using grand or high-flown language. *Magniloquent* and *grandiloquent* are virtually interchangeable. From the Latin *multus*, meaning "many" or "much," comes *multiloquent* (muhl-TIL-uh-kwint), using many words, talking up a storm; and from the Latin *brevis*, meaning "short," comes the word *breviloquent* (bre-VIL-uh-kwint), speaking briefly.

When you speak in an urbane, sophisticated manner, you are *suaviloquent* (swah-VIL-uh-kwint). When you speak like a scholar or an expert on some subject, you are *doctiloquent*. When you speak solemnly or of sacred matters, you are *sanctiloquent* (sang-TIL-uh-kwint). And if you talk in your sleep, you are *somniloquent* (sahm-NIL-uh-kwint).

Word 36: LUGUBRIOUS (luh-GOO-bree-us)

Mournful and gloomy; expressing sadness or sorrow, often in an exaggerated, affected, or ridiculous way.

Synonyms of *lugubrious* include *dismal*, *melancholy*, *dreary*, *funereal* (fyoo-NEER-ee-ul), *doleful*, *dolorous* (DOH-luh-rus), *disconsolate* (dis-KAHN-suh-lit), *plaintive* (PLAYN-tiv), *woeful*, *lachrymose* (LAK-ri-mohs), and *saturnine* (SAT-ur-nyn).

Antonyms of *lugubrious* include *cheerful*, *jubilant*, *joyous*, *gleeful*, *mirthful*, *jovial* (word 19 of Level 5), and *sanguine* (SANG-gwin, word 21 of Level 10).

Lugubrious comes ultimately from the Latin *lugere*, to mourn or lament. The word was coined about 1600 and was at first merely a grandiloquent synonym for *mournful* and *sorrowful*. By the 1800s, however, it had come to suggest mournful, dismal, or gloomy in an exaggerated, affected, or ridiculous way.

According to the second edition of *Webster's New International Dictionary* (1934), the words *lugubrious* and *doleful* "have weakened from their original meaning, and are often used with a half-humorous connotation." For example, *lugubrious* music is mournful or gloomy to an extreme; the expression "Woe is me" is now a lugubrious cliché; the mournful howling of a dog may be lugubrious; and if the expression on a person's face is lugubrious, it is sad or sorrowful in an affected, almost ludicrous way. The corresponding noun is *lugubriousness*; the adverb is *lugubriously*, as "He spoke lugubriously about the company's financial condition."

Word 37: INFINITESIMAL (IN-fin-i-**TES**-i-mul)

Too small to be measured or calculated.

Synonyms of *infinitesimal* include *tiny*, *minute*, *microscopic*, and *minuscule*. And speaking of *minuscule*—and strictly speaking—this word is traditionally and properly pronounced with the stress on the second syllable: mi-NUHS-kyool. The pronunciation **MIN**-uh-SKYOOL, now common among educated speakers, probably came about as a result of the persistent misspelling of the word as *miniscule*, as though it began with the prefix *mini-*. This misspelling is now so widespread that most current dictionaries list it as a variant without comment, and many also give priority to the pronunciation with first-syllable stress. I would argue, however, that the alternative spelling and pronunciation not only are at variance with the word's history but are also, quite frankly, idiotic.

Minuscule comes from the Latin *minusculus* (stress on *-nus-*), somewhat small. Look in any dictionary and you will see that the noun *minuscule* refers to a small, cursive script used in medieval manuscripts. From that sense it came to denote either a small or lowercase letter or something printed in lowercase letters. The adjective *minuscule* originally meant pertaining to that small medieval script or consisting of small letters; its antonym in this sense is *majuscule* (muh-JUHS-kyool), which means written in capital letters. By natural extension *minuscule* also came to mean tiny, very small.

Our misspellings often mimic our mispronunciations, and in this case the evidence suggests that *minuscule*—probably from association with the words *minimum*, *minimal*, and *miniature*—came to be mispronounced **MIN**-uh-SKYOOL and then later misspelled with the prefix *mini-*, which means small.

Today the variant **MIN**-uh-SKYOOL is so popular that I can't in good conscience tell you that it's wrong, but I can at least admonish and implore you to spell the word properly. There is no *mini-* in *minuscule*, and even if you choose to say **MIN**-uh-SKYOOL, for goodness' sake remember that when you write the word it should be spelled like *minus* plus *-cule*.

Well, now that we've straightened out that *minuscule* but not insignificant point of usage, I'm afraid that we've lost track of our keyword, *infinitesimal*. Of course, that's not surprising because this rather large, thirteen-letter word means infinitely small and applies to that which is smaller than you can imagine. Unlike the words *tiny*, *minute*, and *minuscule*, which simply mean very small, and unlike *microscopic*, which means too small to be seen without a microscrope, *infinitesimal* is smaller still, and means specifically too small to be measured or calculated.

Occasionally you will come across a writer or speaker who is unaware of the specific meaning of *infinitesimal* and who uses it loosely. For example, in your local newspaper you might see a sentence like this: "Scientists detected an infinitesimal amount of mercury and lead in the city's tap water." Because *infinitesimal* properly applies to that which is too small to be measured or even detected, that sentence should read like this: "In a test of the city's tap water, scientists determined that if mercury and lead were present, the amounts were infinitesimal."

Word 38: GOAD (GOHD, rhymes with *road*)

To prod or urge to action, stimulate, arouse, stir up.

Synonyms of the verb to *goad* include to *egg on*, *spur*, incite, *impel*, and *instigate* (**IN**-sti-GAYT). Antonyms of *goad* include soothe, *pacify*, *appease*, *assuage* (uh-SWAYJ, word 37 of Level 2), and *mollify* (**MAHL**-uh-FY).

The noun a *goad* is a pointed stick used to prod animals and get them to move. From that sense *goad* also came to mean a stimulus, spur, incitement, anything that urges or drives something on. The verb to *goad* literally means to prick and drive with a goad; hence, to prod or urge to action. Someone can goad you to work harder, goad you to admit a fault or mistake, or goad you to the point of irritation or anger. In *Measure for Measure*, Shakespeare writes, "Most dangerous is that temptation that doth goad us on. . . ."

Word 39: MALINGER (muh-LING-gur)

To pretend to be sick or incapacitated so as to avoid work or duty; to shirk or dodge responsibility by feigning illness or inability.

Don't be misled by the presence of the word *linger* in *malinger*. Despite what some people mistakenly believe, to *malinger* does not mean to linger, loiter, or hang around in a shiftless or threatening way. Although you might hear or read about "drug pushers malingering near schoolyards" or "homeless people malingering downtown," don't believe it. Those people may be loitering, but they are definitely not malingering, for *malinger* means to pretend to be sick or incapacitated so as to avoid work or duty.

The verb to *malinger* comes from a French word meaning sickly, ailing, infirm, and is apparently related to the word *malady* (MAL-uh-dee), which means an illness or affliction. The corresponding noun is *malingerer* (muh-LING-gur-ur), a person who malingers.

When *malinger* and *malingerer* entered English in the early 1800s, they were used of soldiers and sailors who shirked their duty by pretending to be sick. Of course, malingering is popular among the entire workforce, not just members of the military, so it wasn't long before *malinger* and *malingerer* came to be used of anyone who dodges work or responsibility by feigning illness or inability.

Word 40: AVER (uh-VUR)

To state positively, declare with confidence.

Synonyms of the verb to *aver* include *assert*, *affirm*, *avow*, *profess*, *contend*, and *asseverate*.

To *state* means to express something in an explicit and usually formal manner. You state your answer or state your opinion. To *declare* means to state publicly or out loud, sometimes in the face of opposition. You declare your intentions, declare your position, or declare your independence. To *assert* means to declare forcefully or boldly, either with or without proof. You assert a belief or assert your rights. To *asseverate* means to declare in a solemn, earnest manner. Lawyers asseverate their claims in court, professors asseverate their theories from a lectern, and preachers asseverate their spiritual advice from the pulpit. To *affirm* means to state with conviction, declare as a fact based on one's knowledge or experience. You can affirm the truth, affirm your presence, or affirm the existence of something. Our keyword, to *aver*, means to state positively and decisively, with complete confidence that what one says is true. You can aver that you have never disobeyed the law; you can aver that you have always paid all your taxes on time; you can aver that you have never used alcohol or drugs; and you can aver that there is life on the planet Mars. Of course, if you aver all that, then other people probably will aver that you are either lying or off your nut, so it's always wise to watch what you *aver*, state positively, declare with confidence.

Let's review the last ten keywords by playing "One of These Definitions Doesn't Fit the Word." In each statement below, a keyword (in *italics*) is followed by three definitions. Two of the three are correct; one is unrelated in meaning. Decide which definition doesn't fit the keyword. Answers appear on page 263.

1. A *peccadillo* is a small sin, small oversight, slight offense.
2. *Supine* means lying on the back, lying faceup, lying prone.
3. *Banal* means inappropriate, unoriginal, ordinary.
4. *Heterodox* means having an unaccepted opinion, having an unconventional opinion, having an unreasonable opinion.
5. *Grandiloquent* means high-minded, high-sounding, high-flown.
6. *Lugubrious* means mournful, gloomy, grotesque.
7. *Infinitesimal* means tiny, invisible, minute.
8. To *goad* means to order, urge, prod.
9. To *malinger* means to pretend to be sick, avoid work or duty, hang around aimlessly.
10. To *aver* means to state positively, promise earnestly, declare confidently.

Some Pointed Remarks About Usage

And now, at this particular point in time, I'd like to take a break from the *Verbal Advantage* vocabulary to discuss several important questions of usage.

Hold on a minute! Did your verbally advantaged ear catch anything unseemly or untoward in that last sentence? (By the way, *untoward*, pronounced uhn-TORD, means improper or inappropriate.) Did you find anything objectionable or erroneous? (*Erroneous*, pronounced i-ROH-nee-us, means wrong, mistaken, based on error.)

As you may already have guessed, the boo-boo occurs right off the bat in the phrase "and now, at this particular point in time." That major Bozo no-no has the dubious distinction of being not only outrageously verbose but also a triple redundancy.

In the second edition of the *Harper Dictionary of Contemporary Usage* (1985), William and Mary Morris astutely point out that during the Watergate investigation in the 1970s, "the phrase *at that point in time*, used by numerous witnesses before the committee, became an instant cliché. Although used in seriousness by those testifying, it was mocked by the public."

People in the 1970s may have mocked the phrase *at that point in time*, but time passes, memories fade, and by the 1990s this redundancy had become part of the national vocabulary. Today you will hear educated speakers everywhere say "at the present time," "at this point in time," and "at this particular point in time" when what they mean and what they should say is "at present," "at this point," "at this time," or simply "now."

And now—not "at this point in time," but *now*—let's take a look at some commonly confused words. First, let's make sure you recall the distinction between *continual* and *continuous*, which we discussed earlier under *incessant* (word 22 of this level). One means happening again and again at short intervals; the other means uninterrupted, unceasing. Do you remember which means which? *Continuous* implies an uninterrupted state or activity; *continual* means occurring over and over at short intervals: "Education is a continuous, lifelong process." "He finally gave in to their continual demands." "His continual interruptions gave her a continuous headache."

At the beginning of this level we also discussed the word *puerile* (keyword 2). Do you remember what it means? Does it mean childish or childlike—or both? No, it doesn't mean both, because careful speakers and writers distinguish between *childish*, which means immature, silly, foolish, and *childlike*, which means simply like a child, characteristic of a child. *Childlike* suggests the favorable qualities of childhood, such as innocence and trust, whereas *childish* suggests the negative qualities, such as silliness and stubborness. *Childish* and *puerile* are synonyms.

Now, what about the difference between *immigrate* (**IM**-i-GRAYT) and *emigrate* (**EM**-i-GRAYT)? Do they both mean to leave a country and settle in another? Yes, they do, but they differ in their emphasis and direction. The *im-* in *immigrate* means "into," and the word means literally to go into a new country, migrate in. The initial *e-* in emigrate is short for *ex-*, which means "out"; to *emigrate* means to leave or go out of one's country, migrate out. *Immigrate* is followed by the preposition *to*. You *immigrate to* a country, go into it to resettle. *Emigrate* is followed by the preposition *from*. You *emigrate from* a country, go out of it, leave it to settle in another. When you emigrate from your native country you immigrate to another. An *emigrant* is a person who emigrates from his native country to another country; he immigrates to the country in which he will resettle. When the emigrant settles in a new country, he becomes an immigrant to it.

Our last pair of commonly confused words is *eminent* (EM-i-nent) and *imminent* (IM-i-nent). The trouble begins with their pronunciation: *imminent* begins with *im-*, like *immigrate* and *imitate*. *Eminent* begins with *em-*, like *emigrate* and *emulate*. Be sure to clearly say *im*minent and *em*inent. Now for their meanings. *Imminent* means about to happen, impending; an imminent event is about to happen; it's threatening to occur. *Eminent* implies loftiness, superiority, or distinction. An eminent person is renowned, distinguished, superior to others; eminent deeds rise above average deeds, and therefore are remarkable, noteworthy; the right of eminent domain refers to the superior right of government to take over private property for public use.

Now—and by that I mean *now,* not "at this point in time"— let's clarify the meanings and proper application of three commonly misused words: *transpire* (tran-SPYR), *condone* (kun-DOHN), and *promiscuous* (pruh-MIS-kyoo-us).

You have probably often heard *transpire* used as a synonym of *happen* or *occur,* as in "He wondered what would transpire next," or "They told us what had transpired while we were gone." This usage, though widespread, is unacceptable to many careful writers and speakers who know the precise meaning of the word. Since the mid-eighteenth century *transpire* has meant to leak out, become known, come to light, pass from secrecy into common knowledge. When you ask "What transpired while I was gone?" you are not asking what happened but rather what became known, what came to light. When you say the newspaper story described all that transpired, you are not saying merely that it told what happened but rather what passed from secrecy into public knowledge.

This precise meaning of *transpire* is useful and should be protected. *Transpire* used as a synonym for *happen* is pretentious. Save *transpire* for when you mean to pass from secrecy into knowledge, come to light, become known: "When the facts about the Watergate scandal transpired, the public realized that the phrase 'at that point in time' was just an equivocal and pompous way of saying 'now.'"

And now let's consider the word *condone.* How would you use the word? Can you think of a synonym for it? Recently *condone* has come to be used as a synonym for *approve* or *accept,* when the proper meaning of the word is to excuse, pardon, forgive, overlook a fault or offense. Properly, when you condone what someone says you pardon or forgive it, and when you condone someone's behavior, you excuse or overlook it.

And now let's undress the word *promiscuous.* In recent years it has been used to mean having sexual relations with numerous partners, and now many people think that is the only meaning of the word. That is not the case, however; the traditional and precise meaning of *promiscuous* is indiscriminate, unselective, haphazard. This narrowing of the meaning of *promiscuous* to apply only to a lack of discrimination in sexual relations is a result of dropping the modifier "sexually" from the phrase "sexually promiscuous." *Sexually promiscuous* means indiscriminate in one's choice of sexual partners. But *promiscuous* by itself has no inherent sexual connotation; it simply means characterized by a lack of discrimination or careful selection. One's choice of friends, one's taste in food, or one's career decisions all can be promiscuous, indiscriminate, haphazard.

Promiscuous is a close synonym of *miscellaneous*. Whereas *miscellaneous* suggests a throwing together of different kinds, *promiscuous* suggests a complete lack of arrangement and selection. Both a miscellaneous collection and a promiscuous collection are varied, composed of different elements. A miscellaneous collection, however, may be well-organized. A promiscuous collection is put together randomly, with no thought for selection or arrangement.

And with that somewhat promiscuous assortment of information on usage, at this point in time . . . just kidding! Now let's return to the *Verbal Advantage* vocabulary for the final ten keywords of Level 6.

Word 41: CACOPHONY (kuh-KAHF-uh-nee)

A harsh, jarring sound, especially a harsh and unpleasant blend of sounds.

Synonyms of *cacophony* include *dissonance* (DIS-uh-nints), *discord* (DIS-kord), *disharmony*, and *stridency* (STRY-den-see). Antonyms include *silence*, *tranquility*, *serenity*, *placidity* (pla-SID-i-tee), and *quiescence* (kwy-ES-ints), the noun corresponding to the adjective *quiescent* (word 22 of Level 3).

Cacophony comes from the Greek *kakos*, bad, and *phoné*, sound, and by derivation means "bad-sounding."

You can see the influence of the Greek *phoné*, sound, in the English words *phonetic* (fuh-NET-ik), pertaining to or representing the sounds of speech; *symphony*, which means literally "sounding together"; and *telephone*, which by derivation means "a voice from afar."

The Greek *kakos*, bad, is the source of the English prefix *caco-*, which appears in front of a number of interesting English words to mean "bad" or "wrong." For example, *cacography* (kuh-KOG-ruh-fee) is bad writing; *cacology* (kuh-KAHL-uh-jee) is bad speaking or a bad choice of words; *cacoepy* (KAK-oh-uh-pee or kuh-KOH-uh-pee or **KAK**-oh-EP-ee) is bad pronunciation, as opposed to *orthoepy* (OR-thoh-uh-pee or or-THOH-uh-pee or **OR**-thoh-EP-ee), good pronunciation; a *caconym* (KAK-uh-nim) is a bad or erroneous name; a *cacodoxy* (**KAK**-uh-DAHK-see) is a wrong or unacceptable opinion (*cacodoxy* is a synonym of *heterodoxy*, which I mentioned earlier in the discussion of *heterodox*, word 34 of this level); *cacoeconomy* (KAK-oh-ee-**KAHN**-uh-mee) is bad economy or bad management; and, last but not least, we have the fascinating word *cacoëthes* (KAK-oh-**EE**-theez).

Cacoëthes combines the Greek *kakos*, bad, with *ethos*, habit, and means a bad habit, incurable itch, or an insatiable urge or desire: "Mary could overlook John's fingernail biting, excuse his excessive smoking and drinking, and forgive his frequent use of foul language, but the one obnoxious habit she could not bring herself to condone was his addiction to channel surfing. That, in her estimation, was his most loathsome cacoëthes."

And now let's return to our keyword, *cacophony*. Any harsh, jarring sound, and especially any harsh and unpleasant blend of sounds, can be described as a *cacophony*: the cacophony of traffic; a cacophony of angry voices; the cacophony created by a major construction project; the cacophony of newborn babies crying in the nursery.

The corresponding adjective is *cacophonous* (kuh-KAHF-uh-nus), having a harsh, unpleasant, jarring sound: "The hungry animals in the barnyard together raised a cacophonous complaint"; "It seemed that every day the tranquility of his well-manicured suburban street was disturbed by a cacophonous orchestra of lawnmowers, blowers, and edgers." Synonyms of *cacophonous* include *dissonant* (DIS-uh-nint), *discordant* (dis-KOR-dint), *raucous* (RAW-kus), and *strident* (STRY-dent).

Word 42: REFRACTORY (ri-FRAK-tur-ee)

Stubborn and disobedient, actively resisting authority or control, unruly, impossible to work with or manage.

Because the human animal is so often stubborn, disobedient, and unruly, English abounds with words for these qualities. Synonyms of *refractory* include *willful*, *headstrong*, *ungovernable*, *rebellious*, *obstinate* (word 34 of Level 1), *intractable* (word 12 of Level 5), *perverse*, *recalcitrant* (ri-KAL-si-trant), *intransigent* (in-TRAN-si-jint, word 4 of Level 8), and *contumacious* (KAHN-t(y)oo-**MAY**-shus).

Antonyms of *refractory* include *obedient*, *submissive*, *compliant*, *deferential*, *malleable* (word 29 of Level 2), *docile* (word 28 of Level 7), *tractable* (see word 12 of Level 5), *acquiescent* (AK-wee-**ES**-int), and *obsequious* (uhb-SEE-kwee-us, word 3 of Level 7).

I know that's a lot of words to stuff in your head, so let's take a moment to clarify some of them.

Refractory, *intractable*, *contumacious*, *intransigent*, and *recalcitrant* all suggest stubborn resistance to control.

Recalcitrant comes from the Latin *re-*, meaning "back," and *calcitrare*, to kick, and means literally to kick back. The recalcitrant person resists direction or control in a rebellious and sometimes violent manner.

Intransigent, both by derivation and in modern usage, means unwilling to compromise. The intransigent person takes an extreme position and will not budge an inch.

Contumacious means stubborn in an insolent way. The contumacious person displays willful and openly contemptuous resistance to established authority. Examples of contumacious behavior would include insulting a police officer and ignoring a summons to appear in court.

Intractable comes from the Latin *tractare*, which means to drag around, haul, and also to manage, control. *Intractable* implies passive resistance to direction. The intractable person refuses to cooperate and must be dragged along. An intractable problem does not respond to any attempt at a solution and stubbornly refuses to go away.

Our keyword, *refractory*, applies to anyone or anything that is stubbornly disobedient and that actively resists authority or control. Horses, mules, machinery, and children are often described as refractory, but the word may also be applied appropriately to many other things, such as materials that are resistant to heat or chemical agents, or a medical condition that resists treatment, as a refractory case of athlete's foot.

Word 43: ICONOCLAST (eye-KAHN-uh-klast)

A person who attacks cherished or popular beliefs, traditions, or institutions; someone who destroys or denounces an established idea or practice.

Iconoclast comes from the Greek *eikonoklastes*, an image-breaker, a person who smashes icons or images. Originally the word referred to a person who destroyed religious images, or who was opposed to the use or worship of religious images. In modern usage *iconoclast* refers to a person who attacks, denounces, or ridicules cherished ideas or beliefs, or to someone who advocates the overthrow or destruction of established customs or institutions.

Synonyms of the noun *iconoclast* include *radical*, *extremist*, *insurgent* (in-SUR-jent), and *firebrand*. The corresponding adjective is *iconoclastic*, attacking or opposing established or popular beliefs, customs, or institutions.

Word 44: ENERVATE (EN-ur-vayt)

To weaken, drain of energy, deprive of force or vigor.

Synonyms of *enervate* include *exhaust*, *deplete*, *devitalize*, and *debilitate*. Antonyms include *energize*, *invigorate*, *stimulate*, *revive*, *enliven*, *animate*, *vitalize*, and *fortify*.

Whenever I am asked to appear on a radio show to discuss language or speak to a group about vocabulary building, I like to point out that the simple act of reading is probably the best yet most underrated method of building word power. If you want to learn more words, then you should read more and study words in context; at the same time, however, when you come across a word you don't know, or a word you think you know, it's essential that you make the effort to look it up in a dictionary, because the context can often be misleading or ambiguous.

To illustrate that point, I like to relate an anecdote about a woman—the mother of a teenager—who came to one of the author signings for my book *Tooth and Nail*, a vocabulary-building mystery novel designed to teach high school students the words they need to know for the Scholastic Assessment Test (SAT).

"I think your idea of teaching vocabulary in the context of a story is great," the woman told me. "I can almost always figure out what a word means from context, and I hardly ever need to use a dictionary."

Whenever people assert that they can guess what a word means or that they rarely need to use a dictionary, I see a big red flag with the words "verbally disadvantaged" on it.

I looked at the woman and said, "I always encourage people to check the dictionary definition of a word, even if it's a word they think they know. It's not always so easy to guess what a word means from context, because the context doesn't always reveal the meaning. May I give you an example?"

"Sure," the woman said, confident of her ability to guess what words mean and unaware of my devilish plot to expose that practice as a fallacy.

"All right," I said. "I'll give you a word in the context of a complete sentence, and you tell me what the word means. Here's the sentence: 'After her exciting night on the town, she felt enervated.' Can you tell me what *enervated* means?"

The woman frowned, realizing that she had volunteered to go wading in verbal quicksand. "Um, well, I guess if her night on the town was exciting, she must have felt stimulated, or keyed-up, or maybe energized. Is that what *enervated* means?"

Coldhearted inquisitor and unflinching defender of the language that I am, I told her the truth. Because *enervate* sounds like *energize*, many people are tempted to think the words are synonymous when in fact they are antonyms. From my sample sentence, "After her exciting night on the town, she felt enervated," if you don't know precisely what *enervated* means there's no way you can guess because the context is ambiguous—it's vague and capable of being interpreted in more than one way.

The point is, as I've said several times before in this program, if you want to build a large and exact vocabulary, don't rely *only* on context or on your intuition or on someone else's definition of a word. When you have even a shred of doubt about a word, look it up. It won't cost you anything to do that, and no one's going to peer over your shoulder and say, "Hey, what's the matter, stupid? You don't know what *enervated* means?" On the other hand, someone might say "Whoa, get a load of *Verbal Advantage*-head digging through the dictionary again."

If something like that should ever happen, you can throw the book at the person—literally—but why ruin a good dictionary? Instead, you can rest easy in the knowledge that the insolent dullard already is eating your intellectual dust—for you, as a verbally advantaged person, know that reading, consulting a dictionary, and studying this book will invigorate, not enervate, your mind.

To *enervate* means to weaken, drain of energy, deprive of force or vigor. The corresponding adjective is *enervated*, lacking energy, drained of vitality or strength.

Word 45: LEVITY (LEV-i̱-tee)

Lightness or gaiety of manner or expression; specifically, a lightness or lack of seriousness that is inappropriate or unbecoming.

Levity comes from the Latin *levitas*, lightness, which in turn comes from *levis*, light, the source also of the familiar words *levitate* and *levitation*. *Levity* occasionally is used literally to mean buoyancy, the state or quality of having little weight, and it is also sometimes used to mean inconstancy, fickleness, or flightiness. In current usage, however, *levity* most often denotes a figurative lack of gravity, a lightness or lack of seriousness unsuitable to the occasion.

Synonyms of *levity* in this most common sense include *silliness*, *foolishness*, *frivolity* (fri-VAHL-i-tee), *flippancy* (FLIP-'n-see), *tomfoolery*, *triviality*, and *jocularity* (JAHK-yoo-**LAR**-i-tee). Antonyms include *seriousness*, *earnestness*, *sobriety*, *solemnity* (suh-LEM-ni-tee), and *gravity*.

When you are trying to fix a word in your mind and make it a permanent part of your vocabulary, it helps if you can associate it with a vivid image or experience. The experience I associate with the word *levity* occurred way back in high school, which in my case was a small coeducational boarding school in western Massachussetts.

One night in the dormitory some friends and I were up late, several hours after "bedcheck," our prepschool term for "lights-out time." We were shooting the breeze, laughing and joking, being loud and boisterous, and generally behaving in a puerile manner, when suddenly the door flew open and one of the English teachers stepped into the room.

Instantly, we all shut up. In the long moment of silence that followed, the teacher looked at each of us like Clint Eastwood trying to decide whether some deadbeat has enough brains to pack his lunch. Finally he spoke. "This is no time for levity," he growled. "Go to your rooms and go to bed."

To this day, when I think of the word *levity* I think of what that teacher said, and with a chuckle I remember that *levity* means foolishness, frivolity, a lightness or lack of seriousness that is inappropriate or unbecoming.

Word 46: EQUANIMITY (EE-kwuh-**NIM**-i-tee)

Composure, calmness, evenness of mind and temper.

Equanimity comes through French from the Latin *aequanimitas*, calmness, which in turn comes from *aequus*, which means "even" or "level," and *animus*, which means "mind" or "spirit." By derivation *equanimity* means precisely what it does today: composure, calmness, evenness of mind and temper.

Synonyms of *equanimity* include *poise*, *self-possession*, *serenity*, *tranquility*, *placidity* (pla-SID-i-tee), *imperturbability* (IM-pur-TUR-buh-**BIL**-i-tee), and *sang-froid* (saw(n)-FRWAH). As I imagine you can tell from its peculiar spelling and pronunciation, *sang-froid* comes from French. Although *sang-froid* means literally "cold blood," it is used figuratively to mean coolness of mind.

Equanimity and *composure* are close synonyms, but they differ slightly in their use. *Composure* implies self-control. We maintain our composure under trying circumstances. *Equanimity* suggests an inherent mental and emotional balance, and applies to a person who stays calm and collected under all circumstances.

Word 47: STRICTURE (STRIK-chur)

A criticism, critical comment, especially an unfavorable or hostile observation or remark.

Synonyms of *stricture* include *reproof*, *censure* (word 28 of Level 3), *condemnation*, *disapprobation* (DIS-ap-ruh-**BAY**-shin), *castigation* (KAS-ti-**GAY**-shin), *objurgation* (AHB-jur-**GAY**-shin, word 12 of Level 7), and *animadversion* (AN-i-mad-**VUR**-zhun). Antonyms include *praise*, *compliment*, *commendation*, *acclamation* (AK-luh-**MAY**-shin), and *plaudit* (PLAW-dit).

Plaudit, *applause*, and *applaud* all come from the Latin *plaudere*, to clap the hands, express approval. A *plaudit* is an enthusiastic expression of approval or praise. It's always pleasant to be on the receiving end of a plaudit, and it's always unpleasant to be on the receiving end of a *stricture*, an unfavorable criticism or hostile remark.

Stricture comes from the Latin *strictus*, the past participle of the verb *stringere*, to draw tight, bind, the source also of the English words *strict* and *stringent*. *Stringent* (STRIN-jint) means tight, constricted, or rigorous and severe.

We often speak of stringent laws, stringent measures, stringent regulations, or a stringent economic policy.

In medicine, *stricture* is used to mean a contraction or narrowing of a duct or passage in the body. *Stricture* is also sometimes used as a synonym of *limitation* or *restriction*, as "to place strictures on imported goods." Most often, though, *stricture* is used to mean a sharply critical comment, especially one that passes judgment or points out a fault in an antagonistic way: "During the debate, he displayed admirable equanimity when responding to his opponent's strictures."

Bear in mind that *stricture* is a noun, not a verb. In other words, you cannot stricture something, but if you have an unfavorable opinion of a person or a thing, you can express your *strictures*, sharp criticisms or hostile remarks.

Word 48: OPULENT (AHP-yuh-lint)

Rich, wealthy, very well-to-do, having substantial means.

Antonyms of *opulent* include *indigent*, *destitute*, and *impecunious*, which are discussed under *indigent*, word 39 of Level 3.

The adjectives *opulent* (AHP-yuh-lint), *affluent* (AF-loo-int—stress the *first* syllable), and *prosperous* all connote wealth and success. *Prosperous* often is used interchangeably with wealthy, but in precise usage *prosperous* means marked by continued success, thriving, flourishing. A prosperous business is a successful, thriving business, and because successful businesses are profitable it is also likely to be an affluent business. *Affluent*, which comes from the Latin *fluere*, to flow, suggests a constant flow or increase of wealth accompanied by free or lavish spending.

Opulent comes through the Latin *opulentus*, rich, wealthy, and *opis*, power, might, ultimately from the name *Ops* (rhymes with *tops*). In ancient Roman mythology, *Ops* was the goddess of the harvest and the wife of Saturn, the god of agriculture who presided over the sowing of the fields. Because of this etymological connection to agricultural abundance, *opulent* is sometimes used to mean ample or plentiful, but in current usage *opulent* most often applies either to a person who possesses great wealth and property or to a luxurious or ostentatious display of great wealth. If your lifestyle is affluent, you are making and spending large sums of money. If your lifestyle is opulent, you already have plenty of moolah and you enjoy showing off what it can buy.

The corresponding noun is *opulence*, great wealth or a display of great wealth. A couplet from the eighteenth-century English satirist Jonathan Swift nicely illustrates this word: "There in full opulence a banker dwelt / Who all the joys and pangs of riches felt."

Word 49: DISPARAGE (di-SPAR-ij)

To belittle, depreciate, discredit, lower in estimation or value, speak of or treat as inferior.

Familiar synonyms of *disparage* include *abuse* (uh-BYOOZ), *ridicule*, *scorn*, *slander*, *defame*, and *censure* (word 28 of Level 3). Challenging synonyms of *disparage* include *denigrate* (**DEN**-i-GRAYT), *malign* (muh-LYN), *vilify* (VIL-uh-fy, word 32 of Level 9), *traduce* (truh-D(Y)OOS, word 42 of Level 9), and *calumniate* (kuh-LUHM-nee-ayt).

You'd never guess from looking at it, but the word *disparage* is related to the noun *peer*, an equal, a person of equal status. *Peer* comes from the Latin *par*, meaning "equal," the direct source of the familiar English word *par*, which is perhaps most often heard in the phrase "on a par with," meaning on an equal footing. The meanings of *par* and *peer* sit quietly in the middle of the word *disparage*, which comes from an Old French verb that meant to marry unequally, marry a person who was not a peer or on a par with your rank in society.

To marry an inferior person, someone beneath one's station, was the meaning of *disparage* when the word entered English in the fourteenth century. Later it came to mean to degrade, lower in dignity or position, as "The prince disparaged himself by helping the servants prepare the meal."

From those now-obsolete senses evolved the modern meaning of *disparage*, to belittle, depreciate, lower in estimation or value. When you disparage someone or something, you speak of it or treat it as inferior: "Some people claim astrology is a legitimate science; others disparage it as foolish superstition."

The corresponding adjective is *disparaging*, as a disparaging remark or disparaging words. The corresponding noun is *disparagement*, as "The city council's plan for economic recovery received only disparagement in the press."

Word 50: DISCURSIVE (dis-KUR-siv)

Rambling, roving, covering a wide range of topics, wandering from one subject to another.

Don't be confused by the presence of the word *cursive* in *discursive*. *Discursive* has nothing to do either with cursing or with cursive script, in which the letters are joined or flow together. *Discursive* comes from the Latin *discursus*, running about, the past participle of the verb *discurrere*, to run to and fro or in different directions. In modern usage, *discursive* applies to speech or writing that runs to and fro or in many different directions.

Discursive, desultory (**DES**-ul-TOR-ee, rhymes with *wrestle story*), and *digressive* (di-GRES-iv or dy-) are close in meaning.

Digressive means straying from the point, wandering away from the topic under consideration. Digressive remarks about what you discussed in your last therapy session don't go over well in a job interview.

Desultory means passing or leaping from one topic to another in an aimless, disconnected way. Conversation at a lively party is often desultory, and many of our dreams have a desultory quality.

Discursive means rambling or roving over a wide range of topics without developing a unified theme or making a central point: "After dinner and a few drinks, Ben's father was prone to indulge in long, discursive monologues that always began with complaints about business and politics, then moved on to observations about sports, and eventually concluded—after several more drinks—with a detailed assessment of the physical attributes of various female celebrities."

Let's review the ten keywords you've just learned. I'll give you the review word (in *italics*) followed by three words or phrases, and you decide which one of those three words or phrases comes nearest the meaning of the review word. Answers appear on page 263.

1. Is a *cacophony* a bad habit, a harsh sound, or a similarity?
2. When someone is *refractory*, does it mean that person is outspoken, unruly, or unimaginative?
3. Would an *iconoclast* be likely to defend, ignore, or attack a popular custom or belief?
4. Does an *enervated* person feel weak, nervous, or stimulated?
5. Does *levity* mean a loss of control, the ability to stay calm, or an inappropriate lack of seriousness?
6. If you display *equanimity*, does that mean you are fair, calm, or undecided?
7. Is a *stricture* a criticism, a punishment, or an obligation?
8. Is an *opulent* person talkative, rich, or overweight?
9. If you *disparage* something, does that mean you evaluate it, regret it, or belittle it?
10. When a speaker is *discursive*, does that mean the person is thoughtful, hostile, or rambling?

Did you answer at least eight questions correctly? If not, review, review, review.

An Assault on *Impact*

Let's wind up this level with a slam-bang assault on the crushing effect of the word *impact*.

If a language genie ever were to appear and offer me one wish, I think I'd ask that we all immediately cease using the word *impact* in place of the nouns *influence* and *effect* and the verb to *affect*.

Stunting the growth of *impact* may not be on your list of priorities for a better world, but I am going a little daft enduring the earsplitting din of this word. Every day, a thousand times a day, something "impacts" something else, and every event has nothing less than a "tremendous impact" on our lives. It's enough to shatter your nerves and rattle your bones. Multiple impacts have made our daily discourse loud and dull, like the sound of ten thousand car horns blowing behind a fender-bender on the freeway.

Where is all this noise coming from? Just tune your brainwaves to the airwaves around you for a moment and you'll hear them, the evil "impactors" who have penetrated every rank of society, intent on "impacting" our malleable minds. Pompous professors and public officials lecture us about the "social impact," the long-winded lawyer dwells upon the "legal impact," the do-gooder is desperate to have "a positive impact," the economist drones on about the "fiscal impact"—everyone is "impacting" everyone else into a quivering stupor.

Are we wholly deaf to the subtlety of language? Why do we insist on using a pile driver when a putty knife would do?

Once upon a time we expressed the influence of something calmly and clearly by saying that it had an *effect*, or that it *affected* something else. Now it is hammered into our heads day in and day out with the word *impact*. The sad thing is that this powerful word, which connotes considerable force, has lost all of its forcefulness through incessant repetition. The only power *impact* has retained is the ability to cause a headache.

Impact is what the celebrated grammarian H. W. Fowler would call a "vogue-word." A vogue word is one that for no apparent reason becomes popular almost overnight. Often it is an unusual or literary word, or one with a precise meaning, that is adopted as a sophisticated substitute for a common, everyday, hardworking sort of word. In Fowler's day—the early 1900s—the verb to *intrigue*, which had meant to plot, scheme, or carry on a clandestine love affair, became a vogue word used to mean to interest or fascinate. That may not raise many eyebrows today, but the point is that as language progresses we must keep a wary eye on these vogue words, charting their influence—or their impact, as the vogue would have it—and passing judgment on their usefulness and force. Words like *unique, parameters, interface,* and *proactive* are mighty popular these days, but are they clear and strong and useful?

Of course, no one can wave a wand and change the course of language, but a little prudence can go a long way. Unless we give the overworked *impact* a well-deserved rest it won't be long before we hear about cars "impacting" on the freeway, an "impactive" piece of legislation, an "impactual" treatment for cancer, or the "impactability" of a new idea.

And now that I've given the odious, banal, and ubiquitous *impact* a thorough pounding, it's time to say good-bye to Level 6. I encourage you to review this entire level at least once before moving on. Careful and consistent review of the material in the *Verbal Advantage* program is the best way to avoid a "positive impact" and ensure a beneficial effect.

Answers to Review Quizzes for Level 6

Keywords 1–10

1. Yes it could, if the takeover was accomplished in a clever, tricky way. *Legerdemain* means sleight of hand, a cleverly executed trick or deception.

2. No. A *puerile* remark is childish, immature, and therefore foolish, silly.

3. Yes. *Complicity* means conspiracy, partnership in wrongdoing, the state of being an accomplice.

4. Yes. To *transmute* means to transform, to change from one state or form into another, especially a more refined or more desirable one.

5. No. Something *abstruse* is difficult to understand, hard to grasp mentally, incomprehensible, unfathomable.

6. No. Eating and sleeping well may make you healthy, but good health won't edify you. To *edify* means to instruct or improve intellectually, morally, or spiritually.

7. No. *Puerile* means childish or foolish. *Supercilious* means haughty, scornful, contemptuous.

8. No, you cover it up or disguise it. To *dissemble* means to conceal under a false appearance; speak or behave hypocritically.

9. No. A *vacuous* look is a blank or vacant look. *Vacuous* means empty; devoid of substance, interest, or meaning.

10. Yes. *Capacious* means roomy, spacious, able to contain or hold a great deal.

Keywords 11–20

1. True. *Mnemonic* means helping or pertaining to the memory, assisting or improving the ability to recall.
2. False. *Sonorous* means resonant; deep, full, and rich in sound; having, or capable of producing, a powerful, impressive sound.
3. False. Parents admonish their children all the time, and it's perfectly legal. To *admonish* means to warn or notify of a fault or error, especially in conduct or attitude; to criticize or reprove gently but earnestly.
4. True. A *paradigm* is an example, model, or pattern.
5. True. *Circuitous* means roundabout, indirect, not straightforward.
6. False. To *vindicate* means to clear from blame, free from suspicion of wrongdoing or dishonor.
7. False. *Bucolic* means rural, rustic, of or pertaining to country life.
8. False. Being ostracized is no fun. To *ostracize* means to banish; send into exile; exclude or reject from a group or from acceptance by society.
9. False. *Plethora* means an excess, surplus, overabundance, oversupply.
10. True. A *proclivity* is an inclination, a strong natural bent or tendency, often toward something objectionable or wrong.

Keywords 21–30

1. Synonyms. *Commensurate* means proportionate, corresponding in amount, measure, or degree; also, equal, of the same size or extent.
2. Antonyms. *Intermittent* means happening at intervals, periodic. *Incessant* means constant, uninterrupted, continuous.
3. Synonyms. A *sycophant* is a flatterer, parasite, toady, fawning follower, hanger-on.
4. Synonyms. *Tangential* means not closely related, only slightly connected, digressive, divergent.
5. Antonyms. *Tenable* means defensible, reasonable; able to be defended, maintained, or upheld.
6. Antonyms. *Tangible* means capable of being discerned by the sense of touch or realized by the mind. *Impalpable* means incapable of being felt or understood, not able to be perceived either by the sense of touch or by the mind.
7. Synonyms. *Odious* means hateful, detestable, offensive, revolting, arousing strong dislike or aversion.
8. Antonyms. *Ubiquitous* means existing or seeming to exist everywhere at the same time.
9. Synonyms. To *ruminate* means to turn over in the mind, think about again and again, consider carefully or at length.

10. Synonyms. *Remuneration* means payment, compensation, reward.

Keywords 31–40

1. *small oversight* doesn't fit. A *peccadillo* is a small sin, slight offense, minor fault or flaw.
2. *lying prone* doesn't fit. *Prone* means lying on the belly, with the face down. *Supine* means lying down on the back, with the face turned upward.
3. *inappropriate* is the inappropriate word in this case. *Banal* means common, ordinary, unoriginal; lacking freshness or zest; flat, dull, and predictable.
4. *having an unreasonable opinion* doesn't fit. When the Italian astronomer Galileo (gal-i-**lee**-oh) affirmed the copernican theory that the earth rotates on its axis and revolves around the sun, it was not scientifically unreasonable; in the early 1600s, however, that theory was considered not only heterodox but heretical, and for expressing agreement with it galileo was imprisoned by the inquisition and excommunicated by the church. *Heterodox* means having or expressing an opinion different from the accepted opinion; not in agreement with established doctrine or belief.
5. *high-minded* doesn't fit. *Grandiloquent* means characterized by lofty, high-flown language; full of grand or high-sounding words.
6. *grotesque* doesn't fit. *Grotesque* means distorted, ugly, outlandish, or bizarre. *Lugubrious* means mournful and gloomy; expressing sadness or sorrow, often in an exaggerated, affected, or ridiculous way.
7. *invisible* doesn't fit. Many things that are invisible to the naked eye can still be measured or counted. *Infinitesimal* means tiny, minute; too small to be measured or calculated.
8. *order* doesn't quite fit. To *order* means to command or instruct. To *goad* means to prod or urge to action, stimulate, arouse, stir up.
9. *to hang around aimlessly* doesn't fit. To *malinger* means to pretend to be sick or incapacitated so as to avoid work or duty.
10. *promise earnestly* doesn't fit. To *aver* means to state positively, declare with confidence.

Keywords 41–50

1. A *cacophony* is a harsh, jarring sound, especially a harsh and unpleasant blend of sounds.
2. *Refractory* means unruly, stubborn and disobedient, actively resisting authority or control.
3. An iconoclast would attack it. An *iconoclast* is a person who attacks or denounces popular or established beliefs, traditions, or institutions.
4. An enervated person is weakened. *Enervate* means to drain of energy, deprive of force or vigor.

5. *Levity* is lightness or gaiety of manner or expression; specifically, a lightness or lack of seriousness that is inappropriate or unbecoming.
6. It means you are calm. *Equanimity* is composure, calmness, evenness of mind and temper.
7. A *stricture* is a criticism, especially an unfavorable or hostile observation or remark.
8. An *opulent* person is rich, wealthy, very well-to-do.
9. *Disparage* means to belittle, lower in estimation or value, speak of or treat as inferior.
10. *Discursive* means rambling, covering a wide range of topics, wandering from one subject to another.

Review Test for Level 6

1. Which word by derivation means the working of miracles?
   (a) prestidigitation
   (b) legerdemain
   (c) thaumaturgy

2. Which word means literally nimbleness with the fingers?
   (a) legerdemain
   (b) thaumaturgy
   (c) prestidigitation

3. Which pair of words contains a word that is *not* a synonym of *puerile*?
   (a) frivolous, inane
   (b) genteel, sophomoric
   (c) callow, asinine
   (d) juvenile, fatuous

4. Which pair of words is antonymous (opposite in meaning)?
   (a) perspicuous, lucid
   (b) cryptic, arcane
   (c) inscrutable, esoteric
   (d) manifest, enigmatic

5. The *-cilious* part of *supercilious* comes from a Latin word meaning
   (a) eyebrow
   (b) proud
   (c) superior
   (d) nose

6. Which word means spacious or comprehensive?

   (a) vacuous

   (b) capacious

   (c) fatuous

   (d) superfluous

7. Who was the goddess of memory in Greek mythology?

   (a) Laodicea

   (b) Athena

   (c) Mnemosyne

   (d) Ops

8. Which pair of words is *not* synonymous?

   (a) sonorous, sinuous

   (b) devious, circuitous

   (c) serpentine, meandering

   (d) labyrinthine, tortuous

9. Which word means to free from blame, remove a burden of guilt?

   (a) disparage

   (b) ostracize

   (c) remunerate

   (d) exonerate

10. What is petalism?

   (a) revenge

   (b) a school of philosophy

   (c) a form of banishment

   (d) flattery

11. Which word is *not* a synonym of *plethoric*?

   (a) turgid

   (b) opulent

   (c) bombastic

   (d) grandiloquent

12. Who was the robber of Attica who tortured people on his infamous bed?

   (a) Procrustes

   (b) Draco

   (c) Pyrrho

   (d) Theseus

13. Which word means skepticism, universal doubt?

   (a) solecism

   (b) Pyrrhonism

    (c) epicureanism

    (d) hedonism

14. Which word is not a synonym of *Arcadian*?

    (a) pastoral

    (b) bucolic

    (c) idyllic

    (d) Boeotian

    (e) agrarian

15. Which word denotes a social impropriety or a grammatical error?

    (a) pejorative

    (b) Pyrrhonism

    (c) solecism

    (d) ostracism

16. Which word is closest in meaning to *incessant*?

    (a) unceasing

    (b) continual

    (c) sporadic

    (d) regular

17. What is a *toady*?

    (a) a foolish person

    (b) an informer

    (c) a fawning follower

    (d) a despised person

18. *Tenacious* and *tenable* come from the Latin *tenere*, which means

    (a) to bite

    (b) to defend

    (c) to propose

    (d) to hold

19. Something easily perceived or felt is

    (a) tangential

    (b) palpable

    (c) imperceptible

    (d) ubiquitous

20. Which set of words contains a word that is *not* a synonym of *odious*?

    (a) abhorrent, abominable, flagitious

    (b) repugnant, loathsome, refractory

    (c) repellent, execrable, obnoxious

    (d) objectionable, heinous, opprobrious

21. *Ruminate* comes from a Latin word meaning
    - *(a)* to boil slowly
    - *(b)* to contemplate
    - *(c)* to make a low, deep sound
    - *(d)* to chew the cud

22. Which word means lying down in a comfortable position?
    - *(a)* recumbent
    - *(b)* malingering
    - *(c)* opulent
    - *(d)* prostrate

23. A *bromide* is a statement or idea that is
    - *(a)* imaginative and pithy
    - *(b)* doleful and lugubrious
    - *(c)* hackneyed and insipid
    - *(d)* grandiose and bombastic

24. The *-dox* in *heterodox* and *orthodox* comes from a Greek word meaning
    - *(a)* thought
    - *(b)* custom
    - *(c)* opinion
    - *(d)* religion

25. Which word comes from a Latin verb meaning "to speak?"
    - *(a)* grandiloquent
    - *(b)* cacoethes
    - *(c)* cacophony
    - *(d)* orthoepy

26. Which set of three words contains a word that is *not* a synonym of the others?
    - *(a)* melancholy, dolorous, plaintive
    - *(b)* woeful, funereal, lachrymose
    - *(c)* doleful, saturnine, disconsolate
    - *(d)* dismal, impecunious, lugubrious

27. An infinitesimal amount of something is
    - *(a)* a substantial amount
    - *(b)* an immeasurably great amount
    - *(c)* a very small but measurable amount
    - *(d)* an immeasurably small amount

28. What do malingerers do?

    (a) they loiter
    (b) they pretend to be sick
    (c) they threaten or intimidate
    (d) they panhandle or steal

29. Which word means to declare in a solemn, earnest manner?

    (a) vindicate
    (b) ruminate
    (c) asseverate
    (d) indemnify

30. Which statement is *false*?

    (a) Something eminent is about to happen.
    (b) Something eminent is remarkable.
    (c) Something eminent is distinguished.

31. By derivation, what does the *phon-* in *cacophony* and *phonetic* mean?

    (a) word
    (b) letter
    (c) speech
    (d) sound

32. Which word means a bad habit, insatiable urge?

    (a) recalcitrance
    (b) cacoethes
    (c) equanimity
    (d) animadversion

33. Which pair of words is *not* antonymous?

    (a) obstinate, malleable
    (b) refractory, intractable
    (c) acquiescent, perverse
    (d) deferential, recalcitrant
    (e) submissive, intransigent

34. Which word is an antonym of *enervated*?

    (a) animated
    (b) bored
    (c) tired
    (d) curious

35. Which word means coolness of mind, composure?

    (a) acclamation
    (b) stricture

(c) sang-froid
(d) levity

Answers

32. b   33. b   34. a   35. c
22. a   23. c   24. c   25. a   26. d   27. d   28. b   29. c   30. a   31. d
12. a   13. b   14. d   15. c   16. a   17. c   18. d   19. b   20. b   21. d
1. c   2. c   3. b   4. d   5. a   6. b   7. c   8. a   9. d   10. c   11. b

Evaluation

A score of 30–35 is excellent. If you answered fewer than thirty questions correctly in this test, review the entire level and take the test again.

Level 7

The Five Types of Abusage

Throughout this level we will examine the subject of "abusage," by which I mean we will discuss some of the most common problems and errors of usage that plague the average educated person.

As I see it, much of the abusage committed by the average educated user of English falls into five general categories: (1) redundancy; (2) the "sounds-like syndrome"; (3) vogue words; (4) "adverbiage"; and (5) jargon. After every set of ten keyword discussions in this level we will explore one of these categories, and I will show you how to recognize and avoid the pitfalls it contains.

Word 1: REDRESS (REE-dres for the noun, ri-DRES for the verb)

Reparation, compensation, satisfaction for a wrong done.

Synonyms of *redress* include *amends*, *recompense* (REK-um-pents), *retribution*, *rectification*, *requital* (ri-KWYT-'l), and *quittance* (KWIT-'ns).

Redress may take the form of a monetary compensation or it may be an act or statement that makes amends, that repairs or compensates for a wrong. One may seek redress for a loss or injury, or one may demand redress for an insult. *Webster's New World Dictionary*, third edition (1997), notes that *redress* "suggests retaliation or resort to the courts to right a wrong."

The verb to *redress* (ri-DRES) means to repair, set right, make amends for, as to redress grievances, to redress one's losses, to redress a wrong.

Word 2: ANOMALOUS (uh-NAHM-uh-lus)

Irregular, abnormal, out of place; deviating from what is usual or expected; not fitting in with a common type or conforming to a general rule.

Synonyms of *anomalous* include *inconsistent, unnatural, eccentric* (ek-SEN-trik), and *aberrant* (a-BER-int).

Anomalous comes from Greek and means literally "not the same." Something that is anomalous stands out because it is not the same; it is irregular, abnormal, or out of place: "Compared with the last five years, these statistics are anomalous." "In that neighborhood full of ticky-tacky houses, the imposing old Victorian mansion was architecturally anomalous." "Sometimes he was reluctant to express his opinion because he thought it would be perceived as anomalous."

The corresponding noun is *anomaly* (uh-NAHM-uh-lee), which means a deviation from the norm, an irregularity: "As the only female executive in a company dominated by men, Harriet was an anomaly." "His penchant for flamboyant clothes made him an anomaly in his conservative profession." "If there is no other life in the universe, then our planet is an anomaly."

Word 3: OBSEQUIOUS (uhb-SEE-kwee-us)

Subservient, submissive, obedient; ready and willing to serve, please, or obey.

Here are some examples of how *obsequious* may be used: "When the king entered, all the members of the court bowed obsequiously." "Bill's supervisor expected the employees to be obsequious, attending to her immediate needs before dealing with anything else." "When his wife found out about his affair, Larry tried everything he could think of to persuade her to forgive him, but she scorned all his obsequious gestures and banished him from her bed."

The corresponding noun is *obsequiousness*, which means subservience, obedience, an eager desire to serve or obey: "Eleanor was disgusted with Michael's obsequiousness whenever they entertained his boss." "Some companies reward obsequiousness rather than initiative and independent work."

Synonyms of *obsequious* include *compliant, servile, slavish, ingratiating* (word 13 of Level 3), *deferential, fawning, toadying, truckling*, and *sycophantic*. Antonyms include *unruly, defiant, intractable* (word 12 of Level 5), *refractory* (word 42 of Level 6), *recalcitrant* (ri-KAL-si-trant), and *intransigent* (in-TRAN-si-jent, word 4 of Level 8).

Word 4: DIDACTIC (dy-DAK-tik)

Instructive, designed or intended to teach.

Synonyms of *didactic* include *edifying, preceptive* (pree-SEP-tiv), *exposi-*

tory (ek-**SPAH**-zi-TOR-ee), *hortatory* (**HOR**-tuh-TOR-ee), and *pedagogic* (PED-uh-**GAHJ**-ik). *Pedagogic* is the adjective corresponding to the noun *pedagogue* (**PED**-uh-GAHG). A *pedagogue* is a teacher, but today the word is sometimes used disparagingly to mean a teacher who is strict, narrow-minded, or dogmatic.

The adjective *didactic* comes from the Greek *didaktikos*, skillful or adept at teaching. In modern usage *didactic* means designed or intended to teach. A didactic paradigm is a model or example that serves to instruct. A didactic treatise is an instructive treatise, one that teaches a lesson, principle, or rule of conduct. The ancient Greek philosopher Aristotle believed that art should be didactic, for one of his famous precepts is that art should "instruct as well as delight."

Didactic often connotes morally instructive or edifying. A great work of fiction may be as didactic as it is entertaining. Sometimes *didactic* has the negative connotation of inclined to lecture others in a tedious or excessively moralistic way: "The members of the committee soon grew weary of Barney's didactic manner of telling everyone how the organization should be run."

The corresponding noun *didactics* means the art or science of teaching. The word pedagogy (**PED**-uh-GOH-jee) may also refer to the art or science of teaching, but more often *pedagogy* means the teaching profession: "Vince and Janet decided that after they were married they would both pursue careers in pedagogy."

Word 5: TRUNCATE (TRUHNG-kayt, like *trunk* + *ate*)

To cut short, shorten by cutting or lopping off.

Synonyms of *truncate* include *condense*, *abridge*, *abbreviate*, and *curtail*. Antonyms include *lengthen*, *extend*, *elongate*, *prolong*, and *protract* (word 25 of Level 3).

Truncate comes from the Latin verb *truncare*, to maim, mutilate, shorten by cutting off, which in turn comes from *truncus*. As an adjective, the Latin *truncus* means maimed, mutilated, cut short or lopped off; as a noun, *truncus* denotes a tree that has been cut down, so that only the stump remains.

Probably because the history of *truncate* contains so much maiming and mutilation, the word usually suggests a more severe or substantial cutting or shortening than its synonyms *condense*, *abridge*, *abbreviate*, and *curtail*. Of all these words, *curtail* comes closest to the severity of *truncate*.

Truncate may refer to a cutting short in number, length, or duration. An editor truncates an article or a book by cutting out large sections of it. A heart attack or severe illness can truncate a life, cut it short early or in its prime. And a company might decide to truncate its workforce, perhaps by cutting out several departments. Of course, company executives would never use the word *truncate*. They would say they were downsizing, which makes it sound as if they're just putting the company on a low-fat diet instead of engaging in an act of corporate mutilation.

The corresponding adjective *truncated* means cut short, abbreviated, terminated abruptly, as a truncated meeting, a truncated explanation, a brief period of economic growth and prosperity truncated by recession.

Word 6: ABSTEMIOUS (ab-STEE-mee-us)

Sparing or moderate, especially in eating or drinking: "The doctor prescribed an abstemious regimen to reduce her cholesterol level." "After six weeks of being abstemious, he lost twenty pounds and felt ten years younger."

Abstemious may also mean characterized by abstinence, not partaking or indulging, especially in alcoholic beverages: "Their abstemious way of life was dictated by their strong religious beliefs."

Abstemious comes directly from the Latin *abstemius*, which means abstaining from liquor. The corresponding noun is *abstemiousness*: "Vegetarianism is a form of abstemiousness."

Synonyms of *abstemious* include *sober*, *temperate*, and *ascetic* (uh-SET-ik). *Ascetic* means rigorously abstemious, practicing strict and extreme abstinence or self-denial.

Word 7: ETHEREAL (i-THEER-ee-ul)

Heavenly, not earthly; hence, very light, airy, delicate, or refined.

Synonyms of *ethereal* include *celestial* (suh-LES-chul), *lofty*, *elevated*, *tenuous* (TEN-yoo-us), *rarefied* (RAIR-uh-fyd), and *sublime* (suh-BLYM). Antonyms include *mundane* (word 22 of Level 4), *terrestrial*, and *sublunary* (suhb-LOO-nur-ee).

In one of its senses, the word *ether* refers to an imaginary substance that the ancients believed filled the upper regions of space. In this primitive cosmology, ether was the lightest and most subtle of the elements, which included earth, water, and fire. At first the adjective *ethereal* meant pertaining to the ether, the upper regions of space, and therefore heavenly, celestial: ethereal beings are heavenly beings, creatures or gods that inhabit the upper regions. Out of this notion of elemental intangibility, *ethereal* came to mean very light, airy, of unearthly delicacy or refinement, as ethereal music, ethereal voices, ethereal beauty, or an ethereal presence or sensation.

Word 8: BOMBASTIC (bahm-BAS-tik)

Pompous, pretentious, inflated, overblown.

Bombastic applies to speech or writing that is pompous, overblown, or pretentious, or to people who express themselves in this way.

Bombastic, *grandiloquent* (word 35 of Level 6), and *turgid* (TUR-jid) all denote extravagant language. *Turgid*, which by derivation means swollen, is used of an inflated style that obscures meaning. *Grandiloquent* suggests a self-conscious effort to be eloquent through the use of high-flown language. *Bombastic* suggests pomposity and pretentiousness that masks a lack of substance; the bombastic person speaks in a verbose and self-important way, but says little or nothing.

The corresponding noun is *bombast* (BAHM-bast). Originally, *bombast* was a soft, silky material used for padding. The word now means verbal padding, speech or writing that is wordy, puffed up, and pretentious.

Word 9: SENESCENT (si-NES-int)

Aging, growing old, on the decline.

The adjective *senescent* comes from the Latin *senex*, which means "old." *Senex* is also the source of *senile*, exhibiting mental impairment due to old age, and *senate*, which means literally "a council of elders."

Senescent may be used of persons, things, or ideas that are growing old, decrepit, or outworn, as a senescent leader, a senescent forest, a senescent custom, or a senescent industry.

The antonym of *senescent* is *juvenescent* (JOO-vuh-**NES**-int), growing younger. The corresponding noun is *senescence* (si-NES-ints), which means the process of becoming old or the state of being old. Wrinkles, hair loss, persistent aches and pains, and the inability to remember what you ate for breakfast are all telltale signs of senescence.

Word 10: PERNICIOUS (pur-NISH-us)

Deadly, fatal, destructive, causing great harm or injury.

Synonyms of *pernicious* include *injurious*, *ruinous*, *deleterious* (word 33 of Level 4), *noxious*, *baneful*, *malign* (muh-LYN), and *noisome* (NOY-sum). Antonyms include *healthful*, *wholesome*, *salutary* (**SAL**-yuh-TER-ee), and *salubrious* (suh-LOO-bree-us, word 48 of this level).

Pernicious comes through the Latin *perniciosus*, destructive, ruinous, and *pernicies*, destruction, disaster, ultimately from *nex*, which means a violent death. By derivation, that which is pernicious leads to destruction, ruin, or death.

In modern usage *pernicious* suggests an insidious, evil, or corrupting influence that harms or destroys by undermining and weakening. The disease called pernicious anemia weakens the body's ability to absorb vitamin B_{12}. A pernicious influence is a deleterious, corrupting, or deadly influence. A pernicious habit is a harmful and potentially fatal habit. A pernicious rumor is insidious or evil. And a pernicious practice is destructive; it undermines the good intentions of others or corrupts society.

Let's review the ten keywords you've just learned. Consider the following questions and decide whether the correct answer is yes or no. Answers appear on page 318.

1. Can someone seek redress for a grievance?
2. In a modern office, would a manual typewriter be an anomalous piece of equipment?
3. Would an obsequious person ever tell the boss to get lost?
4. If something is didactic, does it teach you a lesson?
5. Can you truncate a piece of writing?
6. When you indulge yourself, are you abstemious?
7. Is an ethereal sound harsh and unpleasant?
8. Is a bombastic speaker pompous?
9. Are teenagers senescent?
10. Can a virus be pernicious?

Did you remember to keep track of your answers and calculate your score?

Say It Again, Sam

Now let's begin our discussion of abusage.

The first and perhaps most common category of abusage is redundancy. As Bergen Evans puts it in *A Dictionary of Contemporary American Usage* (1957), the adjective "*redundant* means being in excess, exceeding what is usual or natural . . . [and] in grammar [the noun] *redundancy* means the use of too many words to express an idea, such as *combine together*, *audible to the ear*, or *invisible to the eye*."

Redundancy is perhaps the most common error in educated usage; it is also the easiest to eschew. Sometimes the problem comes from not knowing the precise meanings of the words we use. For example, when you realize that *shuttle* means "to go back and forth," you see immediately that the common phrase "to shuttle back and forth" is a ludicrous redundancy. In most cases, however, redundancy occurs because we are not listening carefully to what we are saying; it is the result of poor concentration. All most of us need to overcome redundancy is a little ear-training to help us hear the repetition of the verbal note in phrases such as "at this point in time" and "audible to the ear." When you train your ear to listen for redundancies, it's easy to correct or eradicate them. And once your ear is tuned in, you'll marvel at how you ever could have been so hard of hearing before, and you'll wonder why so many people can't hear the redundant phrases phrases in their speech speech.

That repetition was obvious, but the verbiage of redundancy is more subtle because it repeats the same ideas but in different words. Remember, from Level 5, my discussion of the advertising cliché *free gift*? When you step back and consider that *free* means you don't have to pay and a *gift* is something given away free, then the phrase *free gift* appears ridiculous. The ubiquitousness of this redundancy makes you wonder—and you should wonder every time you hear it—whether there's a catch. If they're promising now to give me something free, then what are they going to ask me to pay for later? In his entertaining book *The Writer's Art* (1984), syndicated columnist James J. Kilpatrick has one word to say about *free gift*: "Aaargh!"

To get your ears warmed up to the pervasive problem of redundancy, allow me to present some choice examples. You will probably recognize many of these redundant expressions because they are so common in everyday discourse.

Repeat again: How many times in your life have you heard someone say, "Could you repeat that again?" How many times have you asked that repetitive question yourself? By the way, those were just rhetorical questions, so please don't answer them; it would pain me too deeply to learn how many times you've profaned the English language by repeating the *repeat again* redundancy.

As any dictionary will tell you, *repeat* means "to say again." There's no need to say "Could you repeat that again?" unless the phrase "that again" is what you wish to hear repeated. To avoid this pernicious redundancy, simply drop the word *again* and say "Could you repeat that?" Adding *please* to your request wouldn't hurt.

Have you ever listened to people *interacting with each other*? I hope not. *Interact* by itself means to act upon one another, affect each other. Are you interested in rapid weight loss? Well, you can instantly lose three-quarters of the four-word phrase "interact with each other" because the word *interact* alone says it all.

Has anyone ever told you to endorse a check on the back? The next time someone says that to you, tell the person to take it back because *endorse* already means to write on the back of. You *sign* a check payable to someone else, and you *endorse* a check payable to you.

Here's another redundancy I hope will not stand the test of time: *past history*. Has there ever been a *future history* or a *present history*? *Past* is an uneventful addition to the word *history* because *history* already means the events of the past.

How about *future plans* or *plans for the future*? Whenever I hear those phrases I wonder if they're the opposite of *past plans* or *plans for the past*. A *plan* is a scheme or method for accomplishing some objective in the future. The all-too-common redundancy *advance planning* is a victim of the same futuristic trap. All planning is done in advance of action, so, taken literally, *advance planning* sounds as if it means planning before you start planning, or planning when you will begin to plan.

Yet another old redundancy is the phrase *new innovation*. If the unoriginal people who say "new innovation" would just stop in their banal tracks for a second and consider that an innovation is a new idea, method, or device, they'd realize that when they say "new innovation" they are saying, literally, a "new new idea." Do you see how a precise word like *innovation* can so easily lose its power when people use it thoughtlessly?

Two other redundancies I'm eager to put a stop to are *continue on* and its partner in crime, *proceed on*. Both *continue* and *proceed* mean "to go on, move ahead"; adding the word *on* is unnecessary because *continue* and *proceed* already imply onward motion. Whenever someone tacks on the word *on* after *continue* or *proceed*, to my ear it's like an oral tic or redundant twitch of the tongue. Moreover, speakers who develop the *continue on, proceed on* habit run the risk of going on and on ad infinitum (AD in-fi-NY-tum, endlessly, to infinity). Even if you are now guilty of committing this redundancy, it's easy to get rid of. Whenever you say "continue" or "proceed," just stop right there and don't go on.

Once you become aware of redundancies, it seems as if they're everywhere. In fact, to use one of our keywords from Level 6, you could say that redundancies are ubiquitous. Here are some more redundant samples you can put in a mental file marked "Say It Again, Sam." I haved culled every one of them from "educated speech and writing." Read carefully now, because I won't repeat these again (just kidding!):

Fellow colleague: Your colleague is your fellow worker.

Cooperate together and *collaborate together*: *Cooperate* and *collaborate* both mean to work together.

Confer together: To *confer* means to get together to exchange views.

Combine together: *Combine* means to mix together.

Recur again: *Recur* means to happen again.

Completely unanimous: *Unanimous* means to be in complete harmony or agreement.

Vacillate back and forth (on an issue, matter, etc.): To *vacillate* means to waver, go from one side to the other or back and forth.

Report back: Eliminate *back*. To *report* means to carry back information and repeat it to someone else.

Return it back (to the store, etc.): To *return* means to give back. Eliminate *back* again.

Ascend upward: *Ascend* means to go upward.

Descend down: *Descend* means to go down.

Dwindle down: To *dwindle* means to decrease or go down gradually.

Passing fad: A *fad* is a brief or passing fashion.

Hoist up and *raise up*: *Hoist* and *raise* mean to lift up.

Real fact or *actual fact*: A *fact* is something real or actual, something demonstrable.

Erupt violently or *explode violently*: *Erupt* and *explode* mean to emerge or burst forth in a violent manner.

Mutual respect for each other: *Mutual respect* says it all because *mutual* means "for each other, given and received by each one."

Compete with each other: *Compete* means to vie with another or others.

Final ultimatum: An *ultimatum* is a final demand.

Visible to the eye and *invisible to the eye*: What else but the eye can something be visible or invisible to—the nose?

Universal panacea or *a panacea for all ills*: If you remember our discussion of *panacea* from Level 4, you'll remember that a *panacea* is a universal remedy, a cure for all ills.

New recruit: A *recruit* is a newly enlisted person.

Temporary reprieve: *Reprieve* means temporary relief.

Necessary requirement: A *requirement* is something necessary.

Final completion and *final conclusion*: *Completion* and *conclusion* both imply finality, so the word *final* is superfluous.

Opening gambit: A *gambit* is an opening move or a remark intended to open a conversation.

Each and every day: Say "each day" or "every day," not both.

From whence: If the folks who say "from whence" looked up the word *whence* in a dictionary, they would see that it means "from where" or "from what place." This redundancy should not go back from whence it came. It should go back whence it came.

But don't you go away, because here are some more common redundant phrases in which one word already says all that is meant: *large in size* means *large*; *small in size* means *small*; *few in number* means *few*; *extend out* means *extend*; *expand out* means *expand*; *radiate out* means *radiate*; *cancel out* means *cancel*; *reduce down* means *reduce*; *a consensus of opinion* means *a consensus*; *a variety of different choices* means *a variety of choices*; and finally, in the phrases *link together*, *merge together*, and *blend together*, the word *together* adds nothing but baggage: Say *link*, *merge*, or *blend*, and throw *together* in the trash.

Some redundancies are so outrageous that it's hard to believe the writer or speaker cannot hear the repetition of meaning. Get a load of these, every one of which I assure you I have either heard on radio or TV or seen in print:

Artificial prosthesis: A *prosthesis* is an artificial device that replaces a missing body part, such as a leg.

Stonecut lithographs: A *lithograph* is an engraving made in stone.

An old antique: An *antique* is something old or old-fashioned.

Prerecorded earlier: Something prerecorded has been recorded earlier. Say "prerecorded" or "recorded earlier."

Previous preconceptions: A *preconception* is a conception or opinion formed in advance, an opinion formed previously.

He was not physically present: Was he spiritually present? Did he have an out-of-body experience? Drop *physically* and say you were not present.

Omniscient knowledge of all things: *Omniscient* (ahm-NISH-int) means all-knowing, having knowledge of all things.

Completely annihilate: *Annihilate* means to destroy completely.

Current incumbent: An *incumbent* is a person currently holding an office. Don't say "present incumbent" either.

Individual person: If a person is an individual and an individual is a person, then "an individual person" must be a person who is a person. Usage expert Theodore M. Bernstein advises that it's best to use *individual* as a noun only when you mean to distinguish a person or persons from a class or category, as the *individual* and *society*, or benefits for *corporations* and *individuals*. In all other contexts, use *person* or *people*.

He wrote an autobiography of his own life: What other life could an autobiography be about but his own? The same goes for "She wrote a biography of his life." A *biography* is the story of another person's life. Make it "She wrote his biography."

They were dressed identically alike: People are either dressed identically or dressed alike, but if they are "dressed identically alike" then they are dressed the same same, if you know know what I mean mean.

In conclusion, let me share with you just a few more ridiculous redundancies that I don't think require any comment. Your laughter and scorn will suffice.

> *He has an appetite to eat.*
> *She is one of two twins.*
> *We have a population of people to feed.*
> *She is quite popular with the people.*
> *Given the current problems right now . . .*
> *It happened unexpectedly without warning.*

Are those redundancies "incredible to believe," or are they simply incredible?

As I said before—and at the risk of "repeating myself again" and making it difficult for us to "interact with each other"—once you become aware of redundancy it's easy to correct because the cure is simple: deletion.

And now, my verbally advantaged, unredundant friend, it's time to say goodbye, so long, and ta-ta-ta to the Land of Redundancy and return to the *Verbal Advantage* vocabulary for the next ten keywords in Level 7.

Word 11: CATHOLIC (KATH-uh-lik *or* KATH-lik)

Universal, all-inclusive, all-embracing, comprehensive; specifically, broadminded, tolerant, or all-embracing in one's sympathies, interests, or tastes.

Catholic, with a capital *C*, refers to the Roman Catholic Church, to the religion of Catholicism, or to a member of the Catholic Church. The word *catholic*, with a small or lowercase *c*, has nothing to do with religion. It comes directly from Latin and Greek words meaning universal, general, and suggests a broadminded, tolerant, all-embracing outlook on life.

Synonyms of *catholic* include *open-minded*, *liberal*, *ecumenical* (EK-yoo-**MEN**-i-k<u>u</u>l), and *latitudinarian* (LAT-i-T(Y)OO-di-**NAIR**-ee-i<u>n</u>). Antonyms include *narrow-minded*, *bigoted*, *biased*, *intolerant*, *dogmatic* (dawg-MAT-ik), and *parochial* (puh-ROH-kee-ul).

Ecumenical and *catholic* both mean universal, general, whole. *Ecumenical* often refers specifically to religious universality, and especially to that which furthers or is intended to further the unity of Christian churches or unity among religions. *Catholic* (with a small *c*) is the general word for universal in one's personal outlook, broad-minded in one's sympathies or tastes. The catholic person is "not narrow-minded, partial, or bigoted," says the *Century Dictionary* (1914), but possesses "a mind that appreciates all truth, or a spirit that appreciates all that is good."

Word 12: OBJURGATION (AHB-jur-**GAY**-sh<u>i</u>n)

A harsh rebuke, vehement scolding or denunciation.

Synonyms of the noun *objurgation* include *reproof*, *reproach*, *upbraiding*, *vilification*, and *vituperation*.

The corresponding verb is *objurgate* (**AHB**-jur-GAYT or uhb-JUR-gayt). To *objurgate* is to rebuke sharply, chide harshly, denounce vehemently. *Objurgate* and *objurgation* come from the Latin *ob-*, against, and *jurgare*, to scold or quarrel. In colloquial terms—that is, in the vernacular—when you are called on the carpet or you are read the riot act, you are on the receiving end of an *objurgation*, a harsh rebuke, vehement scolding or denunciation.

Word 13: EFFUSIVE (<u>i</u>-FYOO-siv)

Gushing, overflowing, overly demonstrative, expressing emotion in an excessive or unrestrained manner.

Synonyms of *effusive* include *exuberant*, *profuse*, *ebullient* (i-BUHL-y<u>i</u>nt or i-BUUL-y<u>i</u>nt), *impassioned*, *ecstatic*, and *rhapsodic* (rap-SAHD-ik). Antonyms of *effusive* include *undemonstrative*, *reserved*, *aloof* (word 20 of Level 1), *indifferent*, *reticent*, *diffident*, *taciturn* (word 2 of Level 3), and *laconic* (word 18 of Level 3).

The adjective *effusive* and the corresponding noun *effusion* come through the Latin *effusio*, a pouring forth, from the verb *effundere*, to pour out or pour forth.

True to its origin, in modern usage *effusion* denotes a pouring or gushing forth. The word may be used of a literal gushing, as an effusion of gas or fluid, or it may be used figuratively of an unrestrained emotional outburst in speech or writing.

Effusive is nearly always used figuratively to mean gushing or overflowing with emotion, overly demonstrative, as effusive praise, effusive greetings, an effusive style of writing: "At the dinner party Dan's effusive host couldn't stop telling everyone at the table what a great guy he was."

Word 14: UMBRAGE (UHM-brij)

Offense, resentment.

Synonyms of *umbrage* include *displeasure*, *irritation*, *indignation*, and *pique* (PEEK).

Umbrage is most commonly used today in the phrase "to take umbrage," meaning to take offense. One takes umbrage at being slighted, either by a real or an imagined insult to one's dignity or pride: "He took umbrage at the criticisms leveled against him in the meeting"; "She took umbrage at his rude manner." You may also feel umbrage, resentment, at something, or give umbrage, offense, to someone else, but these constructions are less common.

Word 15: VICISSITUDE (vi-SIS-i-t(y)ood)

A change, variation.

Synonyms of *vicissitude* include *alternation*, *fluctuation*, and *mutation*.

By derivation, *vicissitude* means "change," and in modern usage a *vicissitude* is a change, variation, or an alternating condition occurring in the course of something. The word is perhaps most often used in the plural, *vicissitudes*, to refer to the changes that occur during the course of something, the ups and downs. We speak of the vicissitudes of daily life, the vicissitudes of the stock market, or of a business surviving the viccissitudes of twenty turbulent years.

Word 16: CONTENTIOUS (kun-TEN-shus)

Argumentative, quarrelsome, ready and eager to argue, bicker, or debate.

Contentious, *litigious*, *pugnacious*, *disputatious*, *belligerent*, and *bellicose* all refer to quarrelsome or hostile parties who are inclined to engage in argument or conflict.

Bellicose (BEL-i-kohs) means having a warlike or hostile nature. The ancient Spartans were a bellicose people.

Belligerent (buh-LIJ-ur-int) may mean either participating in fighting or provoking a fight or a war. A belligerent nation either engages in conflict or pro-vokes a conflict. A belligerent look or a belligerent remark can lead to a fight.

Pugnacious (puhg-NAY-shus, word 8 of Level 5) by derivation means ready to fight with the fists; it suggests a temperamental inclination to fight or quarrel: "As a child Melvin was unruly, as a teenager he was deviant, and as an adult he became a pugnacious barroom brawler."

Disputatious (DIS-pyoo-**TAY**-shus) means inclined to dispute, and usually applies to people who engage in formal arguments or to anything involving for-mal debate. Scholars are often disputatious, and it goes without saying that politics is disputatious.

Litigious (li-TIJ-us) means tending to engage in lawsuits or litigation. Although it is entirely appropriate to say that the legal profession is litigious, meaning that its business is to engage in lawsuits, in current usage *litigious* often implies an overeagerness to settle every minor dispute in court.

Contentious (kun-TEN-shus) comes from the Latin *contentio*, striving, ef-fort, and ultimately from *contendere*, to strain or strive against another. From the same source we inherit the verb to *contend*, to struggle, fight, strive in op-position, and the noun *contention*, which may mean either a struggle, opposi-tion—"They were in contention for the job"—or an assertion made in an argu-ment: "It was his contention that if the company wanted to remain solvent, it should truncate its workforce."

The adjective *contentious* means always ready and willing to quarrel, and suggests a persistent inclination to pick fights or arguments. You can be in a contentious mood, meaning you are in an argumentative mood; you can have a contentious coworker, one who is quarrelsome; or you can make a con-tentious comment, one intended to provoke an argument.

Antonyms of *contentious* include *peaceable*, *obliging*, *civil*, *tolerant*, *ami-able*, *amicable* (AM-i-kuh-buul), *benevolent* (buh-NEV-uh-lent), *equable* (EK-wuh-buul), and *forbearing* (for-BAIR-ing).

Word 17: OBEISANCE (oh-BAY-sints—recommended—*or* oh-BEE-sints)

A gesture of respect or submission, or an attitude of respect and submission.

Synonyms of *obeisance* include *deference*, *homage* (HAHM-ij; pronounce the *h*), *adoration*, *reverence*, and *veneration* (VEN-uh-**RAY**-shin).

Obeisance comes from French and means literally obedience. It was once used to mean obedience, or the power or right to demand obedience, but these senses are obsolete. *Obeisance* now means a respectful, submissive attitude or a deferential gesture, one that shows respect for the superiority of another.

Obeisance is used chiefly of formal situations in which respect or homage is paid to a god, a ruler, a religious leader, or a person of great influence or power. A bow, a curtsy, and a genuflection (JEN-yuu-**FLEK**-shin), a deferential bending of the knee, are all examples of obeisance, a gesture or attitude of respect and submission.

Word 18: ASSIDUOUS (uh-SIJ-oo-us)

Hardworking, industrious; done with persistent, careful, and untiring attention.

Synonyms of *assiduous* include *diligent*, *painstaking*, *persevering*, *unremitting*, *indefatigable* (IN-di-**FAT**-i-guh-buul), and *sedulous* (SEJ-uh-lus).

Antonyms include *lazy*, *shiftless*, *indolent* (IN-duh-lent), *languid* (LANG-gwid), *phlegmatic* (fleg-MAT-ik, word 33 of Level 9), and *otiose* (**OH**-shee-OHS, last syllable rhyming with *dose*).

Assiduous comes from the Latin *adsiduus*, which means sitting continuously in one place, engaged in an occupation, and ultimately from the verb *sedere*, to sit down, the source also of the English words *sedate* (suh-DAYT) and *sedentary* (**SED**-'n-TER-ee). By derivation, *assiduous* means sitting down and working diligently until a job is done.

In modern usage *assiduous* means done with persistent, careful, and untiring attention, constant in application or effort. We speak of assiduous efforts, an assiduous reader, an assiduous student, or an assiduous worker.

The corresponding noun is *assiduousness*: "Pamela was delighted that her assiduousness earned her a promotion."

Word 19: DUPLICITY (d(y)oo-PLIS-i-tee)

Deceit, cunning, double-dealing, hypocritical deception.

Synonyms of *duplicity* include *trickery*, *dishonesty*, *fraud*, *guile* (GYL, rhymes with *mile*), *chicanery* (shi-KAY-nur-ee), *casuistry* (KAZH-oo-is-tree), and *mendacity* (men-DAS-i-tee).

The noun *duplicity* comes through the Latin *duplicitas*, doubleness, and *duplicare*, to double, ultimately from *duplex*, twofold, double. Literally, *duplicity* means doubleness of heart or speech; in modern usage it refers to double-dealing, an act of deception in which one uses hypocritical or misleading words or actions to hide one's true intentions: "Steve was astounded at the duplicity of some of the salespeople, who seemed willing to say anything to close a deal."

The corresponding adjective is *duplicitous* (d(y)oo-PLIS-i-tus), which means two-faced, deceitful. The duplicitous person pretends to entertain one set of feelings while acting under the influence of another.

Word 20: INSOUCIANT (in-SOO-see-int)

Carefree, nonchalant, lightheartedly unconcerned or indifferent, free from worry or anxiety, calm and unbothered.

The French phrase *sans souci* (SA(N) soo-SEE) means without care or worry. The English word *insouciant* combines the privative prefix *in-*, meaning "not," with the French *souci*, care, worry, to mean literally not caring, free from worry, lightheartedly unconcerned: "Nanette dismissed Albert's contentious interruption with an insouciant wave of her hand and went on with what she was saying." *Insouciant* sometimes implies a carefree indifference or lack of concern for consequences: "Jim drove with an insouciant disregard for the speed limit and the hazards of the road that Paula found frightening."

The corresponding noun *insouciance* means lighthearted indifference, nonchalance, a carefree lack of concern: "Basking in Angelina's ethereal presence, Peter experienced an insouciance he had never allowed himself to feel before."

Let's review the ten keywords you've just learned. Consider the following statements and decide whether each one is true or false. Answers appear on page 318.

1. A person can have catholic interests, and an idea can have catholic appeal.
2. When you agree with something, you express your objurgation.
3. Effusive speech or writing is restrained and concise.
4. When you take umbrage at something, you take offense.
5. The vicissitudes of life are its problems and challenges.
6. A contentious person enjoys engaging in arguments or debates.
7. An obeisance is a display of disobedience or disrespect.
8. An assiduous worker is inclined to be lazy or careless.
9. Duplicity is a sign of a responsible, loyal person.
10. An insouciant manner is a carefree, unconcerned manner.

The Sounds-Like Syndrome

Now let's examine the second general problem of abusage, which I like to call the "sounds-like syndrome."

The sounds-like syndrome manifests itself when a word, usually one just a bit more refined that most people can handle, becomes confused with and then used as a pretentious substitute for another word that is similar in sound but different in meaning. If the error is repeated by enough people, often the result is that we lose one perfectly good word with a deserving role in the language and wind up with two words that mean the same thing—one the common word that has quietly done its job all along, the other an ostentatious and officious upstart.

In short, the sounds-like syndrome refers to pairs of words that are consistently confused because of their similar sound, with one word tending to eclipse the meaning of the other. Let me give you a few examples of these commonly confused words. As you read them, ask yourself if you can distinguish their meanings: *fortuitous* and *fortunate*; *apprise* and *appraise*; *comprise* and *compose*; *deprecate* and *depreciate*; *enormity* and *enormousness*; *precipitous* and *precipitate*; and *parameter* and *perimeter*.

All right, are you confused enough yet?

In each example given, the two words do not have the same or even a similar meaning. Yet every day one member of each pair is wrenched from its proper place in the language and forced to do the work of the other, as if it were a nut or bolt in a piece of machinery that could fit here or fit there, and serve as well holding one part together as another. But words are not like nuts and bolts—mass-produced, nondescript, interchangeable. They are more like the people who use them—individual, distinct, and irreplaceable.

Why do such confusions happen? First, because people make mistakes and appropriate the errors of others without realizing it. I am not a member of the school that maintains there is a conspiracy at work to corrupt the English language. No one is out there plotting to spread bad usage. What happens is that people hear or read something, and because they respect the person who said or wrote it, or they like the way it sounds, they think it must be right. Then they leave it at that, unaware that what they have just assimilated may be a solecism. (As you may recall from the discussion in Level 6 of words derived from Greek names, a *solecism* is a gross error of grammar or usage.)

The second reason these confusions happen may be attributed to human nature. Because people get bored using the same old words to say the same old things, and because they fear they will appear boring to others if they use the same old words everyone else uses, they start looking for novel ways to express themselves. This restless eagerness to impress others often leads people to substitute an ostensibly more elegant word for a familiar one, or to experiment with an unusual word they have not taken the trouble to learn. For example, they think, "*Fortuitous* looks like *fortunate* and sounds like *fortunate*, so it probably means pretty much the same thing. If we slip it in when we mean *fortunate*, we'll sound more intelligent and no harm done, right?" I'm sorry, but that kind of logic just doesn't wash. The arbitrary substitution or appropriation of a word, whether intentional or not, almost always has a deleterious effect upon the language.

Fortuitous means happening by chance, accidental, unexpected. Though we usually use *fortuitous* to refer to what the dictionaries like to call "happy accidents," and though we rarely use it to refer to a chance event of an unfortunate nature (for instance, you wouldn't say "a fortuitous earthquake"), the fact remains that in precise usage *fortuitous* is not interchangeable with *fortunate*. Allow me to give you an example that I think will illustrate the point. It's not unreasonable to infer from the phrase "a fortuitous meeting" that the meeting may be a fortunate, or lucky, one. But consider how the meaning of *fortuitous* becomes clear when I finish the sentence in this way: "A fortuitous meeting with Mr. Percival Sneed was the cause of his death." There's no way you can use *fortunate* in that sentence, unless you are trying to be droll. (If you need to remind yourself of the precise meaning of *droll*, it's word 36 of Level 5.)

Now let's take a moment to distinguish the other pairs of words I mentioned earlier as examples of the sounds-like syndrome.

Apprise (uh-PRYZ) and *appraise* (uh-PRAYZ): To *apprise* means to inform. To *appraise* means to evaluate or estimate the worth of. You apprise a coworker of what went on in the office while she was away. You appraise antiques, rare books, and works of art.

Comprise and *compose*: As I noted way back in Level 2, *comprise* properly means to include, contain, or consist of. It should not be used to mean *compose*, which means "to make up." The rule for *comprise* is that "the whole comprises its parts; the parts compose the whole." Do not say the United States is comprised of fifty states, or that fifty states comprise the United States. Say the United States comprises fifty states, or the United States is composed of fifty states.

Deprecate (**DEP**-ri-KAYT) and *depreciate* (di-PREE-shee-ayt): To *deprecate* means to express disapproval of. To *depreciate* means to belittle, disparage, lessen in value. When you deprecate something you show your disapproval of it; a deprecating look is a disapproving look. When you depreciate something you belittle it, treat it as inferior or of little value; a depreciating remark is a disparaging remark, one that shows a lack of appreciation for something.

Enormity and *enormousness*: Many people erroneously use *enormity* to mean *enormousness*. *Enormousness* means the state or quality of being enormous, extremely large or great. We speak of the enormousness of the Rocky Mountains or the enormousness of a project, not the enormity of them. *Enormity* refers to something morally outrageous or appalling, a monstrous evil or offense. We speak of the enormity of a crime, or the enormity of Adolph Hitler's diabolical "final solution."

Precipitous (pri-SIP-i-t<u>u</u>s) and *precipitate* (pri-SIP-i-tit): *Precipitous* means steep, like a precipice. *Precipitate* means rash, reckless, hasty, or sudden, abrupt, unexpected. The problem occurs when *precipitous*, steep, is used in place of *precipitate*, rash or abrupt, in such constructions as "a precipitous decision to change jobs," or "an escalating crisis heading precipitously toward war." A sudden or unexpected decision should be a precipitate decision, and a crisis that moves with reckless haste toward conflict should head precipitately toward conflict. Use *precipitous* only when you mean steep. A steep rise in profits is a precipitous rise. A precipitous decline in unemployment is a steep decline.

Parameter and *perimeter*: Most people who use *parameter* have no idea that it's an obscure mathematical term that has been pressed into service not only as a substitute for *perimeter*, which means a limit or boundary, but also as a pretentious synonym for *characteristic* and *feature*. And so today we hear and read such enormities of English prose as "We have to work within certain parameters," and "The design has several new parameters," when clearly what is meant is that the work must go on within certain limits (perimeters) and the design has several new features or characteristics. To me, the word *parameter* sounds extraterrestrial, and ought to be shot on sight. To borrow a quip from the respected language authority Bergen Evans, who borrowed his quip from one of the greatest quipsters, Mark Twain, you could start building a very expressive vocabulary just by leaving *parameter* out.

In closing this discussion of the sounds-like syndrome, I should note that if you look up these or other commonly confused words in a dictionary, you may find them listed as synonyms, often without comment. Don't be bamboozled by that: their equation in the dictionary does not necessarily justify interchanging the words or substituting one for the other; it is simply a reflection of their continual misuse by people who are not aware that careful writers and speakers take pains to preserve their distinctions in meaning. Keep in mind that dictionaries, being descriptive rather than prescriptive documents, eventually will recognize common errors of usage, even though careful writers and speakers continue to eschew those errors and criticize them.

And with that verbally advantageous admonishment, let's proceed with the next ten keywords in Level 7.

Word 21: MYRMIDON (MUR-m<u>i</u>-dahn *or* MUR-m<u>i</u>-d<u>u</u>n)

A loyal follower, faithful servant or subordinate, especially someone who is unquestioningly obedient.

In ancient Greek legend, the Myrmidons were a people of the region of Thessaly (THES-uh-lee) who fought in the Trojan War under their king, the great warrior Achilles (uh-KIL-eez). Brewer's *Dictionary of Phrase and Fable* notes that the Myrmidons "were distinguished for their savage brutality, rude behaviour, and thirst for rapine." (Now there's an interesting word: *rapine* (RAP-in) means pillage, plunder, the act of seizing and carrying off property by force.)

The *Oxford English Dictionary* traces Myrmidon back to the year 1400, and shows that by the seventeenth century it had come to be used in a general sense to mean "an unscrupulously faithful follower or hireling; a hired ruffian." The Myrmidons were perhaps in Alfred, Lord Tennyson's mind when he composed the famous lines in his 1855 poem "The Charge of the Light Brigade": "Theirs not to make reply / Theirs not to reason why / Theirs but to do and die / Into the valley of Death / Rode the six hundred."

In current usage, a *myrmidon*, with a small *m*, is a loyal follower or an obedient servant, a person who follows orders or executes commands without question and, if necessary, without scruple.

Word 22: NASCENT (NAS-int—recommended—*or* NAY-sint)

Beginning to exist or develop; in the process of being born or begun; coming or having just come into being.

Synonyms of *nascent* include *emerging*, *dawning*, *developing*, *commencing*, *embryonic* (EM-bree-**AHN**-ik), *incipient* (in-SIP-ee-int), and *inchoate* (in-KOH-it, word 35 of this level).

Antonyms include *ancient*, *extinct*, *outworn*, *outmoded*, *antiquated*, *obsolete*, *senescent* (word 9 of Level 7), and *antediluvian* (AN-tee-di-**LOO**-vee-in). *Antediluvian* means of the time before the Deluge (DEL-yooj), the great flood described in the first book of the Bible, Genesis; hence, extremely old or old-fashioned: "The horse and buggy is an antediluvian mode of transportation"; "Bob's father still prefers to write on an antediluvian manual typewriter."

There is nothing antediluvian about the word *nascent*, which comes from the Latin verb *nasci*, to be born. By derivation, *nascent* means in the process of being born, beginning to exist or develop. We speak of a nascent idea, a nascent republic, a nascent relationship, nascent anxiety, or nascent hope. The corresponding noun is *nascency* (NAS-in-see or NAY-), which means birth or beginning: "The year 1776 marks the nascency of American democracy."

Word 23: ACCEDE (ak-SEED)

To consent, yield, give in or agree to.

Synonyms of *accede* include *comply*, *submit*, *assent*, *concur* (word 18 of Level 1), and *acquiesce* (word 31 of Level 4). Antonyms include *resist*, *disagree*, *oppose*, *protest*, *contradict*, *dispute*, *dissent*, *wrangle*, and *cavil* (word 29 of Level 3).

The verbs *accede*, *acquiesce*, *assent*, *concur*, and *consent* all suggest agreement. *Consent* implies voluntary agreement: You consent to another's wishes. *Concur* implies agreement reached independently: When you concur with a statement, you agree on your own without pressure from the person who made it. *Assent* implies agreement reached after careful consideration or deliberation: When you assent to a plan, you agree to it after discussion or careful thought. *Acquiesce* implies agreement offered despite tacit reservations: the person who acquiesces often is unwilling to agree but lacks the will or the energy to resist.

Accede, our keyword, comes from the Latin *accedere*, to approach, come near. *Accede* implies agreement in which one person or party gives in to persuasion or yields under pressure. When you accede, you yield your position and give in to a demand or request, often under pressure: "They acceded to the proposal on certain conditions"; "After renegotiating various points, we acceded to the terms of the contract"; "The union refused to accede to the company's demands."

Accede may also be used to mean to attain or assume an office or title, as to accede to the throne, to accede to the presidency.

Word 24: MAGNANIMOUS (mag-NAN-i-mus)

Noble, honorable, generous in overlooking injury or insult, high-minded, unselfish.

People with an abiding faith in the goodness of human nature believe that we are noble, unselfish, and generous more often than we are ignoble, selfish, and grasping. The English vocabulary, however, suggests otherwise. In a language comprising well over a million words, there is a dearth of synonyms for *magnanimous*. Chalk up the words *noble*, *honorable*, *generous*, *unselfish*, and *high-minded*, and the list is almost exhausted; if you stretch things a bit you can add *courageous*, *exalted*, and *lofty* for the noble, high-minded connotation of *magnanimous*, and *charitable*, *altruistic* (AL-troo-**IS**-tik), and *beneficent* (buh-NEF-i-sint) for the generous, unselfish connotation.

On the other hand, the language abounds with antonyms for *magnani-*

mous. Browse through any thesaurus and you will find a cornucopia (KOR-n(y)uh-**KOH**-pee-uh) of these ignoble, selfish words. Here is a selection of my favorites: *vile*, *contemptible*, *malicious*, *despicable* (traditionally and properly DES-pik-uh-buul), *ignominious* (IG-noh-**MIN**-ee-u̱s), *covetous* (KUHV-uh-tu̱s), *avaricious* (word 40 of Level 2), *mercenary* (word 14 of Level 3), *venal* (VEE-nu̱l), *vindictive* (word 39 of Level 5), *churlish*, *sordid*, *abject* (word 50 of Level 4), *servile*, *sycophantic* (SIK-uh-**FAN**-tik), and finally, because we can't go on with this forever, we have the utterly ignoble word *pusillanimous* (PYOO-si̱-**LAN**-i̱-mu̱s), which means cowardly, weak, and mean-spirited. We will discuss *pusillanimous* further in Level 9.

The noble word *magnanimous* comes from the Latin *magnus*, great, and *animus*, spirit, and means literally great-spirited. In modern usage *magnanimous* means having or displaying a noble and generous soul; specifically, showing noble generosity in overlooking injury or insult. It applies either to persons who possess a generous, lofty, and courageous spirit, or to persons or actions that are unselfish, high-minded, and free from pettiness or vindictiveness.

Noble and *magnanimous* are close in meaning. According to the *Century Dictionary*, *noble* expresses that which "in character and conduct . . . is appropriate to exalted place," and "admits no degree of the petty, mean, base, or dishonorable." *Magnanimous* "describes that largeness of mind that has breadth enough and height enough to take in large views, broad sympathies, [and] exalted standards. It generally implies superiority of position: as, a nation so great as the United States . . . can afford to be magnanimous in its treatment of injuries or affronts from nations comparatively weak."

The corresponding noun is *magnanimity*, noble generosity, greatness or dignity of mind or heart: "He is a man of such magnanimity that he will do everything in his power to aid a worthy cause, no matter how unpopular it may be."

Word 25: NONAGE (NAHN-ij)

Immaturity, youth; especially the period of legal minority, the state of being a minor in the eyes of the law.

Nonage comes through Middle English from Anglo-French, the language of the Normans, who conquered England in 1066. *Nonage* combines the prefix *non-*, meaning "not," with the word *age* to mean literally "not of age."

Nonage may be used either generally to refer to any period of immaturity, or specifically to mean the state of being a minor. People in their nonage are under the lawful age for doing certain things such as marrying, making contracts, driving a motor vehicle, voting, or buying alcoholic beverages.

Word 26: INVECTIVE (in-VEK-tiv)

Vehement or abusive language involving bitter, scathing accusations or denunciations.

Synonyms of *invective* include *slander*, *defamation*, *aspersion* (uh-SPUR-zhun), *objurgation* (word 12 of this level), *billingsgate* (**BIL**-ingz-GAYT), *vituperation* (vy-T(Y)OO-puh-**RAY**-shin), and *obloquy* (AHB-luh-kwee).

Antonyms of *invective* include *praise*, *commendation*, *adulation* (AJ-uh-**LAY**-shin), *eulogy* (YOO-luh-jee), and *encomium* (en-KOH-mee-um).

Let's take a closer look at the words *billingsgate*, *vituperation*, and *obloquy*, which, like *invective*, denote various forms of abusive language.

Billingsgate comes from the name of one of the ancient gates of the city of London, near which stood a fish market. Apparently, not only did this market smell foul, as fish markets often do, but legend has it that the vendors and patrons also stunk up the place by exhibiting a proclivity for foul language. From those foul beginnings, *billingsgate* has come to mean abusive language that is filthy and obscene.

Vituperation has no such odorous etymology. *Vituperation* comes from a Latin verb meaning to scold or blame, and today denotes either a prolonged and vicious scolding or harsh, abusive language that violently scolds or blames.

Obloquy comes from the Latin *ob-*, meaning "against," and *loqui*, to speak. *Obloquy* refers to abusive language—and particularly abusive speech—whose express purpose is to defame or disgrace. If someone tries to ruin your reputation by abusing you either in conversation or in print, that's obloquy. And when obloquy strikes, you can react with *equanimity* (word 46 of Level 6), which you will recall means "composure, calm indifference," or you can respond with *invective*, bitter, vehement accusations or denunciations.

In *Synonyms Discriminated*, published in 1879, Charles Johnson Smith explains that "*Abuse* . . . is . . . personal and coarse, being conveyed in harsh and unseemly terms, and dictated by angry feeling and bitter temper. *Invective* is more commonly aimed at character or conduct, and may be conveyed in writing and in refined language, and dictated by indignation against what is in itself blameworthy. It often, however, means public abuse under such restraints as are imposed by position and education."

More than a hundred years later, Smith's distinction still holds: When someone uses coarse, harsh, or obscene language to disparage or intimidate another, we call it verbal abuse. When the abuse occurs in a public context, and takes the form of a bitter, vehement verbal attack that remains just barely within the bounds of decency, we call it invective. Thus, today we speak of a newspaper editorial full of invective; the invective exchanged in a bitter political contest; a snubbed author hurling invective at his critics; or an opinionated radio talk show host who issues a stream of invective against his ideological foes.

Invective comes ultimately from the Latin verb *invehere*, which means to attack with words. From the same source comes the English verb to *inveigh* (in-VAY). Like its Latin ancestor, to *inveigh* means to attack violently with words, protest furiously or express angry disapproval. *Inveigh* is always followed by *against*, as to inveigh against authority; to inveigh against an unfair company policy; to inveigh against an abuse of First Amendment rights.

Word 27: MACHINATION (MAK-i-NAY-shin)

A crafty or treacherous plot, malicious scheme, cunning design or plan to achieve a sinister purpose.

Synonyms of *machination* include *stratagem*, *conspiracy*, *contrivance*, *ruse* (properly ROOZ, rhyming with *lose* and *shoes*), and *cabal* (kuh-BAHL or kuh-BAL).

Machination comes from the Latin verb *machinari*, to plot, devise, contrive to do evil, which comes in turn from the noun *machina*, a device or contrivance for performing work. From the spelling of the Latin *machina* it's easy to deduce that it is also the source of the familiar and versatile word *machine*, something devised to perform work.

The Latin *machina* also appears in a phrase that has been taken whole into English: *deus ex machina* (DAY-uus eks MAH-ki-nuh), which means literally "a god out of a machine." In his delightful book *Amo, Amas, Amat: How to Use Latin to Your Own Advantage and to the Astonishment of Others* (1985), Eugene Ehrlich translates *deus ex machina* as "an unlikely and providential intervention," and explains that the phrase "describes an unexpected occurrence that rescues someone or something from an apparently hopeless predicament." Although *deus ex machina* is Latin, Ehrlich tells us that "the expression has its origin in ancient Greek theater. . . . When the complexities of plot and character appeared incapable of resolution, a god was set down on stage by a mechanical crane to sort out things and make them right."

Our keyword, *machination*, means a crafty plot, malicious scheme, cunning plan to achieve a sinister purpose, as a machination to seize power. In current usage the singular form is less common than the plural, *machinations*: "Ralph's deviousness enabled him to climb the company ladder, but when his machinations finally were exposed he found himself demoted to the mailroom."

You might think that machinations are confined to the crafty worlds of business and politics and to the sinister arena of international espionage, but the word is also sometimes used in a literary or metaphorical way, in such phrases as "the machinations of love," which can often be a treacherous business, or "the machinations of our dreams," which are often devious, or "the machinations of destiny," which may seem to plot against us.

I shall conclude this crafty lesson with an important pronunciation tip. Certain educated speakers, probably misled by the sound of the *ch* in *machine*, have adopted the pronunciation *mash*ination. This beastly *mash*ination is a classic example of what happens when people learn the meaning of a word but don't bother to check the pronunciation in a dictionary. They simply looked at *machination*, saw the word *machine* inside, and decided to say *mash*ination, blithely assuming that their false analogy was right without pausing to consider that the pronunciation they have just invented might not be the one most educated speakers prefer. That, in a nutshell, is how eccentric pronunciations are born—and the worst thing about it is that the mispronouncers often flaunt their inventions, as if to show that they have placed their personal stamp on the language by making up a bizarre way to say a word.

Some dictionaries now recognize *mash*ination, but list it after the preferred pronunciation, in which the *ch* is pronounced like *k*: (MAK-i-**NAY**-shin).

Word 28: DOCILE (DAHS-'l)

Submissive, obedient, compliant; easy to direct, manage, or supervise; following instructions.

Synonyms of *docile* include *amenable, deferential, malleable* (word 29 of Level 2), *tractable, acquiescent,* and *obsequious* (word 3 of this level).

Antonyms include *willful, wayward, headstrong, obstinate* (word 34 of Level 1), *intractable* (word 12 of Level 5), *intransigent* (in-TRAN-si-jint, word 4 of Level 8), and *refractory* (word 42 of Level 6).

Docile comes through the Latin *docilis,* teachable, from *docere,* to teach, instruct. From the same source comes the word *docent* (DOH-sint). A docent is either a teacher at a university who is not a member of the faculty, or a lecturing tour guide in a museum, cathedral, or some such place of cultural interest. By the way, in your travels through museums and the like, you may hear the phrase "docent guide," which is redundant. A docent guide is a "guide guide," because *docent* means a guide trained to lecture on what is being viewed. Think of me as your docent in the museum of the English language.

Our keyword, *docile,* by derivation means teachable. In modern usage *docile* has two closely related senses. It may mean easy to teach or instruct, as a docile pupil, or it may mean submissive, obedient, as a docile pet, or a docile employee—which is not to imply that employees in general are analogous to pets, but only that some employees are docile, easy to direct, manage, or supervise.

The corresponding noun is *docility*: "A dictatorship or totalitarian state derives its power only from the docility of the people."

Occasionally you may hear docile pronounced DOH-syl. DOH-syl is the preference of British and Canadian speakers. The preferred American pronunciation is DAHS-'l.

Word 29: REDOUBTABLE (ri-DOW-tuh-buul)

Formidable, fearsome, arousing awe or dread; hence, worthy of or commanding respect.

Redoubtable comes through Middle English from an Old French verb meaning to fear or dread, and ultimately from the Latin *dubitare*, to doubt, waver in opinion or action, the source also of the words *dubious*, which means doubtful or questionable, and *dubiety* (d(y)oo-BY-i-tee), which means doubtfulness, uncertainty, wavering.

Perhaps because the things we find dubious or that make us waver are often the same things we find disturbing or frightening, *redoubtable* has come to apply to that which we fear and respect because we doubt our ability to match, oppose, or overcome it. In modern usage, *redoubtable* means fearsome, formidable (stress on *for-*, remember?), commanding respect, and may apply either to people or to things.

We speak of the legendary Hercules as a redoubtable hero; of drug abuse as a redoubtable social problem; of AIDS as a redoubtable disease; of the redoubtable genius of Albert Einstein; of a rivalry between two redoubtable football teams; or of small airline companies facing redoubtable competition from the big carriers.

In current usage *redoubtable* sometimes is used to achieve a humorous, gently mocking effect. For example, back when Johnny Carson was host of "The Tonight Show," on which the actress Shelley Winters was a frequent guest, I remember Carson once cut to a commercial with this quip: "Don't go away, because we'll be right back with the redoubtable Shelley Winters."

Word 30: PROGNOSTICATE (prahg-NAHS-ti-kayt)

To predict; especially, to predict from signs, symptoms, or present indications.

Synonyms of *prognosticate* include *foretell*, *forecast*, *foresee*, *prophesy*

(**PRAHF**-i-SY), *presage* (pri-SAYJ), and *vaticinate* (va-**TIS**-i-NAYT).

Prognosticate comes through Latin from Greek, and by derivation means "a knowing beforehand, foreknowledge." From the same source we inherit several related words.

Prognostic (prahg-NAHS-tik), used as a noun, means an indication of something in the future. Used as an adjective, *prognostic* means pertaining to or serving as the basis of a prediction, as prognostic powers or prognostic evidence.

The noun *prognostication* (prahg-NAHS-ti-**KAY**-shin) means a prediction, prophecy, forecast, as the prognostications of economists are not always reliable.

Prognosticator (prahg-**NAHS**-ti-KAY-tur) is a lofty word for "a person who makes predictions." If you want to be grandiloquent, you could say the reporter who does your local weather forecast is a prognosticator, or that a coworker who is always making predictions about affairs in the office is the office prognosticator.

Finally, the useful noun *prognosis* (prahg-NOH-sis) means a prediction of the probable course and outcome of a disease or medical condition.

Prognosis and *diagnosis* should be sharply distinguished. A *diagnosis* is an assessment of a medical condition. When you ask your doctor, "What's the diagnosis?" you are asking for the doctor's opinion of what is wrong based on a clinical analysis of signs and symptoms. When you ask your doctor, "What's the prognosis?" you are asking the doctor to predict the likely course and outcome of the condition based on whatever treatment is administered—in other words, to tell you whether the problem will get better or worse. In short, a *diagnosis* describes the nature of the medical condition; a *prognosis* predicts its likely course and outcome.

Our keyword, *prognosticate*, means to make a prognosis or prediction. *Prognosticate* applies especially to the act of predicting from signs, symptoms, or present indications. Political pundits attempt to prognosticate the outcome of an election. Financial analysts prognosticate trends in the stock market. Your horoscope in the newspaper purports to prognosticate from the alignment of the planets what may lie in store for you that day.

Let's review the ten keywords you've just learned. I'll give you two words, and you decide if they are synonyms or antonyms. Answers appear on page 318.

1. *Antagonist* and *myrmidon* are . . . synonyms or antonyms?
2. *Nascent* and *senescent* are . . .

3. To *accede* and to *consent* are . . .
4. *Ignominious* and *magnanimous* are . . .
5. *Nonage* and *immaturity* are . . .
6. *Commendation* and *invective* are . . .
7. *Plot* and *machination* are . . .
8. *Intractable* and *docile* are . . .
9. *Formidable* and *redoubtable* are . . .
10. To *prognosticate* and to *predict* are . . .

If you answered fewer than eight of the questions correctly in this quiz, remember to reread the last ten keyword discussions before moving ahead in the program.

Are You in Vogue?

Now let's discuss the third category of abusage: vogue words. By "vogue words" I mean words that for some reason suddenly become fashionable, and that people use constantly without considering whether they have any useful purpose or force. Vogue words may be old or new, long or short, but the one thing they have in common is their popularity, which leads to their being worn out by "excessive and mechanical repetition," as Wilson Follett puts it in *Modern American Usage* (1966). In short, vogue words are the words that lazy writers and speakers reach for when they are trying to sound intelligent and original but don't have anything interesting to say.

As you may recall from my tirade in Level 5, *unique* is a prime example of a vogue word. Have you noticed how everything is "so very unique" these days? Apparently, the time has passed when something was just unusual or uncommon. To top it off, the precise meaning of *unique* is not simply "unusual" or "uncommon" but "one of a kind, matchless, without peer." Once you know that, it doesn't make sense to qualify *unique* with such words as *very*, *most*, or *somewhat*. How can something be very unique or somewhat unique if it already is peerless, one of a kind?

You may also recall, from the end of Level 6, my objurgation regarding the vogue word *impact*. In *The Writer's Art* (1984), James J. Kilpatrick says *impact* has "fastened like fatty tissue to the arteries of our language." He's right. No longer can something have a plain *effect*; it must have a dull *impact*. No longer can we say that something *influenced* or *affected* us—the banal vogue demands we say it *impacted* us. In my vocabulary, your teeth or your bones can be *impacted*, wedged together; and an *impact* is a collision or violent blow. But those who follow the vogue have taken all the force out of this word and used it as a feeble substitute for *influence* or *effect*. Today we are bombarded with environmental impact studies, warnings about the impact of inflation, and vicissitudes that may adversely impact the stock market.

As if that's not enough to make a verbally advantaged person contemplate the impact of a bullet on the brain, the *impact* virus now is mutating into even more pernicious forms! For example, I have come across the word *impactful* in print, in an ad for a laptop computer that said, "Presentations are impactful. Engaging. Impressive."

Why did that tin-eared writer use *impactful*? What's wrong with saying the presentations are engaging and impressive—or for that matter, effective, outstanding, striking, splendid, gripping, stunning, sensational, or electrifying? Why invent such an ugly word when so many attractive ones are available? Please, dear reader, for the health and welfare of the English language I implore you to abstain from using *impact* or any of its odious offspring.

Our next vile vogue word is *viable*. The precise meaning of *viable* is able to live, able to take root and grow, capable of independent existence, as a viable plant, a viable fetus, a viable culture, or a viable industry. Today, however, people are using *viable* to mean "possible, workable, doable." When I hear about "viable plans" and "viable alternatives," I wonder where they're going to live, who's going to put them up. If you want a fancy word for *possible*, try *conceivable*, and if you want a fancy word for *workable* or *doable*, try *practicable*—pronounced in four syllables: PRAK-ti-kuh-buul.

Next in the Top 40 of Vogue we have "The Ize Brothers": *maximize*, *finalize*, *prioritize*, *concretize*, *sensitize*, *optimize*, *secretize*, *incentivize*, and many more awkward and pretentious verbs ending in *-ize*. In *The Appropriate Word* (1990), J. N. Hook notes that *-ize* is "an unbeautiful verb ending, often criticized by writers on usage, yet frequently necessary, as *criticize* itself illustrates." In *The Careful Writer*, Theodore M. Bernstein wisely comments that the suffix *-ize* can either help the language grow in a wholesome way, or make it grow "stuffy and grotesque."

Criticize, *sterilize*, *socialize*, and *hospitalize* are useful because they streamline expression. A coinage like *incentivize* is not only ugly and outlandish but also unnecessary, because the language already contains words that express its meaning, such as *excite*, *encourage*, and *stimulate*. Remember, if you hear a strange buzzing in your ears, watch out for a pompous and promiscuous use of the suffix *-ize*.

According to devotees of the vogue, people don't talk, speak, or converse anymore. Instead they *dialogue*, as "We dialogued about it for an hour over lunch." I'm sorry, but it's high time to put a muzzle on that one. Other horrifying vogue words include *interface*, which should not be allowed to show its face outside of computer science; *methodology* used to mean method; *decisioned* used to mean decided; and *proactive*, which the dictionaries now tell us means "acting in anticipation" of something but which the voguesters in business and government all seem to use to mean either "acting to show that we're acting" or "acting as if we know what we're doing."

The poet W. H. Auden once claimed that "nine-tenths of the population do not know what 30 percent of the words they use actually mean." I would wager that most people use words like *impact*, *prioritize*, *methodology*, and *proactive* not because they're trying to use the right word but because they're trying to appear with it or smart. As H. W. Fowler remarks in his classic guide, *Modern English Usage* (1926), vogue words are "words owing their vogue to the joy of showing one has acquired them."

Finally, there are the catch phrases that are so often repeated that they lose whatever shred of meaning or force they might have had. Think about how often you have heard—and perhaps used—these phrases: *calculated risk, cautiously optimistic, credibility gap, communication gap, the bottom line, quantum leap, phase out, cutting edge, state of the art, meaningful dialogue, peer group, considered judgment, factors to be considered, decision-making process, learning experience, positive consequences, it remains to be seen*, and *in regard to*—or worse, the illiterate *in regards to*.

Those are just a handful of the scores of fashionable but vapid or nebulous expressions that the careful writer and speaker rephrases or avoids. Keep your eyes and ears open, and whenever you suspect that a word or phrase is becoming weak from overwork, it's a good bet that it's been bitten by the vogue.

In *The Writer's Art* (1984), columnist James J. Kilpatrick relates an anecdote about former secretary of commerce Malcolm Baldrige, who was so infuriated with the gobbledegook and doublespeak of the Washington bureaucracy that he issued a memo "demanding 'short sentences and short words, with emphasis on plain English, using no more words than effective expression requires.' Thus, for starters," writes Kilpatrick, Baldrige "banned from departmental correspondence and papers such words as *maximize*, *institutionalize*, and *interface*," along with such phrases as "*bottom line* and *serious crisis* and *material enclosed herewith*." I can just see all the bureaucrats "interfacing" and "dialoguing" around the coffee maker, being "cautiously optimistic" about "maximizing" their "bottom line." Somebody had to "impact" their "parameters," right?

There are two lessons to be learned here: Look hard before you leap on the verbal bandwagon, and beware the ostentatious allure of the popular but enervated word. As Wilson Follett writes in *Modern American Usage* (1966), "When repeated use has worn down the novelty, the word we hear and the associations we sense are not what they were at first. . . . Skill in expression consists in nothing else than choosing the fittest among all possible words, idioms, and constructions."

And with that fitting piece of advice on vogue words, let's return now to the *Verbal Advantage* vocabulary for the next ten keywords in Level 7.

Word 31: ENGENDER (en-JEN-dur)

To bring about, bring into being, give rise to, cause to exist, sow the seeds of. Synonyms of *engender* include *produce* and *generate*. Antonyms include *prevent*, *suppress*, *subdue*, *quell*, and *quash* (rhymes with *squash*).

Engender comes through Middle English and Old French from the Latin *generare*, to beget, produce, bring to life. Originally, *engender* meant to beget by procreation, which is a fancy way of saying sexual intercourse. (And who told you *Verbal Advantage* wasn't a sexy program?) Dictionaries still list *beget*, *procreate*, and *propagate* as synonyms of *engender*, but the sense of breeding offspring has fallen by the wayside, and since at least Shakespeare's day *engender* has meant to bring forth, give rise to, cause to exist. A rally in the stock market may engender hope among investors that the economy is improving. An exchange of invective between nations can engender war.

Word 32: FETID (FET-id)

Stinking, foul-smelling; having an extremely offensive odor, as of something rotten or decayed.

In *Hamlet*, Shakespeare could just as well have written "Something is fetid in the state of Denmark," except that if he had, probably no one would quote the line today.

Challenging synonyms of *fetid* include *rank*, *rancid*, *malodorous*, *putrid* (PYOO-trid), *noisome* (NOY-sum), *mephitic* (me-FIT-ik), and *graveolent* (gruh-VEE-uh-lint). Antonyms include *fragrant*, *scented*, *perfumed*, *aromatic*, and *redolent* (RED-uh-lint).

Fetid comes through the Latin *fetidus*, which means "stinking," from the verb *fetere*, to stink, have a bad smell. In current usage, *fetid* is not used of any old bad smell but is usually reserved for an extremely offensive odor, such as that produced by rotting or decay. For example, bad breath makes you wrinkle your nose; *fetid* breath makes you gag. When your garbage is odorous, it smells; when it's malodorous, it smells bad; when it's rank, it's really going sour; and when it's fetid, you'd better get rid of it before your neighbors call the health department.

And now, because I can read your twisted, puerile mind and I know you are waiting for me to get to this: yes, it's also true that a fart (which in this dignified program—stop giggling now!—we call "a gaseous flatus expelled from the anus") can also be *fetid*, foul-smelling.

I shall end this malodorous lesson with a pronunciation tip. You may occasionally see our keyword spelled *foetid*, and you may occasionally hear it pronounced FEE-tid. That's the British spelling and pronunciation. In American English we spell it *fetid* and prefer a short *e*: FET-id.

Word 33: PEDANTIC (pe̱-DAN-tik)

Absurdly learned; scholarly in an ostentatious way; making an inappropriate or tiresome display of knowledge by placing undue importance on trivial details, rules, or formalities.

After that definition, you're probably thinking that your guide through *Verbal Advantage* sometimes is pedantic about language. All right, it's true. As we pedantic types like to say, *mea culpa* (MAY-uh KUUL-puh), which is Latin for "my fault." On the other hand, I am also erudite, which as you learned in Level 3 means scholarly, possessing extensive knowledge acquired chiefly from books. That's not such a bad combination for someone whose job is to help you navigate the stormy sea of English words.

So, my verbally advantaged friend, if you want to emulate my grandiloquent erudition, then please pardon my pedantry as I explain that the adjective *pedantic*, and the corresponding nouns *pedant* (PED-'nt) and *pedantry* (PED-'n-tree), come through Italian and Latin from the Greek *paidagogos*, a tutor of children, the source also of the word *pedagogue* (**PED**-uh-GAHG), which may mean simply a teacher, or a teacher who is narrow-minded, dogmatic, and— you guessed it—pedantic.

If we further break down the Greek *paidagogos*, we see that it is composed of *pais*, *paidos*, a boy or child, and *agein*, to lead or conduct, and means literally a leader or conductor of youngsters. For the significance of that derivation, let's turn to the erudite and only occasionally pedantic *Century Dictionary* (1914). "Among the ancient Greeks and Romans," says the *Century*, "the pedagogue was originally a slave who attended the younger children of his master, and conducted them to school, to the theater, etc., combining in many cases instruction with guardianship."

This servile tutor of classical antiquity eventually rose to become the modern pedagogue, a teacher or schoolmaster, but a stigma of pedantry—mean ing a slavish or dogmatic attention to rules and minor details of learning—remained on the word. Perhaps that explains why, when certain members of the teaching profession went looking for a more dignified word for themselves than *teacher*, they eschewed *pedagogue* and settled on three terms: *educator*, which is a good alternative; *educationist*, which is a pompous one; and *educationalist*, which is preposterous. But unless you happen to be a pedagogue, that's neither here nor there, and being the verbose pedant that I am, I digress.

A *pedant* was originally a pedagogue or teacher, but that sense soon fell into disuse and a *pedant* became, as the *Century Dictionary* puts it, "a person who overrates erudition, or lays an undue stress on exact knowledge of detail or of trifles, as compared with larger matters or with general principles." The noun *pedantry* refers to the manners or actions of a pedant. According to the eighteenth-century Irish essayist and dramatist Sir Richard Steele, "Pedantry proceeds from much reading and little understanding." Jonathan Swift, the author of *Gulliver's Travels*, defined *pedantry* as "the overrating of any kind of knowledge we pretend to." And the poet Samuel Taylor Coleridge (KOHL-rij, two syllables) wrote that "pedantry consists in the use of words unsuitable to the time, place, and company."

The adjective *pedantic* means absurdly learned; scholarly in an ostentatious way; making an inappropriate or tiresome display of knowledge by placing undue importance on trivial details, rules, or formalities.

Word 34: CAPITULATE (kuh-PICH-uh-layt)

To yield, surrender; specifically, to surrender on specified terms or conditions.

The verbs to *capitulate* and to *decapitate* both come ultimately from the Latin *caput, capitis*, which means "the head." *Decapitate* sticks literally to its root and means to cut off the head. *Capitulate* has sprouted from its root and means to list the terms of surrender under various headings in a document.

Although some current dictionaries define *capitulate* as "to surrender unconditionally or on stipulated terms," in precise usage *capitulate* means to yield or surrender only on stipulated terms, although the terms do not necessarily have to be drawn up in a document.

When armies or nations capitulate, they specify the conditions under which they will surrender. When people accused of a crime accept a plea bargain, they capitulate by stipulating the terms under which they will yield to the prosecution and accept a conviction. And when two parties come to terms in a dispute, you can be sure that one party is the victor and the other has capitulated.

The corresponding noun is *capitulation*, the act of surrendering or yielding on specified terms or conditions.

Word 35: INCHOATE (in-KOH-it)

Just begun; in an early stage of development; partly in existence; not fully formed; undeveloped; imperfect; incomplete.

Synonyms of *inchoate* include *elementary*, *preliminary*, *nascent* (word 22 of this level), *rudimentary*, and *incipient* (in-SIP-ee-int).

Inchoate comes from the Latin *incohatus*, just begun, not finished, incomplete; *incohatus* is the past participle of the verb *incohare*, to begin, take in hand, start work on.

Since the sixteenth century, when *inchoate* entered English, the word has been used of that which has just begun or is in an early stage of development, and which is therefore imperfect or incomplete. An inchoate state is an initial, undeveloped state; an inchoate idea is an idea not yet fully formed; an inchoate project is a project that is just getting off the ground.

Word 36: EXPONENT (eks-POH-nint)

A person who stands or speaks for something, a representative or advocate.

Exponent comes from the Latin *exponere*, to put forth, put on view, display. The Latin *exponere* is also the source of the English verb to *expound*, which means to explain, interpret, set forth point by point, as to expound an idea or to expound the principles of business management. An exponent may be a person who expounds, an explainer, interpreter, or commentator, but in current usage *exponent* more often applies to a person who stands or speaks for something, someone who represents, advocates, or promotes some idea or purpose: The leader of a political party is the exponent of its principles and goals; the pontiff is the exponent of Roman Catholicism; the framers of the U.S. Constitution were exponents of democracy and individual liberty; and Carry Nation, the austere and abstemious nineteenth-century temperance crusader who chopped up saloons with a hatchet, was a radical exponent of abstinence from alcoholic beverages.

Word 37: MENDACIOUS (men-DAY-shus)

Not truthful, lying, false, dishonest, deceitful.

Mendacious comes through the Latin *mendacium*, a lie, from the adjective *mendax*, which means lying, deceitful. By derivation *mendacious* means given to lying, disposed to falsehood or deceit. A mendacious person is a dishonest person, one who is prone to lie or deceive; a mendacious statement is an untruthful statement, a deliberate falsehood or a lie.

Synonyms of *mendacious* include *fraudulent*, *hypocritical*, *disingenuous* (DIS-in-**JEN**-yoo-<u>u</u>s), *evasive*, *equivocal* (i-KWIV-uh-k<u>u</u>l), *duplicitous* (d(y)oo-PLIS-<u>i</u>-t<u>u</u>s), and *prevaricating* (pri-**VAR**-<u>i</u>-KAY-ting).

Antonyms include *truthful*, *honorable*, *upright*, *ethical*, *virtuous*, *scrupulous*, and *veracious* (v<u>e</u>-RAY-sh<u>u</u>s). The corresponding noun is *mendacity* (men-DAS-<u>i</u>-tee), untruthfulness, lying, deceit.

Word 38: STRIDENT (STRY-d<u>i</u>nt)

Loud and harsh-sounding, grating, shrill.

Synonyms of *strident* include *earsplitting*, *screeching*, *discordant*, *clamorous*, *cacophonous* (kuh-KAHF-uh-n<u>u</u>s), *vociferous* (voh-SIF-ur-<u>u</u>s), and *stentorian* (sten-TOR-ee-<u>i</u>n).

Antonyms include *faint*, *subdued*, *melodious*, *dulcet* (DUHL-sit), and *euphonious* (yoo-FOH-nee-<u>u</u>s).

Strident comes from the present participle of the Latin verb *stridere*, to make a harsh noise. Apparently, *stridere* was a versatile word in Latin, for ancient Roman poets and writers such as Vergil (VUR-j<u>il</u>), Lucretius (loo-KREE-sh<u>u</u>s), and Ovid (AH-vid) used it to describe many sounds, not all of them harsh: the grating of metal on metal; the whistling of the wind; the scraping or whining of a saw; the creaking of a wagon, a rope, or a hinge on a door; the whirring of a rock or an arrow propelled through the air; the braying of an ass; the trumpeting of elephants; the grunting of a pig; the hiss of a snake; and even the humming of bees.

The words that English has inherited from the Latin *stridere* are not so versatile, and stick more closely to the core meaning of this ancient verb: to make a harsh noise. For instance, the noun *stridor* (STRY-dur) may mean a harsh grating or creaking sound or, in medicine, a harsh sound made when breathing in or out that indicates obstruction of the respiratory tract. The adjective *stridulous* (STRIJ-uh-l<u>u</u>s) means making a harsh or shrill noise. And the verb to *stridulate* (**STRIJ**-uh-LAYT) means to make a shrill, high-pitched grating or chirping sound. Crickets and various other insects stridulate by rubbing certain body parts together.

Our keyword, *strident*, applies to any sound or noise that is disagreeably loud, harsh, and shrill: a piercing scream, the screeching of brakes, the grinding of gears, the whining of a power tool, the wailing of a baby, or any loud, gruff voice that grates on your ears can be described as strident.

Word 39: OLIGARCHY (AHL-uh-GAHR-kee)

Government by a few; rule or control exercised by a few persons or by a small, elite group.

Oligarchy comes from the Greek *oligos*, few, little, and *archein,* to govern, rule, and by derivation means "government by the few." *Oligarchy* may denote rule or control exercised by a few people, a state or an organization run by a few people, or the few dominant people themselves, and the word often suggests the hoarding of power for corrupt or selfish purposes. Thus we speak of an oligarchy within organized crime; an oligarchy of the rich; or the oligarchy of the former Soviet Union.

For the corresponding adjective, both *oligarchic* and *oligarchical* are acceptable.

Here's a pronunciation tip: You may hear some speakers pronounce *oligarchy* with a long *o*: OH-ligarchy. This recent variant is listed second in two current dictionaries; all other authorities, past and present, do not recognize it. Properly, the initial *o* is short, as in *olive* and *college.*

Word 40: REFULGENT (ri-FUHL-jent)

Shining brightly, brilliant, radiant, resplendent.

Additional synonyms of *refulgent* include *gleaming*, *blazing*, *sparkling*, *luminous*, *incandescent*, *scintillating*, and *coruscating*. In case you're wondering about those last three, allow me to explain.

Incandescent (IN-kan-**DES**-int) means extremely bright or glowing with heat. It may sound peculiar to say so, but a light bulb, a person's mind, and a spiritual truth all can be described as incandescent. *Scintillating* (**SIN**-ti-LAY-ting) means throwing off sparks, sparkling or twinkling. You can have scintillating thoughts, scintillating conversation, or observe scintillating stars in the summer sky. *Coruscating* (**KOR**-uh-SKAY-ting or **KAHR**-) means giving off flashes of light, flashing or glittering. An impressive display of fireworks is a coruscating display; a flashy or brilliant performance can be described as a coruscating performance.

Antonyms of *refulgent* include *dull*, *dim*, *obscure*, *gloomy*, and *murky*, all of which I know you know, so I think I'll commit an unpardonable act of pedantic obfuscation by muddling and bewildering you with these mind-boggling antonyms: *tenebrous* (TEN-uh-brus), which means dark and gloomy; *umbrageous* (uhm-BRAY-jus), which means shady or overshadowed; *subfuscous* (suhb-FUHS-kus), which means dusky or somber; and—do you have room upstairs for one more?—*crepuscular* (kri-PUHS-kyuh-lur), which means pertaining to twilight, hence, characterized by dim, waning, or glimmering light.

Our brilliant keyword, *refulgent*, comes from the present participle of the Latin verb *refulgere*, to shine brightly, which comes in turn from *re-*, meaning "back," and *fulgere*, to shine, flash, or gleam. You may use *refulgent* literally to mean gleaming or shining brightly; for example, someone can give you a refulgent smile, or you can explore a cave with the refulgent beam of a powerful flashlight. You may also use *refulgent* to mean figuratively brilliant or radiant; for example, you may know someone with a refulgent wit, or a person of refulgent beauty.

The corresponding noun is *refulgence* (ri-FUHL-jents), brilliance, radiance, resplendence.

Let's review the last ten keywords by playing "One of These Definitions Doesn't Fit the Word." In each statement below, a keyword (in *italics*) is followed by three definitions. Two of the three are correct; one is unrelated in meaning. Decide which definition doesn't fit the keyword. Answers appear on page 319.

1. To *engender* means to bring about, bring up, give rise to.
2. *Fetid* means ugly, rotten, stinking.
3. *Pedantic* means showing off one's knowledge in an inappropriate way, in an impressive way, in a tiresome way.
4. To *capitulate* means to yield, admit, surrender.
5. *Inchoate* means completed, undeveloped, just begun.
6. An *exponent* is an advocate, a representative, an adversary.
7. *Mendacious* means lying, bitter, false.
8. *Strident* means bold, harsh, loud.
9. *Oligarchy* means control by a small group, rule by a dictator, government by a few.
10. *Refulgent* means luxuriant, radiant, brilliant.

Are You Addicted to Adverbiage?

Now it's time to take a look at the fourth category of abusage, which I call "adverbiage."

Adverbiage is the overuse or awkward use of adverbs, words that modify verbs—or to put it in nongrammatical terms, words that tell you how an action is performed. Most, though not all, adverbs end in *-ly*. For example, in the sentence "They listened carefully," *carefully* is the adverb modifying the verb to *lis-*

ten. In the sentence "He used the word properly," *properly* is the adverb modifying the verb to *use*.

There is nothing inherently wrong with adverbs—as you can see from my pointed use of *inherently* in that statement. (And by the way, *inherent* is properly pronounced in-HEER-int, not in-HAIR-int or in-HER-int.) Adverbs can perform a useful service in expressing nuances of quality or manner. The "adverbiage" problem occurs when the adverb is part of a cliché, or hackneyed phrase; when it is an awkward creation, such as "procedurally," "constructionally," "experientially," or "opinionatedly"; or when adverbs are overused, as in this sentence: "As the report clearly states, the only thoroughly and completely effective method for increasing sales rapidly is to competitively engineer and efficiently market our products." That horrendous sentence commits all three errors—hackneyed use, awkward use, and overuse.

Moral: Adverbiage always weakens what you have to say.

In his stylebook *Simple and Direct* (1985), Jacques Barzun offers these examples of adverbial clichés: *to seriously consider*, *to utterly reject*, *to thoroughly examine*, *to be absolutely right*, *to make perfectly clear*, and *to sound definitely interested*. In each case the adverb is superfluous; nothing is lost by removing it. In fact, each phrase is strengthened as a result. "I will consider it" conveys more promise of serious attention than "I will seriously consider it." "I reject the allegation" is firmer and more confident than "I utterly reject the allegation." "To be right" is unimpeachable compared with "to be absolutely right," which suggests that there are degrees of rightness. And "let me make one thing clear" is a stronger statement than "let me make one thing perfectly clear," because inserting the adverb *perfectly* makes you sound either condescending or defensive.

Take a look at the following passage, which I culled from the sales brochure of a company specializing in "instructional technology"—by which they mean, in plain English, "training programs." See if you can discern why and how the writing is flawed:

> [We] understand the critical need for instruction that truly teaches what people need to know. People learn best when the instruction is designed so that it facilitates the learning process and when they thoroughly enjoy the learning activity.

That is terrible writing; unfortunately, it is typical of the thoughtless and careless way many educated and otherwise articulate people use the language. Did you hear the vogue word, catch phrases, and adverbiage? In two sentences containing just thirty-eight words, the writer used the vogue word "facilitates"; the catch phrases "learning process," "learning activity," and "critical need"; and two blundering bits of adverbiage: "truly teaches" and "thoroughly enjoy."

The verb *facilitate* has been in the language for almost four hundred years; it's a decent word that comes in handy every so often. The problem is that in trying to pump up their prose, people have overworked *facilitate* nigh unto death. Why must we always facilitate something when the words *help*, *support*, *assist*, and *encourage* are there to help, support, assist, and encourage us? Likewise, can't we just enjoy learning without making it a process, an activity, or an experience? And why is a need always critical? Will someone die if it isn't satisfied? If you said "I have a critical need to go to the bathroom," the person you said it to probably would burst out laughing. Yet in a world where a crisis must be a "serious crisis" to merit attention, we fear a need will be ignored unless we say it's a "critical need."

Finally, we have the adverbiage problem. The writer of those two miserable sentences tried to sound enthusiastic and convincing by using the phrases "truly teaches" and "thoroughly enjoy" but wound up being verbose and trite. In a colloquial exchange with a coworker about a movie you had seen, it would be natural for you to say you "thoroughly enjoyed" it and found it "truly interesting." That's because speech is more informal, more wordy, and less precise than writing, which should be simple and direct—especially if it's a sales pitch.

Good, tight writing has no superfluous words; the practiced writer learns to cut them out, and the first ones to go are always adverbs. What does *thoroughly enjoy* say that *enjoy* can't convey by itself? Likewise, *truly* does nothing for the verb to *teach*—you either teach or you don't teach. In fact, *truly* is so often used insincerely that it's hard to believe it contains any more enthusiasm than it does in the complimentary close of a letter, "yours truly." *Truly*, along with the adverbs *actually*, *basically*, and *really*, are filler words that carry little or no weight by themselves; they are common in everyday, informal conversation, but in writing they should be used with caution, or not at all.

The lesson here is don't overwrite. Avoid overused words and overblown expressions. Delete wherever possible. Strive to be clear and terse. Strong writing does its work unencumbered by hordes of adverbs, or, as in the case of "critical need," by phrases exaggerated or overused to the point of meaninglessness.

And now it's time for another infusion of powerful words that will help you make your expression more muscular.

Word 41: NEPOTISM (NEP-uh-tiz-'m)

Favoritism shown to relatives.

Nepotism comes through French and Italian from the Latin *nepos, nepotis*, a nephew or grandson. According to the *Century Dictionary* (1914), "the word was invented [in the seventeenth century] to characterize a propensity of the popes and other high ecclesiastics in the Roman Catholic Church to aggrandize their family by exorbitant grants or favors to nephews or relatives."

In current usage *nepotism* denotes favoritism shown to any relative, and the word usually applies to situations in business and public life where relatives are shown preference over nonrelatives and receive privileges or positions that they may not necessarily deserve. Thus, if you give your niece money to help her buy a house or persuade a friend to hire your unemployed brother, it's not nepotism. However, when you hire your brother the bricklayer as vice president of your sporting goods company, and when you give your niece—the high-school dropout who can't type—a secretarial job and six months later promote her to office manager, those are flagrant acts of nepotism.

The corresponding adjective is *nepotistic* (NEP-uh-**TIS**-tik).

Word 42: RIBALD (RIB-<u>u</u>ld)

Humorous in a mildly indecent, coarse, or vulgar way.

Here's what three leading American dictionaries have to say about our humorously indecent keyword: The third edition of *The American Heritage Dictionary* (1992) says that *ribald* implies "vulgar, coarse, off-color language or behavior that provokes mirth." *Merriam-Webster's Collegiate Dictionary*, tenth edition (1998), says that *ribald* "applies to what is amusingly or picturesquely vulgar or irreverent or mildly indecent." And *Webster's New World Dictionary*, third college edition (1997), says that *ribald* suggests "mild indecency or lewdness as might bring laughter from those who are not too squeamish," and refers especially to that which deals with sex "in a humorously earthy or direct way."

Ribald has an appropriately earthy etymology. It comes from an Old French noun meaning a lewd or wanton person; this wanton noun comes in turn from an Old French verb meaning to be sexually abandoned; and this loose verb is related to an Old High German word that meant figuratively to copulate and literally to rub. Although Hamlet's oft-quoted line "Ay, there's the rub" is not a reference to his ribald fantasies about Ophelia, many of Shakespeare's plays contain ribald jokes and puns whose mildly coarse and indecent sexual overtones have provoked laughter from audiences for more than four hundred years.

Synonyms of *ribald* include *gross*, *indelicate*, *lewd*, *immodest*, *sensual*, and *obscene*. Bear in mind, however, that *obscene* suggests lewdness or indecency that is strongly offensive, whereas *ribald* applies to coarse vulgarity that is humorous and only mildly indecent.

Antonyms of *ribald* include *refined*, *decent*, *polite*, *tasteful*, *cultured*, *polished*, *cultivated*, *decorous* (DEK-ur-<u>us</u>), and *urbane* (ur-BAYN).

The corresponding noun is *ribaldry*, which means language or behavior that is humorous in a mildly indecent or vulgar way.

Let me conclude this discussion with a pronunciation tip: Some speakers have adopted the indelicate spelling pronunciation RY-bawld, and certain dictionaries that cater to the gross whims of the vulgar masses now record RY-bawld. I urge you to eschew this unrefined variant, and also to avoid the equally uncultivated RIB-awld. There is no *rye* and there is no *bald* in *ribald*. The word should rhyme with *scribbled* and *dribbled*.

And speaking of rhyme, for your verbal advantage, edification, and delight, I have composed a ribald limerick to help you remember the proper pronunciation of the word:

> William Shakespeare, whenever he scribbled,
> Used a quill that incessantly dribbled;
> When his pen leaked a lot,
> It made Willy quite hot,
> And he wrote something suitably ribald.

Word 43: AVUNCULAR (uh-VUHNGK-yuh-lur)

Like an uncle, pertaining to an uncle, or exhibiting some characteristic considered typical of an uncle.

The noun *uncle* and the adjective *avuncular* both come from the Latin *avunculus*, a mother's brother. You may use *avuncular* to describe some characteristic of your own or someone else's uncle, but the word most often applies to anything suggestive or typical of an uncle. We speak of an avuncular smile, an avuncular slap on the back, avuncular concern, avuncular generosity, and avuncular advice. "I want you for the U.S. Army" is the finger-pointing, avuncular injunction of Uncle Sam.

Word 44: SUPPLICATE (SUHP-li-kayt)

To ask, beg, or plead for humbly and earnestly.

Synonyms of *supplicate* include *entreat*, *petition*, *importune*, and *beseech*.

The verb to *supplicate* comes from the Latin *supplicare*, to kneel, get on one's knees, which in turn comes from *supplex*, kneeling, on one's knees. By derivation, to *supplicate* means to beg or plead for something on bended knee. From the same source we also inherit the word *supple* (SUHP-'l). Occasionally *supple* is used to mean yielding, compliant, or obsequious, but it is now most often used either literally or figuratively to mean bending easily, limber, flexible, as a supple bough or a supple mind.

The corresponding noun *supplication* (SUHP-li-**KAY**-shin) means either a humble and earnest request or the act of begging or pleading for something humbly and earnestly. A person who supplicates or who makes a supplication may be called either a *suppliant* (SUHP-lee-int) or a *supplicant* (SUHP-li-kint).

Word 45: IRASCIBLE (i-RAS-i-buul *or* eye-RAS-i-buul)

Easily angered, hot-tempered, extremely irritable or touchy.

Synonyms of *irascible* include *cranky*, *testy*, *peevish*, *petulant* (PECH-uh-lint), *irate*, *cantankerous* (kan-TANGK-uh-rus), *contentious* (word 16 of Level 7), *snappish*, *choleric* (KAHL-ur-ik), *captious* (KAP-shus), and *splenetic* (spli-NET-ik).

Antonyms include *calm*, *unruffled*, *placid*, *amiable*, *affable*, and *equable* (EK-wuh-buul).

Irascible and *irate* (eye-RAYT) both come from the Latin verb *irasci*, to be angry, which comes in turn from *ira*, anger, wrath. This Latin *ira* is also the direct source of the English word *ire* (like *tire* without the *t*).

A person who is full of *ire*, anger, may be either irate or irascible. *Webster's New International Dictionary*, second edition (1934), explains that an irate person "is at the moment angry or incensed"; an irascible person "is by temperament prone to anger." Thus, when something infuriates you, you are seized by ire, anger, and you become irate, temporarily enraged. However, if ire burns within you constantly, if you are by nature easily provoked to anger, then you are irascible. *Irascible* may also apply to that which displays anger or extreme irritability:

"Steve put up with Randy's incessant stream of irascible remarks for as long as he could, but eventually enough was enough, and he became irate."

Word 46: INEXORABLE (in-EK-sur-uh-buul)

Relentless, unyielding, merciless; not able to be stopped, changed, or moved by entreaty or persuasion.

Synonyms of *inexorable* include *unrelenting, unswerving, inflexible, immovable, uncompromising, intransigent* (in-TRAN-si-jent, word 4 of Level 8), *obdurate* (AHB-d(y)uu-rit), and *implacable* (im-PLAK-uh-buul).

Antonyms include *flexible, compromising, obliging, compliant, docile* (word 28 of this level), *tractable, acquiescent* (AK-wee-**ES**-int), and *complaisant* (kum-PLAY-zint).

Inexorable comes from the Latin adjective *inexorabilis,* not moved by entreaty or supplication. By derivation *inexorable* means not responsive to earnest pleas or humble prayers, and therefore relentless, unyielding.

Inexorable and *implacable* are close in meaning. *Implacable* is the stronger of the two; it applies to feeling, and means incapable of being pacified or appeased. An irascible person might express implacable hatred or implacable resentment. *Inexorable* means incapable of being moved or changed by petition or persuasion, deaf to all pleas.

According to the *Century Dictionary* (1914), *inexorable* "expresses an immovable firmness in refusing to do what one is entreated to do, whether that be good or bad." It may apply to a person: "Joe pleaded with his manager to give him an extra day of vacation, but his manager was inexorable." It may also apply to a thing, as "an inexorable campaign to squash the competition and dominate the industry." It may also be used figuratively, as "The inexorable hand of fate, the inexorable voice of necessity, the inexorable drifting of the sands of time, and the inexorable winds of war all led him to his inexorable doom." And in my ability to produce clichés to illustrate this word, I am also *inexorable,* relentless, unyielding, merciless.

Word 47: PARVENU (PAHR-vuh-n(y)oo)

An upstart; specifically, a person who suddenly acquires wealth and power and rises to a higher class, but who is not accepted by the members of that class.

Parvenu comes from a French verb meaning to succeed, and means literally "a person newly come into success." *Parvenu* almost always is used in a negative sense of a person who gains wealth and standing, but who cannot gain the social acceptance of the wealthy and powerful. In the eyes of the established elite, the parvenu is an upstart—undeserving, uncultured, immodest, and often pretentious.

Those masters of the fine art of condescenscion, the French, have condescended to give English another useful term for this sort of person: *arriviste* (AR-ee-**VEEST**). As you may have deduced from that spelling, *arriviste* means literally "a person who has recently arrived." The word crossed the English Channel into the language about 1900, and is used today of someone who attains social prominence or a position of power sometimes by unscrupulous means and always without paying the necessary dues.

Both the parvenu and the arriviste are upstarts, but the difference between them is this: The parvenu usually acquires wealth and status by an accident of fate—for example, through an unexpected inheritance, a business windfall or promotion, or by cleaning up at Las Vegas. Once arrived, the parvenu makes an awkward or pretentious attempt to gain social acceptance from the members of the class into which he has risen. The arriviste, on the other hand, is a vulgar and often ruthless social climber who has clawed his way to the top and doesn't care what anyone thinks or says about it.

Word 48: SALUBRIOUS (suh-LOO-bree-us)

Healthful, wholesome, favorable or conducive to well-being.

Antonyms of *salubrious* include *insalubrious*, *deleterious* (word 33 of Level 4), *pernicious* (word 10 of this level), *noxious*, *baneful*, *malign*, and *noisome* (NOY-sum).

Salubrious, *salutary*, and *wholesome* all mean good for your health. *Wholesome* refers to that which benefits or builds up the body, mind, or spirit, as a wholesome diet, wholesome recreation, or the wholesome effects of building your vocabulary. *Salutary* (**SAL**-yuh-TER-ee) refers to that which has, or is intended to have, a corrective or remedial effect upon the health or general condition of someone or something, as salutary advice or a salutary proposal to revitalize the inner city. *Salubrious* refers to that which is healthful, invigorating, or promotes physical well-being, as salubrious air, a salubrious climate, or salubrious exercise.

Both *salutary* and *salubrious* come from the Latin *salus*, health. The noun corresponding to *salubrious* is *salubriousness*.

Word 49: HYPERBOLE (hy-PUR-buh-lee)

Exaggeration in speech or writing; especially, extravagant exaggeration that is intentional and obvious.

The corresponding adjective is *hyperbolic* (HY-pur-**BAHL**-ik), or, less often, *hyperbolical* (HY-pur-**BAHL**-ik-ul).

Occasionally, you will hear an educated speaker who has learned this word from reading, but who has not bothered to check its pronunciation in a dictionary, say *hyperbowl*. Any sports fan will tell you that there's a Super Bowl, a Sugar Bowl, a Cotton Bowl, and a Rose Bowl, but there is no Hyper Bowl. The only recognized pronunciation is hy-PUR-buh-lee, and anything else is downright beastly.

Hyperbole comes from a Greek word meaning an excess, something that overshoots the mark. This Greek word comes in turn from a verb meaning to exceed or throw beyond. By derivation, hyperbole is extravagant language that exceeds what is necessary or overshoots the mark.

As Bergen Evans explains in his *Dictionary of Contemporary American Usage* (1957), "*Hyperbole* is the term in rhetoric for obvious exaggeration. There is no intent to deceive. The extravagant language is for emphasis only."

Because hyperbole heightens the effect of what we say without obscuring its meaning, it's a popular rhetorical device, and many of the most shopworn expressions in the language are hyperbolic. Here are just a few examples of hackneyed hyperbole: *I owe you a million thanks*; *she waited for an eternity*; *he was eternally grateful*; *we are forever indebted to you*; *I am so tired I could sleep for a week*; *they ran faster than lightning*; *he's as strong as an ox*; *your briefcase weighs a ton*; *my feet are killing me*; *he said he'd do it or die trying*. These and many more hyperbolic expressions are acceptable in informal speech and excusable in the most casual forms of writing, but in situations that demand more formal and precise expression, or in which an exaggerated effect would be inappropriate, they should be scrupulously avoided.

Not all hyperbole is cliché. There are many memorable statements, withering insults, and powerful speeches that manifest an original, effective, and often striking use of hyperbole. In *The Elements of Speechwriting and Public Speaking* (1989), Jeff Scott Cook defines *hyperbole* as "an exaggeration used to emphasize a point," and offers the following examples, among others:

Former Texas senator, vice-presidential candidate, and secretary of the treasury Lloyd Bentsen once said, "The thrift industry is really in terrible shape. It's reached the point where if you buy a toaster, you get a free savings and loan."

Faye Wattleton, former president of Planned Parenthood, once said, "Those 'just say no' [to sex] messages are about as effective at preventing [teen] pregnancy as saying 'have a nice day' prevents chronic depression."

And the actor Robert Redford once quipped hyperbolically, "If you stay in Beverly Hills too long, you become a Mercedes."

Some of the finest English poetry ever written also makes stunning use of hyperbole. One of Shakespeare's most glorious and hyperbolic passages occurs in *Antony and Cleopatra*, when Enobarbus describes the wondrous, irresistible beauty of Cleopatra, who has sailed down the river Cydnus on an opulent barge. Here is a selection from that passage:

> The barge she sat in, like a burnished throne,
> Burned on the water: the poop was beaten gold;
> Purple the sails, and so perfum'ed that
> The winds were lovesick with them. . . .
>   The city cast
> Her people out upon her; and Antony,
> Enthroned i' th' marketplace, did sit alone,
> Whistling to th' air; which, but for vacancy,
> Had gone to gaze on Cleopatra too,
> And made a gap in nature.

Word 50: SANCTIMONIOUS (SANGK-ti-MOH-nee-us)

Self-righteous; holier-than-thou; characterized by insincere or affected righteousness, virtuousness, or religious piety.

Sanctimonious comes from the Latin *sanctus*, holy, sacred, and the word was once used to mean holy or sacred. In modern usage, however, *sanctimonious* refers to insincere, affected, or hypocritical holiness or righteousness. People who are sanctimonious come off as self-righteous and holier-than-thou but do not practice what they preach.

The corresponding noun is *sanctimony* (**SANGK**-tuh-MOH-nee), righteousness or virtuousness that is affected or hypocritical.

Let's review the ten keywords you've just learned. I'll give you the review word (in *italics*) followed by three words or phrases, and you decide which one of those three words or phrases comes nearest the meaning of the review word. Answers appear on page 319.

1. Is *nepotism* a fascination with violent crime, a devious plot, or favoritism shown to relatives?
2. Is a *ribald* remark foolish, indecent, or straightforward?
3. If someone has an *avuncular* manner, is it like a parent, like an uncle, or like a teacher?

4. Does a *supplicating* person make excuses, make a humble plea, or make a contribution?
5. Is an *irascible* person hard to please, easily angered, or quick to take action?
6. Is an *inexorable* force relentless, powerful, or unpredictable?
7. Is a *parvenu* a beginner, an expert, or an upstart?
8. Is a *salubrious* environment wholesome, unsanitary, or clean?
9. Does *hyperbole* mean anxiety, exaggeration, or deception?
10. Is a *sanctimonious* person self-righteous, impatient, or inconsiderate?

A Paucity of Information, a Plethora of Words

Now let's examine the fifth and final category of abusage: jargon (JAHR-gun, rhymes with *bargain*). As you may recall from our discussion of this word early in the program, *jargon* (word 46 of Level 1) denotes a specialized, abstruse vocabulary or any pretentious language that is unnecessarily difficult to understand.

Jargon is the worm in the apple of expression; it is the refuge of the timid writer and the smokescreen of the self-important one. The dense, inscrutable vocabulary of jargon excludes the average reader or listener. Whenever you read or hear jargon, you may reasonably assume that somebody doesn't want you to understand what's being expressed or is trying to disguise the dearth of content in the words.

Let me give you some examples. Here's the second sentence from the sales brochure passage I quoted earlier in our discussion of adverbiage: "People learn best when the instruction is designed so that it facilitates the learning process and when they thoroughly enjoy the learning activity." That twenty-three-word sentence, translated into simple and direct English, can be expressed in seven words: "People learn best when learning is fun."

The pernicious thing about jargon is that once you start using it, it warps your mind—or, to borrow a line from one of my favorite folk songs, "it will form like a habit and seep in your soul." If some clearheaded person had suggested that seven-word clarification to the writer of the brochure, the writer probably would have said, "No, that's too plain. It doesn't have enough oomph. We need to make the company and its courses sound more important. Hey, I know! Suppose I throw in the word *facilitate*? That's a big favorite among educators. And let's make learning sound more technical and scientific by calling it 'the learning process' and 'the learning activity.' Then if I refer to what we teach as 'designed instruction'. . ."

Ah, me oh my. Such is the self-deluding sophistry that leads us, as usage expert Theodore M. Bernstein puts it, "to wrap a paucity of information in a plethora of words."

Later in the same brochure the writer shifts into high-flown gear and we find this pseudoscientific, jargon-infested sentence: "Analysis," it reads, "involves scoping the nature of the instructional requirements and specifying the tasks, the logistical support, and the instructional management system necessary to achieve goals within the unique constraints of the client's environment."

Can you believe this stuff? In plain English, all that means is "We create courses that fit your needs."

Everyone agrees that the best writing is simple and direct, but when it's time to put our thoughts on paper, most of us become like the person who shakes salt on his food before tasting it. We overseason our sentences with jargon, vogue words, redundancies, adverbiage, and clichés, until our ideas lose their natural flavor and our expression becomes flat, verbose, and dull. As the poet Donald Hall once wrote, "In our culture, lethargic prose is taken as evidence of seriousness or sincerity. The heavier the subject, the paler the prose."

To illustrate Hall's point, let's take a familiar passage from I Corinthians, Chapter 13, in the King James Version of the Bible: "Though I speak with the tongues of men and of angels, and have not charity, I am become as sounding brass, or a tinkling cymbal."

Here's how those poetic words would be expressed in today's nebulous, unmetaphorical, bombastic, and jargon-riddled English: "Despite the fact that my communication skills have been test-marketed and proven to be completely effective in a variety of goal-oriented management environments, if I have not developed the crucial ability to personally interact with fellow colleagues in a highly sensitized manner, nonterrestrial data suggest that my interactive verbal processing ability will not have a positive impact outcome-wise at this point in time, even in a win-win situation."

I hope that outrageous mishmash of overwriting and abusage made you chuckle. The problem is, many educated people write and even speak like that. But enough said. I'm sure that by now you get the point: Eschew jargon and say what you mean.

And with that succinct counsel—and I trust you pronounced *succinct* suhk-SINGKT, with the *cc* like *k-s*—we come to the end of Level 7. I know that all along I've been drumming the importance of review into your head, but another nudge in the right direction never hurts. To ensure full comprehension and retention of what you have learned, do yourself a favor and review this entire level at least once before moving on.

Answers to Review Quizzes for Level 7

Keywords 1–10

1. Yes. *Redress* means reparation, compensation, satisfaction for a wrong done.
2. Yes. *Anomalous* means irregular, abnormal, out of place, deviating from what is usual or expected.
3. Absolutely not. *Obsequious* means subservient, submissive, obedient; ready and willing to serve, please, or obey.
4. Yes. *Didactic* means instructive, designed or intended to teach.
5. Yes. *Truncate* means to cut short, shorten by cutting or lopping off.
6. No. *Abstemious* means sparing or moderate, especially in eating or drinking.
7. No. *Ethereal* means heavenly, not earthly; hence, very light, airy, delicate, or refined.
8. Yes. *Bombastic* means pompous, pretentious, inflated, overblown.
9. No. Senior citizens are senescent. *Senescent* means aging, growing old, on the decline.
10. Yes. *Pernicious* means deadly, fatal, destructive, causing great harm or injury.

Keywords 11–20

1. True. *Catholic* means universal, comprehensive; specifically, broad-minded, tolerant, or all-embracing in one's sympathies, interests, or tastes.
2. False. An *objurgation* is a harsh rebuke, vehement scolding or denunciation.
3. False. *Effusive* means gushing, overflowing, overly demonstrative, expressing emotion in an excessive or unrestrained manner.
4. True. *Umbrage* means offense, resentment.
5. False. The *vicissitudes* of life are its changes or variations, its ups and downs.
6. True. *Contentious* means argumentative, quarrelsome, ready and eager to argue, bicker, or debate.
7. False. *Obeisance* means a gesture of respect or submission, or an attitude of respect and submission.
8. False. *Assiduous* means hardworking, diligent, industrious; done with persistent, careful, and untiring attention.
9. False. *Duplicity* means deceit, cunning, double-dealing, hypocritical deception.
10. True. *Insouciant* means carefree, nonchalant, lightheartedly unconcerned or indifferent.

Keywords 21–30

1. Antonyms. An *antagonist* is an opponent. A *myrmidon* is a loyal follower, faithful servant or subordinate.
2. Antonyms. *Senescent* means aging, growing old. *Nascent* means beginning to exist or develop; in the process of being born or coming into being.
3. Synonyms. *Accede* means to consent, yield, give in or agree to.
4. Antonyms. *Ignominious* means shameful, dishonorable, contemptible. *Magnanimous* means noble, honorable, high-minded, unselfish, generous in overlooking injury or insult.
5. Synonyms. *Nonage* means immaturity, youth; especially the the state of being a minor in the eyes of the law.
6. Antonyms. *Invective* is vehement or abusive language involving bitter, scathing accusations or denunciations.
7. Synonyms. A *machination* is a crafty or treacherous plot, malicious scheme, cunning plan to achieve a sinister purpose.
8. Antonyms. *Intractable* means hard to manage or control. *Docile* means submissive, obedient, compliant; easy to direct, manage, or supervise.
9. Synonyms. *Redoubtable* means formidable, fearsome, worthy of or commanding respect.
10. Synonyms. To *prognosticate* means to predict from signs, symptoms, or present indications.

Keywords 31–40

1. *Bring up* doesn't fit. To *engender* means to bring about, bring into being, give rise to, cause to exist.
2. *Ugly* doesn't fit. *Fetid* means stinking, foul-smelling; having an extremely offensive odor, as of something rotten or decayed.
3. *In an impressive way* doesn't fit. *Pedantic* means absurdly learned; scholarly in an ostentatious way; making an inappropriate or tiresome display of knowledge.
4. *Admit* doesn't fit. *Capitulate* means to yield, surrender; specifically, to surrender on specified terms or conditions.
5. *Completed* doesn't fit. *Inchoate* means just begun; in an early stage of development; not fully formed; undeveloped.
6. *An adversary* doesn't fit. An opponent is an adversary. An *exponent* is a person who stands or speaks for something, a representative or advocate.
7. *Bitter* doesn't fit. *Mendacious* means not truthful, lying, false, dishonest, deceitful.
8. *Bold* doesn't fit. *Strident* means loud and harsh-sounding, grating, shrill.

9. *Rule by a dictator* doesn't fit. A dictator rules alone. *Oligarchy* means government by a few; rule or control exercised by a few persons or by a small, elite group.
10. *Luxuriant* doesn't fit. *Refulgent* means shining brightly, brilliant, radiant, resplendent.

Keywords 41–50

1. *Nepotism* is favoritism shown to relatives.
2. It's indecent. *Ribald* means humorous in a mildly indecent, coarse, or vulgar way.
3. It's like an uncle. *Avuncular* means like an uncle, or exhibiting some characteristic considered typical of an uncle.
4. A supplicating person makes a humble plea. To *supplicate* means to ask, beg, or plead for humbly and earnestly.
5. An irascible person is easily angered. *Irascible* means hot-tempered, extremely irritable or touchy.
6. *Inexorable* means relentless, unyielding, merciless; not able to be stopped, changed, or moved by entreaty or persuasion.
7. A *parvenu* is an upstart; specifically, a person who suddenly acquires wealth and power and rises to a higher class, but who is not accepted by the members of that class.
8. A salubrious environment is wholesome. *Salubrious* means healthful, wholesome, favorable or conducive to well-being.
9. *Hyperbole* means exaggeration in speech or writing; especially, extravagant exaggeration that is intentional and obvious.
10. A sanctimonious person is self-righteous; holier-than-thou. *Sanctimonious* means characterized by insincere or affected righteousness, virtuousness, or religious piety.

Review Test for Level 7

1. Something that deviates from the norm is
   (a) abstemious
   (b) analogous
   (c) anomalous
   (d) hyperbolic
   (e) pernicious
2. Which word is *not* a synonym of *didactic*?
   (a) pedagogic

(b) preceptive

(c) expository

(d) ascetic

(e) hortatory

3. Which word is *not* an antonym of *obsequious*?

   (a) recalcitrant

   (b) intractable

   (c) sycophantic

   (d) refractory

   (e) intransigent

4. Which word is a synonym of *rarefied*?

   (a) bombastic

   (b) ethereal

   (c) effusive

   (d) senescent

   (e) catholic

5. Which word is an antonym of *pernicious*?

   (a) malign

   (b) deleterious

   (c) salubrious

   (d) baneful

   (e) noisome

6. Which phrase is *not* redundant?

   (a) cure for all ills

   (b) passing fad

   (c) consensus of opinion

   (d) from whence it came

   (e) opening gambit

7. Which word best describes a *catholic* person?

   (a) latitudinarian

   (b) docile

   (c) dogmatic

   (d) parochial

8. *Reticent*, *diffident*, and *taciturn* are antonyms of

   (a) refulgent

   (b) effusive

   (c) laconic

   (d) irascible

9. Which word is *not* a synonym of *contentious*?

   (a) disputatious
   (b) belligerent
   (c) litigious
   (d) mendacious
   (e) pugnacious

10. Which word is a synonym of *assiduous*?

    (a) indolent
    (b) languid
    (c) sedulous
    (d) phlegmatic
    (e) otiose

11. *Chicanery* and *casuistry* are synonyms of

    (a) invective
    (b) nepotism
    (c) duplicity
    (d) bombast
    (e) supplications

12. What is a genuflection?

    (a) a blessing
    (b) a bending of the knee
    (c) making the sign of the cross
    (d) an act of deception
    (e) a prayer

13. Which word means to inform?

    (a) appraise
    (b) apprise

14. Which word means rash, reckless or abrupt, sudden?

    (a) precipitate
    (b) precipitous

15. In the Trojan War, who was king and commander of the Myrmidons?

    (a) Hector
    (b) Odysseus
    (c) Procrustes
    (d) Achilles
    (e) Draco

16. Something antediluvian is

    (a) inscrutable or impenetrable

    (b) fearsome and unstoppable

    (c) amusingly eccentric

    (d) old or old-fashioned

17. Which word by derivation means great-spirited?

    (a) catholic

    (b) magnanimous

    (c) pusillanimous

    (d) avuncular

    (e) sanctimonious

18. Which word denotes abusive language that is filthy and obscene?

    (a) invective

    (b) obloquy

    (c) billingsgate

    (d) vituperation

19. Which word means to attack violently with words, express angry disapproval?

    (a) coruscate

    (b) objurgate

    (c) bombast

    (d) inveigh

    (e) capitulate

20. Which two words are synonyms of *prognosticate*? (This question has *two* correct answers.)

    (a) scintillate

    (b) vaticinate

    (c) supplicate

    (d) presage

    (e) inchoate

21. Which phrase does *not* properly apply to a deus ex machina?

    (a) unexpected resolution

    (b) sinister plot

    (c) divine intervention

    (d) unlikely occurrence

22. What is a *docent*?

    (a) an itinerant teacher
    (b) a friendly, agreeable person
    (c) a lecturing tour guide
    (d) an assistant or servant

23. Which word is an antonym of *fetid*?

    (a) redolent
    (b) putrid
    (c) graveolent
    (d) mephitic
    (e) noisome

24. In the phrase *mea culpa*, what does *culpa* mean?

    (a) fault
    (b) belief
    (c) mistake
    (d) responsibility

25. Someone who makes an inappropriate or tiresome display of knowledge is

    (a) an exponent
    (b) a docent
    (c) a parvenu
    (d) a pedant
    (e) a myrmidon

26. Which word is a synonym of *inchoate*?

    (a) insouciant
    (b) refulgent
    (c) nascent
    (d) senescent

27. Which set of three words contains a word that is *not* a synonym of the others?

    (a) scrupulous, upright, ethical
    (b) mendacious, veracious, disingenuous
    (c) hypocritical, equivocal, duplicitous
    (d) evasive, prevaricating, deceitful

28. Which two words are synonyms of *strident*? (This question has *two* correct answers.)

    (a) stentorian

(b) euphonious

(c) vociferous

(d) tenebrous

(e) irascible

29. Which word means pertaining to twilight?

(a) inchoate

(b) subfuscous

(c) crepuscular

(d) umbrageous

30. Which is the traditional and proper pronunciation of *ribald*?

(a) RY-bawld

(b) RIB-uld

(c) RIB-awld

31. Which two words pertain to a family member? (This question has *two* correct answers.)

(a) nepotism

(b) machination

(c) parvenu

(d) avuncular

(e) nonage

32. What is an *arriviste*?

(a) a convert to a religion or cause

(b) a vulgar and often ruthless social climber

(c) an ostentatiously learned person

(d) a faithful servant or subordinate

33. Which three words are synonyms?

(a) unrelenting, implacable, obliging

(b) compliant, compromising, obdurate

(c) inexorable, acquiescent, intransigent

(d) tractable, complaisant, docile

34. Which two hackneyed expressions are examples of hyperbole? (This question has *two* correct answers.)

(a) happy as a clam

(b) between a rock and a hard place

(c) eternally grateful

(d) to fight tooth and nail

(e) to do it or die trying

    (f) pain in the neck

    (g) to throw up one's hands

35. Which word does *not* precisely apply to a sanctimonious person?

    (a) hypocritical

    (b) disingenuous

    (c) unctuous

    (d) redoubtable

    (e) affected

Answers

34. c & e 35. d

1. c 2. d 3. c 4. b 5. c 6. a 7. a 8. b 9. d 10. c 11. c 12. b 13. b
14. a 15. d 16. d 17. b 18. c 19. d 20. b & d 21. b 22. c 23. a
24. a 25. d 26. c 27. b 28. a & c 29. c 30. b 31. a & d 32. b 33. d

Evaluation

A score of 30–35 is excellent. If you answered fewer than thirty questions correctly in this test, review the entire level and take the test again.

Level 8

In this level the going gets even tougher, but the tough keep on going. Are you ready for a real word-power workout?

If you've been adhering to a daily routine of reading and reviewing the material, as I recommended in the introduction, then by now you have approximately tripled your normal rate of vocabulary growth by adding dozens of new words to your active vocabulary and resurrecting others from your passive vocabulary.

If you haven't been sticking to a routine, however, don't be discouraged. Even if you've been reading off and on and occasionally neglecting to review, it's still likely that since you began studying this book you've assimilated many more words than you would have in the same amount of time without the benefit of a disciplined, graduated program. And the fact that you've made it this far indicates that you're serious about improving your verbal skills and making a commendable effort to expand the boundary of your vocabulary.

So, can you feel your verbal muscles getting firmer? Have you been test-driving some of your new words in your writing and conversation? I hope so, and I also hope that each time you try out a new word you will make sure to double-check its definition and pronunciation in a dictionary to verify that you are using and saying it right.

Now let me tell you what you can expect from the last three levels of *Verbal Advantage*. The keywords, synonyms, antonyms, and related words that you will learn in Level 8 fall approximately between the 80th and 90th percentile of the English vocabulary. The words in Levels 9 and 10 range from the 90th to 99th percentile. What that means is that from here on in, we will be covering a selection of the most intellectually demanding words in the language, which are understood and used by the best-educated and most well-read members of society.

So prepare to be challenged by what you're about to learn in these last three levels, and hang on to your hat, or your seat, or something firm nearby, because the leisurely segment of our linguistic tour is over. From here on I intend to proceed with celerity, and I hope you will follow me with alacrity.

If you're already hurrying to keep up with the words *celerity* and *alacrity*, don't worry, because I'm going to tell you about them right now, as we begin our first set of ten keyword discussions.

Word 1: ALACRITY (uh-LAK-ri-tee)

Cheerful readiness, eagerness, or promptness in action or movement: "The duty of the firefighter is to answer every alarm with alacrity."

Synonyms of *alacrity* include *quickness*, *liveliness*, *briskness*, *enthusiasm*, *animation*, *zeal* (ZEEL), and *celerity* (suh-LER-i-tee)

According to *Funk & Wagnalls Standard Handbook of Synonyms, Antonyms, and Prepositions* (1947), *alacrity* denotes "that cheerful and hearty willingness from which *quickness* and *promptness* naturally result; hence, a prompt response. *Alacrity* springs from some demand from without; *eagerness* is spontaneous, springing from within; *eagerness* to act may produce *alacrity* in responding to the call for action."

Alacrity and *celerity* are close in meaning. Both suggest "quickness in movement or action," says *Webster's Ninth New Collegiate Dictionary* (1993). *Celerity* "implies speed in accomplishing work; *alacrity* stresses promptness in response to suggestion or command." Because *celerity* emphasizes swiftness, you cross a busy street, complete a project, or run from danger with celerity. Because *alacrity* emphasizes eagerness, liveliness, or promptness, you meet a challenge, return a telephone message, or respond to a call for help with alacrity.

Word 2: OBVIATE (AHB-vee-AYT)

To prevent, make unnecessary, meet and dispose of, clear out of the way.

Obviate comes through the Latin verb *obviare*, to prevent, from the adjective *obvius*, in the way, the source also of the familiar English word *obvious*, which means literally "lying in the way." The verb to *obviate* suggests preventing a problem or difficulty from arising by anticipating it and taking effective measures to meet and dispose of it or clear it out of the way. You can obviate trivial objections by coming straight to the point. You can obviate a trial by settling out of court. The necessity of attending a meeting can be obviated by a timely phone call.

Word 3: EMOLUMENT (i-MAHL-yuh-mint)

Wages, salary, payment received for work.

Synonyms of *emolument* include *compensation*, *recompense* (**REK**-um-PENTS), and *remuneration*, word 30 of Level 6.

Emolument comes from the Latin *emolumentum*, the fee a miller received for grinding grain, which comes in turn from the verb *emolere,* to grind out. By derivation, *emolument* means "that which is ground out by one's exertion." In the daily grind of the modern world, *emolument* has come to mean wages, pay, compensation for one's labor. *Webster's New International Dictionary*, second edition (1934), notes that *emolument* "applies to whatever profits arise from office or employment, as 'the emoluments of a profession.'"

Now that you know the meaning of *emolument*, and also the keywords *perquisite* from Level 3 and *commensurate* from Level 6, I presume that the next time you consider a new position you will make sure that the perquisites are attractive and that the emolument is commensurate with your experience and ability.

Word 4: INTRANSIGENT (in-TRAN-si-jent)

Uncompromising, refusing to come to an agreement, unwilling to modify one's position or give ground.

Synonyms of *intransigent* include *irreconcilable, unyielding, diehard, hidebound, obstinate* (word 34 of Level 1), *resolute* (REZ-uh-loot), *tenacious* (te-NAY-shus), *recalcitrant* (ri-KAL-suh-trint), *intractable* (in-TRAK-tuh-buul), *refractory* (word 42 of Level 6), and *obdurate* (AHB-d(y)uu-rit).

Antonyms include *compromising, flexible, obliging, submissive, compliant, malleable* (word 29 of Level 2), *docile* (word 28 of Level 7), *tractable, deferential, acquiescent* (AK-wee-ES-int), and *complaisant* (kum-PLAY-zint).

Intransigent combines the privative prefix *in-*, meaning "not," with the Latin verb *transigere*, to come to a settlement, and means literally refusing to settle, unwilling to come to an agreement, uncompromising.

Resolute, tenacious, obstinate, intractable, refractory, obdurate, and *intransigent* suggest firmness or fixity in ascending intensity. The *resolute* person is firmly settled in opinion, resolved to pursue a course of action. *Tenacious*, which comes from the Latin *tenere*, to hold, suggests holding firmly; the tenacious person adheres persistently and sometimes doggedly to a belief or course of action. *Obstinate* implies stubborn adherence to an opinion or purpose and strong resistance to contrary influence or persuasion. *Intractable* means hard to lead or manage; the intractable person stubbornly resists direction. *Refractory* means stubborn and disobedient; a refractory person actively resists authority or control. *Obdurate* means stubbornly hardhearted; the obdurate person cannot be moved by appeals to the emotions.

Our keyword, *intransigent*, combines the firmness of *resolute*, the persistence of *tenacious*, the stubborn resistance of *obstinate, intractable,* and *re-*

fractory, and the hardheartedness of *obdurate*. The intransigent person takes an extreme position and will not compromise or back down under any circumstances.

Word 5: MORDANT (MOR-di̱nt *or* MORD-'nt)

Biting, cutting, keen, sarcastic, scathing.

Additional synonyms of *mordant* include *incisive* (in-SY-siv), *caustic* (KAW-stik), *trenchant* (TRENCH-i̱nt), *virulent* (VIR-(y)uh-li̱nt), and *acrimonious* (AK-ri-**MOH**-nee-u̱s).

When you think of *mordant*, think of gnashing teeth. *Mordant* comes from Old French and Latin words meaning to bite, cut into, nip, or sting. Today *mordant* is chiefly used of speech or writing that is biting or cutting in a bitterly sarcastic way. We speak of mordant satire, mordant wit, mordant criticism, or a mordant cross-examination.

Word 6: SAGACIOUS (suh-GAY-shu̱s)

Wise, shrewd, perceptive; showing sound judgment and keen insight, especially in practical matters.

Synonyms of *sagacious* include *insightful*, *discerning*, *astute* (word 3 of Level 4), *judicious* (word 16 of Level 5), *percipient* (pur-SIP-ee-i̱nt), *sage* (rhymes with *page*), *sapient* (SAY-pee-i̱nt), and *perspicacious* (PUR-spi-**KAY**-shu̱s).

Antonyms of *sagacious* include *undiscriminating*, *undiscerning*, *simple-minded*, *witless*, *inane* (i-NAYN), *gullible*, *credulous* (KREJ-uh-lu̱s), *obtuse* (uhb-T(Y)OOS), and *addlepated* (**AD**-'l-PAY-tid).

The corresponding noun is *sagacity*, wisdom, shrewdness, keen insight or discernment.

Sagacious comes from the Latin *sagax*, having keen senses, especially a keen sense of smell. In its early days in the language, *sagacious* was used of hunting dogs to mean quick in picking up a scent. That sense is long obsolete. By 1755, when Samuel Johnson published his famous dictionary, *sagacious* had come to mean, as Johnson puts it, "quick of thought; acute in making discoveries." To illustrate the expanded sense, Johnson quotes the philosopher John Locke: "Only sagacious heads light on these observations, and reduce them into general propositions." Over the years since then, *sagacious* continued to acquire dignity, perhaps by association with the adjective *sage*, which means having or showing great wisdom. Today, says the third edition of *The*

American Heritage Dictionary (1992), *sagacious* "connotes prudence, circumspection, discernment, and farsightedness."

That's a far cry from the hunting hounds of yore. Yet, as those words reveal, a faint odor of quick-sniffing canine instinct still clings to the word. In current usage, the sagacious person is no brooding scholar or musing philosopher but a shrewd, sharp-eyed, keen-witted person who displays instinctive wisdom, swift insight, and sound judgment regarding mundane or practical matters. Thus we do not speak of a sagacious treatise on the meaning of life, but rather of a sagacious comment on human nature, a shrewd lawyer who asks sagacious questions, or a business executive known for making sagacious decisions—in other words, wise and keenly perceptive decisions.

Word 7: ACERBIC (uh-SUR-bik)

Sour, bitter, and harsh in flavor, tone, or character.

Synonyms of *acerbic* include *tart*, *caustic* (KAW-stik), *pungent* (PUHN-jint), *astringent* (uh-STRIN-jint), *acrid* (AK-rid), and *acidulous* (uh-SIJ-(y)uh-lus).

The direct antonym of *acerbic* is *sweet*.

Acerbic comes from a Latin word meaning sour or bitter like unripe fruit. *Acerbic* may be used literally to mean sour or bitter tasting, as the lemon is an acerbic fruit. However, the word *acidic* probably is more often used in this literal sense, and *acerbic* usually is used figuratively to mean sour, bitter, and harsh in tone or character: An acerbic mood is a sour mood; acerbic words are bitter words; and someone who is acerbic has a harsh, unpleasant personality.

Word 8: VARIEGATED (**VAIR**-ee-uh-GAY-tid)

In a broad sense, varied, diverse, showing variety of character or form; in a strict sense, spotted, streaked, or dappled; having marks or patches of different colors, as a variegated quilt, a variegated cat, or a variegated design.

The verb to *variegate* is now often used figuratively to mean to give variety to, diversify. The adjective *variegated* is also frequently used in this way to mean varied, diverse, or multifaceted, as variegated interests, a variegated selection, or variegated accomplishments.

Word 9: SUCCOR (SUHK-ur, like *sucker*)

To aid, help, relieve, give assistance to in time of need or difficulty, as to succor the wounded or succor the sick.

The noun *succor* means help, aid, relief, assistance in time of need or distress, as to give succor to the homeless on Thanksgiving.

Both the verb and the noun come from a Latin verb meaning "to run to the aid of." Although *succor* and the slang verb *sucker* have the same pronunciation, they are not related and are virtually opposite in meaning.

Word 10: IMPORTUNE (IM-por-T(Y)OON)

To trouble or annoy with requests or demands, make urgent or persistent entreaties or solicitations.

To remember the meaning of the verb *importune*, think of some annoying person who interrupts your life at an inappropriate moment and urgently asks you to do something you don't want to do. Salespeople importune you on the telephone when you're not interested and have better things to do. Panhandlers importune you on the street to beg for a handout. Children are experts at importuning parents when they are preoccupied with work or some pressing domestic chore, like cooking or paying bills.

The corresponding adjective is *importunate* (im-POR-chuh-nit), troublesomely demanding, persistent in a vexatious way.

Let's review the ten keywords you've just learned. Consider the following questions and decide whether the correct answer is yes or no. Answers appear on page 361.

1. If someone said, "You have a call from a fellow named Ed at Publishers Clearinghouse," would you respond with alacrity?
2. Can diplomatic negotiations sometimes obviate war?
3. Do volunteers receive emolument for their services?
4. Is it reasonable to expect an intransigent person to capitulate?
5. Is a mordant remark a flattering remark?
6. Is a sagacious business decision a smart decision?
7. Would an acerbic person say that life is sweet?
8. Could a stock portfolio, the population of a city, and a horse all be described as variegated?
9. Can you succor a sick child?
10. When you're working hard trying to meet a deadline on a project and people keep calling or interrupting you to ask you to do something for them, are they importuning you?

Did you remember to keep track of your answers and calculate your score?

How Do You Feel?

Now let's take a moment to talk about feelings.

Loose-lipped speakers and permissive writers may call me a fusspot, a nitpicker, or even an acerbic pedant, but I am nothing less than intransigent when it comes to how I feel. In other words, I make a clear distinction between feeling *bad* and feeling *badly*. When I am sick or distressed, I say I feel *bad*, and when the dentist gives me a shot that makes my mouth numb, I say my mouth feels *badly*.

In his book *The Writer's Art* (1984), syndicated columnist James J. Kilpatrick offers this explanation of the distinction: "If you feel *badly*, something is wrong with your sense of touch; your fingers may be numb, or calloused, or gloved—who knows? If you feel *bad*, you're ill, depressed, worried."

Kilpatrick also notes that "the same distinction applies to other [linking] verbs, such as *smell* and *taste*. If you smell *badly*, perhaps your nose is stopped up. If you smell *bad*, try a hot soapy shower."

Mr. Kilpatrick and I are far from alone in our disdain for those who say they feel *badly* when they mean they feel *bad*. When the editors of the second edition of the *Harper Dictionary of Contemporary Usage* (1985) polled the members of their distinguished usage panel on this question, three-quarters of the panelists preferred "I feel bad" and rejected "I feel badly," although a number of them admitted that they avoided the sticky issue altogether by saying "I feel terrible, awful, lousy, like death," and so on. Many panelists voiced extremely bad feelings about "I feel badly," calling it everything from "a bit pedantic" to a "dainty-ism" to downright "godawful." The novelist and professor Isaac Asimov had this to say: "'Feeling badly' is the mark of an inept, dirty old man." The compilers also quote this bit of drollery from the literary critic and editor Clifton Fadiman: "Don't feel bad when you hear the broadcaster say he feels badly. Just remember that all men are created equally."

The handbook of SPELL, otherwise known as the Society for the Preservation of English Language and Literature, of which I am a vice president, contains this pithy, prescriptive advice on the use of *bad* and *badly*: "It is incorrect to say 'I feel badly' unless you are referring to the act of feeling. If you want to describe your physical condition, 'I feel bad' is preferred."

Would you like a mnemonic device to help you distinguish between *bad* and *badly*? In *Grammar for Smart People* (1992), Barry Tarshis offers this "memory key": "We feel bad when we perform badly."

Now that you know that you will feel bad when you perform badly, I don't feel bad about saying that learning the next ten keywords in Level 8 will make you feel good.

Word 11: PALLIATE (PAL-ee-AYT)

To lessen the severity of, gloss over, make something seem less serious or severe, as to palliate suffering, to palliate an offense, or to palliate your troubles with drink.

Synonyms of *palliate* include *soften*, *diminish*, *mitigate*, and *extenuate*. Antonyms include *worsen*, *intensify*, *aggravate*, and *exacerbate* (ig-**ZAS**-ur-BAYT). *Exacerbate* and *acerbic*, keyword 7 in this level, come from the same Latin root, and both suggest bitterness or harshness. The adjective *acerbic* means sour, bitter, or harsh in flavor, tone, or character. The verb *exacerbate* means to increase in bitterness or severity, as to exacerbate a problem or exacerbate a conflict.

The verb to *palliate* comes through the Latin verb *palliare*, to cloak or conceal, from the noun *pallium*, a cloak. *Palliate* was once used to mean to cover as if with a cloak, to shelter, hide, conceal. This meaning is now obsolete, and today *palliate* means to conceal or cloak the seriousness of something, make it appear less severe or offensive than it is, as to palliate a social indiscretion or palliate the enormity of a crime.

In modern usage, *palliate* often connotes glossing over or disguising the seriousness of something by making excuses or apologies: "Her press agent issued a statement in an attempt to palliate her role in the scandal."

Word 12: WIZENED (WIZ-'nd)

Dried up, shriveled, withered, shrunken and wrinkled.

The verbs to *wither*, to *shrivel*, and to *wizen* all imply drying up. *Webster's New World Dictionary*, second college edition (1988), explains that *wither* suggests a loss of natural juices: "The grapes were left to wither on the vine." *Shrivel* suggests shrinking and curling as from exposure to intense heat: "With a heavy sigh, Scott removed the shriveled steak from the barbecue." *Wizen* (WIZ-'n) suggests shrinking and wrinkling from advanced age or malnutrition.

Although the verb to *wizen* now is somewhat rare, its past participle, *wizened*, is still often used of persons or parts of the body to mean shrunken and wrinkled, dried up by age or disease: An old person's face may be wizened, or someone's body may be wizened by cancer.

Here is a passage from my vocabulary-building mystery novel, *Tooth and Nail*, in which the context attempts to illustrate the meaning of *wizened*: "An ancient, wizened man shuffled into the room, supporting his stooped and shriveled frame with a stout oaken staff . . . His face was sallow and deeply wrinkled; his cheeks were sunken and his crown was entirely bald. But for his eyes, which twinkled roguishly, he was a picture of death."

Word 13: CAPTIOUS (KAP-shus)

Faultfinding, quick to point out faults or raise trivial objections.

Synonyms of *captious* include *carping*, *quibbling*, *caviling*, *censorious* (sen-SOR-ee-us), and *querulous* (KWER-uh-lus).

Critical, *carping*, and *captious* all mean "inclined to look for and point out faults and defects," says *Webster's Ninth New Collegiate Dictionary* (1993).

Critical, though often used in a negative sense, is in fact a neutral word: the critical person tries to judge something fairly and objectively by weighing its merits and faults. Strictly speaking, a critical assessment is a fair, impartial assessment, and a critical examination may result in a supportive conclusion. *Critical* is so often used of harsh or unfavorable judgment, however, that the neutral sense of the word has nearly been lost; it would be nice if we took pains to preserve it.

Carping, says *Webster's Ninth*, "implies an ill-natured or perverse picking of flaws." *Captious*, which comes from the Latin *captus*, the past participle of the verb *capere*, to take or seize, "suggests a readiness to detect trivial faults or raise objections on trivial grounds."

Here's an idea: The next time you find yourself about to use *critical* in a negative sense, how about giving *carping* or *captious* a try instead?

Word 14: EMENDATION (EE-men-DAY-shin)

A correction, alteration, change made to correct or improve, especially a change made in a piece of writing to correct an error or restore the text to its original state.

The verb to *emend* (ee-MEND) means to make corrections in a text.

Emendation may mean the act of emending, correcting and improving a piece of writing, or it may mean a correction made in a text.

Word 15: TRUCULENT (TRUHK-yuh-lint)

Fierce, ferocious, especially in a brutal, bullying, threatening, or aggressively defiant way.

The corresponding noun is *truculence* (TRUHK-yuh-lints), fierceness, ferocity, brutal aggression.

Synonyms of *truculent* include *pugnacious* (puhg-NAY-shus), *belligerent*, *malevolent* (muh-LEV-uh-lint), *rapacious* (ruh-PAY-shus), and *feral* (FEER-ul).

Antonyms include *humane*, *merciful*, *compassionate*, *benevolent* (buh-NEV-uh-lint), and *clement* (KLEM-int), all of which suggest mercy or mildness, and also *timid*, *demure* (di-MYOOR), *diffident* (DIF-uh-dint), *apprehensive*, and *timorous* (TIM-ur-us), all of which suggest shyness or fear.

Truculent descends from Latin words meaning savage, fierce, cruel, or grim. In current usage *truculent* applies to fierce, savage, or ferocious people or to behavior that is brutal, threatening, bullying, or aggressively defiant: A truculent nation is a hostile, belligerent nation. A truculent look is a pugnacious or threatening look. A truculent philosophy of business is a brutal, aggressive, rapacious, winner-takes-all philosophy of business. In his *Dictionary of Contemporary American Usage* (1957), Bergen Evans offers this sentence to illustrate the meaning of *truculent*: "One of my superiors was a truculent fellow who would have loved being a storm trooper under Hitler."

Truculent is now also used of speech or writing to mean scathing, vicious, or vitriolic (VI-tree-**AHL**-ik), as a truculent retort, a truculent editorial, or a truculent political advertisement.

Word 16: EXPURGATE (EKS-pur-GAYT)

To cleanse by removing offensive material, free from objectionable content.

Synonyms of *expurgate* include *censor*, *purge*, and *bowdlerize*.

The verbs to *expurgate* and *bowdlerize* are close in meaning. (*Bowdlerize* may be pronounced BOWD-luh-ryz, first syllable rhyming with *loud*, or BOHD-luh-ryz, first syllable rhyming with *towed*. Historically the weight of authority favors BOWD-luh-ryz, which I recommend.)

Thomas Bowdler (BOWD-lur) was an English editor who in the early 1800s published expurgated, or cleansed, editions of the Bible and Shakepeare's works. People did not appreciate Bowdler's expurgation of the Good Book and the bawdy Bard, so they took his name and made a nasty word: *bowdlerize*. To *bowdlerize* is to remove material considered risqué, offensive, or obscene, but it connotes doing so out of a prudish or squeamish sense of morality.

Expurgate comes from the Latin *expurgare*, to cleanse, purify, and by derivation is related to the verb to *purge*, to free from impurities, and the adjective *pure*. To *expurgate* means to cleanse by removing that which is objectionable.

When something is *bowdlerized*, that which is considered morally offensive has been deleted. When something is expurgated, that which is considered objectionable for any reason has been deleted. You can bowdlerize Shakespeare by taking out the ribald humor, and you can bowdlerize D. H. Lawrence's novel *Lady Chatterley's Lover* by removing the passages about sex; but you cannot bowdlerize a textbook because presumably it does not contain anything ribald, erotic, or obscene. However, if people charge that a textbook displays a bias or draws conclusions that they find objectionable, they may attempt to expurgate it, cleanse it by removing the offensive material.

Word 17: REPROBATE (**REP**-ruh-**BAYT**)

Thoroughly bad, wicked, corrupt, morally abandoned, lacking all sense of decency and duty.

Synonyms of *reprobate* include *unprincipled*, *shameless*, *base*, *vile*, *degenerate*, *depraved*, *irredeemable*, and *incorrigible*. Antonyms include *virtuous*, *pure*, *righteous*, *honorable*, *chaste*, *unsullied*, and *exemplary*.

Reprobate comes from the Latin *reprobare*, to reprove, disapprove of strongly. In theology, the adjective *reprobate* means damned, predestined for damnation, and the noun a *reprobate* means a person rejected by God and excluded from salvation.

In general usage, the noun a *reprobate* means a corrupt, unprincipled person, a scoundrel, and the adjective *reprobate* means morally abandoned, bad-to-the-core, lacking all sense of decency and duty.

Word 18: SPURIOUS (SPYUUR-ee-<u>us</u>)

False, counterfeit, artificial; not true, authentic, or genuine.

Synonyms of *spurious* include *sham*, *bogus*, *phony*, *fictitious*, *fabricated*, *fraudulent*, *illusory* (i-LOO-suh-ree), *apocryphal* (uh-PAHK-ri-f<u>ul</u>), and *supposititious* (suh-PAHZ-i-**TISH**-<u>us</u>). Antonyms include *genuine* (there is no *wine* in *genuine*; say JEN-yoo-in), *authentic*, *valid*, and *bona fide* (BOH-nuh FYD).

Spurious by derivation means "false, illegitimate." *Spurious* was once used to mean of illegitimate birth, bastard, and although dictionaries still list this sense, it is now rare. Since it came into the language about 1600, and most often today, *spurious* is used to mean false, counterfeit, not authentic or genuine.

Spurious applies to that which is not what it claims or is claimed to be. A spurious document is not authentic or original, and may have been forged; spurious gems are counterfeit, not real or genuine; spurious statements are fabricated, made up; spurious feelings are affected or artificial; and a spurious charge is false, trumped-up, and should be repudiated.

Word 19: VOLITION (voh-LISH-un)

Will, choice, decision, determination.

In Latin, the verb *velle* means to will or wish, and the word *volo* means "I will." From these words comes the English noun *volition*, which may refer either to the power of using the will or the act of exercising it in making a conscious choice or decision.

"He seems to lack volition" implies that he is weak and unable to make a choice or determination. "She came of her own volition" implies that she exercised her will independently, decided on her own to come.

Word 20: INTERPOLATE (in-TUR-puh-LAYT)

To insert, introduce; specifically, to insert words into a piece of writing or a conversation.

The corresponding noun is *interpolation*, an insertion of words into a piece of writing or a conversation.

The verbs to *interpolate*, *interject* (IN-tur-**JEKT**), and *interpose* (IN-tur-**POHZ**) all mean to insert or place between. To *interpose* suggests the insertion of either a literal or figurative obstacle. You may interpose yourself between two people who are quarreling, or circumstances may interpose an impediment or stumbling block that hinders your progress toward a goal. To *interject* suggests an abrupt insertion, and usually refers to speech. You interject an opinion, an idea, or a suggestion. To *interpolate* suggests a deliberate, careful insertion of words into a piece of writing or a conversation. Word-processing programs make it easy to delete or interpolate material and reformat what you have written. *Interpolate* sometimes suggests altering a text by inserting something spurious, unrelated, or unnecessary: Lawyers may insist on interpolating clauses in a contract, or an author may object to an editor's interpolation.

Let's review the ten keywords you've just learned. Consider the following statements and decide whether each one is true or false. Answers appear on page 361.

1. You can palliate an offense or a troublesome situation.
2. A wizened old man is a wise, sagacious old man.
3. A captious comment is an insightful, discerning comment.
4. Editors often make emendations in a manuscript.
5. Truculent people are hostile, brutal, and defiant.
6. When you expurgate something, you speed it up.
7. A person who is reprobate is stubborn and uncooperative.
8. A legal charge, a work of art, and a statement can all be spurious.
9. When you do something of your own volition, you do it independently and willingly.
10. To *interpolate* means to explain or restate the meaning of something.

Let's continue pumping up your word power with the next ten keywords in Level 8.

Word 21: ADDUCE (uh-D(Y)OOS)

To offer or cite as a reason, as evidence, or as authority for an opinion or course of action.

By derivation *adduce* means to bring forward. In modern usage, *adduce* means to bring forward or cite something as a reason, as an example, or as proof in a discussion, analysis, or argument. Lawyers adduce evidence to bolster their case. Politicians adduce facts to justify their position on an issue. Scholars and scientists adduce the results of their research to prove their theories. In writing a report proposing a new marketing plan for a company, an executive might adduce examples of similar marketing strategies that worked for other companies.

Word 22: MISCREANT (MIS-kree-int)

An evil, unscrupulous, vicious person; someone without principles or conscience; a villain, criminal.

Because the world contains so many evil, unscrupulous, vicious people, the language abounds with synonyms for the noun *miscreant*, including but not limited to *scoundrel*, *rascal*, *rogue*, *hoodlum* (HUUD-lum or HOOD-lum), *hooligan* (HOO-li-gun), *ne'er-do-well*, *varlet*, *rapscallion*, *blackguard* (BLAG-urd or BLAG-ahrd), *desperado*, *scapegrace* (SKAYP-grays), *scofflaw* (SKAHF-law), *malefactor* (**MAL**-uh-FAK-tur), and *reprobate*, word 17 of this level.

Miscreant, which entered English in the fourteenth century, comes through Old French from Latin, and combines the prefix *mis-*, which means "bad" or "not," with the Latin *credere*, to believe. By derivation a *miscreant* is someone who does not believe.

For several centuries the word was used to mean a heretic, a person who rejects or flouts religious principles, but this sense is now archaic and since at least the time of Shakespeare *miscreant* has been used to mean a morally bad person, a vile wretch, detestable scoundrel. The adjective *miscreant*, pronounced the same way, means villainous, evil, destitute of conscience.

Word 23: QUIXOTIC (kwik-SAHT-ik)

Foolishly impractical or idealistic, especially in an extravagantly chivalrous or romantic way; inclined to pursue lofty, unreachable goals or far-fetched, unworkable schemes.

Synonyms of *quixotic* include *fanciful*, *whimsical*, *visionary*, *utopian*, *impracticable* (im-PRAK-ti-kuh-buul, five syllables please), and *chimerical* (ki-MER-i-kul). Antonyms include *realistic*, *practical*, *pragmatic*, and *utilitarian*.

Quixotic comes from Don Quixote (kee-HOH-tee), the hero and title of a seventeenth-century satirical romance by Miguel de Cervantes (sair-VAHN-tays). Don Quixote is an old man passionately devoted to the ideals of chivalry—fighting evil and rescuing the oppressed. The Don does not realize that his code of honor has become outworn and been replaced with far less lofty, mercenary goals. With his credulous but pragmatic squire, Sancho Panza (English: SAN-choh PAN-zuh; Spanish: SAHN-choh PAHN-sah), he sets forth on a quest to save the world from wickedness. The world, however, holds only ridicule for the visionary Don, who winds up tilting at windmills and making speeches to the wind.

Today the adjective *quixotic* refers to a person who is extravagantly idealistic or romantic, like Don Quixote, or to an idea or goal that is so impractical and far-fetched as to seem foolish.

Word 24: SUPPURATE (SUHP-yuh-RAYT)

To fester, form or discharge pus.

This unusual word applies to wounds, boils, ulcers, or other lesions that become infected and discharge pus. (By the way, *lesion*, pronounced LEE-zhun, means a wound, injury, infection, or harmful change in some part of the body.)

When a lesion suppurates, discharges pus, it is called *suppuration*; and suppuration, if untreated or unchecked, may lead to a state of putrefaction (PYOO-truh-**FAK**-shin). The verb to *putrefy* (PYOO-truh-fy) means to rot or decay; the adjective *putrid* (PYOO-trid) means rotten, foul-smelling, fetid; and the noun *putrefaction* means rotting, decomposition, foul-smelling decay.

Okay, you can stop holding your nose now because this suppurating, putrid lesson is over and we're moving on to . . .

Word 25: MARTINET (MAHR-ti-**NET**)

A strict disciplinarian, taskmaster, rigid enforcer of rules and regulations.

Martinet comes from General Jean Martinet, a seventeenth-century French drillmaster who became legendary for subjecting his troops to harsh discipline and for his rigid adherence to military rules and regulations. In modern usage, *martinet* may refer to a strict military disciplinarian, or more generally to any rigid, authoritarian enforcer of rules and regulations.

Word 26: COMPUNCTION (kum-PUHNGK-shin)

A twinge of regret caused by an uneasy conscience; a pang of guilt for a wrong done or for pain that one has caused another.

Synonyms of *compunction* include *remorse*, *misgiving*, *scruple*, and *qualm* (KWAHM, the *l* is silent). A stronger synonym is *contrition*, word 9 of Level 5, which means repentance, deep and devastating sorrow for one's sins or for something one has done wrong.

Compunction comes through the Late Latin *compunctio*, a pricking of conscience, ultimately from the Latin verb *pungere*, to prick, sting, pierce, or stab. The Latin *pungere* is also the source of the English words *puncture*, meaning to prick, pierce, or stab; *pungent*, which means piercing or stinging to the smell or taste, as a pungent aroma; and *poignant* (POYN-yint), which means piercing or penetrating to the senses, the emotions, or the intellect.

When you feel the prick or sting of conscience or a twinge of regret for something you have done wrong, or when you feel a pang of guilt for causing pain to another person, that is a compunction: "After a year, Ned still had compunctions about ending his relationship with Suzy." If your conscience is clear and you have no regrets, you lack compunction: "Vanessa grew sick and tired of working for a martinet, and when she finally decided the time was right to quit her job, she did so without compunction."

Word 27: MERCURIAL (mur-KYUUR-ee-ul)

Quick to change moods or change one's mind, having an unpredictable temperament.

Synonyms of *mercurial* include *flighty*, *impulsive*, *fickle*, *capricious* (which properly rhymes with *delicious*; it's word 11 of Level 1), *volatile* (word 47 of Level 4), *erratic*, and *protean* (PROH-tee-in).

Antonyms include *stable*, *fixed*, *steadfast*, *invariable*, and *immutable*.

Does anything about the word *mercurial* sound familiar? Can you guess its derivation? If you're thinking that *mercurial* is related to the word *mercury*, then you are a sagacious person, both in the current sense of wise, shrewd, perceptive, and in the obsolete sense of quick in picking up a scent—in this case, an etymological scent.

The ancient Roman god Mercury, known to the Greeks as Hermes (HUR-meez), was the messenger or courier of the gods, but he had many other responsibilities as well. He was the deity (DEE-i-tee) who conducted the souls of the dead to the underworld, and also the god of commerce, travel, eloquence, and thievery. (Those ancient Greeks and Romans covered all the bases, didn't they?)

Mercury is usually depicted wearing a winged helmet and winged sandals to show his fleet-footedness, and as Hermes he also carried a winged staff with two serpents coiled around it. That staff, which now serves as the symbol of the medical profession, is called a *caduceus* (kuh-D(Y)OO-see-us).

I'm sure that doctors today view the caduceus as a symbol of their devotion to providing swift, efficient health care, but I must confess I find it nothing short of hilarious that the medical profession has chosen a symbol from an ancient god who governed commerce, travel, eloquence, and thievery, and who escorted the dead to their final resting place.

Because of the various hats worn by the god Mercury, the adjective *mercurial* has been used to mean everything from swift, quick-witted, and eloquent to shrewd, clever, and thieving. Dictionaries still list these words under the definition "having the characteristics attributed to the god Mercury," but in current usage the word most often is used to mean like the element mercury, which is also called quicksilver. As you know, mercury is used in thermometers, and it is highly reponsive to changes in temperature. Like the mercury in a thermometer, that which is mercurial is changeable, fickle, or capricious. The mercurial person has an unpredictable temperament and is quick to change moods.

Word 28: NOSTRUM (NAHS-trum)

A quack remedy or medicine; a panacea; hence, a dubious or dishonest plan or scheme for curing a social or political problem.

Nostrum comes from the Latin *noster,* which means "our." In days of yore, the charlatan and the mountebank—two unsavory types that I discussed in word 17 of Level 4—would sell their panacea or cure-all by calling it a *nostrum*, meaning literally "our remedy." As a result, the word *nostrum* came to mean a medicine whose ingredients are kept secret and whose preparer makes exaggerated claims about its effectiveness, which has not been proved.

That definition is still in good standing, as a trip to any health-food store will prove. Because quack remedies can be applied not only to the ills of the body but also to the ills of the body politic, in modern usage *nostrum* has also come to mean a dubious or dishonest plan or scheme for curing a social or political problem. Throughout society today, from the bars to the talk shows to the hallowed halls of government, you can hear quacks, eccentrics, and downright weirdos proposing their nostrums for the ills of the world.

Word 29: PROPITIATE (pruh- *or* proh-PISH-ee-ayt)

To appease, gain or regain the goodwill or favor of, cause to become favorably inclined.

Synonyms of *propitiate* include *conciliate, pacify, mollify, placate,* and *assuage* (word 37 of Level 2). Antonyms include *alienate, offend, antagonize, estrange,* and *disaffect.*

The corresponding noun is *propitiation,* appeasement, conciliation, the act of getting into the good graces of.

The verb to *propitiate* comes from Latin and means literally to soothe, appease, render favorable. From the same source comes the adjective *propitious* (pruh-PISH-us), which refers to favorable conditions or a favorable time for doing something, as a propitious time for buyers in the real estate market.

In modern usage, to *propitiate* means to cause to become favorably inclined, to win the goodwill of someone or something despite opposition or hostility. Typically, you propitiate a higher power, such as your boss, your parents, the Internal Revenue Service, or your god.

Word 30: EFFICACY (EF-i-kuh-see)

Effectiveness; the power to produce a desired effect or result.

Efficacy applies to things that have the power to produce an intended effect. We speak of the efficacy of a drug, a scientific method, or an advertising campaign. The corresponding adjective is *efficacious* (EF-i-**KAY**-shus), which means effective, capable of producing a desired effect or result, as an efficacious law, an efficacious policy, or an efficacious marketing plan.

Let's review the ten keywords you've just learned. I'll give you two words, and you decide if they are synonyms or antonyms. Answers appear on page 362.

1. To *cite* and to *adduce* are . . . synonyms or antonyms?
2. *Malefactor* and *miscreant* are . . .
3. *Pragmatic* and *quixotic* are . . .
4. To *fester* and to *suppurate* are . . .
5. *Pushover* and *martinet* are . . .
6. *Compunction* and *regret* are . . .
7. *Capricious* and *mercurial* are . . .
8. *Panacea* and *nostrum* are . . .
9. *Alienate* and *propitiate* are . . .
10. *Uselessness* and *efficacy* are . . .

If you answered fewer than eight of the questions correctly in this quiz, remember to reread the last ten keyword discussions before moving ahead in the program.

Name That Word

Let's take a short break now from the keyword discussions for an excursion into the wonderful world of eponyms. Do know what an eponym is?

Eponym (EP-uh-nim) comes from Greek and means literally "named after." An *eponym* is a word derived from a name, or a name that becomes a word. The corresponding adjective is *eponymous* (i-PAHN-uh-mus)

So far in Level 8 you have learned four eponymous words, words derived from names: *bowdlerize*, which comes from Thomas Bowdler, the prudish expurgator of Shakespeare and the Bible; *quixotic*, which comes from Don Quixote, the romantic dreamer; *martinet*, which comes from General Jean Martinet, the rigid disciplinarian; and *mercurial*, which comes from the fleet-footed, unpredictable Roman god Mercury.

You may recall that in the discussion of *prodigious*, keyword 48 of Level 5, we covered four more eponymous words: *gargantuan*, from Rabelais' character Gargantua, the gluttonous giant; *herculean*, from the mighty hero Hercules; and two eponyms that come to us from Jonathan Swift's *Gulliver's Travels*: *Lilliputian*, which means like the tiny inhabitants of the mythical land of Lilliput, and *Brobdingnagian*, which means like the gigantic inhabitants of the mythical land of Brobdingnag.

Finally, in Level 6 you also learned several eponyms from ancient Greece, including *Procrustean*, which comes from Procrustes, the brutal robber who stretched people's bodies or cut off their limbs to make them conform to the size of his bed; *draconian*, which comes from Draco, the authoritarian statesman whose code of laws was so severe that it imposed the death penalty for nearly all crimes, great or small; *epicurean*, which comes from the philosopher Epicurus, who advocated the pursuit of pleasure through the practice of virtue; *Pyrrhonism*, which comes from Pyrrho, the exponent of absolute skepticism; and *solecism*, which comes from the rude and foul-mouthed inhabitants of Soloi. In modern usage, a *solecism* is a gross grammatical error or social indiscretion.

As the words *Lilliputian*, *Brobdingnagian*, and *solecism* illustrate, eponyms can be formed from the names of places or whole populations as well as from the names of individuals.

Among the thousands of eponyms in the English language, two of the most familiar are *sandwich* and *silhouette*.

It is said that the word *sandwich* was born when John Montagu, the fourth earl of Sandwich, grew hungry after a long night at the gaming table and instructed his servant to fetch him a snack consisting of slices of roast beef placed between two pieces of toasted bread.

The word *silhouette* comes from Etienne de Silhouette, a French minister of finance in the eighteenth century who imposed severe luxury taxes and stringent austerity measures in an attempt to revive the French economy after the Seven Years' War. According to Robert Hendrickson, in his *Dictionary of Eponyms: Names That Became Words* (1972), because Silhouette "cut expenses to the bone until they became mere shadows of their original selves," his name inspired the phrase *à la silhouette*, meaning "on the cheap," and the phrase was applied to pants made without pockets, to coats made without folds, and to the inexpensive shadow portraits that happened to be in vogue in Paris at the time.

Would you like an all-American eponym? The useful word *maverick* comes from the surname of Samuel Augustus Maverick, a gentleman rancher in nineteenth-century Texas who neglected to brand his cattle. The unbranded cows came to be called *mavericks*, and later the word was applied to any person who stands apart from the herd, a nonconformist.

The moral censorship exercised by the editor Thomas Bowdler was nothing compared with the campaign against vice waged by the man who gave his name to the word *Comstockery* (**KAHM**-STAHK-ur-ee). In his *Dictionary of Eponyms*, Robert Hendrickson explains that Anthony Comstock, who lived from 1844 to 1915, was the founder of the New York Society for the Suppression of Vice and "a self-appointed crusader against immorality in literature." After helping to secure passage of the so-called Comstock Laws, which outlawed "objectionable matter from the mails," Comstock became a special agent of the Post Office, a position in which he "had the power of an inquisitor." According to Hendrickson, Comstock "is said to have arrested three thousand persons over a forty-odd year career," and destroyed "about 160 tons of books, stereotyped plates, magazines, and pictures" that he deemed obscene. "The crusader particularly objected to [George Bernard] Shaw's play, *Mrs. Warren's Profession*, and [in 1905] Shaw coined the word making good clean fun of his name." Today, *Comstockery* means "narrow-minded, bigoted, and self-righteous moral censorship."

I'd like to conclude this excursion into the world of eponyms by telling you the story of the word *chauvinism* (**SHOW**-vuh-NIZ-'m). Nicolas Chauvin was a veteran of the Napoleonic wars, and a fervent follower of the emperor. After the defeat and exile of Napoleon, Chauvin became so zealous in his demonstrations of patriotism and allegiance to the fallen emperor that people began to ridicule him. Robert Hendrickson notes that Chauvin would have escaped national attention if several dramatists hadn't decided to mock him in their plays, and eventually Chauvin became the laughingstock of all of France. The French coined a word for his blind love of country, which soon made its way into English. Today *chauvinism* means overzealous patriotism, and a chauvinist is a superpatriot, a person unreasonably and militantly devoted to his country.

Those are still the meanings of these words today. Since the 1970s, however, the phrase *male chauvinism* has been used to mean a zealous and obnoxious belief in the alleged superiority of men over women. In recent years, people have begun to drop the word *male* and use *chauvinism* to denote a supercilious attitude of men toward women, and *chauvinist* to mean a man who treats women as inferior.

That usage is unfortunate, for today many people think *chauvinism* means only male chauvinism, and the original meaning of the word is now in jeopardy. There is nothing wrong with adding a new sense to a word when there is clear need for it, but the addition ought not to be at the expense of an older meaning that still has a useful and precise function in the language. Now that you know the story of Nicolas Chauvin, I hope you will take care to specify *male chauvinism* when that is meant, and reserve the word *chauvinism* to mean superpatriotism, overzealous devotion to one's country.

And now it is time to leave the land of eponyms and return to the *Verbal Advantage* vocabulary.

Word 31: TANTAMOUNT (TAN-tuh-MOWNT)

Equivalent; having equal force, effect, or value.

Tantamount comes from an Anglo-French phrase meaning "to amount to as much, be equal to," and ultimately from the Latin *tantus*, which means "so much" or "so great." In modern usage, when one thing is tantamount to another, it amounts to as much as the other, adds up to the same thing.

In his *Dictionary of Contemporary American Usage* (1957), Bergen Evans notes that the words *paramount* and *tantamount* "look deceptively alike but they mean very different things. *Paramount* means supreme in rank, preëminent [now written *preeminent*, without the dieresis]. *Tantamount* means equivalent, as in value, force, effect, or significance. It is usually followed by *to* (*Your statement is tantamount to a confession*). *Tantamount* is properly applied to acts and statements but not to material things."

Word 32: PARIAH (puh-RY-uh)

An outcast; a person despised or rejected by society.

Pariah entered English in the early 1600s from *Tamil* (TAM-ul), one of the languages of India. In the traditional social system of India, people were divided into classes called *castes* (pronounced like *casts*). Unlike in the United States, where there has always been a great deal of class mobility, downward as well as upward, until recently the Indian caste system was rigid, and the pariah caste was one of the lowest on the social ladder. Its members worked chiefly as agricultural and domestic laborers and as servants to the British when India was a British colony. The third edition of *The American Heritage Dictionary* (1992) notes that until 1949 the pariahs "were also known as untouchables."

From this sense of social inferiority, the word *pariah* came to be used in English of any person despised or rejected by society, an outcast. Although *pariah* is often used to describe criminals, outlaws, degenerates, and derelicts, the word does not always connote lawlessness, abject poverty, or antisocial behavior. Young people can become pariahs at school if they don't wear the right clothing or do what is considered "cool." In the 1960s, the hippies became pariahs in the eyes of the establishment because of their disdain for traditional values and opposition to the Vietnam War. And in the 1950s, during Senator Joe McCarthy's infamous witchhunt for Communist subversives, many people who worked in the Hollywood film industry were blacklisted and treated like pariahs, social outcasts.

Word 33: GERMANE (jur-MAYN)

Relevant, fitting, appropriate, precisely to the point.

Synonyms of *germane* include *pertinent*, *suitable*, *applicable* (AP-li-kuh-bul), *apposite* (AP-uh-zit), and *apropos* (AP-ruh-**POH**).

Antonyms include *inappropriate*, *unsuitable*, *irrelevant*, *inapplicable*, *alien*, *extraneous*, *incongruous* (in-KAHNG-groo-wus), and *malapropos* (MAL-ap-ruh-**POH**).

Germane comes through Middle English and Old French from the Latin *germanus*, which means "having the same parents." When you have the same parents, you are closely allied by blood, and so related or akin. Out of this notion of family affinity grew the modern meaning of *germane*, having a close relationship to the subject at hand, closely tied to the point in question.

Germane, *apposite*, *pertinent*, and *relevant* are close in meaning.

Relevant is the weakest of the group and means simply related, connected, bearing upon a subject: "The chair of the meeting asked the participants to keep their comments relevant and to refrain from bringing up tangential issues." *Pertinent* implies immediate, precise, and direct relevance: "Emily made several pertinent suggestions during the meeting that helped us focus on the problem." *Apposite* implies relevance that is particularly appropriate, timely, or suitable to the occasion: "Emily made some apposite observations about the competition that made us reconsider our marketing strategy." Our keyword, *germane*, implies a close connection or natural relationship that is highly fitting or appropriate: "Emily also presented a great deal of germane information in her report"; "The judge chided the defense attorney for voicing opinions that were not germane to the case."

Word 34: LICENTIOUS (ly-SEN-shus)

Sexually abandoned; lacking moral restraint, especially in sexual conduct.

Apparently there is something sensual about the letter *l*, because there are no fewer than nine synonyms of *licentious* that begin with *l*: *lewd, loose, lustful, lecherous* (LECH-ur-us), *lascivious* (luh-SIV-ee-us), *libertine* (**LIB**-ur-TEEN), *lubricious* (loo-BRISH-us), *lickerish* (LIK-ur-ish), and *libidinous* (li-BID-'n-us). Additional synonyms of *licentious*—and believe me, I'm selecting only the more challenging ones—include *bawdy, wanton, ribald* (word 42 of Level 7, rhymes with *scribbled*), *prurient* (PRUUR-ee-int), *debauched* (di-BAWCHT), *dissolute* (DIS-uh-loot), *salacious* (suh-LAY-shus), and *concupiscent* (kahn-KYOO-pi-sint).

Had enough sexy words? All right, here are three antonyms of *licentious* to quell your lust: *pure, chaste,* and *virtuous*.

Licentious comes from the Latin *licentia*, freedom, leave, liberty, the source also of the English word *license*. By derivation *licentious* means taking license, and the word implies doing something one is not supposed to do, especially something sexually immoral. Dictionaries will tell you that *licentious* may be used to mean unrestrained by law, morality, or rules of correctness or propriety, as a licentious poet or a licentious rap musician. But the truth is that in current usage licentious almost always connotes unrestrained sexuality. Licentious poets write lewd or lustful poems, and licentious rap musicians hip-hop through their sexual escapades. A licentious person is someone who displays a lack of moral restraint regarding sexual conduct.

Word 35: SUPERANNUATED (SOO-pur-AN-yoo-AY-tid)

Retired because of age, weakness, or ineffectiveness; old and worn out; outdated, outmoded, obsolete.

Synonyms of *superannuated* include *timeworn, antiquated* (**AN**-ti-KWAY-tid), *decrepit* (di-KREP-it), *passé* (pa-SAY), and *effete* (i-FEET).

Superannuated combines the prefix *super-*, meaning "beyond," with the Latin *annum*, a year, and by derivation means beyond the useful years. That which is superannuated is too old for use, work, or service. The word may be used of a person who has reached the age of retirement, or of anything that has outlived its usefulness, that is old and worn out, as a superannuated car, a superannuated custom, a superannuated technology, or a superannuated idea.

Word 36: EGREGIOUS (i-GREE-jus)

Conspicuously bad, remarkable or outstanding for some undesirable or offensive quality.

Synonyms of *egregious* include *flagrant*, *outrageous*, *excessive*, *shocking*, *gross*, *monstrous*, *notorious*, *grievous* (GREE-vus, two syllables please), and *arrant* (AR-unt).

Egregious comes from the Latin *egregius*, not of the common herd, and therefore select or outstanding. *Egregious* was once used to mean outstanding or remarkable, but this sense is long obsolete, and for at least three hundred years the word has most often been used to mean outstanding or remarkable in a bad way, conspicuously bad, offensive, or undesirable.

When you think of how many remarkably bad things there are in the world, it's surprising that *egregious* isn't used more often. Here are a few possible applications: an egregious crime, an egregious lie, an egregious insult, an egregious fool, an egregious oversight, an egregious mistake, and an egregious breach of human rights.

Word 37: VAPID (VAP-id, rhymes with *rapid*)

Lifeless, dull, boring, flat, stale; lacking spirit, interest, or flavor.

Synonyms of *vapid* include *unsavory*, *insipid*, *unpalatable*, *trite*, *prosaic* (word 16 of Level 4), *pedestrian*, and *jejune* (ji-JOON, word 1 of Level 10).

Antonyms include *lively*, *vigorous*, *vivid*, *animated*, *robust*, *vivacious* (vi-VAY-shus), and *emphatic*.

Vapid comes from the Latin *vapidus*, which means spiritless, spoiled, flat. The word has remained true to its Latin root, and in modern usage *vapid* still applies to that which is lifeless, boring, or stale. Today we speak of vapid conversation, vapid beer, a vapid remark, or a vapid look in a person's eyes.

Word 38: CROTCHET (KRAHCH-it, rhymes with *watch it*)

An odd notion or whim that one clings to stubbornly.

The corresponding adjective is *crotchety*. A crotchety person is full of crotchets, and therefore stubbornly eccentric. *Crotchety* is often applied to cantankerous old people who are set in their eccentric ways.

Crotchet comes from a Middle English word meaning a staff with a hook at the end. It is related to the familiar word *crochet* (kroh-SHAY), the form of needlework in which thread is looped with a hooked needle. *Crotchet* was once used to mean a reaping hook or a hooklike instrument. In modern usage, however, the most common meaning of *crotchet* is an odd notion or whim that hooks you or that you cling to stubbornly, as if with a hook.

   Webster's New World Dictionary, third edition (1997), says that *crotchet* "implies great eccentricity and connotes stubbornness in opposition to prevailing thought, usually on some insignificant point." A crotchet may appear insignificant to others, but if it's *your* crotchet, it's far from trivial. Think of all the eccentric people you know, young or old, who cling to some odd notion or peculiar way of doing something and you will see that to the people who hold them, crotchets are heartfelt convictions.

   In *The Writer's Art* (1984), James J. Kilpatrick includes a long chapter in which he lists, without excuses or apology, one hundred of his crotchets about usage. "Every one . . . is as dear to me," he writes, "as Audrey, the country wench, was dear to Touchstone. She was an ill-favored thing, sir, but his own. If I am tetchy about the placement of *only*, that's it. I'm crotchety."

   And before your verbally advantaged guide gets crotchety about usage too, let's move on to the next word.

Word 39: EPIGRAPH (EP-i-GRAF)

An inscription; especially, an inscription on a building or monument, or a brief quotation at the beginning of a literary composition that suggests or is germane to its theme.

   Epigraph, *epigram*, and *epitaph* are close in meaning but sharply distinguished in usage.

   An *epitaph* (**EP**-i-TAF) is an inscription on a gravestone or tomb in memory of the person buried. In *The Devil's Dictionary*, a classic work of satirical lexicography, the acerbic and crotchety humorist Ambrose Bierce defined *epitaph* as "an inscription on a tomb, showing that virtues acquired by death have a retroactive effect." Dorothy Parker, another American writer famous for her quick, mordant wit, once proposed these two epitaphs for herself: "Excuse my dust" and "This is on me."

   Epigram (**EP**-i-GRAM) has two meanings. Originally it referred to a short, witty poem—for example, this two-line ditty by Ogden Nash: "I like eels / 'cept as meals." Later *epigram* also came to mean a short, pointed saying that displays terse wit or a clever twist of thought. One of the greatest epigrammatists (EP-i-**GRAM**-uh-tists), or writers of epigrams, who ever lived was the nineteenth-century poet and playwright Oscar Wilde. Here are three examples of Wilde's epigrams: "When people agree with me I always feel that I must be wrong." "The only way to get rid of a temptation is to yield to it." "[A cynic is] a man who knows the price of everything and the value of nothing."

Our keyword, *epigraph*, is formed from the prefix *epi-*, meaning "on" or "above," and the Greek verb *graphein*, to write. This Greek verb has influenced many English words, including *electrocardiograph*, an instrument for recording the beating of the heart; *orthography*, correct spelling; *polygraph*, otherwise known as a lie detector; and *graphology*, the study of handwriting. Whenever you see a word containing *graph*, you can reasonably assume that it has something to do with writing.

An *epigraph* by derivation means a writing on or above something; hence, an inscription. When you see words engraved on a building, a monument, or a statue, that's an epigraph. When you see a brief quotation placed at the beginning of a book, a chapter, a poem, or the like, that is also an epigraph.

Word 40: EXPATIATE (ek-SPAY-shee-ayt)

To elaborate, speak or write at great length.

Synonyms of *expatiate* include *discourse* (dis-KORS), *expound* (ek-SPOWND), and *descant* (des-KANT).

The verb to *expatiate* comes from the Latin *expatiari*, to wander. *Expatiate* originally meant to wander or walk about freely, but this sense is now rare. In current usage *expatiate* suggests wandering at will over a subject. When you expatiate on something, you elaborate, go into detail, speak or write about it at great length. The corresponding noun is *expatiation* (ek-SPAY-shee-**AY**-shin).

Let's review the last ten keywords by playing "One of These Definitions Doesn't Fit the Word." In each statement below, a keyword (in *italics*) is followed by three definitions. Two of the three are correct; one is unrelated in meaning. Decide which definition doesn't fit the keyword. Answers appear on page 362.

1. *Tantamount* means equal, balanced, equivalent.
2. A *pariah* is an unlucky person, a social reject, an outcast.
3. *Germane* means fitting, relevant, interesting.
4. *Licentious* means sexually immoral, sexually inhibited, sexually abandoned.
5. *Superannuated* means old and worn out, highly exaggerated, obsolete.
6. *Egregious* means conspicuously out of place, conspicuously offensive, conspicuously bad.
7. *Vapid* means lifeless, boring, unpleasant.

8. A *crotchet* is a bad idea, an odd whim, a stubborn notion.
9. An *epigraph* is an inscription on a building, a quotation at the beginning of a book, something written on a gravestone.
10. To *expatiate* means to go into detail, to explain briefly, to elaborate.

Did you remember to keep track of your score? Do you need to review before continuing?

Here are the final ten keywords in Level 8:

Word 41: SINECURE (SY-nuh-KYOOR—recommended—or SIN-uh-KYOOR)

A position that provides a good income or salary but that requires little or no work; in colloquial terms, a cushy job.

Sinecure comes from the Latin phrase *beneficium sine cura*, which means "a benifice without cure." And what does that mean, you ask? A *benefice* is an endowed church position or office that provides a member of the clergy with a fixed income or guaranteed living. A "benefice without cure" means a paid position for a member of the clergy that does not require pastoral work—in other words, the curing of souls. Pastors, vicars, rectors, and the like who were granted sinecures by their church did not have a congregation, and they were paid well to do little or nothing.

Sinecure is such a useful word that it was soon adopted by the laity to mean any position or office that has no specific duties or work attached to it but that provides an income or emolument.

Word 42: PREDILECTION (PRED-i-LEK-shin)

A preference, partiality, preconceived liking, an inclination or disposition to favor something.

Synonyms of *predilection* include *fondness*, *leaning*, *bias*, *prejudice*, *predisposition*, *affinity* (word 46 of Level 4), *penchant* (word 9 of Level 3), *propensity*, and *proclivity*.

Predilection comes through French from the Medieval Latin verb *praediligere*, to prefer. Unlike the words *bias* and *prejudice*, which are often used negatively, *predilection* has either a neutral or positive connotation and is used as a stronger synonym of *preference* and *partiality* (PAHR-shee-**AL**-i-tee). According to the third edition of *Webster's New World Dictionary* (1997), a *predilection* is "a preconceived liking, formed as a result of one's background, temperament, etc., that inclines one toward a particular preference." You can have a predilection for anything you are naturally partial to or inclined to like, as a predilection for ice hockey, a predilection for solving crossword puzzles, a predilection for country music, or a predilection for Italian cuisine.

Word 43: IMBROGLIO (im-BROHL-yoh)

A complicated or intricate situation; a difficult, perplexing state of affairs; also, a misunderstanding or disagreement of a complicated and confusing nature.

Synonyms of *imbroglio* include *entanglement*, *embroilment*, *predicament*, and *quandary* (word 27 of Level 3).

Imbroglio comes through Italian and Old French from Latin and means by derivation to entangle, confuse, mix up, embroil. When *imbroglio* entered English in the mid-1700s, it meant "a confused heap," but this sense is now rare. The great *Oxford English Dictionary* shows that by the early 1800s *imbroglio* had come to mean "a state of great confusion and entanglement; a complicated or difficult situation; a confused misunderstanding or disagreement." The unraveling of an imbroglio is a common plot in many plays, novels, and operas, but there are plenty of imbroglios in real life as well. Open the newspaper on any given day and you will find stories of political imbroglios, financial imbroglios, marital imbroglios, and criminal imbroglios.

Word 44: INEFFABLE (in-EF-uh-buul)

Inexpressible, unable to be expressed or described in words.

Synonyms of *ineffable* include *unutterable*, *unspeakable*, and *indescribable*.

Ineffable comes from the Latin *ineffabilis*, which means unutterable, not able to be spoken. Once upon a prudish time, when Thomas Bowdler was bowdlerizing Shakespeare and the Bible and Anthony Comstock was committing Comstockery on the U.S. Mail, the more refined members of polite society would call the legs of a piano "limbs" and refer to a man's trousers as "ineffables." My, how times change. Today women also wear trousers, and hardly anything is ineffable, especially on late-night TV.

Dictionaries note that *ineffable* may mean too sacred to be spoken, as the ineffable name of a deity (DEE-i-tee) or an ineffable curse, but this sense is now infrequent, and in current usage *ineffable* almost always means inexpressible, unable to be expressed or described in words. *Webster's New International Dictionary*, second edition (1934), notes that *ineffable* usually applies to "good or pleasant things," as ineffable beauty or ineffable joy, but it may occasionally apply to something unpleasant that is inexpressible, as ineffable disgust.

Word 45: STOLID (STAHL-id)

Not easily moved, aroused, or excited; showing little or no feeling or sensitivity; mentally or emotionally dull, insensitive, or obtuse.

Synonyms of *stolid* include *unemotional*, *unresponsive*, *sluggish*, *apathetic*, *impassive*, *indifferent*, and *phlegmatic* (fleg-MAT-ik), word 33 of Level 9.

Stolid comes from the Latin *stolidus*, stupid, dull, unmoving. According to *Webster's New World Dictionary*, third college edition (1997), *stolid* applies to a person "who is not easily moved or excited," and suggests "dullness, obtuseness, or stupidity." Unlike stoic people, who display firmness of mind and character in their thick-skinned, unflinching indifference to pain and suffering, people who are stolid are not easily moved because they are oafs, dolts, louts, or half-wits. In other words, a stolid person shows little feeling or sensitivity because the light's not on upstairs.

Stolid is sometimes also applied figuratively to behavior or things that are unresponsive, insensitive, or not easily moved. A stolid countenance or expression is unresponsive. A stolid bureaucracy is dense and insensitive to the needs of individuals. And stolid opposition is not easily moved.

Word 46: OFFAL (AWF-ul, like *awful*—recommended—*or* AHF-ul)

Waste, garbage, refuse, rubbish.

Offal comes from Middle English and is a combination of the words *off* and *fall*. Originally the word applied to anything that fell off or was thrown off in the process of doing something—for example, wood chips in lumbering or carpentry, or the dross or scum that forms on the surface of molten metal. Since the early 1400s, *offal* has also been used of the waste parts removed in the process of butchering an animal. From that unsavory sense, the meaning of *offal* broadened to denote waste or garbage in general, anything thrown away as worthless. In *Julius Caesar*, Shakespeare writes, "What trash is Rome? What rubbish, and what offal?"

Dictionaries still define *offal* as the waste parts, and especially the entrails, of a butchered animal, and if you are fond of sausages, as I am, I hope it won't disturb you to know that many of them are made from *offal*. However, the more general definition of the word—trash, refuse, rubbish—is now probably more common. Today we dispose of our offal in sewers and landfills, and the offal of society gets sent to jail.

Word 47: LISSOME (LIS-<u>u</u>m)

Limber, flexible, moving with ease and grace.

Synonyms of *lissome* include *nimble*, *agile*, *supple*, and *lithe* (L<u>YTH</u>, rhymes with *writhe*).

Lissome, *lithe*, and *limber* are close synonyms. *Limber* suggests moving or bending easily, as limber muscles, or a limber bough. *Lithe* and *lissome* suggest moving with nimbleness, agility, and grace; of the two words, *lithe* is more literal, *lissome* more poetic. We speak of a lithe runner; a lithe deer; a lissome dancer; a lissome tongue.

Word 48: MELLIFLUOUS (muh-LIF-loo-<u>u</u>s)

Flowing smoothly and sweetly, like honey.

The adjective *mellifluous* comes through Middle English from Latin and means literally flowing like honey. The word has stuck like honey to its root, and in modern usage *mellifluous* means honeyed or honey-toned, flowing smoothly and sweetly.

Mellifluous often applies to sounds or words, as a mellifluous voice, mellifluous music, a mellifluous speaker, or mellifluous writing.

Word 49: SURFEIT (SUR-fit, like *surf it*)

To supply, fill, or feed to excess, especially to the point of discomfort, sickness, or disgust.

Synonyms of *surfeit* include *sate* and *satiate* (**SAY**-shee-AYT), which may mean either to fill or supply to satisfaction or to fill or supply beyond what is necessary or desired. Additional synonyms include *stuff*, *cram*, *glut*, *gorge*, *choke*, *inundate*, and *cloy*.

The verb to *surfeit* is derived from Middle English and Old French words meaning to overdo, exceed, and in modern usage *surfeit* means to feed, fill, or stuff to the point of discomfort, sickness, or disgust. You can surfeit yourself on a Thanksgiving feast. You can surfeit yourself with booze. You can watch episodes of the "Three Stooges" until you are surfeited with slapstick humor. Or you can read *Verbal Advantage* until your brain is surfeited with words.

The corresponding noun *surfeit*, pronounced the same way, is most often used to mean an excess or oversupply, as a surfeit of praise or a surfeit of products on the market.

Word 50: BLANDISHMENT (BLAN-dish-m<u>e</u>nt)

Flattering or coaxing speech or action; an ingratiating remark or gesture.

Blandishment comes through Middle English and Old French from the Latin verb *blandiri*, to flatter, caress, coax, which comes in turn from the adjective *blandus*, which means flattering, fondling, caressing. By derivation, *blandishment* means speech or action that flatters, fondles, coaxes, or caresses in an attempt to win over or persuade a person.

In current usage the word is usually employed in its plural form, *blandishments*, which the second edition of *Webster's New International Dictionary* (1934) defines as "soft words and artful caresses." Unlike flattery, which is generally perceived as self-serving, blandishments are not necessarily insincere. They may be expressions of honest affection, kindness, or desire. When you offer blandishments to your boss, to a friend, to your spouse, or to your lover, you are using gentle flattery and kind words to butter that person up.

The corresponding verb is *blandish*, to coax with flattering or ingratiating statements or actions.

Let's review the ten keywords you've just learned. I'll give you the review word (in *italics*) followed by three words or phrases, and you decide which one of those three words or phrases comes nearest the meaning of the review word. Answers appear on page 363.

1. Is a *sinecure* a period of unemployment, a job with many responsibilities, or a position that requires little or no work?
2. Is a *predilection* a preference, a dislike, or an uneasy feeling?
3. Is an *imbroglio* a devious plot, a complicated situation, or an elaborate plan?

4. Are *ineffable* feelings private, overwhelming, or inexpressible?
5. Is a *stolid* person unemotional, reliable, or stubborn?
6. Does *offal* mean immorality, despair, or waste?
7. If something is *lissome*, is it limber, delicious, or soft?
8. Are *mellifluous* words dishonest, smooth, or foolish?
9. Does *surfeit* mean to shut down, to skip over, or to feed to excess?
10. Does *blandishment* mean flattery, foolishness, or deceit?

If you answered eight or more questions correctly, read on. If not, review.

There Is No *Noun* in *Pronunciation*

We shall wind up Level 8 with a look at a few commonly mispronounced words.

First, the word *query*. The noun *query* means a question or inquiry; the verb to *query* means to ask questions about, especially to resolve a doubt or obtain authoritative information. The noun and verb are now so often mispronounced KWAIR-ee (rhymes with *hairy*) that this variant has made its way into a few current dictionaries. Until quite recently, however, dictionaries gave only one pronunciation, which I recommend as preferable: KWEER-ee (rhymes with *leery*).

Now let's look at *consul* and *consulate*. A *consul* (KAHN-sul) is a diplomat, a person appointed by a government to live in a foreign city and serve his country's citizens and business interests there. *Consulate* (KAHN-suh-lit) refers either to the office or to the residence of a consul. These words are often mispronounced like *counsel* and *counselate*, as if the first syllable were *coun-* instead of *con-*. There is no *counsel* in *consul* and *consulate*, and these words have nothing to do with counseling. So the next time you journey abroad and need help from a representative of your government, go to the *con*sulate and ask to see the *con*sul.

When you want to borrow a book, do you go to the public library or the public *liberry*? Let's hope you go to the public library (LY-brer-ee), because there is no such thing as a *liberry*. The beastly mispronunciation *liberry* is "heard from less educated and very young speakers, and is often criticized," says the second, unabridged edition of *The Random House Dictionary of the English Language* (1987). Unless for some reason you wish to appear less educated or very young, remember there is no *berry* in *library*.

Now for something *irrevelent* about *jewlery* that may help you avoid several *grievious* errors of *pronounciation*. That egregious sentence contained no fewer than four grievous errors of pronunciation, all of which are signs of a sloppy speaker.

First, we have the problem of transposed letters and sounds. In the word *irrelevant*, be careful not to transpose the *l* and *v* and say *irrevelent*. I don't think I'm being irreverent by averring that the proper pronunciation is i-REL-uh-vint. In the word *jewelry*, don't transpose the *l* and the *e* in the second syllable and say JOO-luh-ree. There is no *joola* in JOO-wuul-ree. To get it right, just say the word *jewel* and then add *-ree*. By the way, in linguistics this transposition of letters and sounds in a word is called *metathesis* (muh-TATH-uh-sis).

Next, we have *grievous*, which is often mispronounced GREE-vee-us, even by educated speakers. These speakers are also prone to misspell the word by interpolating a spurious *i*: *grievious*. The correct spelling has one *i*, *grievous*, and the proper pronunciation has two, not three, syllables: GREE-vus.

Now let's talk about *pronounciation*, which of course should be *pronunciation*. I can't tell you how many times I have been a guest on a radio talk show, fielding questions on language, when someone calls in to complain about some horrendous mispro-*noun*-ciation and rail about how people mispro-*noun*-ciate words. Alas, modern medicine has yet to discover a cure for Boeotian ears, which you may recall is an eponymous expression for "ears unable to appreciate poetry or music." There is no *noun* in *pronunciation*, but there is a *nun*: pro-nun-*ciation*. And there are also no such verbs as *pronounciate* or *mispronounciate*. Either you *pronounce* a word properly, or you *mispronounce* it. When you *pronounce* words properly, you have good *pronunciation*; and when you *mispronounce* them, you are guilty of *mispronunciation*.

If you want to hear rampant mispro*noun*ciation, all you have to do is turn on your radio or television. Lately I have heard numerous broadcasters mispronounce the words *siege*, *refuge*, and *refugee* as SEEZH, REF-yoozh, and REF-yoo-**ZHEE**. Gee whiz! The problem here is the letter *g*, which should sound like the *g* in *cage* and *regiment*, not like the *g* in *collage*. Be careful to say SEEJ, REF-yooj, and REF-yoo-**JEE**. (Also acceptable is **REF**-yoo-JEE, with the primary stress on the first syllable.)

How do you pronounce *succinct*? What about *flaccid*? If you say suh-SINGKT (as if the word were spelled *sussinct*) and FLAS-id (as if the word were spelled *flassid*) go directly to the *liberry*, do not pass "GO," and learn how not to mispro*noun*ciate your words. If you said suhk-SINGKT and FLAK-sid, you have my eternal gratitude and respect. (Did you catch that hyperbolic use of *eternal*?)

Now, why are suhk-SINGKT and FLAK-sid correct, you ask? Because the rule for pronouncing double-*c* in a word says that the first *c* sounds *k*, the second like *s*; together they create the sound of *k-s*, as in the name *Jackson*. Thus for *success* we say suhk-SES, not suh-SES; for *accident* we say AK-si-dent, not AS-si-dent; for *accept* we say ak-SEPT, not uh-SEPT; for *eccentric* we say ek-SEN-trik, not e-SEN-trik; and for *accede*, word 23 of Level 7, we say ak-SEED, not uh-SEED. The same rule holds for *succinct* (suhk-SINGKT), brief, concise, and *flaccid* (FLAK-sid), soft and limp. And that goes for the word *accessory*, too—don't let me catch you saying uh-SES-uh-ree. It's ak-SES-uh-ree.

Considering that I've been laying down the law about saying it right, I shall conclude my expatiation on pronunciation by covering three words pertaining to the legal profession: *juror*, *vendor*, and *defendant*. In the courtroom, pompous lawyers and judges often pronounce these as JOOR-or, VEN-dor (or ven-DOR), and dee-FEN-dant (note the final syllable in each case), and many members of the laity are now imitating them. There ought to be a law against using these pretentious variants. What's wrong with the common, everyday pronunciations JOOR-ur, VEN-dur, and di-FEN-dint? They have been heard for centuries and are intelligible to everyone. There is no need to overpronounce these words.

Remember, I'm giving you all this good advice because proper pronunciation is my forte—a word that is traditionally and properly pronounced in one syllable, FORT, just like *fort*. Yup, that's right. The popular two-syllable pronunciation FOR-tay—or worse, for-TAY—is erroneous.

The musical term *forte* comes from Italian and is pronounced in two syllables with the accent on the first syllable, like the Italian: FOR-tay. *Forte* is a musical direction meaning "loud," as opposed to *piano*, which means "soft." The English *forte*, one's strong point, expertise, comes from the French *fort*, strong. This French *fort* entered English in the seventeenth century, and in the eighteenth century a final *e* was tacked on to the word by mistake. That spurious final *e* made the word identical to the Italian musical direction *forte*; hence, the eventual confusion in pronunciation. But most modern authorities continue to stand by the traditional distinction: FOR-tay for *forte* the musical term, FORT for *forte* meaning one's expertise or strong point.

If you'd like to make cultivated pronunciation your forte and learn about more beastly mispronunciations you should avoid, I recommend my tome on the subject, *The Big Book of Beastly Mispronunciations* (Houghton Mifflin, 1999), which you should be able to find at your local bookstore or public library.

And with that flaccid bit of self-promotion, we come to the end of Level 8.

By now your head should be surfeited with importunate admonitions on usage and pronunciation and overflowing with brave new words. I also hope that your dictionary is beginning to show some signs of wear and tear. Before moving on to the most difficult words in the program, you may want to spend some extra time reviewing, just to make certain you have assimilated all the keywords and additional information and are well prepared for the erudite and abstruse vocabulary coming up in Levels 9 and 10.

Answers to Review Quizzes for Level 8

Keywords 1–10

1. Yes indeed you would, if you think you might be the next million-dollar winner. *Alacrity* means cheerful readiness, eagerness, or promptness in action or movement.
2. Yes. To *obviate* means to prevent, make unnecessary, meet and dispose of, clear out of the way.
3. No. *Emolument* means wages, salary, payment received for work.
4. No. To *capitulate* means to yield under specified terms or conditions. *Intransigent* means uncompromising, refusing to come to an agreement, unwilling to modify one's position or give ground.
5. No. *Mordant* means biting, cutting, keen, sarcastic, scathing.
6. Yes. *Sagacious* means wise, shrewd, perceptive; showing sound judgment and keen insight, especially in practical matters.
7. No, not on your life. *Acerbic* means sour, bitter, and harsh in flavor, tone, or character.
8. Yes, they could. In a broad sense, *variegated* means varied, diverse, showing variety of character or form; in a strict sense, variegated means spotted, streaked, or dappled; having marks or patches of different colors.
9. Yes. To *succor* means to aid, help, relieve, give assistance to in time of need or difficulty.
10. Yes, they certainly are. To *importune* means to trouble or annoy with requests or demands, make urgent or persistent entreaties or solicitations.

Keywords 11–20

1. True. To *palliate* means to lessen the severity of, gloss over, make something seem less serious or severe.
2. False. *Wizened* means dried up, shriveled, withered, shrunken and wrinkled.
3. False. *Captious* means faultfinding, quick to point out faults or raise trivial objections.
4. True. An *emendation* is a correction, alteration, especially a change made in a piece of writing to correct or improve it.
5. True. *Truculent* means fierce, ferocious, especially in a brutal, bullying, threatening, or aggressively defiant way.
6. False. To *expedite*, word 49 of Level 4, means to speed up, hasten the progress of. To *expurgate* means to cleanse by removing offensive material, free from objectionable content.

7. False. The adjective *reprobate* means thoroughly bad, wicked, corrupt, and the noun *reprobate* means a person who is morally abandoned, who lacks all sense of decency and duty.

8. True. *Spurious* means false, counterfeit, artificial; not true, authentic, or genuine.

9. True. *Volition* means will, choice, decision, determination.

10. False. To *interpolate* means to insert, introduce; specifically, to insert words into a piece of writing or a conversation.

Keywords 21–30

1. Synonyms. To *adduce* means to offer or cite as a reason, as evidence, or as authority for an opinion or course of action.

2. Synonyms. Both words describe criminals or wrongdoers. A *malefactor* is a person who has done something bad or illegal. A *miscreant* is an evil, unscrupulous, vicious person; someone without principles or conscience.

3. Antonyms. *Pragmatic* means practical, realistic. *Quixotic* means foolishly impractical or idealistic; inclined to pursue lofty, unreachable goals or far-fetched, unworkable schemes.

4. Synonyms. To *suppurate* means to fester, form or discharge pus.

5. Antonyms. *Pushover* is an informal but useful word for someone who is softhearted and easily manipulated. A *martinet* is a strict disciplinarian, taskmaster, rigid enforcer of rules and regulations.

6. Synonyms. *Compunction* is a twinge of regret caused by an uneasy conscience, a pang of guilt for a wrong done or for pain that one has caused another.

7. Synonyms. *Mercurial* means quick to change moods or change one's mind; having an unpredictable temperament; capricious, volatile, fickle.

8. Synonyms. A *panacea* is a cure for all ills. A *nostrum* is a quack remedy or medicine, or a dubious or dishonest plan or scheme for curing a social or political problem.

9. Antonyms. To *propitiate* means to appease, gain or regain the goodwill or favor of, cause to become favorably inclined.

10. Antonyms. *Efficacy* means effectiveness, the power to produce a desired effect or result.

Keywords 31–40

1. *Balanced* doesn't fit. *Tantamount* means equivalent; having equal force, effect, or value.

2. *An unlucky person* doesn't fit. A *pariah* is an outcast, a person despised or rejected by society.

3. *Interesting* doesn't fit. *Germane* means relevant, fitting, appropriate, precisely to the point.

4. *Sexually inhibited* doesn't fit. *Licentious* means sexually abandoned; lacking moral restraint, especially in sexual conduct.

5. *Highly exaggerated* doesn't fit. *Superannuated* means retired because of age, weakness, or ineffectiveness; old and worn out; outdated, outmoded, obsolete.

6. *Conspicuously out of place* doesn't fit. *Egregious* means conspicuously bad, remarkable or outstanding for some undesirable or offensive quality.

7. *Unpleasant* doesn't fit. *Vapid* means lifeless, dull, boring, flat, stale; lacking spirit, interest, or flavor.

8. *Bad idea* doesn't fit. A *crotchet* is an odd notion or whim that one clings to stubbornly.

9. *Something written on a gravestone* doesn't fit. An *epitaph* is something written on a gravestone. An *epigraph* is an inscription on a building or monument, or a brief quotation at the beginning of a literary composition.

10. *To explain briefly* doesn't fit. To *expatiate* means to elaborate, go into detail, speak or write at great length.

Keywords 41–50

1. A *sinecure* is a position that provides a good income or salary but that requires little or no work; in colloquial terms, a cushy job.

2. A *predilection* is a preference, partiality, preconceived liking, an inclination or disposition to favor something.

3. An *imbroglio* is a complicated or intricate situation; a difficult, perplexing state of affairs; also, a misunderstanding or disagreement of a complicated and confusing nature.

4. Ineffable feelings are inexpressible. *Ineffable* means unable to be expressed or described in words.

5. A stolid person is unemotional or unresponsive. *Stolid* means not easily moved, aroused, or excited; showing little or no feeling or sensitivity; mentally or emotionally dull, insensitive, or obtuse.

6. *Offal* means waste, garbage, refuse, rubbish.

7. *Lissome* means limber, flexible, moving with ease and grace.

8. Mellifluous words are smooth and sweet. *Mellifluous* means flowing smoothly and sweetly, like honey.

9. To *surfeit* means to supply, fill, or feed to excess, especially to the point of discomfort, sickness, or disgust.

10. *Blandishment* means flattering or coaxing speech or action; an ingratiating remark or gesture.

Review Test for Level 8

1. Which word comes from a Latin word meaning "the fee a miller received for grinding grain"?
   - (a) remuneration
   - (b) perquisite
   - (c) emolument
   - (d) commensurate

2. Which three words are synonyms?
   - (a) hidebound, complaisant, tenacious
   - (b) intransigent, obdurate, recalcitrant
   - (c) intractable, refractory, malleable
   - (d) obstinate, resolute, acquiescent

3. Which word is *not* a synonym of *sagacious*?
   - (a) percipient
   - (b) sapient
   - (c) credulous
   - (d) perspicacious
   - (e) judicious

4. An importunate person is
   - (a) bitter
   - (b) miserable
   - (c) rude
   - (d) demanding

5. *Alacrity* connotes all of the following except for
   - (a) quickness
   - (b) liveliness
   - (c) promptness
   - (d) eagerness
   - (e) suddenness

6. Which word is an antonym of *palliate*?
   - (a) mitigate
   - (b) expurgate
   - (c) exacerbate
   - (d) propitiate

7. A captious person could reasonably be all of the following except
   - (a) mordant

(b) acerbic

(c) acrimonious

(d) reprobate

(e) querulous

8. Which verb means to make corrections in a text?

(a) expurgate

(b) interpolate

(c) emend

(d) bowdlerize

9. *Apocryphal* and *supposititious* are synonyms of

(a) plausible

(b) spurious

(c) quixotic

(d) sagacious

10. Which word comes from a Latin verb meaning to will or wish?

(a) succor

(b) volition

(c) obviate

(d) truculent

11. Which words are *not* synonyms?

(a) malefactor, pariah

(b) reprobate, varlet

(c) rapscallion, scofflaw

(d) blackguard, miscreant

12. Which word is a synonym of *quixotic*?

(a) ethereal

(b) chimerical

(c) mercurial

(d) vapid

(e) utilitarian

13. What is *putrefaction*?

(a) confusion

(b) purity

(c) disagreement

(d) decay

14. The Greek god Hermes carried a winged staff with two serpents coiled around it. This staff now serves as the symbol of the medical profession. What is it called?

(a) a nostrum
(b) a sinecure
(c) a martinet
(d) a caduceus

15. *Compunction*, *poignant*, and *pungent* all come from a Latin verb meaning

    (a) to hurt or break
    (b) to annoy or bother
    (c) to prick or sting
    (d) to sense or feel

16. Which word is an antonym of *estrangement* and *disaffection*?

    (a) propitiation
    (b) suppuration
    (c) compunction
    (d) expatiation

17. Which set of words contains a word that is *not* eponymous?

    (a) martinet, maverick, chauvinism
    (b) gargantuan, tantamount, epicurean
    (c) quixotic, sandwich, herculean
    (d) mercurial, silhouette, draconian

18. Which word means narrow-minded, bigoted, and self-righteous moral censorship?

    (a) Pyrrhonism
    (b) intransigence
    (c) expurgation
    (d) Comstockery

19. Which word entered English from Tamil, one of the languages of India?

    (a) offal
    (b) cavil
    (c) pariah
    (d) jejune

20. Which word is a synonym of *germane*?

    (a) apposite
    (b) prosaic
    (c) incipient
    (d) pernicious
    (e) stolid

21. Which word is *not* a synonym of *licentious*?

    (a) libidinous
    (b) lubricious
    (c) libertine
    (d) lickerish
    (e) lissome
    (f) lascivious

22. Which word means outdated, old and worn out?

    (a) vapid
    (b) inefficacious
    (c) superannuated
    (d) wizened

23. Which phrase is *not* an appropriate use of the word *egregious*?

    (a) an egregious fool
    (b) an egregious success
    (c) an egregious lie
    (d) an egregious mistake

24. What is an *epigram*?

    (a) an inscription on a gravestone or tomb
    (b) a short, witty poem or a short, pointed, clever statement
    (c) an inscription on a building or monument or a brief quotation at the beginning of a literary composition

25. Which word is a synonym of *expatiate*?

    (a) descant
    (b) variegate
    (c) mollify
    (d) blandish
    (e) adduce

26. By definition, which of the following accompanies a sinecure?

    (a) compunction
    (b) obsolescence
    (c) emendation
    (d) emolument
    (e) predilection

27. Which of the following statements does *not* properly apply to something stolid?

    (a) It is intransigent.

(b) It is apathetic.

(c) It is impassive.

(d) It is phlegmatic.

28. Which word is a synonym of *imbroglio*?

(a) cacophony

(b) machination

(c) duplicity

(d) quandary

29. Which of the following can be mellifluous?

(a) obeisance

(b) blandishment

(c) invective

(d) refulgence

(e) admonishment

30. Which words suggest moving with nimbleness, agility, and grace?

(a) limber, lithe

(b) lissome, limber

(c) lithe, lissome

(d) lissome, limber, lithe

31. What did Thomas Bowdler do to the Bible and Shakespeare's works?

(a) He palliated them.

(b) He expurgated them.

(c) He emended them.

(d) He made interpolations in them.

(e) He made them quixotic.

32. *Sated* and *satiated* are synonyms of

(a) ineffable

(b) incessant

(c) surfeited

(d) superannuated

(e) spurious

33. Which statement is correct?

(a) *Consul* is properly pronounced KAHN-sul.

(b) *Consul* is properly pronounced KOWN-sul.

(c) *Consul* is properly pronounced KAHN-sul or KOWN-sul.

34. Which mispronunciation is an example of metathesis?

(a) GREE-vee-us for *grievous*

(b) JOO-luh-ree for *jewelry*

(c) LY-ber-ee for *library*

(d) pro-*noun*-ciation for *pronunciation*

35. Which two statements are false? (This question has *two* correct answers.)

(a) *Siege* is properly pronounced SEEZH.

(b) *Irrelevant* is properly pronounced i-REL-uh-vint.

(c) *Library* is properly pronounced LY-ber-ee.

(d) *Flaccid* is properly pronounced FLAK-sid.

(e) *Refugee* is properly pronounced REF-yoo-**JEE**.

Answers

1. c 2. b 3. c 4. d 5. e 6. c 7. d 8. c 9. b 10. b 11. a 12. b 13. d
14. d 15. c 16. b 17. b 18. d 19. c 20. a 21. e 22. c 23. b 24. b
25. a 26. d 27. a 28. d 29. b 30. c 31. b 32. c 33. a 34. a 35. a & c

Evaluation

A score of 30–35 is excellent. If you answered fewer than thirty questions correctly in this test, review the entire level and take the test again.

Level 9

Let's dispense with my usual wordy, tiresome, long-winded, boring, and verbose introduction, because this level begins with . . .

Word 1: PROLIX (PROH-liks)

Wordy and tiresome, long-winded and boring, verbose, using far too many and a great deal more words than are necessary and essential to get the point, such as the point may be, across, despite the fact that . . .

All right, already! Now that was a prolix definition if you ever saw one—not to mention redundant.

Challenging synonyms of *prolix* include *circumlocutory* (SUR-kum-**LAHK**-yuh-tor-ee), *tautological* (TAW-tuh-**LAHJ**-i-kul), and *pleonastic* (PLEE-uh-**NAS**-tik).

Antonyms of *prolix* include *concise, terse, pithy, succinct* (suhk-SINGKT, not suh-SINGKT), and *sententious* (sen-TEN-shus).

Prolix comes from the Latin *prolixus,* widely extended. *Prolix* applies to longwinded speech or writing that is tediously discursive, desultory, or protracted. If someone in a meeting talks on and on in a monotonous, boring way, that person is being prolix.

Word 2: APOCRYPHAL (uh-PAHK-ri-ful)

Not genuine, counterfeit, illegitimate; specifically, of doubtful authenticity or authorship.

Spurious (SPYUUR-ee-us, word 18 of Level 8) is a close synonym of *apocryphal.* Other synonyms include *unauthorized, unauthenticated, fabricated, fraudulent,* and *supposititious* (suh-PAHZ-i-**TISH**-us).

Antonyms include *genuine* (JEN-yoo-in), *authentic, valid,* and *bona fide* (BOH-nuh FYD).

The *Apocrypha* (uh-PAHK-ri-fuh) are fourteen books of an early translation of the Old Testament into Greek called the Septuagint (SEP-t(y)oo-uh-jint). The authenticity of these books was called into question, and they were subsequently rejected by Judaism and considered uncanonical, or not authoritative, by Protestants. However, eleven of the fourteen Apocrypha are accepted by the Roman Catholic Church. Today, *apocrypha* (with a lowercase *a*) refers to any writings of doubtful authenticity or authorship, and the adjective *apocryphal* means not genuine, counterfeit, spurious: an apocryphal document, an apocryphal statement, or an apocryphal story.

Word 3: CUPIDITY (kyoo-PID-i-tee)

Greed, a strong desire for wealth or material things.

Synonyms of *cupidity* include *avarice*, *acquisitiveness*, *covetousness*, and *venality* (vee-NAL-i-tee).

Cupidity comes from the Latin *cupidus*, which meant desirous, longing, eager, and also eager for power or money, avaricious. The corresponding Latin noun *cupido*, which means "desire," is the source of Cupid, the cherubic (che-ROO-bik) god of love in Roman mythology, usually represented as a baby or chubby young boy with wings and a bow and arrow. Although Cupid and the English noun *cupidity* are related etymologically, in modern usage *cupidity* does not denote love or desire but rather an excessive love of money, a strong desire for wealth or material things.

Word 4: VERNAL (VUR-nul, rhymes with *journal*)

Pertaining to spring, occurring in the spring; also, having the qualities of spring: fresh, warm, and mild.

Vernal has two challenging antonyms: *hibernal* (hy-BUR-nul) and *hiemal* (HY-uh-mul). *Hibernal* and *hiemal* both mean pertaining to winter, wintry. The ancient Romans gave Ireland the name *Hibernia* because the Emerald Isle seemed so cold and wintry to them. The familiar verb to *hibernate* means to spend the winter either in a dormant state, after the manner of bears, or in a place with a milder climate.

Would you like some words for your next summer vacation? *Estival* (rhymes with *festival*) means pertaining to summer, like summer, or belonging to summer, as estival flowers or an estival holiday. The verb to *estivate* (ES-ti-vayt), which means to pass the summer, is the opposite of *hibernate*, to pass the winter. And moving right along through the year, we have *autumnal* (aw-TUHM-nul), which means pertaining to autumn, to the fall.

Our keyword, *vernal*, means pertaining to spring. The vernal equinox (EE-kwi-nahks), which occurs in March and marks the beginning of spring, and the autumnal equinox, which occurs in September and marks the beginning of fall, are the times during the year when the sun crosses the equator and day and night are approximately the same length.

Word 5: TEMERITY (tuh-MER-i-tee)

Recklessness, rashness, foolhardiness; reckless disregard for danger, risk, or consequences.

Synonyms of *temerity* include *nerve*, *cheek*, *gall*, *audacity*, *heedlessness*, *imprudence*, *impetuosity*, *presumptuousness*, and *effrontery* (i-FRUHN-tur-ee).

Antonyms include *timidity*, *bashfulness*, *faint-heartedness*, *sheepishness*, *apprehension*, *diffidence* (DIF-i-dints), and *timorousness* (TIM-ur-us-nis).

The corresponding adjective is *temerarious* (TEM-uh-**RAIR**-ee-us). When George Washington led his troops across the Delaware River, at the time it must have seemed temerarious, but history has since proved it was a sagacious military maneuver.

Temerity comes from the Latin *temere*, rashly, blindly, heedlessly, and by derivation refers to rash or foolish boldness, a reckless bravado that underestimates the danger or consequences of an action. Do you remember the end of the movie *The Graduate*, when Dustin Hoffman runs into the church, bangs on the glass, stops the wedding in progress, and then jumps on a bus with Katherine Ross, the intended bride? That was an act of temerity.

Word 6: RAPPROCHEMENT (RA-prohsh-**MAW(N)**)

Reconciliation, a reestablishing of friendly relations: "She helped bring about a rapprochement between the hostile parties"; "In 1993, there was a historic rapprochement between Israel and the PLO, and in 1994, an equally significant rapprochement between Israel and Jordan."

Rapprochement comes from a French verb meaning to bring together, and means literally to approach again. The word has been used in English since the early nineteenth century, but it still retains its French flavor in pronunciation: *ra-* as in *rap*; *-proche-* with an *sh* sound as in *potion*; and *-ment* like *maw* with *-aw* stopped in the nose: RA-prohsh-**MAW(N)**.

Word 7: DISQUISITION (DIS-kwə-ZISH-ən)

A formal discussion of or inquiry into a subject; a discourse.

General synonyms of *disquisition* include *treatise*, *critique*, and *commentary*. More specific synonyms include *lecture*, *thesis*, *oration*, *homily* (HAHM-i-lee), *tract*, *monograph*, and *dissertation*.

Discourse, *dissertation*, and *disquisition* all refer to formal discussions of or inquiries into a subject. *Discourse*, which may refer either to writing or speech, means a formal treatise, lecture, or conversation. *Dissertation* may mean any lengthy discourse in writing, such as Noah Webster's *Dissertations on the English Language*, published in 1789; however, in current usage *dissertation* most often refers to a formal thesis written by a candidate for a doctoral degree. *Disquisition* applies to any formal treatment of a subject, usually but not necessarily in writing.

Word 8: PROSCRIBE (proh-SKRYB)

To prohibit, forbid, outlaw: "The city council passed an ordinance proscribing the sale or possession of handguns"; "In certain societies, the practice of bigamy is not proscribed."

Synonyms of *proscribe* include *ban*, *denounce*, *disallow*, *condemn*, *censure*, *ostracize*, *expatriate* (eks-PAY-tree-ayt), and *interdict* (IN-tur-**DIKT**). Antonyms include *permit*, *tolerate*, *legalize*, *authorize*, and *sanction*.

Proscribe comes from the Latin *proscribere*, to post or publish the name of an outlaw or a person to be banished or put to death. By derivation, that which is proscribed is outlawed, not permitted, denounced, or condemned.

Be careful to distinguish the verbs to *proscribe* and to *prescribe*, which are opposite in meaning. *Proscribe* begins with *pro-* and is pronounced proh-SKRYB. *Prescribe* begins with *pre-* and is pronounced pri-SKRYB. A doctor may prescribe a certain drug, advise you to take it, or proscribe saturated fats, advise you to eliminate them from your diet. A prescription is an order to do something. A proscription is an order not to do it, a prohibition.

Word 9: MUNIFICENCE (myoo-NIF-i-sints)

Great generosity, lavish giving.

Synonyms of *munificence* include *philanthropy*, *liberality*, *benevolence*, *bountifulness*, *bounteousness*, *beneficence* (buh-NEF-i-sints), and *largess*, traditionally pronounced LAHR-jis but now more often pronounced lahr-JES.

Either way, the *g* in *largess* should be said like the *g* in *large*. Do not soften or Frenchify the *g* and say lahr-ZHES; this particular affectation is regrettably popular today. The word is sometimes spelled *largesse*, after the French, but the preferred spelling is *largess*, without a final *e*.

Antonyms of *munificence* include *stinginess*, *miserliness*, *close-fistedness* (KLOHS- as in *close*, near), *penuriousness* (puh-NYUUR-ee-<u>us</u>-nis), and *parsimony* (**PAHR**-s<u>i</u>-MOH-nee). We will discuss the noun *parsimony* and the adjective *parsimonious* (PAHR-s<u>i</u>-**MOH**-nee-us) in the next set of keywords in this level.

The noun *munificence* and the corresponding adjective *munificent* (myoo-NIF-<u>i</u>-s<u>i</u>nt) come through the Latin *munificus*, generous, liberal, bountiful, from *munus*, a gift, present, or favor. *Munificent* means characterized by great generosity, as a munificent donation. The noun *munificence* suggests liberal or lavish giving, and may refer to the generous giving of money, favors, or hospitality.

Word 10: PROBITY (PROH-b<u>i</u>-tee)

Honesty, integrity; fairness, straightforwardness, and sincerity in one's dealings with others.

Synonyms of *probity* include *uprightness*, *trustworthiness*, *scrupulousness*, *veracity* (vuh-RAS-i-tee), and *rectitude* (REK-ti-t(y)ood).

Antonyms include *improbity*, the direct opposite of *probity*, and also *dishonesty*, *deceitfulness*, *unscrupulousness*, *duplicity*, *malfeasance* (mal-FEE-z<u>i</u>nts), and *perfidy* (PUR-fi-dee). *Perfidy* means a breach of faith, treachery.

Honesty implies truthfulness and an unwillingness to lie, deceive, or do wrong. *Integrity* implies trustworthiness, reliability, and moral responsibility. *Probity* implies unshakable honesty and integrity; the man or woman of probity has been put to the test and found to be incorruptibly honest and upright, through adherence to the highest principles of conduct.

Let's review the ten keywords you've just learned. Consider the following questions and decide whether the correct answer is yes or no. Answers appear on page 401.

1. Do prolix speakers keep their comments short and sweet?
2. Can a book, a painting, and a story all be apocryphal?
3. Is it an act of cupidity when someone marries for money?
4. Are skiing and ice skating vernal activities?

5. If you display temerity, are you being wise and cautious?
6. Can two belligerent nations seek a rapprochement?
7. When you distribute a brief memorandum in the office, is it a disquisition?
8. Are certain drugs proscribed by law?
9. Would living in an opulent mansion be a display of munificence?
10. Can you trust a person of probity?

Did you remember to keep track of your answers and calculate your score?

A Brief Disquisition on *Convince* and *Persuade*

Let's take a moment to discuss an endangered distinction in the language that is worth preserving.

Many educated people have trouble distinguishing between the verbs to *convince* and to *persuade*. So many people now fail to make the proper distinction in their speech and writing that these words are now often used interchangeably and the fine difference between them is in danger of becoming lost.

If you hear nothing wrong in the sentences "I couldn't convince him to agree with me" and "She convinced him to go," then I urge you to pay close attention to what I'm about to tell you.

The handbook of SPELL (Society for the Preservation of English Language and Literature, of which I am a vice president) explains that "to *convince* someone is to bring the person to your point of view. To *persuade* someone is to induce the person to do something." For example, if you are *convinced* that *Verbal Advantage* is a worthwhile program, then I don't have to *persuade* you to finish it.

In *Common Errors in English and How to Avoid Them* (1943), Alexander M. Witherspoon, who taught English at Berkeley and Yale, writes that "*persuade* emphasizes the idea of winning over. *Convince* emphasizes the idea of proof by argument." Witherspoon offers these examples: "They persuaded me to go home with them. They convinced me that their candidate was the best by showing me his record, and persuaded me to vote for him."

In *The Writer's Art* (1984), syndicated columnist James J. Kilpatrick offers three examples of the egregious misuse of *convince* for *persuade*: "The court 'ruled Monday against a leukemia victim who is trying to convince a woman to donate bone marrow'"; "She recently convinced him to take her to Monte Carlo'"; and "If Venezuela can convince its banks to convert many of the short-term debts . . .'"

"Yeccch!" writes Kilpatrick. "In each instance, the proper verb was *persuade*."

Here's a good way to remember the distinction: *Persuade* usually takes an infinitive, meaning it is often followed by *to*: You persuade someone *to* do something. *Convince* is never followed by an infinitive. You don't convince me *to* do something; you persuade me *to* do it. *Convince* should be followed by either *of* or *that*: You are convinced *of* the truth, or convinced *that* something is important.

As Kilpatrick puts it, "An argument that is persuasive may not be convincing. But once we are convinced of something, persuasion has done its job." I hope that my attempt to persuade you to preserve this distinction in the language has left you convinced that making it in your own speech and writing is the right thing to do.

And now, my verbally advantaged friend, I'm convinced that I won't have to persuade you to return to the vocabulary and learn the next ten keywords.

Word 11: PUISSANT (PYOO-i-sint *or* pyoo-IS-int)

Powerful, mighty, strong, forceful.

Synonyms of *puissant* include *vigorous*, *potent*, *dynamic*, and *stalwart* (STAWL-wurt). Antonyms include *weak*, *feeble*, *infirm*, *debilitated*, *enervated*, *flaccid* (FLAK-sid, not FLAS-id), and *valetudinarian* (VAL-i-T(Y)OO-di-**NAIR**-ee-in).

In the seventeenth-century play *The Alchemist*, Ben Jonson writes: "I will be puissant, and mighty in my talk to her."

Puissant comes through Middle English from an Old French word meaning powerful. Because it is used chiefly in old poetry and scholarly disquisitions, current dictionaries sometimes label *puissant* poetic, literary, or archaic. That doesn't necessarily mean you should avoid using it. *Puissant* is a lovely word that if used in the right place at the right time can add flair and a dash of style to your expression. The corresponding noun is *puissance* (PYOO-i-sints or pyoo-IS-ints), power, strength, might.

There is also authority for the pronunciation PWIS-int for *puissant* and PWIS-ints for *puissance*. But to my ear, these two-syllable variants sound *pwissy* and are best avoided. You are better off with one of the three-syllable pronunciations sanctioned above, which most modern authorities favor.

Word 12: PECULATE (PEK-yuh-layt)

To steal, embezzle; specifically, to steal or misuse money or property entrusted to one's care.

To *peculate* and to *defalcate* (de-FAL-kayt) both mean to embezzle, to steal from or appropriate that which has been entrusted to one's care.

Defalcate by derivation means to cut off with a sickle; hence, to misappropriate funds by fraudulently deducting a portion of them for one's own use.

Although *peculate* comes from the Latin *peculium*, which means "private property," in current usage the word usually refers to the embezzlement of public or corporate funds, or property entrusted to one's care: "For twenty-five years old Barney balanced the books for the city, and just when he was about to retire with a good pension they caught him peculating from the public trough."

The corresponding noun is *peculation* (PEK-yuh-**LAY**-shin), the act of peculating.

Word 13: DIFFIDENT (DIF-i-dint)

Shy, timid, bashful, lacking in self-confidence, hesitant to speak or act.

Diffident comes from the Latin *dis-*, which in this case means "not," and *fidere*, to trust, put confidence in. *Diffident* was once used literally to mean distrustful, but that sense is archaic, and *diffident* now suggests lacking trust or confidence in oneself to speak or act. Diffident people have difficulty asserting themselves or expressing their opinions.

Word 14: VENAL (VEE-nul)

Corruptible, bribable, capable of being bribed or bought off, able to be obtained for a price.

Venal and *mercenary* (word 14 of Level 2) are close in meaning.

Mercenary means done for payment only, motivated by greed or a desire for personal gain: "A mercenary writer writes not for love but for the money"; "When Jim discovered that Alice had three ex-husbands who were all affluent plastic surgeons like him, he concluded that her interest in him was mercenary and called off their engagement."

Venal comes from the Latin *venalis*, for sale, and means literally able to be sold. The word is used today to mean able to be bribed, corrupted, or bought off, or characterized by corrupt, mercenary dealings. A venal judge is corrupt, capable of being bribed; a venal politician is corruptible, able to be influenced by money or favors; a venal administration or a venal business deal is riddled with corruption and bribery.

The corresponding noun is *venality* (vee-NAL-i-tee), a venal state or act.

Venal and *venial* are often confused. *Venial* (VEE-nee-ul, three syllables) comes from the Latin *venia*, grace, indulgence, and means excusable, forgivable, minor, as a venial sin, a venial offense, or a venial error. *Venal* (VEE-n<u>u</u>l, two syllables) means corruptible, capable of being bribed or bought off.

Word 15: PARSIMONIOUS (PAHR-s<u>i</u>-**MOH**-nee-<u>us</u>)

Stingy, miserly, extremely tight with money.

Antonyms of *parsimonious* include *generous*, *liberal*, *open-handed*, *bountiful*, *beneficent* (buh-NEF-<u>i</u>-s<u>i</u>nt), *magnanimous* (mag-NAN-<u>i</u>-m<u>us</u>, word 24 of Level 7), and *munificent* (discussed in word 9 of this level).

Synonyms of *parsimonious* include *grasping*, *money-grubbing*, *penny-pinching*, *close-fisted* (KLOHS- as in *close*, near), *penurious* (puh-NYUUR-ee-<u>us</u>), and *niggardly* (NIG-urd-lee).

Please note that *niggard* (NIG-urd) and *niggardly* are very old words of Scandinavian origin; other than an unfortunate resemblance in sound, they have nothing whatsoever to do with the offensive and derogatory term used by racists to insult African-Americans. A *niggard* is a miser; *niggardly* means stingy, begrudging every nickel and dime.

The noun *parsimony* (**PAHR**-s<u>i</u>-MOH-nee) means excessive or unnecessary economy or frugality. The adjective *parsimonious* means very sparing in expenditure, frugal to excess. The eighteenth-century English essayist Joseph Addison wrote, "Extraordinary funds for one campaign may spare us the expense of many years, whereas a long parsimonious war will drain us of more men and money."

If you've ever known someone who wanted you to do a demanding job and grudgingly offered to pay you half of what it was worth, and not a penny more, then you know well what *parsimonious* means.

Word 16: PUSILLANIMOUS (PYOO-si-**LAN**-i-mus)

Cowardly, lacking courage, timid, fainthearted, irresolute.

Pusillanimous is used of cowardly persons or actions that are especially ignoble or contemptible: a pusillanimous deserter of a cause; a pusillanimous surrender; a mean-spirited and pusillanimous leader. The corresponding noun is *pusillanimity* (PYOO-suh-luh-**NIM**-i-tee).

Word 17: EXTANT (EKS-t<u>i</u>nt, rhymes with *sextant*, *-ant* as in *relevant*)

Existing, still in existence, not extinct, not lost or destroyed.

Extant comes from the Latin *exstare*, to stand out, which comes in turn from *ex-*, meaning "out," and *stare*, to stand. *Extant* originally meant standing out, but this sense is now archaic, and in modern usage *extant* means standing out through time, still in existence, not lost or destroyed: "That law is no longer extant; it's not on the books"; "She was surprised and pleased to find several extant relatives in the village where she was born"; "The only extant writings by this early Greek philosopher may in fact be apocryphal"; "Although Shakespeare's plays have been performed and enjoyed for more than four hundred years, nothing in his handwriting has survived—not one extant manuscript."

Word 18: MERETRICIOUS (MER-uh-**TRISH**-u̲s)

Tawdry, gaudy; attractive in a flashy or cheap way; falsely alluring; deceptively enticing.

By derivation, *meretricious* means pertaining to or like a *meretrix* (MER-uh-triks), a prostitute. This unusual *meretrix* comes directly from Latin and has been in the language for nearly five hundred years, but it is so rare today that you won't find it listed in most dictionaries.

Meretricious is still sometimes used in its literal sense, but most often the word refers to someone or something that has the gaudy appearance or tawdry qualities of a prostitute, especially in a false or deceptive way.

Meretricious eyes are falsely alluring; a meretricious idea is deceptively attractive; a meretricious style is cheap, flashy, and insincere.

Meretricious and *meritorious* (MER-uh-**TOR**-ee-u̲s) are often confused, but they are nearly opposite in meaning. *Meritorious* means worthy of merit, deserving praise; a meritorious action is a commendable action. *Meretricious* actions are falsely alluring, superficially attractive, flashy but insincere.

Word 19: XENOPHOBIA (ZEN-uh-**FOH**-bee-uh)

Fear or hatred of strangers or foreigners, or of anything strange or foreign: "Their xenophobia and temerity led them headlong into war."

Xenophobia entered English at the beginning of the twentieth century. Its antonym, *xenomania* (ZEN-uh-**MAY**-nee-uh), an inordinate attachment to anything or anyone foreign, was coined thirty years earlier but is rarely used today. However, *xenophilia* (ZEN-uh-**FIL**-ee-uh), which came into the language in the 1950s, is still in good standing; *xenophilia* means love for or attraction to foreigners, foreign cultures, or foreign customs.

Xenophobia combines the prefix *xeno-*, which means alien, strange, with the suffix *-phobia*, which means fear. By derivation, *xenophobia* is fear of anyone or anything alien or strange. A *xenophobe* is a person who fears or hates strangers: "An exclusive community filled with vigilant xenophobes who fear any unfamiliar face." The adjective *xenophobic* means affected with xenophobia: "During times of national crisis, people have a tendency to become hostile and xenophobic."

Many educated speakers—and for some reason, especially the highly educated ones—pronounce *xenophobia*, *xenophobe*, and *xenophobic* with a long *e*: ZEE-*nophobia*, ZEE-*nophobe*, and ZEE-*nophobic*. These pronunciations were not recognized by dictionaries until the 1980s, and although all current dictionaries now list them, not one lists them first.

So take my advice and ignore those overeducated, innovative mispronouncers, who are probably foreign spies. Take a Zen approach and pronounce these words with a short *e*. Say ZEN-*ophobia*, ZEN-*ophobe*, and ZEN-*ophobic*.

Word 20: QUOTIDIAN (kwoh-TID-ee-in)

Daily, recurring every day or pertaining to every day, as a quotidian ritual; a quotidian record of events; a quotidian update or report; the quotidian call to order.

Quotidian, *daily*, and *diurnal* (dy-UR-nul, from the Latin *diurnus*, of the day, word 49 of Level 2) are synonyms.

Quotidian comes from the Latin *quotidianus*, daily, of every day. Because something that recurs daily soon becomes routine and ordinary, *quotidian* has also come to mean of an everyday nature, and therefore ordinary, commonplace, trivial: "The first presentation was eloquent, but the second was dull and quotidian." "As he walked he heard the quotidian clamor of the marketplace, where money is forever changing hands."

Let's review the ten keywords you've just learned. Consider the following statements and decide whether each one is true or false. Answers appear on page 402.

1. A puissant opponent is weak and inferior.
2. If you are caught peculating, you could go to jail.
3. Diffident people never hesitate to speak their minds.
4. A venal person can be influenced by money.
5. It's hard to persuade a parsimonious boss to give you a raise.

6. When the chips are down and you need a friend, you can be sure that a pusillanimous person will support you.
7. Dinosaurs are no longer extant.
8. Something meretricious is praiseworthy or commendable.
9. *Xenophobia* means dislike of one's neighbors.
10. A quotidian duty is a duty performed every day.

Now it's time for a respite (pronounced RES-pit, remember?) from your quotidian task of vocabulary building. While you're refueling your brain with oxygen, let's take a look at a few foreign words and phrases.

Here are six useful expressions that English has borrowed from French: *faux pas*; *bête noire*; *bon mot*; *élan*; *qui vive*; and *coup de grâce*. Do you recognize any of them? (By the way, all but the last, *coup de grâce*, are usually printed in roman rather than italic type: this is roman; *this is italic*.)

A *faux pas* (foh-PAH) is literally a false step. In English this phrase is used to mean an error or blunder, especially a social blunder, such as a tactless act or rude remark: "Did you see his faux pas at the party last night?" "I think her criticism of the boss's idea was a faux pas." The plural is spelled the same, but pronounced foh-PAHZ.

Bête noire (bayt- or bet-NWAHR) means literally a black beast, and means someone or something one especially dislikes, fears, or wants to avoid. "Math was my bête noire in high school." "He is my bête noire in this organization." The plural is *bêtes noires*, pronounced bayt- or bet-NWAHRZ.

Bon mot (baw(n)-MOH) means literally a good word. In English it is used to mean a witty or clever remark. The plural, *bons mots*, is pronounced baw(n)-MOHZ.

Élan (ay-LAH(N) or ay-LAHN) means spirited self-assurance, verve, vivacity: "Her work shows élan." "We like the new manager's élan." "He plays the piano with élan."

There is an excellent Yiddish word for the negative side of élan that English has recently adopted: *chutzpah* (or *chutzpa*), pronounced KHUUTS-pah with a raspy, guttural *ch*. *Chutzpah* means nerve as opposed to verve, shameless self-assurance, audacity, impudence, gall. Someone who walks in, takes over, and tells everyone what to do has chutzpah. In *The Joys of Yinglish* (1989), Leo Rosten relates the story of the defendant accused of murdering his parents who throws himself upon the mercy of the court, crying, "I am an orphan." That's chutzpah.

But back now to the French. *Qui vive* (kee-VEEV) is the sentry's challenge, "Who goes there?" In English we use the expression "on the qui vive" to mean on the alert, ready and watchful, as "She was on the qui vive for a better job."

Finally, we have the *coup de grâce* (KOO-duh-**GRAHS**). The word *coup* (KOO) means a blow, stroke—especially a brilliant stroke, a sudden, successful move or action. A *coup d'état* (KOO-day-**TAH**) is a sudden, successful overthrow of a government. *Coup de grâce* means literally a stroke of mercy; specifically, it refers to the finishing stroke, the death blow, that brings a merciful end to something or someone: "After the failure of its last major product and a precipitous decline in the price of its stock, Faux Pas Corporation is almost bankrupt. All people are wondering now is how and when the *coup de grâce* will be delivered."

Now let's take a brief look at six phrases from Latin that have made their way into the English vernacular: *ad infinitum*; *pro tempore*; *sine qua non*; *quid pro quo*; *caveat emptor*; and *pro bono publico*. Do you recognize any of them? (By the way, all these phrases, when not being presented as phrases to be defined, are usually printed in roman type.)

Ad infinitum (AD-in fi-NY-tum) means to infinity, endlessly, without limit: "The meeting went on ad infinitum." (Now there's hyperbole for you.)

Pro tempore (PROH TEM-puh-ree) means temporarily, for the time being; it is often abbreviated *pro tem* (PROH-TEM), as in an official title: John Doe, Chairman of the Board pro tem.

Sine qua non (SIN-ay kwah NOHN) means literally "without which not"; it refers to something absolutely necessary or indispensable: "Their cooperation was the sine qua non in the success of this project"; "His testimony was the sine qua non of the case for the defense."

A *quid pro quo* (KWID proh KWOH) is something given in return for something else, an equal exchange, a tit for tat: "They said they wouldn't close the deal without a reasonable quid pro quo."

The word *caveat* (KAY-vee-at or KAV-ee-at) is used in a general sense to mean a warning, caution, admonition. A *caveat emptor* (EMP-tor) is a *caveat*, warning, to the *emptor*, the buyer; it means literally, "Let the buyer beware." In business, *caveat emptor* refers to the principle that the seller of a product cannot be held responsible for defects in quality or workmanship unless the product carries a warranty.

Pro bono publico (PROH BOH-noh POO-bli-koh or PUHB-li-koh) means "for the public good." The phrase is often shortened to *pro bono* and used as an adjective. For example, pro bono attorneys are those who forgo their customary professional fees to represent the indigent or seek redress for public grievances. Pro bono services are volunteer services, done for the good of the people and donated without charge.

And now, *fortiter in re, suaviter in modo*, which is Latin for "resolutely in action, gently in manner," let us proceed to the next ten keywords in Level 9.

Word 21: EXIGENCY (EK-si-jen-see)

An urgency, pressing need; a situation demanding immediate attention or action.

Exigency comes from the Latin *exigere*, to demand, force or drive out, and by derivation means something one is demanded, forced, or driven to do. In current usage we speak of an unforeseen exigency; a financial exigency; front-page newspaper stories focusing on the exigencies of the moment. The corresponding adjective is *exigent* (EK-si-jint), urgent, pressing, demanding immediate attention or action.

According to the *Century Dictionary* (1914), an *exigency* is a situation of sudden urgency, in which something needs to be done at once. An *emergency* is more pressing and therefore less common than an *exigency*. For example, every day the federal government deals with exigencies in foreign affairs, but only occasionally must it respond to a national emergency. A crisis is an emergency on which the outcome of everything depends, as a midlife crisis, or an economic crisis.

Word 22: PULCHRITUDE (PUHL-kri-T(Y)OOD)

Beauty, loveliness, attractiveness.

Pulchritude comes directly from the Latin word for beautiful. In his famous and influential dictionary, published in 1755, Samuel Johnson defined *pulchritude* as the "quality opposite to deformity."

Pulchritude is a literary word that is usually applied to persons or things that have great physical beauty or external appeal: a woman of pulchritude; the pulchritude of nature. Occasionally it is used of something whose beauty manifests itself in a more subtle way, as the pulchritude of the soul. What seems meretricious to you may possess pulchritude for another, for as the saying (sort of) goes, "Pulchritude is in the eye of the beholder."

The corresponding adjective is *pulchritudinous* (PUHL-kri-**T(Y)OOD**-'n-us), physically beautiful or lovely.

Word 23: DENOUEMENT (DAY-noo-**MAW(N)**—nasalized *n*, silent *t*)

The unraveling or resolution of a plot, as of a novel or a drama; the outcome or resolution of any complex situation.

As you can tell from its vowel-laden spelling and nasalized final syllable, *denouement* comes from French. The word means literally "an untying," as of a knot. Since its introduction into English in the mid-1700s, *denouement* has been used to mean the untying or unraveling of a narrative or dramatic plot, the final sequence of events leading to a resolution of the story.

The *Century Dictionary* offers this illustrative quotation from the *Saturday Review*: "The end, the climax, the culmination, the surprise, the discovery, are all slightly different in meaning from that ingenious loosening of the knot of intrigue which the word *denouement* implies." In current usage, *denouement* has also come to apply to the outcome or resolution of any complex situation, as the denouement of a sensational trial, or the denouement of the negotiations.

Word 24: FUGACIOUS (fyoo-GAY-sh<u>u</u>s)

Fleeting, passing quickly away.

Synonyms of *fugacious* include *transient* (TRAN-sh<u>i</u>nt, word 31 of Level 2), *ephemeral* (<u>i</u>-FEM-uh-r<u>u</u>l, word 12 of Level 4), *transitory* (**TRAN**-si-TOR-ee *or* **TRAN**-zi-TOR-ee, word 4 of Level 5), and *evanescent* (EV-uh-**NES**-<u>i</u>nt).

The words *fugacious* and *fugitive* come from the same Latin source, the verb *fugere*, to flee, fly away. As a noun, *fugitive* refers to a person who flees, especially from the law; as an adjective, *fugitive* may mean either fleeing, running away, or passing away quickly, not permanent, temporary. In this last sense it is an exact synonym of the more difficult word *fugacious*, fleeting, passing swiftly, lasting but a short time.

Word 25: TURBID (TUR-bid)

Literally, muddy, clouded, roiled, murky, as if from stirred-up sediment; figuratively, muddled, obscure, confused, not lucid.

Turbid is often used of liquids to mean muddy or clouded from having the sediment stirred up: a turbid river; turbid wine. It may also apply to air that is thick or dark with smoke or mist. Figuratively, *turbid* means muddled, disturbed, or confused in thought or feeling.

In this figurative sense, *turbid* sometimes is confused with the words *turgid* (TUR-jid) and *tumid* (T(Y)OO-mid).

Both *turgid* and *tumid* mean swollen, inflated, and both may be used literally or figuratively. However, *tumid*, perhaps because of its relation to the word *tumor*, usually is used literally to mean swollen or distended. *Turgid* usually is used figuratively of language or style that is inflated, pompous, pretentious, bombastic.

Turbid never suggests swelling or inflation, but rather muddiness, cloudiness, disturbance, or confusion, as in the nineteenth-century poet Matthew Arnold's line "the turbid ebb and flow of human misery."

Word 26: INDEFEASIBLE (IN-di-FEE-zuh-buul)

Not capable of being undone, taken away, annulled, or rendered void.

The words *defeasance*, *defeasible*, and *indefeasible* come down to us through Anglo-French and Middle English. They were used in Old English law and are chiefly legal terms today. *Defeasance* is the oldest of the three; it means either the annulment or voiding of a deed or contract, or a clause within a deed or contract that provides a means for annulling it or rendering it void. *Defeasible* means capable of being invalidated, undone, or rendered void. Our keyword, *indefeasible*, which employs the privative prefix *in-*, meaning "not," means not defeasible, not capable of being undone, annulled, or rendered void.

Inalienable and *indefeasible* are close in meaning and are often used interchangeably. According to the second edition of *Webster's New International Dictionary* (1934), "that is indefeasible which one cannot be deprived of without one's consent; that is inalienable which one cannot give away or dispose of even if one wishes."

For example, the U.S. Constitution guarantees all citizens certain inalienable rights, such as personal liberty, freedom of speech, freedom of religion, and so on. When you pay off a mortgage on a house and own it outright, you have an indefeasible title to the house, although you may give up or transfer that title by selling your home or putting the deed in someone else's name.

Inalienable means not able to be given away or transferred. *Indefeasible* means not able to be taken away, undone, or made void.

Word 27: DISINGENUOUS (DIS-in-JEN-yoo-us)

Insincere, crafty, sly, not straightforward or frank.

Synonyms of *disingenuous* include *wily*, *subtle*, *slippery*, *deceptive*, *hypocritical*, *fraudulent*, and *mendacious* (men-DAY-shus).

The direct antonym is *ingenuous*, sincere, open, straightforward, without artifice or guile. Other antonyms include *truthful*, *frank*, *candid*, *unselfconscious*, *unaffected*, and *guileless*.

The corresponding noun is *disingenuousness*.

Disingenuous combines the prefix *dis-*, meaning "not," with the Latin *ingenuus*, which means freeborn, of free birth; hence, noble, honorable, upright.

From the Latin *ingenuus*, by way of French, English has also acquired the word *ingénue* (**AN**-zhuh-N(Y)OO), which the *Century Dictionary* defines as "a woman or girl who displays innocent candor or simplicity; specifically, such a character represented on the stage, or the actress who plays it."

An ingénue is an ingenuous woman. An ingenuous person is a woman, man, or child who is free from restraint or reserve, and therefore innocent, straightforward, and sincere. A disingenuous person is not sincere or straightforward. Disingenuous words are crafty, subtle, or deceptive.

Word 28: SCURRILOUS (SKUR-i-lus *or* SKUH-ri-lus)

Foul-mouthed, obscene; using or expressed in language that is coarse, vulgar, and abusive.

Synonyms of *scurrilous* include *shameless*, *indelicate*, *lewd*, *smutty*, *ribald* (word 42 of Level 7), *irreverent*, *insolent*, *disparaging*, *derisive* (di-RY-siv), and *contumelious* (KAHN-t(y)oo-**MEEL**-ee-us).

Antonyms of *scurrilous* include *polite*, *refined*, *tasteful*, *cultured*, *sophisticated*, *cultivated*, *decorous* (DEK-ur-us), and *urbane* (ur-BAYN).

The adjective *scurrilous* comes from the Latin *scurrilis*, mocking, jesting, or jeering like a buffoon. *Scurrilis* comes in turn from *scurra*, a jester, comedian, buffoon, especially one employed to entertain a rich person. By derivation, *scurrilous* means talking like a buffoon.

And what precisely is a buffoon, you ask? Any dictionary will tell you that a buffoon is a person who amuses or attempts to amuse others by clowning around and cracking jokes; however, the savvy lexicographers, or dictionary editors, at Random House include a second definition: "a person given to coarse or offensive joking." That sort of buffoon is the one implied by the word *scurrilous*, which means, as the second edition of *Webster's New International Dictionary* puts it, "using, or given to using, the language of low buffoonery; containing low indecency or abuse." Scurrilous language is coarse, vulgar, and abusive. A scurrilous rogue is a foul-mouthed joker who spouts insolent obscenities.

There are two corresponding nouns, *scurrility* (skuh-RIL-i-tee) and *scurrilousness*; both may refer to coarse, vulgar, and abusive language, or to an expression of foul-mouthed verbal abuse.

Word 29: RECRUDESCENCE (REE-kroo-DES-ints)

A revival, renewal, fresh outbreak after a period of inactivity or quiescence (kwy-ES-ints).

Recrudescence comes from the Latin *recrudescere*, to become raw again, break out again, open afresh. In medicine, *recrudescence* is used of a wound or sore that partially heals and then reopens, or of a fever that abates and then breaks out again.

Does *recrudescence* strike you as a word you'd never use because you can't imagine how you'd apply it? Well, let me give you a few suggestions.

How about sports for the weekend warrior? "Whenever Ken played basketball or softball without warming up properly, he suffered from a recrudescence of lower back pain."

Now let's try economics: "Analysts disagree on whether the recrudescence of inflation will affect the stock market."

Are you in the retail business? Try this: "Booksellers are delighted with the recrudescence of interest in high-priced coffee-table volumes, which accounted for a 20 percent increase in sales this holiday season."

Now let's take a stab at the fine arts: "Some critics are disturbed by the recrudescence of classical themes in contemporary literature and art, though others applaud it."

And let's not forget fashion: "Madonna may have revolutionized our concept of fashion by turning underwear into outerwear, but it's unlikely that she alone can effect a recrudescence of that most alluring of all exterior female garments, the miniskirt."

And finally, we have romance: "Seeing John again after all these years, Sally felt a recrudescence of the love for him that she had suppressed since high school."

You see? *Recrudescence* isn't such an obscure, useless word after all, now is it?

The corresponding verb is *recrudesce* (REE-kroo-**DES**), to break out again, show renewed activity after an inactive period. The corresponding adjective is *recrudescent* (REE-kroo-**DES**-int), breaking out afresh, as a recrudescent epidemic or a recrudescent revolt.

Word 30: DEFENESTRATE (dee-FEN-uh-STRAYT)

To throw something or someone out of a window.

I include this humorous but useful word in the event that you may be experiencing a recrudescent urge to give up building your vocabulary and defenestrate *Verbal Advantage* from a swiftly moving vehicle.

The verb to *defenestrate* combines the prefix *de-*, meaning "out," with the Latin *fenestra*, a window. The corresponding noun *defenestration* means the act of throwing something or someone out of a window.

Let's review the ten keywords you've just learned. I'll give you two words, and you decide if they are synonyms or antonyms. Answers appear on page 402.

1. *Exigency* and *urgency* are . . . synonyms or antonyms?
2. *Ugliness* and *pulchritude* are . . .
3. *Development* and *denouement* are . . .
4. *Fugacious* and *fleeting* are . . .
5. *Turbid* and *clear* are . . .
6. *Indefeasible* and *voidable* are . . .
7. *Candid* and *disingenuous* are . . .
8. *Scurrilous* and *polite* are . . .
9. *Recrudescence* and *revival* are . . .

We'll have to skip *defenestrate* because it is the only word in the language that means to toss out of a window, and to my knowledge there also is no antonym.

If you answered seven or more questions incorrectly in this quiz, you may either defenestrate this book or read the keyword discussions again. If you answered at least seven questions correctly, consider yourself verbally advantaged enough to move ahead in the program.

Word 31: DILATORY (DIL-uh-TOR-ee)

Delaying, causing or intended to cause delay; also, slow, tardy, characterized by delay or procrastination.

Dilatory comes through the Latin *dilator*, a delayer, procrastinator, loiterer, from *dilatus*, the past participle of the verb *differe*, to delay, put off.

In current usage, *dilatory* has two senses. First, it may mean causing or intended to cause delay: The purpose of a dilatory tactic is to delay action; the aim of a dilatory policy is to gain time; and unforeseen circumstances may have a dilatory effect on a project, causing postponement or delay.

Second, *dilatory* may mean characterized by delay or procrastination. When you put off doing something until the last minute, you are being dilatory; when someone responds to your urgent telephone message two days later, that's a dilatory response; and if you pay a bill a month after it's due, that's a dilatory payment.

Word 32: VILIFY (VIL-i-fy)

To defame, slander, attack with vicious, abusive language.

Synonyms of *vilify* include to *disparage*, *denigrate*, *stigmatize*, *malign*, *revile*, *vituperate* (vy-**T(Y)OO**-pur-AYT), *calumniate* (kuh-**LUHM**-nee-AYT), and *traduce* (truh-D(Y)OOS).

Antonyms include to *praise*, *commend*, *laud*, *extol*, *glorify*, *eulogize*, and *venerate*.

Vilify comes ultimately from the Latin *vilis*, cheap, worthless. The word *vile*, in one of its senses, means of little value, and *vilify* was once used to mean to make vile, render worthless, cheapen, degrade, but this sense is now obsolete. In current usage, *vilify* means to take cheap shots, make degrading or defamatory statements, render vile or worthless by attacking with vicious, abusive language.

Vilify is most often used of persons but it may also apply to things. A racist may vilify a certain ethnic group. A xenophobe may vilify foreigners or a particular foreign nation. And in America, the inalienable right of free speech allows a citizen to vilify the president, and most citizens seem to take advantage of that right at one time or another.

The corresponding noun is vilification (VIL-i-fi-**KAY**-shin), which means either the act of vilifying or a deliberate, vicious, and defamatory verbal assault: "Politicians and celebrities often find themselves subjected to vilification in the media."

Word 33: PHLEGMATIC (fleg-MAT-ik)

Calm and unemotional; having a sluggish, apathetic temperament; difficult to move to emotion or action.

Phlegmatic comes from the Greek *phlegmatikos*, pertaining to the humor *phlegm* (FLEM, silent *g*). This *phlegm* is different from that slimy stuff you cough up when you have a cold.

In ancient and medieval physiology, there were four humors, or bodily fluids, thought to determine a person's health or disposition: *blood*, also known as the sanguine humor, which made you upbeat, cheerful, and confident; *choler* (like *collar*), also known as yellow bile, which made you passionate or irascible; *melancholy*, also known as black bile, which made you gloomy or dejected; and *phlegm*, which made you either cool and indifferent or dull and sluggish.

From this humor *phlegm* we inherit the adjective *phlegmatic*, which by derivation means full of phlegm; hence, having a sluggish, apathetic temperament, calm and unemotional, difficult to move to emotion or action.

Word 34: ADVENTITIOUS (AD-ven-**TISH**-us)

Accidentally or casually acquired, not belonging naturally to something, associated by chance, not inherent or integral.

Synonyms of *adventitious* include *foreign*, *extrinsic*, *incidental*, *extraneous*, *fortuitous*, and *supervenient* (SOO-pur-**VEE**-nee-int).

Adventitious comes from the Latin *adventicius*, which means "coming from without or from abroad," and by derivation is related to the word *advent*, which means an arrival, specifically the arrival or birth of Jesus Christ or the season preceding the celebration of His birth.

Adventitious suggests something added or imposed from without, something external or extrinsic that is accidentally or casually acquired. Adventitious information is additional and often unrelated information that you acquire casually or by chance in the course of investigating something. Adventitious blindness is caused by an accident, as opposed to blindness occurring at birth. Adventitious income or wealth is fortuitously acquired, and comes to you from some source other than wages or an inheritance.

Word 35: DESICCATED (DES-i-KAY-tid)

Dried or dried up, dehydrated, deprived of moisture.

The adjective *desiccated* is also the past participle of the verb to *desiccate*, to dry thoroughly. Both words come from the Latin *desiccare*, to dry completely.

Desiccated may apply to food that has been preserved by drying or dehydration, such as fish, cereal, soup, or fruit. It may apply literally to anything that has been thoroughly dried or deprived of moisture, as a desiccated plant, a desiccated mummy, or a steak desiccated on the barbecue. It may also be used figuratively of something that is dried up or deprived of vital juices, as a desiccated affection, a desiccated culture, or a desiccated mind. The corresponding noun is *desiccation*, the act of drying or dehydrating.

Word 36: COMITY (KAHM-i-tee)

Courtesy, civility, politeness, respectful and considerate behavior.

Comity comes through the Latin *comitas*, courtesy, friendliness, from *comis*, courteous, kind, polite.

Comity may be used of courteous relations between spouses, roommates, neighbors, coworkers, and so on, but it is perhaps most often used in the expression *comity of nations*, which means courteous and friendly relations between nations involving recognition and respect for each other's laws and institutions.

Word 37: SPECIOUS (SPEE-sh<u>u</u>s)

Appearing to be true, genuine, or correct but actually false or deceptive; superficially just or reasonable but not so in reality.

Specious comes through Middle English from the Latin *speciosus*, beautiful, splendid, handsome. *Speciosus* comes in turn from *species*, outward appearance, and the verb *specere*, to look at. By derivation, something specious has an outward appearance that is beautiful, splendid, or handsome to look upon but that underneath is false, deceptive, or flawed.

In current usage, we speak of a specious argument, specious reasoning, a specious excuse, or a specious answer, meaning that these things seem reasonable, genuine, or true on the surface but in reality they are intended to mislead or deceive.

Specious and *plausible* are close in meaning but not quite synonymous. *Webster's New International Dictionary*, second edition (1934), explains that "*specious* implies a fair appearance assumed with intent to deceive; that is *plausible* which is superficially reasonable or pleasing, with or without deceit."

The third edition of the *American Heritage Dictionary* (1992) says "a specious argument is not simply a false one but one that has the ring of truth. [There is] a certain contradiction in hearing an argument described as *obviously specious* or *specious on the face of things*; if the fallaciousness is apparent, the argument was probably not plausible-sounding to begin with."

Word 38: NOISOME (NOY-s<u>u</u>m)

Harmful to health or well-being, unwholesome, dangerous, destructive; also, foul-smelling, offensive, disgusting.

Synonyms of *noisome* in the sense of "harmful to health or well-being" include injurious, *ruinous, deleterious* (DEL-i-**TEER**-ee-<u>u</u>s), *noxious, baneful, malign*, and *pernicious*.

Synonyms of *noisome* in the sense of "foul-smelling, offensive, disgusting" include *rank, rancid, putrid* (PYOO-trid), *fetid* (FET-id), *malodorous* (mal-OH-dur-<u>u</u>s), and *mephitic* (muh-FIT-ik).

Antonyms of *noisome* in both senses include *salutary* (**SAL**-yuh-TER-ee) and *salubrious* (suh-LOO-bree-<u>u</u>s).

Noisome comes from Middle English and by derivation means harmful, injurious, unwholesome, as a noisome pestilence, a noisome habit, or noisome beliefs. That has been the meaning of the word since it came into the language in the fourteenth century. Perhaps because it is related to the verb *to annoy*, by the sixteenth century noisome also came to mean foul-smelling, offensive, disgusting, as a noisome stench or noisome breath.

Word 39: CALUMNY (KAL-um-nee)

Defamation of character, slander, a false and malicious statement or accusation meant to injure a person's reputation.

Synonyms of *calumny* include *backbiting*, *denigration*, *obloquy* (AHB-luh-kwee), and *vilification* (VIL-i-fi-**KAY**-shin).

The noun *calumny*, the adjective *calumnious* (kuh-LUHM-nee-us), and the verb to *calumniate* (kuh-**LUHM**-nee-AYT) all come through the Latin *calumniare*, to accuse falsely, from *calumnia*, a trick. By derivation, and in current usage, *calumny* means a tricky, nasty, false, and malicious accusation designed to hurt someone's reputation.

In 1751, Samuel Johnson wrote that "to spread suspicion, to invent calumnies, to propagate scandal, requires neither labour nor courage." And 150 years earlier, in *Hamlet*, William Shakespeare wrote, "Be thou as chaste as ice, as pure as snow, thou shalt not escape calumny."

Word 40: EXCORIATE (ek-**SKOR**-ee-AYT)

To strip, scrape, or tear off the skin; hence, to rebuke or denounce harshly and severely.

Synonyms of *excoriate* in the sense of "stripping off the skin" include *abrade*, *chafe*, *scalp*, *gall*, and *flay*. Synonyms of *excoriate* in the sense of "rebuking or denouncing harshly" include *censure*, *castigate*, and *vituperate* (vy-**T(Y)OO**-pur-AYT).

To *excoriate*, which comes from Latin, and to *flay*, which comes from Anglo-Saxon, are close in meaning. Both mean by derivation to strip off the skin, and in modern usage both have also come to mean to rebuke or denounce harshly, to attack or criticize in a severe and scathing manner.

Flay also means to whip or lash the skin. If you flay an animal, you either strip off its skin or whip the hide off it. If you flay a person, you whip that person either literally, with a whip, or figuratively, with harsh and scathing words. If you excoriate an animal, you strip off its skin. If you excoriate your knee, you have skinned your knee; you have an abrasion. And if you excoriate a person, you figuratively strip that person's skin off by delivering a harsh or severe rebuke or denunciation.

The corresponding noun is *excoriation*.

Let's review the last ten keywords by playing "One of These Definitions Doesn't Fit the Word." In each statement below, a keyword (in *italics*) is followed by three definitions. Two of the three are correct; one is unrelated in meaning. Decide which definition doesn't fit the keyword. Answers appear on page 403.

1. *Dilatory* means delaying, unwilling, procrastinating.
2. To *vilify* means to expose, slander, defame.
3. *Phlegmatic* means calm and unemotional, sluggish and apathetic, tedious and boring.
4. *Adventitious* means accidentally acquired, not belonging naturally, happening at the right time.
5. *Desiccated* means dehydrated, dried up, defunct.
6. *Comity* means courtesy, generosity, civility.
7. *Specious* means apparently true, superficially reasonable, unquestionably correct.
8. *Noisome* means harmful, foul-smelling, unmanageable.
9. *Calumny* means defamation of character, a terrible mistake, a false and malicious statement.
10. To *excoriate* means to reject completely, rebuke harshly, denounce severely.

Are you weary of all these difficult words? Have I dessicated your brain with adventitious verbal information? Has your routine of reading and reviewing become dilatory? If you answered yes to any of those questions, then I think you will appreciate . . .

Word 41: LASSITUDE (LAS-i-T(Y)OOD)

Weariness, fatigue; a weak or exhausted state or feeling; a sluggish relaxation of body or mind.

Synonyms of *lassitude* include *listlessness*, *lethargy* (LETH-ur-jee), *debility*, *indolence* (IN-duh-li̱nts), *inertia* (i-NUR-shuh), *enervation* (EN-ur-**VAY**-shi̱n), *torpor* (TOR-pur), and *languor* (LANG-gur).

Would you like an ultragrandiloquent synonym for *lassitude*? How about *oscitancy*? *Oscitancy* (AHS-i̱-tin-see) comes through the Latin *oscitare*, to yawn, gape, open the mouth, from the Latin *os*, the mouth. Literally, *oscitancy* means the act of yawning or gaping; figuratively, it means sleepiness, drowsiness, or sluggishness.

The Latin *os*, meaning "the mouth," is the source of another delightful grandiloquent word that is entirely unrelated to this discussion—but you don't mind if I'm desultory, do you? (As I mentioned in the discussion of *discursive*, word 50 of Level 6, *desultory*, pronounced **DES**-u̱l-TOR-ee, means skipping or leaping from one subject to another in a disconnected way.) At any rate, this Latin *os*, the mouth, is also the source of the unusual English word *osculation* (AHS-kyuh-**LAY**-shin). *Osculation* denotes a pleasant act, something we all enjoy. With that clue, and knowing that this act has something to do with the mouth, can you guess what *osculation* means? If you're thinking the act of kissing, then you are a sagacious word sleuth indeed.

Now let's get back to our keyword, *lassitude*, which comes from the Latin *lassitudo*, weariness, exhaustion. In modern usage, *lassitude* denotes a weak or exhausted state or feeling; a sluggish relaxation of body or mind. Surfeiting yourself at the dinner table can cause lassitude, and on sultry summer days we often experience lassitude.

Fatigue, *weariness*, and *lassitude* are close in meaning. *Fatigue* usually is the result of physical or mental exertion; you feel fatigue after ten or twelve hours of assiduous labor. According to the *Century Dictionary* (1914), *weariness* is "the result of less obvious causes, as long sitting or standing in one position, importunity from others, delays, and the like. *Fatigue* and *weariness* are natural conditions," says the *Century*, "from which one easily recovers by rest." *Lassitude* is "the result of greater fatigue or weariness than one can well bear, and may be of the nature of ill health. The word may, however, be used in a lighter sense." To illustrate that lighter sense, the *Century* quotes these lines from the eighteenth-century British poet, essayist, and physician John Armstrong: "Happy he whose toil / Has o'er his languid, pow'rless limbs diffus'd / a pleasing lassitude."

Word 42: TRADUCE (truh-D(Y)OOS)

To publicly disgrace or humiliate by making false and malicious statements; to make a mockery of; expose to public ridicule or contempt.

Synonyms of *traduce* include *defame*, *slander*, *denigrate*, *malign* (muh-LYN), *vituperate* (vy-**T(Y)OO**-pur-AYT), *calumniate* (kuh-**LUHM**-nee-AYT), and *vilify*, word 32 of this level.

Antonyms of *traduce* include *praise*, *compliment*, *laud*, *extol*, and *adulate* (**AJ**-uh-LAYT).

Traduce comes from the Latin *traducere*, to lead across or lead in front of others; hence, to exhibit as a spectacle, expose to ridicule, disgrace or humiliate in public. In modern usage, *traduce* applies chiefly to making false, malicious, and humiliating statements about people, as to traduce someone's honor, or a scathing editorial that traduces the mayor. Those gossipy newspapers with the sensational, ridiculous headlines that you see in the supermarket checkout line specialize in scandalous stories that traduce well-known people.

The noun *traducement* means the act of traducing, and a *traducer* is a person who traduces, who makes false, malicious, humiliating statements.

Word 43: DISHABILLE (DIS-uh-BEEL)

The state of being partly clothed; partial undress.

Dishabille may also mean the state of being casually or carelessly dressed, as in one's night clothes or lounging attire.

Dishabille comes from a French verb meaning to undress, which explains why it has all those silent letters. *Dishabille* entered English in the late 1600s, and as you can imagine, the word usually has a slightly sexy or titillating connotation.

Here are a few examples cited in the *Oxford English Dictionary*, which specializes in displaying the language in historical dishabille. From 1684: "To surprise his mistress in dishabille." From 1708: "What would she give now to be in this dishabille in the open air?" From 1796: "His lady made a thousand apologies for being [caught] in such a dishabille." From 1861: "The easy, confidential intercourse of her dishabille in the boudoir" (BOO-dwahr, a woman's bedroom or private dressing room). And from 1885: "The shortcomings of English costume pale before the dishabille of the Dutch colonial ladies."

Little could the writer of that last example have imagined the sometimes shocking dishabille, partial undress, that is commonplace in the worlds of entertainment and publishing today. And now, seeing as we've just discussed a rather prurient word (*prurient*, pronounced PRUUR-ee-int, means characterized by or arousing lust), it seems fitting to invite you to learn . . .

Word 44: SATURNALIA (SAT-ur-**NAY**-lee-uh)

An orgy, licentious merrymaking, unrestrained revelry.

Saturnalia, with a capital *S*, denotes the seven-day festival of Saturn celebrated in December by the ancient Romans. According to Brewer's *Dictionary of Phrase and Fable* (1894), the Saturnalia was "a time of licensed disorder and misrule. . . . During its continuance no public business could be transacted, the law courts were closed, the schools kept holiday, no war could be commenced, and no malefactor punished." (A *malefactor*, pronounced **MAL**-uh-FAK-tur, is a criminal, outlaw, evildoer.)

That week of abandon in ancient Rome has led to a second sense of the word. When spelled with a small *s*, *saturnalia* means any period or occasion of unrestrained revelry or licentious merrymaking; hence, an orgy. Among American college students, the saturnalia is celebrated during the vernal equinox, and goes by the name of "spring break."

Word 45: EXTIRPATE (**EK**-stur-PAYT)

To pull or dig up by the roots, root out, exterminate, abolish or destroy completely.

Although *extirpate* means to root out, it has stayed close to its roots, for it comes from the Latin *extirpare*, to tear up by the roots, which comes in turn from *ex-*, meaning "out," and *stirps*, which means the stem and roots of a plant. The word may be used literally, as to extirpate a tree, or figuratively, as to extirpate evil or a heterodox belief.

Extirpate has two close synonyms: *eradicate* (i-**RAD**-i-KAYT) and *deracinate* (di-**RAS**-i-NAYT). Both these verbs come from the Latin *radix*, the root of a plant. By derivation and in modern usage, *eradicate* and *deracinate* also mean to pull up by the roots, uproot, and so to obliterate, annihilate, get rid of completely.

Deracinate suggests a violent uprooting or annihilation. You can deracinate your hair; a despotic government can deracinate dissent; and a war can deracinate a population. *Eradicate* suggests resistance from the thing being uprooted or destroyed. Campaigns to eradicate drug abuse and organized crime often fall short of expectations.

Extirpate suggests the intentional uprooting or extermination of something deeply entrenched. Self-styled defenders of society, like the zealous antivice crusader Anthony Comstock, are always on the lookout for some pernicious influence to extirpate—obscenity, drugs, subversives, heretics, or heterodox beliefs. The corresponding noun is *extirpation* (EK-stur-**PAY**-shin).

Word 46: FLAGITIOUS (fluh-JISH-u̱s)

Extremely wicked; shamefully and scandalously criminal, vice-ridden, or corrupt.

Synonyms of *flagitious* include *atrocious*, *egregious* (word 36 of Level 8), *heinous* (HAY-nus), *diabolical*, *nefarious* (ne̱-FAIR-ee-u̱s), *odious* (OH-dee-u̱s), and *execrable* (EK-si-kruh-buul).

Flagitious comes through the Latin *flagitiosus*, shameful, disgraceful, infamous, from *flagitium*, a shameful crime, disgraceful action.

Flagitious may be used of persons who are grossly wicked and guilty of atrocious crimes or vices. For example, in different ways and on a different scale, Jack the Ripper and Joseph Stalin were both flagitious monsters. *Flagitious* may also be used of actions or things to mean shamefully wicked, villainous, or evil, as a flagitious crime, a flagitious obsession, flagitious thoughts. The Holocaust was one of the most flagitious events in history.

Word 47: PERIPATETIC (PER-i̱-puh-TET-ik)

Walking about, going from place to place on foot.

Synonyms of *peripatetic* include *ambulating* and *itinerant*.

Peripatetic comes from Greek and means literally walking about. When spelled with a capital *P*, *Peripatetic* refers to the ancient Greek school of philosophy founded by Aristotle, who expounded his theories while strolling in the Lyceum (ly-SEE-u̱m) in Athens.

When spelled with a small *p*, *peripatetic* means walking about, traveling on foot, as peripatetic exercise, a peripatetic police officer, or a grassroots political campaign that succeeded because of the peripatetic efforts of volunteers.

Peripatetic may also be used as a noun to mean a peripatetic person, a pedestrian or itinerant, someone who walks or moves about on foot.

Word 48: CACHINNATE (KAK-i̱-NAYT)

To laugh loudly and immoderately, laugh convulsively or hysterically.

To *chuckle*, *giggle*, *cackle*, *chortle*, *titter*, *snicker*, and *snigger* all suggest moderate, restrained, or self-conscious laughter.

To *guffaw* suggests loud, boisterous, unrestrained laughter.

To *cachinnate* takes the joke one step further. When you cachinnate, you shake with laughter, split your sides. Can you think of the last joke you heard that made you cachinnate?

The verb to *cachinnate* comes from the Latin *cachinnare*, to laugh aloud. The corresponding noun is *cachinnation* (KAK-i̱-**NAY**-shi̱n), immoderate, convulsive, or hysterical laughter.

My earnest hope is that at least once in the course of *Verbal Advantage*, something I've written will catch your funny bone off guard and induce a cachinnation.

Word 49: MANUMIT (MAN-yuh-**MIT**)

To set free, liberate, emancipate, deliver from slavery or bondage.

Synonyms of *manumit* include *unshackle*, *unfetter*, *enfranchise*, and *disenthrall*.

Antonyms include *enslave*, *enthrall*, *subjugate* (word 43 of Level 1), *shackle*, *fetter*, *manacle* (MAN-uh-k<u>u</u>l), and *trammel* (TRAM-<u>u</u>l).

The verb to *manumit* comes through Middle English and Old French from the Latin *manumittere*, to free a slave, which comes in turn from *manus*, the hand, and *mittere*, to send, let go.

To *manumit*, to *emancipate*, and to *enfranchise* are close in meaning. According to the *Century Dictionary* (1914), to *enfranchise* "is to bring into freedom or into civil rights." In the twentieth century, American women gained the right to vote, gained economic and professional influence, and in many other ways became enfranchised. To *emancipate* "is to free from a literal or figurative slavery." You can emancipate someone from bondage or emancipate someone's mind with knowledge. *Manumit* has often been used interchangeably with *emancipate*, but it usually suggests a literal deliverance from bondage or slavery. Abraham Lincoln's Emancipation Proclamation manumitted American slaves. If you get fired from a crummy job, consider yourself manumitted.

Word 50: EXPIATION (EK-spee-**AY**-sh<u>i</u>n)

Atonement; reparation for a sin, crime, or offense.

Expiation comes from the Latin *expiare*, to atone for, purify, engage in a ritual cleansing. The corresponding verb is *expiate* (**EK**-spee-AYT), to atone for, make amends for.

Have you done anything wrong lately? Alienated a loved one? Offended a coworker? Told a lie? Broken a law? If you're feeling guilty about anything, if you have a compunction (word 26 of Level 8), a twinge of regret caused by an uneasy conscience, then Dr. Elster has the verbal cure for you: *expiation*, the act of atonement or reparation for a wrong done. Depending on the nature and severity of your offense, your expiation may require an apology, a punishment, or the wearing of sackcloth and ashes.

Let's review the ten keywords you've just learned. I'll give you the review word (in *italics*) followed by three words or phrases, and you decide which one of those three words or phrases comes nearest the meaning of the review word. Answers appear on page 403.

1. Does *lassitude* mean weariness, restraint, or freedom?
2. Does *traduce* mean to compel by force, make false and malicious statements, or to infer from evidence?
3. Is a person in *dishabille* dirty, partly clothed, or at a loss for what to say or do?
4. Is a *saturnalia* a feast, a diversion, or an orgy?
5. Does *extirpate* mean to pull up by the roots, make an educated guess, or keep away from?
6. Is something *flagitious* very insulting, totally unnecessary, or extremely wicked?
7. Does *peripatetic* mean taking one's time, walking about, or asking questions?
8. Does *cachinnate* mean to object, to ridicule, or to laugh loudly?
9. Does *manumit* mean to excuse, to liberate, or to allow?
10. Is *expiation* acceptance, rejection, or atonement?

What's Afoot with *Effete*?

Let's wind things up with a vocabulary quiz involving only one word: *effete* (i-FEET, almost like *a feet*). Do you know the precise meaning of this word?

Here are five possible synonyms: *(a) womanly; (b) worn out; (c) elegant; (d) snobbish; (e) pseudointellectual.* Take your pick and read on. The answer may surprise you.

Effete comes from the Latin *effetus*, worn out by bearing children, unable to produce offspring, which comes in turn from *ex-*, out, and *fetus*, productive. *Effete* formerly was used of animals to mean past bearing, and of soil or land to mean barren. These applications are now uncommon, though not archaic, and today precise usage most often employs *effete* in the figurative sense of exhausted, having the energies worn out, barren of results, ineffective or unproductive. "If they find the old governments effete," wrote the British statesman Edmund Burke, "they may seek new ones." The correct answer, therefore, is *(b) worn out.*

Do you remember, from Level 4, my discussion of the "sounds-like syndrome"? *Effete* is one of its victims, and its case is particularly complicated because it is commonly confused not with one but with two similar-sounding words.

The first word people confuse with *effete* is *effeminate*. Some years ago I was listening to a literary radio show hosted by a syndicated columnist. The columnist asked his guest, the author of a biography of Margaret Mitchell, who wrote *Gone with the Wind*, whether Mitchell's fiancé was *effete*. Do you think she thought he meant worn out, exhausted, spent? Not for a minute. Going right along with the confusion, the biographer replied, "Yes, Mitchell's fiancé had many effeminate qualities."

Effeminate is a disparaging term applied to men to mean womanish, unmanly, not virile. In *Troilus and Cressida*, Shakespeare writes, "A woman impudent and mannish grown / Is not more loath'd than an effeminate man."

The second word people confuse with *effete* is *elite* (ay-LEET or i-LEET). By derivation *elite* means the choice or best part; the word is most often used of a group or class of persons. "The elite of society" comprises persons of the highest social class, sometimes referred to colloquially as "snobs."

I heard a good example of the confusion between *effete* and *elite* in another radio interview, this time on National Public Radio's "All Things Considered." The interviewer was speaking with the editor of the notoriously stuffy and esoteric *New York Review of Books*, and at one point she asked him if he thought his publication was effete. Did he think she meant exhausted, ineffective, washed up? Hardly. He replied that although the *Review* was highbrow fare, it did not intend to be snobbish or exclusive and was undeserving of any such reputation it might have.

For those who already think *effete* means womanly, delicate, or overrefined, compounding that erroneous notion with the equally erroneous suggestion of snobbery or supercilious self-indulgence requires no great leap of the imagination. For millions of Americans, the confusion of *effete* with *elite* was implanted in the 1970s by Richard M. Nixon's otherwise unmemorable vice president, Spiro Agnew, when, in a speech assailing opponents of the Vietnam War, he uttered the words "an effete corps of impudent snobs."

Almost overnight, "effete snob" became a catch phrase in the war controversy, used by the "hawks," who favored involvement, to disparage the "doves," who were against involvement. As a result of this phrase's hasty dissemination by the media and its subsequent absorption into the nebulous national vocabulary, *effete* now often suggests elitism and snobbery, an association entirely divorced from its true meaning: depleted of energy or vigor, worn out.

What does it mean when some of the most prominent writers, editors, broadcasters, and politicians in the country fall prey to the "sounds-like syndrome"? Is this a Humpty Dumpty case of "a word means whatever I choose it to mean"? Should we just lie back—that's right, *lie*, not *lay*—and say, "As long as we communicate, what difference does it make?"

That, my verbally advantaged friend, is what is called a rhetorical question, to which you already know my answer is a resounding no.

So what can we conclude is afoot with *effete*? Though weakened by the presence in current dictionaries of such incongruous synonyms as *effeminate*, *decadent*, *degenerate*, and *overrefined*, the precise sense of this useful word is not entirely *effete*, exhausted, ineffective, washed-up. Now that you know the story of how the "sounds-like syndrome" has infected *effete*, you must play doctor and decide how you are going to treat the word. And the next time you hear *effete* used effeminately, or by an impudent snob, perhaps you will pass along this word to the wise.

And while we're at it, here's another word to the wise: Before forging ahead with the final level—the denouement, so to speak, of *Verbal Advantage*, after which you will be manumitted—try to snap out of your pusillanimous lassitude and display your puissance and probity by reviewing this entire level. Don't be dilatory or diffident or disingenuous with yourself. Life is too fugacious to be phlegmatic. Do it now!

Answers to Review Quizzes for Level 9

Keywords 1–10

1. No. *Prolix* means wordy and tiresome, long-winded and boring, verbose, using more words than necessary to get the point across.
2. Yes. *Apocryphal* means not genuine, counterfeit, illegitimate; specifically, of doubtful authenticity or authorship.
3. Yes. *Cupidity* means greed, a strong desire for wealth or material things.
4. No. Skiing and ice skating are *hibernal* activities, meaning winter activities. *Vernal* means pertaining to spring, occurring in the spring; also, having the qualities of spring: fresh, warm, and mild.
5. No. *Temerity* means recklessness, rashness, foolhardiness; reckless disregard for danger, risk, or consequences.
6. Yes. *Rapprochement* means reconciliation, a reestablishing of friendly relations.
7. No. A *disquisition* is a formal discussion of or inquiry into a subject; a discourse.
8. Yes. To *proscribe* means to prohibit, forbid, outlaw.

9. No. Donating your mansion to a nonprofit organization would be a display of munificence. *Munificence* means great generosity, lavish giving.
10. Yes. *Probity* means honesty, integrity; fairness, straightforwardness, and sincerity in one's dealings with others.

Keywords 11–20

1. False. *Puissant* means powerful, mighty, strong, forceful.
2. True. *Peculate* means to steal, embezzle; specifically, to steal or misuse money or property entrusted to one's care.
3. False. *Diffident* means shy, timid, bashful, lacking in self-confidence, hesitant to speak or act.
4. True. *Venal* means corruptible, bribable, capable of being bribed or bought off, able to be obtained for a price.
5. Very true. *Parsimonious* means stingy, miserly, extremely tight with money.
6. Absolutely false. *Pusillanimous* means cowardly, lacking courage, timid, fainthearted, irresolute.
7. True. *Extant* means existing, still in existence, not extinct, not lost or destroyed.
8. False. *Meritorious* means praiseworthy, commendable. *Meretricious* means tawdry, gaudy; attractive in a flashy or cheap way; falsely alluring; deceptively enticing.
9. False. *Xenophobia* means fear or hatred of strangers or foreigners, or of anything strange or foreign.
10. True. *Quotidian* means daily, recurring every day or pertaining to every day; also, of an everyday nature, and so ordinary, commonplace, trivial.

Keywords 21–30

1. Synonyms. An *exigency* is an urgency, pressing need; a situation demanding immediate attention or action.
2. Antonyms. *Pulchritude* means beauty, loveliness, attractiveness.
3. Antonyms. *Denouement* means the unraveling or resolution of a plot, as of a novel or a drama; the outcome or resolution of any complex situation.
4. Synonyms. *Fugacious* means fleeting, passing quickly away.
5. Antonyms. Literally, *turbid* means muddy, clouded, roiled, murky, as if from stirred-up sediment. Figuratively, *turbid* means muddled, obscure, confused, not lucid.
6. Antonyms. *Indefeasible* means not capable of being undone, taken away, annulled, or rendered void.
7. Antonyms. *Disingenuous* means insincere, crafty, sly, not straightforward or frank.

8. Antonyms. *Scurrilous* means foul-mouthed, obscene; using or expressed in language that is coarse, vulgar, and abusive.
9. Synonyms. A *recrudescence* is a revival, renewal, fresh outbreak after a period of inactivity or quiescence (kwy-ES-ints).

Keywords 31–40

1. *Unwilling* doesn't fit. *Dilatory* means delaying, causing or intended to cause delay; also, slow, tardy, characterized by delay or procrastination.
2. *Expose* doesn't fit. To *vilify* means to defame, slander, attack with vicious, abusive language.
3. *Tedious and boring* doesn't fit. *Phlegmatic* means calm and unemotional; having a sluggish, apathetic temperament; difficult to move to emotion or action.
4. *Happening at the right time* doesn't fit. *Adventitious* means accidentally or casually acquired; not belonging naturally to something; associated by chance; not inherent or integral.
5. *Defunct* doesn't fit. *Defunct* means dead, extinct. *Desiccated* means dried or dried up, dehydrated, deprived of moisture.
6. *Generosity* doesn't fit. *Comity* means courtesy, civility, politeness, respectful and considerate behavior.
7. *Unquestionably correct* doesn't fit. *Specious* means appearing to be true, genuine, or correct but actually false or deceptive; superficially reasonable or just but not so in reality.
8. *Unmanageable* doesn't fit. *Noisome* means harmful to health or well-being, unwholesome, dangerous, destructive; also, foul-smelling, offensive, disgusting.
9. *A terrible mistake* doesn't fit. *Calumny* means defamation of character, slander, a false and malicious statement or accusation meant to injure a person's reputation.
10. *Reject completely* doesn't fit. *Excoriate* means to strip, scrape, or tear off the skin; hence, to rebuke or denounce harshly and severely.

Keywords 41–50

1. *Lassitude* means weariness, fatigue; a weak or exhausted state or feeling; a sluggish relaxation of body or mind.
2. *Traduce* means to publicly disgrace or humiliate by making false and malicious statements; to make a mockery of; expose to public ridicule or contempt.
3. *Dishabille* means the state of being partly clothed; partial undress.

4. A *saturnalia* is an orgy, licentious merrymaking, unrestrained revelry.
5. To *extirpate* means to pull or dig up by the roots, root out, exterminate, abolish or destroy completely.
6. Something *flagitious* is extremely wicked; shamefully and scandalously criminal, vice-ridden, or corrupt.
7. *Peripatetic* means walking about, going from place to place on foot.
8. To *cachinnate* means to laugh loudly and immoderately, laugh convulsively or hysterically.
9. To *manumit* means to set free, liberate, emancipate, deliver from slavery or bondage.
10. *Expiation* is atonement; reparation for a sin, crime, or offense.

Review Test for Level 9

1. Which word is an antonym of *prolix*?
    (a) sententious
    (b) tautological
    (c) pleonastic
    (d) circumlocutory

2. Which word is a synonym of *apocryphal*?
    (a) ineffable
    (b) fugacious
    (c) spurious
    (d) scurrilous

3. Which word is an antonym of *cupidity*?
    (a) avarice
    (b) munificence
    (c) covetousness
    (d) venality

4. Which word means pertaining to summer?
    (a) hibernal
    (b) vernal
    (c) estival
    (d) hiemal
    (e) quotidian

5. Which words are antonyms?
    (a) temerity, imprudence
    (b) apprehension, timorousness

(c) impetuosity, audacity

(d) effrontery, diffidence

6. Which word is a synonym of *proscribe*?

    (a) extol

    (b) interdict

    (c) obviate

    (d) manumit

7. Which words are synonyms?

    (a) scrupulousness, malfeasance

    (b) uprightness, perfidy

    (c) probity, rectitude

    (d) veracity, duplicity

8. Which phrase misuses *convince*?

    (a) convinced her to do it

    (b) convinced him of the truth

    (c) convinced her that it was important

9. Which word is an antonym of *puissant*?

    (a) opulent

    (b) stalwart

    (c) parsimonious

    (d) enervated

10. Which word is a synonym of *peculate*?

    (a) importune

    (b) defalcate

    (c) supplicate

    (d) desiccate

    (e) excoriate

11. Which word means excusable, forgivable, minor?

    (a) venial

    (b) venal

12. Which words are antonyms?

    (a) beneficent, bountiful

    (b) niggardly, generous

    (c) penurious, stingy

    (d) grasping, parsimonious

    (e) liberal, munificent

13. What is a meretrix?

    (a) an award
    (b) a liar
    (c) a prostitute
    (d) a measuring device

14. What does the prefix *xeno-* mean?

    (a) wood
    (b) animal
    (c) abnormal
    (d) strange

15. Which word is *not* a synonym of *quotidian*?

    (a) frequent
    (b) ordinary
    (c) commonplace
    (d) daily

16. Which phrase denotes something absolutely necessary or indispensable?

    (a) bon mot
    (b) quid pro quo
    (c) faux pas
    (d) sine qua non
    (e) pro bono publico

17. Which phrase denotes something given in return for something else?

    (a) bête noire
    (b) quid pro quo
    (c) sine qua non
    (d) coup de grâce
    (e) bon mot

18. Which phrase denotes someone or something one especially dislikes or fears?

    (a) faux pas
    (b) caveat emptor
    (c) bête noire
    (d) sine qua non
    (e) quid pro quo

19. Which phrase means an error or blunder?

    (a) bon mot
    (b) caveat emptor
    (c) faux pas

(d) bête noire
(e) sine qua non

20. Which word is an antonym of *meretricious*?

(a) pusillanimous
(b) indefeasible
(c) diffident
(d) pulchritudinous

21. Which of the following means the unraveling or resolution of a plot?

(a) disquisition
(b) denouement
(c) coup de grâce
(d) deus ex machina

22. *Ephemeral* and *evanescent* are synonyms of

(a) mellifluous
(b) fugacious
(c) inexorable
(d) ubiquitous
(e) peripatetic

23. Which words mean swollen, inflated?

(a) turgid, tumid
(b) turbid, turgid
(c) tumid, turbid
(d) turgid, turbid, tumid

24. Which word means using coarse, vulgar, insolent language?

(a) flagitious
(b) disingenuous
(c) scurrilous
(d) recrudescent
(e) cachinnating

25. Which word means causing or characterized by delay?

(a) exigent
(b) miscreant
(c) phlegmatic
(d) dilatory
(e) temerarious

26. Which of the following is *not* one of the four humors?

    (a) blood
    (b) phlegm
    (c) choler
    (d) apathy
    (e) melancholy

27. Which word is an antonym of *desiccated*?

    (a) phlegmatic
    (b) succulent
    (c) turbid
    (d) wizened

28. Which word connotes an intent to mislead or deceive?

    (a) specious
    (b) plausible
    (c) both specious and plausible

29. *Pernicious* and *putrid* are synonyms of

    (a) noisome
    (b) salubrious
    (c) mephitic
    (d) deleterious

30. Four of the following five words are related in meaning. Which word has a different, unrelated meaning?

    (a) traduce
    (b) vilify
    (c) calumniate
    (d) expiate
    (e) excoriate

31. What is *osculation*?

    (a) yawning
    (b) kissing
    (c) watching
    (d) eating

32. To be in dishabille is to be

    (a) in a state of disorder
    (b) slightly intoxicated
    (c) partly clothed
    (d) at one's wit's end

33. Which words are *not* synonymous?

   (a) atrocious, odious

   (b) execrable, heinous

   (c) egregious, pusillanimous

   (d) flagitious, nefarious

34. Which word is associated with a school of philosophy founded by Aristotle?

   (a) pariah

   (b) peripatetic

   (c) saturnalia

   (d) lyceum

35. Which two words mean to uproot, abolish, annihilate? (This question has *two* correct answers.)

   (a) manumit

   (b) defenestrate

   (c) cachinnate

   (d) extirpate

   (e) deracinate

Answers

1. a 2. c 3. b 4. c 5. d 6. b 7. c 8. a 9. d 10. b 11. a 12. b 13. c
14. d 15. a 16. d 17. b 18. c 19. c 20. d 21. b 22. b 23. a 24. c
25. d 26. d 27. b 28. a 29. a 30. d 31. b 32. c 33. c 34. b 35. d & e

Evaluation

A score of 30–35 is excellent. If you answered fewer than thirty questions correctly in this test, review the entire level and take the test again.

Level 10

A Verbal Pat on the Back

I know how much time and effort you've been putting in reviewing and working hard to absorb all the challenging words and information I've been presenting, and you deserve a big verbal pat on the back for making it this far. Believe me, your assiduousness will pay off down the line, for you will find the world opening up to you in wonderful, unexpected ways through your newfound insight into words.

I am also honored and delighted that you have stuck with the program and decided to accompany me on the final leg of this journey into the ethereal regions of the language. Only the most intrepid verbal explorers have the courage and the stamina to climb this high. Only the most stalwart and redoubtable ones have the determination to go on when the path becomes rocky and the air grows thin.

We are now going to ascend to the acme of the English vocabulary. Although I can't say we will "boldly go where no man has gone before," I can say we will boldly go where ninety-five out of every hundred people have never gone, for the words you are about to learn are known by fewer than one in ten educated adults. So be bold, be brave, step lively, and above all, stay awake. The last level was tricky, but this one is downright treacherous. If you want to reach the peak of *Verbal Advantage*, then you must give this final part of the journey your full attention.

Follow me carefully now as we traverse our first ten keywords.

Word 1: JEJUNE (ji-JOON)

Dull, uninteresting, or unsatisfying; devoid of nourishment, substance, or significance.

Synonyms of *jejune* include *flat*, *stale*, *arid*, *insipid*, and *vapid* (word 37 of Level 8).

Jejune comes from the Latin *jejunus*, fasting, hungry, barren, dry. From the same source comes the anatomical term *jejunum* (ji-JOO-n<u>u</u>m), the middle section of the small intestine, between the duodenum and the ileum. The jejunum took that name, the dictionaries tell us, because in postmortem dissections it was found barren of digestive contents and therefore believed to be empty after death.

The adjective *jejune* was once used to mean hungry, fasting, without food, but that sense is obsolete and in modern usage *jejune* is used figuratively to mean barren of interest, dull and unsatisfying, devoid of nourishment, substance, or significance. A jejune diet lacks nourishment; jejune food is tasteless and unsatisfying. A jejune idea or a jejune method lacks appeal because it is devoid of substance or significance. A jejune movie or jejune novel is dull, uninteresting, insipid.

If you look up *jejune* in a current dictionary, you will also see another definition of the word: youthful, childish, immature, puerile, as jejune behavior or a jejune response to a serious question. Whence comes this sense of the word, which is so clearly unconnected to the root meaning, barren of substance or appeal?

For an answer let's turn to William Safire, the language maven of *The New York Times*, who writes a column for that paper's Sunday magazine called "On Language." On October 16, 1994, Safire reported that he had queried Jacques Barzun, one of the world's foremost authorities on English usage, about this extended sense of the word, and the venerable professor responded that "the meaning 'youthful, childish' for *jejune*" had gotten into the dictionaries "only as a concession to the misusers."

According to Safire, "the original meaning of *jejune*—'empty of food, meager'—led to its modern sense of 'dull, insipid.' Probably because the word sounded like *juvenile*, it picked up a meaning of 'puerile, childish,' which," Safire asserts, "is the way it is most commonly used today." (Yet another example of the insidious sounds-like syndrome at work.)

Safire then poses the eternal question regarding capricious usage: "Should we stand with the prescriptivists, as Barzun suggests, and hold fast to the 'proper' meaning? Or do we go along with the language slobs, adopting as 'correct' a mistake merely because it is so frequently made?"

Here's how Safire answers his own question: "At a certain point, what people mean when they use a word becomes its meaning. We should resist its adoption, pointing out the error, for years; mockery helps; if the meaning persists, though, it is senseless to ignore the new sense. I say *jejune* means puerile now," Safire concludes.

I disagree with Mr. Safire, and stand with Mr. Barzun on the side of reserving *jejune* for the meaning "devoid of nourishment, substance, or significance." That is my crotchet, and I'm proud of it. However, although few people know the word *jejune*, I will concede that many of those who do now use it to mean childish or immature; and therefore, as Mr. Safire suggests, resistance to this change in meaning may now be *effete*, and further mockery of it may be jejune—which you may take as meaning either dull, insipid, or juvenile, immature.

Welcome to the war of words, my verbally advantaged friend. What will be *your* strategy for this controversial word *jejune*?

Word 2: PAUCITY (PAW-si-tee)

An insufficiency, scarcity, especially a serious or extreme one, a dire lack.

Synonyms of *paucity* include *dearth* (word 12 of Level 3), *shortage*, *deficiency,* and the challenging word *exiguity* (EK-si-**GYOO**-i-tee). The noun *exiguity* and the adjective *exiguous* (eg-ZIG-yoo-us or ek-SIG-yoo-us) come through the Latin *exiguus*, small, scanty, from *exigere*, to measure out, demand. *Exiguous* means extremely meager or scanty; an exiguity is an extremely small or scanty amount. *Exiguity* and *paucity* are close synonyms and are virtually interchangeable.

Paucity comes through the Latin *paucitas*, fewness, scarcity, from *paucus*, few. In modern usage, *paucity* may mean simply a scarcity or insufficiency, as a paucity of words, but it often suggests a serious or extreme insuffiency, a dire lack. We speak of a paucity of supplies; a paucity of information; a paucity of funds; a paucity of natural resources in the region; or a paucity of orders leading to the decision to take a product off the market.

Antonyms of *paucity* include *superabundance*, *superfluity* (SOO-pur-**FLOO**-i-tee), and *plethora* (word 19 of Level 6).

Word 3: MINATORY (MIN-uh-TOR-ee)

Threatening, menacing; having a threatening or menacing aspect or nature.

Minatory and the even more unusual adjective *minacious* (mi-NAY-shus) are synonymous and may be used interchangeably. Both words come from the same source—the Latin *minari*, to threaten—and are related to the word *menace*. Minatory clouds have a threatening aspect, indicating heavy rain or snow. Minatory people are menacing by nature. A minatory look is a menacing look. Minatory words are threatening words.

Word 4: PUTATIVE (PYOO-tuh-tiv)

Supposed, reputed, commonly considered or regarded as such; deemed to be so but not proved.

Antonyms of *putative* include *certain*, *definite*, *unquestionable*, *indisputable*, *indubitable*, *incontrovertible*, and *irrefragable* (i-REF-ruh-guh-buul).

Putative comes from the Latin *putare*, to consider, believe, think, suppose. That which is *putative* is commonly thought to be so, generally considered true but not conclusively proved. We speak of someone's putative parents; the putative perpetrator of a crime; a putative leader or a person with putative authority, meaning the person believed to be in control; and a putative discovery, meaning a discovery generally attributed to someone without proof. We might also speak of Zsa Zsa Gabor's putative age, the age she is commonly thought to be—but who can say for sure?

Word 5: LUCUBRATION (LOO-kyoo-**BRAY**-sh<u>i</u>n)

Nocturnal labor; study, writing, or work done late at night.

Lucubration comes from the Latin *lucubrare*, to work by candlelight. The corresponding adjective, *lucubratory* (**LOO**-kyoo-bruh-TOR-ee) means literally done by candlelight; hence, pertaining to nocturnal study or labor. The corresponding verb to *lucubrate* (**LOO**-kyoo-BRAYT) means to work, study, or write into the wee hours.

To use a vernacular expression, *lucubration* means burning the midnight oil. College students often engage in lucubration, and meeting a deadline for an important project may require an eleventh-hour bout of diligent lucubration.

In current usage, the verb to *lucubrate* may also be used to mean to compose with laborious effort, and especially to write in a scholarly or pedantic fashion, as a professor of political science who lucubrates abstrusely from her ivory tower. The noun *lucubration* has also come to be used of anything produced by laborious study or effort, especially an elaborate, pedantic, or pretentious piece of writing.

Word 6: TROGLODYTE (**TRAHG**-luh-**DYT**)

A cave dweller; also, a person who lives or behaves in a primitive manner, or who lives in seclusion. The corresponding adjective is *troglodytic* (TRAHG-luh-**DIT**-ik), pertaining to or characteristic of a troglodyte.

Troglodyte comes from a Greek word meaning "one who creeps into holes." In modern usage, *troglodyte* may be used in three ways. It may refer specifically to a prehistoric cave dweller, as the Neanderthals (nee-**AN**-dur-TAWLZ) were troglodytes. In a broader sense, *troglodyte* may refer to anyone who lives in a primitive, degenerate, or debased manner or condition, or who is primitive, brutish, and displays a crude lack of sophistication regarding intellectual or cultural matters: "Simone couldn't talk to her coworkers about the novels, plays, concerts, and exhibits she enjoyed because all the people she worked with were couch potatoes, soap opera junkies, mall rats, and troglodytes." *Troglodyte* may also refer to a person who chooses to live in seclusion, a hermit, recluse. The billionaire Howard Hughes was a notorious—and notoriously eccentric—troglodyte.

Would you like two challenging synonyms for a person who lives in seclusion? Try *anchorite* (**ANGK**-uh-RYT) and *eremite* (**ER**-uh-MYT).

Word 7: ALEATORY (**AY**-lee-uh-TOR-ee)

Depending on luck, chance, or on some contingent event; hence, uncertain, unpredictable.

In law, an aleatory contract is an agreement whose conditions depend on a contingency, an uncertain event. An aleatory sale is one whose completion depends on the outcome of some uncertain event. Aleatory music leaves certain sounds up to the performer or up to chance.

Aleatory comes from the Latin *aleator*, a gamester, thrower of dice, crapshooter, which comes in turn from *alea*, a game of dice. *Aleatory* means literally depending upon the throw of the dice. In current usage, *aleatory* may mean gambling or pertaining to gambling, as Las Vegas is the mecca of aleatory activity, but the word is probably more often used to mean depending on luck or chance, uncertain, unpredictable. Aleatory investments are risky investments; an aleatory business needs good luck to succeed.

Word 8: FARRAGO (fuh-RAY-goh *or* fuh-RAH-goh)

A mixture, especially a confused or jumbled mixture.

Synonyms of *farrago* include *conglomeration*, *medley*, *mishmash*, *hodgepodge*, *miscellany*, *potpourri*, *pastiche*, and *salmagundi*.

Farrago comes from a Latin word meaning mixed fodder for animals, a jumbled assortment of grains. In modern usage, *farrago* may be used literally or figuratively of any mixture, especially a confused, jumbled, or miscellaneous assortment of things: "A computer is an amazing tool for storing or sorting through a farrago of information"; "Every day, the psychiatrist listens to an astonishing farrago of hopes, fears, dreams, wishes, doubts, and resentments."

The corresponding adjective is *farraginous* (fuh-RAJ-i-nus), mixed, jumbled, miscellaneous, heterogeneous, as a farraginous collection of notes or ideas.

Word 9: CYNOSURE (SY-nuh-SHUUR)

A center of attention or interest, focal point.

Cynosure comes from the Greek *kynosoura*, a dog's tail, from *kynos*, a dog. From the corresponding Greek adjective, *kynikos*, we inherit the English adjective *cynical*, which means literally like a dog.

Pardon me if I digress for a moment, but the words *cynical*, *cynic*, and *cynicism* have an interesting history that I'd like to share with you.

Cynicism was a school of ancient Greek philosophy founded by Antisthenes (an-**TIS**-thuh-NEEZ) of Athens, a pupil of Socrates. "The chief doctrines of the Cynics," says the *Century Dictionary* (1914), "were that virtue is the only good, that the essence of virtue is self-control, and that pleasure is an evil if sought for its own sake. They were accordingly characterized by an ostentatious contempt [for] riches, arts, science, and amusements."

The most famous exponent of Cynicism was Diogenes (dy-**AH**-ji-NEEZ) of Sinope (si-NOH-pee), who took cynicism to an extreme. In his disdain for human selfishness and his pursuit of a simple life, Diogenes is said to have slept in a tub, thrown away his only utensil, a cup, when he saw a peasant drinking from his hands, and wandered through the streets at midday with a lantern, telling those who asked what he was doing that he was searching for an honest man. According to the third edition of the *American Heritage Dictionary* (1992), Diogenes is also "said to have performed such actions as barking in public, urinating on the leg of a table, and masturbating on the street." Apparently as a result of this doglike behavior, Diogenes was nicknamed *kynos* or *kyon*, meaning "a dog," and the nickname was extended to the philosophy of Cynicism and its adherents. Today when we call people cynical, we mean they are scornful or skeptical of people's motives or that they believe human beings are motivated only by selfishness—in short, that people are dogs.

You will recall that our keyword, *cynosure*, comes from the Greek *kynosoura*, a dog's tail. When spelled with a capital *C*, *cynosure* refers to the constellation Ursa Minor or to Polaris, the North Star, also called the polestar, which is part of this constellation. The North Star is the outermost star in the handle of the Little Dipper, which the Greeks apparently perceived as a dog's tail.

Since ancient times the North Star has been used as a navigational guide. Thus, *cynosure* first came to mean anything that guides or directs, and then came to mean anything or anyone that is the center of attention or interest, a focal point: "He was the cynosure of the party"; "This issue is the cynosure of the campaign."

Word 10: BADINAGE (BAD-i-NAHZH *or* BAD-i-NAHZH)

Banter; playful, teasing talk; good-natured joking or gently mocking conversation.

Synonyms of *badinage* include *repartee* (REP-ur-**TEE**), *raillery* (RAYL-ur-ree), and *persiflage* (**PUR**-si-FLAHZH).

The words *banter, badinage, persiflage,* and *raillery* all suggest "good-humored jesting," says *Webster's New International Dictionary,* second edition (1934). *Banter* implies light, playful mocking or ridicule; *badinage* suggests "more trifling and delicate" teasing or jesting; *persiflage* refers to "frivolous or flippant" talk or writing; and *raillery* implies playful mockery that is "keener and often more sarcastic."

Let's review the ten keywords you've just learned. Consider the following statements and decide whether the correct answer is yes or no. Answers appear on page 442.

1. Can a person's writing be jejune?
2. If there is a paucity of evidence against a defendant, does that suggest the prosecuting attorney's case may be weak?
3. Would you like to receive a minatory letter from a lawyer?
4. Are a company's putative financial assets the assets it is commonly thought to have?
5. Does lucubration mean the act of making investments that turn a profit?
6. Would you like your daughter to marry a troglodyte?
7. Is the success of an aleatory enterprise guaranteed?
8. Can someone have a farrago of thoughts or feelings?
9. Is a cynosure something trivial that's likely to be ignored?
10. Do good friends ever engage in badinage?

Let's hit the verbal trail again with the next ten keywords in Level 10. (Did I mention that I'm a poet and you didn't know it?)

Word 11: HIERATIC (HY-uh-RAT-ik)

Priestly; pertaining to or used by priests; reserved for holy or sacred uses.

Synonyms of *hieratic* include *clerical*, *ministerial*, *pastoral* (PAS-tur-ul), *ecclesiastical*, and *sacerdotal* (SAS-ur-**DOH**-tul).

The prefix *hiero-*, often shortened to *hier-*, comes from Greek and means sacred, holy, divine. This prefix appears in several interesting English words. *Hierocracy* (HY-uh-**RAHK**-ruh-see) means rule by priests, ecclesiastical government. *Hierarch* (**HY**-ur-AHRK) means a person who rules over sacred things, a high priest, and also a person who occupies a high position in a hierarchy. *Hierarchy* (**HY**-ur-AHRK-ee) may denote religious rule or the organization of a religious order into ranks and grades, as the Roman Catholic hierarchy, but today *hierarchy* commonly refers to any organized body or system strictly arranged in order of rank, power, or class.

Hieratic means pertaining to priests or to the priesthood, as hieratic vestments or hieratic rituals. *Hieratic* may also designate a form of ancient Egyptian writing in which the traditional hieroglyphics took on a more cursive, or flowing, form. The hieratic style was opposed to the demotic style.

Demotic (di-MAHT-ik) comes from the Greek *demos,* the people, and means of the people, popular. From the same source comes *democracy*, which means literally rule by the people, popular government. The words *demotic* and *vernacular* are synonymous. In ancient Egypt, the demotic style of writing was used by the people, the laity; the hieratic style was used by the priesthood. In modern usage, *demotic* may refer to speech or writing that is vernacular, popular, characteristic of the people. *Hieratic* writings are priestly, sacred, holy.

Word 12: SATURNINE (SAT-ur-NYN)

Gloomy, sullen, or somber in appearance, manner, or temperament.

Synonyms of *saturnine* include *grave*, *melancholy*, *morose*, *taciturn* (word 2 of Level 3), and *phlegmatic* (word 33 of Level 9).

Saturnine means literally of or pertaining to the planet Saturn; in astrology, it means born under the influence of Saturn. Apparently this is not a happy influence, for today *saturnine* is most often used figuratively to mean having a gloomy, sullen, or somber appearance or disposition.

Antonyms of *saturnine* include *mercurial* (word 27 of Level 8), and *sanguine* (word 21 of this level).

Word 13: EXECRATE (EKS-uh-KRAYT)

To denounce vehemently, declare hateful or detestable; also, to loathe, abhor, detest utterly.

The verbs to *curse* and *damn* mean to denounce violently, specifically to call down evil upon out of a desire for revenge. *Execrate*, which by derivation means to put under a curse, suggests a furious or passionate denunciation, prompted by intense loathing: "The opposition execrates everything she stands for." "Citizens angry over the rise in violent crime gathered in the park to hear speakers execrate drug pushers and gangs." "When the dictator couldn't execute his enemies, he execrated them."

The corresponding adjective is *execrable* (**EKS**-uh-kruh-bul), which means abominable, abhorrent, loathsome, utterly detestable. The corresponding noun *execration* (EKS-uh-**KRAY**-shin) means a vehement denunciation or the act of execrating, declaring hateful or detestable.

Word 14: VITIATE (VISH-ee-AYT)

To corrupt, spoil, ruin, contaminate, impair the quality of, make faulty or impure; also, to weaken morally, defile, debase.

Vitiate comes from the Latin *vitium*, a fault, vice. That which is vitiated may be literally faulty, defective, or spoiled, or it may be corrupt in a moral sense, vice-ridden, debased. Illogical thought can vitiate an argument; editorial interpolation can vitiate a manuscript; noisome smog vitiates the air; a pernicious habit can vitiate a person's life. In law, a vitiated contract or a vitiated claim has been corrupted or violated and is therefore invalid, rendered ineffective.

The corresponding noun is *vitiation*, corruption, spoliation, the act of vitiating or the state of being vitiated.

Word 15: VENIAL (VEE-nee-ul)

Excusable, forgivable, pardonable, able to be overlooked.

Venial comes from the Latin *venia*, grace, indulgence, and means excusable, forgivable, minor or trivial enough to be overlooked. A venial offense can be pardoned; a venial error can be overlooked; a venial insult can be forgiven; and venial negligence can be excused.

In theology, *venial* is opposed to *mortal*. Venial sins are committed without full awareness or consent, and therefore are pardonable. Mortal sins exclude one from grace, and cause the death of the soul.

Do you remember the word *venal*, keyword 14 of Level 9? Be careful not to get *venal* confused with *venial*. *Venal* (VEE-nul, two syllables) means corruptible, capable of being bribed or bought off. *Venial* (VEE-nee-ul, three syllables) means excusable, able to be overlooked.

Word 16: RISIBLE (RIZ-i-buul)

Provoking or capable of provoking laughter.

Synonyms of *risible* include *laughable*, *amusing*, *ludicrous*, *hilarious*, *ridiculous*, and *droll* (word 36 of Level 5).

Risible, *ridicule*, and *ridiculous* all come from the Latin *ridere*, to laugh at. To *ridicule* is to laugh at, make fun of. *Ridiculous* means extremely laughable, preposterous, absurd. And *risible* means provoking or capable of provoking laughter, amusing, as a risible thought; a risible face; a risible speech: "When Ted's supervisor told him that his risible remarks during staff meetings no longer would be tolerated, Ted decided that if his supervisor couldn't see that a staff meeting was one of the most risible forms of human interaction, then he would simply quit and take his sense of humor elsewhere."

Word 17: LIONIZE (LY-uh-NYZ)

To treat a person as a celebrity or as an object of great interest or importance.

One meaning of the noun a *lion* is an important, famous, or especially interesting person. "He is a lion in his profession" does not mean he is ferocious but that he is of great interest or importance. A lion of industry is a prominent industrialist. A literary lion is an important, celebrated writer.

The verb to *lionize* means to treat a person either as a celebrity or as an object of great interest or importance: "If you want to be respected by millions, win a Nobel Prize. If you want to be lionized by millions, become a movie star." "Despite all their scandals and foibles, the members of England's royal family are lionized more often than they are vilified."

Word 18: CONTRETEMPS (KAHN-truh-TAH(N))

An embarrassing, awkward, unexpected situation or event; a sudden mishap or hitch; an inopportune occurrence.

In colloquial terms, a *contretemps* is something that happens in the wrong place at the wrong time, which leaves you high and dry: "There was a contretemps at the party last night when John got soused and started yelling at his wife." "The company can survive a contretemps, but it must avoid a scandal at all costs."

Contretemps comes from French and by derivation means something "against the time" or "out of time"; hence, something unexpected or inopportune. The *Oxford English Dictionary* shows that when the word entered English in the late seventeenth century it applied to the sport of fencing and meant "a pass or thrust . . . made at a wrong or inopportune moment." That meaning disappeared by the eighteenth century, and since then *contretemps* has meant something unexpected that occurs at an inopportune moment and creates an awkward or embarrassing situation.

Because it is an unusual word, not often used in conversation, its pronunciation has never been fully anglicized—that is, made to conform to English ways. Current dictionaries generally prefer the half-anglicized **KAHN**-truh-TAH(N). The plural is spelled the same but pronounced **KAHN**-truh-TAH(N)Z.

Contretemps may vary in severity, but they are never on the same scale as a scandal or a crisis. Contretemps are the common stuff of newspaper stories, for they occur frequently in politics and business. Sitcoms and romantic comedies also rely on contretemps to generate laughs and move the plot. The workplace usually is good for one or two juicy contretemps a month, and if you like to socialize or get together with members of your family, then chances are you already are intimately acquainted with that utterly unexpected, embarrassing, and awkward situation known as the contretemps.

Word 19: RODOMONTADE (RAHD-uh-mahn-**TAYD** *or* -m<u>u</u>n-**TAYD**)

Arrogant boasting or bragging.

Equally challenging synonyms of *rodomontade* include *bluster, braggadocio, vainglory, gasconade, fanfaronade,* and *jactitation*.

Rodomontade comes from Rodomonte, a boastful warrior king in Boiardo's *Orlando Innamorato* and Ariosto's *Orlando Furioso*. The name comes from the Italian *rodomonte*, which means literally one who rolls away mountains. By derivation, rodomontade is the arrogant boasting of someone who claims he can move mountains.

Word 20: HEBETUDE (HEB-<u>i</u>-T(Y)OOD)

Stupidity, dullness, obtuseness, lethargy of mind or spirit.

The corresponding verb is *hebetate* (**HEB**-<u>i</u>-TAYT), to make or become dull, blunt, or obtuse. The corresponding adjective is *hebetudinous* (HEB-i-**T(Y)OO**-di-n<u>u</u>s), dull, stupid, obtuse.

   Hebetude, *hebetate*, and *hebetudinous* all come ultimately from the Latin *hebes*, blunt, dull. They are great words to use superciliously, when you want to be haughty and make someone else look dumb—but don't tell anyone I told you that.

Let's review the ten keywords you've just learned. Consider the following statements and decide whether each one is true or false. Answers appear on page 442.

1. Hieratic writings are priestly, sacred writings.
2. A saturnine person is cheerful and optimistic.
3. When you execrate someone, you forgive a fault or offense.
4. Smog can vitiate the air, and smoking can vitiate your body.
5. A venial indiscretion is an inexcusable indiscretion.
6. A risible statement is an unbelievable statement.
7. Movie stars and pop musicians are often lionized in the media.
8. A contretemps is a favorable or fortunate outcome.
9. It's pleasant to listen to rodomontade.
10. Hebetude is the sign of a sharp mind.

   Did you remember to keep track of your answers and calculate your score?

Frightful Words

To rouse you from your hebetude, let's take a moment to talk about fear.

   When fears are exaggerated or unnatural, they are known as phobias. *Phobia* (FOH-bee-uh) comes from the Greek *phobos*, fear, dread, horror, flight. As a combining form it can be joined with other elements to form a word meaning the fear, dread, or extreme dislike of something. The antonym of the combining form *-phobia* is *-philia* (FIL-ee-uh), from the Greek *philein*, to love. *Bibliophilia* is love of books; *bibliophobia* is fear or hatred of them.

   For whatever you fear, there is, or can be, a phobia. Common phobias include *claustrophobia* (KLAW-struh-**FOH**-bee-uh), fear of enclosed space, and *agoraphobia* (AG-uh-ruh-**FOH**-bee-uh), fear of open spaces, public places, or crowds. (*Agoraphobia* combines *-phobia*, fear, with *agora*, a marketplace or public square in ancient Greece.) You will recall that those fearful of strangers or foreigners, or of anything foreign or strange, suffer from *xenophobia* (word

19 of Level 9).

Xenophobia has a number of specific forms: *Francophobia* (FRANG-kuh-) and *Gallophobia* (GAL-uh-) mean fear of the French; *Germanophobia* (JUR-muh-nuh-) is fear of the Germans; *Japanophobia* (juh-PAN-uh-) is fear of the Japanese; *Grecophobia* (GREK-uh-) is fear of the Greeks; *Russophobia* (RUH-suh-) is fear of the Russians; and *Anglophobia* (ANG-gluh-) is fear of the English.

Among the many phobias with easily discernible meanings are *bacteriophobia* (bak-TEER-ee-uh-**FOH**-bee-uh, fear of germs); *demonophobia* (DEE-muh-noh-**FOH**-bee-uh, fear of demons); *pharmacophobia* (FAHR-muh-kuh-**FOH**-bee-uh, fear of medicine or drugs); *syphilophobia* (SIF-i̯-luh-**FOH**-bee-uh, fear of syphilis, or fear that one is infected with it); *pyrophobia* (PY-ruh-**FOH**-bee-uh, fear of fire); *zoophobia* (**ZOH**-uh-FOH-bee-uh, fear of animals); and *neophobia* (NEE-uh-**FOH**-bee-uh, fear of anything new).

More abstruse phobias include *aeronausiphobia* (AIR-uh-**NAW**-suh-), fear of airplanes (*aviatophobia*, AY-vee-**AT**-uh-, is fear of flying in them); *sitiophobia* (SIT-ee-uh-), fear or dread of food; *ablutophobia* (uh-BLOO-tuh-), fear of bathing; *sophophobia* (SAHF-uh-), fear of learning; *allodoxaphobia* (AL-uh-DAHK-suh-), fear of others' opinions; *thanatophobia* (THAN-uh-tuh-), fear of death, from the Greek *thanatos*, death; *ataxiophobia* (uh-TAK-see-uh-), fear of disorder; *dysmorphophobia* (dis-MOR-fuh-), fear of deformity or anything misshapen; and *dermatophobia* (DUR-muh-tuh-), fear of skin. Don't say "gimme skin" to a dermatophobe.

There are also plenty of thoroughly outrageous phobias. For example, phobiologists (FOH-bee-**AHL**-uh-jists—it's a real word) have identified *dustophobia* (DUHS-tuh-), also known as *rupophobia* (ROO-puh-), a dread of dirt; *dishabillophobia* (DIS-uh-BIL-uh-), fear of disrobing in front of someone (formed from *dishabille*, word 43 of Level 9); *philemaphobia* (fi-LEE-muh-), fear of kissing; and Dracula's hangup, *staurophobia* (STAW-ruh-), fear of crucifixes.

Then, of course, there's *pantophobia*, fear of everything.

I could go on forever with these frightful words (hyperbole!), but I'm afraid my time is up. (Oh, no. That's *chronophobia*, fear of time, pronounced KRAHN-uh-.) I shall leave you with the ultimate fear—*phobophobia*, the fear of those who have nothing to fear but fear itself.

Now let's move on to the next set of keyword discussions, beginning with the utterly unfearful . . .

Word 21: SANGUINE (SANG-gwin)

Confident, cheerful, hopeful, optimistic.

As you may recall from the discussion of *phlegmatic* (word 33 of Level 9), in ancient physiology there were four humors, or bodily fluids: blood, phlegm, choler (also called yellow bile), and melancholy (also called black bile). Early physicians believed that a person's health and disposition were determined by the relative proportions of these humors.

Sanguine originally meant having blood as the dominant humor in one's system; hence, having a ruddy, healthy complexion and a warm temperament. Eventually this sense evolved into the current meaning: confident, cheerfully optimistic.

Sanguine and *sanguinary* (**SANG**-gwi-NER-ee) are sometimes confused because of their common derivation, the Latin *sanguis*, blood. *Sanguinary* means either bloody, accompanied by bloodshed and slaughter, or blood-thirsty, eager for bloodshed. *Sanguine* either means blood-colored, ruddy, red, as a sanguine complexion, or, more often, filled with the uplifting humor of blood, and therefore confident, cheerful, optimistic.

Word 22: DEIPNOSOPHIST (dyp-NAHS-uh-fist)

An adept conversationalist, especially one who enjoys conversing at the table.

You'll need to check a hefty unabridged dictionary to find the unusual words *deipnosophist*, *deipnosophistic* (dyp-NAHS-uh-**FIS**-tik), and *deipnosophism* (dyp-**NAHS**-uh-FIZ-'m), which come from the Greek *deipnon*, a meal, and *sophistes*, a wise man. Like the word *symposium* (sim-POH-zee-um), which means literally a drinking party, and comes from the title of a Platonic dialogue, *deipnosophist* comes from the *Deipnosophistai* of the Greek writer Athenaeus (ATH-uh-**NEE**-us), in which he details the conversation of a group of learned men who are dining together. For your next symposium, whether you plan to cook a gourmet meal or have a potluck, try inviting a few deipnosophists to liven up the conversation.

I have known many deipnosophists, I am something of one myself, and in my book they fall into three categories: the preprandial (pree-PRAN-dee-ul) deipnosophists, who excel at conversation over cocktails before dinner; the postprandial (pohst-PRAN-dee-ul) deipnosophists, who hit their stride and wax eloquent after the plates have been cleared away; and the vulgar deipnosophists, who talk incessantly through the meal, usually with their mouths full.

Word 23: FRANGIBLE (FRAN-ji-buul)

Breakable, fragile, frail, delicate, easily damaged or destroyed.

Fragile applies to something so delicately constructed that it is easily broken. *Frangible* adds to this the idea of a susceptibility to being broken, even if the object in question is not inherently delicate. The solid steel of a car is frangible if struck by another car. The heart of a brave and sanguine person might be frangible in an especially sad and poignant situation. The unusual word *friable* (FRY-uh-buul) means easily crumbled, crushed, or pulverized. Dried herbs are friable, as are the stiff, yellowed pages of an old book.

Word 24: APODICTIC (AP-uh-**DIK**-tik)

Absolutely certain, necessarily true, proved or demonstrated beyond a shadow of a doubt.

Synonyms of *apodictic* include *incontestable*, *incontrovertible*, and *irrefragable* (i-REF-ruh-guh-buul).

Apodictic is chiefly a technical term used in logic of a judgment that asserts its own necessity. "Such judgments," cautions the *Century Dictionary*, "may be false." *Apodictic* is a lovely word, so much more forceful and decisive than certain or true, yet I wonder what in life honestly can be called *apodictic*, absolutely certain, necessarily true. Can you think of anything that is unarguably apodictic? Perhaps only death and taxes.

Word 25: FULMINATE (**FUHL**-mi-NAYT *or* **FUUL**-mi-NAYT)

To explode, especially to explode with invective and denunciations; to shout forth condemnation and censure.

The verb to *fulminate* and the corresponding noun *fulmination* come through the Latin *fulminare*, to strike with lightning, from *fulmen*, a stroke of lightning, thunderbolt. *Fulminate* was once used to mean to strike with lightning, but this sense is obsolete and in modern usage *fulminate* suggests the throwing of verbal thunderbolts, and *fulmination* suggests a thundering verbal explosion: "The speaker fulminated against corruption and vice"; "The dispute between the two nations has not reached the point of war, but there have been fulminations from both sides."

Word 26: SCARIFY (**SKAR**-i-fy)

To wound the feelings of; make cutting remarks about; distress by criticizing sharply.

Synonyms of *scarify* include *lacerate* (word 35 of Level 1), *flay*, *castigate*, *vituperate*, and *excoriate* (word 40 of Level 9). The corresponding noun is *scarification*.

The verbs to *scarify* and *scare* are similar in spelling and sound but they are entirely unrelated in derivation and meaning.

Scarify comes through Latin and Greek words meaning to scratch, ultimately from the Greek *skariphos*, a pencil or stylus. In modern usage, *scarify* has three senses, the first two literal and the third figurative. *Scarify* is used in medicine to mean to make a series of shallow cuts or punctures in the skin; certain vaccinations are administered by scarification. *Scarify* is also used in agriculture to mean to cut into the ground, loosen or break up the soil either to aerate it or in preparation for planting. Out of these literal senses, which suggest scratching and scraping, *scarify* came to be used figuratively to mean to scratch with words; hence, to wound the feelings of, make cutting remarks about, distress by criticizing sharply.

Word 27: HEBDOMADAL (heb-DAHM-uh-dul)

Weekly; pertaining to a week or seven-day period.

The adjective *hebdomadal*, and the corresponding noun *hebdomad* (**HEB**-duh-MAD) come from the Latin and Greek words for the number seven. The noun *hebdomad* may mean a group of seven; for example, a seven-member commission or board is a hebdomad. *Hebdomad* may also mean a seven-day period, a week. The adjective *hebdomadal* means weekly: hebdomadal duties are weekly duties; a hebdomadal occasion is an occasion that occurs once a week.

Word 28: DIVAGATE (DY-vuh-GAYT)

To wander, ramble, or drift about; hence, to digress.

The verb to *divagate* and the corresponding noun *divagation* (DY-vuh-**GAY**-shin) come from the Latin *divagari*, to wander about, which comes in turn from *dis-*, meaning "apart," and *vagari*, to wander, ramble, roam. In modern usage, *divagate* is a grandiloquent synonym for wander or digress, and *divagation* is a loftier word for a digression or the act of wandering or rambling. You may divagate literally, as to spend a summer divagating across the country. Or you may divagate figuratively: "Leroy dreaded his eighty-year-old mother's hebdomadal phone call, because she would jabber and scold and divagate for an hour."

Word 29: IATROGENIC (eye-A-truh-JEN-ik)

Caused by medical examination or treatment.

Pathological, which means pertaining to or caused by disease, is the antonym of *iatrogenic*.

The word *iatric* (eye-A-trik) means pertaining to medicine or medical doctors. The combining form *iatro-* comes from the Greek *iatros*, a physician; in English *iatro-* means "medical" or "medicine." The combining form *-genic* means "producing" or "generating." By derivation, that which is iatrogenic is produced by a medical doctor or generated by medical treatment.

Iatrogenic is used of ailments, maladies, or symptoms caused by medical treatment, especially one caused by a drug or surgery. An iatrogenic disorder may be cause for a malpractice suit against the doctor whose treatment induced it.

Word 30: TERGIVERSATION (TUR-ji-vur-SAY-shin)

Desertion; specifically, the act of deserting something to which one was previously loyal, such as a cause, a party, or a religious faith.

Synonyms of *tergiversation* include *abandonment* and *defection*.

The noun *tergiversation* and the corresponding verb *tergiversate* (**TUR**-ji-vur-SAYT) come from a Latin word meaning "to turn one's back." When you tergiversate, you turn your back on something to which you were previously loyal and become a deserter or a renegade. When *tergiversate* denotes the desertion of a religious faith or creed, it is synonymous with *apostatize* (uh-**PAHS**-tuh-TYZ). *Tergiversation* means the act of desertion, and the word usually applies to the abandonment of a cause, a party, or a religion.

These words may also be used figuratively of language that is shifty and evasive, that does not take a firm stand. In this sense, *tergiversate* is a synonym of *equivocate*, which means to speak in a subtle and evasive manner; and the noun *tergiversation* is a synonym of *equivocation*, which means a shifty or evasive statement, language that does not come straight to the point or take a firm stand.

Let's review the ten keywords you've just learned. I'll give you two words, and you decide if they are synonyms or antonyms. Answers appear on page 442.

1. *Saturnine* and *sanguine* are . . . synonyms or antonyms?
2. *Conversationalist* and *deipnosophist* are . . .
3. *Indestructible* and *frangible* are . . .
4. *Doubtful* and *apodictic* are . . .
5. To *whisper* and to *fulminate* are . . .
6. To *lacerate* and to *scarify* are . . .
7. *Quotidian* and *hebdomadal* are . . .
8. To *digress* and to *divagate* are . . .
9. *Iatrogenic* and *pathological* are . . .
10. *Loyalty* and *tergiversation* are . . .

Go Figure

Are you a number-cruncher? No, I don't mean an accountant or a computer. I mean a person who abuses the word *number* by not observing the proper distinction between the words *number* and *amount*.

Would you say "the *amount* of people at the party" or "the *number* of people at the party"? Would you say "the *amount* of things I have to do today" or "the *number* of things I have to do today"? If you chose *number*, then you've called the right *number* this time. If you chose *amount*, you won't amount to much unless you follow my advice.

Number refers to things that can be counted, itemized, or enumerated; in other words, considered separately or individually. We speak of the number of people at an event, a number of things to do, a number of problems to solve, the number of grocery items in a bag, the number of papers on your desk, or the number of volts in an electric current.

Amount refers to things that are considered collectively, in other words, as a mass or whole. We speak of the amount of sugar in a recipe, the amount of trouble we are having, the amount of food we buy at the store, the amount of paper on your desk.

The word *number* gives educated speakers and writers trouble in one other way; namely, when you hook it to a plural noun, should you use a singular or a plural verb? Here's a quiz to test your *number* literacy:

- Would you say a number of boxes *was* sent or a number of boxes *were* sent?
- Would you say the number of boxes *are* small or the number of boxes *is* small?

- Would you say a low number of crimes *was* committed or a low number of crimes *were* committed?
- Would you say the number of tasks on my to-do list *are* small or the number of tasks on my to-do list *is* small?

If you chose the second sentence in each case, your *number* literacy is excellent. Here's the rule for using *number* with singular and plural verbs: When *number* is preceded by the indefinite article *a*, as *a* number, the construction is plural and requires a plural verb: *a* number of things *were* done; *a* number of people *are* here; *a* number of new employees *have* joined the health club (not *has joined*).

Now, when *number* is preceded by the definite article *the*, as *the* number, the construction is singular and requires a singular verb: *the* number of things left to do *is* overwhelming; *the* number of people in attendance *is* fifty; *the* number of members in the organization *has* decreased (not *have decreased*).

Remember, *a number* is always plural; *the number* is always singular.

Word 31: NACREOUS (NAY-kree-us)

Pearly, consisting of or resembling mother-of-pearl.

Synonyms of *nacreous* include *iridescent* (IR-i-**DES**-int), which means having or displaying lustrous, rainbowlike colors, and the unusual word *margaritaceous* (MAHR-guh-ri-**TAY**-shus).

Random House Webster's College Dictionary (1999) defines *mother-of-pearl* as "a hard, iridescent substance that forms the inner layer of certain mollusk shells, used for making buttons, beads, etc." *Mother-of-pearl* also goes by the name *nacre* (NAY-kur). The adjective corresponding to the noun *nacre* is *nacreous*, pearly, made of or resembling mother-of-pearl.

Word 32: FAINEANT (FAY-nee-int)

Lazy, idle, sluggish, good-for-nothing: "When her thirty-year-old son refused to get a job and demanded more money as an allowance, Mrs. Jones decided that enough was enough and it was time to kick her faineant offspring out of the house."

Common synonyms of *faineant* include *do-nothing*, *shiftless*, *slothful*, and *lackadaisical*, which is often mispronounced LAKS-adaisical. There is no *lax* in *lackadaisical* (LAK-uh-**DAY**-zi-kuul).

More challenging synonyms of *faineant* include *lethargic*, *indolent*, *somnolent*, *torpid*, *otiose* (**OH**-shee-OHS), and also *hebetudinous* (HEB-uh-**T(Y)OO**-di-nus), the adjective corresponding to the noun *hebetude* (**HEB**-i-T(Y)OOD), word 20 of this level.

Faineant comes from a French phrase meaning "to do nothing." *Faineant* may be used as an adjective to mean lazy, good-for-nothing, or as a noun to mean a lazy person, an idler, sluggard. The corresponding noun is *faineance* (FAY-nee-ints). *Faineance* means idleness, inactivity, indolence, or the lazy, do-nothing attitude of a faineant person.

If you look up *faineant* in a current dictionary, you may find it spelled with an accent, fainéant, and find the French pronunciation, fay-nay-AH(N), listed first or even listed alone. Frankly, I find that perplexing, because two of the twentieth-century's most respected arbiters on pronunciation, the second edition of *Webster's New International Dictionary*, published in 1934, and Kenyon and Knott's *Pronouncing Dictionary of American English*, published in 1949, both prefer the pronunciation FAY-nee-int.

Faineant entered English in the early 1600s. After nearly four hundred years, it's expected and sensible to anglicize a word, make it conform to English custom. And when an anglicized pronunciation has existed in educated speech for a half-century or more, it doesn't make sense to retain or revive the foreign pronunciation. It's one thing to use a twenty-dollar word in conversation; it's quite another thing to use it with a pretentious (and especially a Frenchified) pronunciation. *Faineant* and *faineance* have earned their place in the language and they cry out for full anglicization. It's high time we spelled them without an accent and pronounced them as assimilated English words.

Word 33: HISPID (HIS-pid)

Covered with stiff hairs, bristles, or small spines; rough and bristly.

Hispid and *hirsute* (HUR-s(y)oot) are close in meaning.

Hispid comes from the Latin *hispidus*, rough, hairy, bristly. Although the *Oxford English Dictionary* contains one figurative citation that refers to "a hispid law," *hispid* is used chiefly in a literal sense of leaves, plants, insects, animals, and occasionally human beings and inanimate objects to mean covered with rough, stiff hairs or bristles. The nettle, with its small, stinging spines, is a hispid plant; although the spines of the porcupine are relatively large, the animal can fairly be described as hispid.

Hirsute comes from the Latin *hirsutus*, covered with hair, rough, shaggy. In botany and zoology, *hirsute* and *hispid* are synonymous. In general usage, however, *hirsute* means extremely hairy or covered with hair: "Abigail told Angela that she did not care for hirsute men."

Word 34: LONGANIMITY (LAHNG-guh-**NIM**-i̱-tee)

Long-suffering patience; the ability to calmly endure hardship or suffering.

Longanimity and *forbearance* are synonyms.

Longanimity comes ultimately from the Latin *longus*, meaning "long," and *animus*, spirit, mind. By derivation, a person who displays longanimity has the strength of spirit and mind to endure hardship or suffering for a long, long time.

Word 35: SCIOLIST (SY-uh-list)

A person who has only superficial knowledge of a subject, or who pretends to have knowledge.

Sciolist and the corresponding noun *sciolism* (SY-uh-liz-'m) come through a Latin word meaning "a smatterer," and ultimately from the Latin *scire*, to know. By derivation, and in modern usage, a *sciolist* is a person who has only a smattering of knowledge, and *sciolism* means superficial or pretended knowledge.

Sciolist may also apply to people who pretend to be more knowledgeable or learned than they are, or who make a pretentious display of what little they know. As the saying goes, "A little learning is a dangerous thing." The sciolist is a person you want to either avoid or watch carefully, because a small mind containing only a smattering of knowledge is likely to think mean, small-minded thoughts.

Word 36: PROPINQUITY (proh- *or* pruh-PING-kwi̱-tee)

Nearness in place or time, proximity (word 50 of Level 1); also, nearness or similarity in nature, kinship, close relation.

In Latin, *propinquitas* means either nearness, proximity, or friendship, relationship. From this Latin word comes the English adjective *propinquity*, which is used to mean either nearness in place or time, or nearness of blood or nature.

According to the second edition of *Webster's New International Dictionary*

(1934), *proximity* "denotes simple nearness," as the proximity of their houses, or living in proximity to downtown. *Propinquity* "connotes close neighborhood" and "personal vicinity," as the propinquity of marriage, the propinquity of brothers and sisters, the propinquity of vice on the mean streets of the big city, or the hebdomadal propinquity of Christmas and New Year's Day. (Remember *hebdomadal*, word 27 of this level? It means weekly or pertaining to a week.)

Word 37: FACTITIOUS (fak-TISH-u̱s)

Not natural or genuine, produced artificially.

Synonyms of *factitious* include *sham*, *contrived*, *bogus*, *fraudulent*, and *spurious* (word 18 of Level 8).

Factitious comes through the Latin *facticius*, made by art, artificial, from the verb *facere*, to make. A factitious word is not genuine; it has been made up. A factitious need is artificially produced. A factitious smile is unnatural and manufactured for the occasion. And when something has factitious value, its value is not genuine or intrinsic but has been artificially created or imposed.

According to the *Century Dictionary* (1914), "an *artificial* or *factitious* demand in the market is one that is manufactured, the [factitious demand] being the more laboriously worked up; a factitious demand exists only in the invention of one and the imagination of another."

Word 38: PLEXIFORM (**PLEK**-si̱-FORM)

In general, complicated or elaborate; specifically, like a plexus or network.

According to *Random House Webster's College Dictionary* (1999), the noun *plexus* (PLEK-su̱s) means "a network" or "any complex structure containing an intricate network of parts," as "the plexus of international relations." In medicine, *plexus* is used to describe various networks of nerves and blood vessels.

Plexus comes from the Latin *plectere*, to braid, intertwine, interweave. The adjective *plexiform* combines *plexus* and the suffix *-form* to mean formed like a plexus or network. *Plexiform* may be used in this sense, as the plexiform nature of computer bulletin boards and online services. However, outside the fields of medicine and science, *plexiform* probably is more often used in a more general sense to mean having the qualities of a complex network, and therefore extremely complicated or elaborate. We speak of the plexiform nature of human relationships; a plexiform bureaucracy; plexiform negotiations; the plex-

iform operations of a multinational corporation; or the plexiform financial structure of Wall Street.

Word 39: SUSURRUS (suu-SUR-us)

A soft, subdued sound; a whispering, murmuring, muttering, or rustling sound.

A *susurrus* and a *susurration* (SOO-suh-**RAY**-shin) are the same thing.
The corresponding verb is *susurrate* (suu-SUR-ayt), to whisper, murmur; and
the adjective is *susurrant* (suu-SUR-ant), softly whispering, rustling, or murmuring. All of these soft-sounding words come from the Latin *susurrare*, to
whisper, murmer, mutter.

A *susurrus* or a *susurration*—pick the soft-sounding word you prefer—can
apply to many things, because so many things create a whispering, murmuring, muttering, or rustling sound. Here are three possible applications: the
susurrus in the library; the sussuration of the trees; as the lights dimmed and
the curtain rose, a susurrus passed through the audience and then died away.

Word 40: TRITURATE (TRICH-uh-RAYT)

To grind, crush, or pound into fine particles or powder.

Synonyms of *triturate* include *pulverize, comminute* (**KAHM**-i-N(Y)OOT),
and *levigate* (**LEV**-i-GAYT).

To *pulverize* and to *triturate* are virtually interchangeable; both words suggest reducing something to fine particles or powder. *Pulverize* comes from the
Latin *pulvis*, dust, and by derivation suggests reducing something to dust.
Triturate comes from a Latin word meaning to thresh grain or tread out corn,
and by derivation suggests a violent beating, bruising, pounding, crushing, rubbing, or grinding action. When used figuratively, *pulverize* is the more violent
word, and means to destroy or demolish completely, as to pulverize an opponent. Used figuratively, *triturate* suggests either a grinding or crushing into small
pieces or a wearing down to nothing by friction: "Her job was triturating all her
creative abilities"; "He triturated his financial assets until he was bankrupt."

The corresponding noun is *trituration* (TRICH-uh-**RAY**-shin).

Let's review the ten keywords you've just learned. I'll give you the review word
(in *italics*) followed by three words or phrases, and you decide which one of
those three words or phrases comes nearest the meaning of the review word.

Answers appear on page 443.

1. *Nacreous* means grimy, pearly, iridescent.
2. *Faineant* means lazy, uncooperative, idle.
3. *Hispid* means bristly, hairy, bumpy.
4. *Longanimity* means patience, endurance, long life.
5. A *sciolist* is a person with superficial knowledge, a person without knowledge, a person who pretends to have knowledge.
6. *Propinquity* means propriety, proximity, nearness.
7. *Factitious* means not natural, not original, produced artificially.
8. *Plexiform* means widespread, complicated, elaborate.
9. A *susurrus* is a whispering sound, a murmuring sound, a bubbling sound.
10. To *triturate* means to grind up, make a mess of, crush into fine particles.

If this review quiz pulverized you, review the last ten keyword discussions. If you answered at least eight questions correctly, read on.

Sizable Words

Some of us are lovers of the long word. We thrill at the sight and sound of the odd, the overblown, and the obscure. Like birdwatchers or butterfly collectors who traverse mountains, penetrate jungles, or trudge through swamps for a glimpse of some rare species, we slog through the daily mire of language hoping to lay eyes on a lexicographic dinosaur or linguistic Loch Ness monster. To us, the short, straightforward words we have been force-fed and made to regurgitate are like so many indistinguishable ants in an endless and tiresome trail of sentences.

If you are a secret or not-so-secret lover of the long word, then perhaps you already know that the long word for long words is *sesquipedalian* (SES-kwi-pi-**DAY**-lee-in). It comes from the Roman poet Horace's phrase *sesquipedalia verba*, which means literally "words a foot and a half long." *Sesquipedalian* may also refer to anything a foot and a half long, such as a sesquipedalian hot dog.

If you enjoy munching on a foot-and-a-half-long word from time to time, here is a smorgasbord of sesquipedalian monsters that should provide enough verbal nutrition to last you for months. I invite you to try them out for size.

From the Fancy Words for Simple Ideas Department come *muliebriety* (MYOO-lee-uh-**BRY**-i-tee), which means femininity, womanhood; *obnubila-*

tion (ahb-N(Y)OO-bi-**LAY**-shin), clouding over, obscuring; *sarculation* (SAHR-kyuu-**LAY**-shin), weeding with a hoe; *immorigerous* (IM-uh-**RIJ**-uh-rus), rude, uncivil, disobedient; and *vivisepulture* (VIV-i-**SEP**-ul-chur), the act of burying someone alive. One of my favorites in this foot-and-a-half-long category is *chryselephantine* (KRIS-el-uh-**FAN**-tin or -teen), which means made of gold and ivory.

From the Utterly Outrageous Department come *bruxomania* (BRUHK-suh-**MAY**-nee-uh), the habit of grinding the teeth, especially in sleep or under stress; *philopatridomania* (FIL-uh-PA-tri-doh-**MAY**-nee-uh), a fanatic case of homesickness; *azygophrenia* (uh-ZY-guh-**FREE**-nee-uh), the psychoneurosis of single life; *uxorodespotism* (uk-SOR-oh-**DES**-puh-tiz-'m), wifely tyranny; *borborygmus* (BOR-buh-**RIG**-mus), the sound of gas passing through the intestines, a gurgling in your gut; *cacophonophilist* (KAK-uh-fuh-**NAHF**-uh-list), a lover of harsh sounds; *sacerdotophrenia* (SAS-ur-DOH-tuh-**FREE**-nee-uh), clerical stage fright, fear of the pulpit, the mere thought of which is enough to make any preacher *horripilate* (hah- or haw-**RIP**-i-LAYT), get goosebumps; and finally, if you are mathematically challenged you can chew on the redoubtable word *zenzizenzizenzic* (ZEN-zi-ZEN-zi-**ZEN**-zik), which means the eighth power of a number.

Perhaps by now you're wondering just how long can you get? Well, pretty doggone long. I'm not going to give you what some say is the longest word in the language—it's an esoteric chemical term that has 1,185 letters and would take almost a minute to pronounce. I will leave you, however, with three of the longest pronounceable words around.

The rare and fascinating word *bathysiderodromophobia* (BATH-ee-SID-ur-oh-DROH-muh-**FOH**-bee-uh) is formed from the Greek *bathy*, meaning "deep," *sidero*, meaning "iron," *dromo*, meaning "a course or track," and *phobia*, which means "fear." By derivation, *bathysiderodromophobia* means "fear of a deep iron course or track"; hence, fear of subways or underground trains.

The risible word *floccinaucinihilipilification* (FLAHK-si-NAW-si-NY-hil-i-PIL-i-fi-**KAY**-shin), which has twenty-nine letters, means the act of categorizing something as trivial or worthless. In his delightful book *Crazy English* (1989), Richard Lederer notes that *floccinaucinihilipilification* "dates back to 1741 and is the longest word in the *Oxford English Dictionary*."

Weighing in at thirty letters is the heavyweight word *hippopotomonstrosesquipedalian* (HIP-uh-PAH-toh-MAHN-stroh-SES-kwi-pi-**DAY**-lee-in), which, appropriately enough, means pertaining to an extremely long word.

Writing down wonderfully worthless words like *bathysiderodromophobia*, *floccinaucinihilipilification,* and *hippopotomonstrosesquipedalian* can give you a bad case of *graphospasm* (**GRAF**-uh-SPAZ-'m), which is the technical term for writer's cramp.

I hope all those big words haven't knocked the wind out of you, but if they have, here's a breath of fresh air: All you have to do is learn ten more keywords and you will have completed the *Verbal Advantage* program and earned an honorary degree in grandiloquence. So rouse yourself now from your hebetude and get ready for the final leg of Level 10.

Word 41: PROTEAN (PROH-tee-in)

Highly variable or changeable; readily assuming different shapes, forms, characters, or meanings.

The adjective *protean* is an eponymous word, a word derived from a name. It comes from *Proteus* (PROH-tee-us), the name of a sea god in ancient Greek mythology who could change his shape at will. That which is *protean* is changeable like Proteus, able to quickly take on different shapes, forms, characters, or meanings. A master of disguise is protean, taking on the appearance of different characters; words can sometimes be protean, taking on different meanings; dreams are often protean, assuming different forms; a person's career can be protean, full of changes; and in my house at least, leftovers are decidedly protean, readily assuming different shapes or forms.

Word 42: CREPITATE (KREP-i-TAYT)

To crackle; make a crackling, snapping, or popping noise.

The verb to *crepitate* comes from the Latin *crepitare*, to crackle, creak, rattle, or clatter. From the same source we inherit the word *decrepit* (di-KREP-it), which by derivation means having bones that creak and rattle from old age, and also the unusual word *crepitaculum* (KREP-i-**TAK**-yuh-lum), the rattle or rattling organ of the rattlesnake.

To *crepitate* means to do what the ads tell us the cereal does: snap, crackle, and pop. The corresponding adjective is *crepitant* (KREP-i-tint), crackling or creaking, as the crepitant stairs of an old house. The corresponding noun is *crepitation* (KREP-i-**TAY**-shin), as the crepitations of firecrackers on the Fourth of July. In medicine, a crepitation is the grating sound or sensation produced by rubbing together the fractured ends of a broken bone.

Ouch! Let's leave that painful image behind and move quickly on to . . .

Word 43: NOCTIVAGANT (nahk-TIV-uh-gint)

Wandering at night.

Noctivagant comes from the Latin *noctivagus*, wandering by night, which comes in turn from *nox*, meaning "night," and *vagari*, to wander about. This Latin *vagari* is also the source of the English adjective *vague*, literally "wandering in thought," *vagabond*, a wanderer, and *vagary* (traditionally vuh-GAIR-ee, now usually VAY-guh-ree). A *vagary* is an odd, whimsical idea or an unpredictable, capricious action or event, as the vagaries of the stock market.

Our keyword, the adjective *noctivagant*, means wandering in the night. Burglars, streetwalkers, and barhoppers are all noctivagant, but I'm sure you can come up with more pertinent applications for this rare but useful word.

The corresponding noun is *noctivagation* (nahk-TIV-uh-**GAY**-shin), the act of wandering in the night.

Word 44: FULIGINOUS (fyoo-LIJ-i-nus)

Sooty, smoky; pertaining to, resembling, or consisting of soot or smoke.

Fuliginous comes from the Latin *fuligo*, soot. The word entered English in the 1600s and since then has been used both literally to mean sooty or smoky and figuratively to mean dark, dusky, or obscure. Fuliginous air is filled with soot or smog. When you clean the windows of your car, you wash off the fuliginous grime. A fuliginous bar is a dark and smoky bar. Fuliginous ideas or thoughts are darkened as if by soot, and therefore are muddled and obscure.

Word 45: HORTATORY (**HOR**-tuh-TOR-ee)

Encouraging or urging to some course of action; giving earnest counsel or advice.

The verb to *exhort*, the noun *exhortation*, and the adjective *hortatory* all come from the Latin *hortari,* to encourage, incite.

To *exhort* (ig-ZORT) means to urge or advise earnestly to do what is deemed right or proper, as public service announcements that exhort people not to drink and drive.

An *exhortation* (EG-zor-**TAY**-shin) is a statement that exhorts, or, as *Webster's New International Dictionary*, second edition (1934), puts it, "language intended to incite and encourage." Adolph Hitler's racist and chauvinistic exhortations led the German people into World War II.

The adjective *hortatory* means characterized by exhortations. A hortatory speech or sermon encourages or urges the audience to some course of action. A hortatory disquisition gives earnest counsel or advice.

Word 46: HELIOLATRY (HEE-lee-**AHL**-uh-tree)

Worship of the sun.

The combining form *helio-* comes from the Greek *helios*, the sun, and is used in English words to mean the sun. For example, *heliotherapy* (HEE-lee-oh-**THER**-uh-pee) is a form of medical treatment involving exposure to sunlight. In astronomy, *heliocentric* (HEE-lee-oh-**SEN**-trik) means regarding the sun as the center of our planetary system, as opposed to *geocentric* (JEE-oh-**SEN**-trik), which refers to the pre-Copernican notion that the Sun revolves around the earth.

The fascinating word *heliotropism* (HEE-lee-**AH**-truh-piz'm) is formed from *helio-*, the sun, and the Greek *tropos*, a turning. *Heliotropism* refers to the tendency of plants to bend or move toward—or in some cases, away from—a source of light.

Our keyword, *heliolatry*, combines *helio-*, the sun, with the Greek *latreia*, meaning "worship." the corresponding noun is *heliolater* (HEE-lee-**AHL**-uh-tur), a sun worshiper, and the corresponding adjective is *heliolatrous* (HEE-lee-**AHL**-uh-trus), sun-worshiping.

Word 47: SCIAMACHY (sy-**AM**-uh-kee)

Shadow-boxing; the act of fighting a shadow or an imaginary enemy.

Sciamachy comes from the Greek *skia*, a shadow, and *mache*, a battle, contest, struggle. This Greek *mache* is the source of the English combining form *-machy*, which, when tacked on to a word, denotes a battle, contest, or struggle. *Theomachy* (thee-AHM-uh-kee) is a battle against or between gods; *gigantomachy* (JY-gan-**TAHM**-uh-kee) is a war or battle between giants or superhuman beings; *logomachy* (luh-GAHM-uh-kee), from the Greek *logos*, meaning "word," is a battle of words; and our keyword, *sciamachy*, is a battle with a shadow, a contest with an imaginary enemy.

Word 48: GLABROUS (GLAB-rus)

Smooth and bald.

Glabrous comes from the Latin *glaber*, without hair, bald, and is used chiefly in biology of something that has a smooth surface without hair, down, fuzz, or other projections. In my humble opinion, a refined word meaning "smooth and bald" has the potential for many applications outside the realm of science. I offer two examples to point you in the right direction: "The amazing Michael Jordan's glabrous head," and "The glabrous bodies of maidens in bikinis practicing heliolatry on the beach."

Word 49: PETTIFOGGER (PET-ee-FAHG-ur)

A mean, tricky lawyer; especially, a lawyer who handles petty cases in an unethical, unscrupulous way.

Pettifogger is synonymous with the more familiar word *shyster* (SHYS-tur). The proverbial ambulance-chaser is also a breed of pettifogger.

The corresponding verb to *pettifog* (**PET**-ee-FAHG) means to carry on a law practice in a petty, tricky, unscrupulous way; by extension, it has also come to mean to engage in chicanery (shi-KAY-nur-ee) or unethical practices in a business of any sort. The noun *pettifoggery* means the unethical, unscrupulous practices of a pettifogger, legal tricks or chicanery.

Word 50: EPICENE (EP-i-SEEN)

Having characteristics or qualities of both sexes.

Epicene comes through Middle English and Latin from a Greek word meaning "in common." By derivation, that which is *epicene* has characteristics in common with both sexes. Many paintings and sculptures, both classical and modern, depict epicene figures.

Because something that displays characteristics of both sexes is, by all rights, not a member of one sex or the other, *epicene* has come to mean not having the characteristics or qualities of either sex, sexless, neuter, as an epicene hairstyle or epicene clothing. And because something sexless lacks sex appeal, *epicene* is also sometimes used disparagingly of style to mean lacking appeal or potency, feeble, flaccid, as an epicene novel or epicene architecture. Finally, when applied to a man—or at least to someone presumed to be a man biologically—*epicene* is always used disparagingly to mean not virile, effeminate.

Hermaphroditic and *epicene* both suggest having characteristics of both sexes, but in different ways.

Hermaphroditic (hur-MAF-ruh-**DIT**-ik) is the adjective corresponding to the noun *hermaphrodite* (hur-MAF-ruh-dyt). *Hermaphrodite* is an eponymous word; it comes from the name *Hermaphroditus* (hur-MAF-ruh-**DY**-tus). In Greek mythology, Hermaphroditus was the son of Hermes (HUR-meez), the messenger of the gods, and Aphrodite (AF-ruh-**DY**-tee), the goddess of love and beauty. While bathing one day, Hermaphroditus was the victim of a contretemps that united him in one body with a water nymph named Salmacis (SAL-muh-sis). In modern usage, a hermaphrodite is a person who has the reproductive organs of both sexes.

Epicene does not usually suggest having both male and female reproductive organs but rather having a range of characteristics of both sexes, emotional as well as physical. *Epicene* may also be used as a noun to mean an epicene person, someone who has characteristics or qualities of both sexes.

Let's review the ten keywords you've just learned. This time I'll give you the review word (in *italics*) followed by three words or phrases, and you decide which one of those three words or phrases comes nearest the meaning of the review word. Answers appear on page 444.

1. Does something *protean* have a powerful influence, assume different shapes or forms, or have indistinct features?
2. Does *crepitate* mean to tremble, to crackle, or to beg?
3. Does a *noctivagant* person wander about on foot, wander about in the night, or wander about while asleep?
4. When something is *fuliginous*, is it wicked, smelly, or sooty?
5. Is a *hortatory* speech encouraging, amusing, or angry?
6. Is *heliolatry* the worship of false gods, worship of celebrities, or worship of the sun?
7. Does *sciamachy* mean a mortal combat, shadow-boxing, or talking to oneself?
8. Is something *glabrous* smooth and bald, rough and bumpy, or soft and lustrous?
9. Is a *pettifogger* an incompetent doctor; a foolish old person; or a mean, tricky lawyer?
10. Does *epicene* mean having deep wisdom, having characteristics of both sexes, or having a delicate, refined sensibility?

Remember to review this entire level at least once before moving on with your life. And while you're at it, why not reread the whole book?

Some Final Pronouncements

Let's finish off the program with a final farrago of fulminations on pronunciation.

I must issue a special reminder here to be on the qui vive regarding the word *nuclear*. Don't say NOO-kyuh-lur, as if the word were spelled *nucular*. I can't tell you how often I hear people vilify this pronunciation (which does not reflect well on the people who use it). It is probably the most recognized and abominated beastly mispronunciation in the language. Don't undermine your newly acquired verbal advantage by mispronouncing *nuclear*. To get it right, think of *nuclear* as a combination of *new* and *clear*: NOO-klee-ur (NYOO- for the first syllable is even more cultivated).

I'm going to run through the rest of the list quickly, so keep your eyes open and prepare your memory banks for rapid assimilation.

Schizophrenia is properly pronounced SKIT-suh-**FREE**-nee-uh, not SKIT-suh-**FREN**-ee-uh.

The accent properly should be on the first syllable in the words *exquisite* (EK-skwi-zit) and *hospitable* (HAHS-pit-uh-buul).

Weather prognosticators who tell us about the *atmos*-FEER-*ic* conditions properly should tell us about the *atmos*-FER-*ic* conditions. The accented syllable should sound like *fer*- in *ferry*, not like *fear*.

How do you pronounce *prelude*? Don't say PRAY-lood; that's a vogue pronunciation. The preferred pronunciation is PREL-yood.

For *envelope* and *envoy* the pronunciations AHN-vuh-lohp and AHN-voy are pseudo-French; these words are thoroughly English and should be pronounced EN-vuh-lohp and EN-voy.

Don't pronounce the *h* in *vehicle* and *herb*, and don't put a *zoo*- in the beginning of *zoology* and *zoologist*, as so many speakers erroneously do. For these *zoo*- pronunciations to make sense, the words would have to have three o's: *zoo-ology*, *zoo-ologist*. The prefix, however, is *zo*-, pronounced zoh- to rhyme with *go*. Say zoh-AHL-uh-jee and zoh-AHL-uh-jist.

Also, don't pronounce the *extra* in *extraordinary*; the word has five syllables, not six: ek-**STROR**-di-ner-ee.

Be sure to clearly pronounce the *h* in *huge* and *human*. Say HYOOJ and HYOO-mun, not YOOJ and YOO-mun.

For the abbreviation *etc.*, take your time and say et-SET-uh-ruh (four clear syllables). It's uncultivated to say et-SE-truh, and it's downright beastly to pronounce *et* like *ek* and say ek-SET-uh-ruh or ek-SE-truh.

You know the eating disorder many people call buh-LEE-mee-uh? Well, guess what? The proper pronunciation of *bulimia* is byoo-LIM-ee-uh. This medical term entered the language in the fourteenth century, and until the 1980s byoo-LIM-ee-uh was the only pronunciation recognized by dictionaries.

It may be disconcerting at first to be the only one in the neighborhood who says byoo-LIM-ee-uh, but you'll get used to it. You will also be right.

What you probably have heard called a SKIZ-'m (for *schism*) is in fact a SIZ-'m. Believe it or not, since the 1700s authorities have preferred SIZ-'m, and it is the first and sometimes the only pronunciation listed in current dictionaries.

Last but not least, how do you pronounce the name of the *Visa* credit card? Do you say VEE-zuh or VEE-suh? The latter pronunciation, with a hard *s* as in *vista*, is incorrect. *Visa* comes directly from French, where a single *s* between vowels is soft, as in *rose*. Traditionally and properly, the *s* in *visa* is soft as in *visor*, *visit*, and *visible*. Say VEE-zuh.

And now, accolades are in order. I want to congratulate you for choosing a challenging vocabulary-building program and sticking with it.

Consider this: In the few pleasant hours you have spent reading this book, you have approximately tripled your normal vocabulary growth rate and learned more about the language than many people do in a lifetime. You have an impressive set of verbal tools now, and I have shown you how to use them. But don't stop now. When it comes to language, there is always room for improvement. I exhort you to review the portions of the program that you found most interesting or difficult, and also to read more, read widely, and make good use of your dictionary.

Remember: With a minimum of effort you can continue to expand the boundary of your vocabulary for the rest of your life, and your diligent study of words will help open the doors to knowledge and success.

I also would like to thank you for accompanying me all the way through this graduated tour of the English language. If you enjoyed *Verbal Advantage* and feel you benefited from it, why not share this book with a friend, relative, or coworker? Now that you're so verbally advantaged, you'll need to find a few people with whom you can deipnosophize grandiloquently and engage in floccinaucinihilipilification. (Say it three times and it's yours!)

By the way, don't forget to take the posttest. When you compare your score on the posttest with your score on the pretest, you will have a reasonable measure of your verbal progress. I think you'll be astonished and delighted when you see how much muscle you have added to your vocabulary.

Now, my friend, it's time for me to say farewell. I've enjoyed being your guide through the glories of the English language, and I hope you've enjoyed the tour.

As the poet and word lover John Ciardi used to say, "Good words to you."

Answers to Review Quizzes for Level 10

Keywords 1–10

1. Yes. *Jejune* means dull, uninteresting, or unsatisfying; devoid of nourishment, substance, or significance.
2. Yes. A *paucity* is an insufficiency, scarcity, especially a serious or extreme one, a dire lack.
3. No, I don't think you would. *Minatory* means threatening, menacing; having a threatening or menacing aspect or nature.
4. Yes. *Putative* means supposed, reputed; commonly considered or regarded as such; deemed to be so but not proved.
5. No. *Lucubration* means nocturnal labor; study, writing, or work done late at night.
6. No. To answer yes, you'd have to be a troglodyte yourself. A *troglodyte* is a cave dweller; also, a person who lives or behaves in a primitive manner, or who lives in seclusion.
7. No. *Aleatory* means depending on luck, chance, or on some contingent event; hence, uncertain, unpredictable.
8. Yes. A *farrago* is a mixture, especially a confused or jumbled mixture.
9. No. A *cynosure* is a center of attention or interest, focal point.
10. Yes, they often do. *Badinage* means banter; playful, teasing talk; good-natured joking or gently mocking conversation.

Keywords 11–20

1. True. *Hieratic* means priestly; pertaining to or used by priests; reserved for holy or sacred uses.
2. False. *Saturnine* means gloomy, sullen, or somber in appearance, manner, or temperament.
3. False. To *execrate* means to denounce vehemently, declare hateful or detestable; also, to loathe, abhor, detest utterly.
4. True. To *vitiate* means to corrupt, spoil, ruin, contaminate, impair the quality of, make faulty or impure; also, to weaken morally, defile, debase.
5. False. *Venial* means excusable, forgivable, pardonable, able to be overlooked.
6. False. A risible statement is amusing, laughable. *Risible* means provoking or capable of provoking laughter.
7. True. To *lionize* means to treat a person as a celebrity or as an object of great interest or importance.
8. False. A *contretemps* is an embarrassing, awkward, unexpected situation or event; a sudden mishap or hitch; an inopportune occurrence.

9. False. *Rodomontade* means arrogant boasting or bragging.

10. False. *Hebetude* means stupidity, dullness, obtuseness, lethargy of mind or spirit.

Keywords 21–30

1. Antonyms. *Saturnine*, word 12 of Level 10, means having a gloomy, sullen, or somber appearance or disposition. *Sanguine* means confident, cheerful, hopeful, optimistic.

2. Synonyms. A *deipnosophist* is an adept conversationalist, especially one who enjoys conversing at the table.

3. Antonyms. *Frangible* means breakable, fragile, frail, delicate, easily damaged or destroyed.

4. Antonyms. *Apodictic* means absolutely certain, necessarily true, proved or demonstrated beyond a shadow of a doubt.

5. Antonyms. To *fulminate* means to explode, especially to explode with invective and denunciations; to shout forth condemnation and censure.

6. Synonyms. To *scarify* means to wound the feelings of; make cutting remarks about; distress by criticizing sharply.

7. Well, not exactly antonyms, but definitely not synonyms. *Quotidian*, word 20 of Level 9, means daily, recurring every day or pertaining to every day. *Hebdomadal* means weekly, pertaining to a week or seven-day period.

8. Synonyms. To *divagate* means to wander, ramble, or drift about; hence, to digress.

9. Antonyms. *Pathological* means pertaining to or caused by disease. *Iatrogenic* means caused by medical examination or treatment.

10. Antonyms. *Tergiversation* means desertion; specifically, the act of deserting something to which one was previously loyal, such as a cause, a party, or a religious faith.

Keywords 31–40

1. *Grimy* doesn't fit. *Nacreous* means pearly, consisting of or resembling mother-of-pearl.

2. *Uncooperative* doesn't fit. *Faineant* means lazy, idle, sluggish, good-for-nothing.

3. *Bumpy* doesn't fit. *Hispid* means covered with stiff hairs, bristles, or small spines; rough and bristly.

4. *Long life* doesn't fit. *Longevity* means long life or the duration of life. *Longanimity* means long-suffering patience; the ability to calmly endure hardship or suffering.

5. *A person without knowledge* doesn't fit. A *sciolist* is a person who has only superficial knowledge of a subject, or who pretends to have knowledge.

6. *Propriety* doesn't fit. *Propriety* means proper behavior or appropriateness, suitability. *Propinquity* means nearness in place or time, proximity; also, nearness or similarity in nature, kinship, close relation.

7. *Not original* doesn't fit. *Factitious* means not natural or genuine, produced artificially.

8. *Widespread* doesn't fit. *Plexiform* means complicated or elaborate; specifically, like a plexus or network.

9. *A bubbling sound* doesn't fit. A *susurrus* is a whispering, murmuring, muttering, or rustling sound. The words *susurrus* and *susurration* are synonymous and interchangeable.

10. *Make a mess of* doesn't fit. To *triturate* means to grind, crush, or pound into fine particles or powder.

Keywords 41–50

1. Something protean is highly variable or changeable. *Protean* means readily assuming different shapes, forms, characters, or meanings.

2. *Crepitate* means to crackle; make a crackling, snapping, or popping noise.

3. A *noctivagant* person wanders about at night. A *somnambulant* person wanders while asleep. A *peripatetic* person wanders about on foot. *Noctivagant* means wandering at night.

4. Something *fuliginous* is sooty, smoky.

5. *Hortatory* means encouraging or urging to some course of action; giving earnest counsel or advice.

6. *Heliolatry* is worship of the sun.

7. *Sciamachy* means shadow-boxing, the act of fighting a shadow or an imaginary enemy.

8. Something *glabrous* is smooth and bald.

9. A *pettifogger* is a mean, tricky lawyer; especially, a lawyer who handles petty cases in an unethical, unscrupulous way.

10. *Epicene* means having characteristics or qualities of both sexes.

Review Test for Level 10

1. Which word is a synonym of *paucity*?
    (a) superfluity
    (b) idiosyncrasy
    (c) proclivity

(d) exiguity

2. Which word means to burn the midnight oil or to write in a scholarly or pedantic fashion?

   (a) expatiate
   (b) lucubrate
   (c) fulminate
   (d) divagate

3. Which is *not* an accepted meaning of *troglodyte*?

   (a) a prehistoric cave dweller
   (b) person who chooses to live in seclusion
   (c) a vain, boastful person
   (d) a brutish, unsophisticated person

4. Which word is a synonym of *anchorite* and *eremite*?

   (a) priest
   (b) hermit
   (c) prophet
   (d) sailor

5. Which word is a synonym of *miscellaneous* and *heterogeneous*?

   (a) plexiform
   (b) aleatory
   (c) farraginous
   (d) protean

6. *Cynosure* and *cynical* come ultimately from the Greek *kynos*, which meant

   (a) dog
   (b) popular
   (c) scornful
   (d) the North Star

7. Four of the five words below are related in meaning. Which word has a different, unrelated meaning?

   (a) badinage
   (b) banter
   (c) raillery
   (d) rodomontade
   (e) persiflage

8. Which word is a synonym of *demotic*?

   (a) pedantic
   (b) vernacular
   (c) dictatorial
   (d) hierarchical
   (e) diabolical

9. Which word is an antonym of *saturnine*?

   (a) aleatory
   (b) taciturn
   (c) sanguine
   (d) phlegmatic

10. The *lion* in *lionize* signifies a person who is especially

   (a) ruthless
   (b) dangerous
   (c) important
   (d) successful

11. Four of the five words below are related in meaning. Which word has a different, unrelated meaning?

   (a) gasconade
   (b) vainglory
   (c) fanfaronade
   (d) fulmination
   (e) jactitation

12. Which word means weekly or pertaining to a week?

   (a) hebdomadal
   (b) hebetudinous
   (c) hortatory
   (d) hieratic

13. The combining form *-philia* comes from the Greek *philein*, which means

   (a) to love
   (b) to worship
   (c) to know
   (d) to fear

14. Which word means the fear of disrobing in front of someone?

   (a) pantophobia

(b) philemaphobia
(c) dishabillophobia
(d) syphilophobia

15. Which word by derivation means a drinking party?

    (a) lassitude
    (b) deipnosophy
    (c) rapprochement
    (d) symposium

16. What does *sanguinary* mean?

    (a) cheerful
    (b) confident
    (c) bloody
    (d) ruddy

17. Which word means easily crumbled or crushed?

    (a) factitious
    (b) fuliginous
    (c) fugacious
    (d) friable

18. Which word is a synonym of *vituperate* and *excoriate*?

    (a) hebetate
    (b) scarify
    (c) triturate
    (d) fulminate

19. Which word is the antonym of *pathological*?

    (a) phlegmatic
    (b) iatrogenic
    (c) apodictic
    (d) hieratic

20. Which word means the abandonment of a cause, a party, or a religion?

    (a) tergiversation
    (b) badinage
    (c) heliolatry
    (d) defenestration
    (e) propinquity

21. Which two phrases show improper usage? (This question has *two* correct answers.)
    (a) the amount of paper
    (b) the amount of trouble
    (c) the amount of people
    (d) an amount of sugar
    (e) the amount of volts

22. Which two words are *not* synonyms?
    (a) torpid, hebetudinous
    (b) otiose, dilatory
    (c) somnolent, lethargic
    (d) faineant, indolent

23. Which word means rough and bristly?
    (a) nacreous
    (b) glabrous
    (c) risible
    (d) hispid

24. *Sciolist* and *sciolism* come from the Latin verb *scire*, which means
    (a) to study
    (b) to pretend
    (c) to deceive
    (d) to know

25. Which word suggests a soft sound?
    (a) fulmination
    (b) cacophony
    (c) susurrus
    (d) cachinnation

26. What does *chryselephantine* mean?
    (a) made of gold and ivory
    (b) belonging to an ancient time
    (c) massive and unwieldy
    (d) extremely generous

27. Which Latin phrase means "words a foot and a half long"?
    (a) verbum sat sapienti
    (b) sesquipedalia verba

(c) verbatim et litteratim et punctatim

28. *Divagate* and *noctivagant* come from the Latin verb *vagari*, which means
(a) to divide
(b) to darken
(c) to wander
(d) to confuse

29. Which word denotes speech that urges or advises earnestly?
(a) rodomontade
(b) exhortation
(c) fulmination
(d) contretemps

30. Which word refers to the tendency of plants to bend or move toward a source of light?
(a) noctivagation
(b) tergiversation
(c) lucubration
(d) heliotropism
(e) crepitation

31. What is *logomachy*?
(a) shadow-boxing
(b) the ability to endure hardship
(c) the act of reasoning or deducing
(d) a battle of words

32. Which word suggests unscrupulousness or chicanery?
(a) meretricious
(b) pettifog
(c) vitiation
(d) faineant

33. Which word means having characteristics or qualities of both sexes?
(a) troglodytic
(b) comminuted
(c) epicene
(d) frangible
(e) protean

34. Which word denotes a vehement denunciation?

(a) exhortation
(b) expurgation
(c) execration
(d) expiation
(e) exoneration

35. Something putative is

(a) thought to be so but not proved
(b) corrupted or contaminated
(c) apparently true but actually false or deceptive
(d) absolutely certain
(e) utterly detestable

Answers

1. d 2. b 3. c 4. b 5. c 6. a 7. d 8. b 9. c 10. c 11. d 12. a 13. a
14. c 15. d 16. c 17. d 18. b 19. b 20. a 21. c 22. b 23. d 24. d
25. c 26. a 27. b 28. c 29. b 30. d 31. d 32. b 33. c 34. c 35. a

Evaluation

A score of 30–35 is excellent. If you answered fewer than thirty questions correctly in this test, review the entire level and take the test again.

Verbal Advantage: Posttest

Directions: Each test word is printed in CAPITAL letters in a phrase or sentence. From the five answer choices directly beneath the phrase or sentence, select the one that comes nearest to the precise meaning of the test word.

1. PARAPHRASE it.
   rewrite   remove   restate   quote   copy

2. Witnessed the CALAMITY.
   entertainment   misfortune   explosion   foolishness   debate

3. Complete CANDOR.
   rudeness   frankness   simplicity   brightness   truth

4. We CONCURRED.
   met   cooperated   agreed   differed   explained

5. He is PLACID.
   excited   capable   confident   discouraged   calm

6. CAPRICIOUS people.
   snobbish   unpredictable   silly   reliable   tasteless

7. That is NEGLIGIBLE.
   unknown   improper   unimportant   untouchable   single

8. A POIGNANT remark.
   relevant   dull   practical   insulting   piercing

9. NEBULOUS ideas.
   unclear   beginning   threatening   serious   marvelous

10. AMBIGUOUS gestures.
    curious   uncertain   complex   obvious   insignificant

11. He is PERSONABLE.
    warm   talkative   understanding   sensible   attractive

12. The DILIGENT worker.
slow   effective   industrious   careless   smart

13. Is it PLIANT?
full   stiff   well done   more than enough   easily bent

14. An ARDUOUS task.
outrageous   serious   harsh   difficult   painful

15. CLANDESTINE circumstances.
special   inevitable   secret   primitive   obvious

16. A CREDULOUS person.
willing   friendly   easily deceived   well-fed   thoughtful

17. He looks HAGGARD.
dirty   worn out   hostile   different   crazy

18. Is it ONEROUS?
painful   truthful   legal   burdensome   workable

19. Her ANIMOSITY.
ill will   loyalty   hospitality   evil deed   cruelty

20. It was DEFUNCT.
impossible   dead   unimportant   lost   bankrupt

21. He is TACITURN.
gloomy   complicated   silent   trivial   changeable

22. A TERSE statement.
unexpected   concise   unpleasant   long-winded   false

23. For the PROLETARIAT.
citizens   aristocracy   slaves   middle class   working class

24. It's a PITTANCE.
small favor   debt   payment   complaint   small amount

25. He is GLIB.
sarcastic   slow-witted   smooth-spoken   deceitful
spontaneous

26. Can you CIRCUMSCRIBE it?
explain   write   repeat   limit   forbid

27. An INGRATIATING remark.
rude   troublesome   flattering   harmful   penetrating

28. This FALLACY.
misunderstanding   first step   new idea   confusion   false idea

29. Tried to EXTEMPORIZE.
improve   waste   rush   discuss   improvise

30. Her VOLUBLE friend.
obnoxious   attractive   talkative   intelligent   shy

31. I will ESCHEW it.
avoid   consider   not allow   investigate   accept

32. Extremely ERUDITE.
rare   learned   old   difficult   peculiar

33. LOATH to do it.
hate   want   not allowed   not inclined   not ready

34. OSTENTATIOUS clothing.
expensive   tattered   new   showy   secondhand

35. A SALIENT feature.
standard   interesting   hidden   conspicuous   unattractive

36. Is it DISCERNIBLE?
available   unusual   reasonable   invisible   apparent

37. SOLICITOUS about it.
pleased   confused   concerned   angry   curious

38. MERCENARY people.
helpless   poor   forgiving   greedy   disloyal

39. To PROTRACT it.
take back   support   revise   dictate   prolong

40. An ASTUTE remark.
shrewd   vicious   curious   obscene   learned

41. GARRULOUS people.
restrained   vulnerable   dangerous   talkative   uneducated

42. She was IMPASSIVE.
stubborn   unsure   exhausted   ineffective   expressionless

43. For the LAITY.
youth   insiders   ministers   nonprofessionals   academics

44. Another CHARLATAN.
salesperson   miser   beggar   fake   expert

45. They were VINDICTIVE.
    tolerant   revengeful   blameless   cheating   judgmental

46. What do you SURMISE?
    wish for   guess   recall   observe   propose

47. A PENSIVE mood.
    thoughtful   irritated   pleasant   nervous   fickle

48. He was RETICENT.
    eager   lonely   reluctant   silent   unhappy

49. MUNDANE affairs.
    worldly   unusual   never-ending   pertinent   annoying

50. Will they EXONERATE her?
    praise   convict   charge   demote   acquit

51. JOVIAL conversation.
    humorous   foolish   merry   friendly   meaningless

52. Another ACCOLADE.
    gift   reprimand   celebration   opportunity   award

53. ESOTERIC information.
    useful   important   private   insignificant   accessible

54. Made MANIFEST.
    powerful   apparent   abundant   permissible   secret

55. This SUBTERFUGE.
    proposal   conflict   turn of events   deception   violation

56. ADMONISH them.
    warn   seize   ignore   reward   punish

57. A PRODIGIOUS accomplishment.
    unusual   enormous   lucky   important   unexpected

58. The PUGNACIOUS man.
    ugly   friendly   stubborn   combative   self-centered

59. An OFFICIOUS coworker.
    hardworking   ambitious   meddlesome   efficient   overbearing

60. Their COMPLICITY.
    respect   maturity   submissiveness   understanding
    conspiracy

61. It will EDIFY you.
instruct   inspire   change   confuse   oppose

62. A CIRCUITOUS route.
roundabout   difficult   unusual   direct   impossible

63. A SUPERCILIOUS look.
hasty   sophisticated   sympathetic   hopeless   haughty

64. Will they be VINDICATED?
criticized   made legal   represented   cleared from blame
omitted

65. An ABSTRUSE conversation.
long and involved   hard to understand   illogical   pointless
secret

66. He was OSTRACIZED.
misunderstood   reprimanded   perplexed   expelled
depressed

67. Quite PUERILE.
insulting   helpful   childish   worthless   intelligent

68. Will they TRANSMUTE it?
debate   change   rise above   exchange   disprove

69. A SONOROUS voice.
sad   high-pitched   resonant   lonely   obnoxious

70. Is he a SYCOPHANT?
maniac   faithful friend   liar   flatterer   fool

71. It was INCESSANT.
intense   useless   constant   annoying   irregular

72. A definite PROCLIVITY.
aptitude   opinion   accomplishment   likelihood   inclination

73. She will TRUNCATE it.
extend   wipe out   cut short   withdraw   summarize

74. OBSEQUIOUS people.
religious   insulting   demanding   subservient   insincere

75. A SAGACIOUS response.
wise   uncalled for   absurd   polite   sarcastic

76. Their ABSTEMIOUSNESS.
moderation   timidity   complexity   inflexibility   respect

77. RIBALD remarks.
stern   foolish   critical   mildly indecent   grossly offensive

78. BOMBASTIC speech.
vehement   disorganized   loud   exaggerated   pompous

79. LUGUBRIOUS music.
joyful   complicated   grand   background   mournful

80. Done with CELERITY.
courteousness   speed   excellence   ease   pleasure

81. This is SPURIOUS.
exceptional   unnecessary   authentic   offensive   false

82. To SUCCOR them.
praise   trick   deny   advise   aid

83. VAPID conversation.
lifeless   lively   intelligent   irrelevant   foolish

84. RISIBLE remarks.
laughable   cutting   irrelevant   serious   obvious

85. TURBID water.
hot   muddy   polluted   bubbling   still

86. MELLIFLUOUS sounds.
indistinct   melodic   beautiful   romantic   smooth-flowing

87. Still NASCENT.
incomplete   unproved   unchanged   possible   beginning

88. PARSIMONIOUS people.
holy   stingy   considerate   hypocritical   generous

89. Her TEMERITY.
cleverness   rashness   pride   ability   shyness

90. TANTAMOUNT to it.
next   unrelated   superior   equivalent   opposed

91. PHLEGMATIC response.
immediate   inappropriate   sluggish   evasive   minimal

92. It was DESICCATED.
dried up   destroyed   saturated   consumed   cut up

93. The PAUCITY of it.
worth   variety   lack   truth   likelihood

94. Was that a SOLECISM?
old saying   correction   blunder   demand   complaint

95. PERIPATETIC people.
thoughtful   argumentative   irrational   traveling on foot
preaching

96. It seems PROTEAN.
changeable   workable   abnormal   supportive   vague

97. A SATURNINE countenance.
gloomy   cheerful   thoughtful   evil   wise

98. It has been VITIATED.
abused   freed   exposed   corrected   corrupted

99. Engaged in HELIOLATRY.
deep thought   criminal activity   sun worship   air travel
scholarly debate

100. HIERATIC writings.
official   ancient   magical   philosophical   priestly

Verbal Advantage: Posttest Answer Key

1. PARAPHRASE: restate
2. CALAMITY: misfortune
3. CANDOR: frankness
4. CONCURRED: agreed
5. PLACID: calm
6. CAPRICIOUS: unpredictable
7. NEGLIGIBLE: unimportant
8. POIGNANT: piercing
9. NEBULOUS: unclear
10. AMBIGUOUS: uncertain
11. PERSONABLE: attractive
12. DILIGENT: industrious
13. PLIANT: easily bent
14. ARDUOUS: difficult
15. CLANDESTINE: secret
16. CREDULOUS: easily deceived
17. HAGGARD: worn out
18. ONEROUS: burdensome
19. ANIMOSITY: ill will
20. DEFUNCT: dead
21. TACITURN: silent
22. TERSE: concise
23. PROLETARIAT: working class
24. PITTANCE: small amount
25. GLIB: smooth-spoken
26. CIRCUMSCRIBE: limit
27. INGRATIATING: flattering

28. FALLACY: false idea
29. EXTEMPORIZE: improvise
30. VOLUBLE: talkative
31. ESCHEW: avoid
32. ERUDITE: learned
33. LOATH: not inclined
34. OSTENTATIOUS: showy
35. SALIENT: conspicuous
36. DISCERNIBLE: apparent
37. SOLICITOUS: concerned
38. MERCENARY: greedy
39. PROTRACT: prolong
40. ASTUTE: shrewd
41. GARRULOUS: talkative
42. IMPASSIVE: expressionless
43. LAITY: nonprofessionals
44. CHARLATAN: fake
45. VINDICTIVE: revengeful
46. SURMISE: guess
47. PENSIVE: thoughtful
48. RETICENT: silent
49. MUNDANE: worldly
50. EXONERATE: acquit
51. JOVIAL: merry
52. ACCOLADE: award
53. ESOTERIC: private
54. MANIFEST: apparent

55. SUBTERFUGE: deception
56. ADMONISH: warn
57. PRODIGIOUS: enormous
58. PUGNACIOUS: combative
59. OFFICIOUS: meddlesome
60. COMPLICITY: conspiracy
61. EDIFY: instruct
62. CIRCUITOUS: roundabout
63. SUPERCILIOUS: haughty
64. VINDICATED: cleared from blame
65. ABSTRUSE: hard to understand
66. OSTRACIZED: expelled
67. PUERILE: childish
68. TRANSMUTE: change
69. SONOROUS: resonant
70. SYCOPHANT: flatterer
71. INCESSANT: constant
72. PROCLIVITY: inclination
73. TRUNCATE: cut short
74. OBSEQUIOUS: subservient
75. SAGACIOUS: wise
76. ABSTEMIOUSNESS: moderation
77. RIBALD: mildly indecent
78. BOMBASTIC: pompous
79. LUGUBRIOUS: mournful
80. CELERITY: speed
81. SPURIOUS: false
82. SUCCOR: aid
83. VAPID: lifeless
84. RISIBLE: laughable
85. TURBID: muddy
86. MELLIFLUOUS: smooth-flowing
87. NASCENT: beginning
88. PARSIMONIOUS: stingy

89. TEMERITY: rashness
90. TANTAMOUNT: equivalent
91. PHLEGMATIC: sluggish
92. DESICCATED: dried up
93. PAUCITY: lack
94. SOLECISM: blunder
95. PERIPATETIC: traveling on foot
96. PROTEAN: changeable
97. SATURNINE: gloomy
98. VITIATED: corrupted
99. HELIOLATRY: sun worship
100. HIERATIC: priestly

Verbal Advantage: Posttest Evaluation

91–100: You're in the top 10 percent. Congratulations!
80–90: Well-above-average vocabulary. Excellent work.
65–79: Good progress. More review will make the difference.
50–64: Decent progress. Rereading the second half of the program will help improve your score.
Below 50: You can do better if you try. Carefully review the entire program. Make sure that you answer at least eight questions correctly in each review quiz before you move on to the next set of keyword discussions. Read an interesting book or magazine for at least twenty minutes every day. Always keep your dictionary handy so you can look up any unfamiliar words.